Because the liturgy stood at the very heart of medieval religious experience, the study of liturgical change is basic to understanding the Middle Ages, its religious life, and its art. In this far-reaching study, Margot Fassler explores currents of liturgical change in twelfth-century France and the extent to which Augustinian canons regular contributed to them.

Concentrating upon the late sequence, Professor Fassler first restores credibility to the medieval myth that this poetic and musical genre was championed at the Abbey of St. Victor in Paris. Placing these magnificent chants in the context of the twelfth-century Victorine church and liturgy, she explains how the texts were joined through the unique use of symbolic melodies, some of which were composed by the Victorines themselves. Through this interrelationship of text and music, designed to stimulate the collective memory of the worshiping community, the Victorines attempted to create a model of the church. This model, based on the writings of Hugh of St. Victor, magnifies the priestly office and the role of liturgy in unifying the church. The highly developed biblical typology commonly found in twelfth- and thirteenth-century church decoration has a counterpart in these religious songs; like the sequences, the art works were designed primarily to inspire and instruct the clergy.

Professor Fassler thus proposes that the sequences provide crucial evidence both for explaining new attitudes toward the liturgy during the twelfth century and for defining those principles in the arts commonly called "Gothic."

CAMBRIDGE STUDIES IN MEDIEVAL AND RENAISSANCE MUSIC

GENERAL EDITORS:

Iain Fenlon, Peter le Huray,
Thomas Forrest Kelly, John Stevens

This series continues the aims of the Cambridge Studies in Music but now focuses on the medieval and Renaissance periods. As with the earlier series, the central concern is to publish books which make an original contribution to the study of music in its widest sense. Thus the relationship of music both to a broad historical and social context and to the other arts is seen as an important feature.

PUBLISHED

The Organ in Western Culture, 750–1250
PETER WILLIAMS

CAMBRIDGE STUDIES IN MEDIEVAL AND RENAISSANCE MUSIC

Gothic Song

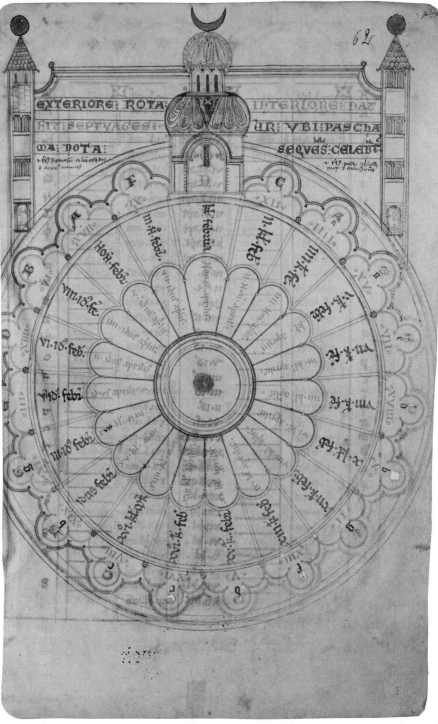

Paris, BN lat. 14673, fol. 62r, from a twelfth-century section of this Victorine source, and part of a computus, a short book demonstrating how to calculate feasts. The church in the upper border seems to rise from the geometrically ordered calendar. Emile Mâle (*Chartres*, 1983, p. 14) explained the figures commonly found on top of church spires as follows: "The tall pyramid terminates in an iron cross, surmounted by a crescent moon, for it is on a crescent moon that the Woman of the Apocalypse rests her feet. The Gothic spire of the other tower bears an image of the sun on its cross to remind us that the Woman of the Apocalypse was dressed in rays of light."

Gothic Song

Victorine Sequences and Augustinian Reform in Twelfth-Century Paris

MARGOT FASSLER

Associate Professor,
Department of Music, Brandeis University

CAMBRIDGE
UNIVERSITY PRESS

Published by the Press Syndicate of the University of Cambridge
The Pitt Building, Trumpington Street, Cambridge CB2 1RP
40 West 20th Street, New York, NY 10011–4211, USA
10 Stamford Road, Oakleigh, Melbourne 3166, Australia

First published 1993

Printed in Great Britain at the University Press, Cambridge

A catalogue record for this book is available from the British Library

Library of Congress cataloguing in publication data

Fassler, Margot Elsbeth.
Gothic Song: Victorine Sequences and Augustinian Reform in
Twelfth-Century Paris / Margot Fassler.
     p.   cm.
Includes bibliographical references and indexes.
ISBN 0 521 38291 2 (hardback)
1. Church music – France – Paris – 500–1400. 2. Church music – Catholic Church – 500–1400.
3. Sequences (Music) – History and criticism. 4. Paris (France) – Church history. I. Title.
ML3027.8.P2F4   1193
782.32'35 – dc20 92–5506 CIP

ISBN 0 521 38291 2 hardback

CE

For Susan Cooper Fassler Babcock and Peter Jeffery

and in memory of Frank B. Fassler

What then is the ark like? Do you desire to know? Bear with me, that I may tell you a few things out of many. This ark is like a storehouse filled with all manner of delightful things. You will look for nothing in it that you will not find, and when you have found one thing, you will see many spread before your eyes. There all the works of restoration are contained in all their fullness, from the world's beginning to its end; and therein is represented the condition of the universal church. Into it is woven the story of events, in it are found the mysteries of the sacraments, and there are set out the stages of affections, thoughts, meditations, contemplations, good works, virtues, and rewards. There we are shown what we ought to believe, and do, and hope . . . There the sum of things is displayed, and the harmony of its elements explained. There another world is found, over against this passing, transitory one; because the things that go through different times in this world exist in that one simultaneously, as in a condition of eternity. There the present does not follow on the past, nor does the future supervene upon the present, but whatsoever is there, is there as in the present.

Hugh of St. Victor,
The Moral Ark of Noah, Book IV
(ca. 1125)

Contents

Illustrations

All plates are published with the consent of the Bibliothèque Nationale, Paris, with the exception of Plates 7.5 and 11.1, which are printed with the consent of the Widener Library, Harvard University

Acknowledgments

The writing of this book began in 1986, during a year on a Morse Junior Faculty Fellowship from Yale University. Just before and after this time, grants from the National Endowment for the Humanities and the American Philosophical Society allowed for trips to Paris to work with liturgical manuscripts, and a grant from the Griswold Fund of Yale University provided for the purchase of the many microfilms needed to prepare this study. I am grateful to the staffs of the Bibliothèque Nationale, the Bibliothèque de l'Arsenal, the Bibliothèque Mazarine, and the Bibliothèque de la Ville de Paris for their kind attention, and to the Bibliothèque Nationale and to Harvard University for permission to publish the plates in this book; librarians in the Yale University Libraries and the Brandeis University Libraries were ever helpful, and I am especially thankful to Brad Short, Vera Deák, Helen Bartlett, Victor Cardell, and Harold Samuels for their many kindnesses, and to Julian Plante and the staff of the Hill Monastic Manuscript Library. Pierre Bizeau, Diocesan Archivist in Chartres, was exceedingly generous with his time, and made many otherwise unattainable documents available for consultation; Madame Christiane Pollin of the Bibliothèque Municipale in Chartres supplied the microfilms I needed for the study of the Chartrian sources, and these, in turn, were funded by another grant from the Griswold fund at Yale University, as administrated by Ms. Sheila Brewer. My visit to Chartres in 1991 was supported by a grant from the Sachar Foundation at Brandeis University. The book was revised completely during 1990–91, when I received a grant from the Howard Foundation, and a leave from Brandeis University. I am deeply grateful to the Howard Foundation and to Brandeis University for the time both to finish the revisions on this book and to begin a second book as well. The musical examples for this book were prepared with the help of my students John Sullivan, George Catalano, and Christopher Mossey, and through grants from the Ford Foundation, which supports the Undergraduate Fellows Program at Brandeis, and the Brandeis University Computer Center. The musical analysis of "O Maria, stella maris," which appears in Chapter 15, is similar in parts to that found in my paper "The Role of the Parisian Sequence in the Evolution of Notre-Dame Polyphony," *Speculum* 62 (1987); pp. 345–374, and is reproduced here with the permission of the Medieval Academy of America.

The various parts of this study were discussed at length with many friends and my colleagues at Yale and Brandeis and Cambridge University Press, and my ideas were often tempered by their criticisms and comments. I would like especially to thank David Hiley and John Stevens, who read an early draft of the book with critical eyes, Penny Souster of Cambridge University Press, whose kindness has been unfailing and whose advice has been of great help, and Lucy Carolan, also of the Press, whose keen perceptions and good sense made the final stages of manuscript preparation a pleasure. Craig Wright was ever supportive of my early work on Adam of St. Victor, and great benefit came from sharing my thoughts about the Parisian liturgy and Victorine sequences with him and Michel Huglo, Edward Roesner, Rebecca Baltzer, Anne Robertson, Joseph Dyer, Jeremy Yudkin, Janet Knapp, Andrew Hughes, George Nugent, David Hughes, Claire Maître, Ruth Steiner, Kenneth Levy, Norman Smith, Lazlo Dobszay, James McKinnon, and, especially, Don M. Randel; my ideas about early sequences and tropes were often tried out upon Professor Alejandro Planchart, with great benefit; David Cohen read and commented upon several early chapters. Conversations with Eric Chafe and Jesse Anne Owens, whose own work in later periods bears certain correspondences with my own, were frequently inspiring, and I am grateful for the bibliographic expertise of my colleague in Near Eastern and Judaic Studies, Marc Brettler.

Because of the interdisciplinary nature of the study, I was often guided by discussions with medievalists from outside my own field: among the historians, I must list Camille Bennett, John Baldwin, Giles Constable, James John, Marsha Colish, and especially James Powell of Syracuse University, who read drafts of Chapters 9 and 10, and made many suggestions for improving the work; among the students of literature: Gunilla Iversen of the Corpus Troporum read and commented upon several chapters of the work, and my esteemed friends Mary Frances Wack, Charles D. Wright, James O'Donnell, and Robert Kaske (before his death in 1989) were always available for consultation; art historians too were involved: Walter Cahn of Yale University and Mark Stansbury-O'Donnell of St. Paul's College read two chapters and their comments were extremely helpful, and I have profited as well from the advice of my colleague Professor Charles McClendon and from consultation with Patricia Stirnemann of the IRHT; in Victorine studies, I have often been helped and encouraged by Reverend Hugh Feiss of Mount St. Angel Abbey, and through my long friendship with Professor Grover Zinn, who has supported my work and the particular directions it took from the very beginning. I offer special thanks as well for the stimulation of my students, singling out from the many Susan Boynton, Matthew Head, Daniel Page, and David Metzer, and to several friends, some of whom were once my students: Katalin Komlos, Marian Smith, Pamela Potter, Judith Ballan, and Margaret Notley. The original inspiration for this book came from Clifford Flanigan, who told me long ago that "someone really ought to have a look at the Victorine sequences"; the style was greatly influenced by Claude Palisca, who convinced me that in a study of this nature I would be better off trying to explain things than to prove them.

The greatest debt of all, however, is owed to my husband, Peter Jeffery, and to my mother, Susan Cooper Fassler Babcock, to whom the book is dedicated. Without their sharing of family responsibilities, and their support and enthusiasm, I could never have written a study of this scope at this particular time in my life. The ideas here were frequently discussed with Peter, and he read two parts of the book carefully and reviewed some of the musical examples, making numerous useful suggestions. My sons, Frank, aged 4, and Joe, aged 7, have had this book as a sibling, and have borne its presence generously and graciously.

Notes on the text

Abbreviations

AH	*Analecta hymnica medii aevi*. Ed. Guido Dreves and Clemens Blume. Leipzig, 1886–1922. 55 vols.
APS–V	*L'Abbaye Parisienne de Saint-Victor au Moyen Age: communications présentées au XIIIe Colloque d'Humanisme médiéval de Paris (1986–1988)*. Ed. Jean Longère. Biblioteca Victorina, I. Turnhout, 1991.
ASSD	*Abbot Suger and Saint-Denis: a Symposium*. Ed. Paula Lieber Gerson. New York, 1986.
BHL	*Bibliotheca hagiographica Latina antiquae et mediae aetatis*. Ed. Socii Bollandiani. 2 vols. Brussels, 1949.
BPH	*Bulletin Philologique et Historique du Comité des Travaux Historiques et Scientifiques*
BSHAL	*Bulletin de la Societé Historique et Archéologique du Limousin*
BSN	*Bulletin de la Société Nivernaise des Lettres, Sciences et Arts*
CCCM	*Corpus Christianorum, continuatio medievalis*. Turnhout, 1964–
CCSL	*Corpus Christianorum, series Latina*. Turnhout, 1954–
CEND	B. Guérard *Cartulaire de l'église Notre-Dame de Paris*. Collection des cartulaires de France, vols. IV–VII. Paris, 1850.
CGP	Robert de Lasteyrie, *Cartulaire général de Paris*. Vol. I. Paris, 1887.
CLLA	Klaus Gamber, *Codices liturgici latini antiquiores*. 2nd edn. 2 vols. Fribourg, 1968.
CSEL	*Corpus scriptorum ecclesiasticorum Latinorum*. Vienna, 1866–
CT	*Corpus Troporum*. Stockholm, 1975–. Seven volumes have appeared; several are listed individually in primary sources.
DMA	*Dictionary of the Middle Ages*. Ed. Joseph Strayer. 13 vols. New York, 1982–89.
DS	*Dictionnaire de spiritualité*. Ed. Marcel Viller *et al.* Paris, 1932–
Dup.-Ag.	Henri Duplès-Agier. *Chroniques de Saint-Martial de Limoges publiées d'après les manuscrits originaux*. Paris, 1974.
JAMS	*The Journal of the American Musicological Society*
JBC	*The New Jerome Biblical Commentary*. Ed. Raymond Brown, Joseph Fitzmyer and Roland Murphy. Englewood Cliffs, NJ. 1990.
LitTrop	*Liturgische Tropen: Referate zweier Colloquien des Corpus Troporum in München und Canterbury*. Munich, 1985.

M&A	Eugène Misset and Pierre Aubry, eds. *Les proses d'Adam de Saint-Victor: texte et musique précédées d'une étude critique*. Paris, 1900.[1]
NG	*New Grove Dictionary of Music and Musicians*. Ed. Stanley Sadie. London, 1980.
NGS	John Emmerich, "Sources, Western Plainchant" In *NG*, 1980.
ODSP	*Obituaires de la Province de Sens*. Vol. I: *Diocèses de Sens et de Paris*. Ed. Auguste Molinier. Paris, 1902.
PL	*Patrologiae cursus completus sive bibliotheca universalis, integra, uniformis, commoda, oeconomica omnium ss. patrum, doctorum scriptorumque ecclesiasticorum qui ab aevo apostolico ad innocentii III tempora floruerunt . . . series [Latina]*. Ed. J.-P. Migne. Paris, 1844–64. 221 vols.
RB	*Revue Bénédictine*
RISM	*Tropen und Sequenzen Handschriften*. Répertoire international des sources musicales, vol. B/VI. Ed. Heinrich Husmann. Munich, 1964.
RTAM	*Recherches de Théologie Ancienne et Médiévale*
SCF	Hugh of St. Victor, *De sacramentis christianae fidei*. PL CLXXVI, cols. 173–618. *On the sacraments of the Christian faith*. Trans. Roy Deferrari. Cambridge, MA, 1951.
SOU	Moines de Solesmes. *Le Graduel Romain: édition critique par les moines de Solesmes*. Vol. II: *Les Sources*. Solesmes, 1957.
TB	*Thomas Becket: actes du colloque internationale de Sedières, 19–24 août 1973*. Ed. Raymonde Foreville. Paris, 1975.
Y1200	*The Year 1200: a Centennial Exhibition at the Metropolitan Museum of Art*. 2 vols. New York, 1970.
Y1200S	*The Year 1200: a Symposium*. New York, 1975.

Quotations from editions and from translations

The policy has been to use the spellings found in each individual edition. Because there is no uniform practice followed in the great variety of editions used, our own text will be inconsistent. In quotations from English translations of Latin works as well, individual translators use many different styles in their works. Here again, our own text will not be stylistically uniform because it has quoted from the work of many translators.

Bibliographic conventions

References in the footnotes are of three kinds. Those consisting of an author's name followed by a short title – e.g. Augustine, *De doctrina christiana* – signify that the relevant entry in the bibliography can be found in the primary sources (pp. 442–446). Those consisting of an author's name followed by a date – e.g. Fassler (1984) – direct the reader to the secondary sources (pp. 446–473). Those consisting of an abbreviation are explained in the list of abbreviations on pp. xix–xx.

Citations from the Bible

The names of Biblical books, and the numberings of chapters and verses, often differ among the many Latin and English editions of the Bible. The major reason for this is that most modern

---

[1] In their edition of the Victorine sequences, Pierre Aubry and Eugene Misset cataloged the individual units of the melodies in the repertory and provided each with a number. They called these units "timbres." When I use the term "timbre number" it refers to the number of the melodic unit as assigned by Misset and Aubry; timbre numbers are abbreviated within the text as e.g. "t. 102."

English translations are based on the original Hebrew and Greek texts, which differ in many respects from the Latin Vulgate. However, even differing editions and translations of the Vulgate are not completely consistent, and no English translation of the Vulgate is entirely adequate. For the sake of consistency, therefore, quotations of the Bible in English are given according to the so-called Douai–Rheims translation of 1582 and 1609, as revised by Richard Challoner (1752, 1763). This has been the most widely used English translation of the Vulgate, and its chapter and verse numberings follow the most common Vulgate system. When the names of Biblical books or the chapter and verse numberings differ from the most widely used English system (originally used with the King James or Authorized Version of 1611), this system is cited in square brackets, following *The New Jerusalem Bible* (Garden City, New York: Doubleday and Co., 1985). Biblical quotations in Latin are given according to *Biblia sacra iuxta vulgatam versionem*, editio minor, ed. Robert Weber *et al.* (Stuttgart, 1984).

The following abbreviations represent books of the Bible (based on the Douai–Rheims names [New Jerusalem Bible names in square brackets].

Apoc. [Rev.]	Apocalypse [Revelation]
Cant.	Canticle of Canticles [Song of Songs]
Col.	Colossians
1 Cor.	1 Corinthians
Dan.	Daniel
Deut.	Deuteronomy
Eph.	Ephesians
Ez.	Ezechiel [Ezekiel]
Heb.	Hebrews
Isa.	Isaiah [Isaiah]
Jon.	Jonas [Jonah]
Lev.	Leviticus
Matt.	Matthew
Ps.	Psalms
Sirach	Sirach [Ecclesiasticus]
Zach.	Zacharias [Zechariah]

Pitch designation

The following conventions are used in the text to designate pitch:

c	one octave below middle C
d	
e	
f	
g	
a	
b	
c′	middle C
d′	
etc.	

Part I

The changing language of the liturgy

1

The study of liturgical change in the Middle Ages: problems and potential

The medieval liturgy: mediator between past and present

During the Middle Ages, liturgical practices were passed on from generation to generation – the texts, the music, the ceremony shaping the minds and hearts of worshiping men and women from early childhood and remaining with them until death. It was in the context of the familiar liturgy that Scripture and the Fathers were learned, religious art was apprehended, the hours, days, and seasons were measured out. Through the liturgy, religious communities found their pasts drawn into the present. God could be experienced again on earth, as Christians once believed he had been centuries before. Through the sacraments, Christians went into the Jordan at baptism, and ate the Last Supper at communion. Through their processions and stational liturgies, cities in northern Europe became Jerusalem and Rome.

Both lay and ecclesiastical leaders were aware of the historical continuity provided by their liturgies, and of the importance of the liturgy in promoting stability and strengthening a sense of unity among their peoples, a unity not only with earliest Christians but with the many communities which followed after them, most significantly with the earliest Christian communities that had existed in their own local regions and dioceses. Feasts of saints whose relics lay beneath church altars were assigned high ranks within those churches, and special texts and music as well; ecclesiastical officials and patrons who had sponsored a church with gifts of money or property, or protected it during times of hardship, were commemorated and prayed for there. Every cleric, monk, or wealthy layperson recorded in the obituary was remembered on the anniversary of his or her death.[1]

Thus liturgies preserved the past, not only through symbolic reenactments of the events of salvation history, but by creating an identity for each individual region, diocese, and church. As a result, medieval men and women were reluctant to

---

[1] For the study of rites and customs associated with remembering the dead within one religious community, see Lemaître (1989).

threaten this link to the past by changing their liturgical practices.[2] The preface of a late-twelfth-century ordinal from the Parisian Abbey of St. Victor exemplifies an attitude of resistance to liturgical change which was held throughout the Middle Ages.

Quoniam ecclesiastici ordinis usus uitio quidem obliuionis per singulos fere annos transmutatus plerumque errorem incurrit abusionis necessarium duximus ordinem quidem antiphonarii non mutantes sed alia ex aliis libris necessaria colligentes annuum usum seriatim describere et quid per totum annum sive de tempore sive de festis sanctorum dicendum sit breuiter annotare. Congruum enim est ut usus ecclesiasticus semper uniformiter teneatur et tocius altercationis molestia in posterum excludatur.[3]

(Because the use of the ecclesiastical estate, corrupted through the vice of forgetfulness almost every year, commonly sustains the error of misuse, we thought it necessary, not indeed changing the order of the antiphonary, but collecting some necessary things from other books, to describe the annual use in order, and to indicate briefly what should be said through the complete year, both of feasts of the time [temporale] and of feasts of the saints [sanctorale]. For it is fitting that the ecclesiastical use ever be kept uniformly and the inconvenience of all dispute be excluded for the future.)

Yet in spite of the importance of the liturgy as a record of the past and of the medieval desire to preserve liturgical traditions, modern study of liturgical sources proves that changes did occur in medieval liturgies, sometimes even changes of great magnitude. The Victorine ordinal quoted above is filled with corrections: some feasts have been scraped carefully from the parchment to be replaced by others, contemporary and near contemporary additions are neatly penned in the margins along with those added more carelessly by later generations, and certain elements of the chant repertory were clearly still in flux during and soon after the time the book was prepared. Comparison of this late-twelfth-century Augustinian ordinal with a Parisian service book from a century earlier, a late-eleventh-century troper-proser which once apparently belonged to the Benedictine Abbey of St. Magloire, reveals changes of a more dramatic sort: during the twelfth century in this city, entire repertories of chants disappeared and many new pieces came into being.[4]

Although each local medieval liturgy had unique features which rooted it in the past and made it impervious to change, the truth is that liturgies belonged ever to the present as well. The liturgy had to be reenacted every day, every season and year, and if certain elements of it no longer either made sense or fitted the self-concept of the community, they might well be changed, or, at least, recontextualized or explained. When the understanding of the relationship between God and man changed, when interpretations of history and tradition changed, and, most importantly, when the clergy arrived at a new self-concept, liturgies and commentaries upon them changed as well. In fact, the liturgy represented the past so profoundly that through altering it, new pasts could be made, and new interpreta-

---

[2] Christian liturgies of the Middle Ages were the voices of institutions. As Douglas (1986, p. 63) has said, "Institutions bestow sameness. Socially based analogies assign disparate items to classes and load them with moral and political content."

[3] See Paris, BN lat. 14506, fol. 267r. This manuscript will be described in greater detail in Chapter 7.

[4] Paris, BN lat. 13252 will be discussed further in Chapter 7.

tions of them offered.[5] Carolingian kings in the eighth and early ninth centuries supported programs of liturgical reform, uprooting the varied branches of the Gallican use and importing more uniform Roman rites, and unifying the various strains of monastic life through the efforts of Benedict of Aniane. In so doing, they gave themselves and the clergy a new history and further empowered themselves.[6] Small-scale liturgical changes with similar purposes can be found throughout the Middle Ages. When the community of Benedictines from the Abbey of St. Martial in Limoges promoted the cult of their patron saint in the early eleventh century, Adémar of Chabannes recast the liturgy so that St. Martial was honored as an apostle, substituting the Mass texts and chants for this saint with others proper to apostles, and writing numerous new pieces as well.[7] In a general statement about the power of tradition in religious life, Paul Vallière describes how major change *could* find acceptance through a fusion of past and present, one which made the new seem to redeem the old. His ideas relate especially well to the medieval liturgy, an aspect of religious life which was strongly traditional and yet subject to change.

Religious traditions are not hostile to change provided that the new can be integrated with the old through the reform or renewal of tradition. In practice, however, such integration is difficult to accomplish, and religious traditions for the most part do not make the effort except when compelled to do so by a crisis of thought, practice, or belief . . . A sense of tradition, allowing for the old to be appreciated as ever new and the new to be received as clarifying or fulfilling the old, provides direction for individuals and groups at such times.[8]

Tensions between past beliefs and modes of thought and new interpretations of history and new religious ideals were constantly resolved in the liturgical forum during the Middle Ages, both through changes in the liturgy itself and through the writings of liturgical commentators and Biblical exegetes. Because significant changes in the liturgy required great amounts of energy to bring about, they were always slow changes. By the time the elements of major changes were fully in place, therefore, the generation that had initiated them had already passed on, and the next generation was already beginning to view the changes as traditional. Thus, the changes in their turn would, perhaps, require explanation, and might themselves become subject to change soon after they were officially in place.

The medieval liturgy was a great wheel turning slowly, just behind the times, and, as it turned, it acquired a momentum all its own, affected by yet independent of other forces. Through it, present generations had to come to terms both with the religious ideals of immediately preceding generations, and with the ideals of the distant past, and this was true in new religious communities as well as older, long-established ones. The dialogue within this forum was always between the living and the dead, and through it each successive generation confronted and

---

[5] Of course, the same thing was done with documents. See Chibnall (1988) and Constable (1983).

[6] For description and discussion of Charlemagne's coronation rite, see Folz (1974), pp. 136–150. Nelson (1971) has discussed changes in the anointing ritual and their signification.

[7] See Callahan (1976) for discussion of Adémar's establishment of the cult of St. Martial. A volume of the *Corpus Chrstianorum* containing the writings of Adémar is now in preparation (ed. Richard Landes, with James Grier, *et al.*).

[8] From the article "Tradition" in *The Encyclopedia of Religion* (ed. Mircea Eliade), vol. XV, p. 13.

redefined its past. Speaking of monastic liturgical practices in the Middle Ages, Giles Constable says:

> There was a constant adjustment between the past and the present, and between the competing claims of conformity and individuality, of structure and community, and of hierarchy and equality. The original purpose and meaning of ceremonies might be forgotten, but new meanings were found, and some of the most creative energy of the Middle Ages went into shaping and interpreting the framework of religious life.[9]

The "constant adjustment between the past and the present" which took place within the liturgy and writings about the liturgy was emphasized during the Middle Ages because of the special character of liturgical books.[10] New material most often circulated first in small, quasi-official collections. These "libelli" were only slowly absorbed into earlier traditions or combined to make new traditions.[11] If the small collections survived, or if transitional manuscripts survived that showed the incorporation of smaller collections into the mainstream, then the historical process would be relatively easy to trace and to study. But they usually have not. What do survive are the books that *replaced* the various small collections and the transitional manuscripts, after the new material had been fully absorbed. The sequences of Notker the Stammerer, for example, were first collected by the poet into a libellus for presentation to Liutward of Vercelli in the 880s. But it was not until the middle of the tenth century that these same pieces were collected into the troper-proser which eventually came to circulate widely in German lands in the eleventh century. There was, as Michel Huglo puts it, "an enormous chronological hiatus" separating the period of original composition of liturgical materials from the periods of standardization and general diffusion, and this was as true for other kinds of liturgical materials as it was for Notker's sequences.[12]

The delayed interaction between past and present taking place within the liturgy and within liturgical sources makes the study of liturgical change difficult, and it is not surprising that liturgical changes are rarely used as evidence by modern historians of the Middle Ages.[13] There is no body of theoretical literature concerning liturgical change, no serious tradition of asking how one studies it, and what can be learned from studying it. Instead, students of the liturgy most often concern themselves with the stability of tradition, and the ways in which liturgical uses resembled those which came before them, or led up to those which came after them. This, too, is not surprising. Whenever one describes change of any sort in the Middle Ages, one must demonstrate that something has happened which is different

---

[9] Constable (1987), p. 774.

[10] For brief discussion, see "The Peculiar Character of Liturgical Manuscripts" in Vogel (1986), pp. 62–64.

[11] For a discussion of the term "libellus" and various demonstrations of its use, see Huglo (1988), pp. 64–75. One of the pioneers in the study of libelli was Niels Rasmussen, who argued that early pontificals consisted of collected libelli for separate rites. See discussion and bibliography in Vogel (1986), pp. 226–239.

[12] An outline of the stages in the diffusion of Notker's works can be found in Huglo (1988), pp. 67–68. Although the textual witnesses are early, the melodies are found only in adiastematic neumes until very late in their history. These difficulties are described at length in the early chapters of Crocker (1977).

[13] An important exception is McCormick (1987), who has both demonstrated how interpretations of imperial victory processions changed over the centuries, and attempted to read these changes as evidence for broader political attitudes.

from what came before it. Claims for innovation are not easily made for an age when a vast fund of traditional materials, from chant formulae to scriptural interpretations, were generally available and in use for centuries. Medieval liturgical texts and music, and the arts supporting and enhancing the celebration of the rites, are, to a significant degree, synthetic; they are made up of preexisting materials arranged or reintegrated in ways that appear either not very different or only somewhat different from what came before them. For this reason, it is rare to find strikingly "new" things in the Middle Ages (or at least things which appear so to us), and this is especially true of the liturgy. Certainly, there is nothing wrong with studying the Middle Ages and its liturgy from the perspective of stability and continuity. Yet without the study of the ways one generation differed from the next, admittedly a subtle and difficult task, the generations may merge too readily into single large groups, with individual distinctions lost.

Liturgies did change in major ways during the Middle Ages, and the changes were not careless, brought about merely through processes of natural and gradual attrition and augmentation (although certainly there was some of this kind of change). Because the tendency was always not to alter the liturgy, major liturgical changes were particularly significant. Understanding them will always offer essential evidence about the period which is not otherwise available. The liturgy was at the heart of the medieval religious experience: when it changed, people, particularly monks and the clergy, and their ideals had changed, too, and in some elemental way.[14] To fail to know when major liturgical changes occurred and who was responsible for them only increases the unfortunate tendency to see each generation of medieval people only as similar to those which came before and after them. In fact, the Middle Ages will not be understood, at least in so far as it was an age of faith, until the major liturgical changes which took place during its many centuries are outlined, accurately situated historically, and explained.

The study of liturgical change: four stages

This book describes a way of studying change in the medieval liturgy. Its thesis is that the creation of numerous new liturgical texts and music usually came within a fairly typical progression of events:

(1) political and religious upheaval of some sort which inspired

(2) a rethinking of traditional religious and liturgical symbols.

(3) Either simultaneously or subsequently new liturgical texts and music were created, which were slowly accepted into actual liturgical practices.

(4) Finally, if the situation warranted, a standardization of the new materials was undertaken through the preparation of new books.

According to this theory of development, new liturgical materials may well have originated only shortly after the time that scriptural exegetes and liturgical com-

---

[14] Vogel (1982), p. 340) has said, "Le point de rupture intervient quand les membres de la communauté ne se reconnaissent plus dans le même praxis."

mentators transformed political and religious ideals into new versions of traditional religious and liturgical symbols; sometimes the same generation and even the same persons were responsible both for reshaping religious symbols within their sermons and liturgical commentaries, and for new liturgical texts and music. But, as explained above, the standardization of the new texts and music and their full implementation within the liturgy was inevitably carried out later. Texts and music had to be tried, modified, rejected and accepted; new books had to be compiled, and copied out by hand. While this happened, one generation would be replaced by another, and even, most likely, another.

Thus the act of liturgical creation was most often a collective endeavor, and the vision which sustained the changes and innovations was a collective vision, each individual generation making its own, identifiable contributions to the process. Medieval liturgical texts and music, like medieval church buildings and building programs, were only rarely made with the kind of control exercised by an individual artist working over a short period of time. The modern study of every major medieval liturgical change requires a range of ideas and theories, therefore, some of which will operate only some of the time, and which will apply only to particular layers of a repertory of texts and music, for example, or to certain parts of a building, rather than to the whole. This situation rises from the very nature of liturgical development during the Middle Ages, and scholars who work with liturgical sources learn not to draw their conclusions too neatly; they come to expect exceptions to their rules. It is possible to develop a critical literature about the study of liturgical change, but the subject will demand that theories be flexible. The medieval liturgical arts, especially the texts and music, are simply not quite like non-liturgical arts, either in the ways they were recorded, or in the ways they grew, developed, and changed.[15] One can learn how to work with the medieval liturgy from studying other subjects, but, as other scholars have recognized as well, the liturgy needs methodologies and critical theories of its own.

This book, therefore, is not organized as a study of how liturgical change happened in the Middle Ages, although, as explained above, it certainly contains many ideas about this subject, and will focus upon and describe one particular change. It is rather organized as an approach to the study of liturgical change, and has five parts, each of which relates what seems to me to be the four essential stages in the study of the subject of change. Although the method of study outlined here has been tested and developed through concentration upon one repertory, the late sequences in twelfth-century France, it is offered as a general method of working, one which, with certain revisions, may be adapted for other repertories of liturgical texts and music as well. Studying how liturgical change happened and learning to interpret the change is, perhaps, best carried out first in later periods of the Middle Ages from which more evidence survives. Subsequently, one can move to the earlier periods where the sources are more scarce. The problems posed by the eleventh, the tenth, and even the ninth and eighth centuries will remain similar to

---

[15] The need for flexibility on the part of modern historians of the Middle Ages is emphasized by Morrison (1982).

those from the twelfth century: for these earlier periods, one will still have, as in the twelfth century, very few sources from the time the changes were actually happening and substantially greater numbers of manuscripts from after the time of full implementation. The challenge will always be to find ways of understanding the period of history between the original bursts of creation and inspiration and the final standardization of repertories of texts and music, and the interaction of past and present which, inevitably, took place during this time of transition.

The general subject of this study is a new style of sequence first written in great numbers in twelfth-century France; the more particular subject is the repertory of late sequences found at the Augustinian Abbey of St. Victor in Paris. These subjects lend themselves well to the study of liturgical change. First, the twelfth century itself was an age of reform and renewal. New religious orders proliferated, and monastic reforms were paralleled by the attempts of popes and church councils to bring new modes of life to the secular clergy of all ranks, from bishops and their canons to parish priests. Second, this was a time during which several repertories of liturgical texts and music either died out or were truncated and modified, and several new kinds of texts and music – rhymed offices, late sequences, versus and conductus, and some styles of polyphonic music – first flourished. Of all the new repertories of liturgical texts and music created during this fervent period, sequences are best suited for the study of liturgical change. They are the only genre of new liturgical texts and music which were written in great numbers before, during, and after the twelfth century; they were also consistently discussed by liturgical commentators during these several periods of time. They have a fuller and more continuous historical tradition, therefore, than any other kind of new liturgical piece from the twelfth century. On the one hand, sequences in the new style seem to have exemplified newness and change for some twelfth- and thirteenth-century commentators.[16] Yet, on the other hand, newer works in the genre remained tied to the traditions of the past.

These long and magnificent pieces, sung just before the reading of the Gospel at Mass, were taken up by all but the strictest of the new religious orders during the twelfth and early thirteenth centuries: canons regular, including the Premonstratensians, had them, as, eventually, did Dominicans, and some Franciscans.[17] By the first half of the thirteenth century, Benedictines, champions of the early medieval sequences, were writing late sequences too, and large repertories of them were being sung in most northern cathedrals, supplementing the repertories of early medieval sequences, some of which remained in place, some of which were removed for the sake of sequences in the new style. Although reformers in the twelfth century had a range of liturgical ideals, for the most part they sought to simplify their liturgical practices, returning in the process to earlier traditions and giving priority to Biblical texts and Gregorian chants; and although the sequence texts are non-scriptural,

---

[16] Sequences continued to be sung in some French cathedrals long after the Council of Trent. Commentary on the sequence was provided by Claude de Vert in the early eighteenth century.

[17] For discussion of the importance of the sequence to Parisian Dominicans, see Becker (1979). Even Cistercians respected them and, although not generally using them in their liturgies, sometimes wrote them: see Benton (1962) and Maître (forthcoming). Carthusians did not adapt sequences for their liturgies.

religious poetry, even a cursory study of these works would suggest that some twelfth-century reformers not only approved of the new sequences, but actually were involved in composing them or, at least, in compiling collections of them. The late sequences belong, then, both to the artistic and stylistic revolutions of the twelfth century, as well as to the movement for religious reform and liturgical renewal. This book seeks to understand which group or groups favored them first, and, most importantly, why they did so, especially given that reformers had a long history of rejecting non-scriptural texts in their liturgical practices. Why did sequences flourish anew in the twelfth century?

Stage 1

The first stage in this study of liturgical change is to consider broad differences in the language used for prayer and praise before and after the introduction of late sequences took place. One asks what was different in a general sense between the texts and music of an earlier period and those which came to replace them later on. In this initial stage of inquiry, one asks not how change happened or why, but rather simply what the nature of the change was. The tradition of studying differences between the prayers of the varied Gallican rite and those from Rome which replaced them during the eighth century serves as an example of this sort of work. Early in the twentieth century, Edmund Bishop used a small sample of Mass prefaces as representative of the essential difference in style between the sensible and sober Roman texts and the long, "slow meander" of the Gallican prefaces. Several scholars following after Bishop have expanded upon his explanation of stylistic difference, using a broader sample of texts, and music as well, but have generally held his ideas to be true.[18]

   I have begun by studying a sample of the kinds of pieces (tropes, prosulae, early sequences) which became less important in the course of the late eleventh and twelfth centuries, in comparison with a late sequence, the kind of piece which came to dominate by the close of the twelfth century. At the same time, I have placed the differences between these pieces in the context of ritual criticism, consulting discussions by medieval liturgical exegetes regarding the Alleluia of the Mass, the sequence, and the nature of praise.[19] With the shifts in religious thinking brought about by the Gregorian reform movement, one finds, not unexpectedly, a new attitude toward the church, the nature of praise, and the purpose of worship. At least some of the new texts and music created in the twelfth century speak with a liturgical voice which is different from that found in liturgical texts written in the ninth, tenth, and, early eleventh centuries; most strikingly, a style of exegesis commonplace in medieval sermons and Biblical commentaries was taken over by sequence poets for the first time. Once this difference is identified and explained in historical context, one begins to understand in a general way the nature of the

---

[18] See Bishop (1918, rpt. 1962), pp. 1–19.

[19] For discussion of the idea, see Grimes (1990). Grimes offers the following definition: "Ritual criticism is the interpretation of a rite or ritual system with a view to implicating its practice" (p. 16).

interdependence among politics, theology and the liturgical arts during the twelfth century. The new liturgical texts and music to be explored in the book, once thought to be primarily the results of changes in poetic taste – a new style of language and a concentration upon religious symbols – became part of larger concerns as well.[20]

Stage 2

The goal of the second stage in the study of liturgical change is to determine as precisely as possible the time during which the original major artistic effort took place and who was responsible. This second stage involves the study of liturgical manuscripts, always and undeniably the primary source materials for understanding liturgical change. There are, at this point in the study of liturgical change, two paths down which one may go, and both may lead to essential information and viable theories about liturgical change. One possibility is to prepare inventories of all the extant manuscripts which pertain to the problem at hand. For major repertories of liturgical texts and music, this is a vast undertaking, requiring years and even decades of a lifetime. Such studies become ends in themselves, and can be, if carefully prepared, reference books of great value. It remains possible to take another path, however, one which involves manuscript study, but of a narrower scope. Here, one examines a small but carefully selected group of manuscripts in great detail, always with certain questions in mind. This kind of analysis is well suited to the study of liturgical change because through it one may focus upon the specific paleographical concerns which are, understandably, often left out of general inventories, but which are necessary for the study of liturgical change. If the selection is well made, conclusions will be sound, and the results can then be tested through comparison with other relevant sources.

It is the second kind of manuscript study which is followed in Parts II and III of this book. Instead of studying all manuscripts of late sequences, I have chosen to study four small groups of manuscripts, each of which allows for the comparison of sequence repertories of different religious establishments, both in different regions of France and at different times during the twelfth and early thirteenth century. Through this work, one gets a view of the differing rates of change within Benedictine, Augustinian, and cathedral liturgies, and can theorize about which religious groups were most directly involved with the production of late sequences, when and where significant numbers of late sequences were first created, and how they made their way into actual liturgical practices. Through this work, I have been able to demonstrate that the Augustinian canons regular were the first great advocates for this new type of sequence, and that, of all houses of canons regular in France, the Abbey of St. Victor stands out as a major force in the creation of this repertory. Thus, the ancient appellation "Victorine sequence" is, to a certain extent,

---

[20] Older discussions of the Victorine sequences such as that of Raby (1953) have been augmented by new works which stress the wider implications of the rhyme schemes (Cunnar [1987]) and the richness of the imagistic language (Hegener [1971]).

justified here, and, for the first time, the mythic connection of this house with the genre is supported by historical facts and close manuscript study.

The connection of Augustinian canons with the late sequences of the twelfth century may well have been suspected by modern music historians of the Middle Ages, especially those who frequently consult Heinrich Husmann's catalog of manuscripts of tropes and sequences.[21] The importance of this connection has, however, apparently not previously been realized. Determining the differences among the various religious orders, and particularly among the reformed orders, is one of the greatest problems posed by the twelfth century. The late sequence repertory of the Victorines offers a unique opportunity to study the political, spiritual, and liturgical goals of the canons regular in France during the twelfth century. Study of the canons regular has rarely been undertaken with liturgical sources as a main focus because it has always been thought that canons regular merely took up the liturgies of the dioceses in which they were located, with little alteration.[22] Parts II and III of this book demonstrate that this was true only in general. Augustinian canons regular throughout France, and in other areas in Europe as well, cared especially about sequences during the twelfth century, enough to change their liturgies from those of the local cathedral in regard to this genre. Although others wrote them as well, Augustinians were the only religious group before the early thirteenth century interested in late sequences to a significant degree. The Victorine sequence repertory only serves to underscore this connection between canons and sequences, for, as has been previously recognized, they wrote their own music for a body of sequence texts which came to be found throughout Paris.[23] Thus not only the texts of the sequences, but also the music and the way the music is used, are especially to be associated with the canons regular, and with the Victorines above all other canons.

Stage 3

The third stage in the study of liturgical change has two main objectives: (1) to explore the political goals and religious ideals of the people previously identified through manuscript study as advocates of liturgical change, and (2) to study the thinkers who turned political and religious ideals into reshaped systems of religious symbolism capable of inspiring new liturgical arts. Accordingly, the third stage of study begins here with a definition of the canons regular as found in an anonymous treatise by a twelfth-century Augustinian from northern France or the Low Countries. Once the spiritual goals of the canons are understood in general, the book moves to Paris to observe the ways in which the Augustinians of this city hoped to turn their spiritual goals into political reality during the first half of the twelfth century. Here one asks how those responsible for religious art and for

---

[21] In fact, I suggested this idea in an article: see Fassler (1984).
[22] Although there is useful information regarding canons regular in King's (1955) study of liturgies of the religious orders, the only full-scale study remains that of LeFèvre (1957) on the Premonstratensians.
[23] See Husmann (1964).

shaping new liturgical texts and music fit into this society, what they struggled for in their lifetimes, and who their allies in the struggle were.

The study of the political situation is the beginning rather than the end of stage three, however. Subsequently, one must identify who facilitated the motion from political struggle and religious ideals to new religious arts and reformed liturgies. In order for political positions to become manifested in the arts, one needs thinkers who are capable of reshaping older religious symbols to represent new viewpoints. Arguments were won and lost in much of the Middle Ages through the re-creation of symbols, and indeed the symbolic mode of thought predominated at least up to the thirteenth century.[24] Even then, when formal logic, as Marcia Colish says, "effected a decisive split between reality, thought, and language," the symbolic mentality remained of major importance in some quarters and especially with thinkers of the Franciscan school.[25] The symbolic mode of thinking about things, which prevailed during most of the Middle Ages, was not less capable as a vehicle of human thought than the rational mode of thought which eventually came to replace it. But it was different. As Chenu has said so well,

> To bring symbolism into play was not to extend or supplement a previous act of the reason; it was to give primary expression to a reality which reason could not attain and which reason, even afterwards, could not conceptualize. Moreover, these symbols claimed to disclose certain intimate relationships – ranging from the psychological import of colors to the sublimated religious value of social acts or to revelations of the divine in nature – which the art of ascertaining multiform truth could not fail to take into consideration.[26]

Because political and theological arguments were made in the Middle Ages through symbols, the liturgy was a major testing ground for ideas and very often a vehicle for propaganda as well. "The art of ascertaining multiform truth" was what liturgies and liturgists always sought to achieve.[27] From its place at the juncture between the unseen past and the visible present, and between knowable human beings and an unfathomable God, the liturgy re-presented, reenacted, and, in order to do so, signified and symbolized. First, it was through the sacraments that the liturgy created a symbolic fusion of the past and the present, creating a timeless unity. Every section in the well-defined cultic celebrations of the medieval liturgy has symbolic meaning growing out of the sacraments. Secondly, as the Christian liturgy developed, the texts of the Old Testament and the New Testament were taken out of their original contexts and rearranged to illustrate the themes of Christian seasons and feasts. Thus the Bible was constantly reordered and reworked within the liturgy. This reworking was part of a larger exegetical dialogue about the

---

[24] Ladner (1979b, p. 245) says "It was one of the fundamental character traits of the early Christian and medieval mentalities that the signifying, symbolizing, and allegorizing function was anything but arbitrary or subjective; symbols were believed to represent objectively and to express faithfully various aspects of a universe that was perceived as widely and deeply meaningful." For general background, see Johan Chydenius and Constable (1990).

[25] Colish (1983), p. 5.

[26] Chenu (1968), p. 103.

[27] For expressions of multiform truth through analogy as developed in medieval literature, see Bogdanos (1983), "Introduction."

texts of Scripture and their meanings, which, like all else within the liturgy, took place between earlier and later exegetes and had to be resolved in the present. Thus the history of Biblical exegesis and the history of the liturgy are inextricably intertwined.[28] Thirdly, through its symbolic powers, the liturgy explained relationships between people, defined the powers of leadership, and represented hierarchies. Through its study, one can learn what bishops, abbots, deacons, and even secular rulers, thought of themselves and their offices, and can get some ideas of real relationships from their formalized counterparts in the liturgy.

In the fourth section of the present book, I have identified Hugh of St. Victor as the thinker in Paris whose writings served to bridge the gap between politics and religious reform on the one hand and the liturgy and religious arts on the other hand. He was a traditional thinker, deeply dependent upon Augustine and Gregory the Great and influenced by the Pseudo-Dionysius as well; yet he was also a committed reformer, having grown up in German lands during the height of the investiture controversy, and having moved to Paris as a young man to join the canons regular at St. Victor during a time of political strife in the city. Although much has been written about Hugh,[29] my approach is different from others because it discusses Hugh's attitudes toward religious art and the sacraments as the work of a reformer in the tradition of the canons regular. Thus his thought is here interpreted in terms of a quest for symbols capable of representing the reformed church, both in its diversity and its unity. He was interested not only in symbols, however, but also in the dynamic process through which humans perceived them and were transformed by them. Hugh's ideas about symbols and their perception are directly relevant to the liturgy and the sacraments, and provide an aesthetic matrix from which new religious arts could grow. In explaining the signs and sacraments of faith, Hugh followed his master, Augustine, and contributed to the emphasis upon teaching and preaching which was characteristic of the twelfth century. Hugh believed, along with Augustine, that "he is a slave to a sign who uses or worships a significant thing without knowing what it signifies."[30] For Hugh, as for Augustine, the best way to understand signs was to know their history. History, for Hugh, was not only to be read about in books, it was to be experienced in the liturgy and through representations of the church.

Stage 4

The fourth stage in the study of liturgical change is to learn how new liturgical texts and music (or, for that matter, new ceremonies or new arts created to serve the liturgy) were integrated into the ritual lives of the communities who chose to adopt them as their own. In the implementation of recently revised or created liturgical texts and music, the immediate past of an institution was reinterpreted by those who

---

[28] See Fischer (1987) for an introduction to this subject. The interaction between Biblical exegesis and the liturgy during the early medieval period is the subject of *Prophecy Mixed with Melody: From Early Christian Psalmody to Gregorian Chant* by Peter Jeffery (forthcoming).

[29] My understanding of him is indebted to the writings of Grover Zinn.

[30] *De doctrina christiana*, Book III, Chapter 9; trans. Robertson, p. 87.

either actually knew the bishops, cantors, and other officials who originally promoted reform, or had first- or second-hand stories about them. In this final stage, one observes how the new things situated historically in Stage 2 and placed in context in Stage 3 were cast into their final forms. Of course, the way this kind of study is carried out will depend upon the nature of the change and the state of the sources. Most typically, however, there will be revision and supplementation of earlier material, sometimes of such magnitude that yet a second change happens. During this stage, the "new" things were actually no longer new; they had, in their own turn, become traditional and needful of explanation. It is useful here, as well, if one can identify the generations and even the specific individuals responsible, and understand the degree to which they continued to read the writers explored in Stage 3, although this will be difficult in many cases.

The Victorine sequences are far easier to examine in this final stage than most medieval repertories of liturgical texts and music. This is, in fact, one of the most appealing things about them, and makes the operation of this repertory of special use to historians. The Victorines reset many of their original texts to new music which, in several cases, they wrote themselves, and added new texts to their repertory as well. Thus, they "changed the changes" in a striking way, and left a strong indication about the importance of the musical dimension of their sequences.

In Part V of the book, I have first explored the ways in which the texts of the sequence repertory fit into the traditional liturgy adapted from the Cathedral of Notre Dame by the Victorines, and then, more specifically, how the texts and the saints chosen for honor complemented the program of altars in the Victorine church and made a statement of Augustinian liturgical ideals. In these final four chapters, I have explained how the repertory was revised by the generations immediately after Adam, probably by Richard and, subsequently, by Godefroy of St. Victor, to become a sounding symbol of ideas found in Augustine's Rule and sermons about praise. My theories about the operation of the Victorine sequence music and the relationships between texts and music will not fit for all the sequences in the repertory, nor would one expect this to be the case. Rather there is evidence that the Victorines of the early thirteenth century had already forgotten how Adam, Richard, and Godefroy thought sequences should work within the liturgy. Later Victorines knew that sequences had been an important part of the early life of their church, so they continued to care about them; but they no longer understood exactly how and why this was true. The myth of Adam's origin, as developed by fourteenth-century Victorines, was an attempt to recapture this lost sense of the past.[31]

The interdisciplinary nature of liturgical study

In this introduction, I have described the medieval liturgy as a mediator not only between past and present, but also between human and divine, as well as between clergy and people. Through its symbolic language of representation, the liturgy

[31] See Fassler (1984).

spoke in many ways: through texts, music, ceremony, liturgical arts, all the way from the ornamented furniture and vestments to stained glass, murals, and sculptures, and the very plans of the churches themselves. Its components were always arrayed in a seemingly haphazard mixture of old things and new things, layer upon layer of texts and music, of walls upon walls, of foundations upon foundations. If the history of each of these things were known, however, they could all be explained. Each succeeding generation added to or subtracted from the whole, yet preserved the past, or sought to create an even earlier past, as best it could. Medieval churches, from small chapels to great cathedrals, were, therefore, community museums where both historical artifacts and ideas about the artifacts were ever on display. Commentaries of various sorts, within the liturgy and without, were written steadily throughout the Middle Ages to explain inconsistencies which, in their turn, had become mysteries.[32] Liturgies also manifested contemporary political situations and ecclesiastical orders of ranking: processions moved forth from the churches, and the Christian community could witness carefully arranged parades of clerics, as well as distinguished visitors, and members of the local nobility. Terrible arguments could and did erupt over the order in which the clergy of individual churches should march, for example, and processions were sometimes boycotted by churches unhappy with the place assigned to them.[33] The actions of the liturgy symbolized present as well as past realities, and through it clergy proclaimed not only who God was but who his ministers were as well.

This book is about the encounter between the old and the new which took place in the medieval liturgy: how to study it, and how to explain it. In my view, such study requires interdisciplinary effort. The liturgy provides, by its very nature, a fabric of interwoven human efforts, the various strands coming from many different directions of medieval society. When one can observe the liturgy, and particularly the changes within it, from many angles, it speaks powerfully about the age that created it. Any of us engaged in such work will be tempted to apologize for often having to leave the disciplines in which we were trained. One risks insulting the specialist with oversimplifications in one section, while losing him or her in yet another part where the material is unfamiliar and its validity cannot be judged. I once presented parts of my work to a group of medieval historians, only to discover that most of them had but little knowledge of what tropes and sequences were; I have also found that some musicologists do not understand why there has to be so much about Parisian politics and Hugh of St. Victor in a book about Victorine sequences.[34] I have tried always, in spite of the difficulties, to write for all medievalists.

[32] For discussion of the importance of unexplainable features of liturgies in creating a sense of mystery see Otto (1958), p. 65.

[33] A detailed description of an argument about the ordering of a grand procession in Paris is found in the early-sixteenth-century diary of Pierre Driart of St. Victor (*Journal*, ed. Bournon, p. 92). Driart believed the confusion to be a cause of "indevocion" for the people of the city.

[34] Kitzinger (1972) has said: "As long as the art historian confines himself to the study of stylistic interrelationships of *ateliers*, schools and individual masters, and the historian to the study of the flow of political, diplomatic and military events, there is scant likelihood of the two finding common ground."

Because the liturgy stands in both of these worlds – it is artistic; it is political and propagandistic – it forms a natural meeting ground for medievalists of all disciplines.

Thus, for example, the first section of the book is meant to serve as an introduction for those who do not usually work with liturgical texts, and particularly with tropes and sequences; much of this material will be familiar to musicologists. Yet even within these early chapters are new ideas about French sequences and the ways in which they changed during the late eleventh and twelfth centuries which may prove of interest to liturgiologists and music historians.

What matters to me is the synthesis that takes place when a liturgical change is followed through its historical trajectory into every aspect of its existence. When the final questions have been answered, one knows at last why certain saints were chosen for celebration, for example, or why particular events in their lives were emphasized; one knows why the texts were fashioned as they were and why certain exegetical themes were chosen from the common fund for special attention. One can hope, to a degree at least, to have ideas about what the music signified as well.[35] Through this kind of study, one begins to sense what the liturgy studied meant to those who sang it and reflected upon it day by day, and, therefore, to know something of the inner life of the worshipers. Through synthesis of a great many kinds of information, a liturgy (or parts of it) becomes again the personal statement of identifiable human beings and, more importantly, of particular communities. It is then that the full force of liturgical evidence, often only the property of a few specialists, becomes available to all who wish to understand the Latin Middle Ages, regardless of their particular disciplines.

[35] A pioneering study into the meanings of liturgical music for the community is Harrison (1972).

2

Liturgical commentators, within the liturgy and without

The nature of liturgical commentary

Some thirty chapters into his *Summa de ecclesiasticis officiis*, the twelfth-century Parisian master Johan Beleth began to expound upon the significance of the various parts of the Mass. At this juncture in his treatise, he paused, as if to gather strength, saying:

> Now let us speak of the ceremony of the altar; and first we must treat of the vestments of priests and of their significance, then what is called the ceremony of the Mass, what the Introit, and what the tropes. But we shall narrate the rest in order briefly and summarily. It is an arduous thing, exceeding the strength of our mediocrity.[1]

Although Beleth's "brief" exposition then occupies him for twenty chapters, his disclaimer must be taken seriously. Given the numerous sources available for the study of the history and meaning of the Mass liturgy, his discussion *is* short, and selecting the details for its presentation must have been difficult. By the twelfth century, every part of the liturgy unfolded in an atmosphere charged by the traditions of centuries. The symbolic associations were well known: a great corpus of liturgical commentary found in patristic sermon literature was read at the office and in the monastic refectory throughout the year. In the sermons of Augustine above all were found a great variety of allegorical interpretations of liturgical events; more obscure liturgical commentators from later centuries remained popular in medieval libraries as well.[2] The most important of all such commentators, the Carolingian Amalar of Metz, although condemned in the ninth century through the efforts of his enemy Agobard of Lyons, was read throughout Europe and exerted a powerful influence on the medieval understanding of the liturgy.[3] In fact, Amalar remained

---

[1] "Nunc de officio altaris dicamus et primo de sacerdotum indumentis et eorundem significatione, deinde quid officium misse, quid introitus quidue tropi nominentur, tractandum occurrit. Cetera uero per ordinem breuiter et summatim perstringemus. Res enim est ardua et modicitatis nostre uires excedens." Johan Beleth, *Summa*, ed. Douteil, Chapter 32, p. 61.

[2] Throughout the later Middle Ages, liturgical commentaries were often written for practitioners, and, in their turn, monks and clerics studied them to learn how to explain and better celebrate their liturgies. See Hoeppner (1984) for discussion of the study of liturgical commentators by religious in the fifteenth century.

[3] In the twelfth-century ordinal from St.-Jean-en-Vallée of Chartres (Paris, BN lat. 1794), for example, one finds texts from Amalar's commentary as part of the description of liturgical practice. For discussion of Amalar's disfavour in Lyons, see McKitterick (1977), pp. 148–149 and H. A. Reinhold (1972).

the most important single source for twelfth-century liturgical commentators such as Johan Beleth.

Although twelfth-century commentators followed the tradition of Amalar, assigning allegorical meanings to ceremonial action as well as to the celebrant, his attendants, the choir, and even the worshiping people, it became increasingly important to them to recreate the events of salvation history within the liturgy.[4] The church year mirrored the ages of time as well as events in the life of Christ; the hours of the day also symbolized historical events as did the structure of the Mass. Adapting these common themes to his purposes, the late-twelfth-century author (Pseudo-Hugh of St. Victor) of the *Speculum ecclesiae*, for example, assigned the various ages of history to the Office hours: matins represented the time from Adam to Moses, terce fom Moses to David, sext from David to the birth of Christ, none from the first Advent to the second coming, vespers the time of repose of souls until the last judgment, and compline the joy of eternity at the end of time.[5] The early-twelfth-century Honorius Augustodunensis drew upon the Carolingian Rabanus Maurus for his comparison of the action of the Mass to events in the life of Christ.[6]

The allegorical interpretations of liturgical commentators are often viewed suspiciously by modern students of the liturgy, many of whom have been reformers themselves in this century and have desired to free their own age from various misunderstood or misapplied medievalisms. Vogel, for example, divides liturgical sources into two categories: (1) "books actually utilized in the course of Christian worship" (liturgical books) and (2) works "that treat of divine worship" (liturgical commentaries).[7] Although he finds the second category of works useful because they "permit us to see the ongoing worship process" and are often all that survives to inform us about liturgies from the remote past,[8] he makes no suggestion that commentators affected liturgical practices, or that liturgical texts and music are often themselves commentaries upon earlier liturgical materials and ideas about them. For music historians and students of the liturgy the emphasis has always been placed upon "liturgical books properly so-called" (Vogel).[9]

No one would doubt the primacy of liturgical books for the study of the medieval liturgy. But the line dividing liturgical books from liturgical commentaries is not clearly defined, and more harm than good sometimes comes from attempting to isolate these two bodies of material from each other. In truth, the liturgical commentaries flourishing throughout the Middle Ages directly affected

---

[4] See the study of Rupert of Deutz by Kahles (1960).

[5] *Speculum ecclesiae, PL* CLXXVII, col. 346.

[6] See *Gemma anima, PL* CLXXII, cols. 571–572.

[7] See Vogel (1986), pp. 9–10.

[8] Vogel (1986), p. 10.

[9] The liturgical commentators have been neglected by modern music historians because their writings are viewed as interpretive rather than descriptive: they simply do not say enough about what happened to satisfy the empirical taste for knowing who stood where and said what (an exception to this is found in the writings of Herbert Douteil). But for the intellectual historian, they provide a feast of information regarding medieval attitudes toward various aspects of the liturgy. In addition, they constantly influenced the making of actual liturgies and liturgical art by those who followed them.

the liturgy itself, and some commentaries were written by men who also created religious texts and music, some of it designed for liturgical use.[10] For this reason, students of liturgical change need to study liturgies as found in liturgical books and in liturgical commentaries together, sifting changes in attitudes found in both, and uncovering parallels when they exist.[11]

The discussion that follows is based upon both kinds of material, commentary written within the liturgy, tropes and sequences, and the writings of liturgical commentators. It demonstrates that the ways in which the liturgical texts operate are often directly reflective of contemporary explanations of these pieces. In fact, the boundaries between liturgical texts and music and liturgical commentators were especially blurred in Frankish lands during the ninth through the twelfth century: most of the new liturgical texts and music created at this time were written as commentaries upon Gregorian chants, and served to redefine the various parts of the Mass and Office liturgies.[12] Commentators such as Amalar explained the chants of the liturgy and their meanings; the poets and musicians explained them too, and offering explanations was their main purpose. To study liturgical change in the Mass from the tenth through the twelfth centuries, then, one looks not to Gregorian chant, but rather to these sung liturgical commentaries, chants whose names are known today only to specialists: prosulae, tropes, sequences. While Gregorian chant was being standardized and transmitted in fixed, written form from at least the mid ninth century, the later ninth through the thirteenth centuries were times of great activity for poets and composers who wrote tropes and sequences.[13] It was in these works rather than in the canonical Gregorian chant that every region in Western Europe developed its own textual and musical style during this time.[14] In these later repertories specific religious communities expressed their own ideals, either by creating new works or, more commonly, by selecting and arranging works from the common fund according to their own tastes and principles.[15]

The analogy between a medieval text with its gloss, most commonly Scripture and legal texts, and Gregorian chant with its "commentary" – the prosulae, tropes, and sequences – is commonplace among music historians.[16] In this analogy, later chants such as the tropes are treated as yet another form of medieval exegesis,

---

[10] From the late eleventh century, one thinks of Bruno of Segni and Peter Damian as examples, both of whom were close associates of reforming popes. On Bruno of Segni, see Stotz (1978) and on Peter Damian, Lokrantz (1964) and the attempts of Blum (1956) to increase the number of works attributed to Peter Damien. For discussion of hymns for St. Peter written during the time of the investiture controversy, see Szövérffy (1957).

[11] One of the most successful attempts to demonstrate how the interpretations of liturgical commentators influence liturgical arts is Reynolds's (1981) analysis of the ivory covers of the Drogo Sacramentary. He argues that the sculptures were influenced by the *Ordines romani* and the commentaries of Amalar. See also Reynolds (1983).

[12] Gunilla Iversen (*Tropes*, p. 21) reveals an attitude similar to that expressed here in her discussion of Sanctus tropes: "Dans les interprétations du Sanctus faites par les Pères et répétées par les auteurs des commentaires et des expositions de la messe entre le IXe et le XIIe siècles sont présentés plusieurs aspects du chant de Sanctus qui sont sans doute d'une grande importance pour ses tropes."

[13] Levy (1987) believes that the Gregorian Mass propers were already being written down by about 800.

[14] The regional natures of these later repertories have long been recognized, although it is only recently that scholars have turned to studying the various dialects and their importances.

[15] See Robertson (1991) on late sequences at St. Denis.

[16] See most recently, for example, Yudkin (1989), pp. 206–208.

liturgical exegesis, created to comment upon the Gregorian chant (whose texts are primarily psalmodic). The simple analogy between gloss and trope needs qualification, however: exegesis within the liturgy has unique properties which separate it from all other forms of textual glosses and Biblical commentary.

(1) Because it is set within the liturgy, it is always conditioned by its place there.[17] Alleluias, for example, have a venerable history, a particular textual and musical style, and a specific function within the Mass. As will be demonstrated below, new works written to supplement an Alleluia, be they text only, melody only, or both text and music, trade upon the traditional meanings ascribed to the Alleluia at Mass.

(2) The liturgical exegesis refered to here is always a sung exegesis. The manner in which the texts unfold is shaped by the mode of performance. The music itself is ripe with meaningful associations operating on many levels, all the way from stylistic considerations to matters of specific quotations from other parts of the liturgy.[18]

(3) Most texts written to explain or expand upon the Gregorian chant have textual and musical traditions which are more variable than those of other kinds of writings.[19] The lack of fixity depends upon a variety of factors ranging from the means of transmission – oral as well as written – to the attitudes taken toward the repertories themselves.[20]

Chapters 2 and 3 of this book demonstrate what the special characteristics of liturgical exegesis outlined above mean for liturgical change during the late eleventh and twelfth centuries. The first part of this chapter analyses a trope and discusses the idea of commentary within the liturgy itself. The rest of the chapter introduces the subject of the Alleluia at Mass and explains various types of early liturgical commentary upon this chant. Because of its position within the Mass and its unique nature as a chant containing many notes but only one word in its opening and final statements, the Alleluia became the focus of an ongoing discussion about the nature of language – angelic, human and divine. From these subjects comes an explanation of medieval views of human language and its expressive powers, one which relates directly to the kinds of changes in these views which have recently been the focus of study in other fields, in communication theory and literary criticism, and in the writings of the art historian Michael Camille.[21]

For the sake of comparison, most pieces discussed in detail and presented in full in

---

17 See Iversen's (1986) discussion of the language found in ordinary tropes for an example of the importance of function as a determinant.
18 The symbolic and representational power of chants and sung commentaries is rarely discussed in modern scholarship. It was of central importance to medieval liturgical commentators for centuries.
19 Leo Treitler has written the most about this subject, viewing the writing down of each trope as the "concretization" of a particular performance. He says (1982, p. 49), "It is as though the notator, in writing down the piece, were saying 'look, this is how it goes,' just as a performer might say that before performing a piece." The unstable nature of trope texts and music and the shifting relationships between the various traditions have inspired Treitler's understanding.
20 Planchart (1988) is the most recent study of changes within the trope repertory and their significance for understanding modes of transmission, oral and written. The bibliography in this article gives an indication of the long struggle scholars have had with the subject of tropes and the relationships between the various Northern European repertories.
21 See especially the writings of Brian Stock, which have influenced the work of medievalists in several disciplines.

this chapter and in Chapters 3 and 4 – an Introit trope, a prosula, and two sequences – have been chosen from the two feasts honoring the cross, the Finding of the Cross (May 3) and the Exaltation of the Cross (September 14). Feasts of the cross came relatively late to the Roman rite and never achieved the importance in the West that they had in Jerusalem and other Eastern centers.[22] In fact, not all of the earliest manuscripts preserving Gregorian chant texts contain feasts of the cross, suggesting that they were not yet well established north of the Alps during the eighth century.[23] As is common with later feasts in the Roman rite, most texts and music of the two feasts of the cross were borrowed from elsewhere in the liturgy – in this case, from Holy Week.[24] And the few chants created by the Carolingians for these feasts, such as the Alleluia "Dulce lignum" discussed below, may well have not been significantly older than the chants belonging to some other genres under the discussion here.[25] Thus tenth- and eleventh-century tropes and other additions written for these relatively new feasts served to establish them and to provide a new context for their chants, which were often taken over from Holy Week services. The twelfth-century sequence discussed last offers a different brand of exegesis and reflects a late-eleventh- and twelfth-century fascination with the power of the cross as symbolic of the teaching, preaching Church. In this sequence, the ancient connection between the Alleluia and the chants and texts written to explain it is still present, but weakened to a significant degree. Thus the sequence, while still claiming its traditional position within the heart of the Mass liturgy, achieves an independence not found in earlier tropes and French sequences.

Exegesis within the liturgy: the tropes

Tropes, additions of both texts and music to a wide variety of preexisting chants, were written in the greatest number for the first antiphonal chant at Mass, the Introit.[26] Not only were Introit tropes the most abundant of all types, they also survived the longest of all proper tropes, enduring into the thirteenth century in some places.[27] Tropes were constructed to comment upon the given lines or sense units of preexisting chants, and thus usually were divided into readily discernible individual elements employed within well-known conventions.[28] Tropes for the

[22] See Jounel (1963), pp. 72–78. The date of May 3 was associated with the finding of the cross in Rome from the beginning of the sixth century, as attested through the legend of Judas Cyriacus. See further *BHL* I, pp. 4163–4177 and II, pp. 7022–3.

[23] See Hesbert, ed., *Antiphonale*, pp. xx and xxiv.

[24] See Jounel (1963), pp. 77–78.

[25] The idea of tropes being roughly contemporary with the chants they embellish applies particularly to ordinary tropes, as first established in detail by Crocker (1969).

[26] For explanations of the various kinds of tropes and the medieval terminology used for them, see Evans (1970), Chapter 1, and Odelman (1975).

[27] Tropes were still being sung for Mass propers (mostly for the introit) in Chartres in the thirteenth century, as will be discussed in Chapter 5; Elizabeth Teviotdale has found new evidence for interest in proper tropes in thirteenth-century England.

[28] Although tropes, along with sequences, constitute the major work of liturgical composers and poets during the ninth through the early eleventh century, the study of tropes is only now coming into its own. Major critical editions, both those of the *Corpus troporum* and editions of individual repertories, are appearing to

Introit, for example, commented on predictable divisions of the Biblical verse or verses making up the antiphon, and sometimes introduced the Psalm verse always intoned after the antiphon, as well as the Gloria patri intoned after the Psalm verse and before the repeat of the antiphon. In many cases, the repeat of the antiphon occasioned a new set of tropes. With the addition of a full complement of tropes, the introit at Mass could become an extravagant work, lasting some five to ten minutes and providing ample time for the magnificent procession of the clergy to the altar on major feasts. These were the works of the Franks, written originally to explain and contextualize the body of received Roman Mass texts imposed upon them by their kings.[29]

The trope below, as found in an early-eleventh-century source from Aquitania, is for the Introit antiphon "Nos autem," its Psalm verse, and the Gloria patri which sealed every introit in the Middle Ages, just before a repeat of the antiphon. "Nos autem," the antiphon, and "Deus misereatur," the Psalm verse, were borrowed as a unit for the feasts of the cross from their original position as the Introit and Psalm verse for the solemn Mass of Holy Tuesday.[30] The addition of this set of tropes to the Introit refashions the earlier piece entirely, situating it in the feast of the Finding of the Cross, both by trading in allusions to medieval cross legends, and through reference to descriptions of the cross in the New Testament. The opening line of the trope forms the expected introduction to the entire work, mentioning the event of the finding of the cross, and charging the faithful to sing out its praises.[31] Thus the trope reinforces the communal message of the chant text, which is a reworking of a passage from Galatians 6:14: "Mihi autem absit gloriari, nisi in cruce Domini nostri Iesu Christi: per quem mihi mundus crucifixus est, et ego mundo."[32]

As the trope unfolds, each of its lines anticipates the chant text: "cruore" occurs in the trope, just before the word "crux" in the chant; "immortality" precedes "saved" and "freed." In a change of mood, the Psalm verse pleading for mercy is introduced by a statement about Christ as victim; the Gloria patri is prefaced by communal acknowledgment that the victory of the cross is glory, and this leads back to the Pauline reference implicit in the opening of the Introit itself. Within this commentary, the familiar, formulaic Gloria patri is reinterpreted as the glory of the cross, mentioned in the Pauline source text as the only source of glory. The Introit antiphon, its Psalm verse, the Gloria patri, and the return of the antiphon are no longer a collection of disparate elements: the trope has melded them into a unified statement about the cross, and placed them in the context of the feast of the day. Old

---

replace the incomplete offerings in *AH* XLIX. For an introduction to the subject of editing tropes, See Iversen (1981) and related topics in Asztalos (1986). The classic catalog of tropes from before the *Corpus troporum* is Planchart's (1977) study and index of the tropes of Winchester.

[29] For an introduction to the function of the introit, see Arlt (1985), and my study "The Meaning of Entrance: Liturgical Commentators and the Introit Tropes," forthcoming in *Prism* and in *The Semiotics of Motion* (ed. Kathryn Ashley).

[30] See Hesbert, ed., *Antiphonale*, pp. 90–91.

[31] According to numerous sources, including Ambrose of Milan, the true cross was discovered by St. Helen, mother of the emperor Constantine, in the early fourth century. See *BHL* I, pp. 4163–4177.

[32] For a discussion of Biblical elements from Psalms and the New Testament in the Easter trope set "Dormivi Pater," see Arlt (1982), pp. 66–73.

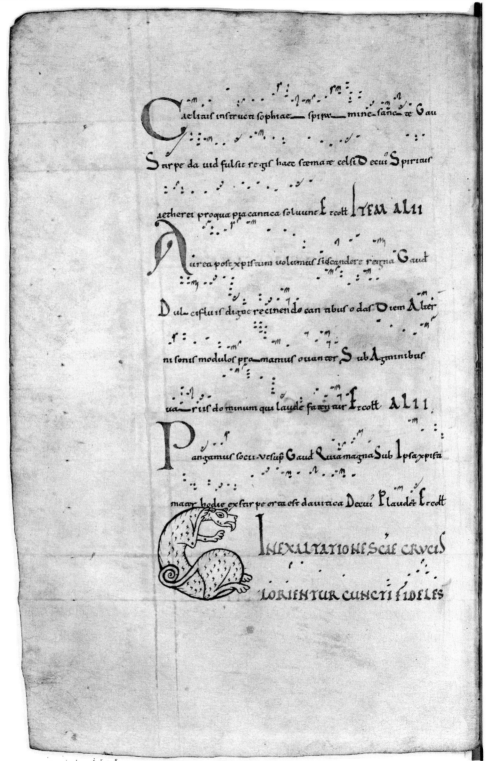

37

xpisti ininuentionis die ligni pretiosi Hosa u i neo quinos pro

prio redemit cruore Incru Cuius complexu deus pater regit

undique mundum Inquo per ipsum induit stolam immortalitatis

er quem AD PSALMVM S e ipsum offerens hostiam immacu

latam deo patri prono bis D s mistere AD GIA Gloria nos seu

crucifesi uictoria etpassur dni ianua Gloria patri Item al

G aelestem xpisti largire benedictionem prono bis fundens

in cruce sanguinem Hosauam Cum caeli pariter plaudentes esse

ministris ordinis accuncenss superis iubila........re beati Incru

Q ui summus pietate polo descendit ab alto uagit er cunis gesta

tis uir........gine matre Per quem AD OFFERENDA

Example 2.1   "Glorientur cuncti fideles," Introit trope for "Nos autem," Paris, BN lat. 1121,
fols. 36v and 37r. (The Introit itself, indicated by textual cues only in the manuscript, has been
supplied from the Aquitanian tradition, as in Paris, BN lat. 903.)

In exaltatione sanctae crucis

Ad Psalmum: Se ip-sum of----fe--rens hos-ti--am im-ma-cu----la---------tam de-o pa---tri pro no-bis.

(Psalm verse: De-----us mi-se--re-a-tur nos-tri et be-ne---di---cat no---bis ... etc.)

Ad Gloriam: Glo-ri---a nos--tra cru-cis est uic---to-------ri----a et pa--ra--dy----si ia--nu----a

Glo---ri-----a (pa-tri et fi--li---o et, ... etc.)

("Caelestem Christi," which follows, is another set of tropes; this second set is only notated at the opening in lat. 1121.)

and New Testament texts are joined, and a moment is created in which God the Father both gazes down upon the Psalmist and yet is one with the person on the cross.[33]

Text for the Introit Trope "Glorientur cuncti fideles" for the Introit "Nos autem" for Feasts of the Holy Cross, as found in Paris, BN lat. 1121, fols. 36v–37r

(Chant text in capitals)
Glorientur cuncti fideles Christi in inuentionis die ligni pretiosi NOS AUTEM GLORIARI OPORTET In eo qui nos proprio redemit cruore IN CRUCE DOMINI NOSTRI JESU CHRISTI, Cuius complexu deus pater regit undique mundum IN QUO EST SALUS, UITA, ET RESURRECTIO NOSTRA; Per ipsum induti stolam immortalitatis, PER QUEM SALVATI ET LIBERATI SUMUS. Se ipsum offerens hostiam immaculatam Deo patri pro nobis, DEUS MISEREATUR NOSTRI ET BENEDICAT NOBIS; ILLUMINET UULTUM SUUM SUPER NOS, ET MISEREATUR NOSTRI. Gloria nostra crucis est victoria et paradysi ianua, GLORIA PATRI ET FILIO ET SPIRITUI SANCTO, SICUT ERAT IN PRINCIPIO ET NUNC ET SEMPER, ET IN SECULA SECULORUM. AMEN. Glorientur, etc.

(Let all the faithful of Christ glory on the day of the finding of the precious wood BUT IT IS FITTING THAT WE GLORY in him who redeemed us by his own blood IN THE CROSS OF OUR LORD JESUS CHRIST, in whose embrace God the Father rules the world from every quarter IN WHOM IS SALVATION, LIFE, AND OUR RESURRECTION, through him we have been dressed in the cloak of immortality, THROUGH WHOM WE ARE SAVED AND DELIVERED. He offering himself, an immaculate sacrifice, to God the Father for us: MAY GOD HAVE MERCY ON US AND BLESS US; MAY HE SHINE HIS FACE UPON US; AND MAY HE HAVE MERCY ON US. Our glory of the cross is victory and the gate of paradise. GLORY BE TO THE FATHER, AND TO THE SON AND TO THE HOLY SPIRIT. AS IT WAS IN THE BEGINNING, NOW AND FOREVER, AND UNTO AGES OF AGES, AMEN. Repeat tropes and antiphon or sing the antiphon with a new set of tropes.)

[33] The history of cosmic cross symbolism is presented in Jean Daniélou (1963).

In creating this new structure, the trope authors have always linked their texts both syntactically and thematically to that of the chant so that the two appear as one unit, however rough the edges between them. The same tendency to fuse new and old may be present in the music as well.[34] But study of the music and the manuscripts in which the piece is contained demonstrates how complicated even a late and geographically contained set of trope elements such as this one can be. In the version of the trope given above, that found in Paris, BN lat. 1121, the music falls into three stylistically unified sections. The first unit of music, "Glorientur," is centered on D and is a tune with sharply articulated phrases.[35] That it is on D but the Introit chant "Nos autem" is on E is consistent with the idea that tropes were often created to form tonal contrasts to the chants they decorated.[36] The next two trope elements, "In eo" and "Cuius complexu," are very different from the opening element: their tonality is less stable and is based on E, the tonality of the Gregorian chant. In addition, these two elements are part of the same musical fabric, both employing the same notes for the final words of their texts. Yet with the fourth element, "Se ipsum," there is a return to the shape and the D tonality of the opening line. A sharp break in the trope follows, however, the last two elements both hovering around A, the central pitch of the Psalm verse and Gloria to come. Both "Se ipsum" and "Gloria nostra" have been constructed as elegant musical prefaces to the intonation formulae of the Psalm verse and Gloria patri.

The music suggests that there are at least three different levels of composition present in this trope. The neatly shaped introductory element represents one layer (perhaps an earlier one). The next three elements may have originated in a different place or at a different time, and two of them were deliberately constructed to emphasize the E mode of the chant. The introductions to the Psalm verse and the Gloria may be part of another layer, here shifting sound again so that trope and chant are even more tightly connected, both textually and musically. The layers are indicated by the state of this trope in the manuscripts as well. It is found in another Aquitanian manuscript, Paris, lat. 909, also from St. Martial. Here, however, only the first four elements are offered, with no tropes for the Psalm verse or Gloria. Instead, the Gloria patri trope "Gloria nostra" is attached to another set of tropes for the same Introit. Two versions of the "Glorientur" set were also found in manuscripts from Nevers, Paris lat. 9449 from the late eleventh century, and Paris lat. n.a.

---

[34] The relationships between the music of Introit tropes and the Gregorian chants to which they are joined are complicated. Apparently, the nature of these relationships varied from center to center and time to time. Ellen Reier has argued that cantors from Nevers deliberately chose to write music that contrasted both melodically and modally with their host chants. See Reier (1981).

[35] In fact, it appears at the beginning of other sets of introit tropes and may well be some popular formula. The study of introductory formulae in the trope melodies is only now beginning. For an introduction to the complexities of the problem see Falconer (1989).

[36] But it must be remembered that "Nos autem" was a tonally ambiguous piece, sometimes assigned to a D-scale and sometimes to an E-scale. Until recently, most scholars, including Paul Evans, held to the point of view that the trope melodies deliberately link up with those of the chant in some way. Richard Crocker and Ellen Reier, however, have argued for the deliberate musical independence of the tropes from the host chants. And Jacobsson and Treitler (1986), while claiming that tropes and chants share a common "grammar," have also argued that the styles of trope melodies and trope texts are substantially different from those of Gregorian chants. The trope repertory is very complicated and often defies generalization. More close studies of individual centers, of individual chants, are needed at the present time.

1235 from the mid twelfth. The first four elements are present in both manuscripts, but the trope elements for the Psalm verse and the Gloria patri have been used instead for the repeat of the antiphon "Nos autem" itself. Clearly, these two trope elements were received later in the Nevers tradition, and their original intention was misunderstood. Perhaps the confusion resulted because the tropes were written down and transmitted in one stage, as tropes occasionally were, without chant cues.[37]

The example above establishes two rules in working with tropes, prosulae, and sequences. First, the pieces exist in many individualized versions, and must be studied case by case. One cannot speak of the piece as if it were a fixed entity, either textually or musically. Instead one has to speak of a piece as sung at Nevers, or a piece as sung at Chartres, etc. Secondly, the force of liturgical tradition determines not only the shapes of pieces, but also the ways in which they were used. The "Glorientur" elements were fitted to the chant one way in Nevers, another way in Limoges. The Limoges version seems to work better, both textually and musically. But the Nivernais cantor who adapted these tropes for the Psalm verse and Gloria patri to the repeat of the antiphon was relying upon the traditional ordering of trope elements as he understood them. This tradition was more important than the musical and textual features of the elements themselves.

The example demonstrates some of the ways in which tropes modified texts and music of an earlier liturgy, one which was, to an extent, an imported liturgy. These later chants were changes begotten by change, yet they changed the original texts and music not by removing them or altering them, but rather by surrounding them. When proper tropes were sung, the Gregorian chants to which they were affixed were recontextualized, both in their words and in their music; at the same time, note for note and word for word, they remained in place. Because of this, the tropes for the proper of the Mass, and for the ordinary as well, developed line by line, always sung in connection with a Gregorian chant. The space in which the trope poets and composers worked was constrained and narrow, and carefully defined by liturgical function, yet this was not allowed to detract from their interpretive powers.[38]

Although later liturgical commentators mention proper tropes from time to time, a tradition of discussing them never materialized.[39] To understand them, one usually works as I have above, letting the texts and music speak for themselves about their purposes. But the second chant studied here, the Alleluia, has not only rich and diverse repertories of texts and music created to supplement it within the liturgy but also a long-standing tradition of medieval commentaries upon both its significance and the significance of its liturgical additions. Tropes for the proper of the Mass,

[37] The eleventh-century troper-proser from St. Magloire in Paris (Paris, BN lat. 13252), has a set of these elements as well. Here, the trope for the Gloria patri falls in the correct position. But the arrangement of the cues demonstrates how easily mistakes could arise. See fol. 10.
[38] This idea of amount of space and the effects of convention in the trope repertory is one I have discussed with Gunilla Iversen.
[39] For discussion of Amalar and tropes, see (Jacobsson) Jonson (1973). The conclusion advanced here is that Amalar did not talk about tropes in his writings. He did however, know about melodic additions to the Alleluia, as will be discussed below.

such as the introit trope discussed above, always remained closely attached to the Gregorian chants. Commentaries upon the Alleluia were sometimes of this type too, but the sequences were written at the close of the chant and were therefore able to occupy a large, individual space within the Mass liturgy and, eventually, to acquire a significant independence from the Alleluia.[40]

The Alleluia and its commentators

Throughout the Middle Ages, at least until the end of the thirteenth century, a musical high point of the liturgical day was surely the first half of the Mass liturgy. It was here, between the readings of the Epistle and the Gospel, that the soloists in the Roman rite poured forth from the steps of the ambo their most striking and elaborate music, the responsorial Gradual and Alleluia. It was here in some churches that an antiphon was sung on high feasts as a preface to the Gospel, and it was at this point in the service that, from the ninth century on, the sequences were sung too. The texts and music of all these chants functioned to herald the ceremonial proclaiming of the Gospel by the deacon. The music prefacing this recitation rendered praise and adoration, underscoring the common belief that the resurrected Christ was soon to be present at Mass as the Word.[41]

This musically charged place in the Mass liturgy began to develop its special character in the Latin rite in the early fourth century. It was Ambrose who introduced responsorial psalmody into the Mass in Milan, and subsequently a variety of responses developed for the people to sing in reply to the soloist, who sang the Psalm verses.[42] In the fourth-century African church of Augustine, the response "Alleluia" was sung at Mass during the fifty days after Easter.[43] This practice of singing Alleluia in the post-Paschal period was of great symbolic importance to Augustine, whose interpretations of the chant as representing the joys of paradise after the end of time were studied throughout the Middle Ages.[44]

Ecce dies isti sancti, qui post resurrectionem Domini celebrantur, significant futuram vitam post resurrectionem nostram. Sicut enim Quadragesimae dies ante Pascha significaverunt laboriosam vitam in hac aerumna mortali: sic isti dies laeti significant futuram vitam, ubi erimus cum Domino regnaturi. Vita quae significatur Quadragesima ante Pascha, modo habetur: vita quae significantur

---

[40] For discussion of the Alleluia in the Roman Easter vespers service, see Van Dijk (1969–70) and Smits van Waesberghe (1976).

[41] For a description of the reading of the Gospel in the Gallican rite, see the Pseudo-Germanus, *Expositio*, ed. Ratcliffe, Epistle II. The attempt by Mensbrugghe (1962) to attribute these letters to Germanus of Paris (†576), has been thoroughly discredited. See Cabié (1972) and Isidore of Seville, *De ecclesiasticis officiis*, ed. Lawson, p. 151*. Pseudo-Germanus quotes extensively from Isidore of Seville (†636) and therefore post-dates him.

[42] See Jeffery (1984).

[43] For a discussion of the situation in other Roman traditions at this time, see Bailey (1983), pp. 4–12.

[44] The "Alleluia" of which Augustine wrote was not the same chant as the later "Alleluia" of Gregorian chant. The actual composers of this later chant probably did not realize this and were able to use his commentaries as guides for their texts and music. For the Alleluia as Augustine knew it see James McKinnon (1990).

quinquaginta diebus post resurrectionem Domini, non habetur, sed speratur, et sperando amatur; et in ipso amore Deus qui promisit ista, laudatur, et ipsae laudes Alleluia sunt.[45]

(These holy days which are celebrated after the Resurrection of the Lord signify the life that is to come after our resurrection. For, just as the forty days before Easter symbolized the life full of suffering in this mortal period of distress, so these joyful days point to the future life where we are destined to reign with the Lord. The life which is signified by the forty days before Easter is our burden now; the life which is symbolized by the fifty days after Easter is not possessed now, but is an object of hope and is loved while it is hoped for. By that very love we praise God who promised this eternal life to us, and our praises are Alleluias.)

For Augustine, the Alleluia represented the song sung both by the angelic choirs in heaven and by worshiping Christians on earth. The idea of a liturgical music that sounds in harmony with the music of the angelic hosts is ancient and of great importance for understanding not only the Alleluia but also the commentaries upon it, both within the liturgy and without it.[46] In his book on the sequences of Notker, Wolfram von den Steinen discussed this concept under the rubric "Una voce," pointing to the several liturgical genres that regularly draw upon it in their texts and liturgical traditions: the Sanctus, the Gloria, the Alleluia, and the hymns and sequences.[47] In an embodiment of this idea that may be as old as the fourth century, the magnificent "Te Deum," the long hymn which closed the matins service in the Roman Office, unites its own praise with the numerous choirs of saints and angels.

> We praise You, O God; we acknowledge You to be the Lord.
> You, the Father everlasting, all the earth does worship.
> To you all the angels, to you the heavens, and all the powers,
> To you the cherubim and seraphim cry out without ceasing: Holy, holy, holy, Lord God
>   of hosts.
> Full are the heavens and the earth of the majesty of your glory.
> You, the glorious choir of the apostles,
> You, the admirable company of the prophets,
> You, the white-robed army of martyrs does praise.
> You, the holy Church throughout the world does confess.[48]

Although most chant traditions in the Western and Eastern rites came to have Alleluias at Mass, it is the chant of the Roman church as imported into eighth-century Gaul, the chant which is called "Gregorian" after Pope Gregory the Great, that developed the largest number of individual melodies for such pieces.[49] From the writings of a certain John, a deacon of Rome in the first half of the sixth century, we can tell that the Alleluia was an important feature of the Roman Mass by this

---

[45] Augustine, Sermon 243. *PL* XXXVIII, col. 1147. Cited in Verbraken (1976), p. 116. Translation in *Sermons*, trans. Muldowney, p. 278.

[46] This idea is part of a larger complex of beliefs about the liturgy on earth as a parallel enactment of the invisible heavenly celebration as found in Hodl (1963). Gunilla Iversen (*Tropes*, pp. 21–23) has discussed the idea as it relates to the Sanctus and its tropes.

[47] See von den Steinen (1948), Darstellungsband, pp. 94–100.

[48] Text and translation from Gaspar Lefebvre, *Saint Andrew Daily Missal* (St. Paul, Minnesota, 1945), p. 1918.

[49] One of the richest such sources is the eleventh-century Gradual, Paris, BN lat. 903; around 150 of the over 300 Alleluias found in this source have been transcribed by Amanda Burt.

time and that it was sung throughout the fifty days after Easter, as it had been in Augustine's church.[50]

It was in the late sixth century that Pope Gregory I extended the use of the Alleluia in the Roman Mass beyond the fifty days after Easter.[51] In the seventh and eighth centuries, therefore, many new Alleluias were composed for the Roman rite to fill the need created by the extension of the form beyond the original fifty-day period; what had originally been a small number of melodies increased dramatically and many early melodies were set repeatedly to different texts.[52] Several chant dialects of the Western or Latin rite, the Gregorian, the Mozarabic, the Old Roman, and the Ambrosian, contain a fairly small number of melodies for the Alleluia and use them repeatedly, seemingly because the number of times they were needed increased. Of all major chant dialects of the Latin rite, however, only the Gregorian developed numerous repertories of chants to comment upon the Alleluia within the Mass liturgy.[53]

By the ninth century, the Carolingian Alleluia, in unadorned form, was a tripartite chant, consisting of the highly melismatic Alleluia statement which has no text other than the word "Alleluia," then the verse (itself always set to a flowing, ornate chant), whose text often comes from the Psalms, and then a repeat of the Alleluia. This chant was capable of representing the sounds of the angels through its style and structure, regardless of what the original reasons for these may have been.[54] As evidence both in the texts to additions to the Alleluia and in the liturgical commentators shows, melismas (musical phrases sung without words) in the Carolingian period represented the angelic sounds of Paradise, of a place where human speech would not be necessary. In the liturgy, the way things were made came to symbolize their history and meaning.[55] As can be seen in "Alleluia dulce lignum" (as it appeared in Paris, BN lat. 903, fol. 87v), much of the piece is textless, making a sheerly musical statement through melismas sung on the final vowel "a."[56] Further, of all chant genres in the Roman rite, the Alleluia preserves the most extensive examples of phrase repetition. In "Alleluia dulce lignum" a short prosula has been created by setting words to the repeated melisma of the "Alleluia" statement, adding emphasis to this feature of the chant.[57] In addition, as in the

---

[50] See Wilmart (1933), for an edition of John's letter. His discussion of the Alleluia is in section XIII, p. 178, and the key sentence is: "Siue enim usque ad pentecosten alleluia cantetur, quod apud nos fieri manifestum est, siue alibi toto anno dicatur, laudes dei cantat ecclesia;"

[51] See Bailey (1983), pp. 15–20.

[52] The ancient practice of using the same Alleluia melody for several feasts is reflected in the fact that most Alleluia melodies for the oldest feasts of the Latin liturgy are adaptations of a small group of melodies, the most popular being "Dominus Dixit," "Dies sanctificatus," and "Excita Domine." See Apel (1958), pp. 381–382, and Wagner (1921), pp. 400ff.

[53] An excellent introduction to the Latin alleluia and its counterparts in various Eastern rites is Martimort (1970).

[54] There are, for example, chants in the Ambrosian office which have similar structures.

[55] This was true in other medieval arts as well. See, for example, Alford (1982).

[56] The geographic origin of the Alleluia "Dulce lignum" remains unknown. But its lack of stability, both musically and textually, in the eleventh century indicates a late date (probably in the tenth century). See Steiner (1969), p. 375.

[57] The text of the Alleluia verse paraphrases part of the hymn "Pange lingua," by Venantius Fortunatus, who died after 600 as Bishop of Poitiers. Stäblein (1975, p. 122), suggests that the music of "Alleluia dulce lignum" contains a quotation from the well-known tune of the "Pange lingua."

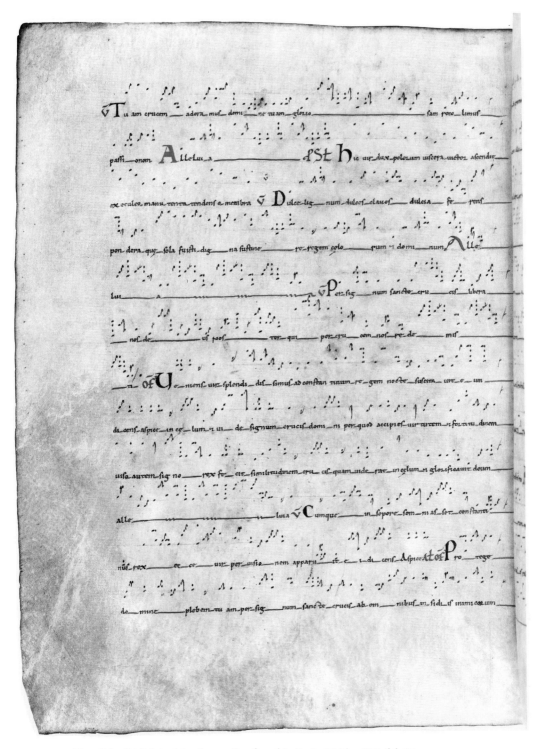

Plate 2.3   "Alleluia dulce lignum" as found in Paris, BN lat. 903, fol. 87v

majority of Alleluias, melismatic portions found in the verses are also repeated. In such music, one might imagine the angels shouting to each other as in the singing of "Sanctus" in Isaiah 6:3: "et clamabant alter ad alterum."[58] This is the song, says the unknown author from the early tenth century quoted below, particularly pleasing to God.

Deinde cantatur "Alleluia," quod ex Hebraeo in Latinum interpretatum sonat, "Laudate Deum"; nam "Allelu" dicitur, laudate: "Ia" nomen Dei est, unum ex decem nominibus, quibus vocatur Deus apud Hebraeos. "Alleluia" autem, primum in Novo Testamento additum est, dicente Joanne: "Audivi vocem in caelo dicentium: Alleluia" (Apoc. 19:6), et quia hac voce Angelos in coelo Deum laudare cognovimus, hujusmodi voce laudationis creditum est Deum delectari. Hoc quoque ideo canimus, ut eumdem Deum nos colere in terra ostendamus, qui etiam colitur ab angelis in coelo, et hoc ante lectionem evangelicam a cantore interponitur, ut laudetur ab omnibus, cuius gratia salvantur omnes . . .[59]

(Next "Alleluia" is sung, which translated from Hebrew into Latin means, "Praise God"; for "Allelu" is said for "praise"; "Ia" is the name of God, one of ten names by which God is called among the Hebrews. "Alleluia," however, was first added to the New Testament when John said: "I heard a voice of those in heaven saying: 'Alleluia'" (Apoc. 19:6), and since we know that the angels in heaven praise God with this sound, it has been believed that God is pleased with the sound of such praise. Wherefore we also sing this so that we may advertise that we on earth worship that same God who is also worshiped by the angels in heaven, and this is placed by the cantor before the Gospel reading so that He may be praised by all, by whose grace all are saved . . .)

In the company of angels: the prosula for the Alleluia

An important function of Introit tropes was to introduce the feast and its major themes, to reinterpret the texts of the Gregorian chant, the great majority of which were taken from the Psalms, in the context of Christian exegesis. All sets of Introit tropes function in the same way: the antiphonal chant was broken up and decorated, unit by unit. The second type of chant examined here, the Alleluia, has three different kinds of liturgical exegesis associated with it, and the styles of the commentaries are conditioned by the nature of the chant itself. Through these commentaries, an inherited repertory of Alleluias was refashioned to make the Alleluia at Mass a symbolic representation of the Carolingian understanding of what an Alleluia was, and to reflect a vision of Paradise as well. Thus all three types of additions to the Alleluia – prosulae, long melodies, and sequences – sought to deepen the liturgical significance of the chant as the musical manifestation of the sounds made by angels. In case after case, be they prosulae, long melodies, or sequences, additions served to make the earthly Alleluia resound with the voices of angels.[60]

Prosulae, the first of the three types of additions to the Alleluia to be considered,

---

[58] This is a matter of supposition on my part. Is. 6:3 is not used as an Alleluia verse, to my knowledge, nor is it customarily cited by liturgical commentators in discussion of the Alleluia.

[59] *Liber de divinis officiis, PL* CI, col. 1250.

[60] See Hammerstein (1962), pp. 39–47.

are even more intimately connected to their chants than are tropes. By definition, prosulae are new texts created for preexisting music, and were added to highly melismatic portions of the chant, and sometimes, as in the examples below, to entire chants. The prosulae reshape the music of the original chants for which they were created through newly imposed textual units,[61] and, in the more elaborate examples, seem to engulf the original text of the chant within a flood of new words and syllables.[62] The prosula below, "Clara et subnixa," which is by no means an extreme example in its expansion of a chant text, is an interpolation of the Alleluia "Dulce lignum" for feasts of the cross.[63] This work reflects the generally high literary quality of most prosulae, its author expanding upon the original chant text with an apparent intention not only of expounding its meaning, but also of clarifying its syntax.[64]

As mentioned above (see n. 56), the Alleluia verse "Dulce lignum" has a text modeled upon a line of the famous passion hymn "Pange lingua" by Venantius Fortunatus: "dulce lignum dulce clavo dulce pondus sustinens."[65] This line of the hymn was changed in the Alleluia verse text from "sweet wood bearing sweet weight with sweet nail" to the confusing "dulce lignum dulces clauos dulcia ferens pondera" ("sweet wood bearing sweet nails and sweet weights (accusative plural)." Through added words of the prosula, this chant text is improved: the nails are fixed to the limbs and a much-needed connective has been added. One can imagine the satisfaction such a new text might have brought to its probable creator, a Novalese cantor, who knew the original hymn and was perhaps troubled by its rough paraphrase in the chant text.[66] His work, the prosula, preserved the chant by making it part of a larger and more meaningful new piece. Yet the notes of both the Alleluia and its problematic verse remain almost the same as in the original, transformed only through the new shapes imposed upon them by the extended text.[67]

The new piece created by adding this prosula to the Alleluia "Dulce lignum" was written in double notation, that is, each line of prosula, be it for the Alleluia statements or the verse, is followed by a line of the original chant. Double notation of this kind has been a source of controversy among music historians and will be

---

[61] For an introduction to the genre as a whole, see Steiner (1969).

[62] The most extreme examples of this tendency to reset chants through prosulae are found in *Les prosules limousines*, ed. Odelman. Here the text of some Alleluia verses almost disappear, making identification of the host chants difficult.

[63] Although prosulae for alleluias were the most common, other groups include prosulae for melismas of final offertory verses, for the Kyrie, for the Gloria (in particular at the "Regnum"), and for the Sanctus (in particular at the "Hosanna"). See discussion in Marcusson *CT* II and (Jacobsson) Jonsson, *CT* I, Odelman in *CT* VI, and Iversen in *CT* VII. Gunilla Björkvall's edition in the *CT* of the offertory prosulae is now in press and is eagerly awaited by the scholarly community.

[64] See Dronke (1985), pp. 1–23.

[65] A ready edition of this hymn is found in Raby (1959), pp. 74–75.

[66] For both a brief history of the Abbey of Novalesa and a description of Oxford, Bodleian Library, Douce 222, see Leach (1986), pp. 7–15 and 47–53.

[67] Johnstone (1986) has demonstrated that the prosulae and the Alleluia melodies in Wolfenbüttel, Herzog August Bibl. Cod. Guelf. 79 Gud. lat. have been provided with melodic cues for the performer, allowing him to adapt the new text to the melody even when numbers of notes and numbers of syllables are not the same.

discussed further later in this book.[68] But here let us take the manuscript at face value and assume what seems the most likely of the several possibilities: that the piece was performed as it is laid out on the page.[69] If this were true, after each statement of the prosula (which transforms the original piece utterly) one would hear a "restoration" of the original. The piece, then, would trade upon a constant interplay between the new and the old, and the improvements found in the new text would be clear. Most important of all, separating out the two musical worlds of "Clara et subnixa" in this way would allow for a statement about the liturgical meaning of the Alleluia itself. In sections of the prosula for the two Alleluia statements, each line of text is followed by a long melisma sung on "a." Not only are the new and the old juxtaposed in these sections, but also the music of the present and the music imagined as appropriate for eternity. The texted lines, perhaps sung by the soloists, are music for humans while the untexted melismas, perhaps sung by the choir, offer glimpses of the angelic music of Paradise where no words will be necessary. Symbolically, here, just before the Gospel, the two "choirs" would offer praise together, echoing back and forth in imitation of the eternal song of heaven.

The Text of the Prosula "Clara et subnixa" as found in Oxford, Bodleian Library, Douce 222, ff. 67v–68v (the text of the Gregorian chant is in italics)

Clara et subnixa cuncta lingua   *Alleluia*
laudes tollat ad sidera grates ac praeclaras   *a* [entire line vocalized]
almo deo, qui sanguine fuso suis uiam pandit claram.   *a* [entire line vocalized]

Dulce et insigne nimis *lignum*   *Dulce lignum*
dulces clauos membris sanctis fixos   *dulce[s] clauos*
dulcia satis gerens atque   *dulcia fe-*
ferens pondera nec non commercia,   *-erens pondera*
[*o crux*] *quae sola fuisti digna* mira, inclita   [*o crux*] *quae sola fuisti digna*
dictione pacis et supernae uirtutis alma, *sustinere*   *sustinere*
regem caelorum omnium regum   *regem caelorum*
et dominum semper sobrium.   *et dominum*
Animas quas redemisti eas sedule custodi.   *um*[70]

Alme mundi   *Alleluia*
omnipotens rex aeterne,
Iesu nazarene,   *a* (entire line vocalized)
populi suscipe preces,

---

[68] How was such a piece performed? Either the soloists sang the prosula simultaneously while the choir sang the chant, or the singing was alternatim, that is, the soloists sang a line of prosula followed by a line of chant sung by the choir, etc. Simultaneous performance is advocated by a long line of scholars including Norberg (1968), pp. 58–64, Elfving (1962), pp. 252–259, and Marcusson (1979), while Kelly (1985) takes the opposing view. Although Kelly's arguments are strong, the traditions he describes are found in late sources, the great majority from after the thirteenth century. (There is, however, important evidence in the Codex Calixtinus.) In question here is a tenth- and eleventh-century practice. There is no a priori reason for thinking that only one of these ways of performing was used throughout the centuries and from region to region; in fact, it is likely that performing traditions for sequences were different east and west of the Rhine. For yet more bibliography, see Jeffery (1984).

[69] For a photograph of "Clara et subnixa" as found in Oxford, Bodleian Library, Douce 222, fols. 67v and 68r, see Stäblein (1975), p. 123, Plate 14a.

[70] The text is edited in *CT* II, p. 47.

clemens ac benigne.   *a* (entire line vocalized)

Translation of prosula text
(Let every tongue, loud and uplifted,
raise praises to the heavens and magnificent thanksgiving
to the nourishing lord, who having poured forth His blood for His own,
opens wide the shining way.
Sweet and most extraordinary wood,
ably bearing sweet nails, fixed to holy limbs,
and carrying the sweet burden, whereby we are redeemed
O Cross who alone were worthy,
celebrated in the speaking of peace,
and nurturing of the highest virtue,
to sustain the king of heavens, of all kings,
and the ever-prudent lord,
guard safely the souls which you redeemed.
Nourisher of the world
eternal, all-powerful king,
Jesus the Nazarene,
clement and benign,
hear the prayers of the people.)

A liturgical change such as that represented by "Clara et subnixa" allows for the creation of a truly new work, and for the preservation of the old, traditional piece as well. Through the new piece, too, the symbolic meaning of the Alleluia as a heavenly song rendered by humans was strengthened and made more dramatic. Liturgical changes in the Middle Ages are often of this type; it was more satisfying to keep things in a different guise rather than to abandon them completely. The Alleluia "Dulce lignum" as refashioned by the prosula is barely recognizable; simultaneously, it both remains the same and is completely changed.

3

Early medieval sequences as Alleluia commentaries

Songs with words and without

In a much-quoted passage, Amalar of Metz describes a melodic elaboration sung by the cantor after the verse of the Alleluia:

Versus Alleluia tangit cantorem interius, ut cogitet in quo debeat laudare Dominum, aut in quo laetari. Haec iubilatio, quam cantores sequentiam vocant, illum statum ad mentem nostram ducit, quando non erit necessaria locutio verborum, sed sola cogitatione mens menti monstrabit quod retinet in se.[1]

(The Alleluia verse touches the cantor inwardly, so that he considers in what way he ought to praise the Lord, or in what to rejoice. This "iubilatio," which the cantors call the sequentia, brings that condition to our mind when the speaking of words will not be necessary, but by thought alone mind will show to mind what it holds within it.)

"Sequentia" here has been identified with the kind of piece specified in the late-eighth- or early-ninth-century gradual from the Anglo-Saxon Abbey of Mount Blandin near Ghent.[2] In a final Alleluia list found in the manuscript, six of the chants are designated "cum sequentia," and Stäblein has demonstrated that all these Alleluias were indeed sung with some kind of addition in later manuscripts.[3] Over a generation after the time of Amalar's description, Notker wrote the preface to his "Liber hymnorum" and described within it the "very long melodies" and the process of setting texts to these embellishments of the Alleluia to help memorize them.[4] Thus, by the mid ninth century at least, the sort of modest pieces mentioned by Amalar and sung at the Abbey of Mount Blandin had, in some places, grown into chants of a large enough dimension to pose difficulties for choirboys.[5]

---

[1] *Liber officialis*, Book III, Chapter 16, in *Opera liturgica omnia*, ed. Hanssens, vol. II, p. 304.

[2] See Hesbert, ed., *Antiphonale*, p. 199 and Gamber, *CLLA*, pp. 504–505.

[3] Stäblein (1961), pp. 4–7. For further discussion, see Crocker (1977), pp. 392–395.

[4] This famous prologue can be found in von den Steinen (1948), pp. 8–10. The passage under discussion here reads as follows. "Cum adhuc iuvenulus essem et melodiae longissimae, saepius memoriae commendatae, instabile corculum aufugerent, coepi tacitus mecum volvere, quonam modo eas potuerim colligare." For discussion and translation, see Crocker (1977), pp. 1–15.

[5] Crocker (1977), pp. 396–397, states that no one knows what exactly happened between the late eighth century and the mid-ninth century in regard to the change in this repertory. He quotes from a later edition of

These "very long melodies" were called by several names in the Middle Ages, most importantly: "sequentiae," "melodiae," "jubili," "pneumae," and in the thirteenth century, "caudae"; in modern times, they have sometimes been called "sequelae."[6] Alleluia melismas are the most substantial group of long, textless melodies from the early Middle Ages. Usually groups of melismas formed closed sets of pieces designed for specific genres of chants (such as pneuma for Office antiphons). Melismas for the Benedicamus domino of the Office and for the Ite missa est for the Mass were borrowed from a wide range of liturgical sources.[7]

Texted versions of the "very long melodies" surely existed before the time of Notker, if his claim is true that he took the idea of adding texts to such music from someone else, and if his teacher already knew how to help him improve his ability to do so. A canon which may have been issued by a council held at Meaux in 845 indicates that cantors in both secular and monastic institutions were adding texts to the melodiae for the Alleluia by this date.

Propter inprobitatem quorundam omnino dampnabilem, qui nouitatibus delectati puritatem antiquitatis suis adinuentionibus interpolare non metuunt, statuimus, ut nullus clericorum nullusque monachorum in ymno angelico, id est Gloria in excelsis deo, et in sequentiis, quae in Alleluia sollempniter decantari solent, quaslibet compositiones, quas prosas uocant, uel ullas fictiones addere, interponere, recitare, submurmurare aut decantare presummat. Quod si fecerit, deponatur.

(On account of the utterly damnable improbity of certain ones, who, seduced by novelties, do not fear to pollute the purity of antiquity with their own added inventions, we decree that none of the clerics or of the monks presume to add, interpolate, recite, murmur, or ring forth any compositions which they call "proses" or any other contrivances in the angelic hymn, that is the "Gloria in excelsis deo," or in the sequences (melodiae) which are wont to be sung solemnly within the Alleluia. If any shall do so, let him be dismissed.)[8]

The passage appears to suggest the practice of interpolating texts into accepted chants was sometimes spontaneous and improvisational, perhaps to condemn it more readily. The idea of adding words to portions of the chant that are usually vocalized without them has long precedent in Christian tradition. In several Eastern liturgies, singers still rely upon conventional nonsense syllables to get them through

---

Amalar which separates out the discussion of the sequence, by giving it a title, and thus demonstrating a change in stature.

[6] For "caudae" see Johannes de Grocheo (c. 1300): "Et [in] alleluia additur cauda quaedam, sicut neupma in antiphonis. Et multoties loco caudae cantatur sequentia, puta cum missa celebratur cum maiori sollemnitate." (And a certain cauda is added to the Alleluia, as the neuma is added to antiphons. And frequently in place of the cauda, the sequence is sung, as when the mass is celebrated with especial solemnity.) *Quellenhandschriften,* ed. Rohloff, p. 162. For "sequelae" see Anselm Hughes (1934).

[7] See Robertson (1988).

[8] Although text may have been issued by a council held at Meaux in 845, its status remains uncertain: this particular passage does not appear in earlier documents from the council and only turns up in tenth-century recensions. It is likely, then, that this canon is a later addition. The passage was brought to the attention of music historians at two colloquia held by the *Corpus troporum* in the early 1980s. For a facsimile as found in an early tenth-century source, see *Lit Trop*, frontispiece. For a discussion of the reasons for holding the canon to be authentic and not a later interpolation, see Falconer (1989), Conclusions. Haug (1991) also believes the passage to be authentic.

long, hard-to-sing passages otherwise without texts.[9] In the West, syllables were added to melismas not only for the obvious purpose of making them easier to sing or as aids to memory, but also to comment upon the meaning of the text and music of the original chant.

The historical and musical relationships between Alleluia, melodia, and sequence have been matters of disagreement among scholars in recent years. Richard Crocker has pointed out that many sequence melodies have no known alleluiatic source and therefore argues that the creation myth of the sequences, which has been the basis of most modern scholarship, is not true:[10]

> This liturgical position, combined with the tradition of calling it *sequentia*, and also the notational practice of writing down the sequence melodies without text, as melismata, each beginning with the text "Alleluia," all projected the image of the sequence as a texted replacement for the *jubilus*; but there are too many discrepancies for the image to be believed.[11]

Although the evidence seems to be on Crocker's side in several cases, still, the "image" of what a sequence was clearly mattered to the Franks. Even when they did not model a sequence upon a particular Alleluia, they at least wanted to create the impression that they had done so:

(1) Sequences from the ninth and tenth centuries are irregular in structure and look like syllables superimposed upon preexisting melodies (which, of course, they sometimes are); the successive couplets also reflect the repeated melodic phrases common in Alleluia melodies.[12]

(2) Unlike the Notkerian sequences, the great majority of sequences written in southern France in the tenth and eleventh centuries sustain the vowel "a" of the Alleluia in the ends of their lines throughout, strengthening the illusion that these pieces are extensions of the Alleluia.

(3) Texts of early medieval sequences from the ninth, tenth, and even eleventh centuries discuss the practice of adding texts to the music of the angels, or to the sound of the organ as a consistent theme. In a typical passage, the Christmas sequence "Nato canunt" refers at the opening to singing "sillabatim."

Nato canunt omnia	(All multitudes are singing devoutly
Domino pie agmina,	to the Lord who has been born,
Sillabatim neumata	By joining the well-proportioned neumes
perstringendo organica.[13]	syllable by syllable.)[14]

---

[9] A comparison between the Byzantine teretismata and Western prosulae is made in Conomos (1974), pp. 284–286.

[10] See Crocker (1977), especially pp. 392–409. Bower (1978), on the other hand, has argued for the importance of the connection between Alleluia and sequence, and has discovered some previously unknown examples.

[11] See Crocker (1990), pp. 258–259.

[12] For this second point, see Handschin (1954) and Husmann (1956). Crocker (1977, pp. 370–379) has provided a range of aesthetic reasons for the use of "doubles" in early sequences, including the generation of more musical material to create a large-scale piece.

[13] See *AH* VII, p. 49.

[14] The traditions standing behind the words "organum" and "organicus" have been explored and summarized in Fuller (1990), pp. 489–492. She says (p. 491) "Praise 'in voce organica' is best construed as being rendered with well-tuned voices, the pitches regulated by exact mathematical proportions as demanded by 'musica,' the fundamental principles of music." For further discussion of this idea, see Reckow (1975).

(4) In the manuscripts, sequences are commonly written with an Alleluia incipit at their opening, even if the opening notes of the piece have no known relationship to a liturgical Alleluia.[15]

(5) The tradition persisted of writing out pieces in two ways, texted and untexted, probably at first because the notation of the untexted piece helped in reading the notation of the texted piece.

Clearly the design of early French sequences promoted the idea that these pieces had a particular history. The dual nature of the sequence kept the repertory joined with the Alleluia and its symbolic musical style and squarely within the context of liturgical commentaries about the Alleluia: early French sequences looked and sounded as if they were some sort of prosulae for Alleluia jubili; as if they were texts added to melodies which, in turn, were related to the Alleluia repertory. It is no wonder music historians cannot be sure where the facts of this history end and invention begins.[16] The state of the sequence melodies is sure evidence that medieval composers took liturgical myths seriously and were inspired by them in the creation of new works. Perhaps the better the sequence embodied the myth, the more successful it sounded to their ears.

The melodic embellishments for the Alleluia of the Frankish Mass and the texted versions of these embellishments are unique in the history of Latin liturgical music: no other liturgical music was written for so long and so consistently in two ways.[17] For centuries, the practice of notating dual versions of the same pieces persisted in both of the separate yet related traditions east and west of the Rhine. In East Frankish sources, the melismas were often written in the margins around the texted versions of the pieces (see Plate 3.1 below);[18] in West Frankish sources, the melodic versions were usually copied in separate fascicles, sometimes labeled with the incipit of the text (see Plates 3.2 and 3.3–3.4 below); in a few manuscripts from the eleventh and early twelfth centuries, one finds sequences written in the same kind of mixed notation used for the prosula described above in Chapter 2.[19] It is difficult to decide what to call these pieces today: in most medieval discussions and liturgical books, texted versions of the long melodies were called either "sequentiae," a name also given to the long melodies themselves, or "prosae," a name also given to the texts alone. Throughout the Middle Ages the use of these terms was variable, and the modern confusion over the proper use of "prosa" (or "prose") on the one hand, and "sequentia" (or "sequence") on the other merely reflects the medieval state of things. In the present age, French scholars usually call the texted versions "proses," and German and English scholars call them "sequences." And although some

---

[15] An extreme example of this is described in the Chartrian sources of Chapter 5.

[16] The idea that the pieces were noted in this way to promote a particular historical understanding of the Alleluia is not found in the scholarship. It is rather usually assumed that the writing down had something to do with performance practice, which, of course, it may have. The way of performing the pieces, however, may also be related to tenth-century views of what they and the Alleluia represented within the liturgy.

[17] For a small collection of plates and discussion of the notational technicalities of this practice, see Haug (1987).

[18] See Stäblein (1975), p. 185, for plates of two versions of the sequence "Congaudeant angelorum." Both show the German practice of placing the melodia in the margin, next to the texted version of the piece.

[19] See, for example, sequences in Paris, BN lat. 1119 as described in RISM, pp. 126–128. The practice of notating sequences was found at Nevers and Cambrai in the late eleventh and early twelfth centuries.

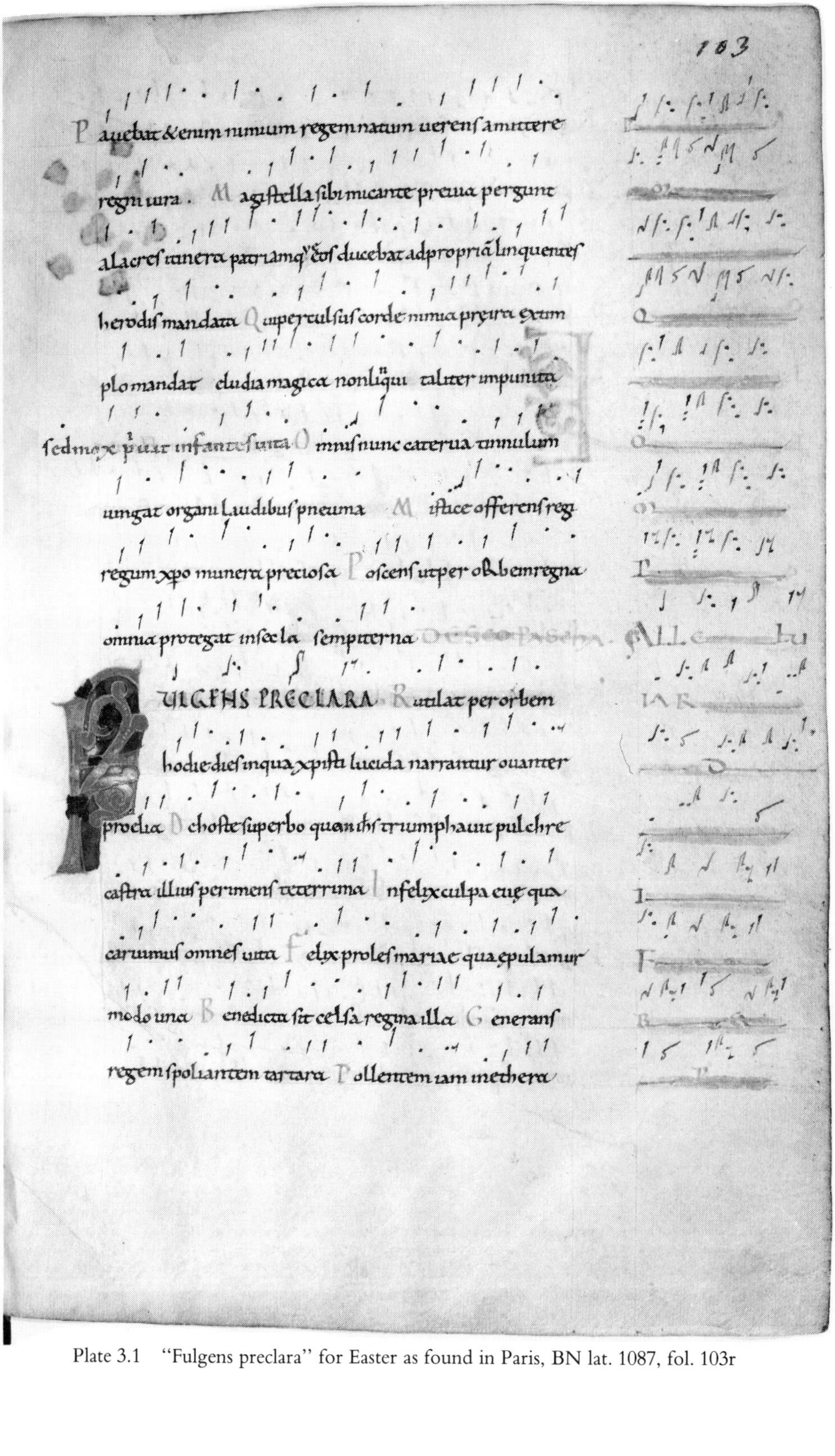

Plate 3.1   "Fulgens preclara" for Easter as found in Paris, BN lat. 1087, fol. 103r

modern scholars have advocated "prosa" for the texted versions and "sequentia" for the untexted, actually the term "prosa" was not used consistently even in French sources until after the thirteenth century. In Paris, for example, the late-twelfth-century liturgical commentator Johan Beleth said that "we call" sequentiae "prosae."[20] But in the same city and same time the Augustinian canons of St. Victor called the same type of piece "sequentia" both in their ordinal and in their customary.

It is a fact of great significance that in the ninth through the eleventh centuries both the texted and the untexted versions of a melody were often called by the same name, that is, "sequentia." But it is too confusing to call them both by the same name today. In this book, the melodic version of the piece sung at the end of the Alleluia will be called either "melodia," as it was in Paris, BN lat. 1087, an eleventh-century Gradual from Cluny, or "pneuma," as it was commonly called by liturgical commentators from the eleventh century on. A texted piece sung at the end of the Alleluia will be called a sequence, a vernacular derivative of the medieval "sequentia," and a term used in English scholarship for generations.[21]

The two traditions of a given sequence, one with text and one without, were sometimes fairly independent: the texted version and the melodic version may not always line up exactly. Plate 3.1 shows the opening of the universally popular Easter sequence "Fulgens preclara" as found in Paris, BN lat. 1087, a Cluniac gradual from the second half of the eleventh century. This is a rare example from the West of the common East Frankish practice of notating the melodiae in the margins. It is a simple matter, even for someone not practiced in working with chant notation, to find the corresponding neumes in the margin for the sequence, and realize that although the melodies are practically the same, they are "imaged" in two very different ways: in the margin, the neumes are ligated (joined) into groups (cues written under the neumes have been blotted out); in the texted sequence, the neumes are broken down into their individual components because of the syllabic character of the piece.

Explanations of praise in early French sequences

Because of its history, the early sequence in France became a place in the liturgy to explore not only the contrast between humans and angels and, particularly, between their very different modes of speech and abilities to praise God, but also the mystery of their concelebration.[22] Through these explanations, the Alleluia was better

---

[20] See Johan Beleth, *Summa*, ed. Douteil, Chapter 38, p. 69: "Deinde sequitur sequentia, quam nos 'prosam' appellamus."

[21] "Prosa" has been rejected here as a term for the texted pieces following the alleluia not only because it originally meant the texts of the pieces only, but also because it refers to the apoetic state of early sequence texts (Crocker says it derives from *prorsus oratio* meaning "straightforward discourse"). A later sequence is not a "prosa," but a "poema." For further discussion, see Odelman (1975), Richard Crocker, "prosa" in *NG*, and Evans (1970), p. 8.

[22] This attempt to study the sequence in the light of the liturgical commentators was presented in early form in my paper on the Victorine liturgy given at the International Congress for Medieval Studies, Kalamazoo

understood by those who sang it. The Pseudo-Dionysius, available in the ninth century through the translation of Eriugena and commented upon by him as well, emphasized the differences between human speech and angelic understanding:

> Now there are two reasons for creating types for the typeless, for giving shape to what is actually without shape. First, we lack the ability to be directly raised up to conceptual contemplations. We need our own upliftings that come naturally to us and which can raise before us the permitted forms of the marvelous and unformed sights. Second, it is most fitting to the mysterious passages of scripture that the sacred and hidden truth about the celestial intelligences be concealed through the inexpressible and the sacred and be inaccessible to the "hoi polloi."[23]

Peter Dronke has explored the poetic themes of Eriugena and has demonstrated parallels between aspects of Eriugena's style of writing and the heightened prose of the sequences.[24]

The understanding of language and its limitations found in early medieval French sequences is directly relevant to the ongoing dialogue between medievalists of various disciplines concerning speech and communication theory. The early medieval sequence was understood as a translation of song into speech, of the wordless into the worded, of the formless into the formed. It imposed the imagery of human utterance upon the freely expressed joy symbolized by the melody, making sound without signification signify.[25] Thus, within their calls to praise, the texts of early sequences often murmur their sounds in the strange syllables which Durandus of Mende would claim in the thirteenth century were typical of their language.[26] Sometimes the poets apologize for their efforts, for the fact that their view of Paradise is clouded by the inevitable human failure to understand the divine.[27] Sometimes the act of singing with the angels can make the singers bold, and great amounts of energy are spent explaining what it means to sing and what the music represents. Finally, the sequence is often a place either for descriptions of historic human encounters with angels described in the Bible or other sacred texts, and for presenting visions of the saints jubilating in Paradise. The early sequence presents not only angelic music, but descriptions of angels as well.

In the tradition of sequences written west of the Rhine, text after text begins with a descriptive exordium, explaining who is singing and how and why they can sing. Then a middle section justifies the act of praise in a number of conventional ways, often related to the feast or season for which a piece is written. At the end, after singing has been introduced and justified, an early French sequence commonly pleads that the praise on earth will be heard along with that of the angels. It is here, at the close, that the praisers, emboldened by their song, address God, Christ or a

---

(1981) and later in my dissertation (Fassler [1983]). The discussion presented here grows well beyond these early works, but owes them its first inspiration. A discussion which mentions some of these same points but develops them in different directions is Van Deusen (1986).

[23] *The Celestial Hierarchy*, Chapter 2; *Complete Works*, trans. Luibheid, p. 149.

[24] See Dronke (1977). Clearly, this subject demands further research.

[25] A catalog of the significance of the Alleluia and its heavenly attributes is found in the tenth-century East Frankish sequence, "Cantemus cuncti melodum," edited in *AH* LIII, pp. 60–61.

[26] See discussion of this passage below, p. 64.

[27] See further, Iversen (1985).

saint directly, and invoke the Trinity. By the end, the song becomes symbolic of unity rather than division between humans and saints.

In any season, David is a model for the human singer, the early sequences constantly using the verb "psallere" and other language evoking the Psalms. Several modern writers have developed the idea of the sequence as a kind of new Psalm, beginning with von den Steinen, who was most interested in finding a model for paired versicles through psalmody.[28] It can certainly be argued that sequence writers in the French sources rely upon David and the Psalms to justify and explain praise of God through the sequence texts, as in "In cithara dauidis" for Sundays of the year. The lyre of David, the human instrument, is that on which we sing the pneumata, in our human fashion, with texts.

In cithara	(On the lyre
dauidis citharoedi	of David the lyre-player
pulchra, rhythmica,	let us sing syllable by syllable
dulcia syllabatim modulemus	the beautiful, sweet, rhythmical,
personora,	resounding,
replicata neumata.[29]	repeating neumes.)

For all major feasts, early sequences develop models for human praise, focusing upon heavenly encounters described in the Bible. At Christmas humans can sing like the shepherds who once joined the angelic choirs and can adore like the Magi. The early-tenth-century "Christi hodierna" for Christmas takes the singer to the stable in Bethlehem.[30] There he watches with shepherds who hear the heavenly host. Subsequently, he sees with Joseph the warning angel of the dream, and Herod, the mad king, is mentioned. He now asks that "we also adore Him," the language here deliberately echoing Matthew 2:2. Thus the singer is made one with the Magi in the final statement of praise and becomes a valid member of the party present at the first Christmas:

Nos quoque	(Let us also
ipsum adoremus	adore Him
ipsumque deprecemur	and all together
simul omnes . . .[31]	implore Him . . .)

In the venerable Christmas text "Celebranda satis nobis est" the worshipers behold the choirs of angels and prophets singing on high of the birth of Christ and then are told again the story of the angel's annunciation from Luke 2. These visions of the

[28] See von den Steinen (1948), Darstellungsband, p. 134 and, most importantly, Crocker's (1977, pp. 372–376) discussion of this passage. Elfving (1962), pp. 217–217, points to several sequences with references to psalm singing. This idea of the sequence as a "new psalm" was developed extensively in von Birkner (1964) and recently discussed in Van Deusen (1986).

[29] *AH* VII, p. 256. See also Elfving (1962), p. 217. References to the cithara, to David, to Psalms, are frequent. Another beautiful example is in "Vox prophetica clara" for advent, *AH* VII, p. 29.

[30] The sequence appears first in Italian and French sources, and its precise region of origin remains a matter of speculation. See *AH* LIII, p. 28.

[31] Here as in *AH* VII, p. 42; for another edition, see *AH* LIII, pp. 25–26. The newcomer to the study of sequences might be confused by the two editions of many of the pieces found in *AH* VII and *AH* LIII. The sequences edited in *AH* VII are those found in the southern French tradition. Sequences in *AH* LIII are early sequences found in other sources, many of which are northern French, English, and East Frankish. Because

angels inspire the poet to ask for the grace of heaven for the crowd of worshipers. The melody of "Celebranda satis" was used for two other Christmas sequences and for one Epiphany text, all of which were found in southern French sources. Together, the works form a family of poems interrelated through common themes and through the use of the same melody.[32]

At Easter, humans may sing because they have been redeemed. An excellent example of this popular theme is found in "Canat omnis turba." Here the people are able to sing directly to Christ with most humble voice along with the Old Testament captives of Hell:

Illico plebs captiva	(At once the captive people,
genua	clasping
amplexans dominica,	the master's knees,
Libera jam effecta	now made free,
exclamat	cry out
voce sic humillima . . . (strophe X).[33]	thus with very humble voice . . .)[34]

In "Clara gaudia," another Easter sequence, the redeemed people sing Alleluia with the angels at the beginning and at the end. In between is a description of the redeeming power of the cross.[35]

A striking example of an angelic encounter is found in the beautiful Easter sequence "Dic nobis," a tenth-century work which may have originated in southern France or in Italy, the opening of which is translated below.[36]

I Dic nobis, quibus e terris nova	(I Tell us, (Alleluia) from which lands
II.1 Cuncto mundo nuntians gaudia II.2 Nostram rursus visitas patriam?	II You again visit our country, announcing new joys to the entire world.
III.1 Respondens placido vultu dulci voce dixit Alleluia: III.2 "Angelus mihi de Christo intimavit pia miracula."	III Responding with a peaceful coun- tenance, the Alleluia sang with a sweet voice, "The angel announced to me holy miracles concerning Christ."

many works in the southern French repertories have concordances in other regions, there is much overlap. In *AH* LIII, the editors sometimes do not supply the full text of pieces already in *AH* VII, just the lemmata.

[32] See *AH* LIII, pp. 37–38.

[33] *AH* VII, p. 59.

[34] The harrowing of hell, described in the early-fifth-century Gospel of Nicodemus, was a popular subject with poets of early French sequences. See further discussion of this subject in Chapter 13.

[35] *AH* VII, p. 66.

[36] For an evaluation of the sources, see *AH* LIII, p. 71; the sequence was also found in tenth-century manuscripts from Winchester, and continued to be sung in England and France until the sixteenth century. The melody of the sequence is also discussed in Crocker (1977), pp. 155–159.

IV.1 Resurrexisse	IV "With voice full of praise
dominum siderum	he sang that the Lord of the heavens
cecinit voce laudanda.	had risen.
IV.2 Mox ergo pennas	Therefore, at once rejoice
volucris vacuas	directing swift wings
dirigens laeta per auras	through the clear air,"
V.1 Redii,	V "I returned,
famulis ut dicam,	so that I might say to the servants
renovatam	that the Old Law
legem veterem	is made new
et novam	and that a new
regnare gratiam.	grace reigns;
V.2 Itaque	therefore,
plaudite, servuli,	applaud, you serving boys,
voce clara;	with a loud voice;
Christus hodie	today Christ
redemit	has redeemed us
nos a morte dira.	from baleful death.")

Here the Alleluia, returning after a long absence during Lent, when it was not sung, is personified and tells of its encounter with an angel who explained the Easter mystery.[37] The Alleluia is like one of the Marys coming back from the tomb on Easter morning, and its servants, the singing men and boys, are like those apostles who must be told the news.[38] In fact, the sequence is a probable source for the later work "Victime paschali laudes," usually attributed to Wipo of Burgundy (d. ca. 1050).[39] This later sequence is, of course, about Mary Magadalene's Easter morning experience, and one of its strophes begins "Dic nobis, Maria."[40] Here the common topos of humility is applied to the singers, the choirboys, who become the servants of the Alleluia in the sequence.

"Alte uox canat": an early medieval sequence for the cross

The sequence "Alte uox canat" for feasts of the cross appears in four different traditions, one from St. Martial, one from Nevers, and one from Chartres, and

---

[37] A short ceremony bidding farewell to the Alleluia at the beginning of Lent was common in Western medieval liturgies (in Eastern churches, however, the Alleluia was sung all year). See Robert (1967). The Alleluia was welcomed back at the Easter Vigil Mass. Paris, BN lat. 1138/1338 contains two sequences hailing the return of the Alleluia, "Jam turma celica" and "Alleluia hoc pium recitat"; the texts for these works are edited in *AH* VII, pp. 56 and 57, respectively.

[38] See Matthew 28, Mark 16, Luke 24, and John 20. In Matthew and Mark, one angel appears at the tomb to Mary Magdalene and the other women; in Luke and John, there are two angels.

[39] In the Norman version of "Dic nobis" as transcribed from Madrid, Bibl. M. 289 by Hiley (1981, p. 731), one finds melodic phrases which resemble several found in "Victime paschali laudes." The melody transcribed by Hiley is different from the one found in Crocker (1977) for "Dic nobis."

[40] "Victime paschali laudes" will be discussed further in Chapter 8.

finally as transmitted to Sicily by the Normans.[41] One can guess from its style that it was created in the late tenth or early eleventh century. It is not an example of the very earliest types of medieval French sequences, but rather is a piece written at a time when texts were becoming versified, and the artful prose of the ninth century and early tenth century was increasingly modified by changing tastes. Like "Victime paschali laudes," "Alte uox" contains a number of strategically positioned rhyming words and phrases linked not only through the similarities of their final vowels, but also through like accents and the same number of syllables. Yet the unusual turns of phrase found in the piece are typical of early sequences from southern France, whose particular vocabulary has been explored by Lars Elfving.[42]

The sequence below is taken from Paris, BN lat. 1121, the early-eleventh-century manuscript from the Benedictine Abbey of St. Martial in Limoges which contained the introit trope discussed above. Although this southern French version of the sequence is quite different from those found in the northern traditions, all versions trade upon the same set of images, and the piece is about singing and how one dares to sing. The opening part of the melody quotes from the Alleluia "Dulce lignum" discussed above. Anselm Hughes reports that its melismatic version was usually the entire Alleluia melody including the verse and merely sung without any text. If this were true, sequences set to this melody would resemble prosulae even more than most, but the observation will not hold for "Alte uox canat."[43]

In Paris 1121 the piece appears in two versions, as would be expected in an early-eleventh-century southern French manuscript. In the section containing melodiae, it appears without any text and is called "Alte uox canat"; in the sequence section, it appears in its texted form, as shown in Plates 3.2 and 3.3–3.4. Comparison of the melodic version of the piece with the texted version reveals that the scribe of the sequence made an error: the ultimate and penultimate sections of the melodia respectively are the penultimate and ultimate sections of the sequence. As can be seen in Plates 3.3–3.4, a correcting hand marked the sequence to indicate that the final two melodic units should be reversed to match the melodia.

The symbolic meaning of the music is the immediate subject of the text: this is the angelic song of the cross, the Alleluia of the sweet wood, here set to words for humans to sing. Perhaps the "loud voice, sweet and pure" is suggestive of a boy soloist, the person most likely to have sung the texted form of the sequence in many churches at this period of history. The choir, composed of a very small group of select singers, would then be responsible for the long melody. Whether the piece was sung by alternating parts or with both chanting at the same time cannot be said for sure, although there are enough references in tenth-century sequence texts themselves to suggest that singing alternatim at least some of the time was likely. In any case, both the "human" and the "angelic" were represented through the two versions of the piece.

[41] See *AH* 7:107. The edition in *AH* accounts for neither the Chartrian nor the Sicilian tradition. Hiley (1981, p. 761) has transcribed the piece as it occurs in the latter, following Madrid 289. His edition of Norman Sicilian sequences is forthcoming.

[42] See Elfving (1962) for parallel expositions of common words and phrases within a large body of sequences.

[43] See Anselm Hughes (1934), p. 37.

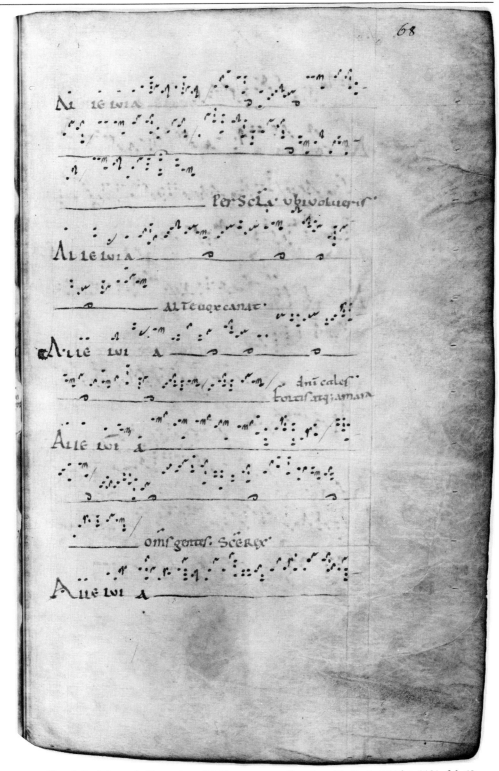

Plate 3.2 The melodic version of "Alte uox canat," as found in Paris, BN lat. 1121, fol. 68r

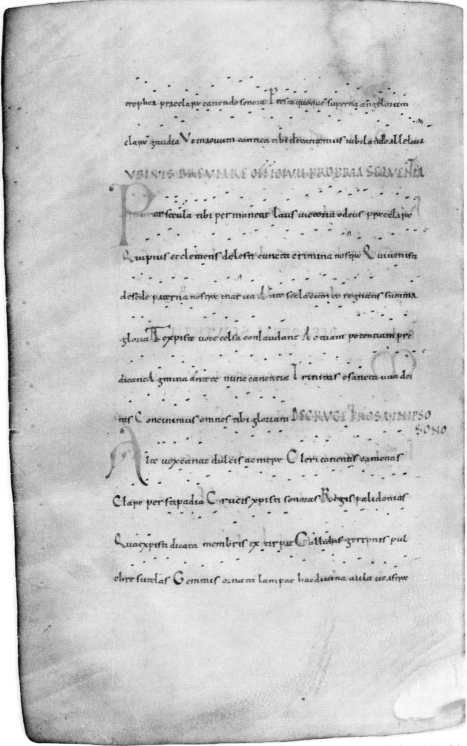

Plates 3.3–3.4   The texted version of "Alte uox canat," as found in Paris, BN lat. 1121, fols. 197v–198r

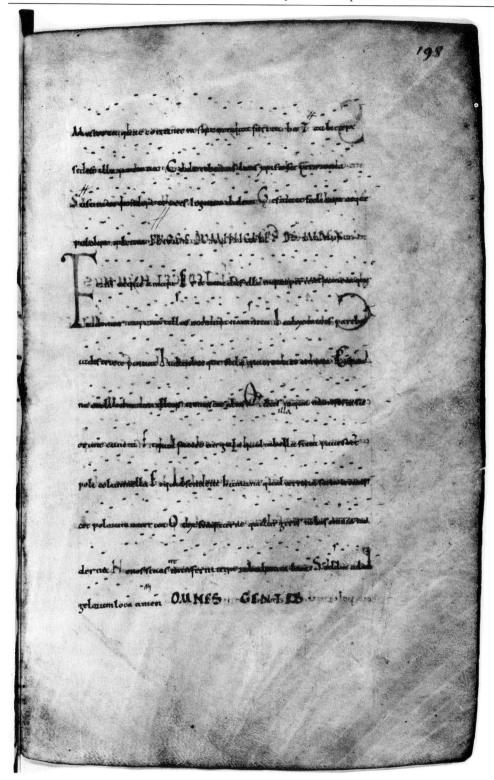

Early medieval sequences have tightly-orgnaized melodies which explore the various levels of a modal range fairly systematically. In a general overview of early French sequence melodies, Richard Crocker says:

The melodies have a clarity and purpose as yet unheard on the medieval scene. They move with strength and grace, avoiding ornamentation on one hand and recitation on the other. They range through relatively broad pitch sets to clearly prepared goals at cadence points. Perhaps the most distinctive feature is a recurrent overall shape, in which relatively shorter phrases at the beginning are gradually extended as the melody ascends into a higher register, reaching a climax in a phrase near the end, followed by a descent for a suitable conclusion. The progress of this shape is explicit: it hides nothing of its operation, but is immediately comprehensible.[44]

Several of the features described above are found in the melody "Alte uox canat" as found in Limoges in the early eleventh century. The opening single line provides the notes from which the next two melodic units are generated. These melodic phrases create the illusion of being alleluia melismas with texts added. Each is a short, repeating, easily remembered group of notes, with a sharply marked cadence of three notes – a single pitch followed by an ascent of a second onto a repeated final note. This cadence often accompanies "a" sounds at the ends of lines, even for the longer lines in the middle part of the piece, causing the phrases to be rhymed with an imagined "Alleluia."

The exploration of various pitch levels is an important feature of sequence music. At their openings, sequences are most likely to explore the middle and lower parts of the range, then they rise up higher and higher, only to descend at the very close. Sometimes, however, as in "Alte uox canat," sequence melodies remain elevated and do not descend to the expected *finalis* of the mode, a situation which defies the commonplace among medieval theorists that chants should end on the *finalis* implied by the opening mode of the piece.[45] When this happens, the final note of the piece is usually a fifth above the *finalis* of the opening scale. Such is the case with "Alte uox canat," which begins in G-plagal, as does the chant "Alleluia dulce lignum," after which the opening is modeled. Interest focuses in the first two lines upon notes the fourth and fifth above g, c' in line 1, and d' in line 2. At "Quae christi" (unit 4), the music begins to shift upwards, but the transition is gradual and makes for an apparent tension in the music, at least to the modern ear. Line 5 centers around d' and the fourth above it, but cadences avoid "finals" and mediant notes, preventing a sense of tonal rest. The upper part of this melody explores the fourth from d' to g', the very notes outlined by the opening leap of the melody in line 1, only an octave higher. Technically, with a final of d' and a range of d' (ornamented by a lower neighbor of c') to g', the second half of the piece is in the D-mode, but with the emphasis upon the fourth between d' and g', it sounds rooted in the G-scale, and one could believe it were the lower fourth of the plagal G-scale

---

[44] See Crocker (1990), pp. 257–258.

[45] The "final" or "finalis" of a mode is the note around which the scale is centered and the note upon which convention decrees the piece should close. For a brief explanation of the church modes see the article "Mode" in *The New Harvard Dictionary of Music*, ed. Don M. Randel (Cambridge, Mass., 1986), pp. 499–501; for fuller discussion see "Mode" by Harold Powers in *NG*.

transposed up an octave. What is one to make of music which defies theoretical rules and behaves in a fashion untypical of most other categories of chants?[46]

This convention of ending a piece a fifth above the final of the opening mode may be yet another way of invoking the common idea of angels and humans singing in consort. There is some reason to suspect that the two ranges of pitch symbolize the two choirs, one on earth and the other in heaven, or at least the convention may have come to be interpreted in this way.[47] The sequence "Ave stella gloriosa," which is discussed further in Chapter 5, contains a description of two choirs: one sings the tetrachord of a scale and the other the pentachord, and together they form the ringing octave of the entire scale.[48] In such a musical analogy, the angels are undoubtedly represented by the high part of the range, and to remain on high at the end of the piece would draw the singers closely to the heavenly experience the early sequences constantly describe.

From "Ave stella gloriosa," middle strophes[49]

Celica et terrea	(Things of heaven and earth,
plaudite symphonia	Clap, and let
plaudat et canora,	the tuneful concord clap,
Hymnizet nectarea	Let it sing in hymns
diatessaron sua	Its nectared fourth
diapente juncta.	With the fifth joining.
Diapason clara	Clear octave
ex his facta	made from these,
surge tinnula	Ascend, ringing,
Dulcis melodia	Sweet melody
et suavis	and pleasant,
ede carmina.	Utter your songs.

Text of "Alte uox canat," sequence for the Cross, as found in Paris, BN lat. 1121, fols. 197v–198r

I Alte uox canat	I–IV Let a sweet and pure voice
dulcis ac mera	sing loudly
II Cleri canentis camenas	through the songs of the singing clergy
Clara per stipendia	chanting with the bright throng
III Crucis christi sonoras	the sonorous carols
Regis palinodias.	of the cross of Christ the King
IV Quae christi dicata membris	which, dedicated to the limbs of Christ,
exstirpat	splendidly roots out the crafty tricks of the idler.
Callidas gerronis pulchre sutelas.	

---

[46] Crocker (1977, pp. 172–173) discusses this phenomenon, saying, in regard to "Congaudent angelorum," "It seems to me that the composer wanted his melody to end higher than it began, with a clear sense of rise to a new region, yet with enough finality for completeness."

[47] How or why it actually began remains unclear at the present time.

[48] See p. 108.

[49] See *AH* IX, p. 165.

Example 3.1   Melody of "Alte uox canat," sequence for the Cross, as found in Paris, BN lat. 1121, fols. 197v–198r

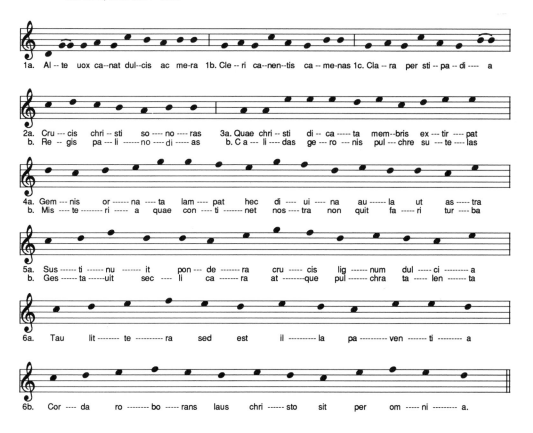

V   Gemmis ornata lampat hec divina aula ut astra.

Mysteria quae continet nostra non quit fari turba.

VI   Sustinuit pondera crucis lignum dulcia

Gestauit secli cara atque pulchra talenta.

VII   Tau litera sed est illa paventia

Corda roborans laus christo sit per omnia.

V–VII   Decorated with jewels this divine court shines like the stars.

The mysteries which it contains our crowd is not able to speak.

The wood of the cross sustained the sweet weight

And bore the dear and beautiful gold of the age.

But Tau is the letter strengthening trembling hearts;

Let there be praise to Christ through all things.)

The well-defined position of the sequence in the Mass liturgy and its dual nature as both an untexted and a texted piece allow for a compressed use of images in early medieval sequences. Although there are frequent illusions to Old Testament types and figures, there is no apparent desire to establish a narrative sequence of events or to relate a history through the typology, as found in some sermons and scriptural commentaries from this period and earlier. Instead this piece, like so many other southern French sequences from the tenth century, allows blinding glimpses of heavenly splendor, but from behind a screen of pleading. In "Alte uox canat" an exordium introduces the singers and the cross with its Devil-defeating powers. But then, in an abrupt switch, the cross is established in the bejeweled court of the heavenly Jerusalem.[50] With this image, the cross would become to all learned men and women the throne of the Lamb, adored by those marked with His name:

The throne of God and of the Lamb will be in the city; His servants will worship Him, they will see him face to face, and His name will be written on their foreheads. (Apoc. 22:3–5)

And then the mortal song of the sequence is brought face to face with its condition. "Our throng" (as opposed to the angelic throng) is not able to give utterance to these mysteries. We come to the door of Paradise, but we cannot enter, we cannot sing with the angels. As in so many early French sequences, the dilemma is about how to praise and how one dares to raise the voice heavenward.

Here resolution is achieved through the "litera," Tau, the cross-shaped letter or sign that empowers mortal praise. Through it, mortal speech is liberated and humans are saved, daring here to add a final strain to the heavenly song. The tau represents that sign marking the heavenly host, the angels who already can sing. The "sign" written on the foreheads of the elect was, according to Jerome's rendering of a parallel passage in Ezechiel, the sign of the cross.[51] "The letter" opens the way for human speech, for praise, for human mingling with the divine.

The movement of the piece is the same as that of so many other early French sequences: after an introduction of angels and humans, a dilemma of separation is introduced; this is solved, usually by reference to Christ as both God and man or through the description of the angels or angelic encounters; then final praise or pleas are offered. The theme of separation, of the gulf between the human and the divine, is, of course, underscored by the music with its two sonic worlds. The single line closing many sequences reflects the unity of praise so commonly achieved at the end.

The antepenultimate couplet of "Alte uox" in Paris lat. 1121 appears in none of the northern versions, which end with a single statement of praise. The couplet is a paraphrase of a line in Fortunatus' hymn discussed above and may have been added to a slightly earlier tradition of the piece. The groups of paired lines form the kind of couplet structure typical of the later sequence, which eschewed single lines throughout. The northern sources suggest that "Alte uox" originally ended with a single line, "Laus Christo sit per omnia" (or a variation thereof), rather than the more modern couplet. The piece as it survives in lat. 1121 reflects the kinds of changing taking place in Aquitanian sequence poetry during the early eleventh century.[52]

The version of "Alte uox canat" in lat. 1121, the manuscript containing writings

---

[50] The twelve walls of the city are each made of a different precious stone, and each has a gate of pearl. See Apoc. [Rev.] 21:15–21.

[51] The seal on the foreheads of the saints is mentioned in Apoc. [Rev.] 7:3 as well, but the source is Ezechiel 9:4: "He called to the man dressed in linen with a scribe's ink-horn in his belt and Yahweh said to him, 'Go all through the city, all through Jerusalem, and mark a cross on the foreheads of all who grieve and lament over all the loathsome practices in it.'"

[52] See also discussion of "Summa culmina" for St. Peter in Chapter 6.

of Adémar of Chabannes, is several decades earlier than that found in Nevers, lat. 9449 from the 1060s.[53] Moreover, it does not appear in the other Aquitanian sources edited by Dreves in *AH* VII, nor is it found in lat. n.a. 1871 from Moissac. In fact, this sequence may have been written at St. Martial, perhaps even by Adémar of Chabannes himself. A legend found in a later chronicle describes his miraculous vision of a fiery cross seen against the sky, a representation of the bejeweled cross of Jerusalem.[54] Adémar was inspired, perhaps by his vision, to make the pilgrimage to Jerusalem, where he died in 1034.[55] It was during his lifetime that Bishop Fulbert of Chartres maintained a close relationship with Duke William V of Aquitaine, and the piece may have migrated between the two centers at this time.[56] As the melodic traditions are very different, it probably circulated first as text alone. The sequence repertory of Chartres Cathedral was very conservative, and may have remained as Fulbert and his students designed it for several decades after his death; thus the piece was more likely to be revised in a southern tradition.[57]

There were many repertories of early sequences written in the ninth through the late eleventh centuries; all major geographical areas in Western Europe had them during these centuries (although the Iberian peninsula, where the Mozarabic liturgy was retained until the late eleventh century, had far fewer than other areas). Here I have explained the central purpose of early medieval sequences from France within the Mass liturgy, and demonstrated how an early sequence in this particular tradition made its meaning.[58] In the process of seeking a general statement about early sequences, I have had to ignore many issues: by concentrating upon French sources, I have not discussed the great differences between individual repertories, nor have I taken time to demonstrate that even within the French sources one finds significant examples of change during this period of time. In Chapters 5 and 6 it will be possible to turn briefly to sequences which were written later in the eleventh century but which grow out of this tradition, and show how change was taking place then as well.

Without this understanding of early medieval French sequences for a point of contrast, however, it would be difficult to say what is "new" about the repertories written in the twelfth century and what made them different from their ancestors written primarily during the tenth and eleventh centuries. These early sequences were, to quote a title of a well-known book, "Songs of Glory," and, like the Romanesque architecture they enhanced and perhaps helped to inspire, focused almost entirely on the mystery of angelic praise.[59] They made their meanings by invoking the heavenly hosts, and never strayed far from the early ideal of commen-

---

[53] This manuscript is mentioned below in Chapter 5.
[54] See Dup.-Ag., p. 47.
[55] The iconography of the jeweled cross of Jerusalem during the Middle Ages is explored in Novelli (1987).
[56] See descriptions of the letters written between Fulbert and the duke in Behrends (1976), pp. lxxxii–xc.
[57] See Chapter 5 for discussion of sources from Chartres.
[58] Bibliography on the early French sequence is sparse. There were no famous poets such as Notker from the tenth and eleventh centuries to draw attention to the repertories written here.
[59] The façade of the church at Angoulême as described by Seidel seems a fitting counterpart for the liturgical themes developed within the southern French sequence repertory. See Seidel (1981), p. 40 and Figure 42.

ting upon the significance of the Alleluia. Although in concept the sequences remained "tropes" for Alleluias, at the same time they carved out a unique position within the Mass liturgy and, unlike tropes and prosulae, came to function independently from the chants with which they were originally associated.

4

An introduction to the twelfth-century sequence

Liturgical commentators and the late sequences

In Book XVI of *The City of God*, Augustine discusses the contrasting ways God speaks to angels and to humans:

And God does not speak to the angels in the same way as we speak to one another, or to God, or to the angels, or as the angels speak to us. He speaks in His own fashion, which is beyond our describing. But His speech is explained to us in our fashion.

Early medieval sequences written in what is now France were most often statements about the angelic "speech" of their music, whose mode of communication was believed superior to that of the texts themselves.[1] In these repertories, texts are magnificently wrought shades, placed for human convenience over the dazzling expressivity of the melodies. Through these texts one imagines angelic hosts and Paradise, and sometimes confronts them directly in most dramatic ways. But late sequences, those first written in significant numbers during the twelfth century, acknowledge along with Augustine that God has a special speech for humans, and that this speech is offered in our own terms. Although God speaks to the angels in ways "beyond our describing," he also addresses us in a language deliberately designed for mortal ears and minds, a language fashioned from the signs and symbols of Scripture. Twelfth-century sequences attempt to talk in this tongue, using the Old Testament typology so often found in sermons and exegesis of the church fathers, but here adapting it for the purpose of praise. Not only is the language of these sequences different from that of the early medieval French sequence; their subjects too have changed. These sequences create histories through the use of typology, but as will be seen below, the histories are of a certain type. Here the kind of scriptural exegesis found in twelfth-century sequences will be studied in two ways, first through liturgical commentators who wrote about

---

[1] For further juxtapositions of divine and human speech, see Resnick (1990). This generalization does not hold as well for the Notkerian sequence, however. The comparative richness of Notker's texts is readily seen in Stäblein's (1964) discussion of the several settings of one popular sequence melody.

sequences, and secondly through the example of the most beloved of all late sequences written in the twelfth century, "Laudes crucis attollamus."

Although the allegorical style of Amalar of Metz was very popular in the writings of twelfth-century liturgical commentators, there are essential ways in which these later works differ from comparable ninth-century treatises. The watershed in the tradition was the eleventh century, and the change was caused by the Gregorian reform movement. It was during the late eleventh and early twelfth centuries, a period when secular rulers were struggling to consolidate ever larger power bases, that the Roman church too felt driven to unify its own wealth and property, and to strengthen its ability to govern the institutions beholden to it.[2] The political goals of this particular reform were many and varied, and not all of them will be discussed here; in chapter 9 there will be a description of one branch of reformers from a particular region, the canons regular in northern France. For now, let it suffice to say that liturgical commentaries written after the late eleventh century were marked by an increasing desire to teach the clergy how to use the liturgy effectively within their churches and to understand the importance of their roles as part of a strong, newly unified ecclesiastical hierarchy. Mary Schaefer has traced the changing relationship between priest and Christ and priest and people in the liturgical commentators, finding differences in the twelfth century between Benedictine/monastic commentators and what she calls "scholastic" commentators. In her view, a Benedictine such as the early-twelfth-century Rupert of Deutz would "cling to the 'old' patristic formulations of the mystery-dimension of the Mass, the direct activity of Christ as liturgist of the Mass, and the integral participation of the faithful in the co-offering of the sacrifice with the priest."[3] But in "scholastic" treatises from the twelfth century, works such as the late-twelfth-century liturgical commentary by the Premonstratensian Richard of Wedinghauser, the Mass is explained "as a means of the priest's obtaining grace."[4] Schaefer claims a sub-group is formed by Ivo of Chartres, Hildebert of Lavardin, Pseudo-Alger of Liège, and Issac of Stella, who place emphasis on "the Mass as commemoration of the Cross."[5] But there were other writers in the twelfth century who seem strongly tied to the cross and its symbolic centrality to the Mass liturgy and, surely, Richard of Wedinghauser must be included among them.[6] Later, in the thirteenth century, the high scholastic commentators do their work, creating repositories of liturgical allegory, the most famous and important of which is the *Rationale divinorum officiorum* of Durandus of Mende. Here the Mass is the official act of the priest, who has been "deputed by ordination to consecrate and to offer sacrifice on behalf of the people."[7]

One of the first liturgical commentaries written under the influence of the

---

[2] See Yves Congar (1983).

[3] Schaefer (1982–83), p. 78.

[4] Schaefer (1982–83), p. 80.

[5] Schaefer (1982–83), p. 81.

[6] "Virtus missae, crux Christi est, quae sacramentum altaris et omnis Ecclesiae sacramenta consecrat et sanctificat." *Liber de canone mystici libaminis*, col. 459.

[7] Schaefer (1982–83), p. 81.

Gregorian reform movement is the *Micrologus* of Bernold of Constance (†1100), which may date from around 1089. In his description of the readings at Mass and the chants between them, Bernold fixes upon the deacon, stating that he reads the Gospel even though he is not a priest. Of course, the deacon was ordained to his particular office and invested with its symbols, as were each of the minor and major orders.[8] But for Bernold, it would be better if the priest read the Gospel for the deacon rather than the other way around.[9] The act of ordination comes up time and again in this passage: Bernold warns that only those specifically ordained for the purpose ought to sing from the pulpitum, sing the Alleluia, and read in church.[10] As the liturgy is a vehicle designed for hierarchically ordered clerics to use in their work, Bernold seeks to protect it from the unordained. One assumes Bernold wanted the clergy to be present in their communities, singing their offices themselves, and not giving them over to vicars to serve in their steads. His attitude toward the laity and especially toward women is also emblematic of a church then seeking to rid itself of lay influence and to abolish the common practice of clerical marriage. Priests, the reformers believed, could best function if they were celibate and beholden to ecclesiastical powers alone.[11]

Although Bernold is more strident and legalistic than many writers on the liturgy, his attitudes often coincide with those of the new type of commentators found in the centuries immediately after him. The intention of the reform movement, was, of course, not only to make the church more powerful in a secular sense. It was also to make it more effective in the salvation of souls. And along with this desire came a new belief in the power of its liturgical voice. Here was a church reborn, a church that could speak once again with the force of the Apostles. One can trace these developments through commentators from the twelfth and thirteenth centuries and their changing understanding of the purpose of the sequence within the Mass liturgy. The interpretations are part of a focus upon history and the ability of the liturgy both to explain and to depict this history, especially the history of liturgical events, of priestly offices, and of the sacraments.

Commentators before the twelfth century speak of the musical addition to the Alleluia only, usually calling it the pneuma. John of Avranches, Bishop of Rouen (†1079) is content to cite Amalar's discussion when he speaks of the pneuma,[12] and Bruno of Segni (†1123) does not mention it at all. But the mid-century Honorius Augustodunensis, the most prolific of all twelfth-century liturgical commentators, has much more to say.[13] His cantors are not soloists who sang the pneuma by themselves, like those of Amalar and subsequently of John of Avranches. These are rather "the apostles who taught the churches the praise of God."[14] Those singing the

---

[8] For an authoritative discussion, see "Ordination, Clerical," by Roger Reynolds in the *DMA*. The bibliography includes references to several of his articles and his book (1978) on the subject.

[9] Bernold of Constance, *Micrologus*, col. 982.

[10] *Ibid.*

[11] See Barstow (1982).

[12] John of Avranches, *De officiis ecclesiasticis, PL* CXLVII, col. 54.

[13] The identity of Honorius remains a problem. For recent views, see Flint (1982), Garrigues (1983) and Crouse (1987).

[14] *Gemma animae*, col. 549.

gradual signify those serving Christ in the active life; those singing the Alleluia represent participants in the contemplative life. But "the choirs will jubilate the sequence alternatim because great numbers of angels and humans will praise the Lord in the house of God for all eternity."[15] If one looks at his other discussions of this chant, it is difficult to tell whether Honorius means a texted or an untexted work.[16] But whatever the case, he thinks of this "sequentia" differently from the way Amalar thought of it. For Honorius, this is a choir piece rather than one for a soloist, and is sung antiphonally, the choirs answering each other back and forth to represent the jubilation of mortals and angels at the end of time. And although the Alleluia represents the joy of angels, the sequence represents the time when mortals will see the face of God.[17]

The writings of Honorius mark a kind of turning point in commentaries on the sequence; in the late twelfth and thirteenth centuries, writers have much more to say about it than in earlier centuries. Clearly the genre has achieved some new and loftier status. Johan Beleth, for example, provides a short history of the sequence, mentioning Notker and Hermannus Contractus and stating that Pope Nicholas (undoubtedly Nicholas I, a ninth-century pope) gave the genre official sanction.[18] The *Speculum ecclesiae*, an anonymous work from the second half of the twelfth century, breathes with the spirit of Victorine mysticism (it was once ascribed to Hugh of St. Victor), all the while emphasizing the role of the clergy as ministers to the people.[19] Here the deacon and the subdeacon walk before the priest at Mass because they represent the prelates of the Church who prepare the way of the Lord. Since the time of Bernold of Constance, there is a new respect for the subdeacons and deacons and their offices. In its lengthy commentary on the chants before the Gospel, one finds a significant change of attitude toward sequences as well. Because themes and modes of expression found here will be important later in this book, the passage is quoted in full.

Hoc ergo gaudium quia nec penitus verbis exprimi, nec penitus taceri potest, Ecclesia quasi demissis verbis jubilando quasi in admirationem prosilit, ac si dicat: Quae vox, quae poterit lingua retexere, etc. Hic enim verba non sufficiunt nec intellectus, nec tamen amor sinit tacere. Sic ergo Ecclesia pneumatizando, dictu mirabile, expressius quodam modo et melius sine verbis quam per verba innuit quantum sit gaudium Dei ubi verba cessabunt. Per pneuma enim, licet non enarretur quantum sit aeternum gaudium, saltem monstratur ipsum esse inenarrabile. Quando autem sequentia sequitur, posterius Alleluia non habet Pneuma, sed chorus in loco ejus sequentiam concinit, quae idem significat, id est aeternae vitae gaudium atque delicias. Unde illa nova solet habere verba et inusitata, quia coeli gaudium secretum est et incognitum mortalibus. Vel sequentia aeternae vitae mysticat laudes. Unde dictum est: "Beati qui habitant in domo tua, Domine, in

[15] "Sequentiam chori alternatim jubilabunt, quia frequentiae angelorum et hominum in domo Dei Dominum in saeculum saeculi laudabunt." (*Ibid.*)

[16] In his *Sacramentarium* Honorius says, "Sequentia ideo dicitur, quia neumam jubili sequitur." But then, "Sequentia ideo jubilamus, quia faciem Domini in jubilo videbimus." (col. 575) Elsewhere in the *Sacramentarium* he says, "Jubilatio, quae sequentia vocatur, significat illum statum, dum necessaria non erit locutio verborum; sed sola cogitatione mens menti monstrabit quod in se retinet." (cols. 788–89)

[17] *Sacramentarium*, col. 575.

[18] Johan Beleth, *Summa*, ed. Douteil, Chapter 38, pp. 68–69.

[19] The treatise remains unascribed to any person, but it clearly belonged to someone living in Victorine circles.

saecula saeculorum laudabunt te" (Ps. 83:5 [84:4]). Huic significationi pulchre convenit quod sequentia verba habet laudiflua et cantum dulcisonum, quia ibi omnia erunt plena laude, et melodia coelestis organi abundabit dulciflua laetitia . . . Et quia laudes aeternae vitae humanis verbis non resonabunt, quaedam ecclesiae mystice pneumatizant sequentiam sine verbis. Nulla enim verborum significatio necessaria, ubi corda singulorum patebunt singulis librum uitae intuentibus.

(Therefore since this joy is neither fully to be expressed with words, nor is fully able to be still, the church, as if jubilating with suppressed words, bursts forth in admiration, as who should say, "What voice, what tongue will be able to tell . . ." etc. For here words do not suffice nor the intellect, but neither does love permit silence. Therefore the church, wondrous to say, by making pneumas, somehow indicates more expressly, and better without words than through words, how great may be the joy of God where words will cease. For through the pneuma, though it is not described how great eternal joy may be, at least it is shown that this joy is indescribable. And when the sequence follows, the later Alleluia does not have a pneuma, but the choir sings the sequence in its place which signifies the same thing, that is the joy and delights of eternal life. Whence it generally has new and unusual words, since the joy of heaven is hidden and unknown to mortals. And the sequence mysteriously represents the praise of eternal life. Whence it is said, "Blessed are they that dwell in thy house, O Lord: they shall praise thee for ever and ever" (Ps. 83:5 [84:4]). It is suited beautifully to this signification that the sequence has praiseful words and a sweet-sounding song, because there all will be full of praise and the melody of the celestial organum will abound with sweet happiness . . . And because the praise of eternal life will not resonate with human words, certain churches pneumatize the sequence mystically without words. For no significance of words will be necessary where the hearts of each lie open to each gazing upon the book of life.)

The chants have become the voice of the church, each with official groups of messages. Thus the pneuma, although still the mortal representation of the heavenly song, is here interpreted as wordless not only because language will not be necessary in Paradise, but also because we do not yet know what Paradise will be like. Yet the song bursts forth, unable to be silent because of the power of its love. This church is not afraid to try to sing in the mode of the angels.

The sequence is seen as a liturgical song in its own right by this anonymous author, capable of standing on its own, without the pneuma sounding along with it. Indeed, the sequence is a substitute for the pneuma; one is not needed when the other is present. And the practice of singing the sequence without text is not viewed as superior to using the words, but rather as the special practice of some churches. The sequence mysteriously represents praise of eternal life, and no apologies are made for its having a text. It is perfectly suited to the job of praising divine praise, for it has mystical, unusual language, a mode of speech typifying the secret and wordless joys of heaven.[20] And its song is particularly sweet, worthy of its purposes. Copious praise of the heavenly state as sung in the sequence just before the Gospel plays a major role in this "mirror of the church." The new importance afforded the genre here carried over into thirteenth-century commentaries as well.

---

[20] This description of language is apparently written with the early sequence in mind. This commentator reveals a new attitude toward sequences in general, but is not describing the "Victorine" sequences in particular. He stands on a ledge between the old and the new.

The *Mitrale* by Sicard of Cremona (†1215) incorporates passages found in the writings of Honorius, Johan Beleth, and the *Speculum ecclesiae* to make up its discussion of the sequence. But Sicard has also added new information. Here the sequence is not only a substitute for the pneuma, it is separated out as different from all the other music sung between the Epistle and the Gospel. For Sicard, the sequence is the special song of victory.

Sequentia vero canticum designat victoriae. Unde plausum victorum cum neumis imitatur; hanc exsultationem praefiguravit tympanistria Maria, quae victoriam liberato populo recitavit, dicens: "Cantemus Domino" [Exodus 15:1, 20–21], cum qua et populus jubilavit.[21]

(But the sequence designates the song of victory, for which reason it imitates through its neumes the beating of the victors' drums. The tambourine player Miriam prefigured this exultation, who announced victory to the liberated people, saying "Let us sing unto the Lord" [Exodus 15:1, 20–21] and with whom the people too rejoiced.)

Sicard too speaks of the sequence as sung in choir, just as did the author of the *Speculum ecclesiae*, but he redirects the emphasis. This is not a song by soloists, like the other chants between the Epistle and the Gospel, but one sung "communiter" by the two halves of the choir. This interpretation of the sequence as a chant different from all others in its joyfulness is also given by the late-thirteenth-century music theorist Johannes de Grocheo, who wrote in Paris. He singled out the sequence, clearly for him the texted piece only, as special in character, and compared it to the ductia, which was performed with sharply marked beats:[22]

Responsorium autem et alleluia decantantur ad modum stantipedis vel cantus coronati, ut devotionem et humilitatem in cordibus auditorum imponant. Sed sequentia cantatur ad modum ductiae, ut ea ducat et laetificet, ut recte recipiant verba novi testamenti, puta sacrum evangelium, quod statim postea decantatur.[23]

(The Gradual and the Alleluia are sung in the mode of the stantipes or crowned song, so that they inspire devotion and humility in the hearts of the listeners. But the sequence is sung in the mode of the ductia, that it may lead and make glad so that, in turn, they may rightly receive the words of the New Testament – that is, the Holy Gospel – which are sung immediately afterwards.)

It is clear from the many commentators studied in this chapter and in earlier chapters, and the wide spread of centuries in which they lived and wrote, that attitudes toward sequences changed from the ninth through the thirteenth centuries. The new interpretations in the writing of twelfth and early thirteenth-century commentators are puzzling at first. Were they writing only about the early medieval sequences, or did they have works in the new style in mind? Two commentators from the second half of the thirteenth century, the Dominican Hugh of St. Cher, and Durandus of Mende, suggest that the answer to this question should be "both." The new attitude toward sequences was probably fostered by the

---

[21] Sicard of Cremona, *Mitrale*, c. 104.
[22] See also Handschin (1929–30 and 1930–31).
[23] See Grocheo, *De musica*, in *Quellenhandschriften*, ed. Rohloff p. 164. A description of the ductia is found in the same treatise on p. 136. The "cantus coronatus," described on p. 130, is solemn song composed in praise of a king or high-ranking official.

significant numbers of pieces written in a new style during the twelfth century. The emphasis upon angelic choirs and unusual language came from reinterpreting surviving examples of earlier styles in light of the new works, for although new sequences often replaced older ones, in many cases the old works survived and were still sung. This distinction between old sequences (so called explicitly) and new ones (called simply sequences) can be found in Hugh of St. Cher:

"Alleluia" repetitur cum neumate, et significat laudem patriae. Significatur autem per sequentiam idem quod per neuma. Unde in antiquis sequentiis sunt verba incognita, quia ignotus est nobis modus laudandi in patria.[24]

("Alleluia" is repeated with neumes, and signifies the praise of the fatherland. The same thing is signified through the sequence that is signified through the neume. Whence in antique sequences are unknown words, because the way of praising in the fatherland [heaven] is unknown to us.)

The sequence means the same as the Alleluia, praise of the homeland, praise of the divine land to which all are called. This is a venerable idea, one met in source after source. But then the interesting part: the "antique" sequences had strange words to indicate that the mode of praising in the fatherland is unknown to us now. The antique sequences, the early medieval sequences, that is, are to be distinguished, we may assume, from those written in the new style of the twelfth century, and not by their poetic style (which does not get mentioned) but rather by the kind of words they used.

The meaning of this passage is clarified in the writing of Durandus of Mende, a canonist trained at Bologna as well as a commentator on the liturgy. Born in the diocese of Narbonne in southern France, William Durandus was an Augustinian canon regular before being called to the bishop's throne at Mende. In his substantial discussion of the sequence, Durandus makes a clear distinction between the antique sequences, with their strange language, and the sequences of his own time. The old sequences, like the pneuma itself, spoke with a voice or sound that did not "signify," thus representing, among other things, that the joy of heaven is secret and unknown. This type of sequence is contrasted with the sequence of his own day: "but today sequences are sung with signifying voice, to note that in the great festival of the eternal life the jubilus will be known fully."[25] The sequence has moved from being a translation of angelic sounds into mortal language to being a proclamation of knowledge about Paradise.

The new song of the twelfth century: the text

A bright new "standard of the king" was lifted in churches throughout France and beyond during the twelfth century: the magnificent sequence "Laudes

---

[24] Hugh of St. Cher, *Tractus super missam*, ed. Sölch p. 18.
[25] "Hodie vero Sequentiae cum voce significativa dicuntur, ad notandum quod in illa magna festivitate vitae aeternae jubilus plene scietur." *Rationale*, IV, 22, p. 199.

crucis.''[26] The piece appears as an addition in several mid-century collections, and by the late twelfth century most churches in France with sequences were singing it. Although surely later than a handful of popular late sequences added to many liturgies by the mid twelfth century (including "Hodierne lux diei" for the Virgin Mary and "Congaudentes" for St. Nicholas), "Laudes crucis," like these, has its own music, in this case a melody which quotes from "Alleluia dulce lignum" in its opening.[27] Although the melody was adapted for dozens of other texts in the twelfth and thirteenth centuries, examples of this particular text existing with another melody are hard to find. The piece may have spread so quickly because it was associated with the victory of the First Crusade, carried out just before the time it must have been written. In fact, some of the martial language found within it and the emphasis on the cross making thousands flee may be an oblique reference to the retaking of Jerusalem by Christian forces in 1099. "Laudes crucis" is a classic representative of the late sequence as written in Paris in the twelfth century, and the most widespread of all twelfth-century sequences. Through study of its text and music one can accurately identify the major characteristics of this style, and also begin to understand why they had such appeal for the epoch.

The relationship between liturgical commentary and liturgical texts and music is particularly clear in the so-called "Victorine" sequences. The texts work in different ways from those of early medieval sequences, and have a function very like those of contemporary commentaries. As the analysis below shows, the poetry alludes to heaven and its mysteries, just as does the early sequence, but its main purpose is to tell a history of events on earth, especially a history of priests and priesthood, of feasts and sacraments.

The sequence text has four clearly discernible sections: (1) an exordium, (2) a history of the cross through Old Testament typology, (3) an expression of the powers of the cross in contemporary life, and (4) a final prayer addressed to Jesus. Although this poem resembles most early medieval sequences in its basic structure, each of the individual parts is different from what would be expected in an earlier piece written west of the Rhine. There is no talk of angels in this exordium. The middle section does not seek to justify praise: this work has been invented to expound mysteries, not to excuse its inability to do so. And just as its purpose is different, so too is its subject and mode of presentation. This is a poem about the cross and its power, flowing through the sacraments of the church to the people. The subject and the mode of treatment are profoundly linked to early-twelfth-century

---

[26] There are many general studies of the late sequence texts found in the standard introductions to Latin religious lyrics. See, especially, Szövérffy (1965 and 1985); Klopsch (1980), Langosch (1969), and Raby (1953). The best study of the texts of the Victorine sequences is Hegener (1971), who reveals the dependency of the Victorine texts on allegory as understood from Augustine's *De doctrine christiana*. These ideas were first expressed in the writings of Hegener's teacher Hennig Brinkmann; see especially Brinkmann (1980), pp. 21–25. For discussion of allegory in the medieval German lyric, see Freytag (1982). My own study is different from other analyses of sequences in two major ways: (1) it studies the sequences in the context of the Victorine liturgy and theology, conceiving of them as the works of a particular community, and (2) it accounts for both the textual and the musical dimensions of the pieces.

[27] Texts for "Hodierne" and "Congaudentes" are found in *AH* LIV.

liturgical commentary upon the meanings of the sacraments.[28] In fact, the *Liber de sacramentis*, a long poem by Petrus Pictor, who was, at one stage in his life, an Augustinian canon of St. Omer in Flanders in the early twelfth century, contains so much of the theological underpinnings of "Laudes crucis" that it can be used as a kind of running commentary upon the sequence, helping to explain the imagery at several turns.[29] Petrus Pictor is the kind of person probably responsible for the origins of this new type of sequence in the early twelfth century. He was a twelfth-century liturgical commentator, but presented a systematic doctrine of teaching about the Mass liturgy in hexameters. Mary Schaefer finds him "motivated by the need of priests to have instruction in sacramental theology and the meaning of liturgical rites so that they in turn can instruct the faithful."[30]

Like the *Liber de sacramentis*, "Laudes crucis" is about the actions of priests and their beneficial effects upon the faithful. The exordium of "Laudes crucis" calls to praise those who exult "by the special glory of the cross." This special group of worshipers believes the sweet wood worthy of the melody they sing. And how comes their music to be so sweet? It is sweet because lives and voices are unified, and the injunction to sing is bound up with the injunction to live well. This exordium explains singing, too, as does that of the early medieval sequence, but the explanation is different. These singers raise their song to God as testaments to service and to the dedication of their lives. Their song is an offering, representative of a special calling to follow the cross. At the end of the exordium, they are encouraged to gaze upon it as the first altar, red with the blood of the Lamb. The theme of sacramental action is introduced: we have been removed to the archetypal early church and the first "Mass." In this service, Christ was the offering, and the blood and water flowing from his side instituted the sacraments.[31] None of the ideas here is a new one. Their presence in a sequence in this particular exegetical mode and with a systematic use of Old Testament typology for the sacraments and priests unifying the entire work, however, is new in sequence poetry.[32]

The differences between this exordium and that in an early sequence, while striking, are not as great as those marking off the rest of "Laudes crucis" from a piece such as "Alte uox canat." In strophe IV the poet tells what this cross is: it is the ladder by which Christians climb to Jesus, and its form teaches that it reaches out

---

[28] For another analysis of this text, see Szövérffy (1976) on hymns of the holy cross.

[29] In the critical edition of Petrus' poems (Petrus Pictor, *Carmina*), L. van Acker tells what little has been surmised about the poet's life using the evidence of the poems themselves and their manuscript traditions. He was exiled from Flanders for some unknown reason and came to make his living as a painter of decorative images.

[30] See Schaefer (1983), p. 5, and Petrus Pictor, *Liber de sacramentis*, Chapter 21, in *Carmina*, ed. van Acker, pp. 38–39.

[31] In Chapter 12 of the *Liber de sacramentis*, Petrus describes the mingling of water and wine in the chalice as representing the effusion of fluids from the side of Christ: "Aqua pariter sanguini admiscetur quia utrumque simul in cruce de latere Salvatoris emanavit, sanguis videlicet redemptionis et aqua baptismatis per quod Ecclesias figuratur." For Petrus, as for many other medieval exegetes, this is the moment when the church and its sacraments were instituted.

[32] The early sequence west of the Rhine was not dependent upon Old Testament typology to a great degree; but the Notkerian sequence was much more so. Szövérffy (1989, p. 33) says of Notker: "The biblical past, the Old and New Testament, and, even the world of legends became for Notker and his generation a firm foundation for the frail human existence . . ."

mystically to all corners of the world.[33] As in "Alte uox canat," an image of the Cross is presented. But in the earlier sequence the bejeweled image shines through powerfully, briefly, as if in a vision, and then disappears from view. In "Laudes crucis," the cross is introduced to be explained through signs which have existed at various times throughout history, and not just as in the apocalyptic glory of Revelation. In the next part of the sequence, the poet rediscovers the sweet wood in the books of the Old Testament. This sequence is not primarily about angels, as early medieval French sequences so often are; it is rather about human beings and their place in salvation history.

Three Old Testament figures are cited, although not in the order they appear in the Bible: Moses, Noah, and the widow of Zarephath. It is crucial that Moses is described as having an "officium," an office through which he performs the special deeds mentioned. In the Vulgate Bible this word is never used to describe the actions of Moses, but it is used twice in Exodus (28:35 and 31:10), each time to speak of Aaron, Moses' brother, whom Moses eventually consecrated as the head Levite or priest. In subsequent books of the Bible, throughout the Old Testament, and in the new as well, "officium" means a special office, that of priest.[34] Through this context, Moses becomes a type of the priests, performing special actions, with God's grace. And the actions ascribed to him are carefully chosen for their sacramental character: he makes bitter water turn sweet by putting wood into it (Exodus 15:25);[35] he brings water from a stone by striking it with his staff (Exodus 17:6); he sees to it that the houses of those for salvation are marked with the blood of the Paschal Lamb (Exodus 12:7).[36] In all cases, according to this sequence text, the miracles were caused by the power of the cross found mystically within the wood or within the blood of the sacrificed. Just as the priest at Mass is believed able to change outer signs into inner realities through the special powers of the office, so too did this ancient priest perform sacramental acts of great symbolic power.[37]

Choosing from a store of conventional cross symbolism, the poet of "Laudes crucis" picks those images which relate to the sacraments of the church.[38] The

---

[33] Esmeijer (1978) provides a detailed discussion of the symbols of the cross in Christian art and exegesis. She mentions the commonplace that the cross harmonized the elements, an idea often expressed by musical imagery (p. 117). The idea of the cross as sustaining a harmony of interrelationships was central to Victorine exegesis and will be explored further in Part V of this book. Ladner (1955, p. 200) says in his discussion of the symbolism of the cross in Gregory of Nyssa: "To sum up Gregory's view, the Cross is for him a visual symbol of the four principal extensions of the universe and of its unity in Christ."

[34] Augustine says in his commentary on Psalm 98[99]:6 "Of Moses it is not there stated that he was a priest. But if he was not this, what was he? Could he be anything greater than a priest? This Psalm declareth that he also was himself a priest: 'Moses and Aaron among his priests.' They therefore were the Lord's priests." (p. 486)

[35] Augustine says, "Through the wood, the water was made sweet, prefiguring the glory and grace of the cross." *Quaestiones*, Chapter LVII, pp. 615–616.

[36] In Chapter 4 of the *Liber de sacramentis*, the making of the sign of the cross by Christians is said to be prefigured by the signs made on the doorposts of the Israelites.

[37] Moses as a type of the priesthood of Christ is found in Petrus Pictor as well: "Quod Christus noster legislator nosterque sit Moyses, qui nobis de diabolica servitute ereptis agnus paschalis immolatus est, quique per huius mundi desertum ad regnum nobis promissum nos introducit." *Liber de sacramentis*, Chapter 16, in *Carmina*, ed. van Acker, p. 33.

[38] For an introduction to the bibliography on medieval cross legends and symbolism, see Kaske (1988), pp. 146–151.

power of the wood is demonstrated again in the ark of Noah, a ship built to save.[39] The waters of the flood baptize those gathered in the ark, offering a sacrament which would later be officially established by Christ.[40] Noah, like Moses above, has been interpreted as carrying out a priestly function; he has been commissioned to baptize. The widow in Zarephath (3 Kings [1 Kings] 17:12) gathered two sticks in the Vulgate Bible (sometimes rendered by modern translators as "a stick or two") to cook a final meal for herself and her son. Because she did as Elijah said, her meal and her oil did not run out, and life was preserved in the midst of famine. The two sticks alluded to here clearly represent the cross. The story introduces two elements necessary for the sacraments in the Christian church: oil, essential for anointings of all sorts, and meal, needed to make communion bread.[41] The widow of Zarephath is like the faithful; because she has hope in her salvation, the physical signs of oil and grain are representative of spiritual realities. In the Christian tradition, faith on the part of the believer is counted essential for the sacrament of communion to work.[42]

In strophe IX, the next major division in the poem occurs with the return of the teaching voice: the good rewards of the cross are hidden under figures in Scripture, and several examples have been explained. But "now" they lie open; this is a poem about the mysteries of scriptural exegesis: it does not just employ standard techniques, it attempts to show how to use them, and it assumes that it is proper so to do. In the time after Christ kings believe, unlike pagan kings, who did not. The oblique reference here to the conversion of Constantine is presented in language equally relevant to the feelings of twelfth-century Christians who would make pilgrimages to the Holy Land. The cross of strophes X and XI is the new tree of life, presented as the source of rejuvenation, rather than of death. Its medicine works as described in strophe XI, through human agents performing deeds in its name. And in strophe XII, another image refers back to the opening of the poem and finishes the framework for the middle sections: Christ is directly addressed as the "consecrator" of the cross, the official who has dedicated it as a bishop would a church.

Besides being the sequence for cross feasts, "Laudes crucis" had other liturgical uses in the twelfth and thirteenth centuries. The "ave" and "vale," "hail" and "farewell," are offered because the piece must have been designed for singing in a church possessing a fragment of the true cross among its major relics.[43] This piece

---

[39] This strophe is now known only in the version in Paris, BN lat. 1086. It is hoped that other versions will be discovered.

[40] The idea of the flood as an archtype is found in the First Letter of Peter, a short treatise thought by some scholars actually to be an early sermon for Christian baptism. See 1 Peter 3:19–21: "In which also coming he preached to those spirits that were in prison: Which had been some time incredulous, when they waited for the patience of God in the days of Noe ['Noah'], when the ark was a building: wherein a few, that is, eight souls, were saved by water. Whereunto baptism being of the like form, now saveth you also . . ." See also 1 Corinthians 10:2: "And all in Moses were baptized, in the cloud, and in the sea."

[41] In Petrus Pictor, Christ is seen as typified by the grain of wheat which comes to life in the ground. See *Liber de sacramentis*, Chapter 18, in *Carmina*, ed. van Acker, p. 34.

[42] The twelfth century was a time of great debate over the meaning of the communion service and the real presence. For an introduction to this subject see Schaefer (1982–83), Mitchell (1982, pp. 137–167), and Browe (1967).

[43] And this might argue for Orléans and be seen as substantiation of Weisbein's theory of origins: see Huglo (1987), p. 210. But Orléans was hardly the only city in France possessing fragments of the true cross in the early twelfth century. As argued by Geneviève Bautier (1971), the Cathedral of Notre Dame received a

might well be sung at the high point of a special procession during vespers to the place where it was displayed, as well as in the Masses for feasts honoring the cross. The sacramental theme of "Laudes crucis" is however, at the very center of this poem. It is no wonder that liturgists in the Middle Ages positioned it in two places where this meaning would have deep significance:

(1) In northern France, most notably in Paris, "Laudes crucis" was sung during the ceremony of the Dedication of the Church at the very point when crosses were drawn by the bishop on the walls of the church, that is, when the church itself was anointed.[44] The significance of this action as a kind of reinterpretation of "Laudes crucis" will be discussed later in this book.

(2) In the diocese of Cambrai (and in other churches as well), during the twelfth century, strophes XI.2 and XII.1 were sung after communion in the Premonstratensian rite. This period of reflection just after receiving the host was well served by a text about the 'Christian medicine," the benefits of the sacraments empowered by the cross.[45]

"Laudes crucis" speaks with a different voice from that typically found in an early medieval sequence, and its subjects and exegetical mode are different. This voice does not go seeking reasons for joining with the angelic hosts. Instead it teaches, confident in its ability to understand the hidden meanings of Scripture, convinced that it is important for humans to express these meanings. In a book on the poetry of late sequences, Hegener has discussed the twelfth-century belief in God's language of signs, a belief in part inspired by renewed study of Augustine's *De doctrina christiana*.[46] Hegener begins his discussion of the Parisian poet Adam of St. Victor with a quotation from the poet's contemporary, Hugh of St. Victor: "Primum fit sermo Dei ad nos, postea sermo noster ad Deum."[47]

God speaks to humans through signs – through things, actions, and characters whose meanings are hidden throughout Scripture.[48] The meanings of these things are revealed through Christ and the miracle of his death and resurrection, and the redemption they offer to humankind. Humans in return speak back to God, making a language that shows understanding, and that speaks in things as well, as God does. "Laudes crucis" is expressed in such a tongue. It first reveals understanding of God's language; it then talks back, describing the cross through tangible properties which show it to be the verdant Tree of Life, the new tree, for a world transformed by the "New Adam." The ability to talk back to God through prayer and praise in the language he chose for humans is in itself an expression of confidence in salvation.

---

fragment in 1120, and Huglo (1987) and, following him, Wright (1989, p. 276) have suggested that this reception was the inspiration for "Laudes crucis," and that the older attribution of the piece to Adam of St. Victor may be correct.

44 See, for example, the thirteenth-century Parisian pontifical, Arsenal 332, fol. 92v, which incorporates the singing of "Laudes crucis" into the ceremony for the Dedication of the Church.

45 See King (1955), p. 255.

46 See Hegener (1971), and Berndt (1991), p .275.

47 For this quotation in context, see Hugh of St. Victor, "De verbo Dei," Book V; xxxx edn., p. 74. It is also found in the *Didascalicon*. "De verbo Dei" is discussed further in Chapter 10 below, pp. 225–227.

48 Hugh says in the *Didascalicon*: "The philosopher knows only the significance of words, but the significance of things is far more excellent than that of words, because the latter was established by usage, but Nature

The influence of renewed study of Augustine is reflected not only in the language of this sequence, but also in the treatment of the subject. "Laudes crucis" contains an historical exposition of the cross, based on exegetical commentary of the sort found in the writings of the fathers, particularly in the writings of St. Augustine and continuously after him.[49] Although written commentaries are found throughout the Middle Ages in sermons and other Biblical commentaries, one does not find this reliance upon typology and three- and fourfold exegesis in French sequences to any degree before the twelfth century. In fact, there is no early medieval French sequence known to me which attempts to write a history in this way.[50] Although the use of Old Testament typology has been mentioned as a feature of Victorine sequences by other scholars, it has usually been seen as part of medieval hermeneutics in general (which, of course, it was), rather than as a change or shift.[51] An important exception to this view is found in the writings of Josef Szövérffy, who has shown in his study of twelfth-century St. Peter sequences that the use of typology and biographical details "are not so generally known from earlier sequences."[52] "Laudes crucis," written early in the twelfth century, suggests that the sequences helped lead the way in the "speculative biblicism" of the century.[53]

"Laudes crucis," a sequence for the feasts of the Finding of the Cross (May 3) and the Exaltation of the Cross (September 14). (The text is transcribed from Paris, BN lat. 1086, a late-twelfth-century source from the Augustinian Abbey of St. Leonard in Limoges. Strophe IX is added from the Victorine gradual, Paris, BN lat. 14819.)

1 Laudes crucis attollamus nos qui crucis exultamus speciali gloria	(I Let us raise praises of the cross We who exult By the special glory of the cross.
II.1 Dulce melos pulset celos dulce lignum dulci dignum credimus melodia	II.1 Let the sweet melody touch heaven. We believe the sweet wood is Worthy of sweet melody.
II.2 Voce uita non discordet cum uox uitam non remordet dulcis est simphonia.	II.2 Let not life be in discord with voice: When the voice does not disquiet life, The harmony is sweet.
III.1 Serui crucis crucem laudent qui per crucem sibi gaudent uite dari munera dicant omnes et dicant singuli aue salus totius seculi arbor salutifera.	III.1 Let the servants of the cross praise the cross, Who rejoice to be given for themselves The gifts of life through the cross. Let all say together and singly, "Hail salvation of the entire race, Salvation-bearing tree."

dictated the former. The latter is the voice of men, the former the voice of God speaking to men." Book V, Chapter 3; Taylor edn., pp. 121–122.

[49] Pontet (1946) says (p. 377): "La croix apparaît donc au bout de toutes les grandes avenues de l'exégèse augustinienne. Puisqu'elle donne le sens même de l'Ecriture, qu'elle l'ouvre, l'unifie, la transforme, il est clair que son importance théologique est, aux yeux du prédicateur, de premier plan." For further discussion of cross symbolism in Augustine, see also Ladner (1955 and 1983), pp. 197–208.

[50] For discussion of the subject of narrative in the medieval lyric, see Edwards (1989).

[51] See, for example, the excellent introduction to typology in the Victorine sequences in Raby (1953), pp. 355–375, and M&A, pp. 57–110. My own work, unlike these, will emphasize the political and educational points of view standing behind the sequences.

[52] Szövérffy (1965), p. 10.

[53] For the term, see Seeberg (1920–33), vol. II, p. 184.

III.2   O quam felix quam preclara
fuit hec salutis ara
rubens agni sanguine
agni sine macula
qui maundauit secula
ab antiquo crimine.

III.2   O how splendid, how beautiful
Was this altar of salvation,
Red with the blood of the Lamb;
Of the Lamb without stain
Who cleansed the world
From the ancient crime.

IV.1   Hec est scala peccatorum
per quam Christus rex celorum
ad se traxit omnia.
IV.2   Forma cuius hoc ostendit
que terrarum comprehendit
quatuor confinia.

IV.1   This is the ladder of sinners
Through which Christ, King of heaven,
Drew up all things to Himself;
IV.2   The form of that which
Encompasses the four regions of the earth
shows these things.

V.1   Non sunt nova testamenta
nec recenter est inventa
crucis hec religio.
V.2   Ista dulces aquas fecit
per hanc silex aquas iecit
moysi officio.

V.1   These are not new signs,
Not recently was this religion
Of the cross invented:
V.2   It made waters sweet,
Through it the rock gave water
By Moses' office.

VI.1   Nulla salus est in domo
nisi cruce munit homo
super liminaria.
VI.2   Nec defusit gaudium
nec amisit filium
quisquis egit talia.

VI.1   No salvation is in a house
Unless a man protects
With the cross on his threshold:
VI.2   None felt the sword
Nor lost a son
Who did so.

VII.1   Archa natans super aquas
saluat formas animatas
quam noe composuit.
VII.2   Archa crucem noe christum
signat unda hunc baptismum
quem christus exhibuit.

VII.1   The ark swimming on the water
Saves the living species
As many as Noah brought together;
VII.2   The ark signifies the cross; Noah, Christ;
The waves this baptism
Which Christ conferred.

VIII.1   Ligna legens in sarepta
spem salutis est adepta
pauper muliercula.
VIII.2   Sine lignis fidei
nec lechitus olei
ualet nec farinula.

VIII.1   Gathering sticks in Zarephath
The poor woman
Obtained the hope of salvation:
VIII.2   Without the sticks of faith
Neither the cruse of oil
Nor the little pile of meal is any good.

[IX.1   Roma naues uniuersas
in profundum uidit mersas
una cum maxentio.
IX.2   Fusi traces cesi perse
sed et partis dux aduerse
uictus ab eraclio.]

[IX.1   Rome saw all ships sunk
In the deep,
Together with Maxentius.
IX.2   Thracians fled, Persians slain,
And the leader of adverse foes
Conquered by Heraclius.]

X.1   In scripturis sub figuris
ista latent sed iam patent
crucis beneficia.

X.1   In Scripture under figures
These benefits of the cross are hidden
But now lie open:

X.2	Reges credunt hostes cedunt	X.2	Kings believe, enemies recede

X.2   Reges credunt hostes cedunt
sola cruce Christo duce
hostis fugant milia.

XI.1   Ista suos fortiores
semper facit et victores
morbos curat et languores
reprimit demonia.
XI.2   Dat captiuis libertatem
uite confert nouitatem
ad antiquam dignitatem
crux reduxit omnia.

XII.1   O crux lignum triumphale
mundi uera salus uale
inter ligna nullum tale
fronde flore germine.
XII.2   Medicina christiana
salua sanos egros sana
quod non ualet uis humana
sit in tuo nomine.

XIII.1   Insistentes crucis laudi
consecrator crucis audi
atque servos tue crucis
post hanc uitam uere lucis
transfer ad palacia.
XIII.2   Quos tormento uis seruire
fac tormenta non sentire
sed cum dies erit ire
nobis confer et largire
sempiterna gaudia.

Amen.

X.2   Kings believe, enemies recede
By the cross alone with Christ leading
One gives flight to thousands.

XI.1   This ever makes its own courageous
And victorious;
Makes well the sick and languishing,
Restrains demons.
XI.2   It gives freedom to the captives,
Confers the newness of life:
The cross restores all things
To the former worth.

XII.1   O cross, triumphant wood,
True salvation of the world, farewell!
Among woods, none is such wood
With leaf, or flower, or seed.
XII.2   Christian medicine
Save the well, make well the sick:
What human power cannot do
Is done in your name.

XIII.1   Consecrator of the cross, hear
Those standing by for praise of the cross,
And, after this life,
Take the servants of your cross
To the palace of true light;
XIII.2   Those whom you are willing to subject
      to torments
Make them not feel the torments;
But when the day of wrath will come,
Confer to us and grant to us
Eternal joys.

Amen.)

The new song of the twelfth century: the music

Late sequences resemble early medieval sequences in that they are organized in paired versicles, each pair having the same music, and thus with a musical form aa, bb, cc, dd,, ee, etc. But it is readily apparent that a sequence such as "Laudes crucis" is strikingly different from its ancestors of the ninth through the eleventh century. Instead of being written to look like syllables added to a melisma, as are the majority of early sequences, the text of "Laudes crucis" is organized into strophes, resembling a hymn. In sources from the twelfth and thirteenth centuries, it is even provided with a brief "Amen."[54]

[54] The Victorine sequences as found in Paris, BN lat. 14819, for example, all have "Amen" at the close. Later in the history of this manuscript, the "Amens" were crossed out or otherwise obliterated.

The poetic strophes are marked by their regularity, as a classical Ambrosian hymn would be, with the same numbers of syllables for matching lines, and a consistent metrical pattern. Each strophe has been organized to fall into two halves or versicles, a form characteristic of sequences even in the early times. Medieval hymns were written in this style of poetry, too. What keeps Victorine or late sequences from being hymns is their music. Unlike hymns, which have the same music for each successive strophe, late sequence melodies change with each successive strophe. In addition, melodies for individual strophes are divided into repeating halves, with the two versicles of an individual strophe set to the same music. Thus, in the late sequence, the music underscores the double-versicle structure of individual strophes.[55] "Laudes crucis" has music organized like that of the early sequence, but its text is like a hymn. It is therefore, a hymn-like sequence, a type of piece not seen before the end of the eleventh century.

Thus "Laudes crucis" has a style and structure reflecting features borrowed from both hymns and sequences, but fused together to make something new. Although its poetic style may make it sound like a hymn, it remains a sequence – not only because of its special structure, but also because of its particular place within the Mass liturgy and the host of associations built throughout the centuries into such a position. In the eleventh century, a new interest in composing rhythmical liturgical poetry rose up, and rhyme, which had always been important in hymn texts, gained in prominence. Raby has defined the chief characteristics of the regular sequences, the most important genre of rhythmical liturgical poetry in the twelfth century, as follows:

1   The rhythm is regular and is based wholly on the word-accent, with occasional transpositions of stress, especially in the short line which ends a strophe.
2   The caesura is regular, and should occur at the end of a word.
3   The rhyme is regular, and at least two-syllabled.
4   The Sequence measure *par excellence* is the trochaic line of eight syllables, repeated one or more times, and followed by a trochaic line of seven syllables. The initial independent strophe is rare, and the recognizable parallelism hardly distinguishes the composition from a hymn.[56]

In the opening of its melody, one can still hear the Alleluia of the sweet wood, and the text makes reference to this mystical song, calling it "dulce melos." Indeed, as analysis will demonstrate, the entire melody has been constructed to keep referring back to the opening with its associative powers.

Many of the things one can say about hymn melodies in general, especially as developed in lands of the Frankish kingdom, can be said about the melodies of these hymn-like sequences:

The hymn strophe offered a framework within which melodic detail (like textual detail) could be precisely located and its effect maximized. Inflections, cadences, ascents and descents, figural repetitions and variations all could be given an emphasis within this framework that could not be achieved in the less regular phraseology of an antiphon or responsory.[57]

[55] An introduction to the melodic style of the Parisian late sequence is found in Fassler (1987).
[56] Raby (1927), p. 348.
[57] Crocker (1990), p. 242.

But, because the piece is through-composed, and the text is very long, a late sequence offers a tightly controlled structure of vast proportions, a framework of set accentual patterns and line lengths, which requires a great amount of music. The sequence texts provided the first extensive rhythmic gridwork against which composers could make music, varying patterns in systematic ways, creating refrains, generating new motives from old ones.[58] Because of the framework, musical variation was displayed with a clarity unknown before, and with a new rhythmic dimension.[59] The interaction between strophic poetry and sequence form which took place beginning in the late eleventh and twelfth centuries was a musical event of great consequence.[60] It was here, in the Parisian sequences, and in other repertories similar to them, that the revolution in music identified with the twelfth century actually began.[61]

Analysis of "Laudes crucis" demonstrates some of the techniques used by composers in the Parisian school of the twelfth century, emphasizing the importance of interplay between phrases made possible by the extensive framework created by the shape of the text.

The opening melodic units of "Laudes crucis" unfold according to the principle of successive variation: each is connected to the unit that comes immediately before it, as well as to the unit following directly after, and this is true not only for these units, but for all that follow after them.[62] Thus, the music of the entire sequence is a chain of individual events, each linked to the other through various kinds of shared material. In fact, much of the melody seems to have been generated from the first melodic unit, or, at least, to embody thematic ideas found there. Melodic units (M&A's "timbres") are made up of phrases, one for every line of a hemistrophe.

As can be seen from the score of "Laudes crucis" (in the anthology, Example A.1, pp. 416–418), the hemistrophes are divided into phrases not only by the rhymes of their texts, but also by the carefully shaped structures of individual musical phrases, each of which has a cadence on g.[63] Thus the melody of unit 1A (t. 61) first moves upward to an ornamented g, then leaps up to c′, for a stepwise descent back to g; unit 1B explores the fourth below g rising at the end back up to this pitch; and unit 1C is a formulaic ornamentation of g. Phrases 2A and 2B (parts of t. 70) are

---

58 For discussion of technical aspects of rhythmic poetry, see Norberg (1988), Fassler (1987a), Camargo (1984), and Davis (1966). The theological implications of rhyme in Victorine poetry have been studied by Cunnar (1987). The themes of sound and silences as found in Augustine and discussed by Colish (1978) are surely relevant as well.

59 See Fassler (1987) for further discussion.

60 The Aquitanian versus too are a part of this development. For studies of this repertory (monophonic and polyphonic) and its sources, see Treitler (1967), Fuller (1969), and Grier (1988).

61 Begins, but does not end. Traditionally the revolution is seen as beginning with Notre Dame polyphony. Although my goal is not to discount the great achievements of the polyphonists, I would argue that their musical ideas had important precedents in contemporary monophonic genres.

62 See the score of "Laudes crucis" in the Anthology, Example A.1 (p. 416). In this discussion, a melodic unit refers to the music for one hemistrophe; a cell or phrase is the music for a single line. The "timbre" numbers are those found in M&A, and are used for identifying melodic units. The strengths and weaknesses in their system are evaluated in Chapter 13.

63 All examples, unless otherwise indicated, have been transcribed from the Victorine sequentiary found in Paris, BN lat. 14819, the earliest surviving witness of this tradition; because the source is incomplete, sequences which fell late in the calendar have been taken from Paris, BN lat. 14452. These manuscripts are discussed further in Chapter 7.

reworkings of the music of phrases 1A and 1B. But although the melodic contours of the phrases 2A and 2B are very much the same as the corresponding phrases of unit 1, the cadences of 2A and 2B avoid the final g found in phrases 1A and 1B. Thus, when 2C begins with music identical to that of 1C, the return to g is powerful. Unit 2 serves not only as an expansion of unit 1, however, but also to introduce the music of unit 3. Phrase 3A resembles phrase 2A, but it is organized around d′, rather than g, leaping upward to d′ at the start and remaining there throughout. Phrase 3B repeats the pitches of the ending of phrase 3A, but spaces them out, and closes with an abrupt leap back down to g, only to be followed by 3C, the same music which closed units 1 and 2. Phrases 3D, E, and F offer yet another version of material from units 1 and 2: the descent from g down to c in 3D is a familiar stepwise melodic contour, resembling that found at the end of phrases 1A and 2A, but the range is low, and the phrase cannot be extended any lower in subsequent development without violating the range of the mode. Thus a further melodic descent, as in 1B or 2B, is out of the question. Instead the music shifts dramatically from c to an ornamented g, which is similar to the cadential formula of 1C.

References back to the phrases of units 1 and 2 can be found throughout the piece: phrases resembling 1A are 4A, 5A, and 8A; phrases resembling 2A are 7A and 9A. Many B phrases have the same contour found in phrases 1B and 2B, most notably, 4B, 6B, 7B, and 9B. Unit 1C is reused exactly as the ending for units 2, the first half of 3, and 4, and versions of it are used to close the second half of unit 3 as well as units 4, 7, 9, 11, and 12.

Although the text forms a predictable rhythmic framework, the music offers its own patterns of sound against it.[64] A counterpoint exists between text and music: on the one hand, they play together always, their caesurae and cadences falling simultaneously, as shown above. But, on the other hand, text and music are independent, the music having a life of its own, one which seems structurally freer than that of its counterpart. A simple example of the constant interplay between text and music has already been described in the discussion of unit 3: a version of the cadential refrain comprising units 1C and 2C comes in at the ends of 3D and 3E, though such a cadential formula would be expected to occur at the end of the unit (i.e. 3F) rather than here. Thus the shift in the usual position of this formula adds variety and an element of suspense not found in the text alone.

Successive variation operates in this music not only because of similarity between phrases, but also because the phrases are made up of a small group of cells, each usually accommodating four syllables of text. Richard Hoppin identified these and demonstrated their constant presence throughout the melody in his analysis of "Laudes crucis."[65] These operate in the first two melodic phrases, each of which is made up of two groups of four notes. In the seven-syllable phrase at the end of each line, the cells are used only infrequently. Instead, a cadential formula of some sort, which often forms a kind of refrain for the entire piece, is used. Although the shape

[64] See Fassler (1987b), pp. 366–389.
[65] See Hoppin (1966).

of the musical line itself is somewhat predictable, and is governed by the tightly patterned text, the melodic cells which make up units 1A and 1B can be seen operating sometimes in the same, sometimes in different, positions in lines throughout the rest of the sequence.

Thus the cell closing phrase 1A, the descent from c′ to g, occurs usually in this position when it is used in other phrases. In phrase 5A, it is transposed up a fourth; in phrase 8A, it begins up a fifth, and the stepwise motion is slightly varied by a small leap in the middle; in phrase 12D, it occurs at pitch. Still, in these examples, the cell is found at the end of the phrase, and in two out of three of them, at the close of a phrase beginning a line. The original position of the cell is of major importance, therefore, and serves to establish the character of the cell almost as much as does its melodic contour. When one or the other of these is altered, the result can be striking, as in phrases 3B, D, E, and F, where the cell (or a variation upon it) has been placed at the beginnig rather than at the end of a phrase.

The attention late sequence composers gave to the units, phrases, and cells of their melodies does not mean that they had no regard for overall structure; quite the opposite. In "Laudes crucis" one finds what appear to be sections arranged in a meaningful order, an order, it should be mentioned, that was respected by Victorine composers in the second half of the twelfth century when they used "Laudes crucis" as a model, adapting its melody to new texts.

The first three units of "Laudes crucis" are not only similar in melodic contour, as demonstrated above. They also are in the same melodic mode, G plagal, the lower of the two scales that have G as their main tonal center. Beginning with the fourth melodic unit (t. 83), the melody shifts to the G authentic mode, the scale that lies a fourth higher in range than the plagal. The first two units in this new mode (t. 83 and t. 84) concentrate upon the upper fourth of the scale, from d′ to g′, with only an occasional dip down to the g at the bottom of the scale, particularly at the ends of phrases. These two units are quiet, their hymn-like phrases lying within small ranges, for the most part, with few leaps and not many melismas.

The three units following them (t. 85, 95, and 102) are more complex in several ways: the lines are more jagged, motion from a higher to a lower part of the range occurring within just a few notes. Melismas are more frequent and longer, and for the first time a single unit (t. 102) moves through both of the G scales, the plagal and the authentic. The sound of this unit is also a world apart from the rest of the piece: B♭ is indicated in the manuscripts, changing the character of the music altogether. It is not uncommon to find B♭ indicated in the Victorine manuscripts, but one can usually tell the reason for the accidental: either (1) F is in immediate proximity, so that without the B♭ a bare tritone would be exposed, or (2) the text mentions Satan or his minions. Unit 102, which is tonally distinct from what follows before and after it, may be so designed because the text describes the enemy, Maxentius, foe of Constantine in the early fourth century, and the Persians and others defeated by Heraclius, defender of the cross, and Byzantine emperor in the early seventh century. This particular melodic unit with its B♭s is a musical hissing at figures believed to be enemies of the cross and, therefore, agents of Satan.[66]

After unit 8 the B♭ does not return, so that the final melodic units of "Laudes crucis" form a placid return to the mode and to the calm melodic contours of the first unit. Unit 9 (t. 96) is the last until the very end of the piece to soar into the upper part of the authentic G mode, and it closes with a plain, formulaic phrase that resembles the ending of unit 1. The next three units (t. 144, 137, and 160), close the piece. They share phrases with each other: 10 (t. 144) and 11 (t. 137) are almost identical throughout, and their B phrase is the same as 12c (t. 160). This music forms a massive cadential statement, the ornamented gs of Unit 1C predominating in phrase after phrase. "Laudes crucis" is more than a series of interconnected melodic bits; it is a piece with a beginning (units 1–3), a middle (units 4–9), and a strongly marked end (units 10–12), and with what seems to be a deliberate balance between the three sections.

"Laudes crucis": text and music

The analysis of "Laudes crucis" offered here provides details about the use of typology in twelfth-century sequence poetry which have not been previously explored. In the past the poem has been depicted as a random catalogue of medieval cross typology; here it emerges as a work constructed by a highly selective poet, one who chose to emphasize ideas of the sacraments as they take place within the church, and the members of the priesthood both as celebrants and as connected to the cross and its meanings through their liturgical powers. In fact, this poet is writing a versified liturgical commentary, using Old Testament typology and describing a communal devotion to the mysteries of the cross. Because the events described are specially chosen as well, with an emphasis upon clerical action, the altar, and the sacraments, they demonstrate the history within the liturgy, and create a liturgical commentary of the type which was so popular during the twelfth century. Each liturgical event stands with a host of Old and New Testament associations behind it; the priest at the altar becomes Moses and Aaron as well as himself: a type of Christ, in the past, the present, and the future. Instead of trying to transport the singer or listener to heaven, this sequence takes him inside the church and up to the holy of holies, and proclaims a long historical tradition standing behind ritual action.

It may seem unfair at first to compare "Laudes crucis" with "Alte uox canat" and the other liturgical texts for the cross discussed in these chapters. "Laudes crucis" may seem to have greater weight just because it is longer. One could argue, however, that both sequence texts discussed here are equally magnificent: the earlier work offers a personal vision of a glorious object pregnant with hidden mysteries – it is a contemplative revery; the later piece explains a history of the cross and its

---

[66] Melodic unit 102, with its B♭s and other characteristics, was not used in other settings of "Laudes crucis" at St. Victor with one exception, "Letabundi iubilemus," for the Transfiguration. This use and its significance will be described below in Chapter 13.

meanings – it is a call to minister and to preach and it serves to explain as much as to inspire. "Alte uox canat" is typical of the early medieval French sequence, and has not been chosen to make "Laudes crucis" seem mightier than it is. Although some other early cross pieces were longer than "Alte uox canat," many were not, and all of them resembled it in style of language and exegetical mode.[67] It is also quite accurate to see "Laudes crucis" against the background of the works discussed here, proper trope, prosula, and early sequence. By the end of the twelfth century, these pieces had either ceased to exist or were diminished in number, but "Laudes crucis" was sung in Mass liturgies throughout Europe, a sequence of international fame.

This new sequence was different too because of its hymn-like features. It was unquestionably a sequence, but the sharply rhythmic text is reminiscent of the traditions of the Ambrosian hymn and the liturgy of the Office: hymns were never sung at Mass in the Latin West during the Middle Ages. With this style of music, the exegesis in the style of Augustine took on new prominence within the very heart of the Mass liturgy. More than this, composers could feel challenged to draw closer to the meanings of the texts, not only to make them sound, but to symbolize them as well. Early medieval sequences had a complicated set of symbols built into their music, as has been suggested. When sequences became hymns, these associations were, to a degree, lost, and new ways of making the music representative of its tradition were required.

Conclusions to Part I

During the ninth through the eleventh centuries, medieval artists created large and varied repertories of new pieces to supplement and otherwise decorate the chants of the Mass liturgy: tropes (both for proper and ordinary chants), prosulae (primarily for the Gloria, the Offertory and the Alleluia), and sequences, in texted and untexted forms. By the middle of the thirteenth century, many of these pieces were gone in most places.[68] In their stead, large new repertories of late sequences existed side by side with the several early medieval sequences which had survived the reforms of the twelfth and early thirteenth centuries, and some ordinary tropes.

In these opening chapters, I have presented examples of the older types of chants which disappeared – a trope, a prosula, and an early sequence – and an example of the type of chant which triumphed after the liturgical upheaval of the late eleventh and twelfth centuries – a late sequence.[69] There are many ways of studying the differences between these kinds of pieces. Here, I have chosen to pay close attention to what medieval commentators said about the Alleluia and the sequence, and three

---

[67] The sequence "Vexilla regis," for example (*AH* VII, p. 105), is a long sequence for the cross written in southern France in the early eleventh century. Its emphasis is upon the mysteries of the cross, the beauty and regal powers it displays throughout the universe. Although the cross depicted here exists throughout time, is sung to by David, and is seen on the last day, the sequence does not write its history through the use of typology.

[68] Proper tropes survived well into the thirteenth century at Chartres. Teviotdale 1991 has discovered interest in proper tropes in thirteenth-century England as well. See also Chapter 5, note 15 (p. 90 below).

[69] And, indeed, in several sources, "Laudes crucis" is a direct replacement for the earlier "Alte uox."

conclusions have emerged from this analysis, all of which will require further examination in subsequent chapters.

(1) Attitudes toward relationships between Alleluia and sequence changed to a great extent over the centuries. In the tenth century through the early twelfth century, the sequence was seen as a kind of extension of the Alleluia, dependent upon it, expressing the same things it expressed. By the late twelfth and thirteenth centuries, the sequence had become an independent piece, still trading on the symbolic meanings of the Alleluia, to be sure, but very different from it in character and having a purpose of its own within the liturgy.

(2) The performance of the sequence must have changed from the ninth to the twelfth centuries. In the early centuries, at least in some places, soloists were involved, as was some sort of wordless vocalizing of the music. By the late twelfth and thirteenth centuries, the sequence had become a choir piece in some places, perhaps a piece for the entire religious community to sing; in fact, except for its musical struture, it had become a hymn.[70] The practice of singing the sequence melody without text died out in the twelfth century, and by the thirteenth century, there is only infrequent mention of it. Instead texts and music were written together, and sometimes followed with an "Amen," as they were in the Victorine books.

The late-twelfth- or early-thirteenth-century Victorine ordinal found in Paris, BN lat. 14506 suggests that the singing of the sequence was a community effort, requiring no soloists. On folio 333v and 334r is found a model for the cantor's tablet.[71] Each Saturday, he would write down major liturgical assignments for celebrating, reading, and singing throughout the week.[72] Thus, the first page provides spaces for names of singers and lectors at Mass, including the celebrant, a lector for the Epistle, two singers for the Gradual (here called the Responsory), two singers for the Alleluia, a lector for the Gospel, and someone to hold the candle in the (Gospel) procession; other readers needed during the day are specified as well. The second page outlines matins, both for a nine-reading day and for a ferial day, when there were only three readings and responsories, with readings and responsories listed in parallel columns. The small group of specialized singers, a choir, commonly referred to in Benedictine ordinals, was apparently not important to the canons.[73] Perhaps they believed that all should participate in the communal liturgy on a regular basis.[74]

(3) Late sequences such as "Laudes crucis" operate in a different exegetical mode from the early medieval French sequence. They work like sermons, emphasizing Old Testament typology and explaining the history of liturgical events in time. In

---

[70] Harrison (1963, p. 67) says of the performance of the sequence in late medieval England: "The rulers, standing in mid-choir, sang the opening phrase, and the choir continued *alternatim*."

[71] For further information on the cantor's role as the supervisor of services and the selector of readers and singers, see Fassler (1985).

[72] This requirement of his office is described in some detail in the *Liber ordinis*, ed. Jocqué and Milis, pp. 81–84 and 138–142.

[73] For discussion of the choir and of the special ceremony where the members were tapped, see Fassler (1985).

[74] The cantor supervised the singing and reading and only chose persons he thought were worthy for the tasks. See the *Liber ordinis*, ed. Jocqué and Milis, pp. 83–84.

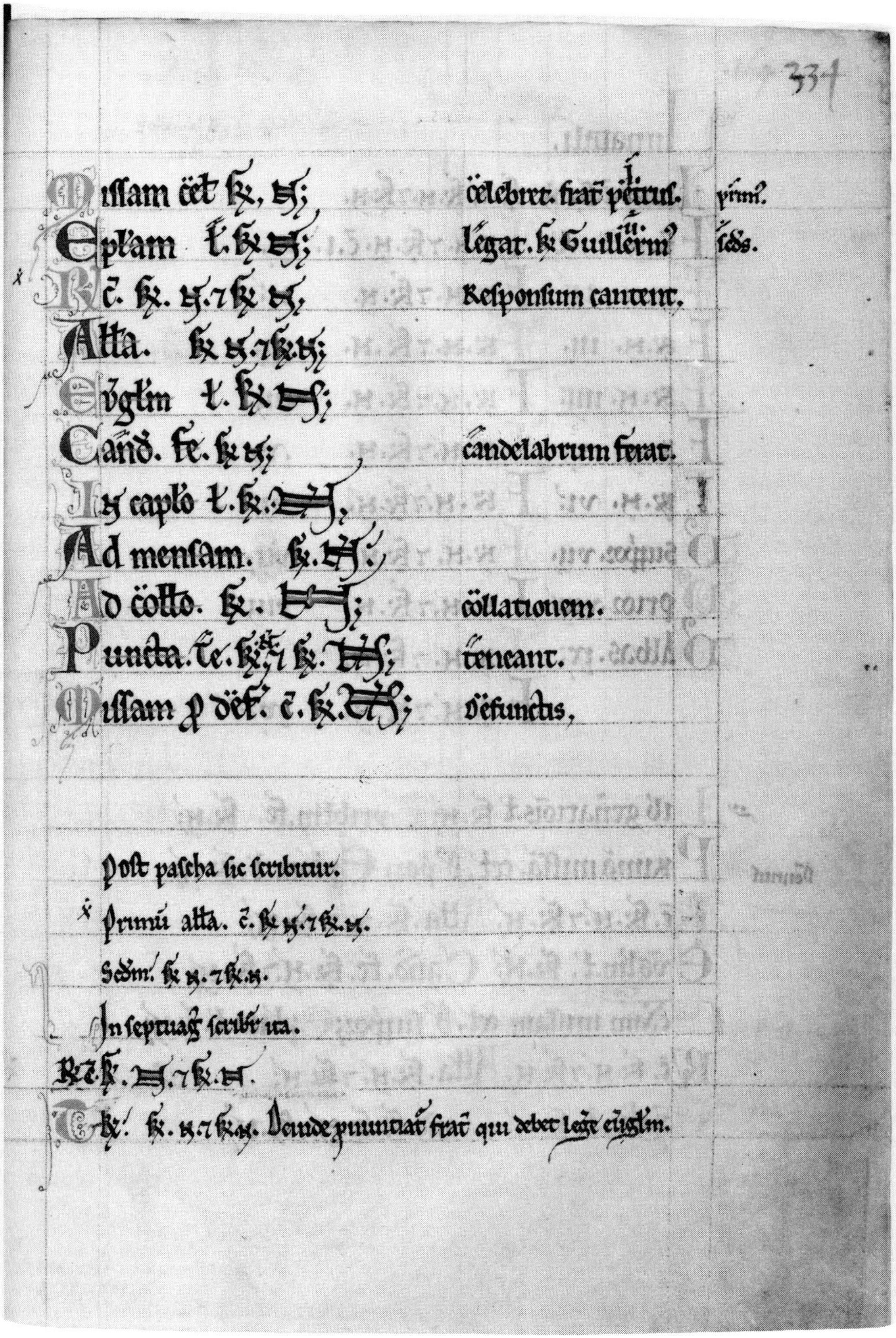

Plates 4.1–4.2   Model for the cantor's tablet from the Victorine ordinal, Paris, BN lat. 14506, fols. 333v–334r

cantor petrus iacob

Inuitat. c. R. v. 7R. vi.

R. v. v. i. v. Fr.v. c. y. R.

R. v. ii. R. vi. ii.

R. v. iii. R. vi. iii.

R. v. iiii. R. vi. iiii.

R. v. v. R. vi. v.

Fr.v. vi. Fr.v. vi.

R.v. vii. R. vi. vii.

R. v. viii. R. vi. viii.

Fr.v. ix. R.v. ix.

frat iohs legat pmã lectione. Galterus canter pmu responsu.

R.v. v. i. v. R. c. i. R.

R.v. ii. R.v. ii.

Fr.v. iiii. R.v. iiii.

Quando duo fres ponuntur in simul in breu

ille qui maioris est ordinis debet psc pnuntiari.

this aspect, they resemble the writings of twelfth-century liturgical commentators, particularly of those who were Augustinian canons regular, and are themselves versified and imagistic commentaries written to be sung within the liturgy itself. The language found in the Victorine sequences, as described by Henig Brinkmann and Eckhard Hegener, draws upon ideas borrowed by Hugh of St. Victor from Augustine's *De doctrina christiana*.

Liturgical changes of this magnitude are usually connected to changes in theological, political, and artistic attitudes with broad implications. In order to identify these, it must first be asked how these changes in sequence repertories took place and if any group or groups of persons were primarily responsible for them in the early stages of their history.

Part II

The rise of the late sequence in twelfth-century France

5

Chartres and Nevers

The importance of comparative study: Benedictines, Augustinians, cathedral canons

In the mind of one poet, the shift in liturgical language represented by "Laudes crucis" had already taken place by the early twelfth century, the date when this sequence was apparently written.[1] But how and when did this sequence and others of its type come into the liturgical practices of churches in France during the twelfth and early thirteenth centuries? What group or groups of people were first interested in them? Which were the first important centers for their production? How were older pieces replaced or supplemented by them, and how long did it take for these kinds of pieces to cease to seem new and to become traditional liturgical fare in their own rights?

These are complicated questions and can best be answered through examination of two kinds of liturgical evidence. In the first place, it is necessary to identify and compare manuscripts from just before and just after the change in sequence repertories took place, as well as manuscripts from the period of transition itself. In the second place, if one wishes to understand the relationship of the change to particular groups of people, it is also crucial to compare manuscripts from a variety of religious establishments: Benedictine, Augustinian, and cathedral. Manuscripts with sequences from the twelfth century, the very time late sequences must first have come into French liturgies, are few, however, compared with the torrent of sources from the thirteenth and fourteenth centuries. By the mid thirteenth century, the new sequences were everywhere in abundance, and liturgists throughout France were standardizing their sequence repertories, incorporating fairly substantial numbers of late sequences, with little apparent regard for their few remaining tropes.[2] There was no need for the traditional manuscripts of the twelfth century or

---

[1] For reasons explained in Chapters 2 and 3, sequences are usually designed for the liturgy, and for a specific place in the liturgy, and not just as religious songs.

[2] The only exceptions to the constant and steady demise of trope repertories which took place in the course of the twelfth and early thirteenth centuries were several genres of ordinary tropes. The recent work of Gunilla Iversen has demonstrated that during the late eleventh and twelfth centuries, some repertories of ordinary

for ancient repertories of tropes and sequences no longer in use and often written in old-fashioned systems of notation. For these reasons, late-eleventh- and twelfth-century trope and sequence manuscripts do not survive in great numbers, and only two twelfth-century collections of proper tropes, one from Chartres and the other from Nevers, survive from central and northern France.

Because the survival rate for twelfth-century sequence manuscripts is comparatively low, there are few centers for which beginning, middle, and later phrases of twelfth-century liturgical changes can be documented directly from extant sources. To study this change, then, one needs to examine manuscripts from various times during the twelfth century, comparing the use of one religious group to that of another, and of one center or region to another. In this way the inevitable gaps in the documentation of one place or use or generation can be filled in with surviving manuscripts from others. The manuscripts to be studied in Part II of this book have been chosen with great care: concentraton is upon centers with two or more sources containing sequences from the very late eleventh, twelfth, or early thirteenth centuries, and only from those places whose surviving manuscripts represent at least two types of religious establishments. Fortunately, these criteria are met in three places in France: Chartres, Nevers, and Limoges, and met imperfectly in yet a fourth place, Paris, where the sources, although excellent, are late. The regional variety offered by the manuscripts and the numbers of religious institutions represented here will provide a dependable overview of changes within sequence repertories during the twelfth century and will allow for the determination of which religious groups favored late sequences during this epoch. In each case, another manuscript from the area and period will be brought into the discussion to give a fuller picture of the differences in attitudes between Benedictines, Augustinians, and cathedral canons in regard to these repertories. Each region studied allows a unique view of liturgical change and of the effect of religious reformers upon the liturgy. In Chartres, one can compare the liturgy of Augustinian canons regular to that of the cathedral in the first half of the twelfth century; in Nevers, a cathedral liturgy untouched by reform for generations (from the mid eleventh to the mid twelfth century) may be compared to a liturgy of reformed Augustinians just after the middle of the twelfth century; and in Limoges, it is possible to view the effects of two reforms, one of Benedictines, the other of Augustinians, upon the local development of sequences. Ideas regarding reform and liturgical change are tested finally in Paris where, although the relevant sources date, for the most part, from the early thirteenth century, several uses – cathedral, two houses of Augustinians, and Benedictines – may be compared.

tropes actually expanded. See especially Iversen (1991) and her article (forthcoming) on Paris, BN lat. n.a. 3126.

The first half of the twelfth century: the Augustinians of Chartres

Sources to be considered

Manuscript location, siglum	*Use and type of book*	*Century*
1 Châteaudun, Arch. Hôtel Dieu 13, fols. 179–201 (abbreviated as OV)	Cathedral rite ordinal	12th (mid)
2 Paris, BN lat. 1794	St.-Jean-en-Vallée (Augustinian) ordinal	12th (mid)
3 Paris, Ste. Gen. 1256 (Prepared for Notre-Dame de Gâtains and very close to lat. 1794)	St.-Jean-en-Vallée ordinal	12th (mid)
4 Chartres, BM 1058 (abbreviated as OC)	Cathedral rite ordinal	12th (second quarter)
5 Provins 12	Cathedral rite gradual with tropes and sequences	12th/13th
6 Chartres 520 (Facsimile edition by David Hiley is forthcoming)	Cathedral rite noted Missal	13th (mid)

Chartres is of special importance for the study of reform and its effects upon the liturgy and liturgical arts during the early twelfth century. For over twenty-five years (1089–1115) the diocese was overseen by Bishop Ivo, one of the most influential religious reformers in France. A canonist of central importance, Ivo left not only his codifications of church law and his letters, but also a significant body of sermons which contains comments about religious art and its purposes. Ivo of Chartres, instrumental in establishing reformed houses of canons in other cities and in his parent house, St. Quentin in Beauvais, was not to allow Chartres to remain untouched by the Gregorian reform movement.[3] During the late eleventh century, he attempted to bring reform to the cathedral canons, and when they rejected his ideas, he reformed the house of seculars at St.-Jean-en-Vallée in 1098, instituting the Rule of St. Augustine.[4] It was here the famous bishop chose to be buried, offering to the church a final gesture of his affection and the perpetual blessing of his remains.

Thus the history of Chartres in the early twelfth century reveals both cathedral canons resistant to the ideas of change and reform, and a newly founded house of Augustinians that had embraced them. It is fortunate for this study that the liturgies of both of these institutions are fully documented in ordinals prepared not long after the time of Ivo's reform of St. Jean. Both of these ordinals, the *Ordo veridicus* (OV) from the Cathedral of Notre Dame in Chartres, and the contemporary ordinal from

---

[3] See Dereine (1948).

[4] The foundation charter is printed in Merlet, ed., *Cartulaire de Saint-Jean-en-Vallée de Chartres*, pp. 2–3.

St. Jean, are early for books of their type and rival in detail the ordinals of Cluny prepared in the late eleventh century.

The contents of the OV probably so named because it had a green cover at one time, exist only through a series of fortunate incidents, each of which negates the results of an even greater misfortune. The original OV from the Cathedral of Notre Dame is lost without a trace, and was surely replaced by the revised ordinal, Chartres 1058, in the second quarter of the thirteenth century.[5] In the third quarter of the twelfth century, however, the OV was copied for the use of the Hôtel-Dieu in Châteaudun, located in the diocese of Chartres.[6] This copy was still extant in the first half of the twentieth century, but has subsequently been either destroyed or, more likely, misplaced.[7] In 1935, however, the dedicated scholar and canon of Chartres Cathedral, Yves Delaporte, made a detailed handwritten copy of the book for his own study.[8] It is his copy which survives today, and photocopies of it have been made available to researchers through the generosity of Pierre Bizeau, Diocesan Archivist of Chartres.[9] Delaporte believed the book to contain the cathedral liturgy as it existed in the late eleventh or early twelfth century: feasts of the temporale and the sanctorale are mixed throughout the book, an early feature; it does not contain the Translation of St. Aignan, instituted in Chartres in 1136. The states of various of its repertories show it to be indeed earlier than Chartres 1058 (OC), the cathedral ordinal from the second quarter of the thirteenth century. The OV has more proper tropes than the OC; it has no late sequences and the OC has several; it has slightly fewer mentions of organa. Delaporte believed its contents to date from the early twelfth century or, perhaps even the early eleventh century, in spite of the fact that it mentions the "porta regia." He thought rather that a door by this name must have existed in the eleventh-century church of Fulbert as well.[10] Because the copy is so late, it would be prudent to adopt the later rather than the earlier part of the span of years proposed by Delaporte – the first decade of the twelfth century, but probably before 1136. This would still place the book before the construction of the present twelfth-century "Porta regia," usually dated to 1145–50, and would mean that the book outlines the Chartrian liturgy as it existed

---

5   If it had still been in use or in existence by the late twelfth century, as is likely, it would probably have been burned in the fire of 1194. Unlike other kinds of books (which were kept in large cabinets in the cloister), liturgical books of both monasteries and cathedrals were customarily kept in the church and, if they were particularly valuable, even in the treasury of the church.

6   The church "L'Hôtel-Dieu" was rebuilt in the first half of the twelfth century and Delaporte believed the copy of the *Ordo veridicus* was made in the third quarter of the twelfth century for the new church. See Delaporte, ed., *L'Ordinaire chartrain*, pp. 12–18 and especially pp. 16–17. A history of Châteaudun is found in the introduction to Merlet's *Inventaire-Sommaire des Archives Hospitalières Antérieures a 1790: Hospices de Châteaudun* (Châteaudun, 1867), pp. i–xvii.

7   There is always hope, but Jean Loup Lemaître was unable to find the volume in his recent search in preparation of his massive *Répertoire des documents nécrologiques français*.

8   Canon Delaporte had his own difficulties in finding the manuscript. Correspondence found today in the Diocesan Archives of Chartres revealed that he searched for it from as early as 1924 and in 1934 was still looking. By the following year, however, he had been able to study it.

9   Through a oversight uncharacteristic of his meticulous work habits, Delaporte supplied no folio numbers in his copy. The numbers cited here for the OV refer to pages in his copy.

10 Delaporte, ed., *L'Ordinaire chartrain* (hereafter OC), p. 17.

within the church begun by Bishop Fulbert in the 1020s and continuously modified throughout the eleventh and early twelfth centuries.[11]

If the contents of the OV may be dated as indicated, then the book is a very near contemporary of the earliest surviving ordinal from the Augustinian Abbey of St.-Jean-en-Vallée. When the canons were newly founded in 1098, they adopted the liturgy of the mother church, Notre Dame de Chartres, but they did not preserve it absolutely unchanged. They reformed it in certain details, and recorded the results of their labors in a new ordinal. The contents of the book date after the time of Ivo's death in 1115: it contains his commemorative Mass and Office, but it does not contain the Translation of St. Aignan. Two nearly identical twelfth-century copies of the ordinal survive; the earlier copy, Ste. Gen. 1256, dates from just around 1150 and was prepared for Notre Dame de Gâtins, an affiliate of St. Jean. Although Paris, BN lat. 1794 was copied after Ste. Gen. 1256 by two hands dating from the third quarter of the twelfth century, the contents of the book are earlier. This ordinal represents the work of the first generation and a half of canons regular at St. Jean, many of whom must have known Ivo himself. Through studying the contents of this collection, one can move near to the liturgical intentions of Augustinian reformers in northern France during the first half of the twelfth century.

How is the Augustinian rite of St. Jean different from that found in the early-twelfth-century ordinal from the cathedral, the OV? How did the Augustinians change the liturgical practices imported from the cathedral?

A major difference between the earliest Augustinian liturgy at St.-Jean-en-Vallée and the contemporary cathedral rite is in attitudes toward proper tropes and organum. Although proper tropes, especially for the introit, were abundant in the early-twelfth-century cathedral rite and organum was in evidence for several major feasts, such pieces have no place in the Augustinian Mass liturgy. This attitude toward tropes and organum at St. Jean persisted, even as organum became somewhat more important at the cathedral in the course of the twelfth century.[12] A comparison of texts for the second Mass of Epiphany exemplifies the situation for major feasts at Chartres. At the cathedral, tropes for the introit and Offertory were sung in the early twelfth century; by the early thirteenth century, although introit tropes remained, those for the Offertory had disappeared (as was the case in most other French centers by the early thirteenth century). But neither of the ordinals representing the use of St. Jean mentions these two tropes, even though they are more detailed in general than the cathedral ordinals. The statement regarding performance of the Gradual ("R. cum organo ut consuetudo est") in the OC suggests that polyphonic performance of this part of the Mass was customary for this feast by the early thirteenth century at Notre Dame of Chartres. (However, although organum is specified for several other feasts in both the OV and the OC, it is primarily in connection with the Alleluia.) By contrast, the Augustinian ordinals

---

[11] The structure was seriously damaged by fire in 1194, and this event occasioned the building of the present cathedral.

[12] In Paris, too, although the sources proving it are later, organum seems to have been the special musical provence of singers in the cathedral. See Wright (1989), p. 257.

never mention organum. Thus whether early or late in the twelfth century, the Augustinians rejected the proper tropes and organum characteristic of the cathedral rite.

The apparent disinclination of Augustinians to allow proper tropes into their liturgy is underscored by the situation regarding the Mass of St. Andrew. When the cathedral canons processed on November 30 to celebrate the Mass with the Augustinians at the nearby church of St. André, they left their trope repertory behind. "Ibi," the cathedral ordinals state, "missa 'Michi autem,' sine tropis et sine laud., sequentia 'Organicis.'"[13] That is, when worshiping with the Augustinian church of St. André, the customary tropes for the feast (and these are preserved in Provins 12) were not sung, nor were the Gloria tropes. The sequence, however, was. The Augustinians at St. André in Chartres were even stricter regarding tropes than the Augustinians of St. Jean: they would not allow the visiting canons this liturgical practice, although it was permitted to them when they visited St. Jean.[14] This Augustinian disavowal of proper tropes at Chartres, demonstrated early in the twelfth century, suggests that instead of merely reflecting a preexisting trend to get rid of tropes, the Augustinian refusal to adapt proper tropes for their liturgy may have been a factor in their demise during the late eleventh and twelfth centuries. If so, however, this was part of a long-established trend: from Cluniacs to Cistercians and, apparently, to Augustinians, religious reformers from the tenth through the thirteenth centuries were not inclined to use tropes, especially proper tropes, in their liturgies.[15]

Epiphany at Chartres: a comparison of the feast in the four ordinals from the twelfth and early thirteenth centuries

1. Cathedral: *Ordo veridicus*
Ad ultimam missam, tropos "Ecclesie sponsus," seq. "Epiphaniam Domino," et in Octavis seq. "Sonent regi nato" uel "Iubilemus," et ad Off. Tropos "Letetur."

2. Augustinian: Lat. 1794
Ad magnam missam dominus abbas. Chorus in capis. Et fit processio cum duobus candelabris turibulis et textu cantor. Ecce advenit. Psalmus Deus iuditium. Kirie fons bonitatis. Collectio Deus qui hodierna. Epistola Surge illuminare. R. Omnes de saba v. Surge. Alleluia Vidimus stellam. Sequentia Epiphaniam domino. Ante ev. fit Processio cum duobus candelabris turibulis textu et cruce a. Tribus miraculis. Ev. Cum natus esset★★. credo in unum. Off. Reges. Pref. Quia cum unigenitus. Sanctus. Communicantes. Agnus dei. Com. Vidimus stellam.

3. Augustinian: Ste. Gen. 1256 (modeled after 1794, script from the mid twelfth century) 54v
Ad magnam missam. Domnus abbas. Fit processio cum candelabris turibulo et textu. [Offin.] Ecce

---

[13] OC, p. 191.

[14] See *ibid.*, pp. 173–174. The description is of the Mass of the Beheading of St. John the Baptist. The canons processed to St.-Jean-en-Vallée where Mass was sung, with tropes. As would be expected, the canons sang tropes at the Benedictine church of St.-Père-en-Vallée. See *ibid.*, p. 162.

[15] The attitude of Cluny toward tropes will be discussed below in Chapter 6. Andreas Haug has identified a generally unknown layer of proper tropes surviving after the twelfth century, and a few of these can be found in Augustinian sources, especially from east of the Rhine; an inventory of these late tropes will appear in his forthcoming musical index to the Corpus Troporum. I am grateful to Dr. Haug for having shared the results of his research with me prior to its publication.

advenit. Ps. Deus iudicium. Kyrie Fons bonitatis. Collecta Deus qui hodierna. et cetera sicut sunt. Seqn. Epiphaniam. Credo. Pref. Quia cum unigenitus. Communicantes.

4.   Cathedral: Chartres 1058 (second quarter of the thirteenth century, modeled after the *Ordo veridicus*)
Ad missam Ecce advenit cum tropis. Kyriel. Kyrie fons bo., R. cum organo ut consuetudo est, sequentia Epiphaniam. Ante. ante evangelium Tribus miraculis.

Although the Augustinians at St. Jean elected to omit proper tropes and organum from their version of the cathedral liturgy, they showed an interest in sequences, an interest which is manifested in several ways. Even the first generation of Augustinians increased their inherited repertory by over a third: they kept all twenty-six sequences found in the OV and added thirteen pieces. At first glance, the additions themselves are not spectacular, mostly chosen from a large repertory of works known throughout France. Nor do the subjects honored with sequences provoke surprise: here are a sequence for John the Baptist, patron of the church, two sequences for St. Augustine, patron of the order, and a sequence for the Virgin Mary. The sequence "Precelsa seculi" for St. Vincent, just coming in at Cluny and elsewhere in France in the late eleventh century, was picked up here at Chartres also, as might be expected.

This core of sequences found at the Cathedral of Notre Dame in Chartres and at St. Jean (with supplements) in the early twelfth century is small, and one wonders at first if the picture of the sequence repertory found in these ordinals is reliable. The consistency with which these sequences appear in the four ordinals studied here, however, attests to their probable reliability in this regard. Several "classic" sequences assumed to have been written in the late eleventh century are not in the twelfth-century ordinals: "Victime paschali laudes" (for Easter), "Congaudentes" (St. Nicholas), and "Letabundus" (usually for Christmas), for example, are not yet found here. This is a conservative repertory, undoubtedly compiled before sequences in the new style of accentual Latin poetry had become popular and were either readily available or accepted. The only pieces in the transitional-verging-on-new or the new style are found in the Augustinian use: "Clara chorus" for the Dedication and "Interni festi" for St. Augustine, of which these manuscripts are the earliest witnesses.[16] "Mane prima" for Mary Magdalene is mentioned in lat. 1794 as well, but the sequence was just coming in: it was sung only if the feast fell on a Sunday. Because the Augustinians at St. Jean adapted the cathedral liturgy in most aspects, the several sequences added by them at this early stage point to a special regard for the genre.

This emphasis on sequences at St. Jean is further attested by their attempt to create a full cycle of sequences for the entire church year, not, in their case, by writing new pieces or selecting from the plentiful repertory of sequences then circulating throughout France, but rather by repeating a small group of pieces again and again.

---

[16] The use of rhyme and regular accentual patterns found in "Clara chorus" is very different from that of "Interni festi," which is fully in the new style. "Clara chorus" was probably written in the mid eleventh century: it was just coming in at Cluny and Cambrai in the late eleventh century, and had achieved great popularity by the early twelfth century.

Table 5.1. *Sequences added to the cathedral repertory by the Augustinians at St.-Jean-en-Vallée in the early twelfth century*

Title	Feast at St. Jean	Century
Nostra tuba	Vigil of Christmas	9th(?)
Nato canunt	Days of Christmas	10th
Precelsa seculi	St. Vincent	11th
Clare sanctorum	Apostles	9th
Clara chorus	Dedication	11th
Gude caterua	John the Baptist	11th
Interna festi	St. Augustine	late 11th
Adest nobis	Octave of Augustine	10th/11th
Alle celeste	Nativity of the BVM	10th
O alma trinitas	St. Martin	10th
Virginis uenerande	One virgin	9th
Mane prima	Mary Magdalene	late 11th
	(If the feast fell on a Sunday)	

The long cycle of Sundays extending from the first Sunday after Pentecost until the first Sunday of Advent was served in most places by Dominical sequences, pieces designed just for these days; some repertories contain one or two such sequences; others have none, making it unclear whether sequences were sung on these days, or which pieces they were.[17] The compilers of Paris, lat. 1794 left none of these Sundays to chance: in their list of Alleluias for Sundays after Pentecost, each chant is paired with a sequence.[18] They had other Sunday cycles as well: Sundays after Epiphany and after Easter are served by small groups of sequences, in each case using some sequences found in the Advent cycle.[19]

The Augustinians at St.-Jean-en-Vallée reacted in different ways to proper tropes on the one hand and sequences on the other. They were not interested in proper tropes: even those for their own patron, John the Baptist, were removed from their liturgy. They seem to have cared especially, however, about sequences, and not only to have increased the number of pieces, but also to have expended effort to insure that the genre was integrated into their Mass liturgy, writing out the cycles noted above by pairing each sequence with an Alleluia. Of course, other churches had ways of supplying their Sunday cycles with sequences, most commonly by singing one or two pieces for Sundays during the year, and others as applicable. It is, however, unusual to find Sunday cycles with sequences all written out in this

---

[17] The cycle for Sundays after Pentecost is found, but incompletely, in Provins 12, a thirteenth-century copy of a twelfth-century Chartrian book. Although Provins 12 represents the cathedral use, rather than the use of St. Jean, it proves that other Chartrian churches knew and used sequence cycles, too, but not to the extent they were found at St. Jean. I have edited the trope repertory in my forthcoming book on the liturgy of the Cathedral of Notre Dame in Chartres.

[18] See Paris, BN lat. 1794, fol. 162.

[19] For a complete list of the sequence cycles at St. Jean, see Fassler (1991).

manner in an ordinal. In fact, I know of no other example. Thus this feature of the ordinal does testify to an interest in sequences.

The relationship between Alleluia and sequence has a long history which has been discussed in Chapters 1 and 2 of this book. It must be noted that these Chartrian Augustinians worked to create an illusory bond between the two genres of chant, a bond which they undoubtedly believed was historically valid and at one time stronger. It was important to them that Alleluias and sequences functioned in pairs, even if a particular sequence was paired with several different Alleluias, and even if, as was usually the case, the chants lacked any semblance of musical relationship. The pairing itself was what mattered. By connecting each sequence to an Alleluia, the Augustinians made a liturgical statement: sequences and Alleluias served a common function in the Mass liturgy and both were central to its celebration; the sequence was an extension of the Alleluia, a commentary upon it. The development of this historical relationship in their liturgy offers the first piece of evidence we have for explaining the attraction that sequences had for the canons regular. The words of such pieces were, of course, commentaries upon the meanings of the Alleluia, the very chant their patron saint, Augustine, had discussed in detail in his sermons.[20] Thus the sequences provided an opportunity for Augustinian canons regular to expand upon the tradition established first by their spiritual father. The sources from Chartres suggest that they realized this already in the early twelfth century.

Taken all together, this evidence suggests that the Augustinians in Chartres had a higher regard for sequences than their contemporaries at the Cathedral of Notre Dame. They did not write new pieces themselves, however; rather, they sought them from the older repertory of sequences. Only "Interni festi," an early-twelfth-century piece for St. Augustine, may have been written at St Jean itself. Yet their interest in the genre indicates the positive attitude of Augustinians toward sequences in early-twelfth-century northern France, and it contrasts with an apparent lesser interest on the part of cathedral canons.[21]

What happened to this Augustinian repertory from Chartres as the century advanced? Many of the sources that could answer this question have been destroyed or mutilated. Rome, Biblioteca Angelica 435, an early-thirteenth-century troper-proser from the Augustinian house of St. Chéron, is incomplete, as is the thirteenth-century gradual from St.-Jean-en-Vallée, Chartres, BM 529.[22] The best evidence one has of the Chartrian sequence repertory in the late twelfth and early thirteenth centuries is as sung at the cathedral and at other secular churches. The cathedral ordinal from Chartres edited by Delaporte, the OC, has thirty-seven sequences, ten more than are found in the OV. Provins 12 contains forty-five sequences, and

---

[20] Liturgists in the twelfth century would not have realized that the Alleluia Augustine described was not the same as the Alleluia found in their Mass.

[21] Although the evidence is not plentiful, it is clear that sequences were not only used at the Mass in Chartres, but sometimes found a place in the Office as well, as substitutes for hymns at vespers or compline. During Easter week, the canons of St. Jean, the cathedral of Chartres, and of other northern cathedrals as well, sang sequences at vespers or compline. Both cathedral ordinals state that the sequence "Rex omnipotens" was to be sung at Ascension and throughout the octave "alternando" at compline. See OV, p. 54 and OC, p. 128.

[22] A microfilm of Chartres 529 survives in the Bibliothèque Municipale, Chartres.

fifteen of these are in the late style, most of the new works appearing in a supplement copied in the main hand.[23] Chartres 520, a mid-thirteenth-century noted missal with sequences, contains forty-six sequences, nineteen of which are in the late style.[24] The sequence repertories of these churches had increased in number by the mid thirteenth century, apparently in two stages: a small number came in during the late twelfth and very early thirteenth centuries, and a yet larger number entered during the second quarter. Were the Augustinians of Chartres the leaders in this change, following through with the emphasis on sequences evident in the first half of the twelfth century? Several of the sequences found in lat. 1794 were taken over by the secular repertories mentioned above. But the evidence to answer this question is lacking at Chartres.

Of course, to complete this picture of the Chartrian liturgy, a Benedictine source with sequences from the mid twelfth century is needed as well. Unfortunately, the scribe of Troyes, BM 894 changed his mind about including sequences in this early-twelfth-century noted missal from the Benedictine house of St.-Père-en-Vallée of Chartres. After copying out the first two sequences, he never even referred to another such piece. For a contemporary Benedictine witness, one must look outside Chartres.

The Benedictine attitude toward sequences in the mid twelfth century: St. Evroult

Manuscript to be considered:

Paris, BN lat. 10508	cantatorium-troper-proser	mid 12th century
SOU:103; NGS:625		

The Benedictine Abbey of St. Evroult was founded in 1050 on the frontier of south-western Normandy. Here, during the first half of the twelfth century, the monk Ordericus Vitalis wrote his thirteen-book *Historia ecclesiastica*, a work which, ultimately, was to insure the fame of his monastery long after its demise in the late eighteenth century.[25] Ordericus, a defender of Benedictine tradition, mentions the chant of his abbey and its importance in this history of St. Evroult. The first abbot, Thierry of Matonville (†1058), taught chant to the monks himself;[26] Robert of Grentsmesnil, the second abbot, supposedly commissioned the music for the Office of St. Evroult from Arnoul, cantor of Chartres and pupil of the great Fulbert. Undoubtedly because it came in unheightened neumes, two monks from St.

---

[23] For an inventory of the manuscript, see David Hiley, "Provins 12 (24), a 13th-century gradual with tropes from Chartres Cathedral" (forthcoming). Professor Hiley kindly supplied me with a copy of his article before its publication.

[24] Although the manuscript was destroyed in 1944, a microfilm survives. A facsimile edition made from this film and edited by David Hiley is now in press. Professor Hiley kindly shared copies of his work with me before publication.

[25] Ordericus Vitalis, *Historia ecclesiastica*, ed. Chibnall.

[26] See Book III, Chapters 20–21; Chibnall edn., vol. II, pp. 18–20.

Evroult traveled to Chartres to get the melody from the mouth of the master.[27] Other monks are mentioned as composers for the troper and the antiphoner,[28] and two monks are cited for their singing: Berengar, son of Arnold of Heugon, and Robert Gamaliel.[29] Here, according to Ordericus, was a chant tradition worthy of importation to monasteries in Italy under Norman control.[30] The historical connection between this Benedictine house and Chartres, and their liturgical music, make it a worthy subject of comparison.[31]

A mid-twelfth-century library inventory attests to a significant collection of chant books at St. Evroult: three antiphoners, three graduals, and twelve prosers.[32] At least one book has survived from St. Evroult which may have been among those listed: Paris, BN lat. 10508, a twelfth-century manuscript collection of Mass music, divided into pieces for the choir (ordinary chants and sequences) and soloists' chants (Graduals and Alleluias).[33] The main hand of the manuscript and the hand of the library inventory are strikingly similar, although not the same.

Two colored lines, a green one usually signifying C and a red one signifying F, are used throughout in Paris lat. 10508, the same as in Provins 12.[34] Pitches can be read without the aid of the memory, unlike those mentioned by Ordericus when discussing the Office for St. Evroult. The notation is up to date in this book, and the sequence repertory is large and more typical of the period than the smaller repertories found at Chartres. The manuscript contains around fifteen sequences which were probably written in the late tenth through the late eleventh century, some of which are found in southern French sources, some of which are found east of the Rhine, and a few of which are found either first or only in this manuscript. This is a less conservative sequence repertory than that found at Chartres Cathedral in the early twelfth century, where only one sequence from the eleventh century, "Sonent regi," probably by Fulbert of Chartres, is found. Although many sequences written in the eleventh century were adopted by these Benedictines when they wrote their sequence repertory, transitional and late-style pieces often assumed to have been written in the late eleventh or early twelfth centuries are not present: "Letabundus" for Christmas, "Clara chorus" for the Dedication, "Mane prima" for Easter week and St. Mary Magdalene, and "Congaudentes" for St. Nicholas are all

---

[27] Book III, Chapter 96; Chibnall edn., vol. III, p. 108.

[28] Book III, Chapter 96; Chibnall edn., vol. II, p. 108.

[29] Book III, Chapter 90; Chibnall edn., vol. II, p. 103, and Book 3, Chapter 86; Chibnall edn., vol. II, p. 96.

[30] Book III, Chapter 91; Chibnall edn., vol. II, pp. 102–103. "So in these three Italian monasteries the liturgy of St. Evroult is chanted and the monastic rule has been observed to the present day, as far as the customs of the region and the allegiance of the inhabitants allow."

[31] Ray (1972) has suggested that one of Ordericus's purposes in writing the *Historia* was to record commemorative features of the liturgy at St. Evroult.

[32] See Delisle (1912), Plate I.

[33] Alençon B.M.135 is also from St. Evroult and is, according to Planchart (1977), vol. II, p. 343) "A Collectanea of Lives of Saints with some hymns and tropes, partly in the hand of Ordericus Vitalis."

[34] For a color plate of Paris, BN lat. 10508, fol. 10r and v, see Stäblein (1975), p. 119. Delaporte (ed., *Fragments*), p. 15, speaks of the "portée chartrain" as consisting of four drypoint lines, with the F in green, and the C in yellow, with some modification. Thus the colors used in both Provins 12 and lat. 10508 are not those used in Chartres itself, where, apparently, red was not common. It is of course, impossible to see the colors in early photographs and microfilms of Chartian manuscripts destroyed in the terrible fire of May 26, 1944.

missing. There is little in the repertory to indicate activity in either the very late eleventh or the early twelfth century.

Most interesting for the study of liturgical change are the sequences added later, mostly at the back of the book. Here one finds an indication of the pieces or kinds of pieces which interested the cantors of St. Evroult in the second half of the twelfth century and the early thirteenth century. These are the sequences they would be experimenting with, trying out in their liturgies to see if they would stand the test of time. There are five of these sequences in various hands at the back.

The first piece added in the back is "Interni festi" for St. Augustine, copied carelessly in a hand contemporary with the main hand.[35] At first, it might seem surprising to find this piece, the hallmark of an Augustinian book, drawn into this Benedictine repertory at mid-century.[36] Its presence testifies that the Benedictines at St. Evroult had an interest in this work, perhaps as exemplifying a new style of sequence, but even more probably because of the close connection between St. Evroult and Chartres, whose Augustinians may well have been responsible for the creation of this piece. Each of the sequences which follows "Interni festi" is in a different hand, and each hand gets later in the twelfth century as one approaches the end of the book. "Luce lucens prefulgida," is written in a script very near in date to the main hand. After it follow two Marian sequences, the twelfth-century "Post partum uirgo" and "Potestate non natura," a twelfth-century sequence which was widespread in sources east of the Rhine and which perhaps originated in Austria with the Augustinians of St. Florian or Seckau.[37] Here, it is without notes. In a very different late-twelfth-century or early-thirteenth-century hand is a copy of "Laudes crucis," the final piece in the book.[38] The text is the traditional version, but the melody is somewhat odd, the cadence patterns not behaving characteristically. Even this famous sequence, which was in general circulation not long after the mid twelfth century, came late to St. Evroult.

Ordericus Vitalis sounds a note of pride when speaking of the traditional chant of St. Evroult. He is far less enthusiastic about the orders of reformed Benedictines around him and their liturgical practices:

From the ides of September to Easter they fast every day except Sunday; their doors are always shut close, and they bury themselves in profound secrecy, admitting no monks belonging to any other religious house into their cells, not allowing them to be present in the chapel at mass or other divine offices. Multitudes of noble champions and learned men joined their society from the novelty of its institutions, and voluntarily submitting to their canonical rigour, rejoiced to chant triumphant anthems to Christ in the *right* way [emphasis mine].[39]

---

[35] See fols. 136v–137r. This sequence and other sequences are written on parchment which is ruled just like the main body of the book; thus the pieces were a part of the book from the start, rather than stray leaves gathered up and bound in at some later date. The scribes who added the pieces to the original, ruled parchment were not careful to use the pages as the original scribe did, and this makes the pieces look tentative and experimental. No rubrics were supplied for any of them. Added elsewhere are "In sapientia" and "Missus Gabriel," both dating from the twelfth century.

[36] This is the earliest full copy of the piece known to me.

[37] See discussion in *AH* LIV, p. 147. The text is edited here as well. See also Prassl (1987).

[38] fols. 134v–135v.

[39] Book VIII, Chapter 26. For commentary upon this famous passage, see Holdsworth (1985).

The passage is somewhat critical of these "new monks," who must keep their liturgies to themselves and who claim to know better than their more traditional brethren not only how to live, but how to chant as well.[40] As elsewhere in this particular section of his vast history, Ordericus doubts whether the novelties of the day are truly superior to the tried and true Benedictine practices in which he was raised. The cantor who prepared lat. 10508 may well have shared these views. He neither got rid of sequences, as the Cistercians would have, nor sought more and newer ones, as the Augustinians in Chartres did; the repertory was already large by the mid twelfth century and sufficed for the needs of the church. Just as Ordericus was content with his life as a Benedictine of the old order, this unknown cantor was content to let his sequence repertory remain as it might have been a generation before him; his work, one can imagine, was to incorporate the several sequences adopted during the second half of the eleventh century, the very kinds of pieces not found at Chartres cathedral. If the later additions made to the manuscript are an indication of the kinds and quantities of new pieces experimented with during the second half of the twelfth century and into the early thirteenth century, then the sequence repertory of St. Evroult did not grow much or in any significant way then.

This study of manuscripts of three separate traditions, but all from the same region, is of sequence repertories put together during the opening decades of the twelfth century. It demonstrates that by the third and fourth decades of the twelfth century sequences in the new style had not come into liturgical books in great numbers. Only the ordinal from the Augustinians at St. Jean has two of these pieces. Examination of other books from the region would reveal a similar state and would promote the conclusion that sequences in the new style were only in the experimental stage during the opening decades of the twelfth century.[41] At this time, sequences such as "Interni festi" for St. Augustine or "Laudes crucis" for the cross would have seemed strikingly different from their ancestors created in the ninth, tenth, and early or mid eleventh centuries, especially in northern regions, where there seems not to have been a significant number of sequences written in the eleventh century. In so far as sequences in the new style were known, they were not yet accepted and were apparently heard as departures from the more traditional sounds of the early sequence. It is easy for the modern scholar, looking back on the twelfth century with knowledge of the great success of late sequences in the late twelfth, thirteenth, and fourteenth centuries, to forget that these works were, at one time, new. The sources suggest that to have great numbers of them in a Mass liturgy at the mid twelfth century would have been very unusual.

---

[40] Although Ordericus is not critical of the canons regular, other Benedictines were. See, for example, Van Engen's (1983, pp. 323–334) discussion of Rupert of Deutz's attitude toward the regular canons.

[41] There are, for example, very low numbers of sequences in the new style in the two Norman-Sicilian manuscripts from just before the mid twelfth century – Madrid, B.N. 288, and Madrid, B.N. Vitrina 20–4 – and in Cambrai 60 (61), a Gradual with sequences dating from the middle of the twelfth century, which represents the use of Cambrai Cathedral.

Nevers during the middle decades of the twelfth century: long-standing tradition and rapid change

Manuscripts to be considered

Location and siglum	Type of book and use	Date
Paris, BN lat. 9449 SOU:102; NGS:616; RISM:140–142	troper-proser Cathedral	1059–61
Paris, BN lat. n.a. 1235 SOU:111; NGS:625	gradual with tropes and sequences Cathedral	mid 12th century
Paris, BN lat. n.a. 3126 NGS:616; RISM:148–149	kyriale-proser Augustinian	mid 12th century

The ancient cathedral town of Nevers is located on the river Loire in the geographical center of France, near to the towns of Auxerre and Autun.[42] Medieval Nevers had two important libraries, one at the Cathedral of St. Cyr and the other at the Augustinian house of St. Martin.[43] As was typical of most monastic and cathedral libraries in France, both these collections were despoiled and dispersed during the Revolution and the years immediately following it, with most of the volumes permanently lost.[44] Yet during the late nineteenth and early twentieth centuries, when French scholars, most notably Crosnier, Boutillier, and de Lespinasse, attempted to recover the history of medieval Nevers, its libraries, architecture, and liturgy, a small collection of Nivernais liturgical manuscripts became known to the scholarly community.[45] In the twentieth century, yet another Nivernais manuscript was found (Paris BN lat. n.a. 3126), the strength of the collection inspiring modern scholars of the chant and liturgy to turn attention once again to medieval Nevers.[46] Altogether four sequence manuscripts survive from Nevers, one from the eleventh century, two from the twelfth century, and one

---

[42] The dependence of the early Nevers liturgy upon that of Autun was described by Crosnier (1868). Reier (1981) has bolstered this view, showing that the Introit repertory of lat. 9449 is highly concordant with, although larger than, the Autun repertory as preserved in Paris, Bibl. Arsenal 1169 (from around 1000).

[43] A ninth-century Evangeliary from Nevers now in the British Library (Harley 2790) contains a book-list bearing the inscription: "Hec sunt nomina librorum qui sunt in armario sancti cyrici."

[44] For surviving inventories of the cathedral library, see Boutillier (1890) and Cahn (1981), p. 65. The devastation of the Nivernais libraries is discussed in Duminy (1900). The destruction began well before the Revolution; pages from dismembered Nivernais liturgical books were commonly used to bind registers in the late seventeenth century. See Huglo (1957), pp. 24–25.

[45] These three and other active members of the Société Nivernaise des Lettres, Sciences et Arts wrote monographs, prepared editions, and offered a stream of articles to the society's *Bulletin*. Unfortunately, this series did not survive World War II.

[46] Although Augustin Crosnier spent his lifetime investigating the Cathedral of Nevers and its liturgy, he worked without the benefits of modern paleographical science. Pioneering work was done in this century by Huglo (1957), who offered an inventory of the sequences found in Paris, BN lat. n.a. 3126 and brief descriptions of other liturgical books from Nevers. Van Deusen (1980 and 1982) has prepared a useful inventory of the Nivernais repertory, using lat. 9449 as a base, and has transcribed texts and music from lat. n.a. 1235 and n.a. 1236. Reier's (1981) thorough and illuminating study of the Introit tropes has significantly advanced understanding of the character of the Nivernais liturgy.

from the fourteenth century, and the earliest three of these are immediately relevant to this study.[47]

The first part of investigation involves comparison of two manuscripts with sequences which are almost 100 years apart and both of which record the sequence repertory of the Cathedral of St. Cyr. Here study is not of change, but of the lack of change. Paris BN lat. 9449 is a troper-proser which dates from around 1060.[48] Crosnier believed that this book was commissioned by Hugh de Champallement, bishop of Nevers from 1013 to 1065 (also called Hugh II and "The Great"), pointing to similarities between it and the much-studied sacramentary from Nevers, Paris BN lat. 17333.[49] Following his lead, lat. 9449 is usually assigned to the Cathedral of Nevers, but although lat. 17333 and lat. 9449 have many saints in common, they do not correspond directly, and books from other churches in Nevers would demonstrate allegiance to these same saints. Two things, however, lend credence to Crosnier's unsubstantiated claims that lat. 9449 was prepared for (or, at least, by) the cathedral. (1) the book is a direct ancestor of the repertory found in the twelfth-century gradual-troper-proser Paris lat. n.a. 1235, a manuscript which seems undoubtedly from the cathedral (and which Crosnier did not know). (2) the book was copied just when Bishop Hugh had finished restoring and rebuilding the Cathedral of Nevers. New buildings and new liturgical books were frequently common partners in furthering the goals of ambitious churchmen. The rebuilding had begun at least by 1029, the year in which Hugh granted the canons two new altars in exchange for rebuilding a wall, the cloister, and the cemetery.[50] On October 26, 1058 the new church was solemnly dedicated by Hugh with two other bishops and a great crowd of clergy and laity present.[51]

Lat. 9449 contains a full repertory of proper tropes and some sixty-five sequences (including a near contemporary supplement at the back) as opposed to the small repertory of twenty-seven sequences found at Chartres Cathedral in the opening of the twelfth century. The book is organized by feast, each having a full complement of liturgically ordered tropes and sequences, as well as incipits for the proper chants and Offertory verses.[52] Perhaps it was easier for proper tropes and sequences to survive when books were organized this way, or perhaps the Cluniac zeal for liturgical reform, which, as will be seen in Chapter 6, cut away proper tropes and

---

[47] See Van Deusen (1982) for a comparative inventory of all four manuscripts; the major points of variance are indicated in later tables.

[48] By studying the acclamations for the king, or the Laudes Regiae, in the manuscript, Delisle discovered the date of the book: the Laudes address both Henry and Philip as king, and thus the source was put together during the short time father and son held the title of king, that is, between May 23, 1059 when King Henry had his son Philip crowned and August 29, 1060, when the older man died. See Delisle (1860) and also Crosnier (1868), p. 105.

[49] See the preface to Crosnier, ed., *Sacramentarium* as well as Crosnier (1868), pp. 104–113.

[50] Lespinasse, ed., *Cartulaire de St. Cyr*, No. 75, p. 103.

[51] *Annales Nivernaises*, p. 90. Hugh's cathedral was destroyed by fire in the early thirteenth century.

[52] A festive Mass included several troped Introits, a troped Kyrie and Gloria, an Alleluia with prosula, one or more sequences, an Offertory with verses and prosula, and a troped Sanctus and Agnus Dei (as well as cues for all proper chants). Only a handful of French books followed the form of organization found in lat. 9449, including Paris, Arsenal 1169 from Autun, Apt 18 and Paris, BN lat. 779 from southern France, but the format was more common in northern Italian sources.

sequences at the Benedictine Abbey of St. Martial, had little effect upon the liturgy of the Cathedral of St. Cyr.[53]

For Nevers was no stranger to reform, especially during the tenure of Hugh II. He restored and rebuilt several monastic churches, and in some cases he promoted restoration by introducing reform: in 1045, the Benedictine Monastery of Saint-Sauveur was given to Cluny by Hugh; in 1059, the famous Abbey of Charité-sur-Loire was handed over to Cluny as well; and in 1063 Hugh reformed the ancient Abbey of St. Stephen, founded originally by Columban, by imposing the Order of Pope Sylvester upon the newly established canons. Hugh's reform of this last institution failed, however, and St. Stephen's too went over to Cluny in the late 1060s, just after Hugh's death. Thus, within ten years either side of 1060 (the date of lat. 9449) every major monastic church in Nevers became a daughter of Cluny.[54] Surely, if some elements of the ancient Nivernais trope and sequence repertory found in lat. 9449 were originally monastic, it would be no wonder to have found them swept into the cathedral of St. Cyr. This may account for the fact that the texts of some sequences, including those for Benedict, were dutifully copied, with no intention of ever being notated (and hence sung in the liturgy).[55] This is one way of promoting change, yet still acknowledging the past; the pieces live on in the record of the book, but they soon cease to be part of the liturgy because they cannot be sung.[56]

In the middle decades of the twelfth century, the cathedral repertory represented by lat. 9449 was reorganized into a new book, the gradual Paris BN lat. n.a. 1235. Yet the process of reorganization was not accompanied by any major changes in the trope of sequence repertories, although both were made somewhat smaller.[57] The scribe of lat. n.a. 1235 instead reorganized the repertory, incorporating it into a gradual, and dividing ordinary tropes and sequences into separate sections at the end.[58] Therefore, although the sequence repertory of lat. n.a. 1235 is a truncated

---

[53] Yet another feature of lat. 9449 makes it seem an older cousin to Paris, BN lat. 1132 (a source representing the Cluniac reforms at St. Martial, which will be discussed in Chapter 6): sequences are written here in the transitional notational style found in Paris, BN lat. 1119: each line of text with neumes above it is followed by a melismatic statement of the music with no text below it. In lat. 1132, this mid-eleventh-century practice had been replaced by the new norm: sequence texts appeared with notes above them, no bows to the tradition of the melodiae being given.

[54] And in 1085, the newly-founded Benedictine priory of St. Victor went over to Cluny as well. See Cottineau (1939–70), vol. II, p. 2066.

[55] The theory that lat. 9449 was compiled from monastic books for the cathedral would help explain some of its problematic features. Lat. 9449 has two feasts for St. Benedict with a full complement of tropes and sequences, one for March 21 and the other for December 4, the date on which the Translation was celebrated in France. Yet neither of these feasts is notated throughout. The sequences were written by the scribe so as not to leave room for the melismas at the end of lines – apparently he never intended to supply them with music. Thus these texts and, one presumes, their music were known in Nevers at the time lat. 9449 was copied, but the cathedral was not particularly interested in them and, in fact, the feasts are not represented in lat. n.a. 1235. (The slightly earlier sacramentary lat. 17333 has but one set of prayers for Benedict.) Yet, with all its emphasis on the patron saint of monasticism, lat. 9449 has no texts or music for Ambrose or Augustine (both of whom are represented in the sacramentary), in spite of the fact that an altar had been recently built for these two saints at the cathedral (to be shared with their fellow confessors Nicholas and St. Jerome of Nevers, bishop of the ninth century).

[56] At least it cannot be sung once no one is still alive who remembers it.

[57] The strongest reason for ascribing lat. n.a. 1235 to the Cathedral of St. Cyr, rather than to some other church from Nevers, is the mention of the bishop in a liturgical role.

[58] A good sense of the extent of the truncation can be gained from Reier's statistics on the Introit tropes in the two manuscripts: of a total of 291 lines in lat. 9449, 223 were retained in lat. n.a. 1235, a very high number,

version of that found in lat. 9449, most deletions are sequences which the scribe of lat. 9449 had already abandoned, copying them in a manner to indicate that he had no interest in ever notating them.[59] Composers, poets, and liturgists at Nevers were not actively involved in altering this ancient repertory, or even in correcting it. There is no evidence of interest in writing new sequence texts for preexisting melodies. A hundred years is a long time to remain content with an entire Mass liturgy, especially during a period of great religious and artistic ferment. Yet, apparently, such was the case here.

Why make a new book at all? The scribe of lat. n.a. 1235 was not a mere copyist: his achievement lay in expressing the ancient trope and sequence repertory of Nevers in a new notational system, replacing the unheightened neumes of lat. 9449, unreadable without precision unless one has the music by memory, with heightened neumes displayed against a drypoint staff with two colored lines (red and yellow), readable to anyone who knows the notation.[60] The scribe of lat. n.a. 1235 also adopted a different practice for writing down sequences. The sequence repertory in lat. 9449 is notated in the mixed style found also in Paris, BN lat. 1119: each individual line is written two ways, once with text and music together and then, immediately following, in neumatic notation with no words. Perhaps this way of representing sequences was transitional, in between the time when they were notated in two separate ways (with text and as melodiae) and the time when they were always expressed as texted pieces, the wordless melodiae having died out. The transition from lat. 9449 to lat. n.a. 1235 suggests that this process of change took place in Nevers, at least: lat. n.a. 1235 contains only texted versions. At Nevers, too, the melodiae passed away altogether. Thus although the components of this sequence repertory changed little during the late eleventh and early twelfth centuries at Nevers Cathedral, the manner in which it was notated and probably how it was performed did change, and in precisely the direction which will be found in Limoges.[61]

given the fact that lat. n.a. 1235 is one of only two twelfth-century French manuscripts to contain proper tropes. See Reier (1981), vol. I, p. 33.

[59] Van Deusen (1982, pp. 50 and 52) provides a list of the sequences found in lat. 9449 without concordance in lat. n.a. 1235. There are seventeen pieces without concordance, a significant number. However, because the scribe did not set up the texts of most of these pieces so that there was room for the melismatic rendering of each line, the way he characteristically wrote out a sequence, it was clear he never intended to notate these pieces. They had, in a sense, died out before lat. 9449 was prepared. About half of these pieces appear in the appendix mentioned above which is contemporary with the manuscript itself. Most often appendices to sequence manuscripts contain the pieces most recently being learned – sung, yes, but not yet incorporated into liturgical order. This is another kind of appendix, one that does occur from time to time: it contains pieces once in use in the area, or at least found in the copies from which the book was being compiled, yet no longer actually in use. Thus it would be a mistake to understand the omission of these particular sequences as a change between lat. 9449 and lat. n.a. 1235; rather, they represent a change between lat. 9449 and the now-lost manuscripts from which it was prepared.

[60] This work should not be diminished by the knowledge that such a transition was happening all over France at this time. At the Abbey of St. Martial in Limoges the switch from unheightened to precisely heightened neumes took place much earlier, in the early eleventh century, the notational differences between lat. 1120 and lat. 1121 proving the point. See, for example, Evans (1970), pp. 47–48.

[61] The steadfast clinging to tradition at Nevers is underscored by the scant number of sequences actually added to the repertory: lat. n.a. 1235 has only two sequences not found in lat. 9499, and neither of these is in late style.

Although the main body of sequences copied in lat. n.a. 1235 is very similar to that of lat. 9449, lat. n.a. 1235 may have remained a book in use in Nevers cathedral for several generations after its production.[62] In the various collections of sequences added to it later, one can get an idea of the kinds of changes that may have been taking place in the sequence repertory of this cathedral during the thirteenth century; these are only indications, however, as none of the additions is part of the original book, although they could have been bound with it at a significantly later date. Sewn in at the beginning of the book is a gathering of four leaves. These were all inscribed by the same mid-thirteenth-century hand and contain a variety of liturgical pieces. The first sequence, for St. Cyr, is "Puer natus est cyricus," which was probably written at the cathedral, and whose presence demonstrates the need felt by thirteenth-century religious communities to have sequences in the new style for their patron saints. Following this is a collection of incipits of sequences which were written in the psalter kept in the choir. On the evidence of this index, a repertory of fifteen new Marian sequences had come into the liturgy of Nevers Cathedral by the mid thirteenth century.[63]

At the end of the book are various other thirteenth- and fourteenth-century additions, which, as can be seen in the inventory, had the purpose of providing texts and music for new or newly upgraded feasts: St. Anne, St. Augustine, and Corpus Christi. If the additions to lat. n.a. 1235 can be taken very cautiously as evidence, they suggest that sequence repertory of the cathedral of Nevers did not grow or change much between the mid twelfth and the mid thirteenth centuries, with one exception: by the mid thirteenth century, a new repertory of sequences for the Virgin Mary was in place. When, how, and the stages by which these pieces arrived cannot be told from this liturgical book.

The Nivernais sequence repertory preserved in the main corpus of lat. n.a. 1235 contrasts sharply with that found in Paris BN lat. n.a. 3126, a Nevers troper-proser which, if later, is only slightly so.[64] Although this newly discovered manuscript has been assumed to be from the cathedral, I believe it was more likely prepared for the Augustinian church of St. Martin.[65] The intensive reform of churches in Nevers witnessed during the 1060s was unrivaled until the mid twelfth century when Bishop Fromont, who had been Abbot of St. Martin's before he became bishop, began to restore his mother church of St. Martin's. He initiated a building program in 1130, attached numerous benefices to the church, and brought the Rule of St. Augustine and the common life to the resident canons in 1143.[66] If my theory is

---

[62] Lat. 9449 was undoubtedly not in use during the late twelfth and thirteenth centuries.

[63] There is also an incipit for "Gaude, sion, que diem recolis" for St. Martin.

[64] Lat. n.a. 1235 is usually assigned to the first half of the twelfth century, lat. n.a. 3126 to the second half, but the notational practices and handwriting styles of the two books push both toward the middle part of the century, making them near contemporaries. Perhaps scholars have wanted to distance them chronologically because their contents are so different; when they can be seen as representing two separate traditions, the pressure to do so lessens.

[65] I proposed this idea to the Chant Study Group of the IMS at the meeting in Pécs, Hungary in September, 1990. Reference to it is made in Fassler (1992).

[66] See Sery (1902), pp. 135–139 and Cottineau (1939–70), vol. II, p. 2066.

correct, lat. n.a. 3126 was prepared by the Augustinian canons for their new church in the first generation after their reform.[67]

There are several reasons for assigning lat. n.a. 3126 to St. Martin's instead of to the Cathedral of St. Cyr. The repertory it contains is very different from that found at the cathedral at the same time or only slightly earlier: the tropes for the proper are gone completely; the tropes for the ordinary are transformed dramatically.[68] More important for arguments made here, lat. n.a. 3126 has a sequence repertory far different from the long-established repertory of the cathedral: although it retains all but three pieces of the ancient repertory, it adds a total of twenty-seven new works, most of which are in the late style, and many of which are found in a supplement written in the main hand. And in later hands, a variety of late sequences have been added to lat. n.a. 3126. Thus, not only are the sequence repertories copied by the main hands of lat. n.a. 1235 and of lat. n.a. 3126 dissimilar; the kinds of later additions made to the two books are different as well, leading to the conclusion that they represent the ongoing liturgical traditions of two different churches.

Specific details point to the church of St. Martin and away from the cathedral as well: the repertory includes the sequence "Interni festi gaudia," for St. Augustine, a sequence which appears almost exclusively in Augustinian books during the twelfth and early thirteenth centuries; two other sequences have been added for St. Martin, giving him greater prominence than any other saint besides Mary and John the Baptist;[69] the feast of the Dedication in this manuscript falls after the feast of St. Martin (Nov. 11) and before the feast of St. Cecilia (Nov. 22) and thus not on October 26, the date of the feast at the cathedral of St. Cyr.[70] Although I have not yet been able to establish the date of the feast of the Dedication at St. Martin, dedicatory feasts were quite often celebrated in the week after the patronal feast. The placement of the feast in lat. 3126, therefore, does promote the case of St. Martin as place of origin.[71]

If the assignment of lat. 3126 to St. Martin is correct, then the Augustinians of Nevers cared a great deal both about sequences and about the place in the liturgy where they were sung. This is the first liturgical manuscript extant with a substantial number of works in the new style. The twelve sequences added to the repertory of the main corpus by the Augustinians are, in three cases, ancient sequences brought in

---

[67] Sery (1902) is very disappointing on the early history of St. Martin. Lat. n.a. 3126 does contain a sequence by Peter the Venerable, and so cannot date much before 1160.

[68] Out of twenty-seven ordinary tropes found in lat. n.a. 3126, only seventeen were in lat. 9449 and lat. n.a. 1235. Also, the total number of ordinary tropes is smaller than that found in the earlier manuscripts. The transformation of the Ordinary trope repertory in lat. n.a. 3126 is now being studied by Gunilla Iversen.

[69] One of these, "Sacerdotem Christi Martinum," is a tenth-century piece. The special status of St. Martin is attested by the fact that this is one of the few times the compiler sought to introduce an ancient sequence previously unknown in Nevers. The other new sequence for St. Martin was added in the thirteenth century: it is "Ecce dies specialis," a piece usually assigned to confessors and here specially adapted for Martin.

[70] There has been minor wrangling in the scholarship over the placement of the Feast of the Dedication in the Nevers manuscripts. In truth, only one of them has this feast on October 26 and that is lat. n.a. 1235, probably the only manuscript of the three which can be assigned absolutely to the cathedral.

[71] See, for example, the sequence list from Paris, BN lat. 10511.

from elsewhere.[72] The other additions are in the late style and several of them are works which were already becoming popular at this time: "Laudes crucis" and the early "Mane prima." Six of the twelve are Marian sequences, and their presence demonstrates that just after the mid twelfth century her cult had grown sufficiently both to have inspired many new sequences, and for those sequences to have won acceptance in liturgical books.

Of even greater interest, however, is the second group of sequences added in the main hand. The order and contents of this group suggests that these were sequences being considered for the permanent canon at the time the manuscript was prepared in the late twelfth century. They are not in liturgical order, and they include some works which fall somewhat on the periphery and are experimental in nature: most notably the planctus of Peter Abelard, included with others of his works.[73] Five of these pieces are for Mary and two for the Dedication; the rest are a mixed group of pieces, some for the sanctorale, some for the temporale, with no apparent thematic ideas standing behind the choices. There are, however, several pieces here which are usually attributed to Adam of St. Victor and the Parisian school of sequence writers, including "Zyma uetus," which is most probably by Adam himself.

Lat. n.a. 3126 demonstrates that these Augustinians had no interest in the venerable repertory of proper tropes still sung at the cathedral at this time, just as their earlier counterparts in Chartres had not. The Augustinians of Nevers did have a special interest in sequences, however. As far as can be told from the surviving evidence, this was a part of their inherited liturgy which they wanted to change to fit their own liturgical ideals and with which they were willing to experiment.[74] They wanted more sequences, and selected some works which technically did not even belong to the genre. They wrote a few new works themselves, but imported most of them, and several are the creations of famous men: Peter the Venerable, Peter Abelard, and Adam of St. Victor.[75]

The manuscript also offers features relevant to the study of liturgical change. If one were going to revise a sequence repertory in around 1160, how would one do it? This manuscript offers an illustration. In lat. 9449, sequences in which there was not strong interest were recorded, but without notation. Subsequently, when lat. n.a. 1235 was prepared these same pieces all disappeared. By contrast, the Augustinians just left out pieces they did not want; they respected the liturgical past of the Cathedral of St. Cyr, but at the same time they wanted to create a liturgy of their own and were bold enough to do so. They also occasionally reversed the order of pieces, putting those they substituted or preferred first.[76] And, of course, they added pieces. The additions are of two types: additions for feasts which already had sequences in lat. n.a. 1235, and additions for feasts which were not so developed in

---

[72] These "new" pieces are for St. Martin, for Apostles, and for Mary Magdalene.

[73] See Waddell (1986) for discussion of the importance of lat. n.a. 3126 in establishing a corpus of sequences for Abelard.

[74] This is also true of the ordinary tropes, a subject I will leave to Gunilla Iversen.

[75] For brief discussion of Peter the Venerable's attitude toward hymn and sequence texts, see Szövérffy (1979). Szövérffy (1985a) reports on a forthcoming dissertation concerning the hymns of Peter the Venerable by Udo Wawrzyniak (Freie Universität, Berlin).

[76] See choices for Epiphany and for the Purification, for example.

lat. n.a. 1235. The first kinds of additions point to those feasts which the Augustinians wished to reinterpret and were not satisfied with as celebrated at the Cathedral. The most heavily revised feast in this category is the Feast of the Dedication of the Church: one sequence, "Obseruanda," has been eliminated; in the supplement, two new pieces have been added. Clearly this feast was important to Augustinians at mid century; we have already seen that three sequences from the late eleventh century added by the Augustinians at Chartres were for the dedication. It is not surprising to find these reformers interested in how to express the idea of the church in their liturgical poetry.[77]

Feasts for which sequences exist only in lat. n.a. 3126 are undoubtedly those which were being upgraded at the Augustinian church of St. Martin – either the community had acquired relics for the saint, or had particular reasons for honoring him or her. Such a saint in this liturgy is St. Cecilia, who inspired one of the few sequences these Augustinians may have written themselves.[78] The piece is not in the new style; rather the text is adapted to the melody "O alma maior" as used for the text "O alma trinitas, Deus es et unitas."[79] The piece is found in the first group of sequences inscribed in the main hand, and had probably been accepted into the liturgy. Thus the only sequence possibly created by the Augustinians at St. Martin's themselves and incorporated into their liturgy was not written in the new style; it was an adaptation of a new text to the melody and form of a sequence probably written in the early eleventh century.

In the supplement, however, one finds two sequences which may also have been written by these canons. The first is for Mary, "Mater clemens ac benigna."[80] This sequence is in the late style, not only in its versification, but in the way it treats its subject. This is a history of Mary as a type of the church created through Old Testament typology. Through such a piece, the Augustinians provided not only a historiated picture of Mary, but also commented upon the church and its nature, a subject which was clearly of interest to them, and they did so in a language reminiscent of the exegesis of their patron saint, Augustine.

Lat. n.a. 3126 contains a repertory quite different in character from that contained in the ordinal of Chartrian Augustinians from the second quarter of the twelfth century. In this younger source from Nevers, late sequences were beginning to make their presence felt, even though most of the repertory written in this style was still in the experimental stage. Clearly, however, the Augustinians were far more interested in sequences at mid century than the cathedral canons of the same town. What of Benedictines in the same region?

---

[77] This subject will be of major importance in the final chapters of this book.

[78] The text for this sequence is printed in Huglo (1957), pp. 14–15. There is no known concordance.

[79] See Huglo (1957), p. 15, notes for the sequence, and Hughes (1934), p. 40. The text for "O alma trinitas" is edited in *AH* VII, p. 239.

[80] See Huglo (1957), p. 17, for the text. This was not one of the Marian sequences listed at the beginning of lat. n.a. 1235.

St. Florentin of Auxerre: a Benedictine house in the vicinity of Nevers

Manuscript to be considered

Paris, BN lat. 10511	gradual with kyriale, processional antiphons and sequences	12th century (3rd quarter)

To find a Benedictine source roughly contemporary with the sequence manuscripts from mid-twelfth-century Nevers, one must consider a manuscript from a neighboring place, the cathedral town of Auxerre, near to, although in a different diocese from, Nevers. Paris, BN lat. 10511 is a little-studied manuscript; no inventory or complete description of it exists, and its exact place of origin has not previously been determined. The main body of this gradual with a kyriale and sequences can be dated through script and notational style to the third quarter of the twelfth century. Unfortunately, there are no saints particularly helpful for dating. Michel Huglo realized that the manuscript was from the region of Auxerre, and suggested the church of St. Laurent, probably because the manuscript has both a vigil and an octave for St. Lawrence in its sanctorale.[81] But, as Huglo stated, this is undeniably a Benedictine source, with two feasts for the saint, as well as a sequence. St. Laurent of Auxerre was an Augustinian church, so lat. 10511 cannot be originally from there.[82]

If one puts the contents of the manuscript in parallel with the known history of churches in Auxerre in the second half of the twelfth century, it is possible to assign this book to a specific church. Comparison of the temporale and sanctorale of the gradual with the noted missal from Auxerre, Paris, BN lat. 17312, which dates from around 1200, reveals a high degree of correspondence between the calendars, and both manuscripts have vigil and octave Masses for St. Lawrence, indicating the high regard in which he was held in this center.[83] The sequentiary following the gradual is more complicated, however. The first part of it is copied in the main hand. At folio 313, just after the sequence "Salue crux," for the feast of the Finding of the Cross, the main hand breaks off. The sequentiary and the rest of the kyriale are completed by another scribe and notator, and their styles appear later than those of the main hand. This continuing sequentiary was copied on leaves of the original book and completes its liturgy. This is not a later supplement of some sort, but a deliberate continuation, written in a hand with later features. One of the sequences added in the continuation does not fit with the main body of the manuscript, but rather upgrades the feast of St. Florentinus. The sequence for this saint (November 7) is followed directly by the sequence for the feast of the Dedication. The main body of the manuscript reveals that this is a Benedictine book, prepared for a church

---

[81] See SOU.

[82] The manuscript is dated to the thirteenth century in *AH* and attributed, through an error uncovered by Michel Huglo, to St. Laurent of Longère.

[83] The chants are usually the same, although there is variation in the kinds of pieces written out. The Alleluia repertories are frequently at variance for feasts of the sanctorale.

from Auxerre; the continuation demonstrates that the book was finished at a later date and adapted for another church, one very likely dedicated to St. Florentinus.

During the mid twelfth century, the priory at St.-Florentin-du-Château, near Auxerre, was made a dependency of St. Germain in Auxerre.[84] Through this action, the church which had been served by canons became Benedictine. The transferral of the church was not smooth and rapid, and there was apparently some difficulty in instituting the new religious group and its use.[85] Lat. 10511 was probably begun during the third quarter of the century in Auxerre, and completed somewhat later for the priory of St. Florentinus. This book is written in the same notational style as lat. n.a. 1235 and lat. n.a. 3126 and is their slightly younger contemporary. It contains the sequence repertory of a Benedictine church from the third quarter of the twelfth century, and it shows how the book was completed soon after.

The sequence repertory, the only part of the manuscript which concerns this study, consists of forty-five pieces, the majority of which were written in the ninth through the eleventh centuries. This repertory is not very different in character from the earlier Benedictine source used for comparison with the Chartrian manuscripts, lat. 10508. Like lat. 10508, it has a layer of sequences which were written in the eleventh century, and these, as in the case of lat. 10508, constitute about one-third of the entire repertory.[86]

"Aue stella gloriosa" for St. George is one of these several sequences probably written in the eleventh century, and may have originated in Auxerre.[87] The text demonstrates features typical of French sequences written in the south of France during the early eleventh century. The "a" sound at the ends of lines connects the poetry to the Alleluia, whose melismas were vocalized on "a;" the subject of the sequence, St. George, is revered not for his deeds on earth or their history, neither of which is described, but for his authority as a martyr in heaven. The opening describes the song of the heavenly choirs and then the symphony of earthly choirs with heavenly choirs. The singing of the sequence is a time for worshipers to experience the union of the church on earth and the church in heaven. As the music and texts try to draw the mortals nearer, a glimpse of the sights and smells of Paradise are offered. The sequence extends the heavenly song of the Alleluia, and imagines what this song might be like and how it might be duplicated. The plea to George as a favored saint is for help in singing.

Aue stella gloriosa	(Hail, glorious star,
Gemma martyrum pretiosa	Precious gem of martyrs
Georgi martyr spes unica.	George, a martyr, a unique hope.

---

[84] For a copy of the bull by Innocent II addressed to Gervais, Abbot of St. Germain in Auxerre, see Maximilien Quantin, ed., *Cartulaire Général de l'Yonne: Recueil de Documents Authentiques*, (Auxerre, 1854), pp. 327–328. The document dates from March 24, 1138.

[85] See Salomon (1859), pp. 328–331.

[86] In Chartres it is primarily the absence of these kinds of pieces which make the cathedral repertory so much smaller than that of St. Evroult.

[87] It is the only witness from the twelfth or thirteenth centuries in *AH* VIII, p. 165. In a later source from Compiègne, the sequence is dedicated to St. Vincent.

Adest hic nunc tibi plebs devota	Here are present now the people devoted to you;
Adesto famulis et cantica	Be present to your servants and make our song
fac Deo digna nostra.	Worthy of God.
Jubilat caterua palliata	The throng in pallia jubilates,
Dulces alternat cantus sonora	It sounds sweet songs back and forth
conjungit et organa.	It joins the sonorous vast choirs.
O te regum rex bone	O good king of kings,
Nos una benedicimus	Single, nourishing Trinity,
semper trinitas alma	We praise you ever
mente deuota.	With faithful mind.
Quam preclara et pulchra	Most outstanding and beautiful
premia sanctorum	Reward of the saints,
uia uita et diadema	The way, the life, the crown,
lux sempiterna.	The perpetual light.
Celica et terrea	Things of heaven and earth
plaudite symphonia	Clap and let
plaudat et canora,	the tuneful concord clap
Hymnizet nectarea	Let it sing in hymns
diatessaron sua	Its nectared fourth
diapente juncta.	With the fifth joining.
Diapason clara	Clear octave
ex his facta	made from these,
surge tinnula	Ascend, ringing
Dulcis melodia	Sweet melody
et suavis	and pleasant,
ede carmina.	Utter your songs.
Nunc te, Georgi	Now, you, George,
dilecta	The beloved throng
precatur turma	begs,
ubique nos guberna	Guide us everywhere,
In angelica curia	In the angelic court
nostra opera excusa fragilia.	excuse our meager works.
Post te nos trahe tua	Draw us after you
manu beata	with your blessed hand
ad eterni	To those celestial
regis regna illa superna.	realms of the eternal king.
Illic albescunt lilia,	There lilies grow white
rubet et rosa	and the rose is red
redoletque	and the happy fatherland
mira balsama	smells of
felix patria.	wonderful balsam trees.

Jesus quo sua	Where Jesus
gaudet cum sponsa	is glad
ejus sola	with His only spouse
summa gratia.	with highest favor.
Illi gloria	To Him be glory,
laus melliflua	sweetest praise
seculorum	throughout the ages
sit in secula.	of ages.
Amen clamemus	Let us shout Amen
uoce magna	With a great sound,
salue celestis	Hail,
margarita.	Pearl of heaven.)

Both Benedictine manuscripts inventoried so far are poor in late sequences. In the older part of the sequentiary in lat. 10511, which contains thirty-seven works, three only are written in the late style; the extension adds two more, "Laudes crucis" and "Congaudentes" for St. Nicholas, making a total of five, or six if one counts a second copy of "Clemens et benigna" which is also found in this section. Even "Adest namque" for St. Florentinus is not in the late style, but in the rhyming hexameters popular in eleventh-century repertories.[88] The interest in late sequences seen in the contemporary Augustinian manuscript from Nevers, lat. n.a. 3126, is not in evidence here. The existence of the Augustinian repertory proves that substantial numbers of late sequences could be incorporated into a Mass liturgy in central France soon after the middle of the twelfth century, but what evidence survives suggests that this was true only of Augustinians. Additions of late sequences to the Benedictine sources studied are few: in lat. 10508 from St. Evroult, the pieces were written carelessly on stray sheets; in lat. 10511, they were written in the main hands, but in very small numbers. To study the situation in greater detail, we will move further south to Limoges where, once again, it is possible to compare the sequence repertories of Benedictines and Augustinians, this time in the very late twelfth and early thirteenth centuries.

[88] For discussion of this poetic meter, see Norberg (1989).

6

Late sequences in southern France during the twelfth century

Manuscripts to be considered

Manuscript	Type of book	Date and use
Paris, BN lat. 1087	gradual with melodiae, a few sequences, and ordinary chants	mid 11th century Cluny: Benedictine
Chailley:MS.L; SOU:97; NGS:615		
Paris, BN lat. 1132	gradual with 2 series of sequences	late 11th or early 12th; second series, mid-12th St. Martial: Benedictine
Chailley:MS.0; Crocker:I,317–326; II,159–161; SOU:99; NGS:616		
Paris, BN lat. 1139	varied contents include 5 collections of sequences	11th; 12th 13th some fascicles are from St. Martial: Benedictine
Marshall (1961); NGS:625; de Poerck (1969); Facsimile ed. Gillingham (1987); Fuller (1979); Grier (1988)		
Paris, BN lat. 1086	ordinary tropes and sequences	late 12th or early 13th St. Leonard: Augustinian
RISM:123		
Paris, BN lat. 778	gradual with ordinary tropes and sequences	late 12th Narbonne: Cathedral
NGS		

Introduction: Bernard Itier, librarian and cantor

Liturgy and history sometimes came together in medieval monasteries (and even in cathedrals in earlier periods) in the person of the cantor. Frequently he was in charge both of the liturgy and liturgical books and of the library and the scriptorium.[1] As the preparation and maintenance of martyologies and obituaries fell to him and his assistants, so too did the writing of death notices and the keeping of the rolls.[2] Because cantors preserved the time, both through the preparation of liturgical calendars and through commemoration of the dead, they were also often chosen to write institutional chronicles. Thus from Helgaud of Fleury, who wrote a life of Robert the Pious, to the early-fifteenth-century works of Thomas Walsingham of St. Albans and Michel Pintoin of St. Denis, medieval cantors were also historians.[3]

Bernard Itier (1163–1225), librarian of the Benedictine Abbey of St. Martial, Limoges in the late twelfth and early thirteenth centuries, is perhaps the only cantor-chronicler who is better known for his work with books than for his histories.[4] The famous collection of liturgical books which was once found at St. Martial is unique: because of it, no other region is so well-represented by liturgical books from the eleventh and twelfth centuries. It survives not only because it was purchased by the Royal Library in the early eighteenth century and thus escaped the Revolution, but also because someone took an interest in beginning it and caring for it during the late twelfth and early thirteenth centuries.[5]

Bernard Itier was involved with the library at St. Martial throughout his lifetime, and was well chosen for the office of armarius. He often noted which books he secured personally, which ones he had bound; one of his library catalogs closes with a listing of the several books he owned himself.[6] In his chronicles, people are occasionally mentioned for the books they gave: "Then Gaufredus de Niolio, subprior, died from whom I had many books," says an entry from 1208;[7] and in 1214, he reports, "we made a monk Peter the Spaniard, priest, for the love of God, and the convent gave to him clothes for his bed and his back, and he gave three small books to us . . ."[8]

Comparison of the library catalog made in the late twelfth century to those made later in Itier's lifetime suggests that during his tenure as subarmarius (by 1195)[9] and subsequently as armarius (1204 until his death in 1225)[10] the library at St. Martial more than doubled, reaching the approximate size it retained throughout the rest of the Middle Ages.[11] Itier's predecessor, undoubtedly the man who trained him for his office, was Peter de Vertuol, who had caused the library to

---

[1] See Fassler (1985).

[2] For a history of the message system used by the monks, see Kahn (1987).

[3] See Helgaud de Fleury, *Vie de Robert le Pieux*, and, on Thomas Walsingham, Galbraith (1937). Michel Pintoin has only recently been identified as the author of a history from St. Denis. See Grevy-Pons and Ornato (1976).

[4] Although generally well known among medievalists, Itier is little studied. For a recent discussion, see Lemaître (1985).

[5] See especially Delisle (1895).

[6] Paris, BN lat. 1085, fol. 104v: "Libri Bernardi Iterii armarii sunt isti." See Dup.-Ag., pp. 338–339.

[7] Dup.-Ag., p. 73.

[8] See Dup.-Ag., p. 90.

[9] "Anno gracie MCXCV, obiit Ademarus junior, vicecomes Lemovicensis. Crux aurea furata est a carpentario nostro. Audoinus erat thesaurarius, ego fui subarmarius." Dup.-Ag., pp. 63–64.

[10] "Anno gracie M CC iii, fuit ultimum Pascha, et ipso anno injunctum est mihi officium armariatus, insuper ut essem prior iii." Dup.-Ag., p. 69.

[11] The catalogs are printed in Dup.-Ag., pp. 323–355.

be built.[12] Subsequently Itier, too, was concerned with housing the collection: in 1217, two new book cabinets were built in the cloister and one in the church, the latter for the work of the children.[13] Clearly, the decades just before and after the year 1200 constituted the great period of acquisition and development for the library at St. Martial, and much of the work must have been carried out by Itier himself.

The collection of liturgical books from the eleventh and twelfth centuries, which were once part of the library of St. Martial, represent, at least to a degree, the interests of Bernard Itier.[14] Medieval library catalogs are usually only of limited use when trying to estimate numbers of liturgical books: because these books were kept in the church rather than in the book cupboards in the cloister, they were often left out of general inventories. The late-twelfth-century catalog from St. Martial found in Paris BN lat. 5243, for example, lists none of the liturgical books found in the later catalogs of Itier. Instead it contains the line: "Hymni, prose, orationes," probably representative of several liturgical books.[15] Lat. 909 and lat. 1121, both eleventh-century books from St. Martial itself, must have been present but in storage, and yet they are not listed independently.[16] Itier's comments on his own catalogs of the collection, on the other hand, demonstrate that he did not wish to ignore liturgical books in his work. He says, "if anyone will bring together all the books in this monastery into one, he will find without doubt around 450, with missals, bibles, and prosers."[17] In the first, he mentions mostly breviaries, reporting there are three in the chapter, two in the sepulchre (of St. Martial), one in the abbot's chapel, one on the altar of St. Benedict, and the armarius has one.[18] In the second catalog, he mentions more liturgical books, often giving small groups a single line: "5 books with song," "4 responsoriales," "ten prosers," "three prosers," etc. Although he thought liturgical books were of a different status than the other volumes in the library, nonetheless, he considered them worthy of enumeration.

Itier's catalogs of the library are not the only sign of his interest in ancient liturgical books from St. Martial and its environs. He not only collected and cataloged them. He also gave some of them new purposes, demonstrating thereby his desire to salvage them. Itier's habits of making extensive notes and actually writing chronicles and catalogs in the margins and on the stray pages (sometimes even between the lines) of the books in his keeping have never been successfully explained, some scholars condemning him for mutilation, others believing that he

---

[12] Dup.-Ag., p. 81. It is not surprising that there was no special room for books until this time. Many monasteries did not have libraries; the cloister served the purpose. The library built by Peter de Vertuol was probably either a part of it or immediately adjacent.

[13] Dup.-Ag., p. 100.

[14] The collection is much studied. See descriptions in Delisle (1896), in Chailley (1957 and 1960), and in Crocker (1957).

[15] Dup.-Ag., p. 327.

[16] See Chailley (1960), pp. 80–81 and 88–92 and Crocker (1957), vol. II, pp. 146–147 and p. 155. The adherence in these liturgical manuscripts to the legend, then prevalent, of St. Martial as an original apostle links them to Adémar of Chabannes and the years 1028–33. Professor James Grier is now preparing a study of Ademar and his work as a liturgist and musician.

[17] Paris, BN lat. 1338, fol. 143r.

[18] Dup.-Ag., pp. 331–332.

was short of parchment.[19] Occasionally at least his practices may have been yet another way of keeping old books around: he reused them to justify keeping them, thereby rescuing them from probable destruction.[20] His attitude toward some of the original books he copied in is revealed in his inscription for Paris, BN lat. 1085: "Bernard Itier, armarius of this place, wrote in this very volume, since this book is not useful for reading, and now will not be without use."[21] He called his annotated copy of the eleventh-century sequentiary Paris BN lat. 1138/1338 "himni cum cronica" ("hymns with histories"), openly acknowledging the dual nature he had forced upon it.[22] By writing important documents in "useless" books, sometimes in liturgical books whose repertories and notational practices were no longer current, Itier made them "useful" again, and thus worthy of keeping. Through his work he preserved two histories of St. Martial, one deliberately in the chronicles, and the other through the manuscripts he collected; occasionally he seems to have been aware of drawing these two together.

All the manuscripts to be studied in this chapter were once in the library of St. Martial. The two Benedictine sources offer a picture of developments in the sequence repertory at the Abbey of St. Martial from the early twelfth through the early thirteenth century, and the later of these can be studied along with Itier's chronicles, which are rich in liturgical observations. Another source crucial for this study was also found in the library at St. Martial: Paris, BN lat. 1086, a late-twelfth-century sequence collection with troped ordinary chants from the Augustinian Abbey of St. Leonard in Limoges. With this source and the collections found in Paris, lat. 1139, one can compare the status of late sequences in two different types of churches from the same town. Although a contemporary manuscript from the Cathedral of St. Stephen in Limoges has not been identified, a late-twelfth-century manuscript with sequences does exist from Narbonne, Paris BN lat. 778. All told, the contents of these sources demonstrate the different ways in which late sequences were used and regarded by Benedictines, Augustinians, and cathedral canons in southern France in the very late twelfth and the early thirteenth centuries.

Sequences at St. Martial from the late eleventh through the early thirteenth century

In 1062–63 monks from Cluny took over St. Martial, undoubtedly superimposing

---

[19] Chailley (1960, p. 61) thinks of him as a man "qui barbouilla d'innombrables manuscrits antérieurs . . ." Henri Duplès-Agier says "Comme le parchemin etait devenu rare et chere au commencement du XIIIe siecle, B. Itier avait place les notes historiques qui la composent sur les marges d'un ancient antiphonaire . . ." (Dup.-Ag., p. xxii). The book is Paris, BN lat. 1138/1338, a sequentiary which once included a proser as well.

[20] Of more than 200 books which survive from the library of St. Martial, around one third have some sort of annotations by Itier.

[21] "Bernardus Iterii, hujus loci armarius, in hoc volumine ideo intitulavit, quia liber iste inutilis est ad legendum, et sic non erit inutilis."

[22] See Dup.-Ag., p. 339.

some of their customs and features of their liturgy.[23] During the eleventh century Cluny, in spite of its reputation for liturgical elaboration, never cultivated tropes and sequences.[24] Naturally, then, tropes, at least, and perhaps sequences too, might be expected to disappear in St. Martial manuscripts copied after 1063 or so, and the reform would explain this change. Comparison of sequence repertories in a source from mid-century Cluny and a source written at St. Martial a generation after the reform suggests that certain aspects of the liturgy at St. Martial were indeed changed by the new order.

Lat. 1087, the source most often consulted by students of the Cluniac Mass liturgy, is a gradual of Cluny probably dating from the third quarter of the eleventh century. It is, then, somewhat later than the famed *Liber tramitis*, a Cluniac customary supposedly written during the time of Abbot Odilo (†1049).[25] Taken together, these two documents provide a picture of the Cluniac liturgy just before and during the time St. Martial was reformed. The customary, the earlier of the two books, mentions only melodiae, the long melismas sung after the Alleluia at Mass, and, at one point, indicates that they were not texted.[26] The gradual lat. 1087 bears out the position suggested by the customary: sequences were not usually sung after the Alleluia at Cluny; instead the melodiae without texts were common for major feasts. There is a collection of some twenty-six *melodiae*, a few being partially texted, and no comparable collection of sequences in lat. 1087. Instead, the manuscript contains a collection of nine sequences, all assigned to a handful of major feasts. The apparent newness of this sequence collection is underscored not only by its size, but also by its mise-en-page: this is the only surviving repertory of sequences from a French center that follows the East Frankish practice of placing neumes for the sequences in the margins. Apparently, sequences had not achieved great stature at mid-eleventh-century Cluny. They had a presence here, however, and this is more than can be said for tropes. The great majority of chants for the ordinary in this manuscript are untroped; there is no evidence for the presence of any proper tropes.

Returning to the St. Martial manuscripts, one can evaluate the pre- and post-reform sequence repertories. An overview of early-eleventh-century sequence manuscripts from the region would demonstrate great activity. For reasons not yet understood, many early sequences no longer appealed to the late-tenth-century religious who inherited them, and, therefore, by the early eleventh century,

---

[23] The reform was not readily accepted by the monks of St. Martial, but rather was imposed by the count of Limoges as a way of getting rid of financial responsibility for the abbey. For an account of the take-over, see de Lasteyrie (1901), pp. 74–80. Resistance to the reform of one institution by another was common throughout the Middle Ages; sometimes the Cluniacs were turned back, as in the case of Baume. See Constable (1985) and Cowdrey (1978).

[24] See Gy (1983), who was the first scholar to propose a "zone anti-trope," to which Cluny belonged. Hiley (1990) has compared the late-eleventh-century Cluniac gradual with tropes and sequences, Paris, BN lat. 1067, to Cluniac customaries of the same period, suggesting that the small repertory of such pieces is indeed all that seems to have been found there. Hiley is in accord with Gy's position that Cluny was essentially anti-trope and perhaps anti-sequence as well, and that the Cluniac reform of St. Martial brought changes to the liturgy of the latter church. One remains puzzled, however, by the apparent continuation of trope repertories at St. Pierre in Moissac, even after the church was reformed by Cluny.

[25] *Liber tramitis*, ed. Dinter.

[26] The feast is the octave of St. Martin: "Missam caelebrent honorifice sicut superius intulimus et sequentiam melodient in eadem die." *Liber tramitis*, ed Dinter, p, 193, lines 17–18.

Aquitanian sequence repertories were in various states of transition.[27] The most important change was in the sequence texts, which were rewritten in large numbers, usually readapted to fit preexisting melodies. Thus lat. 1138/1338, the large collection of sequences from the first quarter of the eleventh century in which Itier wrote his chronicle, is comprised of two series of sequences. One of these contains earlier works, but the other is labeled as containing new pieces: "Facta sunt prosas novas."[28] It is among the "new proses" that one finds the retexted sequences which were the primary creative work of the late tenth and early eleventh centuries.

By the mid eleventh century, however, the activity demonstrated in lat. 1138/ 1338 seems to have ceased at St. Martial. Instead, the liturgical trends found here are in general conformity with the mid-century practice at Cluny, with its respect for melodiae and its apparent disregard for tropes and sequences. Indeed, tropes do drop out some in mid-century Aquitanian manuscripts, three of these surviving with only collections of melodiae without accompanying sequences of any kind. But whether this was their original state has not yet been determined.[29] Changes were taking place, and apparently in the direction away from the tropes and sequences and toward the untexted melodiae. Whether these particular changes postdate 1063 and were, as seems likely, the result of reform cannot yet be told until further paleographical and codicological study of the Aquitanian sequence manuscripts has been done.

For one manuscript, however, it is possible to be more precise. Paris BN, lat. 1132 is a late-eleventh-century gradual from St. Martial. The post-Pentecostal Alleluia series matches that of Cluny exactly, yet differs from that of earlier manuscripts known to be from St. Martial. Therefore, lat. 1132 was prepared for St. Martial itself after the reform.[30] Both of its major sections, the gradual and the first collection of sequences, are in the same hand. Here is the repertory of sequences sung at St. Martial in the very late eleventh century, after the monastery had been taken over by Cluny.

> Major sections in Paris, BN lat. 1132, from St. Martial
>
> c1   fols. 1–4: Fragment of a breviary with notes by Bernard Itier
> c2   fols. 5–107v: a gradual, dating from the late eleventh or early twelfth century
> c3   fols. 113v–131: A sequence collection, written in the same hand as the gradual, preceded by a few ordinary tropes for common of saints.
> c4   fols. 132–144: A second sequence collection dating from the mid twelfth century

[27] These changing trends are best described in Crocker (1957). Their significance for the history of the Middle Ages has never been explored in any detail.

[28] See discussion in Crocker (1957), vol. II, pp. 127–137.

[29] The three manuscripts are Paris, BN lat. 1133, 1134, and 1135. The post-Pentecostal Alleluia list in lat. 1134 is almost identical to that found in lat. 1087. However, Chailley, who does not use Alleluia lists in his work, doubted that the manuscript was from St. Martial.

[30] As pointed out in SOU, p. 97. A simple way of monitoring whether or not a given eleventh-century Limousin manuscript was influenced by the reformers is by comparing its Alleluia lists for Sundays after Pentecost to that from Cluny (as found in lat. 1087). As students of the liturgy have long recognized, Alleluias for Sundays after Pentecost were established late in the history of Gregorian chant. Thus, although basically the same group of Alleluias was used everywhere, each center had its own order for these pieces. Sometimes, they can provide a kind of liturgical fingerprint, capable of linking particular manuscripts to certain regions or centers.

It can be no coincidence that this book stands as a watershed among the eleventh-century sequence manuscripts from St. Martial and the surrounding area: it is the first of them to combine tropes (for the ordinary) and sequences with a gradual.[31] Even more importantly it is the first of them to do away completely with the pneumae, the untexted melodies of the sequences. Thus, although the sequence repertory appended to the gradual is small, twenty-five in number (most of them select pieces for major feasts from the earlier repertory), this later source is somewhat different from Cluniac traditions at mid century. Lat. 1087 had but nine sequences; this manuscript has almost three times that number, with none of the sequences in favor at Cluny. Lat. 1132 also has a second collection of sequences, copied almost two generations later, and containing nineteen pieces, bringing the total to over forty. It seems that even though several other genres of liturgical music for the Mass faded at St. Martial during the eleventh entury, including tropes for the proper, tropes for the ordinary, and even the melodiae themselves, the sequences remained, and their small number had begun to increase by the mid twelfth century.

The second group of sequences in lat. 1132, which probably dates from the second quarter of the twelfth century, shows the ways in which this growth took place. Six of this series of nineteen were composed in the late eleventh or early twelfth century; of these, five are written in rhythmic, accentual verse, and all but two of them were widespread throughout France and in other areas as well.[32] But there is little evidence that new sequences in any style – early, transitional, or new – were being created in great numbers at St. Martial or in the immediate vicinity during the late eleventh and early twelfth centuries. The great activity in sequence writing witnessed by lat. 1138/1338 in the early eleventh century appears not to have had a counterpart in the late eleventh or early twelfth centuries.[33]

The chronicles and library catalogs of Bernard Itier offer a kind of evidence not available for the earlier period in Limoges, providing, when studied along with contemporary manuscripts, a view of the sequence during the late twelfth and early thirteenth centuries at St. Martial. During this time interest in sequences had gained greater momentum than earlier in the twelfth century. Several monks at St. Martial created or at least owned sequence collections: Itier lists prosaria as belonging to William de Laia, who died in 1213,[34] and to Helie Guitberti, whose unfortunate death in 1200 was recorded in the chronicle.[35] A third sequence collection is recorded in the chronicle as made by P. Passerau, who was subarmarius in 1209, thus serving directly under Itier. Apparently Itier commissioned Passerau to make the book, paying him 50 solidos.[36] A fourth proser at St. Martial was that of William La

---

[31] See Crocker (1957), vol. II, pp. 159–161. One cannot agree, however, with Crocker's statement that the two series of sequences are contemporary.

[32] The pieces probably written in Limoges or its vicinity during the eleventh century are "Omnis mundus letabundus" for St. Martial and "Sacra Vincentii" for St. Vincent. See *AH* VIII, pp. 176–177 and 223–224.

[33] This is not to say that there was a lack of activity, however. The repertories of versus and polyphony attest to the production of new music in the area.

[34] Dup.-Ag., p. 352.

[35] Dup.-Ag., p. 352 and pp. 66–67.

[36] See Dup.-Ag., p. 102.

Concha, also a contemporary of Bernard Itier.[37] This last collection is identifiable as a libellus found in Paris, BN lat. 1139, fols. 9v–31.[38]

Lat. 1139 is a much-studied manuscript, famous for its drama and its monophonic and polyphonic versus repertories.[39] Bound within it are several collections of sequences, one of which, as noted above, can be linked directly to St. Martial itself:

> Sequences in Paris, BN lat. 1139
>
> (Collections are numbered by the order in which they occur in the present manuscript)
>
> c1   fols. 1–8: A small, catch-all group of sequences in various hands, most dating from the mid thirteenth century
>
> fol. 9: An inventory of the sequences in the manuscript by Bernard Itier
>
> c2   fols. 9v–31: The proser of William la Concha, dating from the early decades of the thirteenth century
>
> c3   fols. 80–118: A liturgically-ordered collection of 16 sequences copied in the mid eleventh century, followed by Kyries and a few additions in later hands
>
> c4   fols. 149–199: A collection of 34 sequences, which is liturgically ordered only at the beginning, from the late twelfth or early thirteenth century
>
> c5   fols. 209v–228: An early-thirteenth-century supplement of sequences in the late style

The state of lat. 1139 meshes well with Bernard Itier's library catalogs and chronicles: five of the six collections were created in the late twelfth or early thirteenth century, during the time Itier was cantor and librarian, and others besides the work of la Concha may well be the libelli he mentions. Furthermore, Itier's inventory, which includes all collections except the later catch-all c1, proves that he knew the sequence collections in the manuscript, and suggests he may have ordered them as they are today.[40] Furthermore, the collection of Marian texts and music found from fol. 119v to fol. 148v has numerous correspondences with Itier's descriptions of Marian music, including the ceremony for raising "the great majesty of the genetrix of God."[41] This evidence, taken with the fact that younger sequence collections in lat. 1139 contain several pieces for St. Martial, binds the manuscript closely to the abbey in the early thirteenth century. The various sequence collections it contains provide an encapsulated history of the development of the sequence at St. Martial and its environs during the late twelfth and early thirteenth centuries.

From these sources it can be told more precisely when various types of sequences within a predictable steady influx of pieces in the late style came into this southern French repertory. Although the early sequences contained in lat. 1132 remain well

---

[37] La Concha was one of the wealthiest and most influential monks at St. Martial during the early thirteenth century. He left the library some twenty volumes and bequeathed numerous other gifts as well. Itier reported him to be among those who gave sermons at St. Martial. He became sacristan in 1216. See Dup.-Ag., p. 313.

[38] The inscription to the collection says: "William la Concha made me and gave me to blessed St. Martial." ("W. la concha me fecit et beato marc[iali] donauit.")

[39] For the best descriptions to date, see Fuller (1979) and de Poerck (1969). The manuscript is also inventoried in Chailley (1960) and Spanke (1931), but most fully in Marshall (1961). See also Gillingham, ed., *Paris, fonds latin 1139*.

[40] See fol. 9r.

[41] See Dup.-Ag., pp. 103 and 105. The raising of an image of Mary and the singing of an Alleluia and sequence is a subject to which I will return in forthcoming Marian studies.

represented in the two chronologically earliest sequentiaries of lat. 1139, these collections from the late twelfth and early thirteenth century are, as one would expect, increasingly dominated by works in the rhythmic style. New additions seem to enter the repertory in chronological layers according to subject. The collection in lat. 1139 called c4 in the list on p. 117 above is the most extensive sequentiary in lat. 1139. Although copied by a single hand, only the opening is liturgically ordered. This late-twelfth-century collection represents an attempt to integrate pieces from throughout the century with older works. All new sequences found in the second and later sequence collection of lat. 1132 are also found in lat. 1139:c4. New sequences in lat. 1132:c2, which dates, it should be remembered, from the mid twelfth-century, were for a variety of feasts: one each for the cross ("Laudes crucis"), the Dedication ("Quam dilecta"), St. Mary Magdalene ("Mane prima"), St. Vincent ("Sacra uincentii"), the BVM ("Aue Maria gratia plena"), and St. Martial ("Omnis mundus"). In comparison with lat. 1132:c2, lat. 1139:c4, reveals a shift in emphasis: in addition to the six late-style pieces found in lat. 1132, there is one piece each for St. John the Evangelist, the Dedication, and St. Martial, but five for the BVM, making a total of fourteen sequences in the new style. At St. Martial, the emphasis on Marian sequences came in the third quarter of the twelfth century, and by the late twelfth century the pieces were recorded in this small collection.

Lat. 1139:c5 is a libellus at the end of 1139:c4, and it contains pieces being created and copied during the very late twelfth century.[42] In lat. 1139:c5, the emphasis has shifted yet again: of fourteen works, one finds only two pieces for the BVM, but four for St. Martial, sequences probably written by the monks themselves. Also in lat. 1139:c5 are found new pieces for major feasts of the temporale: "Patrum natum" for the Trinity, "Salue dies dierum" for Easter, as well as "Postquam hostem" and "Qui procedis" for Pentecost. Several of these pieces were common in Paris at about the same time, but were already part of large, standardized collections. Their presence in lat. 1139 demonstrates an incipient interest in sequences written in the North.

Still another phase of development is recorded in lat. 1139:c2, the proser of William la Concha, a libellus dating from the first decades of the thirteenth century, a collection which was cataloged by Bernard Itier. This group of nine sequences is the only libellus (aside from a few somewhat later pieces in lat. 1139:c1) not written in the notational style characteristic of Limoges and the surrounding region.[43] William la Concha may have learned to notate music elsewhere. There is only one new piece here for St. Martial, the greater portion of works (four altogether) being for the Apostles. These pieces are found in the first Parisian repertories as well and in all later Parisian books from the thirteenth century, and are quite likely of Parisian origin. Thus la Concha worked primarily as a transmitter of a northern sequence tradition to his own monastery in the south of France.

---

[42] As far as the physical make-up of the manuscript is concerned, c5 is not a "libellus." Its first sequence is copied in the middle of a gathering and it ends in yet another gathering.

[43] The sequence collection of William la Concha begins on a new gathering of parchment and ends mid-way in a second. The stray leaves at the end are filled with writings of Bernard Itier.

Lat. 1139:c1, a loose collection consisting merely of various sequences copied at various times on blank leaves, contains three works written in the mid thirteenth century, two of which are for St. Francis. On folios 6v–7r is a copy in a mid-thirteenth-century hand of the Parisian sequence "Prunis datum" for St. Lawrence, a piece probably by Adam of St. Victor. Once the piece had been written out, a notator began to set it to the melody "Hodierne lux diei," the same melody used for the text by William la Concha.[44] The copy suggests how medieval musicians worked, first copying texts on stray leaves of parchment, and then reaching into their own and their institution's funds of melodies for inspiration.

In most cases, it is impossible to tell from the sources the extent to which new pieces in the youngest libelli of lat. 1139 were actually replacing or supplementing time-honored sequences within the liturgy at this time. One does have, however, Itier's own observations as a general guide regarding attitudes toward new pieces and liturgical change at St. Martial, and indications of how change took place there during this period. When his chronicle begins to report events in his own lifetime, it becomes filled with observations about the liturgy. In the eyes of a thirteenth-century cantor, God could be experienced in church at any moment, his presence underscored by some near-miraculous turn of events. Thus when the monks sang the antiphon "Spiritus sanctus in te descendet, Maria" in the subterranean church during Advent, "such a light illuminated the church that all present were amazed."[45] In an unrelated incident from the same year (1203), the day after the excommunicated clerics and priests had sung on Palm Sunday, the wall fell in where they had been standing.[46] The connection of new texts and music with events such as these sometimes helped win their acceptance into the liturgy; miraculous tales provided context and made the new materials seem more than mere texts and music. Such was the prayer which Itier reports was "given by Blessed Mary last year during quadragesima to a certain Cistercian monk . . . instructing him that this collect should be said frequently.'[47] Itier quotes the prayer in full, just before reporting the miracle, and was undoubtedly introducing the prayer into St. Martial at this time.

The greater part of Itier's liturgical descriptions, however, is concerned with reporting both newly accepted features of the liturgy and texts and music which were apparently still on trial. Thus he commonly relates when feasts are raised in degree or newly instituted, and, more rarely, notes when an innovation had some sort of official sanction. As cantor, he seems to have been involved in most minor liturgical changes: in 1211, he says "At Easter we changed the accustomed Kyrie eleison; we began to celebrate the octave of Easter as a double."[48] One senses from reading his contemporary chronicles that he had a certain amount of freedom to reshape liturgical events. On the one hand, it is clear that changes were often carefully introduced: when the rank of the Annunciation was raised in 1211, for

[44] See fols. 15r–16r.
[45] Dup.-Ag., p. 68.
[46] *Ibid.*
[47] Dup.-Ag., p. 78.
[48] Dup.-Ag., p. 77.

example, the feast seems to have been celebrated with special dignity, and Raymundus Gaucelmi, who had just been made a priest, celebrated the Mass.[49] On the other hand, cultic events could arise spontaneously from special circumstances: in 1215, an earthquake in the night drove the monks from choir and civilians from their beds; the next day, the monks made a special procession to the church of St. Mary de Arenis.[50] In the same year, an especially joyful celebration with a corea by the monks on the octave of St. Martial inspired a similar, yet even greater, celebration in the town on the feast of the Finding of St. Stephen.[51]

Although little of what Itier has to say about the liturgy relates specifically to sequences, it does demonstrate the atmosphere in which the new works were being introduced. His description of the visit to St. Martial in 1212 by Alberic, Archbishop of Rheims, proves that he was using at least one of the sequences found in the collection of William la Concha by this date.

Domnus Albericus, Remensis archiepiscopus, remeans de obsidione *de Moichac*, ubi nepos ipsius occisus fuit, missam priuatam celebrauit in sepulcro de apostolo Marciale, et diximus prosam "Exultamus" et fuit in capitulo, ubi fecit sermonem de apostolo satis diserte, et commendans se nostris orationibus, apud Grandimontem perrexit.[52]

(Lord Alberic, Archbishop of Rheims, coming back from the siege of Moissac, where his nephew was slain, celebrated a private mass in the sepulchre of St. Martial, and we sang the prose [sequence] "Exsultemus"; and he was in chapter, where he preached a sermon on the apostle most eloquently, and, commending himself to our prayers, continued on to Grandmont.)

The archbishop celebrated his mass in the tomb of the saint and preached about him to the assembled monks. The sequence, seemingly "Exsultemus sic" for St. Martial, would have served to praise the merits of the apostle of Gaul in his own tomb, and to bring elements of his vita into the Mass liturgy. Because Itier mentions the sequence, its singing was a special event, and probably, as in so many other cases, a newly introduced liturgical work.

It is very likely that "Exsultemus sic" and others of the late sequence in la Concha's collection were just earning places in the liturgy at St. Martial. The same can also be said of one of the late-twelfth-century pieces in 1139:c4. Itier mentions the singing of "Celeste organum," at the Mass "De luce" of the Nativity.[53] This sequence in the late style was mislabeled in lat. 1139:c4 as a sequence for John the Evangelist, indicating unfamiliarity with the text and its use.[54] It is worthy of notice that the piece was already established with the Augustinians of Limoges at the same time.[55]

It is possible to sketch a brief history of the sequence at St. Martial from the various collections in the manuscripts lat. 1132 and lat. 1139, both of which were

---

[49] Dup.-Ag., p. 77.
[50] Dup.-Ag., pp. 94–95.
[51] Dup.-Ag., p. 93.
[52] Dup.-Ag., p. 86.
[53] Dup.-Ag., p. 82.
[54] See fol. 151r in the inventory.
[55] See the inventory of lat. 1086.

connected with the abbey. Clearly the sequence as a genre had diminished in importance during the late eleventh century. The first collection of sequences found in lat. 1132 is small and made up of generally widespread works which were composed in the tenth century.[56] The growth in this repertory is represented by the second collection in lat. 1132 from the mid twelfth century: late sequences were not particularly important to its development, and the six pieces chosen for inclusion were popular and were slowly coming into sequence repertories throughout France at this time. Although this is a less conservative repertory than that of its contemporary from St. Evroult, lat. 10508, it does not show the great interest in late sequences found in its somewhat younger contemporary from Nevers, lat. n.a. 3126. It was not until the very late twelfth and early thirteenth centuries that large numbers of late sequences are found at St. Martial, and only then had the monks begun to write new works in this style themselves. Even by this time, as far as can be told from the surviving sources, there was no organized attempt to order the new sequences by feast and integrate them into the liturgy in some permanent way. The primary intention of the majority of the new sequences is either to venerate St. Martial or to add to the significant repertory of Marian texts and music then coming into the liturgy of the abbey.

The Augustinians of Limoges

No evidence suggests the presence at St. Martial of a fully organized, standardized collection of sequences in the late twelfth or early thirteenth century, and there are several indications that sequences were in a state of flux at this time. The situation was entirely different, however, in a neighboring church, St. Leonard of Noblat, just outside Limoges, a house of Augustinian canons regular. Commitment to the common life had been reestablished at St. Leonard by an act of the Bishop of Limoges, Itier Chabot, in 1062.[57] Although documents are scarce, the chapter apparently grew increasingly independent from the Cathedral of St. Stephen in Limoges during the course of the twelfth century and acquired several dependencies both near and far during this time. The great popularity of the patron saint, St. Leonard, in England perhaps helps account for the churches there put under sway of this church. In 1911 the Bishop of Limoges ordered the crypt at St. Leonard to be closed, claiming that the great revenues brought by flocking pilgrims caused trouble to the church.[58] At this time, there were twenty-three canons in residence under a prior.[59]

Lat. 1086, never studied in any detail, has long been assigned to the house of Augustinian canons regular in residence at the church of St. Leonard. There is no

---

[56] Leaving size to one side, however, the repertories have much in common: only six of the twenty-five sequences found in lat. 1132 are not in lat. 9449.

[57] See Becquet (1960), pp. 229–231, and (1974), pp. 76–86.

[58] St. Martial seems always to have been the favored house of the cathedral canons. The chronicles demonstrate a close relationship. Bernard Itier never mentions the Augustinians of St. Leonard.

[59] See Becquet (1974), p. 86.

reason to dispute this assignation or the traditional date for the manuscript: the late twelfth or very early thirteenth century, a date placing the book during the era of great devotion to St. Leonard and of prosperity for his church, as well as during the lifetime of Bernard Itier. Lat. 1086 is a fully organized, liturgically ordered book: a kyriale or collection of music and texts for the ordinary of the Mass (some of which are troped) and a full proser. The format here, which puts the sequences after the Glorias and before the Sanctus and makes the sequences seem yet another category of the kyriale, had become common by the early thirteenth century. A kyriale with a proser in its midst almost always followed a gradual or noted missal, as, indeed, the collection from St. Leonard originally may have done.

This is an Aquitanian book. The notation is characteristic; older sequences here are, for the most part, found also in lat. 1132.[60] The proser begins with the prologue "Precamur nostras," typical of so many books from the region.[61] In case after case, textual variants between the two manuscripts line up and the melodic use is the same.

Yet the parallels between lat. 1086 and sequence collections found in lat. 1139 must not be too sharply drawn. Lat. 1086 has no special sequences for St. Martial, an unusual omission for a book from this area. It has two pieces for St. Leonard, probably written in Limoges, as well as the widespread "Interni festi" for St. Augustine, a piece not commonly found in Benedictine books. Musical details do not match consistently: although there was a shared melodic use between sequences in lat. 1086 and the collections found in lat. 1139, that is, the same melody was used for the same given text in each place, the melodies themselves are not identical and variants are rampant. Even texts are not always the same: "Prunis datum" for St. Lawrence appears twice in lat. 1139, once at the beginning in an early-thirteenth-century hand, and again in the proser of William la Concha. Both times the text is a truncated version of the piece. But in lat. 1086, the text is complete. The famous "Laudes crucis" for feasts of the cross has a strophe in lat. 1086 that does not appear in the collection from St. Martial.[62] But the difference in the make-up of the book as a whole is what truly separates lat. 1086 from its contemporary, lat. 1139:c4. With fifty-eight sequences, the collection is far larger than c4 or any single collection found in lat. 1139. Here new sequences are not experiments recorded in libelli; they have become part of the canon of works regularly used in the liturgy. Of the fifty-eight sequences found here, thirty-nine, or well over half, are in the late style. Although eighteen of these works are also found in one or another collection from lat. 1139, they are all organized here in liturgical order, a condition which indicates their acceptance and regular performance at an earlier time than at St. Martial. The Parisian pieces found in 1139:c5 and in the collection of William la Concha (lat. 1139:c2) are already in place here. Perhaps this was how the monks of St. Martial learned about them.

[60] "Christi hodierna," assigned in lat. 1086 to the octave of the Epiphany, is an exception of sorts: the manuscript does not follow the version established in Limoges, but rather that found in Narbonne and a variety of French and Italian centers. See *AH* VII, pp. 42–43 and LIII, pp. 25–28.
[61] See *AH* VII, p. 27.
[62] The version of "Laudes crucis" found in lat. 1086 is transcribed in Chapter 4.

The compiler of lat. 1086 took pieces from the various historical stages discussed in the analysis of lat. 1139 and combined them into a whole, fleshing them out where needed with eighteen sequences in the new style which are not found in any of the collections of lat. 1139. The new pieces found in lat. 1086, but not in other collections from Limoges, are the clearest indication what aspects of their liturgy the canons wished to emphasise. Of nine Marian sequences, for example, only two are not also found in lat. 1139. One of these is the very popular "Verbum bonum et suaue," found as an addition in lat. 778, and also as an addition to lat. 903 in a hand similar to that of Itier. The other sequence, "Salue mater saluatoris," a work usually attributed to Adam of St. Victor, was also found in the South, at Narbonne, in the late twelfth century (but, not, it must be noted, in the main body of the manuscript).[63] When lat. 1086 was put together, its compilers were content to use pieces already in Limoges or, in one case, at nearby Narbonne, for Marian feasts. These pieces were arranged and assigned rubrics in several cases, and an apparent octave for the Assumption is in place (although rubrics were not supplied). No piece has been assigned to the Nativity of the BVM (September 8). Ratios are similar in regard to new pieces for the temporale and for later saints: there are few new pieces not found elsewhere in Limoges and surrounding regions. The situation is quite different for the Apostles and other early disciples of Christ (including John the Baptist), however: of eleven such pieces, seven are not present in lat. 1139. Although two of the seven ("Superne matris" [assigned here to St. Mark or other Apostles], and "Iocundare plebs" [for the Evangelists]) were common in the North and are probably imports to this southern repertory, five others are not, and may have been written at St. Leonard itself. In this late-twelfth-century manuscript, emphasis is upon the Apostles and other disciples of the early church.

In Limoges it has been possible both to take a long view of the sequence at the Benedictine Abbey of St. Martial, and then to compare sequence repertories of two institutions during the same period – the late twelfth century. Just before the turn of the thirteenth century, the Augustinians of this town had greater numbers of late sequences than did the Benedictines (and, more importantly, had organized them into a liturgical book), whereas, according to the chronicles of Bernard Itier, the kinds of sequences found in the later collections at St. Martial were just beginning to come into the liturgy there in the early thirteenth century. In Limoges, the Augustinians were demonstrably more interested in making late sequences part of their official liturgy at an earlier date than were their Benedictine counterparts, and this is true even though the genre was highly valued at St. Martial as well. As Table 6.1 below illustrates, the Augustinians in Limoges not only had a great *number* of late sequences than the Benedictines, but also devoted a far greater proportion of their repertory to them. The explosion of new sequences in a traditional style (with modifications) written in southern France in the eleventh century was of little interest to them. The force of tradition may have demanded that early sequences composed in the ninth and tenth centuries remain in place for major feasts, but

---

[63] See Appendix 4, Inventory of lat. 778, fol. 184r (pp. 375–389).

Table 6.1. *The sequences at the Augustinian church of St. Leonard*

Total number	Early	Eleventh century	New style	In liturgical order
58	9	8	41	All

when that force was not present, new sequences were substituted. This repertory is comparable to the Augustinian one found in lat. n.a. 3126, except that attitudes toward late sequences are even more positive in the later source. Here the late sequences are fully integrated and have triumphed as the predominating feature of the liturgy.

Sequences in Narbonne Cathedral in the late twelfth century

There is no surviving late-twelfth-century manuscript from the Cathedral of St. Stephen in Limoges.[64] To find a manuscript representative of southern cathedral use in this precise period, one must travel to Narbonne, some 200 miles from Limoges, and close to the border of Spain. The Rite of Narbonne was romanized in the late eighth and early ninth century, and the Archbishop of Narbonne was given authority over a large territory. Elements of the Hispanic Rite practiced in Narbonne until the romanization persisted throughout the Middle Ages, however, and have recently proved of interest to liturgists.[65]

The liturgy of the Cathedral of Narbonne was celebrated in the late twelfth century with an abundance of ordinary tropes and sequences.[66] Lat. 778 from the Cathedral of St. Just dates from the twelfth century, and is a contemporary of both lat. 1086 from St. Leonard in Limoges and lat. 1139:c4. The manuscript is a troper-proser (ordinary tropes only), and contains one of the most extensive surviving repertories of ordinary tropes from the twelfth century.[67] It also contains many more sequences than are usually found in the repertories of twelfth-century French churches, and harks back to the great numbers of sequences found in certain Aquitanian sources from the early and mid eleventh century, lat. 1118, or lat. 1138/1338, and Paris, BN lat. n.a. 1871, perhaps from Moissac.[68] Comparison of numbers of sequences found here with those sung in cathedrals further north to this date reveals that Narbonne had more pieces, sometimes considerably more.[69]

---

[64] Although some idea of the close relationship between the cathedral and St. Martial may be gained from Becquet (1982 and 1983).

[65] See especially Gros (1976 and 1982).

[66] There is, however, no evidence of proper tropes, probably because of the late date of the source.

[67] For an inventory, see Iversen, *Tropes*, pp. 309–314.

[68] Lat. 1118 contains 140 sequences and lat. 1138/1338 contains 140, divided into two separate series. Both manuscripts are inventoried in Crocker (1957), vol. I. Lat. n.a. 1871 has just over 120 sequences, with several additions in later hands.

[69] The repertory of Chartres Cathedral in the early thirteenth century (which contained 37 sequences according to the ordinal, Chartres 1058) seems particularly small by comparison. There were over 100

Table 6.2. *The Sequences found in lat. 778 from Narbonne Cathedral*

	Main hands Liturgical order	Suppl. A Hand I Liturgical order	Suppl. B Hand I No order	Other hands at end	Overscribed in later hands
Dates	late 12th	late 12th	late 12th	13th	13th
Totals	110	9	7	8	4
Late style	9	1	7	8	4

What types of sequences made up the extensive Narbonnais repertory and when were the various layers composed? About half of the 119 sequences contained in the main body of the collection and its liturgically ordered supplement are from the ninth and tenth centuries, sequences found throughout southern France and often established east of the Rhine as well. But around forty of these sequences represent later development, the creative work of the late tenth, eleventh, and even early twelfth centuries. Some works in this layer are found also in lat. 1138/1338 and in lat. n.a. 1871, and date from the eleventh century. Others are not found in these sources, and may represent a group of sequences composed further south, around Narbonne and Toulouse.[70] Just under half of the forty works probably composed in the eleventh or early twelfth century are not found in the other southern French sources accounted for in *AH* VII or in lat. n.a. 1871. Many of these sequences demonstrate an interest in rhyme and accentual patterns of words, and several of them are long works. The great interest in writing sequences as found earlier in some southern French centers seems to have continued in Narbonne, and there was a great respect for eleventh-century and early-twelfth-century sequence repertories in this cathedral liturgy. What need was there for sequences in the new style of rhythmic poetry when the kinds of works written in the eleventh century were still flourishing in the early twelfth century as well?

"Summa culmina apostolica," for the feast of St. Peter's Chains, was probably written in the twelfth century in Narbonne or a neighboring church. The sequence shows many features typical of earlier southern French sequences from the eleventh century: its subject is Peter in heaven, the song appropriate for him, and his role as keeper of the sheep, gatekeeper of heaven, and the saint given the power on earth to bind and loose, hence to forgive sins. Not only does the text look heavenward in its subject, it is designed so that each short phrase ends with "a," creating a link with the vocalized sound of the Alleluia jubilus. But the picture of Peter presented here is not

---

sequences at Laon in the late twelfth century, but many of these are in a special supplement for the Christmas Octave found in Laon 263; the special pieces are not in the ordinal, Laon 215.

[70] Hitherto, a lack of research in this area has made it impossible to reach any firm conclusion. The extensive catalog of sequence incipits and excipits now being produced by Nancy Van Deusen will undoubtedly shed much light on this problem.

only of the saint in heaven, as is the sequence for St. George discussed above. Here he is assigned his customary heavenly attributes, as in other sequences from the eleventh century, . . . there is also an attempt to describe events in his life, and to point to some of the ironies of the historical situations: Herod the tyrant locks up the gatekeeper of heaven; the broken chains of Peter represent the freedom his ministrations offer to the worshipers.

For the feast of St. Peter's Chains

Summa culmina apostolica	(The apostolic church now joyfully makes
Leta pertonat nunc ecclesia	The topmost peaks resound
Petrus digna turpi turba quia gerit sceptra	Because Peter bears the rod needed for the base throng,
Ab ipso percepta uerbigena gregis cura.	Having received from the Word – born one Himself the care of His flock
Cujus pia merita die patent ista sublima	Whose loyal merits Are made plain On this lofty day,
Qui per sua soluta uincula dat nostra libera.	Who through loosening his own chains makes ours unbinding.
Pulchra decet illum camoena lausque digna	A beautiful song suits him and proper praise,
Cui coelica dat deus regna conseruanda.	To whom God gave the heavenly kingdom to keep.
Que ligat in arva in aethra solida manent ipsa.	Things which he binds in the plains in the air themselves remain firm.
Infera supera fores ualue cuncta sunt soluta.	Below, above gates, doors, all are set free.
Agnorum summa adepta custodia santique capta spiraminis gratia ovium plurima congerens milia per pascua uite sancta duxit ad ouilia.	Having received the highest guardianship of the sheep, and having obtained the grace of the holy spirit, gathering together many thousands of sheep, he led them through the pastures of life to the holy sheepfolds.

Hunc inuidia	With envy
ob tanta negotia	On account of such great deeds,
Herodes arta	Herod thrust
trusit in ergastula	in a narrow jail
claudit qui celica	him who closes and unlocks
reserat et regna	The heavenly dominions;
quem diuina	the highest divine power
uirtus summa	sets him free
laxa soluit catena.	loosening the fetter.
Solamina per angelica	Through angelic ministrations
Ad socia redit agmina.	He returned to the throngs of his companions [Acts 12:1–11]
Maxima hec festa	These very great festivities
restant atque salutifera	and salvation bearing
remedia	remedies demonstrate
Quod nostra	That our chains
sunt uincla	are made loose
per sacra Petri absoluta	Through the holy bonds
ligamina.	of Peter.
Pura paterna	You, who restrain
ampla qui per arua	throughout the cleared, wide,
ac poli supera	plains of the Father
celsa	and the lofty heights of the heavens
tenes a deo cessa	by God's orders, stay,
Laxa ligata	Loosen the things bound,
reseraque clausa	And unlock the closed,
crimina laua	Wash away all faults,
cuncta	With the power
potestate commissa.	entrusted to you.
Olim tua	Once
sunt umbra omnia	all sick bodies
egra tacta reddita	placed near your way
ualida	Having touched your shadow
uiam juxta	were restored
corpora posita.	to health. [Acts 5:15]
Ita nostra	Thus put to flight our
facinora magna	great and sickly crimes
que sunt in uia eius ac	which are in his path
morbida	with the touch
tactu fuga	which, with the hem of a garment,
qui sat fimbria.	is sufficient,
Quo cepta	So that the path begun
tendat semita	may reach
ad regna secura,	safe realms,

Ac septa	and the
ouium turma	crowd of sheep
subeat astrea.	may rise to the starry fold.
Nostra iam turba	Now produce the heavenly
cantica	song
edita regia	given forth by our throng
fac in aula almisona.	in the gracious-sounding hall.
Culpa soluta	With sin dismissed
per jura	by judicial decisions,
tibimet tradita	Unlock the heavenly gates
superna claustra resera.	Given up to you.
O summa Petre columna	O Peter, lofty pillar,
nixa qua stat ecclesia,	on which the church stands leaning,
Et gregi fer auxilia	Bring assistance to the flock,
quo in pacis ouilia	whereby it may enter in
Diuina subeat	The sheepfolds of peace
fouendus gratia.	favored with divine grace.)

Lat. 778 demonstrates a cathedral liturgy highly decorated with sequences; it seems that for generations new pieces were added here, and yet there was no tendency to reform the repertory and to discard earlier works. Sequences are advocated for vespers on seven major feasts; one of these pieces is written in mixed notation, probably indicating alternating performance between texted and untexted lines.[71] One suspects that selection may have been made from the numerous pieces listed for other major feasts for vespers as well, even when none was specifically assigned. In a repertory such as this, a great variety of sequences was available for many feast days, but late sequences were usually not among the selections; out of 119 sequences in the first series and the liturgically ordered supplement, only ten are in the new style, and several of these were written in the late eleventh century. Late sequences predominate only in the final supplement in a main hand, a collection representing the kinds of pieces being tried out at the Cathedral of Narbonne just before the beginning of the thirteenth century, and in later additions. Time and again, when there is more than one piece for a feast, the newer works are listed last: this is the case with Christmas, for example, and with several saints' feasts. Only when a late sequence had great popularity was it capable of bumping an early work out of first place, as in the example of "Laudes crucis."

The inventories of lat. 778 and lat. 1086 in the appendix allow for comparison between these two contemporary repertories from the same region, one for a cathedral, one for an Augustinian church. The Augustinians had far fewer sequences, just about half as many as the cathedral canons, but for them one late sequence had the ability to replace several works written in the ninth, tenth, and eleventh centuries. For many well-established feasts in southern France there would

---

[71] See "Aue dei dilecte," for John the Baptist at Vespers, fol. 174r.

have been several sequences written in the tenth and eleventh centuries of a type comparable to "Alte uox canat," the early sequence studied in Chapter 3. In an Augustinian repertory they might all disappear for some feasts, one can find instances where a choice of several earlier sequences for a particular feast has been replaced by a single late sequence. There is no intention here to claim that the late sequences were superior to earlier sequences; but they were different, not only in poetic style but also in content, and they did have a particular attraction for Augustinians in the twelfth century, early, middle, or late.

Conclusion to Part II: liturgical change and the late sequences in twelfth-century France

The kinds of change to be encountered in these two chapters can, without too much forcing, be placed into three simple categories, and some manuscripts may show two or even three types of change at one time, depending upon the pieces under consideration. The first category of change is slow and on a small scale. Pieces came in at the back of liturgical books (sometimes without music), either to be used immediately or to pass through a trial period, awaiting incorporation into the main corpus the next time the book needed to be replaced; other pieces in the main body of the manuscript might be left without music or assigned to second or even third place within a feast after the most favored piece or pieces, subsequently dropping out when a new version of the book was prepared. This kind of change is represented here by a group of untexted sequences found in the earliest manuscript with sequences from Nevers, Paris, BN lat. 9449 from the late eleventh century. These pieces are not found in Paris BN lat. n.a. 1235 from the first half of the twelfth century, and have dropped out of the repertory. The minor differences between two sources from Cambrai, Cambrai 78 and Cambrai 60, from the late eleventh and mid twelfth century, are also of this type. The later additions to Paris BN lat. 10508, from the Benedictine Abbey of St. Evroult in Normandy, are fine examples of slowly acquired repertory as well. There are many reasons for small changes or alterations within a repertory, and they are difficult to generalize about without intense study of the particular region involved.

The second type of change is more dramatic, and sometimes only the degree of change distinguishes this type of change from the first type. Here significant new groups of pieces come in or significant reordering of pieces takes place. But, in spite of these additions, rearrangements, or changes in format, an original corpus is retained, with very few older pieces actually disappearing. As far as format is concerned, the second Nevers manuscript falls into this category: although repertorial changes are relatively minor (as indicated above), the repertory here has been completely rearranged and its tropes and sequences transcribed into a new notational system. The differences between the two cathedral ordinals from Chartres, the first from the early twelfth century (the OV), the second (the OC) from the thirteenth century, show changes of this type. These are not mere matters of careless attrition or addition, as the first type may be. Instead they are caused by some shift in religious or artistic taste, some essential change in the way music was performed or notated, or some powerful person's perceived need for liturgical change, perhaps related to architectural change as well.

The third type of change, as the reader by now may have surmised, is of the major sort. Here large numbers of pieces drop out, or major shifts of emphasis occur. The differences between Paris BN lat. 909 and Paris BN lat. 1132, both eleventh-century manuscripts from St. Martial in Limoges, are evidence of this type of change. So are those between Paris BN lat. n.a. 1235 and Paris BN lat. 3126, both from Nevers. Although there is no specific earlier manuscript to measure it against, clearly the imported repertory added to Aix 13 from Aix-la-Chapelle represents change of this sort as well.[72] Major changes such as these usually indicate that something has happened to alter theological or political opinions, and that the liturgy has been reformed to express these new ideas.

Who brings about liturgical change? Changes of the first type are often difficult to ascribe to any particular person or group of persons, but one can assume that the cantors, monastic or cathedral, or other persons such as succentors or magistri puerorum – all officials with certain responsibilities regarding singing and cere-mony – were involved in some decisions. The occasional abbot, prior or bishop or other official with an interest in music could also effect such change. Cantors, as has been demonstrated, had many duties beyond supervising liturgical music. Among other things, they were often responsible for recording deaths in the rolls and for translating received news into the chronicles of their own monasteries.[73] Thus, the innumerable messengers who traveled from place to place for the express purpose of keeping these obituary rolls up to date, created an ever-present pipeline of infor-mation from cantor to cantor.[74] Pieces could be sent from place to place in this way, and undoubtedly were. Although little evidence regarding the details of trans-mission has yet come to light, there is no doubt that such a message system existed and that cantors were usually responsible for it.[75] The repertories investigated here will prove one thing for certain, however: any sequence *could* be found almost anywhere in France, and its absence does not mean it was unknown or unavailable. It means it was not selected for use. Cantors undoubtedly knew many more sequences than they actually copied or had copied in the service books placed in their keeping, and they sometimes kept private anthologies of such works, perhaps as a matter of professional interest.[76]

Changes of the second and, especially, of the third types, however, are often directly attributable to major figures or movements within the life of a particular church or diocese, and when they are found with some consistency from place to place, they represent major transformations, capable of being associated with widespread shifts in theological movements or political circumstances. The most

---

[72] Aix 13 is discussed further below, on pp. 132–133.
[73] See Kahn (1987).
[74] See Fassler (1985).
[75] See Fassler (1985).
[76] Paris, BN lat. 1871 may be such a book.

important catalysts for liturgical change of the second stage were ambitious bishops or abbots who wanted to remodel their churches through new building programs and upgrade or even update their liturgical books, hoping to improve the quality of the singing and the power of the ceremony.[77] Theodaldus of Arezzo, bishop from 1024–1033, was undoubtedly such a man.[78] In the introduction to a treatise dedicated to Theodaldus, the famous music theorist Guido of Arezzo says:

Just as you created, by an exceedingly marvelous plan, the church of St. Donatus, the bishop and martyr, over which you preside by the will of God and as his lawful vicar, so likewise, by a most honorable and appropriate distinction, you would make the ministers of that church cynosures for all churchmen throughout almost the whole world. In very truth it is sufficiently marvelous and desirable that even boys of your church should surpass in the practice of music the fully trained veterans of all other places; and the height of your honor and merit will be very greatly increased because, though subsequent to the early fathers, such great and distinguished renown for learning has come to this church through you.[79]

Buildings and chants must have changed in Arezzo during the first half of the eleventh century, and one can guess why: the bishop wanted to improve them, giving himself and his diocese greater stature in the process. Time and again, when new buildings and new books appear (and there is often evidence of both at about the same time) in a medieval cathedral town or in an established religious house, the chronicles report the tenure of a particularly energetic bishop or abbot.

Changes of the third type, however, occur for somewhat different reasons. Usually, it is true, there is an outstanding bishop or abbot, prince or queen involved with them, at least in the initial stages, and this person has an agenda of some kind, a political or religious statement he or she wants to make. Major liturgical upheaval in any institution or center is a sure sign of religious reform, whether inaugurated by forces from outside or by insiders linked to some larger religious group or institution, monks from Cluny for example, or Augustinians, or Cistercians. The machinations of Ivo of Chartres in the late eleventh and early twelfth century, first in Beauvais and later in Chartres itself, demonstrate this type of change. Ivo founded new institutions, and gave them sets of laws for their internal governance. The liturgy of one of these places differs from that of the local cathedral.

The kinds of change taking place in sequence repertories during the twelfth century are of all three types. Change as it came into most Benedictine repertories, at least until the very late twelfth century, was of the first or second type: either a few new pieces were added, and a few pieces in the late style came in; or, late in the twelfth century, a number of late sequences were under consideration. Although some Benedictine repertories had grown by significant numbers in the eleventh century, this kind of change was not taking place in the twelfth century.[80]

---

[77] See Crozet (1967).

[78] The concerns of bishops in the first half of the eleventh century, before the Gregorian reform, are studied by Fanning (1988).

[79] This translation from the *Micrologus* is by Warren Babb, and found in *Hucbald, Guido and John*, ed. Palisca. For discussion see Palisca's introduction to the treatise and Smits van Waesberghe (1953), pp. 13ff. Smits van Waesberghe reports that Bishop Theodaldus commissioned the architect Adalbertus Maginardo to build the new cathedral.

[80] The change in southern French Benedictine sequence repertories will be the subject of a forthcoming study.

By the late twelfth century, the Benedictines of St. Martial were considering substantial numbers of late sequences for their liturgy, and this was probably because the new style had become sufficiently popular in southern France to make such sequences desirable. The same situation was found with the sequence repertory of the Cathedral of St. Just in Narbonne: late sequences had not been of major importance during the twelfth century itself, but by the very late twelfth century, they were beginning to come in, not yet as part of the major collection copied at this time, but at the back, some in the main hand, others added in the first half of the thirteenth century. I would call these processes changes of the second type.

The only twelfth-century sequence repertories with major changes are those shaped by religious reformers. In the eleventh century, when Cluny reformed St. Martial, the sequence repertory became suddenly much smaller; the proper tropes apparently disappeared. The only twelfth-century sequence repertories with major changes were those of Augustinians, or, perhaps, of cathedrals with strong Augustinian affiliations (as in the case of Paris, discussed in Chapter 7). Although communities of canons regular consistently adopted the liturgy of the local cathedral for their own use, they changed this body of inherited texts and music when they wished, and always with an emphasis upon their sequence repertories. Thus, before any other religious institutions caught on to them, Augustinians had incorporated large numbers of late sequences into their Mass books, and not in small, unorganized libelli, but rather in the kind of order indicating actual, official sanction.

There are indications in both later Augustinian repertories examined here that sequences from Paris, works which were probably written by Adam of St. Victor and his school, were among those brought in during the second half of the twelfth century; by the very late twelfth century elements of the Parisian repertory were coming into St. Martial, on the one hand, and the Cathedral of St. Just, on the other. Yet another sequence manuscript from the early thirteenth century demonstrates the influence of Parisian sequences upon other repertories. Aix 13 from Aix-la-Chapelle (Aachen) is an unusual book, a gradual with two sequence repertories, one French/Parisian and the other German, each with its characteristic notational style.[81] This repertory is, of course, representative of the geographical position of Aix-la-Chapelle, situated in the midst of what was once Charlemagne's kingdom.[82] But, beyond this, the Augustinian canons at St. Mary's church in the early thirteenth century looked not only westward, but rather specifically to Paris for many of their French sequences.[83] Although a few of the late sequences included in the "French" section of the sequentiary were actually written by Augustinians in Austria, most probably at St. Florian and Klosterneuburg, and others were generally in circulation in various French centers, a substantial group of works are undoubtedly of Parisian origin and appear at Aix-la-Chapelle with either Victorine or cathedral melodies. In

[81] Although the "French" is somewhat odd, and certainly not like contemporary square notation in Paris.
[82] Hesbert (*Le Prosaire d'Aix-la-Chapelle*) argues convincingly that the compiler of the manuscript interrelated the two repertories, deliberately leaving out some feasts in one that were covered by the other, etc.
[83] The chapter of the cathedral, dedicated to the Virgin Mary, was founded by Charlemagne in 796 and followed the Rule of St. Augustine from the beginning. See L. Boiteux, "Aix-la-Chapelle," in *Dictionnaire d'histoire et de géographie ecclésiastique* (1912–), vol. I, pp. 1245–1270.

the rubrics for "Ecce dies triumphalis," St. Victor is called "of Paris."[84] These canons showed their particular interest in sequences by borrowing works, both texts and melodies, from the Parisian tradition. This is yet further proof that there was a special repertory of late sequences at one center in France and that other churches wanted to adopt works from it.

The early thirteenth century was a time of great prosperity for the canons at Aix-la-Chapelle.[85] An indication of the interest taken in the church and its liturgy is manifested by a letter from Pope Innocent III in 1211 asking the canons to sing the "Te Deum" and the Gloria on the feast of the Annunciation because their church was the "magistra" of all churches dedicated to Mary.[86] Fourier Bonnard has cited the fourteenth-century chronicler Jean de Paris (Jean Bouin) as the source for his belief that Innocent III was a champion of the Victorine sequences and gave them special commendation at the Fourth Lateran Council in 1215.[87] According to Bonnard, papal promotion was chief among the reasons that several churches, including Aix-la-Chapelle, incorporated Victorine sequences into their liturgies just after this date. Bonnard may be right about the pope's affection for Victorine sequences; the style had become popular even in Rome, and the gradual from Aix-la-Chapelle is proof that Paris and the Victorines were known at this time for their sequence repertories.[88] As has been demonstrated here, however, interest in the sequence repertory from Paris predated the Fourth Lateran Council.

Sources from outside Paris in the twelfth century suggest that the late sequence as it developed in France was, at the beginning, an Augustinian sequence. That is not to say that Benedictines and cathedral canons did not write sequences during that century; of course they did. But during the twelfth century, only Augustinians worked to incorporate large numbers of the new sequences into their liturgies. From the evidence presented so far, it is possible to hypothesize about why the Augustinians favored sequences when other groups of reformers in the twelfth century did not.

First, the sequences were Alleluia commentaries, and Augustine wrote extensively about a chant which canons from the twelfth century would have assumed was the Alleluia of the Mass liturgy; he also wrote about the "jubilus," a word which would have been associated in the twelfth century with the melismatic endings of Alleluia phrases.[89] Secondly, the Augustinians turned their sequences into hymn-like songs, perhaps in order to follow the only command regarding music in

---

[84] Of course, the saint is St. Victor of Marseilles. His appellation at Aix reveals an emphasis on the saint as celebrated in Paris at the Abbey of St. Victor, the place of origin of the sequence.

[85] See *Dictionnaire d'histoire et de géographie ecclésiastique* (1912–), vol. I, p. 1266.

[86] See Meuthen (1972), p. 245, for the text of this document.

[87] Bonnard (1904–07, vol. I, p. 130) says: "Nous n'avons pas à rapporter ici les multiples affaires qui occupèrent cette imposante assemblée. Bornons-nous à constater avec Jean de Paris que le Pape y donna son approbation formelle aux ouvrages de saint Anselme, de saint Bernard, de maître Hugue, Maître Adam et maître Richard de Saint-Victor." See Jean de Paris, *Memoria*, Paris, BN lat. 15011, fol. 428. I have not been able to find references to Adam of St. Victor in surviving documents from the council itself.

[88] See Van Dijk (1960), p. 395.

[89] For a convenient collection of passages regarding the Alleluia from Augustine's letters and sermons, see McKinnon (1987), pp. 163–167. There is further discussion of the Alleluia as interpreted by Augustine in Roetzer (1930).

the Rule of St. Augustine: "When you pray to God in psalms and hymns, turn over in your heart what your voice is uttering."[90] Augustine's own conversion was advanced by the hymns sung in Milan and composed by his master Ambrose:

How much I wept at your hymns and canticles, deeply moved by the voices of your sweetly singing church. Those voices flowed into my ears, and the truth was poured out in my heart, whence a feeling of piety surged up and my tears ran down. And these things were good for me.[91]

The sequences favored by the twelfth-century canons regular combined these two ideas: they were Alleluia commentaries, in the form of the Ambrosian hymns. Thirdly, as demonstrated in the analysis of "Laudes crucis" in chapter 4, they contained powerful images of the church, and thus offered a precedent for discussing issues of ecclesiastical reform. Fourthly, texts of the late sequences examined thus far were dominated by the exegetical techniques championed by Augustine and other church fathers. As far as can be told from the surviving sources, it was the canons regular who were responsible for bringing this change of style to sequence poetry. Fifthly, of course, Augustine wrote a treatise on the art of poetry, and an example of poetry in the rhythmic style.[92] Sixthly, as shown above in Chapter 4, a late sequence such as "Laudes crucis" incorporates a rhythmical grid against which its meaning unfolds. Such a work of art is reminiscent of certain mnemonic systems devised in the twelfth century. Mary Carruthers has translated the scheme found in the preface to Hugh of St. Victor's *Chronica*, a small selection of which is offered below:

The first means of classifying is by number. Learn to construct in your mind a grid numbered from one on, in however long a sequence you want, extended as it were before the eyes of your mind. When you've heard enumerated a group of items of a certain numerical size, get in the habit of quickly turning your mind there [on your mental grid] where the sum-total [of items enumerated] is marked off . . . Make this method of thinking and this way of imagining it practiced and habitual, so that you conceive visually of the extent and limit of all numerical groups, just as though [they were] placed in particular places.[93]

The twelfth-century sequences of St. Victor, like the moralized Bibles and other rhythmical, didactic literature from the period, were cast in such modes, so that the information and ideas they contained became might be more readily learned. This emphasis upon learning and teaching, which will be discussed in Chapter 9, was at the heart of the twelfth-century Augustinian canons' call to reform.

This liturgical tour through twelfth-century France has one stop left, Paris. Paris is the only place visited from which Benedictine, Augustinian, and cathedral sources survive. Here, the hypothesis that the late sequence was, originally, an "Augustinian sequence" may be tested further. But the sources are, with one exception, from the early thirteenth rather than from the twelfth century. Thus the history provided in Chapters 5 and 6 will serve as a guide for understanding the Parisian books and the sequences they contain.

---

[90] See Zumkeller (1987), p. 290.
[91] From *Confessions*, Book IX, Chapter 6, as translated by McKinnon *Music in Early Christian Literature*, p. 154.
[92] See Vroom (1933) and Lambot (1935).
[93] Carruthers (1990), p. 262.

Part III

The rise of the late sequence in Paris

7

Paris: first major center for the late sequences

Introduction

Although many of the sequence repertories discussed above in Chapters 5 and 6 are without a strong tradition of secondary literature, literary scholars have long turned attention to the sequences of medieval Paris.[1] In the nineteenth and early twentieth centuries, several attempts were made to edit the sequences from St. Victor, and, more recently, the Parisian repertory of the Cathedral of Notre Dame, as found at the Ste. Chapelle in the mid thirteenth century, has been editied in facsimile by Hesbert.[2] The best studies concerning the nature and scope of the Parisian sequences have been done by Hans Spanke, whose work on late medieval Latin poetry and correspondences with vernacular traditions remains central, and Heinrich Husmann, the first scholar to identify the two separate melodic traditions of the Parisian sequence repertories.[3]

There are two parallel studies one must undertake to understand the history of the Parisian sequence repertories and the relationships between them. One is to study the manuscript sources, and the other is to identify and subsequently to study the persons responsible for creating the texts and music found in the sources and for developing the ideas embodied within them. As might be expected from the discussion in Chapter 1, the manuscripts will be significantly later than the original time of creation. In Parts III and IV of this book, I will offer reasons for believing that a large group of sequence texts was written in Paris during the middle decades of the twelfth century, that several of these are very likely by the poet Adam of St. Victor, and that some of the melodies for these texts were also probably by Adam as well. The prominence given at the Abbey of St. Victor to a small group of interrelated melodies suggests that the music too may originate with this famous

---

[1] Music history books are usually organized so that Gregorian chant, tropes and early sequences, and some early polyphony are studied first; the emphasis shifts in the study of the twelfth century to polyphony and remains there. With but few exceptions most repertories of late medieval and Renaissance chant – sequences, late liturgical drama, rhymed offices – have not been studied.

[2] A list of editions of Victorine sequences, texts and music, is found in the bibliography (p. 442). None of these is a critical edition.

[3] See Spanke (1941) and Husmann (1964).

figure.[4] Information about the sources and the historical circumstances of Adam's life presented later in Part IV indicates that the creation of the first Parisian sequences occurred just before and during the time of the building of Gilduin's church at St. Victor, and the rebuilding of St. Denis by Suger; the redaction of the Victorine sequence repertory took place in the decades immediately after this time.[5] According to this dating, the Parisian sequence repertory becomes the first major musical endeavor of the famed Notre Dame school, and as such it forms the proper historical preface to the polyphonic repertories of later generations.[6] Thus the late sequences grew up with the architectural style known as "Gothic," which came to dominate in the Capetian realm during the late twelfth and thirteenth centuries.[7] Wherever this style went, late sequences went too.[8] Yet, as will be demonstrated in chapters to come, the first large, liturgically organized repertory of these texts and music can be traced first to one group of poets and musicians, and the ideas underlying them tied to a particular school of thinkers. Thus, the late sequences are of great value in understanding developments in the liturgical arts in France during the middle two quarters of the twelfth century.

I have begun discussion of the Victorine sequences with the earliest manuscript sources from Paris. Their study follows logically after the discussion of sources from outside Paris found in Chapters 5 and 6. In fact, because of the nature of the Parisian sources, the study of sequence repertories in other centers will prove crucial. Not one of the large number of liturgical books with sequences which must have existed in twelfth-century Paris has survived.[9] Many of these manuscripts were undoubtedly replaced during the thirteenth century by books with standardized collections of sequences.[10] The earliest Parisian sequence manuscript dates from the late eleventh century and was compiled for the Benedictine Abbey of St. Magloire. Some of the additions to this book were made in the twelfth century and thus offer a glimpse of the kinds of pieces coming into this particular Parisian liturgy during the

---

[4] The Victorine melodic tradition is discussed in Chapter 13.

[5] Suger's major building campaign took place between 1140 and 1144. The first stages of Abbot Gilduin's church at St. Victor just have been well under way, if not completed, by this time. The complete destruction of the Victorine church (for more information on this subject, see Chapter 11) has long been lamented by art historians. It is now assumed by scholars that St. Denis incorporates architectural features which were prevalent in other early Parisian churches, none of which survive. Before his untimely death, Stephen Gardner was writing a monograph on this subject, studying features of now destroyed buildings from early lithographs and other records.

[6] See Fassler (1987).

[7] A history of the term "Gothic" is provided by Jan van der Meulen in the article "Gothic architecture," *DMA*, vol. V.

[8] Alain Michel (1976, p. 165) agrees with this assessment: "Et voici qu'au moment où s'établit le style nouveau de l'architecture, le vieux langage des tropes et des séquences trouve son extrême accomplissement chez Adam de Saint-Victor, dans la discipline très élaborée de ses strophes rhythmiques."

[9] Along with the twelfth-century additions to the St. Magloire manuscript, one does have the few autographs of Godefroy of St. Victor (for which see Gasparri [1982 and 1985] and Ouy [1982]). But these works, in addition to the works mentioned in the writings of Godefroy and Richard of St. Victor, do not prove that these sequences were part of any Parisian liturgy. For that, one would need ordinals or graduals.

[10] David Hiley (1989) argues that Rouen 249, a late-twelfth-century gradual with sequences, represents a twelfth-century Parisian use. Whereas it is true that the manuscript shows Victorine influence, the late date of the sequence collection in this book (fourteenth-century) is disturbing. The variants, both textual and melodic, in the sequence collection in Rouen 249 are very complicated, and I will save discussion of these problems for another time. I am grateful to David Hiley for sharing his thoughts about the manuscript with me, and other materials pertaining to its study as well.

twelfth and thirteenth centuries. None of these is a work associated with Adam of St. Victor, however, and after this source, there are no relevant manuscripts until around 1200, the first being a Victorine ordinal, Paris, BN lat. 14506.

Here an attempt will be made to understand the nature of the twelfth-century Parisian tradition – early and late – through thirteenth-century manuscripts. Theories developed in Chapters 5 and 6 concerning the twelfth-century sequence and the differences between the various religious orders and their willingness to embrace the new genre will be tested here as well. If one looks exclusively at the earliest Parisian sources, are there apparent differences between the Benedictine, the cathedral, and the Augustinian attitudes toward sequences? Does the fame of Paris as a center for late sequence production have a basis in the history of the manuscripts and their repertories?

The earliest sources from the Abbey of St. Victor

Manuscripts to be considered

1 Paris, BN lat. 14506	ordinal from St. Victor	ca. 1200
BON I, 132 ("not after 1206")		
2A Paris, BN lat. 14452	Victorine gradual	c.a. 1200
2B	sequentiary	1220–35
SOU, 107; NGS, 630		
3A Paris, BN lat. 14819	fragment of a gradual	1140–60
3B	sequentiary	1220–35

It is possible to sketch a history of the Victorine sequence repertory from the small group of Mass manuscripts and the ordinal which survive from the twelfth and early thirteenth centuries.[11] Some of these books fit into the history of book preparation at the abbey.[12] Taken together, the books testify that the Victorine liturgy, and particularly the sequence repertory, developed significantly during this period. It is particularly important to discuss the Victorine sequence books in some detail because they have been misdated for generations, and this has bolstered the opinion that the Victorines were not really important in the early history of the late sequence in France.[13]

---

[11] Although the Victorine graduals discussed here are well known to chant scholars, paleographic study of their various parts has not before been carried out; the change of hands in lat. 14452, for example, has not been recognized before. The Victorine ordinal has not previously been studied in any detail, and theories about additions and corrections of this book are my own.

[12] Patricia Stirnemann of the Institut de Recherche et d'Histoire des Textes in Paris is now writing a history of book production at the Abbey of St. Victor in the twelfth and thirteenth centuries. A brief report on her forthcoming work may be found in *APS–V*, pp. 140–141; her article (1990) provides samples of Parisian flourished initials from the mid twelfth through the early fourteenth centuries. I am grateful to Madame Stirnemann for sharing the results of her research with me and for having verified the approximate dates I have established for the Victorine liturgical manuscripts discussed below.

[13] The manuscripts Paris, BN lat. 14819 and 14452 were dated to the late thirteenth century or early fourteenth century in *AH* and this dating has sometimes been assumed in subsequent scholarship. See for example, discussions of the Victorine manuscripts in Huglo (1987), p. 212, note, and van Deusen (1987),

The earliest Victorine Mass book is the fragmentary gradual found in Paris, lat. 14918.[14] This book was prepared by the Victorines themselves during their first campaign of book preparation, a burst of activity which Patricia Stirnemann dates from between 1140 and 1160.[15] Eleven manuscripts have thus far been identified as belonging to this era, and two of them are liturgical books, the gradual fragment described here, and also a lectionary, Paris, lat. 14280.[16] The gradual fragment in lat. 14819 survives perhaps because it includes the feasts for the temporale, the part of the Mass liturgy least subject to change during this period; sequences are not indicated by incipit, as they were in later graduals, and this too made it possible for the book still to be useful late in the twelfth century, and even after.[17] The rest of the book, however, does not survive, and one can imagine why: the sanctorale would have been at something of a rudimentary stage in the mid twelfth century, especially regarding Marian feasts;[18] the sequence repertories once probably included at the close of the book would have undergone dramatic change as well, and would have required recopying. The survival of this fragment demonstrates that the Victorines, like any other religious order, did not recopy books unless it was necessary. Here was the part of their liturgy that was relatively stable by the mid twelfth century, and, therefore, they retained this early copy of it. (See Plate 7.1.).

The next surviving books date from the second major campaign of book production at St. Victor, dated by Stirnemann to between 1185 and 1205.[19] One of these is a gradual, Paris lat. 14452, whose flourishing and script place it right within a few years of 1200.[20] More of this gradual survives than of its earlier counterpart: both the temporale and the sanctorale remain. The only part of the kyriale which survives is that falling just before the sequentiary, and it contains an important complement of Kyries and Glorias none of which, it should be noted, is troped. Just after the final Gloria the sequentiary begins, and it too is in the main hand. But then, just after "Iubilemus omnes" for the fourth Sunday of Advent, the main hand stops. A leaf in a late-fourteenth-century hand intervenes, and then the sequence repertory begins in order, written now in a hand dating from the third decade of the

p. 217. M&A (pp. 23–26) dated the two Victorine sources to "before 1239" because neither of them contains the sequence "Regis et pontificis" for feasts of the Holy Crown (instituted throughout Paris in 1239).

[14] This book is mentioned by Bonnard (1904–07) in his brief list of Victorine liturgical manuscripts. It is the earlier of the Parisian Mass books with notation surviving from the twelfth century, the other being Paris, Bibliothèque Ste. Geneviève 93, usually dated to the late twelfth century.

[15] Gasparri (1973) has identified the major scribe of this campaign, and discussed the hand further (1976 and 1979). The capitals are very plain and probably indicate an early rather than late date in the campaign. For other examples from the period, see Stirnemann (1990), p. 60.

[16] The rest of the manuscripts identified by Stirnemann (personal communication) as falling into this group are Paris, BN lat. 14290 (Augustine on the Psalms), 14363 (saints' lives), 14471 (St. Jerome), 14480 (writings of St. Augustine), 14487 (writings of St. John Cassian), 14505 (writings of Hugh of St. Victor), 14858 (writings of Augustine and others), 15082 (writings of Augustine), and Arsenal 250 (writings of Augustine). About half of these books are copies of the writings of St. Augustine, testifying to the Victorine attitude toward the patron saint of their order. For more detailed descriptions of contents, see Delisle (1869).

[17] A late cursive hand has written the sequence incipits in the margins, suggesting that the book remained a working copy for centuries after its preparation.

[18] Some sense of the sparse Victorine calendar at the mid twelfth century can be gained from studying the early Victorine lectionary Paris BN lat. 14280.

[19] Françoise Gasparri has also worked extensively on the second campaign. See also Cahn (1982), pp, 278–279.

[20] See also Branner (1977), p. 201, and Stirnemann (1990), p. 63.

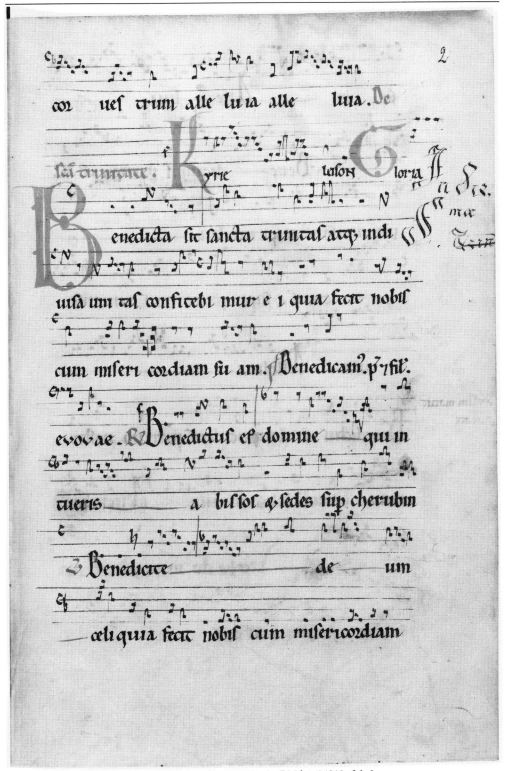

Plate 7.1   Victorine gradual, earlier part. Paris, BN lat. 14819, fol. 2r

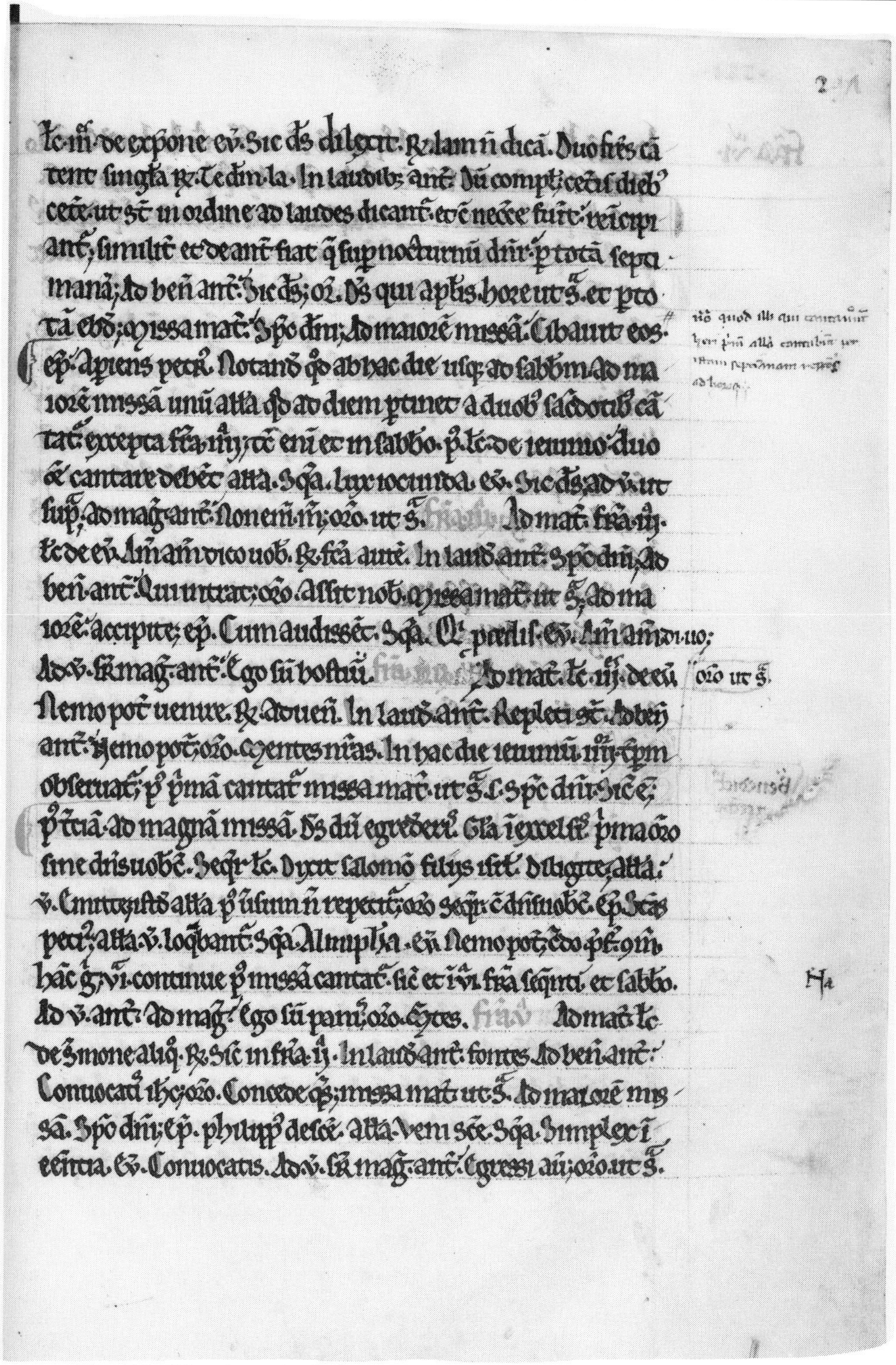

Plate 7.2   Victorine ordinal of ca. 1200, with corrections in a hand of ca. 1210–20. Paris, BN lat. 14506, fol. 297r

thirteenth century. The same reasoning followed in evaluating the condition of lat. 14819 applies here as well: the Victorines could use an entire gradual prepared in 1200 for centuries to follow because both the feasts of the temporale and the sanctorale were standardized and well-established by this date. Their ordinary chants were fixed as well. But changes were still being made in the sequence repertory and it could not be used later on in its late-twelfth-century state.[21]

This description is verified by a second liturgical book dating from around 1200 and also part of the second campaign of book production at St. Victor, the ordinal, Paris, BN lat. 14506. This book proves that the Victorines had a large repertory of sequences in place by the year 1200. The original hand has left space for their incipits in feast after feast and written the abbreviation "seq" just before the title was to appear. But the ordinal also shows that there was still some confusion about which pieces should be sung and for what feasts. Indeed, most of the actual incipits have been written in a second hand, and often this hand seems to have corrected what was there before.[22] (See Plate 7.2.)

Ordinals speak with a kind of authority that troper-prosers or even graduals with sequences at the back do not.[23] The twelfth-century author of lat. 14506 says he has compiled the book "alia ex aliis libris colligentes . . . ut usus ecclesiasticus semper uniformiter teneatur." It is impossible to say precisely when this introduction was originally penned, but, in spite of its admonitions, significant changes were introduced into this very book in the decades immediately after its copying.[24] Ordinals did not prevent change, but they did slow it down, and their presence signifies that a particular church had a liturgical tradition it consciously wished to preserve.[25] The Victorine cantor who amended the sequence incipits in this book in the early thirteenth century carried out his work so as not to violate the page, the margins, or the script. And the changes are easy to miss, especially if one works with a microfilm copy.[26] For example, corrections have been made on folios 297v and 298r and the sequence "Profitentes" is among the additions; on folio 313, the feast of the Transfiguration has been reworked, and the sequence "Letabundi iubilemus" added. Other changes are more obvious and certainly later than these: on folio 313v,

---

[21] The book is very tightly bound, making it difficult to count the gatherings.

[22] The rubbing away of parchment is so skillfully done and so thorough that even with the use of an infra-red lamp one cannot discern the earlier incipits.

[23] For a thorough introduction to the subject of ordinals, evaluations of modern scholarship, and a list of editions of medieval ordinals, see Martimort (1991). Both Martimort and Foley (1988) attempt to define the term "ordinal," and demonstrate the usefulness of this particular type book for students of medieval liturgy and ceremony. Further bibliography concerning printed ordinals may be found in Oury (1971 and 1972) and in DuFrasne (1959), who has prepared a catalog of all secular ordinals found in the Bibliothèque Nationale.

[24] In fact, so carefully have the earliest emendations been added that they are difficult to discern from a microfilm copy. Fol 313v contains the addition of the Feast of the Holy Crown, instituted in 1239. The page has been carefully scraped and every attempt made to fit the text within the margins and to duplicate the original hand.

[25] Foley (1990) suggests that the first ordinal from St. Denis was prepared because architectural changes meant that sequence change was imminent.

[26] When I first wrote about the ordinal in 1984, I had not yet understood the extensive nature of the corrections.

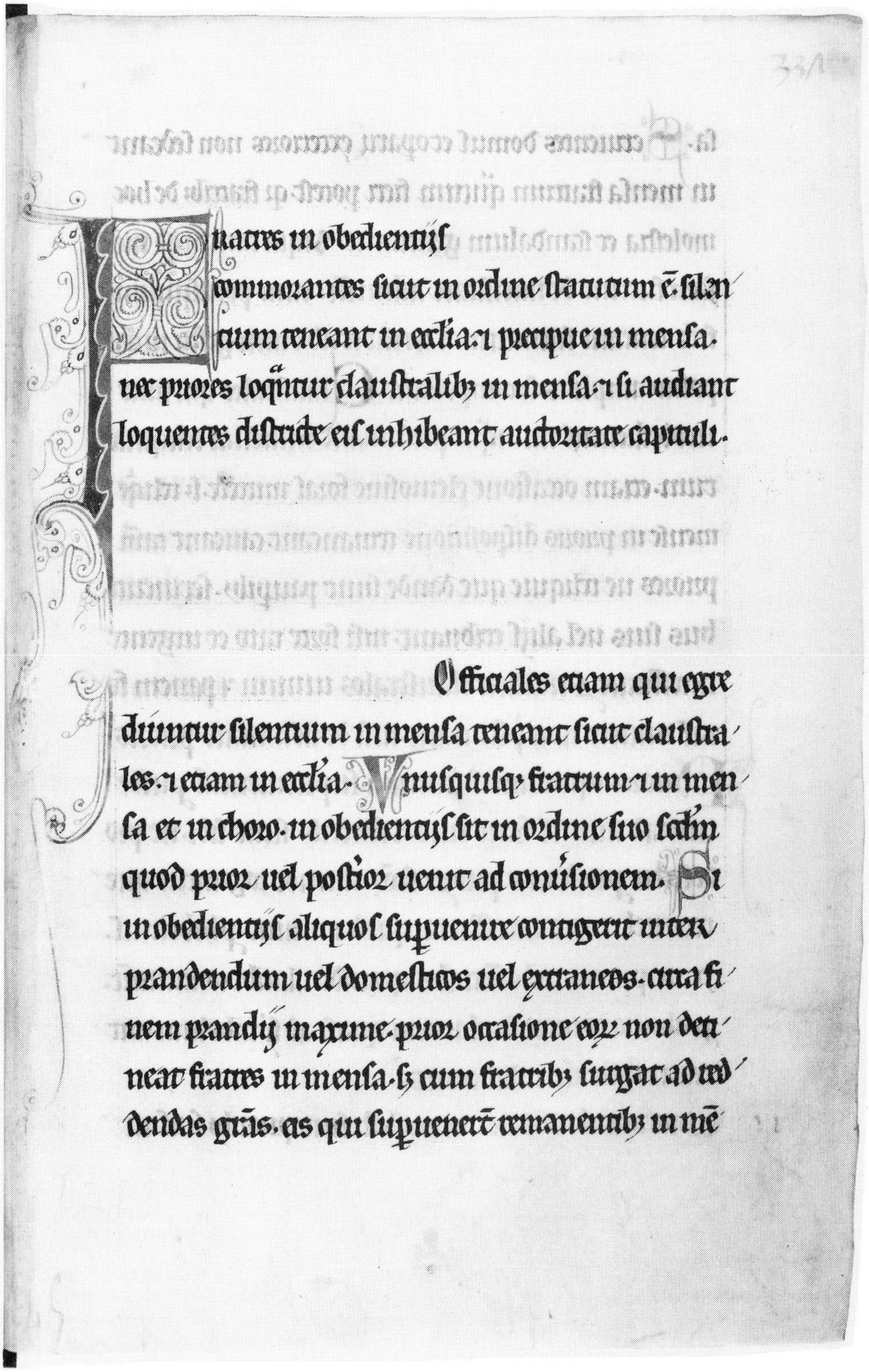

ratres in obedientiis
commorantes sicut in ordine statutum e silen
cium teneant in eclia · precipue in mensa ·
nec priores loquntur claustralib; in mensa · si audiant
loquentes districte eis inhibeant auctoritate capituli ·

Officiales etiam qui egre
diuntur silentium in mensa teneant sicut claustra
les · et etiam in eclia · Vnusquisq; fratrum · in men
sa et in choro · in obedientiis sit in ordine suo sctm
quod prior uel postior uenit ad confusionem · Si
in obedientiis aliquos supuenire contigerit inter
prandendum uel domesticos uel extraneos · citra fi
nem prandii maxime · prior occasione eos non deti
neat fratres in mensa · s3 cum fratrib; surgat ad red
dendas gras · eos qui supuenerit remanentib; in me

Plate 7.3   Addition to the Victorine ordinal in the hand of the corrector of ca. 1210–20. Paris, BN lat. 14506, fol. 337r

for example, the Translation of the Holy Crown has been added in a hand which must date from around 1240, just after the feast was instituted.[27]

The most extensive campaign of additions to this ordinal was carried out by one scribe and with one purpose: to upgrade the sequences and place them in final order. I have been able to date this hand with some precision because I believe it is the hand which copied a small supplement to the ordinal found on folios 337–341.[28] Patricia Stirnemann has verified that this hand appears to be slightly later than the main hand of the ordinal, the large initial on folio 337 showing characteristics of flourishing as found ca. 1210–20.[29] (See Plate 7.3.) Thus the state of the ordinal suggests strongly that the Victorine sequence repertory underwent its final standardization during the second decade of the thirteenth century, soon after the time of the second campaign of book production, and just after, as will be shown in Chapter 11, other additions were made to the architecture of the church which undoubtedly necessitated additions to the sequence repertory.[30]

The final books to be mentioned here date from just after the period of revision reflected in the ordinal. They are, of course, the two fully noted sequentiaries already referred to above and found in lat. 14819 and lat. 14452. These books are near contemporaries; lat. 14452, the only complete collection, is perhaps slightly later than its brother. Their scripts and flourishing are very similar and enable one to date them to the third decade of the thirteenth century (the most helpful characteristic for dating is the swirled infilling of the flourished capitals.[31] The books contain a repertory of sequences that very nearly matches that of the ordinal, and therefore not much change took place in the repertory between the revision of the ordinal and the copying of these books.

The two surviving Victorine sequentiaries fall at the end of a period of intense

---

27 The liturgical books from the Abbey of St. Victor discussed here contain few feasts useful for dating; no other information concerning institutions of particular feasts during the twelfth century has been found in the archives. The history of the abbey as written by later Victorine historians would doubtless prove useful to the liturgiologist, but work on this vast quantity of material has not been undertaken by modern scholars. Fourier Bonnard knew these histories and other documents well, but he often does not provide references for his conclusions.

28 Its most telling characteristics are the serifs which trail off to the left in rather long lines at the tops of tall letters. See Plate 7.4.

29 I believe that this is also the hand which added the feast of St. Catherine to the ordinal; this would suggest that the sequence "Vox sonora" came in (along with the feast) between the years 1210 and 1220. See folio 322. The great devotion to St. Catherine in early-thirteenth-century Paris is demonstrated by the Val des Écoliers, founded in the early thirteenth century. These men patterned their customs and liturgy after St. Victor, and a branch of their order was established in Paris in 1229. Their church in Paris was Ste. Catherine de la Couture.

30 Feasts of particular importance for dating Parisian liturgical manuscripts from the first half of the thirteenth century are listed in Branner (1977), p. 197: St. Eloi (1212), St William of Brouges (1218), St. Francis (1228), St. Dominic (1234), St. Fiacre (1234), St. Elizabeth (1235), the Crown of Thorns (1239), St. Edmund (1247), St. Peter of Verona (1253). None of these are of help with Paris, BN lat. 14452, which is earlier than all of them, and the Victorines did not write sequences for any of them either. The status and dates of the feasts of the Visitation and of the Transfiguration can also be useful.

31 The large "S" on folio 37v is perhaps an imperfectly rendered copy of an earlier style. It is clumsily made, and one finds no other such capital or flourishing in the rest of the sequentiary. This "S" is in the style of flourishing found in Paris BN lat. 16200, a manuscript copied at St. Victor in 1213. See Stirnemann (1990), cat. 20, p. 65. The other flourished initials in this sequentiary are made in a style falling between Stirnemann's catalog examples 21–25, which would give them a range of dates from 1220–1234. See Stirnemann (1990), pp. 65–67.

Plate 7.4   Victorine gradual, later part. Paris, BN lat. 14819, fol. 96v

activity in two different spheres: the creation of sequences and the standardization of sequences into a liturgically ordered book. Investigation of the sources suggests that whatever sequence repertory was put together during the first period of book production (and this repertory would have been found at the end of the fragmentary gradual in lat. 14819) was revamped. None of the collection survives as part of this book. The ordinal, lat. 14506, prepared during the second major period of book production, was designed to include incipits for a very large repertory: apparently these sequences had been incorporated into the Victorine liturgy in large numbers by the year 1200. The gradual in 14452 contains the beginning of the sequence repertory as it existed in about 1200. But the sequentiary breaks off abruptly after the first four pieces. More work was needed for the repertory to satisfy those who sang it during the first decades of the thirteenth century. But by the third decade of this century, the Victorine repertory was fixed and ordered. Thereafter, there was no reason to change it in any major way. Paris, Bibliothèque de l'Arsenal 197, which dates from the final quarter of the thirteenth century, shows only one addition to the sequences in its main corpus, a sequence for the feast of the Translation of the Holy Crown.[32] A few other additions are added in the main hand, but only after the copying of the core repertory as found in lat. 14819 and 14452.

Other early Parisian sources

Manuscripts to be considered

Paris, BN lat. 13252	troper-proser from St. Magloire	late 11th
Paris, BN lat. 1112	noted missal with sequences from Notre Dame	ca. 1220
Paris, Ste. Gen. 1259	noted missal with some sequences from Ste. Genevieve	second quarter of the 13th
Paris Bibl. Maz. 526 Robertson (1984, 1991); Foley (1990)	ordinal from St. Denis	1234–36

St. Magloire

In sheer numbers of sources, the medieval Parisian liturgy is perhaps the best documented in all of France, and, for the sake of its twelfth- and thirteenth-century polyphony, the most studied by modern scholars.[33] Yet manuscript sources from before the thirteenth century are sparse indeed.[34] The search for the twelfth-century

---

[32] For description of a later Victorine missal from Bristol, see Atchley (1900). Arsénal 197 is described briefly in Bernard, ed. (1974).

[33] For a brief introduction to the sources and background of Notre Dame polyphony written for the non-specialist, see Fassler (1987b).

[34] The only other twelfth-century Parisian source with notation from the twelfth century, besides the Victorine gradual fragment in lat. 14819, and the St. Magloire manuscript to be studied here, is Paris, Ste. Geneviève, 93. For discussion, see Bernard's catalog of notated manuscripts from this library and SOU, p. 112.

Parisian sequence tradition begins at St. Magloire. This Benedictine abbey, founded in the tenth century on the site of a chapel dedicated to St. Bartholomew and then reformed in the late tenth century, lived through tumultuous times in the late eleventh and early twelfth centuries.[35] In the late eleventh century, it was reformed by Marmoutier, the famous house of reformed Benedictines in Alsace, sometimes called "The Cluny of the East"; and in the first half of the twelfth century, the entire establishment was moved from its original location in the heart of the city to a new site to the north, outside the city walls.[36]

Lat. 13252 is thought to be from St. Magloire primarily because of similarities between it and Paris, Bibliothèque de l'Arsenal 623, a fifteenth-century manuscript known to be from St. Magloire.[37] There is an enormous decorative capital beginning the trope series for St. Magloire in the earlier manuscript, which demonstrates that it was indeed for a house honoring this particular saint.[38] But there has been a problem with the attribution: the tropes for both St. Magloire and St. Bartholomew, the patrons of the church, are out of liturgical order; although written in the main hand, they are apparently additions to some original series, and there is no sequence or other special material for either of them elsewhere in the manuscript. A likely solution to this problem may be that the manuscript was prepared at another church for use at St. Magloire.[39] Comparison with Paris, Ste. Gen. 93, a noted missal which probably dates from the third quarter of the twelfth century,[40] and with the fragmentary gradual in Paris, BN lat. 14819, reveals that the post-Pentecostal Alleluia list in 13252 is not the same, but this could be explained by the change which took place in the Parisian Alleluia repertory during the late eleventh and early twelfth centuries.[41]

A comparison between the early sequence repertories found in thirteenth-century Parisian manuscripts and the repertory in lat. 13252 reveals no clear parallels. The chart of Parisian sequences in Appendix 5 shows that although some of the pieces found in lat. 13252 are present in sources from the early thirteenth century, substantial numbers are not. The sequence repertory of lat. 13252 has strong ties, however, with the repertories studied in Chapter 5, those of Nevers and St. Evroult.[42] Most of the sequences not present in the early layers of the thirteenth-century Parisian manuscripts (about half of the total) occur at either Nevers or St. Evroult (although often not in both), testifying to the northern French eclecticism observed earlier in Chapter 5. The relationship of lat. 13252 to the later sources

---

[35] On the foundation of St. Magloire in the tenth century, see Merlet (1895).

[36] See Auvray (1892), Tanon (1883), and the Chronicles of St. Magloire in *Recueil des historiens de la France*, vol. XXII, pp. 4–7, 81–87.

[37] See RISM, vol. VI, p. 144.

[38] For discussion of this initial, see Deslandres (1955).

[39] Recently proposed in a forthcoming paper.

[40] The manuscript is incomplete, containing no feasts for the sanctorale. It has not been possible to assign it to a particular church or religious order. It is hastily and carelessly written and notated.

[41] Of course, as Michel Huglo has cautioned, one must not make too much of the evidence of Alleluia lists. It is difficult to interpret their evidence. The change in Parisian Alleluia repertories is discussed briefly in Wright (1989), p. 66.

[42] Charts of correspondences between the introit repertories found in Reier (1981) also demonstrate this affiliation.

suggests, however, that there may not have been a single "Parisian" sequence repertory in the tenth and eleventh centuries, at least not in the way there appears to have been a "Chartrian" repertory.[43] Instead there may have been a Benedictine tradition at St. Magloire, another tradition at the Cathedral of Notre Dame, and yet another tradition at St. Denis.

The additions to lat. 13252 provide an indication of the types of sequences in which these Parisian Benedictines took an interest during the course of the twelfth and thirteenth centuries. Any expectation of being able to observe the works of Adam of St. Victor slowly coming into this house of reformed Benedictines is thwarted here. In various twelfth-century hands one finds: "Ecce dies digna," for St. Peter's Chains; "Clara chorus," for the Dedication; "Alma cohors," for St. John, Evangelist; "Celeste organum," for Christmas, and two pieces for St. John the Baptist, "Gaude caterua" and "Sancti baptiste Christi." None of these sequences are late in style.[44] Two other additions are the only newer works: "Hodierne lux diei," an eleventh-century piece in the late style, and "Mundi etate," also in the late style, but written in the late eleventh or early twelfth century. As Appendix 5 shows, some of these pieces are found in early-thirteenth-century Parisian sources, others are not. There is no steady march of "Parisian" sequences coming into this repertory and no great influx of works in the late style. The twelfth-century Benedictines at St. Magloire appear far more interested in early sequences than in late ones, and they were just as likely to pick up pieces not found generally within Paris as they were to adopt pieces found in the city.

The Cathedral of Notre Dame

The kind of information the Victorine ordinal (and the later copies of this book from the fourteenth century and after) provides is not available for Notre Dame cathedral and, as scholars have often lamented, this lack cannot be fully compensated for, even by the study of processionals and archival materials.[45] We will simply never know as much about the liturgy of the Parisian cathedral in the twelfth century as we do about Chartres or Laon or St. Victor or other places with ordinals and customaries from the century itself.[46] But lat. 1112, a noted missal representing the use of the cathedral, provides texts and music for the sequence repertory of around 1220.[47] Compared with the other surviving thirteenth-century French manuscripts with sequences (the majority of which date from the second half of the thirteenth century), this is an early source, dating from not long after Aix 13. And, in fact, it is the earliest Parisian manuscript with full texts and music for the late

---

[43] And it must be remembered that the Chartrian repertory was found at the Cathedral and in churches dependent upon it. We do not know what it was like in the Benedictine houses as Chartres and, indeed, it may well have been considerably different.

[44] See Appendix 5 (pp. 390–409).

[45] For an introduction to some of these materials for the cathedral, see Wright (1989) and Baltzer (1988).

[46] For a catalog of secular ordinals in the Bibliothèque Nationale, see DuFrasne (1959).

[47] The manuscript has been dated by Branner (1977), p. 206.

sequence repertory.[48] Its repertory of some eighty-five pieces is large for a northern cathedral in the early thirteenth century, rivaled in numbers only by the sequence repertory of Laon, as found in Laon 263. But whereas about sixty of the sequences found in lat. 1112 are written in the late style, Laon 263 contains only around fifteen late sequences. Thus, for numbers of late sequences, collections found at St. Victor at the beginning of the thirteenth century are comparable.

At first glance, it appears that late sequences were as important to the cathedral liturgy as they were to the Augustinian liturgy of St. Victor, and if this were true, it would challenge the primacy of the twelfth-century Augustinians in the champion-ing of sequences as seen in Nevers and Limoges. But even the statistics presented here show that, although the repertory at the cathedral is larger than that of St. Victor, the number of late sequences within these repertories is essentially the same. Thus the Victorines have a greater proportion of such works. The fact that the Victorines developed their own melodic tradition for many of these works puts them in a class of their own. The relationship between the bishops of Paris and the Abbey of St. Victor, which will be explored later in this book, will offer further reasons for the large repertory of late sequences found at the cathedral in the twelfth century.

St. Denis and Ste. Geneviève

A gap of almost twenty years separates the missal of Notre Dame from the next Parisian source, Bibliothèque Mazarine 526, an ordinal from the ancient Abbey of St. Denis. Anne W. Robertson has dated this manuscript to 1234–36.[49] Its early date makes it particularly useful to this study because the monks at St. Denis modernized their sequence repertory dramatically in the later thirteenth century, just after this book was prepared. Paris, BN lat. 976, an ordinal dating from around 1258 or perhaps slightly earlier,[50] for example, is quite different in character from Maz. 526, even though only two decades (or less) elapsed between their copyings.[51]

The sequence repertory represented in Maz. 526 is very different from that found at the Abbey of St. Victor and the Cathedral of Notre Dame. Even though the Victorine and cathedral sources are significantly earlier than the first St. Denis source with sequences, they are much larger. At St. Denis in the 1230s there was a repertory of just around forty sequences, less than half the number found at Notre Dame over two decades earlier. And the proportion of new works is different as

---

[48] The manuscript was not used by the editors of *AH* for vols. LIV and LV, even though it is the earliest and most reliable witness of the Parisian cathedral tradition. It was used to prepare the edition of "Ecce magno sacerdoti," for St. Gendulf, but is said to date from the fifteenth century. See *AH* XL, p. 193.

[49] See Robertson (1984), pp. 326–327; and (1991), pp. 373–375. I have relied upon Professor Robertson's inventory of this manuscript and of other St. Denis sources. Foley (1990) has inventoried Maz. 526 as well, listing sequences with hymns, pp. 727–731.

[50] For the dating of lat. 976, see Robertson (1984), pp. 332–333; and (1991), pp. 379–380.

[51] For a table of the sequences in the thirteenth- and fourteenth-century sources from St. Denis, see Robertson (1984), pp. 496–504; and (1991), p. 278. There was a great burst of activity in the second third of the thirteenth century. Robertson lists the repertory of late sequences probably written at St. Denis in the thirteenth century. Only two of these appear as additions to Maz. 526; the rest are not present at all.

Plate 7.5   The twelfth-century church of Ste. Geneviève, from an illustration in the Atlas of Jean-Baptiste de Saint-Victor, "The ancient church of Ste. Geneviève"

well. Well over half of the sequences at St. Victor and the cathedral were new-style pieces; at the Benedictine Abbey of St. Denis, well over half were early medieval sequences. Even though the Benedictines at St. Denis had some late sequences, and new sequences were being created nearby, during the twelfth and early thirteenth century they did not choose to incorporate great numbers of late sequences. It was only in the second half of the thirteenth century that they brought in large numbers of late sequences from the Parisian repertories and came to create an important body of sequence texts themselves.[52]

Paris, Bibliothèque Ste. Geneviève 1259 (Gen. 1259), the last manuscript to be considered here, dates from the second quarter of the thirteenth century: it was almost certainly copied after 1228, the date of the canonization of St. Francis, whose feast the manuscript contains, but before 1238–39, the date of the institution of the feast of the Holy Crown (August 11), which is present only as an addition to the calendar.[53] The notation, script, and flourishing all support a dating of sometime in the late 1230s. In spite of its late date, the manuscript exhibits conservative traits. Although it is a noted missal, the sequences for the temporale were written along with other chants for individual feasts, not collected at the end as would be expected in a Parisian source from the mid thirteenth century. For the sanctorale, the plan of the book is different: here only incipits are provided for sequences. Thus they must have been collected elsewhere and the fascicle lost. In any case, the full texts and melodies of many sequences in this early version of the repertory from Ste. Geneviève are no longer extant.[54]

The Abbey of Ste. Geneviève was inhabited by secular canons in the first half of the twelfth century. At mid century, it was reformed by the Victorines, and Odo, the Prior of St. Victor, became abbot, bringing a group of twelve Victorines to help him establish control.[55] The original canons rebelled against the reform, resisting the imposition of the Victorine liturgy and customs. Nonetheless, with Abbot Suger of St. Denis administering the reform, the Victorines carrying it out, and the Pope demanding it, there was ultimately little they could do. Augustinians they became and remained. Gen. 1259 was prepared some eighty or ninety years after this reform was initiated, yet it bears both the marks of the reform and of the resistance to it. This is an Augustinian book, with a sequence ("Interni festi") and a high-ranked feast (duplex) for St. Augustine. But it is hardly a book representing the Victorine use: there is a feast for St. Victor, but no sequence for him. Sometime after the reform at mid century, the canons at Ste. Geneviève broke off from the Abbey of St. Victor and developed a Mass liturgy of their own, retaining, as one might expect, features both of their ancient original use and of the Victorine reforms.[56]

---

[52] This repertory is found in Paris, BN lat. 1107.

[53] Bernard (1965) suggested that Gen. 1259 was only adapted for the use of Ste. Geneviève. In an unpublished paper on the manuscript (1989), David Metzer has refuted Bernard's claim, pointing to the three principal feasts for Ste. Geneviève (nameday, translation, and miracles), as well as feasts for her associates Ste. Clotilde and Ste. Aude, a feast for Cerranus (the twenty-fifth bishop of Paris who was buried at the abbey), and for William of Eskill, a member of the abbey, who was canonized in 1224.

[54] Many of these are available in later manuscripts from Ste. Geneviève, however.

[55] For a study of this reform, see Feret (1883), vol. I, pp. 89–147.

[56] The Victorine Stephen of Tournai was abbot of Ste. Geneviève until 1176 until 1192, when he departed to become bishop of Tournai. The next abbot, John of Toucy, who reigned from 1192 to 1222, may have been associated with St. Victor early in his life. But the abbots following him were apparently not connected with the Abbey of St. Victor. See Feret (1883), vol. I, pp. 149–154 and Vulliez (1990). Despite these ongoing signs of affiliation in the late twelfth and early thirteenth centuries, relations between St. Victor and Ste. Geneviève were strained during these decades. Perhaps because they were neighbors, there were many bones of contention between them, including the rights to certain streams and mills. Indeed, immediately after the reform, St. Bernard interceded to see that water rights from an important spring on land belonging to Ste. Geneviève would be given to St. Victor.

The sequence repertory consists of fifty pieces and is thus somewhat larger than the contemporary repertory at the Benedictine Abbey of St. Denis, yet far smaller than the repertory of St. Victor or of the Cathedral of Notre Dame. About half of the sequences are in the late style, but just under half were written in the tenth century or earlier, transitional pieces from the eleventh century filling out the rest. Because of its conservative cast, one might think that the repertory of early sequences at Ste. Geneviève could represent some sort of Parisian "ur-repertory," a collection of pieces found throughout the city and its environs before the reforms of the twelfth century pushed much of the repertory away. But this is not the case: only a handful of the early sequences found at Ste. Geneviève were found at St. Magloire, St. Denis, and Notre Dame. The rest are spread out unevenly, and although Ste. Geneviève has more old pieces in common with St. Denis than any other place, the numbers are still not impressive, the three Masses for Christmas being the most important examples of concordances between the two repertories.[57] Once again, it seems that if there was a uniform Parisian sequence use in the tenth and eleventh centuries, it was not powerful enough or shared by enough institutions to insure its survival into the late twelfth century. The new sequences in this repertory behave differently, however: of the some twenty-five late sequences at Ste. Geneviève, almost half are found at St. Victor and the cathedral and five more are found at St. Victor, the cathedral, and St. Denis. Only three twelfth-century pieces, "Genouefe translatio," for the patron saint, "Martyris egregii," for St. Vincent, and "Mundo christus oritur," for St. Thomas of Canterbury, were not found in other early Parisian sources.[58] Even though the repertory of late sequences at Ste. Geneviève is small, there is far greater uniformity between sources from Ste. Geneviève, St. Victor, and the Cathedral in the late repertory than in the surviving early repertory.

This introduction to the first Parisian sources has emphasized the absence of any apparent core repertory of early sequences, although most of the pieces were found in northern France.[59] But by the time all of these sources were written numbers of late sequences had come in already, even to St. Denis, and at the cathedral and St. Victor late sequences dominated the repertory. The only seasons for which one gets something of a picture of the way sequences existed in Paris in the early twelfth century are Advent and the Nativity. At Easter, new pieces at the Cathedral had pushed almost all others out, but at Christmas this was not the case.

As Appendix 5 shows, all churches had the same four pieces for Advent Sundays, with the exceptions of St. Magloire (which shows none and may be incomplete) and St. Denis where "Gaudia mundo" instead of the customary "Salus eterna" is found. If one studies the Chartrian sources and the sources for Laon, one finds that the four advent pieces are not firmly in place there either. Chartres too was slow to insti-

---

[57] As can be seen in Appendix 5 (p. 391), both St. Denis and Ste. Geneviève have the same sequences for the first, second and third masses of Christmas. Two of these pieces are not found in the other early Parisian manuscripts.

[58] "Geneuese translatio" was probably composed at Ste. Geneviève; "Mundo christus oritur," however, is an English piece. Only the incipit of "Genouefe" is found in Gen. 1259.

[59] Except for a handful of surprises from St. Magloire.

tute the full cycle of four pieces (they are not all found in Advent in the OV), Cambrai did not have them, and Laon had its own series, several of which were probably written in Laon. St. Denis, then, is the only Parisian source that reflects the lack of uniformity found in northern Advent sequences from the twelfth century. The set of four was not brought in immediately, and the monks wrote their own sequence for the first Sunday in Advent.[60]

For Christmas day, with its three masses, the Parisian sources show an array of different sequences. At the cathedral, the canons were content to repeat Advent pieces for the first two masses.[61] At St. Denis and Ste. Geneviève, two tenth-century pieces and an eleventh-century piece were used, and in the same order. At St. Victor, all the early sequences available for Christmas day were scrapped and a single late work, "In natale saluatoris," sufficed. Once again, St. Denis appears to be the best representative of an early tradition of sequence singing within the environs of Paris.[62]

It must be remembered here that the sequence and trope repertories at Chartres Cathedral were very small in the early twelfth century, and that the large repertory of tropes and sequences at Nevers Cathedral appeared first in a Benedictine guise. Here in Paris, too, the cathedral sequence repertory of the early thirteenth century is surprisingly short of early examples, and there is no evidence of either a strong connection between the shreds of this early repertory and other Parisian churches or of any creative force writing early sequences at the cathedral in the centuries before the twelfth. One is left to wonder if, indeed, the tenth- and eleventh-century liturgy at the cathedral of Paris came anywhere near rivaling the ceremony and music found at St. Denis during the same period. Perhaps French cathedrals before the twelfth century only rarely expended energies upon their liturgies with the fervor of their Benedictine brethren.

The number of late sequences written in Paris

By the end of the twelfth century, the demand for late sequences throughout France exceeded the supply of new works available. With houses of Augustinian canons and nearby cathedral chapters requiring ever greater numbers of these works for their liturgies, local poets were often unwilling or unable to write the pieces fast enough. Thus, as it has been shown in Chapters 4 and 5, in Nevers, in Limoges, in

---

[60] The text of "Gaudia mundo" is edited in *AH* 37:13, using Paris, BN lat. 1107 from St. Denis and two sources from St. Corneille in Compiègne. In 1150 Suger and the monks from St. Denis reformed this monastery, imposing their own liturgy and customs. Robertson (1984) has written about the strong ties between the two institutions before the reform. The presence of this sequence in these sources and not in other sources consulted by the editors of *AH* is an indication that it might well have originated at St. Denis.

[61] In the OV from Chartres, the order for Christmas Day is: first Mass, "Salus eterna"; second Mass, "Sonent regi"; third Mass, "Lux fulget."

[62] Two other sequences are candidates for consideration as works from St. Denis: "Laudis odas resonemus" (which appears at St. Magloire and in the Compiègne manuscripts), and "Super armonie uastam," for St. Denis. The appearance of this second piece at both St. Magloire and St. Evroult shows an affinity between northern Benedictine houses.

Aix, in Narbonne, and elsewhere as well, significant groups of new pieces were imported from Paris in the late twelfth and early thirteenth centuries. The most obvious reason other places looked to Paris to provide late sequences in the late twelfth century was because it had more of them than any other French center at this time. And the fact that it had two distinct traditions of sequences so early, one at the Cathedral of Notre Dame, the other at the Augustinian Abbey of St. Victor, suggests that it had long been an important center. To evaluate the Parisian late sequences and their significance, however, one first needs some idea of how many pieces were created there during the twelfth century. Were these pieces just collected there in great numbers, or were they actually written in Paris, as tradition has long held?

Until more and better editions of late sequences have been made and a catalog of sequence melodies completed, the information to answer this question must be gleaned from the editions of late sequence texts found in *AH*, primarily in volumes X, LIV, and LV.[63] There are problems with these editions: crucial manuscripts were missed (Paris lat. 1112, for example, is rarely cited), the dates of manuscripts given are usually too late or imprecise, and pieces which are additions are sometimes not listed as such. The editors did not study ordinals, Parisian or otherwise (although one should not fault them for this), yet the information ordinals contain about the presence or absence of sequences is invaluable for understanding dating and transmission.[64] In spite of these problems, *AH* will give a fairly accurate picture of the general status of many late sequences, if one takes account of the most important neglected manuscripts. Because late printed books were regularly consulted, the ongoing presence of a piece in Paris can be tested in *AH* as well. Many of the pieces traditionally thought to be Parisian do appear with great consistency only in Parisian sources and those dependent upon them only, sometimes even only in Victorine sources.[65] There are a few early sources from outside the city that consistently have these pieces – Aix, St. Leonard's of Limoges, some of the later fascicles of lat. 1139, and Assisi 695 – and their very consistency argues that these sources were drawing upon some Parisian stream of influence, rather than feeding pieces into Paris. There is a consistent pattern of sources for a great majority of these sequences, and it is often obvious when it is violated. If a piece turns up in great numbers of other places early on as well – in England, in German or Austrian centers, in Italy – then it is much riskier to call the sequence "Parisian," even though, of course, it still could be.

In this chapter and in Tables 7.1 and 7.2 below (pp. 158–160), decisions have been on the cautious side every time, and, unless there is other evidence (such as the testimony of Richard of St. Victor or Alan of Lille), pieces are called "Parisian/

---

[63] In Chapter 13, there is an evaluation of the various efforts to catalog and study late sequence melodies in past scholarship.

[64] As stated above, the Victorine manuscripts 14819 and 14452 are listed as being from the late thirteenth century, and the ordinal 14506 was not consulted. Therefore, the Victorine witness to many of these texts appears late, when it is usually the earliest.

[65] Aix 13 and Assisi 695 are the only non-Victorine manuscripts to contain great numbers of uniquely Victorine texts. Rouen 249 from Eu was prepared from Victorine exemplars and has a few "Victorine" sequences as well.

Victorine" only if they show up exclusively in Parisian sources from the thirteenth century, in the sources cited above (Aix, Assisi 695, Lat. 1086), and in no more than one other center.[66] As the label "Parisian/Victorine" indicates, it is difficult to say from the evidence presented in this chapter which church, the cathedral or the abbey, had these pieces first. Sequences labeled "Parisian" were probably written first at the cathedral; sequences labeled "Victorine" were created at the Abbey of St. Victor, and did not make their way into the cathedral liturgy. Sequences are called "Probably Parisian" if they are found consistently in a great number of thirteenth-century Parisian sources, early and late, in Aix, Assisi 695, etc., and in no more than three other French thirteenth-century sources. Late sequences found in Paris which do not meet these requirements or which are found in more than two witnesses in other regions outside France are listed at the end of Table 7.1b.

Following this method of determination, we can list almost sixty sequences written in Paris in the twelfth century and in existence long enough to have found their way into service books by the third decade of the thirteenth century; and of course this group consists only of those which have survived. Many more than this must have been written in Paris which were either not accepted into any liturgy by this early date or eventually discarded altogether. Thus Paris had four to five times more native late sequences than any other center at this time, and the flourishing of late sequences there constitutes a small renaissance in late medieval poetry and music. There had been small numbers of late sequences written in the late eleventh and early twelfth centuries, and they circulated rapidly throughout Europe. During the second half of the twelfth century, many churches began to import small repertories of Parisian sequences, but only Augustinian churches had large numbers of them officially in place. By the early thirteenth century, many works from the Parisian sequence repertory had been established in churches throughout France. After this time, hundreds of pieces would be written on Parisian models, and the late sequence became the "classic," not only in its poetic form, but also in content and exegetical mode.

The statistics presented in Table 7.2 have a further message: fifteen Parisian sequences appear only at the Abbey of St. Victor and eleven only at Notre Dame, sixteen more are found only at St. Victor and Notre Dame, and nine are found at Notre Dame, St. Victor, and Ste. Geneviève. Thus in the late twelfth century the great majority of Parisian sequences appears only at Notre Dame or St. Victor, or both. St. Denis did not have these works, for the most part, and even Ste. Geneviève had only a small collection of them. If the repertory had been widely accepted in all Parisian churches by the late twelfth century, one would certainly expect to find more of it at Ste. Geneviève.

Of all late sequence repertories created in twelfth-century France, the repertory of Paris is the largest, both in the number of imported works and in the number of works created within the city itself. Perhaps it is because late sequences were so important in twelfth-century Paris that little remains of the original repertory of

---

[66] More often than not, however, it is not necessary to invoke this "single exception" escape clause.

early sequences within the city, making it difficult to regain a sense of what this repertory may have been like. Comparison of the early repertories at St. Denis, Ste. Geneviève, and the cathedral with the repertories of St. Magloire and other twelfth-century northern sources, including books from St. Evroult, Chelles, Chartres, and Nevers, do not reveal convincing patterns of concordances. What little evidence there is, however, suggests that St. Denis may have been more interested in the cultivation and preservation of a tradition of early sequences than was the cathedral of Notre Dame, and that this Dionysian repertory would have had more in common with that of other northern Benedictine houses than with the eleventh-century sequence practice of the cathedral (whatever it may have been).

As has been shown above, study of the earliest sources demonstrates that only the cathedral and St. Victor had large numbers of late sequences in the twelfth century, and that neither Ste. Geneviève, the first representative of secular Parisian churches within the city, nor St. Denis, the representative of Benedictine churches just outside the city, had significant numbers of late sequences or of late specifically-Parisian sequences during the twelfth century. The late-twelfth- or early-thirteenth-century manuscript from Chelles, just outside Paris, also contains very few late sequences; none of the pieces added to the St. Magloire manuscript are Parisian pieces in the late style. In fact, there were more Parisian sequences in places such as Aix-la-Chapelle and St. Leonard of Limoges, Augustinian churches which sought them specifically, than in uninterested Parisian churches of the late twelfth century. By the mid thirteenth century, however, this picture changed, and all Parisian churches began to adopt the large repertory of sequences sung at the Cathedral of Notre Dame. The monks of St. Denis embraced the new genre to such an extent as to write a significant body of late sequences themselves during the second half of the thirteenth century.[67]

The twelfth-century Parisian sequence repertory originated at the cathedral and St. Victor; that much is clear. But when in the century was it written and which institution, if any, had priority over the other in the beginning? To answer these questions one needs to contrast the distinct traditions of sequences found at the Augustinian Abbey of St. Victor with the repertory of Notre Dame Cathedral.

Abbreviations used in Tables 7.1 and 7.2

VIC	found in the contemporary Victorine sources lat. 14819 and 14452
ND	found in lat. 1112 from the Cathedral of Notre Dame
Gen	found in Bibl. Ste. Geneviève 1259
Den	found in Paris, Bibl. Mazarine 526 from St. Denis
Mag	lat. 13252 from St. Magloire
add	as an addition to the source, but no later than the early 13th century

---

[67] For discussion of these sequences, see Robertson (1984 and 1991).

Table 7.1a. *Sequences written in Paris in the twelfth century (in calendar order)*

Title	Origin	In early Parisian sources
Temporale		
In natale salvatoris	Victorine	Vic
Splendor patris	probably Parisian	ND, Vic
In excelsis canitur	Parisian/Victorine	ND, Vic
Nato nobis saluatore	probably Parisian	ND
Virgo mater saluatoris	Victorine	Vic
Zima uetus	Parisian/Victorine	ND, Vic, Gen
Ecce dies celebris	Parisian/Victorine	ND, Vic, Gen
Lux illuxit dominica	Parisian/Victorine	ND, Vic, Gen
Sexta passus feria	Parisian/Victorine	ND, Vic
Mundi renouatio	Parisian/Victorine	ND, Vic, Gen
Salue dies dierum	Parisian/Victorine	ND, Vic, Gen
Postquam hostem	Parisian/Victorine	ND, Vic
Lux iocunda	Parisian/Victorine	ND, Vic, Gen
Simplex in essentia	Parisian/Victorine	ND, Vic, Gen
Qui procedis	Parisian/Victorine	ND, Vic
Sanctorale		
Genouefe sollempnitas	Parisian/Victorine	ND, Vic, Gen: add
Animemur ad agonem	probably Parisian	ND
Ecce dies preoptata	Parisian	ND, Vic
Iubilemus . . . qui	Victorine	Vic
Corde uoce	Parisian	ND, Vic
Templum cordis	Victorine	Vic
Lux aduenit	Parisian	ND
Regina uirginum	unknown	ND
Gaude prole grecia	Parisian/Victorine	ND, Vic, Gen, Den
Gaude turma	Dionysian	Den
Lux illuxit triumphalis	Parisian	ND
Ex radice caritatis	Victorine	ND
Mundi etate	Parisian	ND, Mag: add
Precursoris	Parisian	ND
Ad honorem	Parisian/Victorine	ND, Vic
Gaude Roma	Parisian/Victorine	ND, Vic, Gen
Corde uoce	Parisian/Victorine	ND, Vic
Roma petro	Parisian/Victorine	ND, Vic
Ecce dies triumphalis	Victorine	Vic
Gaude superna	Parisian	ND
Letabundi iubilemus	Victorine	Vic
Prunis datum	Parisian/Victorine	ND, Vic
O Maria, stella maris	Parisian/Victorine	ND, Vic
Aue uirgo . . . mater	Parisian/Victorine	ND, Vic
Vergente mundi	probably Parisian	ND
Aue uirgo . . . porta	Victorine	Vic
Gratulemur in hac die	Victorine	Vic
Laudemus omnes	Parisian/Victorine	ND, Vic

Precursorem summi regis	Parisian	ND
Res est admirabilis	probably Parisian[a]	ND
Aue mater ihesu christi	Parisian	ND
Salue crux arbor	Parisian	ND
Laus erumpat	probably Parisian	ND, Vic
Cordis sonet	Victorine	Vic
Geneuefe translatio	St. Geneviève	Gen
Gaude syon que diem	Parisian/Victorine	ND, Vic
Ecce magno sacerdoti	probably Parisian	ND
Vox sonora	Parisian	ND, Vic: add
Exsultemus et letemur	Parisian	ND, Vic
Congaudeant hodie	Victorine	Vic
Heri mundus	Parisian/Victorine	ND, Vic
Gratulemur ad festiuum	Parisian/Victorine	ND, Vic
Gaude syon et letare	Victorine	Vic
Iubilemus . . . quem	Victorine	Vic
Rex salomon	Parisian/Victorine	ND, Vic
Stola regni	Victorine	Vic
Cor angustum	Victorine	Vic

[a] Later sources thinner than usual

Table 7.1b. *Late sequences in Paris by the early thirteenth century, but not exclusively in Parisian sources*

Title	Sources in Paris			
Ante torum	ND			
Mane prima	ND	Vic	Gen	Den
Veni sancte	ND	Vic	Gen	
Laudes deo			Gen	
Profitentes	ND	Vic		Den
Martyris egregii			Gen	
Salue mater saluatoris	ND	Vic		
Aue maria gratia	ND			
Laudes crucis[a]	ND	Vic	Gen	Den
Stola iocunditatis	ND		Gen	Den
Aue mundi	ND			
Interni festi		Vic	Gen	
Promat pia	ND			
Iocundare	ND	Vic		
Virginis egregie	ND			
Psallat chorus	ND			
Congaudentes	ND	Vic	Gen	
Quam dilecta	ND	Vic		
Sancte Syon	ND			
Superne matris	ND	Vic	Gen	Den

[a] Hard to tell by these criteria because it is so widespread

Table 7.2. *Concordances within the Parisian late sequence repertories*

Source	Parisian	Probably Parisian	Not Parisian
Numbers of works in one source only			
Vic only	15	0	0
ND only	7	4	6
Gen only	1	0	0
Den only	1	0	0
Numbers of works in two sources			
ND, Vic	19	1	2
ND, Vic: add	2	1	1
Vic, Gen	0	0	1
Gen, Den	0	0	1
ND, Mag: add	1	0	0
Numbers of works in three sources			
ND, Vic, Gen	9	0	3
ND, Vic, Gen: add	1	0	0
ND, Vic, Den	1	0	0
ND, Gen, Den	0	0	1
Numbers of works in four sources			
ND, Vic, Gen, Den	1		3
ND, Vic, Gen, Mag: add			1

8

Contrafacta in the Parisian sequence repertories: an introduction

The two Parisian sequence repertories

Although the first Parisian sequence manuscripts date from the very late twelfth or early thirteenth centuries, several repertorial features already observed suggest that these sequences had existed long before the first surviving manuscripts were copied: this is an exceedingly large repertory, it was already liturgically ordered by the late twelfth century at the Abbey of St. Victor (and probably at the cathedral too), and it existed in two related but unique traditions by this time as well. Here, in the city where the late sequences first flourished, a house of canons regular developed a sequence tradition apart from that of its mother church, the church from which it originally inherited its liturgical books and first drew its membership during the early twelfth century. No other town or city in France had a dramatic split in its sequence use at this early date, and the existence of these dual traditions is one of the striking musical facts of the twelfth century. In this chapter it must be asked what the nature of this separate Victorine tradition was.

One begins to explore the Victorine repertory by comparing it with the sequence repertory of Notre Dame and other Parisian churches, taking the idea of making contrafacta, that is, of resetting new texts to already existing melodies, as a starting point. The subject is essential to introducing the Parisian sequence repertories on two counts: (1) contrafacta are, as has long been recognized, basic to the composition of sequences, and this is true for earlier as well as twelfth-century repertories; (2) and, as Husmann observed, the Victorines had a particular interest in contrafacta.[1] It is surprising how little attention has been paid to the medieval art of contrafactum, given that it was fundamental to the work of liturgical poets and musicians for centuries, and, of course, to poets who wrote in the vernacular languages as well.[2] Too often, modern scholars have thought of the re-utilization of popular melodies by medieval poets and musicians as only mechanical, perhaps

---

[1] See Husmann (1964).

[2] Most interest in contrafacta has focused upon vernacular settings of hymns and sequences; see particularly Spanke (1932); also Lehmann (1922), Szövérffy (1983b), and several of the articles of Bruno Stäblein, particularly (1962).

suggestive of artistic impoverishment.[3] In reality, medieval poets and composers developed many approaches to contrafacta, ranging from the simple to the complex, and some artists used the technique as a means of interrelating their texts.[4] By focusing attention upon the contrafacta techniques found in a particular group of Parisian sequences, it is possible to distinguish how the Victorine sequence repertory was different from all the others, and to demonstrate the special emphasis the Victorines placed upon the musical dimension of the repertory.

Because the making of contrafacta is central to the formation of both major traditions within the Parisian sequence repertory, it is especially useful to study it within what may well be an early layer of Parisian sequence texts, looking for clues about the natures of the deep divisions within the Parisian use. Here I will concentrate, out of the large repertory of some sixty sequences written in Paris in the twelfth century, upon those eight works found at three churches in the early thirteenth century, Notre Dame, St. Victor, and Ste. Geneviève, adding to these the one Parisian late sequence found in all four sources: (the three already mentioned and the Abbey of St. Denis): "Gaude prole grecia" for St. Denis.[5] Tangentially, variants from later manuscripts from other Parisian churches will be considered as well. The close connections between these three institutions during the first half of the twelfth century have already been mentioned, and will be discussed at greater length in Chapters 9 and 10: the Abbey of St. Victor, which began unofficially in 1108 and received its foundation charter in 1113, was originally founded by secular canons from the cathedral who left with William of Champeaux to follow the Rule of St. Augustine. Of course, the very early liturgy of St. Victor must have been the liturgy of the Cathedral of Notre Dame. The Victorines, in turn, growing immensely in power and prestige during the first decades after their founding, were responsible for reforming the Abbey of Ste. Geneviève during and just after 1148. They imposed their customary and liturgical practices, which certainly might have included their sequences. One would expect the liturgies of these three institutions to be somewhat ingrown. But the relationships between them have a complex history throughout the twelfth century, as the varying states of their earliest surviving late sequence repertories show.

Out of the large repertory of some sixty sequences written in Paris in the twelfth century, only these nine were found in all three of the earliest sources, those from St. Victor, the Cathedral of Notre Dame, and Ste. Geneviève. It is likely, therefore, that this small group of pieces forms an early layer of sequences, a layer representing those pieces which were accepted into the liturgy already at mid-century, perhaps before the time the Victorines reformed Ste. Geneviève. In this early layer, one finds undoubtedly some works by Adam of St. Victor. The concentration of all but two

---

[3] The pervasive use of contrafacta in late sequence repertories has been criticized as a flaw by modern scholars: see, for example, the history of sequences by Nicholas de Goede in his preface to de Goede, ed., *The Utrecht Prosarium*. For the suggestion that the contrafacta found in the late sequences are of equal interest to those found in the early sequences, see Diehl (1985), p. 89.

[4] For comparison of the use of one early sequence melody in several different traditions, see Stäblein (1964).

[5] A further sequence, "Genouefe sollempnitas," appears in three sources. Because it is only an addition to Ste. Gen. 1259, however, it is not of the same stature as the others.

Table 8.1. *Parisian sequences found at Notre Dame Cathedral, St. Victor and St. Geneviève in the early thirteenth century*

Title	Feast at			Melody at		
	ND	Vic	Gen	ND	Vic	Gen
Zima uetus	All within the Easter octave			Laudes crucis	Zima uetus	Zima uetus
	Fer3	Oct	Oct			
Ecce dies celebris	All within the Easter octave			Mane prima	Mane prima	Mane prima
	Fer4	Fer2	Fer3			
Lux illuxit	All within the Easter octave			Superne matris	Superne matris	Interni festi
	Fer5	Fer3	Fer4			
Salue dies dierum	All within the Easter octave			Salue	Salue	Salue
	Oct	Fer4	Fer6	ND	ND var	Vic
Mundi renouatio	All within the Easter octave			All settings of Victime paschali		
	Sab	Sab	Fer5			
Lux iocunda	All in Pentecost octave			Lux iocunda	Laudes crucis	Laudes crucis
	Fer3	Fer2	Fer2	ND		
Simplex in essentia	All in Pentecost octave			Mane prima	Mane prima	Mane prima
Ad honorem	All for John the Baptist (Nativity)			All set to Congaudentes		
	No. 2	Only	Only			
Gaude prole	St. Denis			All set to Mane prima (Included also at St. Denis)		

fer = feria; oct = octave; sab = in sabbato

of these sequences in two weeks within the church year suggests further that the Octaves of Easter and Pentecost were of primary concern to Parisian liturgists of the mid twelfth century. Certainly, finding new sequences for these feasts was important at Ste. Geneviève, which does not have great numbers of new pieces for other occasions. But even within this group of texts one finds many areas of disagreement, and enough evidence to suggest that even if the texts are all early, the musical settings are not part of the same cloth. To begin with, the Octaves of both Easter and Pentecost are arranged differently in regard to sequences in all three places. Of greater importance is the fact that each institution has its particular way of singing the texts: sometimes all agree on the melody, sometimes Notre Dame has one use and St. Victor another, with Ste. Geneviève apparently caught in between the two traditions. "Zima vetus" is set to the "Laudes crucis" melody at Notre Dame, but to a melody written specially for it at St. Victor and Ste. Geneviève. "Lux iocunda" was set to its own melody at Notre Dame, but to "Laudes crucis" at St. Victor and Ste. Geneviève. And both traditions had their own melody for "Salue dies dierum," Ste. Geneviève following the cathedral use. This last melody is of particular interest because the Victorines respected the cathedral melody enough to quote it in the opening of their own, only to veer off in a unique direction after this opening statement.[6]

"Victime paschali" and "Mundi renouatio"

Within these nine texts, one finds ample material both for an introduction to contrafactum techniques employed in the late sequences of Paris and for an exploration of what differentiates the Victorine repertory from the others. An initial overview, provided through analysis of "Mundi renouatio," demonstrates one of the many ways in which Parisian composers reworked older sequences in their new pieces: in this sequence the tradition of the original piece is preserved not only through the text, which is an Easter poem, like its model, but also through the music, which has been reshaped through a new style of poetry, yet retains the characteristic melody of the original.

The text of "Mundi renouatio" is about two gardens of Eden, the one created at the beginning of the world and the other through the power of the resurrection. The sequence bursts open without formal salutation, emphasizing throughout the idea of renewal, of "renovatio": the joys are "new," the elements conspire to express them – sky, sea, wind, and land revivified by the Easter miracle. Death is ice melted, representing the frozen world of sin ruled over by Satan and now released from his dominion. At the end, this newly verdant earth becomes the Paradise regained through Christ's actions, as the angel barring entrance to the descendants of Adam and Eve drops his sword, and the garden is now open to those released from the ancient crimes of Adam and Eve.[7] This idea of two creations, one by the Father (with the Son as agent) and the other by the Father through the Son, stands behind *De sacramentis christiane fidei* by Hugh of St. Victor, the leader of the Victorine school in the first half of the twelfth century.[8] The idea is central in the writings of Hugh's mentor, Augustine, who developed it most fully in his *Confess-*

---

[6] See discussion of Family IVD in Chapter 13, pp. 311–315. The text "Gaude, syon, que diem" for St. Martin is set to this melody in the Anthology (Example A.7, pp. 434–435). "Salue dies dierum" was also sung to this melody at St. Victor.

[7] See Genesis 3:23–24. "He banished the man, and in front of the garden of Eden he posted the great winged creatures and the fiery flashing sword to guard the way to the tree of life." The poet here next refers obliquely to Apoc. [Rev].22:14–15. The angel describing the Heavenly Jerusalem says its gates will not be open to sinners.

[8] The major themes of Hugh's writings are discussed at length in Chapter 10.

ions and in his Genesis commentaries, but who often spoke of the parallels between creation and re-creation in his sermons to the people as well. In his sermon on Psalm 95 [96], for example, Augustine described the new Adam who recreates from the elements of the first creation:

Ipse ergo Adam toto orbe terrarum sparsus est. In uno loco fuit, et cedidit, et quodam modo comminutus impleuit orbem terrarum; sed misericordia Dei undique collegit fracturas, et conflauit igne caritatis, et fecit unum quod fractum erat. Nouit illud facere artifex ille; nemo desperet: multum quidem est, sed qui sit artifex, cogitate. Ille refecit, qui fecit; ille reformauit, qui formauit.[9]

(Adam therefore hath been scattered over the whole world. He was in one place, and fell, and as in a manner broke small, he filled the whole world: but the mercy of God gathered together the fragments from every side, and forged them by the fire of love, and made one what had been broken. That artist knew how to do this; let no one despair: it is indeed a great thing, but reflect who that artist is. He who made, restored: He who formed, reformed.)

In the sequence there is a fusing of Old Testament and New Testament time, which creates a typological history of creation and re-creation, and provides a commentary upon both events. Like the text of "Laudes crucis," analyzed in Chapter 4, this late sequence text too has the presentation of a dramatically visualized history as its major goal. Here one experiences sensually the second spring.

The text of "Mundi renouatio," as found in Paris, BN lat. 14819[10]

I.1   Mundi renouatio noua parit gaudia;

I.2   Resurgenti domino conresurgunt omnia;

I.3   Elementa seruiunt et actoris sentiunt quanta sit potentia.

II.1   Celum fit serenius et mare tranquillius spirat aura mitius uallis nostra floruit;

II.2   Reuirescunt arida recalescunt frigida postquam uer intepuit.

III.1   Gelu mortis soluitur princeps mundi fallitur et eius destruitur in nobis imperium;

III.2   Dum tenere uoluit in quo nichil habuit ius amisit proprium;

III.3   Vita mortem superat homo iam recuperat quod prius amiserat paradysi gaudium;

III.4   Viam prebet facilem cherubin uersatilem amovendo gladium.

IV.1   Christus celos reserat et captiuos liberat quos culpa ligauerat sub mortis interitu;

IV.2   Pro tali uictoria patri proli gloria sit cum sancto spiritu.

(I   The renewal of the world spawns new joys. The Lord rising again, all things rise again together. The elements serve and feel how great is the power of the creator.

II   The sky is made clearer and the sea more tranquil; the wind breathes more gently; our valley has bloomed. Dry things grow green again; frozen things warm up, now that spring has grown warm.

III   The ice of death is melted, the prince of the world is deceived and his dominion over us is destroyed. While he wished to reign over that to which he had no claim, he lost his own right. Life

---

[9] Augustine, *Enarrationes in Psalmos* 95, CSEL XXXIX, pp. 1352–1353; Coxe trans., *Expositions* pp. 474–475.
[10] For the Latin original and the music, see the anthology (Example A.2, pp. 419–420).

conquers death; man now regains the joy of paradise which formerly he had lost. The angel makes the road easy by removing the opposing sword.

IV   Christ unlocks the heavens and frees the prisoners, whom sin had bound under the destruction of death.[11] For such a victory let there be glory to Father, to the Son, and to the Holy Spirit.)

"Mundi renouatio" makes its meaning first through the power of its poetry, but secondly because it was set to a version of the melody for the Easter sequence "Victime paschali laudes," which was probably created in the first half of the eleventh century.[12] In the copy of "Mundi renouatio" found in the anthology (Example A.2, pp. 419–420), the melodies of "Mundi renouatio" and "Victime paschali" (in smaller staves) are constantly juxtaposed, so that the technique of recomposition used by the Parisian artist may be more readily observed. The new melody follows its model in the arrangement of lines, and of melodic units within the lines. In fact, the entire shape of the original piece is adhered to closely, and one might, at first, wonder why such an obvious repeating of the same melody is worthy of notice. It is useful, however, to see the techniques of Parisian contrafactum employed in so direct and clear a fashion. One can tell how the composer altered notes when he had to, firm in the knowledge that this is indeed a reworking of an older piece. In other sequences, the parallels are not so exactly made, and one must argue harder to verify borrowings.

Whenever the text lines have an identical number of syllables, the same music was used for both of them. When this is not the case, the composer reworked the music of the earlier piece. He tried to make the new music resemble its model in melodic contour and kept the notes the same at the beginning and end of phrases, making changes in the middle notes. Thus, as Example A.2 in the anthology shows, the end of the second melodic unit (phrase 2C) in "Mundi renouatio" is an adaptation of two phrases in "Victime paschali." First the new phrase 2C has the same two opening notes as "Victime paschali," 2D and the same closing note, but the middle portion has been expanded to accommodate a longer text. Yet the melodic shape of the phrase "Mundi renouatio," 2C resembles that of "Victime paschali," phrase 2C. In writing phrase 2C, the Parisian composer alluded to two phrases in the model simultaneously. In "Mundi renouatio," phrase 4B, the opening note of the model ("Victime paschali," 4B) is in place, as are the last three notes; the contour of the line resembles that of the model, but the middle notes have been slightly altered. In "Mundi renouatio," melodic phrases 4c' and 4c", one can observe a reworking of "Victime paschali," melodic phrase 4C. The composer of the Parisian sequence has turned the opening of the model phrase 4C into phrase 4c' of the new piece, and the end of the model phrase 4C into phrase 4c" of "Mundi renouatio."

The text of the later sequence exemplifies a new poetic style: lines are regular in length, and accentual patterns and end rhymes prevail. The artist changed the music

---

[11] A reference to the harrowing of hell.

[12] "Victime paschali" was one of the most heavily contrafacted sequences in the entire medieval chant repertory. For discussion of several versions, neither of which mentions "Mundi renouatio," see Szövérffy (1973) and Lehmann (1922).

Table 8.2. *Sigla for selected thirteenth-century Parisian graduals or noted missals with notated sequences, usually in a collection at the back of the manuscript (a few of these MSS have small numbers of ordinary tropes)*

	Siglum	Use	Century
A	Paris, BN lat. 14819	St. Victor	13th (third decade)
B	Paris, BN lat. 14452	St. Victor	13th (third decade)
C	Paris, Bibl. de l'Arsenal 197	St. Victor	13th (final quarter)
D	Paris, BN lat. 1112	Cathedral	ca. 1220
E	Paris, Bibl. Ste. Gen. 1259	Ste. Geneviève	13th (third decade)
F	Bari 1	Ste. Chapelle	ca. 1250
G	Paris, BN lat. 15615	Cathedral	mid 13th
H	Paris, BN lat. 830	St. Germain	13th (third quarter)
I	Paris, BN lat. 1107	St. Denis	1259–1275

of the new piece to suit his text, yet preserved the familiar contours of the melody so that it could easily be recognized, even though reshaped within a new poetic framework. Together, the new text and the older, reworked melody create a sonorous duet of Easter themes: the sounds of "Victime" bring the original text to mind at the same time the new text unfolds.

Thus the Easter morning scene of Mary Magdalene found in "Victime paschali" plays out in parallel with the re-creation of the world expressed in "Mundi renouatio." As the saint proclaims the mystery indirectly through the power of the melody, the elements proclaim it as they form a new Eden. There are numerous other examples of deliberately planned interaction between existing melodies and late sequence texts in the Parisian repertory, and a knowledge of these techniques is basic to an understanding of many late sequences found in twelfth-century Paris, and especially at the Abbey of St. Victor.[13] "Mundi renouatio" is a simple pairing of a well-established Easter melody with a new Easter text, but it is also an example of how text and music illuminate one another.

"Mundi renouatio," as we have said, contains the music of an earlier sequence in its melody, and in fact the melodies for both "Mundi renouatio" and its model "Victime paschali" are found in the earliest surviving sequence manuscripts from the Abbey of St. Victor, the Cathedral of Notre Dame and the Abbey of Ste. Geneviève. By comparing select variants of both the texts and melodies within these three uses, one may gain a surer sense of the early history of this sequence in Paris. The major melodic variants of "Victime paschali" are shown in Example 8.1 and those of "Mundi renouatio in Example 8.2, using the melody as found at the Abbey of St. Victor as a base. Looking first at Example 8.1, it can be seen that the three manuscripts disagree in the same places, and that there is roughly the same amount

---

[13] The most complicated examples of this technique in the twelfth-century sequence repertories are discussed in Chapter 13.

Example 8.1   Major melodic variants of "Victime paschali," as found in the three earliest Parisian sequence traditions

Victorine version: Paris, BN lat. 14819

Other versions
MS D   MS E

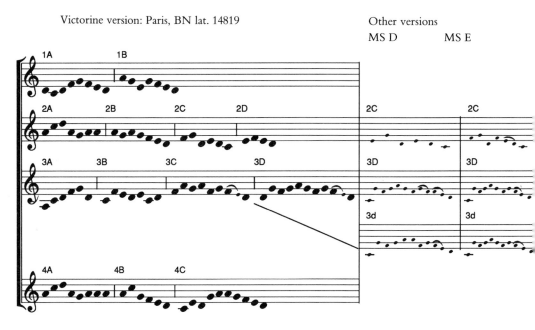

of disagreement between any two. The kinds of variation are simple – thirds are filled in, passing notes are left out, there is disagreement when notes are low in pitch, and hence fall below the staff – and are precisely those which would creep in during copying from late-twelfth-century musical notation. There is no suggestion from such material as to which church had the sequence first.[14]

The melodic variants of "Mundi renouatio" for the three earliest Parisian sources (MSS A, D and E above) are more illuminating. When studying them, one can compare differences between the melodies for the later sequence as well as the way in which the earlier melody is used, and make decisions as to the stability of the three versions. As Example 8.2 shows, the later piece is not uniformly varied: variants in the Victorine version of the melody stand to one side, whereas there is fairly close agreement between the two sources from the cathedral and Ste. Geneviève. The Victorine adaptation of "Victime paschali" as used for "Mundi renouatio" is closer to the model in four places. Unit 1B as found in the "Mundi renouatio" corresponds exactly to "Victime paschali," unit 1B; the version found in MS D and MS E is off by one note. Unit 3D in the Victorine "Mundi renouatio" corresponds to unit 3D in "Victime paschali" (although the notes are ligated differently); unit 3D in "Mundi renouatio" from MSS D and E lacks the characteristic upward leap found in all versions of the original unit in "Victime paschali," and has a slightly different cadential pattern. Unit 4B of "Victime paschali" was the same in all versions of the

---

[14] Textual variants place the poem as found at Ste. Geneviève to one side. Ms D from the cathedral has "quem" for "quam" in the final strophe, clearly an error, and one not found in any of the sources collated for the edition of the text in *AH* LIV, p. 13.

Example 8.2   Major melodic variations of "Mundi renouatio," as found in the three earliest Parisian sequence traditions

melody; when it became unit 4B of "Mundi renouatio," the Victorines kept the contour of the line, but filled in some of the intervals with passing notes and ornamental notes. In the other two versions, unit 4B of "Mundi renouatio" is different each of the three times it occurs; hence, although the basic shape is preserved, the stability found in the Victorine version is missing. Unit 4cc as found at St. Victor also keeps the upward leap of a third characteristic of Unit 4C of "Victime;" in the other versions, the opening leap is gone. The flavor of the model is better retained in the Victorine version than in the other two versions. In the one place where the cathedral version is closer to the model, the resemblance is of a minor sort: in unit 2C of the Victorine "Mundi renouatio," the initial note f is ornamented, whereas at the cathedral it was not, and this is like the opening of 2C in "Victime paschali."

Textual variants of "Mundi renouatio" do not sort out as readily as the melodic variants. There are three major variants: in one place MS E is against MS A and MS D; in one place MS D is against MS A and MS E; and in one place MS A is against MS D and MS E. Of these three major variants, only one affects the sense of the text: in strophe III.4, the Victorine and Genevivien readings are "viam" (accusative case for "way") and the cathedral reading is "vitam" (accusative case for "life"). The former reading makes better sense because the angel has moved the sword guarding the *way* to paradise.

Whereas one cannot draw conclusions from the major melodic and textual variants of a single late sequence, the information presented here points to the unique nature of the Victorine sequence repertory, and other examples could be provided. From an analysis of the variants in "Victime paschali," we can deduce that it is likely to have come into all churches at about the same time. With "Mundi renouatio," too, despite the variants discussed above, there is no major disagreement as to how the text should be set, and it seems that this sequence came in with the same music to all three places. Nevertheless, as the analysis of the melodic variants showed, the Victorines were more interested than the other churches in preserving the connection between "Victime paschali" and the later melody, and the text found at St. Victor and Ste. Geneviève was found to be slightly superior to that of the cathedral. If the composer's goal was to write a new sequence with clearly established connections to "Victime paschali," the Victorine version is superior. The version from Ste. Geneviève seems to have been influenced by both the Victorine and the cathedral traditions, and perhaps is suggestive of an early but now lost stage of the Parisian sequence repertory, of a time when the cathedral and St. Victor were closer in their sequence uses than the surviving manuscripts show them to be at present.

Variants in the early contrafacta of "Mane prima sabbati"

In Chapters 5, 6 and 7 it became clear that late sequence texts sometimes circulated from place to place without their melodies.[15] This was probably true in Paris as well, at least in an early stage of repertorial development. With great numbers of sequences invented during a relatively short period of time during the twelfth century, many works were designed to be contrafacta. Sometimes late sequence poets appear to have created their texts with certain melodies in mind, and the textual plan could provide an indication as to which melody should be used (given, of course, that one knew the melodic tradition for which a particular poet wrote). It would have been clear to any liturgical poet or musician in twelfth-century Paris when certain texts were written for the distinctive melody "Superne matris," for example.[16]

---

[15] New pieces at the back of liturgical books appear without notes frequently enough to indicate that they were often received as texts first. In regard to the Parisian sequences, the great anthology of works found in Assisi 695 is instructive. This manuscript contains the Parisian textual tradition, but not the melodic tradition.

[16] As Appendix 5 shows, this sequence was used repeatedly throughout Paris for whatever saint it was needed for. The melody was so popular that other texts as well were set to it in twelfth-century Paris. Texts written for this melody have a peculiar shape: all strophes consist of eight syllables per line and two lines for each half-strophe:

Strophe I

Superne matris gaudia
representet ecclesia

Dum festa colit annua
suspiret ad perpetua.

(Let the church represent
the joys of the supreme mother

Sequence texts set to a particular preexisting melody would require no change in the original music if the number of strophes, number of lines per strophe, and number of syllables per line were the same as those of the original. As soon as this was not the case, however, changes had to be made in the original melody so it would fit the new text.[17]

Late medieval sequence melodies were pliant, loosely connected sets in interrelated smaller units, each of which served to accommodate a given strophe of text and the lines within it. The melodies were, therefore, modular, and melodic units and individual cells or phrases could be modified or even lifted out and replaced when necessary. Composers and poets came to each of the popular melodies with their own tools and ready to exercise their artistic wills, yet, as will be demonstrated in this chapter and in subsequent discussion, one can identify some general rules which were apparently followed by Parisian composers and poets in the process of adaptation. Because the basic plan of the original melody and its several melodic units created an overall structure, freedom was more likely to be exercised in the smaller details of the melody.

The main part of the discussion to follow will concentrate on the largest group of sequences from the nine pieces listed above (p. 163), the three texts set to the melody "Mane prima sabbati": "Ecce dies celebris," "Simplex in essentia," and "Gaude prole grecia." Although the settings are fairly straightforward, nonetheless, they and the variants within their texts and music go further in distinguishing the repertory of St. Victor from the repertories of other Parisian churches.

"Mane prima," a sequence honoring Mary Magdalene and probably written in the late eleventh century, had come to be sung consistently throughout France at Easter time by the late twelfth century.[18] It depicts Magdalene's vision of the risen Christ outside the tomb, concentrating upon her "blessed eyes," the first to see and understand the miracle:

O beati oculi	(O blessed eyes
quibus regem seculi	by which the first woman saw
morte iam deposita	the king of all time
prima est intuita.	when He had thrown off death.)

Although this sequence is written in the new style of accentual poetry with consistent use of end rhyme, the subject and its mode of treatment have more in common with eleventh-century sequences than with the twelfth-century poetry of the Parisian sequence writers.

Because "Mane prima" was well established early in the history of the late sequence in France, it came to serve as a model for poets and composers working in the twelfth century. Texts written following its pattern and using its melody

---

While it celebrates the yearly feasts,
Let it yearn for perpetual things.)

[17] As was the case with "Mundi renouatio."
[18] The edition of the text in *AH* LIV, pp. 214–218 attests to its widespread acceptance. The sequence retains the early feature of having a single line at the beginning and end. Great variance existed in the text of the short, final line.

Table 8.3. *Plans of texts set to "Mane prima sabbati" in both the Cathedral and the Victorine uses*

Strophe number	Melodic units (Aubry numbers)	Poetic form (line per strophe and syllables per line)	Strophe number	Melodic units	Poetic form
Mani prima sabbati			*Ecce dies celebris*		
I	t. 183	ABC 777	I	t. 183	ABC 777
II	t. 183	ABC abc 777 777	II	t. 183	ABC abc 777 777
III	t. 33	ABC abc 777 777	III	t. 33	ABC abc 777 777
IV	t. 114	ABCD abcd 7777 7777	IV	t. 114	ABCD abcd 7777 7777
V	t. 34	ABC abc 887 887	V	t. 34	ABC abc 887 887
VI	t. 47	ABC abc 887 887	VI	t. 47	ABC abc 887 887
VII	t. 119	ABCD abcd 8888 8888	VII	t. 119	ABCD abcd 8888 8888
VIII	t. 118	ABCD abcd 8887 8887	VIII	t. 118	ABCD abcd 8887 8887
IX	12.11	AB 77	IX	12.11	AB 77
Simplex in essentia (Victorine version)			(*Cathedral version*)		
I	13.38	ABC abc 777 777	(Strophes I–IV same as Victorine)		
II	13.39	ABC abc 887 887			
III	t. 33	ABC abc 777 887			
IV	t. 114 var	ABC abc 777 777			
V	t. 10	AB ab 87 87	V		made of t. 34
VI	t. 34	ABC ABC 887 887	VII		t. 47
VII	t. 47	ABC abc 887 887	VII		t. 119 var
VIII	t. 119 var	ABC abc 887 777	VIII		t. 119
IX	t. 118	ABCD abcd 8887 8887	IX		t. 118

Gaude prole grecia
(*Victorine version*)

(Cathedral version, also in other
Parisian churches, with the exception
of St. Denis, which has its own version)

I	13.38	ABC abc 777 777		(Strophes I–VI same as Victorine)	
II	13.39	ABC abc 777 777			
III	t. 33	ABC abc 777 777			
IV	t. 114	ABCD abcd 7777 7777			
V	t. 114 var	ABCD abcd 7777 7777			
VI	t. 34	ABC abc 887 887			
VII	t. 47	ABC abc 887 887	VII	t. 118	
VIII	t. 119	ABCD abcd 8888 8888	VIII	t. 119	
IX	t. 120	ABCD abcd 8887 8887	IX	t. 120	
X	t. 118	ABCD abcd 8887 8887	X	t. 129 var	
XI	12.12	AB 77	XI	12.11	

apparently had an authority welcomed by poets and composers working in the new tradition. As is the case with all popular late sequences, however (with the exception of "Laudes crucis," which is more stable than most), melodic units occurring early in a piece are much more fixed than later ones, each major region having its own version of the melody at the end. "Mane prima" circulated in early-thirteenth-century Paris in a fairly stable version having only a few major variants in text and melody. It was used for many sequence texts in Paris and the table above illustrates how the particular text plans of the pieces to be studied here were adapted to its melody. As in the melody for "Mundi renouatio," the numbering system for melodic units ("timbres") used in Misset and Aubry's edition have been retained. Units without timbre numbers have been assigned new numbers, e.g. 12.11. Letters refer to individual lines with strophes.

Table 8.3 depicts two different kinds of contrafacta. "Ecce dies celebris" is an Easter text which has been deliberately constructed following "Mane prima sabbati." Every strophe, line, and syllable of these two sequences line up, a situation which did not happen by coincidence. The poet created a new Easter text with "Ecce dies celebris" and set it to a familiar Easter melody, much as was done for "Mundi renouatio." In this case, however, the correspondences are exact and the

Table 8.4. *Major textual variants in a late-eleventh-century sequence and its earliest Parisian contrafacta*

16:	Mane prima sabbati			
ABC		DEFGHI		
ABCDEFGHI		DF		
ABCDEFGHI		DF		

13:	Ecce dies celebris			
ABCH		DEFG		
ABCH		DEFG		

25:	Simplex in essentia			
ABCEG		DFH		
ABCEG		DFH		
ABC		DEFGH		

49:	Gaude prole grecia (Full text not in MS E)			
ABCG		DFHI		
ABCHI		DFG		
ABCDFGH		I		
ABCFI		DGH		
ABCG		DF	H	I
ABCI		DFGH		

poetic styles similar. It is rather the treatment of the subject which is different in the later sequence. "Mane prima" relates the experience of Magdalene on Easter morning and then helps to raise the saint's stature by comparing her with the Virgin Mary. "Ecce dies celebris" describes the Easter mystery in terms of Old Testament typology, and introduces other themes as well which are typical of "Victorine" sequences and which will be discussed further in Part V of this book.

"Simplex in essentia" for Pentecost and "Gaude prole grecia," although fitting conveniently with "Mane prima sabbati," were not necessarily originally designed with this famous melody in mind. In both cases, adaptations must be made in the music to make the new texts fit the older melody. In "Simplex in essentia" strophe V consists of hemistrophes of two lines each, rather than three lines, as in "Mane prima sabbati"; the final strophes as well consist of different numbers of lines from those found in "Mane prima sabbati." In both cases, the Victorines and the cathedral musicians came up with different solutions to these problems, and the other Parisian churches followed the use of the cathedral. The same situation occurs in "Gaude prole grecia," where the final strophes do not exactly fit the melody of "Mane prima sabbati." Here, too, the two institutions had different solutions, and, once again, the cathedral setting was adopted throughout Paris, except at St. Denis, where yet another solution was found. It could be concluded that the texts of "Simplex in essentia" and "Gaude prole grecia" came into St. Victor and the Cathedral of Notre Dame as texts and after the two institutions no longer shared their musical tradition. All Parisian churches had the same understanding, however, of which melody these texts should be set to.

The textual and melodic variants of these four pieces offer yet other clues about their early histories. In all four texts, major variants almost always have the texts of St. Victor on one side and of the Cathedral of Notre Dame on another. Other Parisian churches, however, may agree with one or the other of these two, and there are few consistent patterns with the exception that MS F from the Ste. Chapelle agrees regularly with the cathedral and is likely to have had its sequence texts directly from this institution. In Table 8.4 above, major textual variants are depicted for each sequence, and manuscripts which agree are grouped together. Letters refer to the manuscripts as designated in Table 8.2.

Major melodic variants in "Mane prima" and sequences set to this melody are much more complicated than textual variants and will not fit into a simple table without great amounts of explanation. Such matters will be discussed at length in my forthcoming edition of the Parisian sequence repertory. One detailed example will serve to illustrate a fact which emerges from the patterns in melodic variants of the entire repertory: there is deep division between St. Victor and the cathedral. And, whereas the textual history shows frequent agreement between St. Victor and other Parisian churches, the melodic variants show the opposite: St. Victor stands out alone with a strong tradition which is always separate from the equally strong tradition preserved in lat. 1112. The Parisian manuscripts studied above come from several different churches and their dates range from the mid to the late thirteenth century. They are always either closer to or in agreement with the cathedral tradition, except for St. Denis and Ste. Geneviève, which sometimes have their own versions and sometimes agree with the Victorine tradition.

In "Mane prima," melodic unit 3B and b, the middle section of Aubry's timbre 33, the Victorine tradition is consistently the same at the opening in all four settings – the motion is always from a to a ligated with b, followed by a descent to g; the cathedral version usually begins on a, rises to c′, and then descends to g. The only variants which resemble the opening of the Victorine version are found for "Mane prima," 3B at Ste. Geneviève, where the unit opens on a, rises to b and descends to g; 3b for "Mane prima" as found at the Cathedral and Ste. Geneviève; and 3b for "Simplex in essentia" as found at the Cathedral of Notre Dame and several other Parisian churches. The ending of this small cell of music for four syllables of text is fairly consistent at St. Victor: the variation found in the Victorine versions is caused by consideration for the sound of the poetry. Thus in "Mane prima," 3B, there is a liquescent neume on the "mag" of "magdalene," but not on the "te" of "morte" in the second statement of the cell in 3b; each time there is an "in," a liquescent neume is used, as is traditional in much of the chant repertory, early and late. Thus, at the ending of this cell, too, the Victorine music is more consistent within its own tradition.

Yet another contrafactum is found among the sequences found in the three earliest Parisian sources listed in Table 8.1: "Ad honorem" for St. John the Baptist. The text was set to the well-known melody for the sequence "Congaudentes

Table 8.5. *Melodic variants from "Mane prima sabbati," unit 3B and its early Parisian contrafacta*

(*The opening of the unit is viewed in all four sequences and the same variants are placed in vertical columns.*)

Unit 3 (t.33) 3B and b, music for first four syllables of text

Mani prima sabbati

| ABC★ | C★ | | D★F★G★ | | HIF★ | E★ | D★E★ | G★ |

Ecce dies celebris

| ABC | | FG★ | | DE★G★H | | E★ | | |

Simplex in essentia

| ABC | | | D★F★ | | H★ | | G★ | D★EF★G★H★ |

Gaude prole grecia

| ABC | D★ | | D★FGHI | | | | | |

Example 8.3   Melodic variations found in "Mane prima," Unit 3B and b, and its earliest Parisian contrafacta

exsultemus," a St. Nicholas sequence probably dating from the late eleventh century.[19] Most of the way through, "Ad honorem" has a text designed to follow the same scheme as "Congaudentes" and there is no problem in adapting it to this melody. But after the tenth strophe, one runs out of music because "Ad honorem" is several strophes longer than "Congaudentes." A comparison of the settings of

---

[19] "Congaudentes" can be found in some early-twelfth-century sources and was coming in everywhere by the second half of the twelfth century.

"Ad honorem" at St. Victor and the cathedral shows great differences between the melodies for the final strophes of the text, that is, when there is no more of the familiar "Congaudentes" melody to be used. Like two of the texts set to "Mane prima," "Ad honorem" probably came into the liturgy of both places after the two repertories had established distinct traditions. The cathedral and St. Victor also have slightly different versions of the "Congaudentes" melody.

Study of the contrafacta with the same melodies in this group of nine sequences leads to several conclusions regarding the Parisian sequence traditions:

First, the cathedral and Victorine repertories were not rigidly set, as they were later, at the time of standardization represented by the surviving thirteenth-century manuscripts. As far as can be told from the surviving evidence, most Parisian churches did not accept large numbers of late sequences during the twelfth century; the repertory was the special property of the cathedral and of St. Victor. When other Parisian churches did adopt these sequences, later in the thirteenth century, they took them from the Cathedral of Notre Dame, rather than from St. Victor. The status of "Mane prima" and its contrafactum "Gaude prole" at St. Denis suggests, however, that there may have been a strong Victorine presence in the very early transmission of these texts and melodies and some sort of affiliation between St. Victor and St. Denis in regard to the sequence "Gaude prole," which is, after all, for St. Denis himself. In the middle decades of the thirteenth century, however, when the cathedral repertory became accepted by many churches in Paris, this Victorine strain of influence had disappeared for the most part.[20]

Secondly, the two firmly established traditions at the cathedral and St. Victor argue for a division between the liturgical practices of the two institutions taking place sometime soon after the death of Adam of St. Victor (1146), perhaps even before the mid twelfth century. Even a late-eleventh-century sequence such as "Mane prima" was sung consistently with uniquely Victorine variants in both its text and melody. Of all thirteenth-century Parisian manuscripts with sequences (and there are over twenty of these), only one non-Victorine source reveals significant affiliation with the melodic tradition found at the Abbey of St. Victor: Gen. 1259 from Ste. Geneviève. Sometime in the twelfth century, the canons at Ste. Geneviève began to bring Parisian late sequences into their Mass liturgy, and when they did, they brought in a tradition which had at least some Victorine influence, although they arranged the sequences in a unique way.

Thirdly, the ways in which several of the texts are contrafacted suggest that some of them came into both traditions without music, but rather with a common understanding of which melodies were to be used for them. Although "Mundi renouatio" is adapted to "Victime paschali" in the same way in all manuscripts, even when the original melody does not fit, this is not the case for three of the other texts: "Simplex in essentia" and "Gaude prole grecia" set to "Mane prima," and "Ad honorem" set to "Congaudentes." The textual tradition of at least some sequences

---

[20] The only exception to this is Paris, BN 830, from St. Germain, which sometimes shows affinities with the use of St. Victor. This affinity is much stronger in textual variants than in melodic variants, however.

was earlier than the melodic tradition, and may have existed independently of it for several years during the mid twelfth century.

Fourthly, variants of the separate melodic tradition at the Abbey of St. Victor are of a different nature from variants in other Parisian traditions. Individual melodies are more stable and used with greater consistency than they are in other churches; there are far fewer variants among the Victorine manuscripts than in the wider tradition which emanated from the cathedral. At the abbey melodies were reset making sure that the example of the original was followed in the new piece, as if the Victorines were aware they were resetting an older melody, and wished to preserve its details. They must have taken the making of contrafacta very seriously, and they must have vigilantly supervised their sequence melodies to keep new variants from coming in.

Families of sequences at the Abbey of St. Victor

Yet another way in which the Victorine sequence repertory stands apart from the tradition at the Cathedral of Notre Dame is in the way melodies were chosen for the sequence texts. As the following list shows, the Victorines had fewer new melodies than the Cathedral of Notre Dame, and arranged their texts into families using their own melodies, families which were of a different character from those found at the cathedral. While concentrating upon the texts and music of the Victorine repertory, the list also indicates major differences between the sequences of St. Victor and of Notre Dame as well. One can tell not only that the Victorines liked to set single melodies several times, but also that they were most interested in sequence music for particular saints: apostles, early members of the ecclesiastical hierarchy, and bishops. Also, as would be expected, they show a growing devotion to Mary, and the way in which this devotion developed at the abbey during the second half of the twelfth century will be a subject of particular interest later in this book.

Melodies are named by the incipit of what is believed to be their original text, hence the melody "O Maria stella maris" is so called because the poem "O Maria stella maris" was undoubtedly the original text for this music. In some cases, the original is not so easily determined; educated guesses have been made as to which text was the original and thus should give its name to the melody. It should be emphasized that only transitional and late or "second epoch" sequences – that is, those works written in the late eleventh and twelfth centuries – are considered, earlier sequences having been discussed in Chapter 7.

Families of late sequences within the Victorine sequence repertory

I.   Families based on "transitional" sequence melodies created before the twelfth century
    A.   "Congaudentes" for St. Nicholas
        1.   Shared texts set to Con at both Vic and ND
            (No other texts set to this melody at ND)
            "Congaudentes" for St. Nicholas
            "Ad honorem tuum" for St. John, Baptist

"In excelsis canitur" for the Circumcision
"Clara chorus" for the Dedication

2. Texts set to a version of Con at Vic
    "Interni festi" for St. Augustine (Not at ND)
    "Lux illuxit" for within the Easter octave (Set to "Superne matris" at ND)

B. "Mane prima sabbati"
    1. Shared texts set to the melody MPS at both ND and Vic
        "Mane prima sabbati" within the Easter octave
        "Ecce dies" within the Easter octave
        "Gaude prole" for St. Denis
        "Simplex in essentia" within the octave of Pentecost
    2. Shared texts set to MPS at VIC and not at ND
        "Exsultemus et letemur" for St. Andrew
    3. Texts set to MPS at Vic and not found at ND
        "Congaudeant hodie" for St. Thomas, Apostle

C. "Hodierne lux diei" for the BVM
    1. Shared texts set to the melody HLD at both ND and Vic
        "Hodierne lux diei"
    2. Texts set to HLD at Vic and not found at ND
        "Iubilemus saluatori qui" for the Conversion of St. Paul
    3. Texts set to HLD at ND and not found at Vic
        "Nato nobis saluatore"

D. "Victime paschali" for Easter
    1. Shared texts set to the melody VP at both ND and Vic
        "Victime paschali" for Easter
        "Mundi renouatio" for within the Easter octave

II. Families based on twelfth-century melodies known at both the cathedral and St. Victor
    A. "Laudes crucis"
        1. Shared texts set to the melody "LC" at both ND and Vic
            "Laudes crucis" for the Cross
            "Corde uoce" for St. Paul
            "Heri mundus" for St. Stephen
            "Laus erumpat" for St. Michael
            "Vox sonora" for St. Catherine
        2. Shared texts set to "LC" at Vic, but to other melodies at ND
            "Lux iocunda" for Pentecost
            "Postquam hostem" for Ascension
            "Profitentes" for Trinity
        3. Shared Texts set to "LC" at ND, but to other music at Vic
            "Gaude syon" for St. Thomas of Canterbury
            "Prunis datum" for St. Lawrence
            "Roma petro" for Sts. Peter and Paul
        4. Texts found at Vic only and set to LC
            "Letabundi iubilemus" for the Transfiguration
        5. Texts not found at Vic and set to LC at ND
            "Ante torum" for the octave of the Nativity

B. "O Maria stella maris"
1. Shared texts set to the melody OM at both ND and Vic (No texts besides these set to OM at ND)
    "O Maria, stella maria" for the BVM
    "Rex salomon" for the Dedication
2. Shared texts set to OM at Vic, but to other melodies at ND
    "Sexta passus feria" within the Easter octave
3. Texts set to OM at Vic and not found at ND
    "Ave Virgo . . . porta" for Sat. in the Assumption octave
    "Iubilemus saluatori quem" for Sun. in the Christmas octave
    "Templum cordis" for the Purification

C. "Superne matris gaudia"
1. Shared texts set to SMG at both Vic and ND
    "Superne matris gaudia" for Common of Saints
    "Genouefe sollempnitas" for Ste. Geneviève
    "Laudemus omnes inclita" for St. Bartholomew

2. Shared texts set to SMG at Vic and not at ND
    "Splendor patris" (a Christmas text) begins by being set to SMG but changes to uniquely Victorine music
3. Shared texts set to SMG at ND but not at Vic
    "Lux illuxit dominica" for within the Easter octave
4. Texts not found at Vic set to SMG at ND
    Gaude superna ciuitas" for St. Marcellus, Bishop of Paris

IV. Sequence texts set to uniquely Victorine melodies

		Melody at ND
A.	Texts set to "Zima uetus"	
	"Zima uetus" for Easter	"Laudes crucis"
	"Gratulemur in hac die" for the Octave of the Assumption	Not present
	"In natale saluatoris" for the Nativity	Not present
B.	Texts set to "Prunis datum"	Melody at ND
	"Prunis datum" for St. Lawrence	"Laudes crucis"
	"Cordis sonet" for St. Leger	Not present
	"Ecce dies triumphalis" for St. Victor	Not present
	"Gaude syon" for St. Thomas of Canterbury	"Laudes crucis"
	"Roma petro" for Sts. Peter and Paul	"Laudes crucis"
	"Stola regni" for Apostles	Not present
C.	Texts set to "Gaude Roma"	Melody at ND
	"Gaude Roma" for Sts. Peter and Paul	"Salve mater"
	"Ecce dies preoptata" for St. Vincent	Unica
	"Ex radice caritatis" for St. Victor	Not present
	"Gratulemur ad festiuum" for St. John the Evangelist	"Salve mater"
	"Cor angustum" for the Apostles	Not present
D.	Texts set to "Gaude syon que"	Melody at ND

"Salue dies dierum" for within the Easter octave		Set to a melody used only
"Gaude syon que" for St. Martin		for these two texts
E.	Texts set to "Iocundare"	
	"Virgo mater" for the octave of the Epiphany	Set to a melody used only
	"Ave uirgo . . . mater"	for these two texts
	"Iocundare" for St. Matthew	Has a melody used only for
		this text

V. Late sequences with singular melodies at St. Victor
    A. Twelfth-century melodies which were set repeatedly at ND but only once at Vic
       "Salue mater saluatoris" Set 6 times at ND
    B. Shared texts whose individual melodies are essentially the same, but with major
       variation at both ND and Vic
       "Quam dilecta" for the Dedication
       "Qui procedis" for within the octave of Pentecost
       "Veni sancte spiritus" for within the octave of Pentecost

The list above confirms what has been recognized since Husmann's article as the primary difference between the Victorine and the cathedral sequence repertories: the Victorines preferred to set individual melodies repeatedly, rather than to compose new melodies for specific texts. Of course they could have thought up new melodies or availed themselves of the repertory of the cathedral whenever they wanted – in the course of putting their repertory together they actually did some of both. But in general it seems that the Victorines simply did not like to restrict each melody to one text only. One cannot conclude that the Victorines were lazy about their sequence music; as discussion of melodic variants above has shown, this clearly was not true. It is more likely that they were interested in creating families of sequence texts that were interrelated through their melodies. Clearly they preferred every text to be a part of a family, and in fact only four late sequences, those at the end of the list (section V), have melodies unrelated to those of any other texts. "Postquam hostem" for the octave of the Ascension exemplifies the Victorine attitude. At Notre Dame Cathedral this text was set to a melody specially designed for it: the opening notes quote the Alleluia "Non vos relinquam," sung, like the sequence, on the Octave of the Ascension.[21] Thus, at Notre Dame, the time-honored connection between Alleluia and sequence was made through this melody. But the Victorines chose not to use it, setting "Postquam hostem" to the melody "Laudes crucis" instead, and thereby making it part of the largest family in their repertory. It meant more to them to situate "Postquam hostem" within their "Laudes crucis" family than it did to connect it with the Alleluia of the day.

Three conclusions can be drawn about the families of sequences created at the abbey:

(1) The Victorines were not particularly interested in expanding the families of sequences united through early melodies. Section I of the list above shows them, in most instances, to follow the same groupings found at the cathedral and only to add

---

[21] See Hesbert, ed., *Le Prosaire de la Sainte-Chapelle.*

a piece or two. Thus the numbers of shared texts are large, four for both "Congaudentes" and "Mane prima," and the proportion of different texts added to these families by the Victorines is fairly small (always less than half).[22] The only area where significant change shows up here is in the settings for "Congaudentes." The Victorines created a new melody based upon the older one and set two texts to it, one of them "Interni festi" for St. Augustine. This kind of attention suggests that the texts receiving the special setting were probably of great significance to the Victorines.

(2) The Victorines were far less satisfied with the way late sequence melodies were used at the cathedral, and made numerous changes and additions. More than half the texts set to "Laudes crucis" by the Victorines are not used with this melody at the cathedral; moreover, one of them, "Letabundi iubilemus" for the Transfiguration, is a uniquely Victorine text. The Victorines clearly cared a great deal about how "Laudes crucis" was set. They were attracted to the melody "O Maria, stella maris" as well: it was set only twice at the cathedral, but the Victorines set it six times, creating a significant group of sequences through its use. "Superne matris," on the other hand, held less interest for them: they were content to use cathedral settings for three texts, and only set one of their own texts to this melody, changing it mid-way to music of their own design. And the beautiful "Salue mater saluatoris," which was set repeatedly at the cathedral, was not of particular importance to the Victorines: they far preferred "O Maria, stella maris" for their Marian texts.

(3) Over a third of the late sequence texts found in the Victorine repertory were set to music that was created by the Victorines themselves. The state of these nineteen texts varies at the cathedral: four of them were set to "Laudes crucis," two were set to "Salue mater," eight were not found at the cathedral, and several others were set to music created there just for them or for a pair of them. The nineteen texts listed in section IV of the list above received special treatment at the Abbey of St. Victor, and one must look especially to them and their music to understand what the Victorines tried to achieve in their sequence repertory. They will be discussed in Chapter 13.

Conclusion to Part III

Study of the manuscripts and patterns of variants in a select group of Parisian sequences and of the families of sequences at the Abbey of St. Victor has added further weight to the idea that many Parisian sequences were actually created a generation or two earlier than their first surviving manuscripts. It is also now clear that the Victorine sequence repertory was not merely a later version of texts and music found originally at the Cathedral of Notre Dame. I once argued that the similarities between the Victorine and cathedral melodies of "Quam dilecta tabernacula" and "Ecce dies preoptata" (for St. Vincent), for example, proved that the two

---

[22] And they felt no need to change the melodies of their early sequence repertory.

churches shared a tradition until quite late in the twelfth century.[23] But this view failed to take into account the possibility that these two pieces were of different dates, and the natures of their variants. "Quam dilecta" may be an earlier piece, probably written just after the mid twelfth century: the Victorine and cathedral versions of its melody are very different, although related. The state of this piece, therefore, like several others studied in this chapter, suggests that the traditions were divided early, perhaps just after mid century.[24] "Ecce dies preoptata," on the other hand, is a much later work, not written by Adam or even by his disciples. It may have come, both texts and melody, from the cathedral to St. Victor, where the regular canons stripped it of its melody and incorporated it into their own use, leaving features of the cathedral melody in place as evidence for their actions.[25]

Given the evidence of the manuscripts, and most importantly of the variants found within them, it seems that many of the Parisian sequence texts may well have been in existence by the middle decades of the twelfth century and, therefore, that some of them could indeed have been written by Adam of St. Victor. It also seems that many of the texts were the common property of both the Cathedral of Notre Dame and St. Victor, with St. Victor perhaps having greater numbers of its own texts, and the cathedral having greater numbers of its own melodies. Early on, there may have been a common understanding of how to sing most of these texts, but sometime, probably while Adam was still alive, the Victorines had already decided to create their own melodic tradition. Adam may have written some new texts for St. Victor and probably a small repertory of melodies as well, but he certainly died before the sequence repertory had evolved into the shape in which it is ultimately found in the Victorine ordinal.

In the generation after Adam's death, the Victorines must have continued to develop their unique sequence repertory and to incorporate more and more of the pieces they knew and esteemed into their service books. A similar process was taking place at the Cathedral of Notre Dame, as each institution assigned melodies to various texts and standardized its repertory. One can guess that each institution had a substantial repertory of late sequences by around 1170, probably including octaves for Easter, Pentecost, and (at the cathedral) the Assumption, as well as many sequences for especially honored saints.[26] And this may be the time the canons at Ste. Geneviève brought a few texts into their repertory, taking cues from both St. Victor and the cathedral. As mentioned earlier, substantial textual and musical variants argue against the repertories having been established much later than this. The variants also reveal that St. Victor had an incorrupt textual tradition for these sequences, further underscoring the idea that Adam may have written some of these sequences himself for the Abbey of St. Victor.

At first, new pieces came into Notre Dame and St. Victor as texts, and each institution developed its own melodic use for the works, given that rules for writing

[23] See Fassler (1984).

[24] As will be seen in Chapter 15, a quotation from the melody of "Quam dilecta" is found in the melody of "Rex salomon," a sequence mentioned by Richard of St. Victor at mid-century.

[25] See Fassler (1984).

[26] The autograph of Godefroy of St. Victor, described in Chapter 14, is evidence for this dating.

contrafacta and tradition within the city would have provided guides as to which melodies should be chosen for certain works. Later, by the last quarter of the twelfth century, the sequences circulated with their melodies and Ste. Geneviève, the third church known to have adopted a small but significant repertory of these works, chose some cathedral melodies, some Victorine melodies, arranging the sequences to suit itself and sometimes creating variant readings of melodies in the process. By the mid thirteenth century, the two melodic traditions were frozen in place and churches desiring late sequences usually took them, both their texts and their melodies, from the cathedral. At this time, the cathedral tradition had become so powerful that one can find the Victorines sometimes correcting versions of their ancient use to match that of the cathedral.[27]

If great numbers of sequence texts were written during the middle third of the twelfth century, as I believe, who was responsible for these works? The editors of *AH* and other scholars have tried to determine which pieces in the Parisian repertory were by Adam of St. Victor through studying style, assuming that his were the most regular, the most thoroughly governed by laws regarding word accent.[28] Attempting to establish authenticity in this way is difficult. Many poets in twelfth-century Paris could have penned regular sequences for this repertory, including Godefroy of St. Victor and Leoninus of Notre Dame and St. Victor. Attempts to prove which works were Adam's reveal a modern preoccupation with "composer's identity" which is foreign to medieval liturgical texts and music. This study has demonstrated that the process of assimilating this great new repertory of texts into the liturgies of Notre Dame and St. Victor involved at least three different generations of composers, poets, and liturgists, and it is particularly important to realize that the two communities, that of the Cathedral of Notre Dame and that of St. Victor, brought the sequences into their liturgies in dramatically different ways.

The repertory of sequences at the Cathedral of Notre Dame stands as an exception to the rule that the first great repertories of late sequences in France were developed by Augustinians. But even this exception is subject to modification: in the first place, the Victorines did have a proportionately greater number of late sequences than the cathedral; in the second place, they managed their sequentiary with great care, as shown by the study of variants in this chapter, and gave strong indications thereby of the significance late sequences had for them. Thus, even in Paris, where there were two distinct and separate sequence uses by the close of the twelfth century, the Augustinians seem to be the group most interested in late sequences. What has been learned in Paris does not then disprove the hypothesis that the late sequences were favored by the Augustinian canons regular, but it does suggest that the situation regarding sequences in Paris is worthy of further study.

---

[27] There are several examples of Victorine corrections in Paris, Bibl. de l'Arsenal 197. Sometimes the late-thirteenth-century Victorines responsible left a melodic unit in its original Victorine rendition in one statement, but altered it to agree with the cathedral tradition in the second statement.

[28] See, for example, the introduction to *AH* LIV.

Part IV

The political and theological contexts of the Parisian
sequences

9

The Augustinians of Paris and the politics of reform

Introduction: who were the canons regular?

Throughout twelfth-century Europe, calls to reform stirred a wide range of people: not only monks and canons, but bishops, popes and the laity as well. Ideals of reform, their sources and their translation into both new and renewed modes of religious life, are subjects central to understanding the period.[1] Historians divide the most important reforms into two main branches: the Gregorian reform (originally named for Pope Gregory VII) sought primarily to reform the secular arm of the church, the bishops and cathedral canons;[2] the monastic reforms led by the Cistercians attempted to restore the original Benedictine way of life and advocated strict adherence to the Rule of St. Benedict. As will be shown below, the canons regular fell in between these two branches and looked to both for inspiration.[3]

Claiming disgust with an apparently decadent secular church and wishing to bring to it the spirit and vigor of Western monasticism, eleventh-century Gregorian reformers such as Peter Damian and Humbert of Silva-Candida initiated legislation encouraging new modes of life among the secular clergy.[4] It seemed the time had come for renewal of the ecclesiastical hierarchy: though the great monastic reforms of the Carolingian era had continued to find new champions in the tenth and the

---

[1] "This dream of renewal after a period of decline came increasingly to seem a reality in the twelfth century. The lives of saints, chronicles, and charters contain countless references to the reform of religious houses by charismatic individuals and groups of monks. The new orders of monks and canons used the imagery of renewal not only to legitimize their reforms but also, beginning in the 1130's, to celebrate the creation of new forms of religious life." Constable (1982), p. 42.

[2] The Gregorian reform movement affected religious life in Europe for generations, beginning in the second half of the eleventh century, and continuing throughout much of the twelfth century. It is difficult, as will be demonstrated below, to say when it ended: on the one hand, many of its goals were achieved, but, on the other hand, the call for reform of lax and worldly clergy never ceased. Tierney (1964) contains a collection of key texts and introductions to them; Tellenbach (1940) is a classic study; invaluable as well are the collected essays of Constable (1979 and 1980) and Blumenthal (1982).

[3] For a general introduction to the canons regular, see especially Dickinson (1950), Bosl (1979), and the collection *La vita comune del clero* (1962). For the canons regular in France, and especially their attempts to reform the secular clergy, see Becquet (1975 and 1985) and Châtillon (1977a).

[4] See Leclercq (1966), Ladner (1973), and Olson (1969). Ladner discusses terminology: Gregory I used *renovare* to refer to his intended reform of the church; Gregory VII used the word *renovatio*.

eleventh centuries,[5] reforms of cathedral canons instituted by Chrodegang of Metz in the mid eighth century had too often failed to catch fire.[6] Clergy in charge of cathedrals were viewed by many reformers as small-time feudal lords, more interested in managing their considerable property and in promoting their near relatives than in serving the spiritual needs of their flocks or in furthering the political power of the church itself.[7] Reformers sought to sever the ancient alliance between high-ranking clergy and the secular rulers who promoted them and secured their offices: simony, the selling of church offices, was singled out as a detested evil, and the struggle over lay investiture came to a head in the early twelfth century in Germany.[8] Clerical marriage and concubinage were also severely restricted during this period, marriage essentially dying out.[9]

Early Gregorian reformers desired nothing less than fundamental change within the clergy. As Ladner says: "What Hildebrand (Gregory VII) and the other reformers of his generation considered as absolutely essential was to make sure that henceforward the *sacerdotium*, the priestly office, from the pope down to the last priest and cleric, would be motivated by spiritual and not by temporal interests."[10] Steady pressure was exerted upon cathedral canons to live chaste lives and to hold all property in common as, it was claimed, did the Apostles of the primitive church, and as had monks for centuries.[11] But it was one thing to ask cathedral canons to live without wives; it was another to ask these men, virtually always rich and powerful members of prominent, if not of noble, families, to relinquish control over their property, abandon their houses, and sleep in common dormitories. Although clergy at a handful of cathedrals were reformed by the early twelfth century, the reformers major work of persuading cathedral canons to adopt the common life still remained to be done.[12]

The new legislation enacted to reform cathedral canons could just as easily be applied to other groups as well, and indeed it was. In an early sign of papal support for clerical reforms, the Lateran councils of 1059 and 1063 had promulgated decrees concerning the formation of new orders of canons:

Those of the above mentioned orders who, in obedience to our same predecessor, have kept their chastity, shall eat and sleep together in the churches to which they have been ordained, as is fitting

---

[5] The most famous and far-reaching were the reforms instituted by the Benedictines at Cluny. For an introduction to the early history of Cluny, see Rosenwein (1982).

[6] Recent scholarship has argued against a total lack of reforming zeal among canons of the tenth and early eleventh centuries. See the seminal works of Dereine (1952) and Siegwart (1962), which oppose the more traditional views of early canons as put forward by Dickinson (1950). Earlier historians such as Dickinson were doubtless swayed in their views of canons before the Gregorian reform movement by the reformers themselves, who may have stacked the evidence against earlier canons to strengthen their own positions.

[7] The bibliography on the Gregorian reform movement and its effects upon the cathedral clergy and the formation of new orders of canons regular is immense. For introductions to the central issues, see Dickinson (1950), Siegwart (1962), Dereine (1952), Petit (1968), Milis (1969), Becquet (1972), Châtillon (1977a), and Bynum (1979). An important collection of articles on the new orders of canons is *La vita comune del clero* (1962).

[8] For early background to the eventual settlement of the Concordat of Worms (1122), see Chodorow (1989).

[9] See Lynch (1976).

[10] Ladner (1971b), p. 548. For discussion of one example of the secular goals which sometimes underlay the promulgation of these ideas, see Chodorow (1989).

[11] See Barstow (1982).

[12] For discussion of reformed cathedral chapters in this period see Becquet (1975).

to religious clerics; and whatever income they derive from the churches they shall hold in common. And we ask and urge that they shall strive with all their might to attain to the apostolic, that is the common, life.[13]

Canons regular were those who chose to live the common life, and it was their mode of life that distinguished them from the secular canons in cathedrals and made them especially able to promote the goals of the Gregorian reform movement. These canons were "regular" because they were "ruled," that is, they lived under a version of the so-called Rule of St. Augustine.[14] Although the Rule is short, it insists clearly upon the common life, firm in the belief that this was the way to achieve a community most like that of the early apostles.

From the opening of the Rule of St. Augustine

1. We enjoin you who are established in the monastery to keep these rules.
2. First, because you have been gathered together as one body, you should live in unanimity in the house, with "one heart and one soul" [Acts 4:32] for God.
3. And you should not call anything your own, but everything should be common property, and your superior should distribute food and clothing [1 Tim. 6:8] to each of you, not the same to everyone, because you have not all the same strength, but rather to each man as he may have need [Acts 4:35]. For this is what you read in the Acts of the Apostles, that "all things were in common to them, and distribution was made to everyone as he had need" [Acts 4:32, 35].
4. Those who owned anything in the world should be willing without begrudging for it to be common property after they have entered the monastery.[15]

For Augustine, "it is precisely apostolic poverty that will make the heart free for God and set aside all hindrances that would oppose a harmonious living together."[16] The ideal of the common life was emphasized in Possidius's life of Augustine, which was written soon after his death and remained popular throughout the Middle Ages:

So, having become a priest, he soon established a monastery within the church, and began with the servants of God to live according to the manner and the rule of the holy Apostles. Above all, no one in this community was to have anything of his own; everything was to be held in common, and there was given to everyone according to his need [Acts 4:32–35].[17]

Because the codification of canon law that was under way during this same period had promoted intense study of Augustine's corpus of writings and an increased respect both for the saint himself and for the rules of common life that

---

[13] Translation modified after Dickinson (1950) p. 321; original text in Mansi, ed., *Sacrorum conciliorum,* vol. XIX, col. 898. For discussion of later councils' actions regarding the common life, see Foreville (1980).
[14] The complicated relationship between the several monastic rules attributed to Augustine is explained in both Dickinson (1950) and Dereine (1952). The entire subject has been reexamined by Verheijen (1967) and a summary of Verheijen's ideas is found in Edward Synan, "Augustine of Hippo," *DMA,* vol. I, pp. 657–658. For recent reevaluation, see Lawless (1987).
[15] Quotation from Zumkeller, *Augustine's Ideal,* p. 289, as are other references to the Rule of St. Augustine. Zumkeller follows Verheijen in his belief that the "Preceptum" is the most primitive and authentic of the several documents belonging to the tradition. Canons in the Middle Ages knew the several Rules and also the numerous writings of Augustine on the religious life. Many of these have been collected and translated by Zumkeller, and these will be used as sources in the discussion to follow.
[16] See *ibid.,* p. 395. The distraction of possessions is a constant theme in Augustine's writings.
[17] *Ibid.,* p. 424.

bear his name, the new orders of canons had in their patron saint a worthy counterpart to St. Benedict, patron of the older orders of monks and of the new order of reformed Benedictines, the Cistercians.[18] During this period Augustine's views on the religious life were vigorously studied, and the canons regular attempted to realize them in their own institutions. According to Augustine, clerics who lived the common life "are the members par excellence of the City of God; their life is its fullest terrestrial realization."[19]

The identity of the canons regular is not hard to establish if one is content to say that they were religious living the common life under a Rule of St. Augustine. But, of course, this document, in either of its two more popular versions, is very short, comparing hardly at all to the much longer Rule of St. Benedict. When Augustinian canons regular had to look elsewhere for their rules and customs, they found them among their Benedictine brethren, particularly with the Cistercians.[20] Thus, because canons regular adopted several aspects of their internal modes of governance from the Benedictines, modern scholars have come to question whether twelfth-century canons regular were different in important ways from their monkish counterparts.[21] For the last few decades, it has seemed that reformed Benedictines and canons regular could, and most often did, share spiritual and theological goals, and this in spite of the fact that certain factions within the two groups waged polemical battles throughout the twelfth century.[22] If a house of Augustinian canons lived according to customs that were similar to (and in fact borrowed from) those of the Cistercians and submitted to a similar program of spiritual renewal, how then were Augustinian canons different from Benedictine monks?[23]

The early writings of Carolyn Walker Bynum, with their comparisons of various commentaries upon rules of life penned by both Augustinians and Benedictines, have opened the subject anew, suggesting that there is indeed more to learn about the differences between the two groups in the twelfth century:

The basic distinction between monks and regular canons, which historians have sought in actual practices, in polemical stance, and in articulated conceptions of the spiritual life, thus seems to lie in the area of attitudes and assumptions. Although frequently living similar lives, regular canons and monks understood in very different ways the significance of what they did and the responsibilities entrusted to them.[24]

---

[18] See Chenu (1968), pp. 202–238.
[19] See Ladner (1971a), p. 59.
[20] For example, the Premonstratensian canons apparently borrowed heavily from Cistercian ordinals and customaries in the making of their own internal laws. For a brief discussion, see Waddell (1982), p. 100.
[21] For comparisons of various modes of governance among the canons regular, see Giroud (1961); a bibliography of Augustinian ordinals is in Dereine (1951 and 1959). Since Dereine's work was published, many more Augustinian customaries have been edited; a recent list of edited Augustinian customaries is in Jocqué (1991), pp. 53–54, note 3.
[22] See especially Leclercq (1962), p. 134.
[23] Ziezulewicz (1986) has shown that "restorations" by St. Forent-de-Saumur, although adding greatly to the financial security of these Benedictines, were carried out under the pretense of reform ideals, in this case, the removal of church property from lay control.
[24] Bynum (1982), p. 57.

Of the "very different ways" in which the two orders understood their missions, Bynum concentrates upon one: the drive of the canons to teach "through word and example." She is cautious in forming her conclusions: differences are found only in "the quality of their (the canons') awareness, their sense of responsibility for the edification of their fellow men."[25] The demonstrable differences in attitudes toward edification found in the particular kind of treatises Bynum studied provoke further questions about the Augustinians and their place in twelfth-century religious life.[26] If it is true that the canons were generally more interested than monks in teaching, why was this so, and how was this attitude realized in the actual circumstances of their lives and especially in their liturgies?

The scholarship of past decades suggests that one should not expect single answers for these questions. It is perhaps better at this time to investigate the situation in particular regions or centers and during particular periods of history, and thereby hasten the day when enough information will be available to write a more general history of the Augustinians throughout late-eleventh- and twelfth-century Europe. Parts II and III of this book have shown that there was a liturgical art form developed primarily by Augustinian canons in the twelfth century and that the leading city for the creation of these works was Paris, with the Abbey of St. Victor playing a major role. The goals of Part IV of this book are:

(1) to offer an explanation of the spiritual goals of the canons regular as provided by the author of the *Libellus de diversis ordinibus et professionibus qui sunt in aecclesia*, a canon who wrote in the mid twelfth century and lived in northern France or the Low Countries,

(2) to illustrate the ways in which these spiritual goals were turned into political action in Paris during the first half of the twelfth century, with particular attention paid to the interrelationships between important Victorines and members of other religious orders,

(3) to situate Adam of St. Victor, whose identity has only recently been established, in the context of Parisian political and religious life, and

(4) to explain, through the writings of Hugh of St. Victor, the major spokesman for the canons regular in Paris, the ways in which the canons' attitudes toward reform in twelfth-century Paris fostered a particular vision of the church, a vision capable of inspiring the religious arts.

A twelfth-century view of the canons regular: *Libellus de diversis ordinibus*

The critical attitudes of Ordericus Vitalis toward the Cistercians described in Chapter 5 were symptomatic of his age. New orders of religious flourished, each thinking of itself as addressing a certain group of concerns; older orders rushed in to defend their traditions. As a matter of course, spokesmen for religious orders of various types were numerous during the late eleventh and twelfth centuries, writing

[25] *Ibid.*, p. 58.
[26] See also Brooke (1985).

their polemical treatises to explain who and what they were, and often attacking the viewpoints of other groups as well. Giles Constable has said of this poorly studied body of literature that, "the authors were usually angry as well and confused, and did not understand the causes of the differences between the forms of religious life they were attacking or defending."[27] The lack of perspective evinced in these treatises does not, however, discount their importance for understanding how twelfth-century religious *felt* about who or what they were. One can feel poor, even with great amounts of money in the bank; early-twelfth-century Benedictines such as Ordericus felt besieged by the new orders even though, as modern scholars have demonstrated, the older orders of black monks remained strong and their houses numerous during this period.[28] The feelings are as important a part of history as the numbers, for they are likely to form the bases for political action.

Libellus de diversis ordinibus et professionibus qui sunt in aecclesia belongs to the polemical literature of the mid twelfth century.[29] The anonymous author is even-handed toward most of the groups he discusses, and demonstrates numerous parallels between reformed Benedictines on the one hand and reformed canons on the other.[30] Nonetheless, this author has a definite point of view, in spite of his gentle tone, and is particularly critical of one religious group's mode of life: writing as a canon regular, he suggests that the secular canons are the religious group most in need of reform. His attitudes, particularly toward canons regular and secular canons, are important here because, as will be shown later, they are the ideas underlying the political stance of the canons regular in Paris during the first half of the twelfth century.

The author of the *Libellus* has two major goals: (1) to promote ecclesiastical unity, especially through adoption of common rules of life, and (2) to encourage religious to demonstrate through their lives what their conversion means. In order to develop the idea that each of the several religious groups discussed have their own place within the church and in God's plan, the author identifies Old Testament and New Testament types for them, making all part of a single design.[31] In this procession of orders, the author begins with the hermits, and puts his own order, the canons, last – a gesture of humility typical of his approach and style.[32] His discussion even of the hermits, men who live by themselves, usually in groups of two and three, shows concern for social meanings, for an understanding of how these solitary dwellers

---

[27] See the introduction to *Libellus de diversis ordinibus*, ed. Constable and trans. Smith. All references are to this edition.

[28] See Van Engen (1986).

[29] For a history and description of the sole manuscript, British Library, Add. 21244, see pp. xiii–xv. From internal evidence, Constable dates the treatise to between the years 1121 and 1161. See p. xv.

[30] Constable says, "The author's perception that the fundamental distinction was not between the orders of hermits, monks, and canons but between the strict, moderate, and lax groups within each order . . . is an insight still not fully appreciated . . ." (p. xxiii).

[31] The only group for whom he has no use (and no typology) are those who call themselves monks, but live without vows and outside a rule. See pp. 54–57. A chart in Constable's introduction (p. xxiv) outlines the orders discussed, the most important scriptural sources drawn upon in the work, and the Biblical typologies.

[32] This plan of organization works well rhetorically, too. The author puts the canons regular, the group he is most interested in and favors, next to last, and then, finally, criticizes the seculars who do not match up either to the monks or to the regular canons.

relate to other men.[33] He cautions the hermits to beware lest they criticize others for living an easier life than their own and of becoming proud of their own asceticism.[34] And then he says:

Love in others what you yourself do not have, so that another shall love in you what he does not have, so that what either does shall be good for both and those shall be joined in love who are separate in works, and each shall become, with the apostle, "all things to all men," so that you shall attain with us to Him who is "all in all."[35]

Hermits are to make sure that their lives complement those of other groups of religious, and they are asked to think about others and to expect that others will look to them for inspiration as well. Readers who might have been tempted to criticize the hermits for the diverse ways in which they live are warned as well. He suggests to critics that they

Be therefore a profitable and chosen vessel in the house of your God, lest through lack of faith and slander of your brother you break into pieces, and like a sherd from the earthen vessel you have a biting edge and have nothing to contain what has been put into you.[36]

For monks who "live close to men, such as Cluniac and the like," that is, for the older orders of Benedictines, he advances the same ideals of unity and instruction, but rephrases the discussion to apply directly to the monks, and, in the process, becomes their advocate.[37] The author knows how easily monks are drawn into arguments about fasting and other internal customs connected to liturgical practice, and cautions them to lay petty differences aside. Instead, he advocates a uniformity of rules and customs for all religious living in one town or area, seeing this as a way of removing strife and increasing fellowship.[38]

He asks that the monks work to convert others to their way of life through both example and preaching.[39] If anyone were to complain that he assigns to monks who live in cities "what is more suitable for clerics and many other of the faithful," he would reply that these monks are like Jesus in the town of Ephrem (John 11:54) a

---

[33] In this attitude he follows Augustine, who says in *The City of God*, Chapter XIX: "A man ought neither to lead such a contemplative life that in his leisure he does not consider the welfare of his neighbors, nor to lead so active a life that he does not seek the contemplation of God . . ." (See Zumkeller, *Augustine's Ideal*, p. 339.)

[34] The attitude toward criticism of other members of a religious community is in keeping with Augustine's own. He says in Letter 210: "Put more of your effort into promoting harmony than in correcting one another; for just as vinegar rots the barrel if it is kept there too long, so anger rots the heart if it lasts overnight." (see Zumkeller, *Augustine's Ideal*, p. 372.)

[35] "Amo ergo in alio quod ipse non habes, ut amet alius in te quod ipse non habet, ut utriusque sit bonum quod uterque fecerit, et coniungantur amore qui disiunguntur opere, et fiat unus quisque cum apostolo 'omnibus omnia,' ut perveniatis nobiscum ad eum qui est 'omnia in omnibus,'" (p. 14).

[36] "Esto ergo uas utile et electum in domo Dei tui, ne propter incredulitatem et fratris detractionem frangaris, et tanquam testa de uase fictili habeas unde tangentem mordeas, et non habeas unde in te missum conserues" (p. 16).

[37] From the heading of Chapter 2. See p. 19.

[38] "I would wish that the monks of the same province, and the canons similarly, should follow each other mutually, so that those who live in one province should fast in the same way and follow the same rule of silence. I am speaking of those who live in cities and towns. Perhaps then both rules would be better maintained and more willingly . . ." See p. 37 (Latin text on p. 36).

[39] "Anyone sharing in the kingdom of heaven and worthy of the divine vocation, seeing God's servants living in this way, accepts the divine love and, joining himself with them in a holy life, tells of the future glory of the chosen . . ." (p. 23).

word meaning "fertile or growth."[40] By withdrawing to a town near the desert, Jesus illustrated to the monks that they should "increase the multiplicity of virtues and the number of [their] brothers."[41]

The advice to accept unity and to live so that others might be inspired is found in the discussion of the Cistercians as well. The author admires their way of life because it promotes unity, and it sounds, as he describes it, like the ideal of the common life.

Look at . . . the monks even of our own day who live similarly, how harmony of mind has been added to spirit, and having one spirit they live together, feel as one, wishing to differ in nothing one from another, eat similarly, adopting one kind of worship and way of life, so that concord of soul should be expressed by an outer consonance of appearance.[42]

Even monks, cloistered away from people and deliberately choosing to live in remote areas, have, according to the author of the *Libellus*, a responsibility to encourage conversion. They are like Jesus in Luke 4:42, who went into the desert and was followed by the multitudes. After they have prayed in solitude and dispelled the multitude of their own vices, the monks should say with the Jesus of Luke 4:43 "To other cities also I must preach the kingdom of God." They should preach to those "who are as yet not of the flock of monks but will be of them."[43] Monks of the "desert" must become strong "to support others weaker and feebler," but in their strength are to feel "united with the humble."[44]

Before beginning his discussion of specific orders of canons, the author defines their work in general, acknowledging with restrained pride that although the order had become tepid, "in our day, thanks be to God, it has now begun to flourish somewhat."[45] The canons have two types in the Bible: first the Apostles, for they, like them, live the common life, and secondly, and even more importantly for this author, the Levites of the Old Testament. Like the Levites as described in Numbers, the canons' tasks are:

to teach the people, take tithes, collect offerings in church, remonstrate with delinquents, reconcile the corrected and penitent to the church, and observe other duties also laid down in the old law which are still kept in the church of our day.[46]

The canons have the responsibility of caring for the altar and the tabernacle: just as it was in the Old Law, they "look after the sacred objects, and carry them and clean them . . ."[47] Their responsibility for the temple means that canons should be of high moral stature: "no one should be admitted to the ministry of the church unless he has lived purely and in accordance with a rule."[48] Canons as defined here and as typified by the Levites and the Apostles have little resemblance to the secular canons found in most medieval French cathedrals.

[40] See p. 25.
[41] See p. 27.
[42] See p. 51 (Latin, p. 50).
[43] See p. 53.
[44] See p. 55.
[45] See p. 57.
[46] See p. 57.
[47] p. 59.
[48] p. 59.

The specific types of canons are three: those who, like the Premonstratensians, live far from men; those who, like the canons of St. Quentin (of Beauvais) and St. Victor, live near towns and cities, and the secular canons who "live among men of the world." Clearly, the author of the *Libellus* is not a Premonstratensian. Although he admires them, he has misgivings about their work in stables and barnyards. They are, after all, priests and the care of the altar should be their primary task. Although he praises such humility, he wonders how those with soiled hands and garments can properly do their jobs. Should not the animal husbandry be left to "others who are not yet suited for the assumption of such duties in the church"?[49] The higher orders of canons are to meditate upon the Scriptures and the meaning of the sacraments. The purpose of their withdrawal from the world is to become the perfect Levites, standing nearest to the inner power of the divinity. Their charge is to let the sacraments work within them: "By eating the flesh and drinking the blood of Jesus Christ, you will change into him and become a member of his body."[50]

Regular canons who live near men receive the fullest treatment from the author of the *Libellus*, for it is here that he speaks of his own order, often using the second person plural in his descriptions. These canons follow the middle road, neither withdrawing completely from men, nor living with them. They choose this position in society because it is their responsibility to win others over through example. With other orders, the hermits, the monks, the Premonstratensians, the author finds ways of incorporating this idea of inspiring others through example into the discussion. But for canons regular such as the Victorines, this idea comes first and is seen as their very *raison d'être*.

They undertake this [mode of life] for the correction of human customs, so that evil men seeing their life should be converted from evil and, being converted, may either enter upon such a life or, if they cannot enter it, in loving it and imitating it as much as they can and in bestowing alms, for the reception of the just, and in giving at the very least a cup of cold water in the name of a disciple, they may accept the reward of both.[51]

The regular canons described here permit several types of lives within an individual house: some are canons of the cloister whose major work is to pray, meditate and perform the sacraments; others care for the house itself, the needs both of the brethren and of their guests; and yet others are sent out to have charge of churches within parishes. Thus the canons regular close to towns look both within and without: they serve the altar and the sacraments, yet they also minister to lay persons.[52] Unlike monks and canons who do menial work, they are specially concerned with cleanliness and purity not only for the sake of the altar, but also as

---

[49] See p. 69. Large groups of lay brothers were present to do the heavier work in many religious communities. See Reinke (1987). Augustine discusses the idea of work in the monastic community in his treatise *The Work of Monks* (ca. 400); for excerpts, see Zumkeller, *Augustine's Ideal*, pp. 323–330. For discussion of lay brothers and servants at the Abbey of St. Victor, see Jocqué (1991), pp. 83–92.

[50] See p. 67.

[51] p. 75 (Latin, p. 74).

[52] See p. 79.

representing the proper human state, and are often in charge of administering penance.[53]

According to the author of the *Libellus* the canons regular live in towns and cities so they can direct, admonish, and inspire others to live like themselves. When he turns, at the very end of the book, to the secular canons, however, he keeps this same definition. Regular canons are what canons truly should be, and secular canons who are not like them fail to live up to their name "canon":

Having examined these matters carefully, you will understand that the name secular does not stem from the fact that many of them live secular lives, but they are called seculars suitably because they must direct and instruct the men of the world among whom they live. They will do well, then, if they live communally, if they cut off superfluous things from their lives, and then they will properly be called canons, that is regulars.[54]

Although the author chooses his words carefully, desiring to avoid "biting reprehension," which would "in no way help the secular canons," nonetheless, he believes that they can only do their work properly if they are reformed to the common life.[55] Throughout the entire discussion of secular canons, he never abandons this theme. In the lengthy comparison of secular canons to the Merarites of Numbers 4:31–32, he claims that they "are ordered to carry the cords of the tabernacle so that they and those committed to them would be bound to each other in mutual charity."[56] He says further on that "their life ought not to differ from the way of life of the canons, that is the regulars, but they should live among secular men as mentors of the people in an orderly and regular fashion."[57] He speaks sorrowfully of the "costly clothing which many of them wear, and houses painted with an excess of ornament, and the secular activities . . ." and, at the end, of the absence of the common life.[58] Some are praised for having common buildings, and the example of Augustine is offered:

From the fact that he instituted near the city of Hippo a church of brothers "according to a rule established at the time of the holy apostles," he is justly called the father of those who are near men; from the fact that when he lived in the bishop's house he lived communally with his brothers, he is properly said to be the father of those who live among the people with a bishop or under a bishop. There are sermons of his on the clerical way of life, where it appears that they who lived with him before he became a bishop, and they who lived with him when he was bishop, lived in a similar manner, communally according to a rule.[59]

---

[53] "For if you examine such canons prudently and consider their calling, you will find that those of them who live in the cloister for these reasons meticulously investigate their own and their companions' actions, lest there should be anything to offend the eye of divine majesty; those also who are sent outside on account either of a dependency or a parish ponder their own actions and those of the people committed to them scrupulously, and above all else they maintain cleanliness in what concerns the service of the altar . . . it would not be absurd if these canons should direct the people, since they know how to discuss their deeds and, by virtue of their office, how to make them clean." See p. 83 (Latin, p. 82).

[54] p. 99 (Latin, p. 98).

[55] "Relicta igitur mordaci reprehensione quae auditoribus forsitan scandalum generaret, et illis canonicis nichil forte prodesset . . ." (p. 100).

[56] p. 105 (Latin, p. 104).

[57] p. 107 (Latin, p. 106).

[58] See first p. 99 (Latin, p. 98) and then p. 115 (Latin, p. 114).

[59] See p. 117 (Latin, p., 106). The author is aware of the problems with authorship posed by the versions of the Rule of St. Augustine, however. see note 1, p. 73.

The author of the *Libellus* believes that canons regular who lived near men were there to inspire others to follow after them, adopting the common life, and that secular canons were the men most in need of this call to conversion.

Reformers in a changing Paris

Late-eleventh-century Paris was one of several important northern French cathedral towns; by the closing decades of the twelfth century, it had become a small, but significantly more cosmopolitan, city of major significance, overshadowing its neighbors in importance.[60] This change in the city's fortunes occurred, in part at least, because the Capetian kings of France, first Louis VI and then his son, Louis VII, made Paris a true royal capital at the very time that the French throne was being strengthened and its power consolidated.[61] The transformations of Paris and the French monarchy in the course of the twelfth century occurred simultaneously, then, and, in the process, the fate of the city and of the monarchy became permanently entwined. In the opening decades of the twelfth century, the new prestige Louis VI gave to his capital precipitated the forming of new alliances, the strengthening of old ties, and, as a predictable consequence, fighting among the various factions present in and around the city.[62] Because the Bishop of Paris and the canons of the Cathedral of Notre Dame were noblemen, the struggles involved clerics as well as laypersons.[63] The recent work of Robert-Henri Bautier depicts struggles between powerful families during the first half of the twelfth century, and places Parisian reformers in roles as allies or enemies of either the Senlis or the Garland families.[64]

The political situation in Paris during the first half of the twelfth century was tied to the actions of religious reformers in the city. Of the several reforming groups found within the city at this time, the most active were apparently the canons regular and their supporters among the secular canons at the cathedral. One does not hear much of Cluniac reformers, Cistercian reformers, early Premonstratensians, or hermits in early-twelfth-century Paris. This was an urban environment, and the religious struggles there were dominated, as would be expected, by canons "who lived close to men." These men were most concerned with keeping the Bishop of

[60] The earlier histories of Paris by Sauval (1724), Félibien (1725) and LeBeuf (1883–93) can be updated by Bautier (1981), Boussard (1976), Fleury (1961), Guérout (1949), and Lombard-Jourdan (1976). The best studies of the political situation in early-twelfth-century Paris are Luchaire (1890) and the recent stimulating essay by Bautier (1981), which, while owing much to Luchaire, supplies greater details concerning the discord among powerful Parisian families.

[61] See Bautier (1976) and Fleury (1961).

[62] The collections of documents most useful for the study of political and religious life in twelfth-century Paris are *CEND*, *CGP*, and *ODSP*.

[63] For a picture of the kinds of struggles found in cathedral towns throughout France as the reform became more powerful, see Chodorow (1972).

[64] See especially Bautier (1981). This article has been criticized by Henri Silvestre in *RTAM* 13 (1984), pp. 617–620. Bautier's theories depend upon the *HC* as an authentic work of Peter Abelard. Although John Benton and Henri Silvestre have both tried to demonstrate that the *Historia calamitatum* is a later work and not by Abelard, their arguments have not yet won wide acceptance.

Paris on the side of clerical reform. Men such as Ivo of Chartres, Gilduin of St. Victor, and Stephen of Senlis did not seek to promote certain candidates for bishoprics and reject others merely because of a desire to increase their own network of power. They wished to see men they liked get key positions – that is only human – but what made them like some men to begin with seems to have been as much a real concern for both the political and the spiritual powers of the church and a perceived need for freedom from secular control as patronization in the hope of self-advancement. The history below concentrates upon the men involved in episcopal elections, and the political ideals of Augustinian canons regular within the city of Paris.

Already at the very opening of the century, the most important reformer in the vicinity of Paris, Ivo, Bishop of Chartres, struggled with the Garland family of Paris over an episcopal election. In 1101 the bishop's throne at Beauvais stood empty, and Stephen of Garland, Archdeacon of the Cathedral of Notre Dame in Paris, with the support of King Philip I, put himself forward for the post. Unfortunately for the king and Garland, his claims were unacceptable to Ivo, whose student Galon had been duly elected to the post. It must have seemed to the king that Ivo's nose was perpetually stuck into the governance of the church and the selection of its bishops.[65] In 1096, for example, he had masterminded the election of his student William as Bishop of Paris, a feat which, as will be shown, he was to repeat with another student.[66] Ivo believed that bishops' seats should be held by men schooled for the job, learned and deeply religious men with reformers' ideals. The thought of the worldly Garland as Bishop of Beauvais struck him as disastrous. Ivo had grown up in Beauvais; this church was his mother, who had nourished him from the beginning.[67] It is clear from reading his many letters concerning Beauvais from this period that he had hopes of bringing the cathedral canons there to the common life and the Rule of St. Augustine.

The argument over Beauvais shows Ivo pressing for a certain kind of person to be bishop and rejecting another kind, and his arguments are squarely within the tradition of the Gregorian reform movement. Garland was, Ivo wrote more than once, "not yet a deacon, illiterate, gaming, skirt-chasing, and infamous because publicly accused of adultery." His student Galon, on the other hand, was "a man honest in life, decorated with bookish studies and ecclesiastical disciplines."[68] In a letter to Pope Paschal II, Ivo criticized the king's role in preventing Galon's assumption of the post, saying that if the king were given his way, any canonical election would be null, except those brought about by simony or violent intru-

---

[65] And sometimes the favor was returned. In 1103, Prince Louis (later Louis VI) intervened to settle a dispute between Ivo and the chapter of Chartres, on the one hand, and the Countess of Chartres on the other. Although Louis decided in favor of Ivo, the bishop was loath to accept his help. See Luchaire (1890), pp. 13–14, no. 23.

[66] See letters in praise of William and his election written by Ivo to Pope Urban II and to Richer, archbishop of Sens. *PL* CLXII, Ep. 43, col. 54 and Ep. 50, col. 62.

[67] *PL* CLXII, Ep. 92, col. 112: "Mater mea Belvacensis ecclesia, quae in Christo me genuit, quae lacte suo me aluit . . ."

[68] *PL* CLXII, Ep. 104, col. 122.

sion.[69] Garland strove to win the position at Beauvais as the king's hand-picked candidate, thereby raising the stakes as far as the reformers were concerned.[70]

The contest ended in a stalemate: the king and his supporters (chief among them members of the Garland family itself) would not accept Galon as bishop in spite of his election, refusing to endow him with the "biens" or monies and properties of the office; Pope Paschal II and Ivo of Chartres, along with other supporting reformers, would not accept Garland and insisted upon the validity of Galon's election. In 1104, the throne in the church of Beauvais still stood empty.[71]

The course of action taken by a early-twelfth-century bishop operating within the principles of the Gregorian reform movement are demonstrated through this incident. Ivo wanted high ecclesiastical posts to be awarded through the efforts of church officials to men well-trained through study, prayer, and long service in the ecclesiastical ranks. He looked to the pope and other bishops to back him up, and relied upon the support of other religious reformers in the area as well. Early in his career, Ivo had helped to establish a new order of canons regular in St. Quentin of Beauvais, becoming their prior in 1078, and helping to design their customary. According to foundation documents, the new canons regular were found to promote the cause of reform in a place where wills were hardened against it.[72] As envisaged by Ivo, the new canons regular of Beauvais would work to convert the secular clergy through the power of their exemplary adherence to the common life.

The debate over Beauvais surely helped prominent reformers in Paris to identify Stephen of Garland as a promotor of "the old order," of simony and of secular control over church offices. Garland was an archdeacon and chancellor of the Cathedral of Notre Dame and, for a short while later in his career, became seneschal to the court of King Louis VI at the same time.[73] It is not historically accurate to portray Stephen of Garland as the only person opposed to reforming the cathedral canons of Paris during the early decades of the twelfth century. But his dual allegiance to the sacred and the secular realms (as an archdeacon and as a chief advisor to the king) and his self-promoting schemes made him particularly unattractive to leading reform clerics, and, therefore, more is known about him than about the many others who joined him from the ranks of the secular clergy during this time. In a much-discussed letter to Suger, for example, Bernard of Clairvaux criticized Garland, saying:

For whose heart is not indignant, and whose tongue does not murmur either openly or secretly to see a deacon equally serving God and Mammon, against the precept of the Gospel heaping up ecclesiastical dignities, so that he seems not to be inferior to Bishops, yet so mixed up in military offices that he is preferred even to dukes. What monster is this, that being a clerk, and wishing at the same time to appear a soldier, is neither? It is equally an abuse that the deacon should serve at

---

[69] See *PL* CLXII, Ep. 105, cols. 123–124.

[70] See Luchaire (1890), p. 10, no. 17.

[71] And thus, although he collected numerous other high ecclesiastical offices, deaconships of Ste. Geneviève in Paris, of St. Samson and of St. Avit in Orléans, and, finally, of the Cathedral of Orléans, Archdeacon Stephen Garland never became a bishop. See Luchaire (1890), p. 34, and Petit-Dutaillis (1936), p. 94.

[72] See Dereine (1948).

[73] The seneschal was the king's leading man. For discussion of this office, its evolution, and its responsibilities, see Bournazel (1975), pp. 95–97.

the table of the King, and that the server of the King should minister at the altar during holy mysteries. Is it not a wonder, or rather a scandal, to see the same person clothed in armour march at the head of armed soldiery, and vested in alb and stole read the Gospel in the midst of the Church; at one time give the signal for battle with the trumpet, and at another convey the orders of the Bishop to the people?[74]

In 1104, the same two persons involved in the dispute over the see of Beauvais argued again, this time over Paris. With the backing of Ivo of Chartres, William of Champeaux and other canons interested in reform, the same Galon who once tried to defeat Stephen of Garland for the bishop's throne in Beauvais was elected Bishop of Paris.[75] Thus Galon took over a see in which one archdeacon was his recent rival, Stephen of Garland, and the other was his ally William of Champeaux.[76] After the election William and Bishop Galon presented a nucleus of power for reform-minded clerics at the cathedral.[77] William was an active reformer, following in the intellectual and spiritual pursuits that reformers considered proper to high ecclesiastical office.[78] Stephen, on the other hand, deservedly or not, stood for the old order in the minds of some reformers. Thus ecclesiastical politics at the cathedral were polarized by reform.

During this early period, Bishop Galon and his reforming archdeacon brought the common life to the city. In 1107, William and Galon reformed the Parisian nunnery of St. Eloi, that is, they essentially took it over, replacing its constitutions and introducing canons regular.[79] The charter singles out the apparent laxity regarding vows of chastity, enforcement of celibacy among clerics and chastity among monks and nuns being a favored theme with early-twelfth-century reformers:[80]

Omnibus igitur notum fieri volumus monasterium Sancti Eligii Parisiensis ordini quidem monacharum antiquitus fuisse deputatum; sed tandem diabolico instinctu, fragilis ille sexus ad tantam turpitudinis prolapsus est miseriam, ut publice secularitati impudenter adhaerens, uoto castitatis rupto, proposito religionis penitus abjecto, templum Dei speluncam fornicacionis effecerit, et uocem nostre ammonicionis et correpcionis nullatenus audierit.[81]

(Therefore, we wish it be made known to all that the nunnery of St. Eloi in Paris had from olden times been given over to the order of nuns; yet, through demoniac impulse of late, that feeble sex has fallen into such great wretchedness of dishonor that, cleaving insolently to public worldliness, the vow of chastity broken and the premises of religion cast away, it has rendered the temple

---

[74] Bernard of Clairvaux, Letter 78; in *Life and Works* ed. Mabillon, trans. Eales, vol. I, pp. 284–285.

[75] Letters were written in support of Galon's candidacy by Ivo of Chartres. See *PL* CLXII, Ep. 144 and Ep. 146, cols. 150–152.

[76] For an introduction to William of Champeaux, see Châtillon (1952), pp. 147–155. Few of his writings have survived, but see Lottin (1959), pp. 189–227, Green-Pederson (1974), and Fredborg (1976).

[77] For the reconciliation of Philip I and his son Louis to this election, see Luchaire (1890), p. 18, no. 29.

[78] William was called a humbug by his enemies, most notably by Abelard, who accused him of using his reform credentials only to gain greater power within the Church. See *Historia Calamitatum*, ed. Monfrin, p. 65. The true worth of this scholar is reevaluated by Jolivet (1991).

[79] The reform was supported by Philip I and Louis. See Luchaire (1890), p. 26, no. 49.

[80] The study of the wording of foundation charters is long overdue and would contribute important information to the views various types of religious had of themselves. See Dickinson's (1950) discussion of the foundation charter of St. George of Troyes, for example.

[81] For the full text, see *CGP*, pp. 161–163.

of God a den of fornication, and in no manner has it heard the voice of our admonition and reproach.)

William and Galon's reform of St. Eloi demonstrates the pattern of action characteristic of Parisian bishops interested in reform to the common life during the first half of the century. With the blessings of the popes in Rome (most of whom were reformers themselves during this era), reform-minded bishops and other high-ranking ecclesiastical authorities such as abbots of reformed monasteries could appropriate monasteries judged worldly or dissolute, and institute their own customs and personnel.[82]

In 1108 Stephen of Garland won important military victories for the king, and, as a consequence, was rewarded with greater ecclesiastical authority.[83] In the same year, the other archdeacon, William of Champeaux, left the Cathedral of Notre Dame to establish a new religious life within the city: his intention from the very start was to found a house of canons regular.[84] William took with him a band of cathedral canons, all of them, apparently, dedicated to the common life. They established themselves on the site of an abandoned hermitage dedicated to St. Victor just outside the city walls and on the left bank of the Seine.[85] It was precisely in such locations that reformers such as Ivo of Chartres established new houses of canons regular: far enough from the city to have land and solitude, yet near enough to make their presence strongly felt within it. Among the departed canons was the talented Gilduin who in 1113 – the date of the foundation charter – became the first abbot of St. Victor, a post he held until his death in 1155.[86] The circumstances of its foundation suggests that the abbey was created not only as a haven for Parisian canons who yearned for the common life, but also as an example for the secular canons at the cathedral.[87] Thus, although St. Victor was a royal abbey from the time of its official foundation,[88] and Gilduin, confessor to Louis VI, was able to win favors from the royal family, the house nevertheless served immediately to promote conversion to a particular mode of religious life.[89] William of Champeaux set up an open school at St. Victor at the start and it continued to be one of the most

---

[82] See Ziezulewicz (1986).

[83] For description of this rebellion against the king by the Rochfort family, see Suger, *Vita*, ed. Waquet, pp. 68–78. Documents describing Archdeacon Stephen's new privileges are found in *CGP*, pp. 166–167.

[84] On the founding of the Abbey of St. Victor, see Bonnard (1904), Chapters 1 and 2, Châtillon (1952 and 1969 [introduction]), Willesme (1977), and Bautier (1991).

[85] In his telling of the events of 1108, Abelard makes it seem that William retreated from Notre Dame to escape the power of Abelard's dialectic. As Bautier would have it, however, William's leaving was politically motivated. See Bautier (1982), pp. 62–63. In a charter of 1108, William gave up certain parts of his income, apparently before his departure for St. Victor. See *CEND*, vol. I, pp. 413–414. A short discussion of the "hermitage" is provided in Bautier (1991); he believes that simple buildings must have been constructed before William's departure. See pp. 29–30.

[86] The charter is edited in *CGP*, pp. 187–189. It was confirmed by Pope Paschal II on December 1, 1114. See *PL* CLXIII, col. 359.

[87] For the details surrounding the charter, its recognition by the pope, and Gilduin's election (which was first as "prior"), see Bautier (1991), pp. 33–35.

[88] See Luchaire (1890), p. clii.

[89] The final confession of Louis VI is reported in Suger's *Vita*, ed. Waquet, pp. 282–286: "Qui nunquam super his improvidus, accito venerabili Parisiensi episcopo Stephano et religioso Sancti Victoris abbate Gilduino, cui familiarius confitebatur eo quod monasterium ejus a fundamine construxerat, et confessionem repetit et exitum suum viatico Dominici corporis muniri devotissime satagit."

important centers of learning in Paris at least through the mid century, offering a style of scriptural exegesis and an approach to the liberal arts which often differed from those of the numerous secular masters flourishing in the city during the same decades.[90] A dynasty of brilliant young men found their way to the Abbey of St. Victor, some to learn and then to leave, others to remain for their entire lives.[91]

From studying the *Libellus de diversis ordinibus et professionibus* one can imagine what the early spirit and intentions of the new canons regular of St. Victor must have been. Here were men who desired both to live the common life following the Rule of St. Augustine and also to live close to the cathedral, their mother church.[92] From this vantage point, they undoubtedly hoped to inspire the bishops and canons of that church, through the examples of their own lives and liturgy, to give up secular pursuits, abandon their lands and houses, and return renewed to their altars and the people entrusted to their care.

It seems that a policy of waiting and watching was in effect during the first decade at St. Victor, formed perhaps, indeed, out of necessity. For over a decade after the military triumphs of Archdeacon Stephen of Garland in 1108, it seemed that he would have the final word with the king on pressing ecclesiastical issues. William of Champeaux left Paris in 1113, having become Bishop of Châlons. Ivo of Chartres died in 1115 and was replaced by Geoffrey, a man of sound reputation but without the commitment to reform and the energy that marked the career of his predecessor.[93] Bishop Galon died in 1116 and was replaced by Gilbert, an old ally of Stephen of Garland.[94] It is Gilbert who Bautier suggests had been the successor three years earlier to William of Champeaux as head of the cathedral school and who offered Abelard his long-coveted teaching position at the cathedral during these years.[95] According to Bautier, it is no coincidence that Abelard, arch-enemy of William of Champeaux, fared well in Paris at the beginning of Gilbert's term as bishop.[96]

---

[90] Within Hugh of St. Victor's *Didascalicon*, for example, are several allusions to the secular masters and the differences between their material and that of teachers in the Victorine school. For more on the founding and longevity of the school itself, see Bischoff (1935) and Ferruolo (1985), pp. 27–44.

[91] Peter Lombard was in residence at the Abbey of St. Victor for over a decade; Otto of Freising probably attended the school there as well. For a discussion of Hugh of St. Victor's influence on Otto of Freising, see Bennett (1985).

[92] There is no detailed study of the role of the Abbey of St. Victor in the political and religious life of twelfth-century Paris, in spite of the fact that the historical events related below are well known and, of course, the importance of the Abbey has long been recognized.

[93] Perhaps Geoffrey of Lèves was sometimes called upon to negotiate between warring Parisian factions because of his moderate stance. Bautier (1991), p. 41, believes that Geoffrey was a protector of both Abelard and Heloise. See further discussion in Fredborg, ed., *Theirry of Chartres*.

[94] It was with Bishop Gilbert's approval that Garland was able to build his own chapel and staff it with two canons. Garland's own prebend was divided and a part given over to finance the new canons. Unlike all other canons, who were nominated by the bishop, these were nominated by and subject to the chapter itself. Bishop Stephen of Senlis complied with Garland's wishes in 1124 by confirming the arrangement set up for this private chapel. See *CEND*, vol. I, 328, 333, and 457; vol. III, 406; and vol. IV, 70.

[95] See Bautier (1982), pp. 62–63.

[96] See Bautier (1981).

The struggle for reform at the Cathedral of Notre Dame: Stephen of Senlis and the Victorines

It was not until the third decade of the twelfth century that there was open fighting between the Victorines and the secular canons of Paris. When Bishop Gilbert died in 1123, Stephen of Senlis was elected Bishop of Paris. The Senlis family had long been opponents of the Garlands; Stephen of Garland had temporarily wrested away the position of bouteiller from the Senlis family and had given the job to a Garland.[97] But not only was Stephen of Senlis from a family long in conflict with the Garlands, he was also a zealous reformer and a champion of the canons regular at the Abbey of St. Victor.[98] When he became bishop, he immediately began to extend the power and influence of the abbey in the city: in 1124 he secured permanent revenues for the abbey from the cathedral;[99] in 1126, Bishop Stephen and others persuaded King Louis VI to assign the revenues and privileges from prebends of eleven churches in and around Paris to St. Victor.[100]

Stephen of Senlis's vigorous support for the Abbey of St. Victor and the ideals of reform threatened those who supported the ancient secular customs of the cathedral chapter. Undoubtedly Garland and other secular canons were reluctant to see the king's favors lavished upon the bishop and his protégés at St. Victor; the archdeacon and certain other canons at Notre Dame feared, and with just cause, that this new bishop would succeed in bringing the common life and the Rule of St. Augustine to the cathedral.

In 1127 one finds a substantial number of charters and letters demonstrating that Stephen of Garland had mounted a several-pronged attack against his bishop and the Victorines. Garland's leading ally in these maneuvers was Thibaut Notier, also an archdeacon at the Cathedral of Notre Dame during these years. In 1127, Thibaut Notier attempted to assert his authority in the governing of the cathedral chapter, checking the bishop's attempts to reform it. Letters were sent to the pope and other ecclesiastical dignitaries by Archdeacon Thibaut Notier and Bishop Stephen of Senlis in attempts to discredit each other, and Honorius II, apparently wearied by this seemingly never-ending strife in Paris, set up a commission to enforce a peaceful settlement.[101]

At the same time as Thibaut was stirring up the canons and attempting to thwart the ecclesiastical power of the bishop, Stephen of Garland went to work on destroying the bishop's relationship with the king. Garland – and, we may assume,

---

[97] See Luchaire (1890), p. 304 and Bournazel (1975), pp. 40–46. The bouteiller was in charge of the vineyards and their revenues. The office came to have political as well as domestic responsibilities during the course of the twelfth century. See Bournazel (1975), pp. 90ff.

[98] Only Stephen's letters survive. See *Recueil des historiens des Gaules et de la France*, vol. XV.

[99] See *CGP*, pp. 222–223 and *CEND*, vol. I, p. cxxxv and p. 334. This action was confirmed by Pope Honorius II in 1125.

[100] See *CGP*, p. 230. Pope Honorius II confirmed this charter in 1126.

[101] The relevant documents are described in *CGP*, pp. 231–233. See further discussion in *CEND*, vol. I, pp. cii–ciii. The charter has been edited in *CEND*, vol. I, pp. 28–29. One copy states that Thomas, Prior of St. Victor, was among the witnesses.

other like-minded men – undoubtedly confirmed the king's suspicions that zealous reformers were asking too much when they wanted lay influence removed from ecclesiastical life. Bishops and canons had long held secular authority and responsibilities and been the allies of secular rulers. The reformers' ideals of the common life were best carried out in monasteries where they would not get in the way of men of action.[102] In an important document from 1127, Louis VI confirmed the privileges of the Chapter of Notre Dame, stating that he would not tolerate the organization to be ruled by any other than its ancient customs. Furthermore, canons regular were not to be allowed to hold a prebend in the cathedral or to otherwise try to introduce themselves into the chapter.[103] Clearly, Bishop Stephen and the Victorines had attempted to install the regular canons into the prebends of the cathedral of Notre Dame, and one can understand that the potential loss of revenue would have threatened the chapter.

The attempt at reforming the cathedral, which must have been going on since 1124, failed. In the year 1127, or shortly thereafter, a charter of peace was drawn up between Stephen of Senlis and the canons of Notre Dame, who agreed to address certain charges of excessively worldly behavior. The reconciliation was effected by Abbot Suger of St. Denis, and Abbot Gilduin and Prior Thomas of St. Victor.[104] This nod in the direction of reform was the best effort Bishop Stephen ever got from his chapter, and it certainly did not mean the struggle to bring reform to the canons was over.

As might be imagined, the peace that came in 1127 was not an easy one.[105] In the next few years, strife between Bishop Stephen and Stephen of Garland remained intense.[106] Garland's and King Louis's efforts to drive the bishop to despair were well known: the bishop's goods were confiscated and he fled to Bernard of Clairvaux.[107] Two anonymous letters written to Stephen of Senlis at this same time suggest that the bishop should fear for his life.[108] It is certainly possible to assume that these letters of warning were written by Adam, Precentor of Paris, the man who had been third in power at the cathedral, just after the bishop and the deacon, since 1107.[109] Adam, himself a long-standing ally of the reform party, must have supported the bishop in the events that dominated cathedral life at this time. Other powerful men tried to help as well: Bernard of Clairvaux attempted to discredit Garland and offered aid to Bishop Stephen; around 1130, Geoffrey of Chartres

---

[102] See Huguenin (1857), pp. 186–194.

[103] The text is printed in *Recueil des historiens des Gaules et de la France*, vol. XV, p. 333.

[104] The text of this document is in *CEND*, vol. I, pp. 338–340.

[105] A charter promulgated in 1128, with the assent of the king and Bishop Stephen, attempts to protect the property and rights of the canons from trouble and demands that restitution be made for devastation. It is clear from the language of this charter that the recent fighting has been fierce. See *CEND*, vol. I, pp. 218–219.

[106] In 1128 Bernerus, deacon of the cathedral, issued a document with the consent of the king and of Bishop Stephen of Senlis to protect church property from the upheavals caused by the warring canons. See *CEND*, vol. I, pp. 218–219.

[107] See Luchaire (1890), pp. 198–199, no. 428.

[108] See pp. 208–209.

[109] See Gérard Dubois (1690–1710), vol. II, p. 25 and Luchaire (1890), p. 198, no. 427. The letters are very emotional and warn Stephen of the grave danger he is in and of the violent natures of his adversaries.

suggested to Senlis that he and Garland submit their difficulties to Bernard of Clairvaux for resolution,[110] and Stephen, Abbot of Cîteaux, wrote to the king objecting to his severe treatment of the bishop;[111] Suger of St. Denis, himself recently "reformed,"[112] actively sought reconciliation between the parties involved.

With so many forces advocating it, a resolution to the conflict emerged – but only slowly and over a number of years. In the years between 1127 and 1131, Stephen of Garland was in disgrace with the king.[113] When Garland had attempted to make the office of seneschal hereditary, the king for once conceded to the Queen's long-standing dislike for Garland, confiscating his property and removing him from office.[114] But by 1131 Garland had recaptured the king's favor.[115] The king wavered back and forth between accepting and rejecting the Bishop of Paris, and Suger became ever more the reformer, and ever more the power closest to the king. The events of the year 1133 described below, however, seem to have brought all difficulties to a head and made the struggles in Paris matters of international concern.

In 1130, Innocent II had become pope, and soon after him the anti-pope Anacletus II also claimed the office. With the backing of his powerful Roman family, Anacletus had driven Innocent out of the city.[116] Innocent toured Europe, slowly picking up support and winning the affections of leading reform clergy. When he became powerful enough to regain his authority in Rome itself (1131–32), he did not forget his friends.[117] Reformers such as Bernard of Clairvaux, Stephen of Senlis, Abbot Suger and Abbot Gilduin of St. Victor had a pope who could be counted upon to support their attempts to reform institutions that had become lax in their vows and customs.[118]

Buoyed by such support, the reformers increased their attempts to extend their influence into the cathedral. In 1132 or 1133, Innocent II invited Bishop Stephen to donate a prebend at the cathedral to St. Victor, and a long list of other gifts came to St. Victor from the hands of the bishop.[119] Following this lead, in 1133, Adam Precentor donated his prebend to the Abbey of St. Victor and eventually left the

---

[110] For a list of editions of this text, see *CGP*, p. 237.

[111] The text of this letter is most readily available in *PL* CLXXXII, col. 149.

[112] See Panofsky's introduction to Suger's writings, pp. 10–11.

[113] Stephen of Garland's difficulties with King Louis VI are mentioned in the *Chronique de Morigny*, ed. Mirot, pp. 42–44.

[114] For discussion of Garland's fall from power and his amazing ability to recoup his strengths for one last time, see Bournazel (1975), pp. 111–122. Well-known is the letter from Hildebert of Lavardin to Stephen, consoling him upon the destruction of his Parisian properties by an order of the queen. See Luchaire (1890), p. 198, no. 426.

[115] Indeed, in 1134 the king promulgated a charter protecting the lands of Stephen of Garland, restoring property that the king, by his own admission, had razed. See *CEND*, vol. I, pp. 268–269.

[116] See Schmale (1961).

[117] Although the schism was truly over only with the death of Anacletus on January 25, 1138.

[118] Innocent II called the Second Lateran Council in 1139 with the purpose of consolidating the goals of the Gregorian reform movement and moving away from "the arid juridical conflicts with the secular authorities to concern with the deeper, wider-ranging reforms which Gregory VII had called for" (*ODSP*, p. 168). For further discussion, see Klewitz (1939).

[119] See *CGP*, pp. 246–247. The actual text of Innocent's letter is in *PL*, CLXXIX, col. 620. This was an action Garland and the king had tried to prevent in 1127.

cathedral to live at the church "he especially loved."[120] It was, of course, not easy for Stephen of Garland and his allies to sit by watching Bishop Stephen and the Victorines win triumph after triumph through the pope's support. When Bishop Stephen and the Victorines marched upon the Benedictine Abbey of Chelles with the purpose of reforming it, and passed near land owned by Thibaut Notier, they were ambushed by relatives of this ally of the Garland family. As the reformers told the story, Prior Thomas of the Abbey of St. Victor was murdered, dying in Bishop Stephen's arms.[121] The murder of Prior Thomas became a *cause célèbre* for outraged clergy throughout Europe. Letters were written in protest by Bernard of Clairvaux, Peter of Cluny, and others, and an episcopal synod was held at Jouarre to discuss what actions should be taken against the miscreants.[122]

In fact, this act of revenge was a miscalculation by Stephen of Garland and his immediate allies in their attempts to turn the king against the reformers. Bautier suggests that it brought great sympathy and revenues from the king to the Abbey of St. Victor.[123] Time was against them as well, however, for when Louis VII became king in 1137, the controversy between Garland and the reformers was officially over. Suger had become the most powerful man in France; Stephen of Senlis dominated the reform movement in Paris; the Abbey of St. Victor was a center of learning, drawing many students from throughout Europe to its school. Archdeacon Stephen, the "cleric" of the Garland family, retired to spend his final years across the river at the Abbey of St. Victor.[124]

Conclusion: Adam of St. Victor in Paris

The first half of the twelfth century, an era that witnessed the rivalry between the bishops of Paris and the secular canons, was also a period of important developments in the arts and writings about the arts. Although the meaning of the word "reform" had become so blurred and general by the mid twelfth century as almost to defy definition, it was still possible for some institutions, at least, to sustain their individual traditions; in Paris, this was particularly true of the canons regular. From the start, their goal was to encourage the common life, and to convert the cathedral canons; beginning with Hugh, the Augustinians at St. Victor had a large and steadily increasing body of writings on Augustine's ideals of the monastic life.

It is a task of some importance to situate Adam of St. Victor in twelfth-century

---

[120] Adam's obituary (*ODSP*, pp. 536–537) in the Victorine necrology reads: "XIX Kal. febr. Ann. sollempne domni Ade, precentoris Parisiensis et nostri canonici, patris et matris ejus, qui ecclesie nostre quam specialiter dilexit utilitati studens, prebendam suam in manu domni Stephani, Parisiensis episcopi, reddidit."
(January 14, solemn anniversary of Lord Adam, precentor of Paris and our canon, and of his father and mother, who, applying himself to the service of our church, which he especially loved, offered his prebend in the hand of Lord Stephen, Bishop of Paris.)

[121] In two letters, one to Geoffrey of Chartres, the other to Innocent II, Stephen of Senlis describes the murder. See *CGP*, p. 248, for a list of sources.

[122] For a bibliography of sources, see *CGP*, pp. 248–250.

[123] See Bautier (1991), pp. 43–44.

[124] See Bautier (1981), p. 77.

Paris, because he has long been thought of as a figure who lived in the second half of the twelfth century, and who died in 1192.[125] Only recently has it been established that Adam of St. Victor is indeed one and the same as Adam Precentor, the cantor of Notre Dame Cathedral from at least 1107.[126] The importance of this identity has not been realized, however. It means that Adam flourished in the first half of the twelfth century; he was a contemporary of Hugh of St. Victor; he was a composer as well as a poet; and he had strong allegiance to two institutions, the Cathedral of Notre Dame and the Abbey of St. Victor. His double affiliation surely helps to explain the state of the Parisian sequence repertories as described in Part III of this book.

Adam, Precentor of Paris perhaps held an office at the Cathedral of Notre Dame as early as 1098. In this year a charter was signed by a certain Subdeacon Adam, who may well be the same person as Adam Precentor.[127] Adam first appears with the title "precentor" in 1107, when he signed the charter reforming the nunnery of St. Eloi.[128] Adam, then, was well established at the cathedral by the year 1107, a colleague of archdeacon William of Champeaux. Because Adam secured a prestigious position at the cathedral as a young man during the time of Bishop Galon and became a leading member of the reform party in Paris, he and William must have found themselves on the same side of many issues.[129]

Because of Adam's title it is certain that he was a musician; at this early date, the position of cantor of Notre Dame had not yet become primarily administrative.[130] Although his family name is not yet known, the necrology of the Cathedral of Notre Dame preserves the names of his parents, Beatrice and Gunther; like most canons at the cathedral, he was doubtless of noble blood.[131] His obituary in both Victorine and cathedral necrologies is lavish.[132] Adam Precentor, as he signed his name on numerous documents throughout the following decades, was a leading figure in the strife that set bishop against deacon and archdeacon against archdeacon at the cathedral in the early decades of the twelfth century. These same documents and the necrologies of St. Victor and the Cathedral of Notre Dame demonstrate that Adam was a loyal and an outspoken member of the reform party in Paris. He would have been not only a disciple of William of Champeaux but also a colleague of Gilduin, first Abbot of St. Victor. And yet he was not among the initial band of

---

[125] See, for example, the discussion by Dreves (1885) and the introduction to *AH* LIV.

[126] See Fassler (1984). I will not repeat the several arguments for Adam's identity here.

[127] See *CGP*, p. 145. The next time the name Adam shows up on a charter from the cathedral, it is followed by the title "precentor."

[128] See *CGP*, pp. 146 and 163.

[129] There is little in the Parisian charters about the election of the cantor. A document describing the office as it existed at the Parisian church of St.-Germain-l'Auxerrois states that the cantor was elected by the deacon and the chapter, with the bishop taking over if the dean and the chapter could not agree. See *CEND*, vol. I, p. 81.

[130] In his discussion of Magister Albertus, who followed Adam as cantor at the cathedral, Wright (1989) brings forth further evidence to support the idea that the cantor was still a practicing musician in the middle of the twelfth century. I would point to a letter by Suger written in 1147 defending the cantor of the cathedral and upholding his right to lead the choir as he saw fit. For sources containing this letter, see *CGP*, p. 310.

[131] See *ODSP*, vol. I, p. 120. "[21 April] XI kal. Eodem die, obiit Gonterus, pro cuius anima et Beatricis, uxoris eius, Adam precentor, filius eorum, dedit nobis quinque arpennos terre et arpennum vinee et dimidium, apud Montem Civriacum, ad vinum quadragesime."

[132] See *ODSP*, pp. 99 and 536–537.

canons from the cathedral who left with William in 1108 to found the abbey.[133] Instead he stayed with his position, providing an ally for the Victorines in the administration of the cathedral.

The first decade and a half of Adam's tenure at the Cathedral of Notre Dame may have been difficult. He served most of these years under Bishop Gilbert who was a friend of Stephen of Garland and an enemy of William of Champeaux and the Victorines. It was a bleak time for reformers. But Adam and other reform-minded clerics must have been encouraged during this period by the foundation of the new Abbey of St. Victor. Because of his close association with the abbey, Adam must have already known Hugh; perhaps they collaborated even at the start.

If Adam and others who wrote sequences in the opening decades of the twelfth century had trouble getting their works accepted by Bishop Gilbert, they certainly could have tried them out at the Abbey of St. Victor. After 1123, however, when Stephen of Senlis became Bishop of Paris, there would have been no barrier to writing new works for the cathedral liturgy as well. It was during this same time that Hugh of St. Victor wrote his first great works of scriptural exegesis and developed his vision of the church in the *Moral Ark of Noah* and the slightly later *Mystical Ark of Noah*.[134] The 1120s were perhaps years of productivity for Adam Precentor as well. He was in the prime of life; a new bishop fully in accord with his political and religious beliefs had just become his immediate superior; the ideals he had served for decades were receiving expression at the Abbey of St. Victor. The works he wrote during these years (and all the years before) could be tried out on major feasts at both the cathedral and the abbey and they could unashamedly promote the causes of reform and of the common life. By the end of the 1120s, a handful of new sequences may have been circulating in Paris, and these works were slowly making their way into the common liturgical practices of the cathedral and the abbey. This was the period in which the cathedral and the Abbey of St. Victor, the first churches in Paris to have these sequences, would have shared a common tradition of sequences, both texts and melodies.[135]

It was in the year that Prior Thomas was murdered, 1133, that Adam Precentor gave up his prebend at the cathedral, consigning all its revenues to the Abbey of St. Victor. Bishop Stephen supported his action, accepting the loss of income it would bring to the cathedral. Such a resignation was not typical at this time, and under most circumstances would have been prevented. The canon yearning for a more pious life would have been released, but his income would have stayed with the cathedral. And although a charter from 1125 had given the Victorines the right to a prebend from a canon leaving to join a reformed order, they constantly had to reassert their claim on Adam's prebend throughout the twelfth and thirteenth centuries.[136] If the two anonymous letters written to Bishop Stephen at this time

---

[133] See Willesme (1979 and 1981).
[134] These writings are discussed in Chapter 10.
[135] See discussion of the repertory in Chapters 7 and 8.
[136] SEe *CGP*, pp. 228–229.

warning him to beware of possible attempts on his life are by Adam, they underscore his commitment to the cause of reform.[137]

The precise date of Adam's actual departure for the Abbey of St. Victor is not known. But probably by the mid 1130s he was often in residence at the place that had captured his affections so long ago. The last charter he witnessed at the cathedral was in 1133, a document giving the small Parisian church of St. Denis of the Cell to St.-Martin-des-Champs.[138] He is also mentioned in a charter from 1133 giving various prebends throughout Paris to the Abbey of St. Victor.[139] One of these prebends, the one given by the cathedral to St. Victor, was Adam's own. And it is difficult to imagine that he would have remained long at the cathedral once his means of financial support had been consigned to the Abbey of St. Victor, although he certainly could have. A Victorine charter, prepared at mid century, is signed by "Adam Precentor," and he is listed fourth, just after the abbot, prior and sub-prior.[140] Clearly, Adam was at St. Victor and serving in some sort of official capacity.

So it was that for the final decade or so of their lives, Adam Precentor and Hugh of St. Victor, the greatest poet-composer and the greatest theologian of mid-twelfth-century Paris, sat in the same cloister. This is the time that the Victorines, with Adam in their midst, must have begun to develop their own liturgical practice. Of course, the crowning jewel of this work was their sequence repertory, and Adam, Hugh, Abbot Gilduin, and others apparently wanted it to be unique, to speak of the special relationship the great poet, the "egregius versificator," had with the Abbey of St. Victor.[141] Several of the sequence texts unique to the abbey may have been written by Adam during these years. But the Victorines consciously and deliberately set their own sequence repertory apart from that of the Cathedral of Notre Dame at some time in the second half of the twelfth century. Adam's presence at the abbey at mid century leads one to suspect that this development began at this time and with the blessings of the poet himself.

The political situation in Paris during the first half of the twelfth century and Adam's place within it demonstrate how it was that the sequences could be products of both the Abbey of St. Victor and the Cathedral of Notre Dame, and yet be in essence the work of Augustinians. The cathedral was led throughout the twelfth century by men who were reformers with strong allegiance to the Augustinian canons regular at St. Victor: Adam Precentor was such a man, as were Stephen of Senlis and the most important bishop of the second half of the twelfth century,

---

[137] See *Recueil des historiens des Gaules et de la France*, vol. XV, pp. 333–334. The attribution to Adam is made by Gérard Dubois (1690–1710), vol. II, p. 25. The author of the letters has had his vineyards torn up by the king because of the author's support for Bishop Stephen.

[138] See *CGP*, pp. 243–244.

[139] See *CGP*, pp. 246–247. Bishop Stephen states that he gives the prebend at Notre Dame to St. Victor with the permission of the dean, Bernerus, and of Adam Precentor, and of the entire chapter. The Abbey of St. Victor is to the cathedral, Stephen states further, as daughter is to mother.

[140] See *CGP*, pp. 330–331. Odo is still prior, so the charter was probably signed before the reform of Ste. Geneviève in 1147.

[141] So the great poet was called by Richard of St. Victor at mid century. See *Liber exceptionum*, ed. Châtillon, p. 384.

Maurice of Sully. If Adam was indeed the first great Parisian sequence poet, one would expect to find his sequences filled with calls to the common life and dedicated to the ideals of the Augustinian canons regular of St. Victor. As far as can be told from the sources, these were the ideals he served throughout his life.

10

Hugh of St. Victor's vision of the church

Introduction

It has been difficult for students of the twelfth century to move from reform and the spirit of reform to artists and works of art.[1] Although it has seemed clear that Cistercian reforms fostered both a Cistercian spirituality and a characteristically Cistercian architecture and liturgy, only rarely have scholars found connections between the art and liturgy that was designed by and for new houses of canons regular or for cathedral chapters with reform-minded bishops and the theology of these reformers.[2] Were there direct lines of influence between the writings of the men who first championed the Gregorian reform movement in France during the first half of the twelfth century, men such as Ivo of Chartres and Stephen of Senlis, and the new cathedrals at Sens or Notre Dame in Paris, or any of the new repertories of liturgical texts and music appearing in cathedrals and houses of canons regular throughout Northern Europe in the late twelfth and early thirteenth centuries? And if it is true that the Gregorian reform movement helped to inspire an artistic renaissance in twelfth-century France, how did the idea that the church was to be reborn, renewed, and not even to look as it did before, become translated into early manifestations of the art often called "Gothic"?[3]

Here it will be argued that although the reform had many strains in the first half of the twelfth century, an Augustinian viewpoint can be identified in Paris through the Victorine writings about the liturgy and liturgical practices. This chapter concentrates upon one writer from the Abbey of St. Victor in the first half of the twelfth century: Hugh of St. Victor. In his works, one finds a bridge between the legalistic concerns of the late-eleventh- and early-twelfth-century reform movement

[1] A brief discussion of romanesque sculpture in relationship to the reformers' devotion to Roman art is found in Hearn (1981): see, for example, pp. 117–118. The first full investigation of the reformers' artistic ideals is Toubert (1990). (The book did not appear in time for me to incorporate its arguments into my work.)

[2] On Cistercian theories of art, see Rudolf (1987) and Hufgard (1990).

[3] The one scholar who has devoted much of his life to asking such questions is Gerhart Ladner. Although he does not work in any concentrated way on Augustinian canons, his writings have been very useful for this study simply because of his strong interests in the subject of reform and reformers' views of the arts.

and the religious art of the mid twelfth century.[4] Hugh was not the only thinker who helped to translate the ideals of the reformers into both interpretations of the liturgy and aesthetic principles: Honorius Augustodunenis, for example, was also a reformer who wrote extensive liturgical commentaries which apparently inspired the visual arts.[5] For Parisian art of the mid twelfth century, and Victorine art in particular, however, Hugh was a major force.

Hugh of St. Victor's importance to twelfth-century religious art has long been recognized. For decades general studies of medieval ideas about art, although rarely exploring Hugh's treatises in great detail or mentioning specific works of art, have pointed to him as a major figure.[6] A recent author states, apparently without feeling the need to justify his opinions, that Hugh's "theory of aesthetics is at the center of the theory of beauty of the Middle Ages."[7] Other scholars have linked Hugh to specific artistic concepts and works of art: Otto von Simpson believed that Hugh's influence upon Suger was undeniable, and both Grover Zinn and, more recently, Conrad Rudolf have begun to study the twelfth-century church at St. Denis in the context of Hugh's thought. Zinn has made a strong case for the pervasive influence of Hugh's writings upon Suger's church and is presently at work on interpreting the surviving windows at St. Denis in the terms of Victorine theology. His analysis of the west portal at St. Denis has introduced the strong possibility of Victorine influence.[8] Of importance too are the studies of Helmut and Heide Buschhausen concerning both the iconography of liturgical objects (especially of processional crosses) and the role of Hugh's ideas (as first transmitted through the Parisian sequences and liturgical objects from St. Denis and as subsequently expressed in other decorative media and in other centers).[9] The art form which one might expect to correspond most closely to Hugh's writings is the Parisian sequence, and especially the repertory found at St. Victor.

The purpose of this chapter is to set forth those aspects of Hugh's thought which were most important to the sequence composers. Hugh's symbolic representations or drawings of the church were of primary importance because they came to underlie his understanding of the sacraments and the liturgy. Furthermore, his understanding of religious art and its purposes was always that of a reformer and of an Augustinian canon regular, with the goals of strengthening the commitments of regular canons in residence at the abbey, and secondarily, of inspiring secular clergy to the common life.[10] During Hugh's life, the Victorines were actively debating how the church should be organized, and how its clergy should be trained and

---

[4] This was true of other writers of liturgical commentary in the first half of the twelfth century, Rupert of Deutz, for example, and Honorius Augustodunensis.

[5] For discussion of a church building perhaps inspired by the writings of Honorius, see Skubiszewski (1988).

[6] See most notably de Bruyne (1946), vol. II, pp. 242–247, and the discussion of Victorine aesthetics in Tartarkiewicz (1970).

[7] Schueller (1988), p. 349.

[8] See Zinn (1986), p. 37.

[9] See especially Heide and Helmut Buschhausen (1983).

[10] The importance of reform to Hugh has long been recognized, but his writings are not usually interpreted with reform of the clergy as a major goal. McGonigle (1977, p. 296) who stresses the importance of reform in Hugh's description of "contemplative ascent," is an exception.

encouraged to live the common life; the years of major crisis and attempts to bring the common life to the cathedral (1124–37) were precisely the years in which Hugh wrote his major treatises. Beginning with Hugh, the body of writings emanating from the Abbey of St. Victor in the twelfth century was, therefore, dominated by the subject of the church and its ministers, its structure and organization, its purpose in contemporary life, and its significance throughout history;[11] it also sought ways of drawing the canons deeper into the Augustinian mode of life as described in the Rule, and heightening devotion to the liturgy by means of commentary.[12] Jean Châtillon has described the mainstream of Victorine thought as follows:

> The ecclesiastical hierarchy, the temples where the Christian cult takes place, the ceremonies that unfold there, the rites accomplished there, the liturgical vestments themselves, all this was studied, analyzed, described and explicated according to an allegorical method which here became a veritable liturgical system of symbols.[13]

This "veritable liturgical system of symbols" is developed in Hugh of St. Victor's writings, and becomes the language of the Victorine sequences as well.[14] Hugh is a thinker whose most complicated ideas seem to spring fully-formed from his brain. Even "early works" such as the *Didascalicon* read as though conceived with "later works" in mind. This sense of Hugh's oeuvre is undoubtedly attributable to the fact that, as he himself says, he put things aside for periods of time and picked them up again (*Commentary on the Celestial Hierarchy*), and that he revised writings-in-progress for many years (*De sacramentis*).[15] These work habits make it difficult to trace the development of major concepts and to establish a firm chronology for Hugh's voluminous writings.[16] Although many problems in chronology are presently unresolved, several of the works either mentioned or discussed in this chapter may be loosely arranged upon a time-line, at least in relationship to each other. From early to late, they are as follows. (1) The *Commentary on the Celestial Hierarchy of the Pseudo-Dionysius*, which was probably, as van den Eynde argued, an early work, revised at least once at a later date. (2) *The Didascalicon*, a work agreed upon by all scholars to be early, and which Hugh mentions as such in *De sacramentis*. (3) *The Moral Ark of Noah* and *The Mystical Ark of Noah*, both probably written in the mid to late 1120s. (4) The "De verbo Dei" and the "De unione corporis et spiritus," two short treatises whose approximate dates remain unestablished, but which also may have been written in Hugh's "middle period," that is in the late

---

[11] One can tell from the early manuscripts in the Victorine library that the writings of Augustine were intensely studied there in the first half of the twelfth century. See discussion in Chapter 7.

[12] The version of the Rule followed at St. Victor is discussed in Jocqué (1991), pp. 66–67.

[13] Châtillon (1949), p. 124.

[14] The ways in which Hugh's ideas underlie the Parisian sequences, and especially the repertory of St. Victor, will be the subject of Part V.

[15] Hugh also apparently wrote small papers encapsulating important ideas and then incorporated them into his larger works. See Weisweiler (1949).

[16] The chronology of Hugh of St. Victor's writings remains a major problem, undoubtedly only to be solved in the preparation of a new edition of his works now under way in the *Corpus Christianorum*. The problems with dating the *Commentary upon the Celestial Hierarchy* are a case in point: van den Eynde (1960) thought it was early (see pp. 58ff.); Baron at first argued that it was late (1958), but then (1963, pp. 134–135), advanced the now accepted opinion that it was a work revised several times.

1120s and early 1130s. (5) The *De sacramentis christiane fidei*, clearly, and by Hugh's own admission, one of his latest works but revised over a long period of time, in part to supersede freely-circulating earlier versions.

In the Victorine crucible of reform theology, a theory of religious art and its purposes was formed, and from three major sources: the writings of the Pseudo-Dionysius, patron saint and supposed apostle of France, the writings of St. Augustine (including the Rule), patron of the Abbey of St. Victor and of canons regular everywhere, and the ideals of the great reformers who lived in the two generations before Hugh of St. Victor, men such as Ivo of Chartres, William of Champeaux, Anselm of Laon, and Rupert of Deutz.[17] Still, the visual model of the church to be described here was apparently Hugh's own; no other contemporary writer created a system closely resembling Hugh's, although certainly many twelfth-century writers drew upon several of the same sources and had similar concerns.[18] Discussion begins with Hugh's model of the church, as described in *The Moral Ark of Noah* and *The Mystical Ark of Noah*. Hugh's model was both microcosm and macrocosm: his explanation of the inner workings of human psychology depends upon it, as does his *magnum opus*, the *De sacramentis christiane fidei*. Hugh's all-encompassing vision of the church is a reformer's church, and for three main reasons.

First, it presents a church which is carefully organized and with the clergy playing the central role as the heirs of the Apostles. The clergy of this church are unified in two directions: both throughout all time, and throughout all levels, from pope to parish priest. The structure of Hugh's church parallels the ideal of a unified church which inspired the Gregorian reform movement from the very beginning.

Secondly, Hugh's picture of the church emphasizes the importance of a clergy which is purified of all secular influence and well-educated. These two were central ideals of the reform movement, and ones in which the Victorines took great interest in the city of Paris.[19]

Thirdly, this vision of the church is offered to the clergy to help them to convert to the common life. Through study of Hugh's picture, clerics can learn greater respect for their appointed tasks and, especially, for their liturgical offices.

The vision of the church that rises out of Hugh's writings is also readily adaptable to artistic programs, to buildings, to any art depicting the church and its liturgical function and power. This is so for three reasons:

First, Hugh applied his theological theories to drawings, or works of art. The drawings themselves do not survive, and one could debate whether they ever really existed at all. The actual existence of the drawings is of little consequence here, however. What matters instead is that Hugh describes them and the creating of

---

[17] See the writings of Jean Châtillon, who has discussed several of the sources of Hugh's thought, and Baron (1957 and 1959). For neoplatonism in St. Augustine and the early church, see several of the essays in Blumenthal and Markus (1981). Although it is common to think of Rupert of Deutz as German, he was originally from Liège, a point emphasized by Van Engen (1983).

[18] An introduction to the standard Patristic sources of Hugh is found in de Lubac (1961), Part II, Vol. I, pp. 287–359.

[19] See Bautier (1981), pp. 66–67, and (1991), p. 39, for description of the conflict in the 1120s over control of the schools in Paris.

them in sufficient detail to allow for understanding his view of religious art and its purposes.[20]

Secondly, several of Hugh's treatises when studied together outline a plan for applying theological principles to the structures of actual buildings. Thus Hugh's constant commentary on the church, which is found in all of his writings, be they early or late, had an immediately practical dimension, making it possible to extend his ideas to artistic representations of the church, and thereby make the works of art themselves representative symbols of higher truths. This attitude toward the purpose of church buildings and how they should be constructed and decorated to achieve that purpose is a defining feature of the changes that began to take place in church art and architecture in the mid twelfth century. It also inspired the development of the sequence in Paris, most particularly at the Abbey of St. Victor. In fact, as will be demonstrated later, the Victorines tried to build a kind of church out of their sequences.

Thirdly, Hugh fused two traditional kinds of books in his *De sacramentis*, a Genesis commentary and a liturgical commentary, and thus made a new kind of book.[21] In Hugh's book, the works of creation, God's initial works, are balanced by the works of restoration created by Christ and carried on by his church. Although this idea is central to Augustine and underlies the *Confessions*, Hugh extends it in ways Augustine did not.[22] With Hugh, the works of restoration always take place inside the church, through the sacramental action of the liturgy. Thus the church and its liturgy became a kind of second world, and are both model and effective agent. This view promotes the importance of the church building, its liturgy, and the members of the ecclesiastical hierarchy. As an Augustinian canon, Hugh wanted to see these instruments of salvation carefully organized and beautifully arrayed to promote spiritual goals.

Hugh of St. Victor was a traditional thinker, deeply dependent upon Augustine and Gregory the Great, as well as the Pseudo-Dionysius. What made him so important to the arts in the early twelfth century, and particularly in the Ile-de-France, where he was much read, were the visual implications of his exegesis, and the appeal of his carefully constructed model of the church.[23] There is nothing in Hugh to suggest that he wished medieval artists would take up his writings as models for their works.[24] Yet it would not be surprising if they had done so, simply because of Hugh's great emphasis on the importance of systematically *visualizing* complicated theological ideas. De Lubac says of Hugh:

---

[20] See Esmeijer (1978).

[21] Honorius Augustodunensis wrote both a Genesis commentary and liturgical commentaries, but did not actually combine these two kinds of treatises.

[22] For further explanation, see discussion of "Mundi renouatio" in Chapter 8.

[23] See Goy for discussion of how many copies of Hugh's writings survive from the Middle Ages, and which kinds of institutions owned them. Hugh was particularly favored by reformers in the twelfth century: canons regular and Cistercians.

[24] Esmeijer (1978, p. 56) doubts that exegetes intended their works for specific artistic projects: "although as teachers Honorius and, more specifically, Hugh of St. Victor often made use of the visual exegetical method, it is stretching matters much too far to see their writings as a sort of vademecum for commissioners and executants of visual exegetic programmes."

Il aime voir et parler aux yeux. Il s'émeut à la beauté des choses visibles, et surtout à celle qui leur vient de leur coloris . . . Il faut d'ailleurs à son dessein symbolique une peinture parlante, ainsi qu'il le dit; ou, suivant une autre expression qui est encore de lui, il a besoin de "visibiles figurationes." Elles ne sont d'ailleurs pas seulement, dans son idée, nécessaires à la connaissance: elles sont généatrices de joie.[25]

As a discussion of several versions of Hugh's "church" below will show, the image was designed to be viewed from many angles. It represented a particular history of Jewish and Christian people, it represented the inner life of the human person, and it represented the building in which the sacraments unfolded.

A model for contemplation

In the *Didascalicon* Hugh of St. Victor displays his love of hierarchy and order, designing arrangements of the arts, rules for study, groups of books, and methods of reading. The result, however, is a panoply of things which threatens to create a kind of disorder through its very inclusiveness.[26] As work after work attests, Hugh was deeply disturbed by the appearance of chaos.[27] In his next textbooks, Hugh sought a single image that would allow him to represent the many concerns of the *Commentary on the Celestial Hierarchy* and the *Didascalicon* all at once, an image that would be capable of sustaining the massive weight of accumulated Christian knowledge, yet, at the same time, be perceivable by humans as a unity. The image was sought as a remedy, as a means of beginning the process of restoration by teaching the mind how to focus inwardly.[28]

Cum sederem aliquando in conventu fratrum, et illis interrogantibus, meque respondente, multa in medium prolata fuissent, ad hoc tandem deducta sunt verba, ut de humani potissimum cordis instabilitate et inquietudine admirari omnes simul, et suspirare inciperemus; cumque magno quidem desiderio exposcerent, demonstrari sibi quae causa in corde hominis tantas cognitationum fluctuationes ageret, ac deinde si qua arte sive laboris cujuslibet exercitatione huic tanto malo obviam iri posset, summopere doceri flagitarent;

(When I was one day sitting with the assembled brethren, and replying to the questions which they asked, many matters came up for discussion. Finally the conversation was so directed that we began with one accord to marvel at the instability and restlessness of the human heart, and to sigh over it. And the brethren earnestly entreated that they might be shown the cause of these unstable

---

[25] de Lubac (1961), Part II, vol. I, pp. 324–325.

[26] The idea of a multitude of things distracting the soul is of primary importance to Augustine. In the *Confessions*, Book 10, he writes "How countless are the things that by different skills and manufactures men have added as enticements for the eyes . . . following outwardly what they have created, men desert inwardly by whom they were created." (Trans. from Zumkeller, *Augustine's Rule*, p. 320.)

[27] Confusion and chaos are symbolic of the fallen condition of humankind. Hugh says in *The Moral Ark*: "when we let our hearts run after earthly things without restraint, a multitude of vain thoughts arises, so that our mind becomes so divided that even the order of our native discrimination is disturbed." Book IV, Chapter 4; trans., pp. 125–126. Subsequent references are to page numbers in the translations.

[28] Like Augustine, Hugh believed that people needed practical demonstrations of beliefs in order to understand. Augustine discusses this idea in the *De magistro*. Augustine's theory of knowledge is discussed in Bubacz (1982).

movements in man's heart, and further particularly begged to be taught if such a serious evil as this could be countered by any skill or by the practice of some discipline.)[29]

Hugh found the image his students needed in the ark of Noah, the great old ship described by Augustine as "a symbol of the City of God on pilgrimage in this world, of the church which is saved through the wood on which was suspended 'the mediator between God and men, the man Jesus Christ.'"[30] Here was a Christo-centric symbol which Hugh could expand to become a model of the church, an edifice rising up from the pages of Scripture, like St. Gregory's "building" referred to in the *Didascalicon*.[31] The ark as Hugh designed it is filled with saints and piloted by the Crucified; it bobs upon the waves of time, defying mortality as it goes.[32] Yet it is much more than a mere image of the church; it is an object for meditation. And it has been designed deliberately to initiate that process by which human beings can uncover the divinity buried within their souls. With his models of the ark, Hugh designed a depiction of the church which was meant to order and strengthen the minds of those who beheld it.

In drawing his pictogram, Hugh joined a long tradition of authors who sought to explain and teach through such devices. Anna Esmeijer says:

The image, the representation, was highly valued for the possibilities it provided of rendering the "historia" in a summary, compressed form, or of perpetuating the "memoria" of saints and martyrs, and also for its power to move and inspire to imitation . . . The contemplation of the image can function as a vehicle for spiritual elevation, leading to the prototype, of which the image is a representation.[33]

The image was, as Mary Carruthers has argued at length, a visual aid to memory, allowing for the storing of great amounts of information within the mind, from whence it could be readily retrieved:

This compositional structure is mnemonic. The rigid steps (*gradus*) in the growth of a tree provide Hugh's heuristic as he composes. To each stage of growth, Hugh has attached a Biblical *dictum* concerning wisdom . . . Each growth-stage with its primary text is the subject of one chapter, and is stated in a rubric at the start. Basically the structure is that of a concordance, or *catena*, in which the parts are associated by key-words, each of which pulls other texts and sayings with it, "compounding with interest," as Hugh's Chronicle preface promises.[34]

Hugh presented the elaborate symbol several times, but describes it as an actual drawing only in his two treatises on the ark of Noah. One of these, the *Mystical Ark of Noah*, explains the drawing's allegorical significance, and the other, the *Moral Ark of Noah*, concentrates upon its tropological meaning. These treatises, written at

---

[29] *The Moral Ark*, p. 45.
[30] See Augustine, *The City of God*, Book XV, Chapter 26. The ark of Noah has been a common symbol for the church throughout the history of Christian exegesis. See de Lubac (1961), Part II, vol. I, pp. 317–328.
[31] See *The Didascalicon*, ed. and trans. Taylor, Book VI, Chapter 3, p. 135.
[32] Zinn (1974b, p. 153) states that Hugh's view of the flood as representative of time is absolute and denies previous interpretations of the waters as not only destructive but also as cleansing.
[33] See Esmeijer (1978), p. 210.
[34] Carruthers (1990), p. 210.

approximately the same time, are profitably studied together.[35] In both of them, Hugh is teacher and artist, creating elaborate drawings representative of the church throughout the ages, as depicted in the Old and New Testaments and in the lives of the saints.[36]

In the *Mystical Ark*, Hugh describes precisely how the picture is made, indicating where he puts the points of the compass, how he marks off lines, where he bisects angles, the very opening of the treatise serving as an example of his working method:

Primum ad mysticam arcae Noe descriptionem, in planitie ubi arcam depingere volo, medium centrum quaero, et ibi fixo puncto parvam quadraturam aequilateram ad similitudinem illius cubiti, in quo consummata est arca, ei circumduco.

(First for an allegorical marking out of the ark of Noah, in the surface where I want to draw the ark, I seek the center in the midst of the whole, and there, having fixed a point, I draw around it a small square, making a representation of that cubit within which the ark was completed.)

Although we cannot know whether he actually made the drawing, Hugh everywhere attempts to make the reader feel as if this were an artistic enterprise: in the first person, he speaks of painting it, planning it, labeling its parts. Even though it could have been one, Hugh does not present this model as an idealized conception, far removed from the drawing board. Indeed, difficult though it might be, it might well be possible to reconstruct Hugh's elaborate model from the directions he left behind, and his work may have inspired the drawings of Richard of St. Victor.[37] Although the extensive drawing instructions found in the *Mystical Ark* are missing in the *Moral Ark of Noah*, in the latter Hugh is more specific about his artistic intentions. Creation of the picture is an action serving to further God's plan, an action not necessary for the plan to succeed, of course, but appreciated by God nonetheless.[38] Hugh's model is a "definite object," created to "engage our attention seriously and to occupy our thoughts.[39] The final sentences of the *Moral Ark of Noah* illustrate that Hugh meant his students to gaze upon his work of art, to contemplate it, and to use it to rise mentally to the invisible reality it represented:

And now, then, as we promised, we must put before you the pattern of our ark. Thus you may learn from an external form, which we have visibly depicted, what you ought to do inwardly, and when you have impressed the form of this pattern on your heart, you may rejoice that the house of God has been built in you.[40]

Hugh's art is meant to initiate transformation, to help remake the observer in God's image, a goal stated in the Rule of St. Augustine: "So all of you live with one soul and one heart, and honor in one another God, whose temples you were made to

---

[35] For an excellent introduction to the ark treatises and the earlier scholarship upon them, see Grover Zinn (1975). Through this article and his earlier Ph.D. dissertation (1969), Professor Zinn opened up a new understanding of Hugh's thought through these two crucial works.

[36] See further discussion in Esmeijer (1978), p. 31.

[37] On the drawings of Richard of St. Victor, see Cahn (1900).

[38] *The Moral Ark*, p. 46: "I know that God would have us work along with Him . . ."

[39] See *The Moral Ark*, p. 126.

[40] See p. 153. The final lines translated here are missing in the version in *PL*.

be."[41] It is the visible stimulation necessary to lead to the invisible and, for its making, it requires the planning skills of a single thinker, one capable of organizing its parts and making sure they rest on the firm foundations of historical knowledge and doctrinal truth. In Hugh's work, the functions of theologian, artist, and teacher are one, and the artistic creation itself is a model of the Christian church. The reformer makes his ultimate statement: the church must be ordered and presented in its ideal form because only in this way can its purposes be known, and only if its purposes are known can human beings begin to become part of it. To know is to love and to love is to know: this art leads from itself to itself.[42] It represents the operation of Wisdom in Biblical history. The drawing is supposed to teach how Christ gathers up the truth from the texts and draws them into the one meaning of Himself. By knowing this, by observing this, Hugh believed the viewer, with God's grace, might be drawn within a spiral of knowledge and love.[43]

Hugh of St. Victor has combined the many goals of his earlier writings, the *Commentary on the Celestial Hierarchy* and the *Didascalicon*, into one purpose in these ark treatises: making an image of the Body of Christ. This image is, of course, dependent upon Hugh's method of Biblical exegesis. Like Origen and Gregory the Great, Hugh worked within a threefold system of scriptural interpretation; for Hugh the three levels of meaning were the historical, the allegorical, and the tropological.[44] The anagogical, that level of interpretation which focuses upon future events, was subsumed into the allegorical in this particular scheme. Hugh of St. Victor made historical understanding the foundation of Biblical study in the *Didascalicon*, but the full implications of this emphasis upon history only become apparent in Hugh's later works, particularly in the ark treatises. Here he reveals that his model of the church is an interpretation of time, an allegorical and tropological view of historical events. It is not, then, that Hugh was interested in an historical understanding of the actual ark of Noah as depicted in Genesis, or in concentration upon the ship and how it was made, or in providing an extensive literal reading of the process of ship-building. As an exegete, he is instead interested in the allegorical and tropological understandings of history, rather than in history itself.[45] He utilizes the Biblical description of the ark in his design, but he is far more concerned with

41   From Part I, section 8 of the version of the Rule of St. Augustine known as the *Praeceptum*; ed. Zumkeller in *Augustine's Ideal of the Religious Life*, pp. 289–300, at p. 289. Zumkeller and Edmund Colledge (who is responsible for the English version) worked from the edition of Verheijen. A concise discussion of the several versions of the Rule which circulated in the Middle Ages may be found in *Augustine's Ideal of the Religious Life*, pp. 283–287. The verison called the *Praeceptum* has priority, and is now thought to have been written by Augustine himself. Augustinian canons in the twelfth century (including those of St. Victor) generally followed the *Praeceptum*, but they knew and studied other versions as well.

42   See *The Moral Ark*, "And to put it more exactly, the Church herself is the ark, which her Noah, our Lord Jesus Christ, the Helmsman and the Haven, is guiding through the tempests of this present life, and leading through Himself unto Himself."

43   Hugh believed that the events of biblical history could lead the reader to God. See McGonigle (1977), pp. 84–85.

44   See discussion in de Lubac (1961), Part II, vol. I, pp. 328–339.

45   De Lubac makes this point at length, in criticism of early writings of Beryl Smalley. See especially, de Lubac (1961), Part II, vol. I, pp. 317–328. For further discussion, see McGonigle (1977), p. 87, and Zinn (1969).

demonstrating how the ark contains all the ages, from the beginning of time until the end of time, not only contains them, but organizes them into a picture of historical events with Christ in the middle. In Hugh's hands, all history worth knowing becomes church history and its agents and explicators, churchmen.[46]

Hugh's history of the world is found in both ark treatises, but in the *Mystical Ark* it is presented person by person and event by event, whereas in the *Moral Ark* it is interpreted as the means by which humans can learn and develop. Thus in the *Mystical Ark* Hugh, following Augustine, states that:

> Longitudo autem Ecclesiae consideratur in diuturnitate temporum, sicut latitudo in multitudine populorum . . . Credimus enim nullum tempus esse ab initio mundi usque ad finem saeculi, in quo non inveniantur fideles Christi . . .[47]

> (The length of the church is seen in the duration of time, just as the width is seen in the multitude of the peoples . . . So we believe that there is no time from the beginning of the world to the end of the ages in which persons faithful to Christ are not found . . .)

Representatives of all people who have believed in Christ are pictured in the ark, beginning with Adam and proceeding up through the present, and in the center is a huge column which is both the tree of life and the Book of Wisdom.[48] This column, which represents Christ, marks off and defines the ages. To one side of it are Adam and the patriarchs, and the genealogy of the tribe of Judah, leading up to Joseph the Nazarene. On the other side is the lineage of the New Adam, beginning with Peter, who has the rest of the twelve Apostles arranged around him, six to his right and five to his left.[49] And then from Peter descends the long line of popes, ending with Honorius (Honorius II, who reigned from 1124 to 1130).[50] And the twelve patriarchs and the twelve Apostles are arranged around the column to resemble the twenty-four elders of the apocalypse.[51] In this arrangement, Hugh pushes the past of the Old and New Testaments through the present and into the future of the apocalyptic Christ in majesty, reigning in the midst of the church.[52]

Hugh's picture of the church is one he deeply desires his students to *see*. The arrangement itself is a visual display, the ordering of which has profound significance and must be taken in by the eyes and contemplated. Many individual elements of the array are themselves depictions: the Lamb in the cubit in the center of the ark – the point toward which the entire edifice tends – is carefully drawn and

---

[46] This point is not made in de Lubac's analysis of Hugh's ark treatises.

[47] *The Mystical Ark*, Chapter III, col. 685.

[48] For discussion of the symbols of book and tree in Hugh's ark treatises, see Zinn (1974a), pp. 150–162. Zinn says, "As Book of Life, Christ chides and illumines; this has to do primarily with his human nature. As Tree of Life, Christ shelters and feeds . . . this has to do with his divine nature." (p. 151).

[49] Tree schemes were common devices in medieval pictograms; see Esmeijer (1978), p. 41. The tree of life in Eden often becomes the Cross in medieval Christian art and exegesis. See Ladner (1979), pp. 257–270. "Trees" are frequently used in pictograms which provide some sort of historical schema.

[50] In placing this emphasis on the popes, Hugh shows himself once again to be a reformer. See Ladner (1947).

[51] *The Mystical Ark* Chapter IV, col. 687.

[52] The similarity between this vision and the Christ in majesty sculpted on the portals of several twelfth-century churches is striking. In a forthcoming paper, Grover Zinn will argue the importance of Hugh's image, explaining it in terms of Is. 6:1, "I saw the Lord sitting upon a throne, high and elevated," expounded by Hugh in the opening book of the *Moral Ark of Noah*.

painted in symbolic colors.[53] The patriarchs of the twelve tribes and the Apostles all have images, the kind of pictures Hugh says the Greeks call "icons."[54] This is a history picture-book, but its story is very selective: here are the leaders of the Israelites, with an emphasis on those who formed the lineage of the ecclesiastical hierarchy; here are the Apostles, and their successors, the popes: these men reach ahead to Christ or forward from Him.[55] They are the churchmen mentioned repeatedly in Hugh's *Commentary on the Celestial Hierarchy*, but here seen progressing through time and moving geographically from east to west. It is by seeing them, arranged in a symbolic historical pattern which, for Hugh, represented reality, that the process of ascent can begin. In his *Mystical Ark* Hugh draws many ladders reaching up toward the top of the ark, demonstrating how humans are to climb from knowledge of history up to moral perfection: he expects this to be done by watching time, by coming to understand its significance, and by finally reducing it to a single meaning within. The time to be watched, is, of course, the history of the church as found in the Old and New Testaments, and manifested through the story of its ministers.

When humans watch time in this particular way, they become most like God. Time, as Augustine argued in his *Confessions*, then collapses in upon itself and ceases to entrap.[56] Hugh's depiction of history is ultimately an antidote to time:

Habent enim quoddam esse suum res in mente hominis, ubi illa etiam, quae in seipsis vel jam praeterierunt, vel adhuc futura sunt, simul subsistere possunt. Et in hoc quodammodo rationalis anima similitudinem sui Creatoris habet, quia sicut in mente divina omnium rerum causae aeternaliter sine mutabilitate, et distinctione temporali substiterunt, ita etiam in mente nostra praeterita, praesentia, et futura per cogitationem simul subsistunt.[57]

(For things have their own kind of being in the mind of man, where even those which, in themselves, are past or yet to come can exist together. And in this respect the rational soul bears a certain resemblance to its Maker. For as in the mind of God the causes of all things have existed eternally without change or temporal differentiation, so also in our minds things past, things present, and things future exist together by the means of thought.)

By knowing the history of the church in time, humans not only become like God in the way they perceive things, but are also inspired with love.

If, then, you have made your thought to range from the world's beginning to its end, and have considered as you went what marvels, what great marvels God has wrought and is still working for His elect, and through them, and by means of them, then you have made the lengthwise measure of your heart three hundred cubits. Again, if you review the Church in thought and,

---

[53] The Lamb in the center of quaternity schemes is a common pictorial device. In an illustration from a twelfth-century lectionary (Stuttgart, Landesbibliothek, Brev. 128), the Lamb is at the center of a cross, and the arms of the cross are made of the four rivers flowing through Paradise; in another illustration in the same manuscript, Christ appears in majesty surrounded by the twenty-four elders. See Esmeijer (1978), figures 58a and 58b.

[54] See *The Mystical Ark*, Chapter IV, cols. 686 and 687.

[55] In his *Chronicon*, a series of historical tables, Hugh of St. Victor gave special place to the priesthood of the old Testament by emphasizing the "four successions" – patriarchs from Adam to Moses, judges from Moses to David, kings from David to the Babylonian captivity, and high priests from the Exile to Christ. The high priests were not found in other medieval schemata since the time of Eusebius. See Zinn (1977) for a full explanation of Hugh's historical tables.

[56] For further discussion of freedom from temporal restraints in Augustine, see Teske (1985).

[57] *The Moral Ark*, p. 73.

having contemplated the believers' way of life, adopt it as your pattern, you stretch your heart to fifty cubits wide. And if you have acquired the science of the Holy Writ, which is comprised in thirty books, you will build your heart up to the height of thirty cubits. This is the ark that you must build.[58]

Beauty is found in representations of the church, of the historical body of Christ, and this beauty is esteemed only because it inspires transformation. Thus to those perceiving Hugh's drawing of the ark of Noah he explains: "You will see there certain colors, shapes, and figures which will be pleasant to behold. But you must understand that these are put there . . . that you may learn wisdom, instruction, and virtue . . ." As teacher and artist, Hugh is only concerned with art as it can help those who see it to understand, to know, and consequently to love God. He remains convinced that people could not love without seeing, without knowing. For Hugh, beauty is found not in lines, shapes, geometric proportions. It is found rather in people, in human beings so ordered and arranged that their representations form Christ's historical body. "So great is the beauty of His loveliness," Hugh says, "that no one who sees Him can fail to love Him."[59] Hugh depicts Christ through the people who have loved and served Him throughout all of history. Hugh's church is not magnificent because of its pillars, its jewels, its arches: it is beautiful for its saints, Old Testament and New. It is a church not made of stones, but of human beings. Its master artificer is not a mason; he is rather an historian.

In Hugh's hands, the ecclesiastical hierarchy is perceived through history, and to perceive it is the first stage in the Dionysian ascent.[60] Thus the very model of the church in time is a hierarchy, and the importance of knowing about it, of viewing it, is central to the process of salvation, not just for clerics but for all humans. Later, in *De sacramentis*, Hugh implies the design was intended primarily for learned clerics. After reading the ark treatises, however, one is left with the impression that *all* must be instructed, *all* must know, to begin the process of recovery possible through meditation. Hugh wished not only to inspire his students to change themselves; he also wished to make them want to change others.[61]

The church within and the church without

Hugh's model of the church was constructed according to his theories of how human beings learn. His interest in this subject would inspire other Victorine thinkers, especially Richard and Godefroy, both of whom employed models of understanding in their exegesis.[62] Of his own model of the church, Hugh said:

[58] *Ibid.*, p. 74.
[59] *Ibid.*, p. 48.
[60] Although Hugh's dedication to concepts of hierarchy comes from long study of the Pseudo-Dionysius, his emphasis upon history comes rather from Augustine.
[61] McGonigle (1977, p. 295) says, "Within the Hugonian perspective, the divine love which makes believers one with Christ in the contemplative experience fills them with Christ's concern for the salvation of others."
[62] For further discusson of images of the church, see Imkamp (1983).

The first [ark] is that which Noah made with hatchets and axes, using wood and pitch as his materials. The second is that which Christ made through His preachers by gathering the nations into a single confession of faith. The third is that which wisdom builds daily in our hearts through continual meditation on the law of God. The fourth is that which mother grace effects in us by joining together many virtues in a single charity.[63]

Yet, for Hugh, Platonist that he was, all the arks have the same structure and reduce to one:

Nevertheless there is in a certain sense only one ark everywhere, for there is only one common ground of likeness everywhere, and that which is not different in nature ought not to be different in name. The form is one, though the matter is different, for that which is actualized in the wood is actualized also in the people, and that which is found in the heart is the same as that which is found in charity.[64]

The analogies made in these quotations are of central importance for understanding Hugh's belief in the power of religious symbols to promote knowledge and conversion. In two short treatises, Hugh developed a more complete explanation of the hierarchical motion within his arks: the first treatise to be discussed here, "De unione corporis et spiritus," demonstrates how human perception works and the important role of symbolism in the process of understanding; the second, "De verbo Dei," uses a framework similar to that found in "De unione," but expands it to show how the Word is likened to the symbol, both within the human person and within the church. Although the ideas encountered in these treatises are found in other works by Hugh, these offer particularly concise statements of them and are thus well worth study.

In "De unione," Hugh describes the hierarchy that constitutes a human person. The body and the senses are the lowest region; above the body is the spirit, and it is divided into two faculties. The lower of these, the corporeal or animating faculty, humans share with beasts. The higher faculty, the rational faculty, is possessed by humans alone. Mediating between the body and the spirit are the senses and sensibility; mediating between the corporeal spirit and the rational spirit is the imagination.[65] Each part of this hierarchy is graded, having higher and lower attributes. And, therefore, although flesh cannot mingle directly with spirit and corporeal and rational faculties cannot unite, a person can move into the upper regions of one realm of being and then, by the process of mediation, ascend to the next one.

Hugh was chiefly interested in the importance of the imagination and received images in the process of ascent. Like Augustine, Hugh believed it was important for each human to rediscover the divinity within her or his own soul. The hierarchy of perception leads from the bestial senses to the supreme goodness inspired by reason,

---

[63] *The Moral Ark*, p. 59.
[64] *Ibid.*, p. 60.
[65] Hugh was true to Augustine in his emphasis on the importance of both the body and the spirit in the formation and salvation of the soul, but took both his hierarchical interpretation and his emphasis on the imagination from the Pseudo-Dionysius. Fruitful comparison may be made between ideas regarding the body and spirit in Augustine, *De musica*, Book VI and Hugh of St. Victor, *Commentary on the Celestial Hierarchy*, Book II.

to the discernment given by God. Hugh describes this ascent by relating what can happen to raw, sensory data:

This is the imagination of the similitude of sense, in the highest part of the corporeal spirit and in the lowest part of the rational spirit, representing the corporeal and reaching to the rational. For sensation, touching the body without, is formed either through sight, through hearing, through smell, through taste, or through touch, and, reducing within that same form conceived from the body by contact, by means of paths disposed for the purpose of sending forth individual senses and calling them back within, collects it [the form] to the mind's imagining chamber, and, impressing it on the purer part of the corporeal spirit, makes the imagination.[66]

The room within the human soul, the "cella phantastica," is the matrix of action in Hugh's description. The force of the imagination formed here, although nothing but a corporeal similitude, can rise up and be loosened, touching the incorporeal, rational realm of the soul. Now, the corporeal substance of the rational is light; and the imagination, in so far as it is an image of the body, is a shadow. Therefore, if a person holds on to the image with worldly love, it will overshadow and blot out the light of the rational.[67] If, however, the person can let go of the image, use it for divine contemplation, then the light will flood down upon it and the divinity within will triumph.

And therefore, after the image has risen to the intellect (ratio) like a shadow coming into light and superimposing itself upon the light, it [the image] is made manifest and definite inasmuch as it comes to the light, but in so far as it superimposes itself on the light, it beclouds it, overshadows it, and enfolds and covers it. If, indeed, the intellect receives the image for the purposes of contemplation only, the image is like a garment which remains outside and about itself, of which it may easily divest or strip itself. But if reason clings to the image with pleasure, the image becomes a skin about it, so that it is painful for reason to strip itself of an image to which it clings with love.[68]

The key to ascent to the divinity within is the properly formed image, an image made for contemplation. A person must not exhibit worldly love for the image, but must rather offer it forth freely with the trust that comes from divinely inspired love. According to this view, then, the best images for contemplation would be, as Richard of St. Victor later said, those representing invisible things.[69] Clearly Hugh's picture of the church was designed to be such an image, a visible representation of the invisible Body of Christ and its journey through time.

In "De unione" Hugh shows how a complicated symbol such as his picture of the church works when taken up by the human person, gathering sensual impressions into a form which can be shaped by the imagination and subsequently stamped upon the intellect. Once this has occurred, a person may move beyond and through the image to the deepest recesses of his mind, glimpsing the brilliance of recovered

---

[66] "De unione," Piazzoni, p. 886; *PL* CLXXVII, col. 287. A background for Hugh's theories can be found in Carruthers (1990), Chapter 2. Surprisingly, she does not discuss "De unione."

[67] Here Hugh reveals a suspicion of images found in both Augustine and the Pseudo-Dionysius. For a brief evaluation of patristic attitudes toward images, see Esmeijer (1978), pp. 1–6.

[68] "De unione," Piazzoni, p. 887; *PL* CLXXVII, col. 288. Translation from Kleinz (1944), pp. 42–43. See further Augustine, *De doctrina christiana*, Book I, Chapter 4, p. 8.

[69] See, for example, *The Mystical Ark*, Book II, Chapter 18; ed. Zinn, pp. 203–204.

light. It is through rightly received symbols and the action of the imagination that humans begin to find the divinity within. And this view of human perception and transformation is a general view, not designed just to describe canons regular or cloistered monks. Hugh is not selective here, and leaves the impression that all who would be restored need symbols of the Body of Christ.

In "De verbo Dei," essentially a commentary upon Hebrews 4:12–16 and 5:1–2, Hugh continues his explanation of crucial features of his hierarchical systems. Here, however, his subject is the Word, the Wisdom of the Father: for Hugh, the force that divides hierarchies into their various units, that shapes them, that holds their elements together, and, finally, that links them one to the other.[70] The concept of Christ as Word lay at the heart of much medieval speculation about language, and Hugh's treatises are no exception.[71] In this particular example, Hugh is concerned first with how speech is interchanged between God and man, and secondly with how this communication forms a model for the actions of hierarchies, both within the soul and within the church.

As the Psalmist says, "God hath spoken once."[72] This utterance, according to Hugh, exists first as the instrument through which God created his works, and second as the Son, clothed in human flesh.[73] Both of these are known today through the human speech of the Bible.[74] But this speech is alive, for, following Hebrews 4:12:

the word of God is living and effectual, and more piercing than any two-edged sword; and reaching unto the division of the soul and the spirit, of the joints also and the marrow, and is a discerner of the thoughts and intents of the heart.[75]

Thus in this treatise, too, the Word makes the invisible visible, but here because it is able to mediate between external appearances and internal realities, penetrating into the deepest human motivations. Thus each layer of the human person corresponds to a part of Hugh's picture of motivation and deeds: the skin is the action; the desires are the flesh; the thoughts are the bones, and the intentions are the marrow. Just as all time is described as present to the eye of God, so too is human action. God can see at once through the layers, looking instantly from action to motivation and understanding both in a way humans cannot. It is through the Word too that humans can best approach the divine understanding of these things, matching words, deeds, and intentions to the model of divine knowledge.

Haec autem omnia sermo Dei diiudicando penetrat, quia ille qui per sapientiam suam intus secreta nostra subtiliter intelligendo discernit, foris per doctrinam suam utiliter nos illuminando eadem intelligere facit.[76]

---

[70] McGonigle (1977, p. 84) says, "For Hugh sacred scripture has a unique function within the process of restoration since the Word-Wisdom, Jesus Christ, is truly present in the *Sacra pagina*." For more on the Victorine emphasis on the presence of the divinity within the Bible, see Zinn (1974a).

[71] See Colish (1983) and Fredborg (1988).

[72] Ps. 61:12 [62:11]. Hugh used this quotation to begin "De verbo Dei."

[73] "De verbo Dei", lines 8–11.

[74] *Ibid.*, lines 19–24.

[75] Hugh uses this verse for the basis of Parts II and III of "De verbo Dei."

[76] "De verbo Dei," lines 159–162.

(Thus the Word of God penetrates all these things by judging, since He who discerns our secrets within by acutely knowing through His own wisdom, makes us understand these same things without by illuminating for our benefit through His own teaching.)

It is the teaching of the Son that reaches through the layers of human action and stops at the gate of the heart, laying bare all intentions and explaining them, offering at the same time a model for correction. Here is the great teacher, who discerns within and explains without, making the deepest secrets of the human mind understood.[77]

In the final sections of "De verbo Dei," Hugh turns from divine speech to human speech, for just as God talks to men, so must they answer. Hugh first describes the ways in which individuals respond, settling upon the image of the book mentioned in Apoc. 20:12: ". . . and the books were opened; and another book was opened, which is the book of life; and the dead were judged by those things which were written in the books, according to their works." First, then, humans respond to God by writing the book of their lives, books which will be read and evaluated at the end of time. In order to write properly, they copy with Christ as exemplar, correcting mistakes through constant comparison with the source.[78] Thus each person is a scribe writing his book in accordance with the *liber vitae.*

But not only do humans speak through their individual books, they also have a collective voice, a voice found in the liturgy. This voice too is heard through a process of hierarchical ascent, the sound going up through a human chain: prelates speak to the Son, who in turn is the primal archbishop, leading the liturgy before the Father. Here, Hugh has returned to a favored subject, the ecclesiastical hierarchy and religious reform, and develops the idea of the Word as high priest. First Hugh argues that through his three utterances over the Son, God established Christ's office as bishop: at baptism, he was elected; at the Transfiguration, he was ordained and vested; and in Jerusalem, soon before the Passion, he was tried and confirmed in his dignity.[79] With the last passage, from the Gospel of John, Hugh claims to draw a parallel between Christ and Aaron, who also was tried and confirmed by God. On the mountain, Christ accepted the vesture of glory in ordination; in his resurrection, he put it on for offering prayers to God for humans.[80]

In the final section of "De verbo Dei," the emphasis is on Christ's workers, the bishops of the church on earth. They are to be like the great archbishop established by God the Father, virtuous within, obedient without. They are the prelates of God's kingdom, ruling it with an authority parallel to, but separate from, the prefects of kings and emperors.[81] In the reformer's political statement expressed

---

[77] This emphasis on psychology was expanded upon by Richard of St. Victor, especially in *The Twelve Patriarchs.*

[78] See lines 221–237.

[79] For this discussion, see "De verbo Dei," lines 251–259. The direct speech of God at the baptism and transfiguration are not found in the Gospel of John, whereas the speech from heaven in Jerusalem (John 12:28) is not found in the synoptic Gospels.

[80] See *ibid.*, lines 261–263.

[81] Hugh did not have a carefully worked out understanding of the relationships between Church and State. Rather, like Bernard of Clairvaux, he "only referred to Church and State when he was concerned with the protection of the Church . . ." See Chodorow (1972), pp. 58–60.

here, the two earthly kingdoms, one the political entity led by a ruler, and the other the church led by the bishops, are both seen as powerful and necessary in governing the people; but they are also plainly interpreted as separated one from the other, each with its own type of leader and its own allegiance, and with the church as superior and more important.[82] There is no room for worldly bishops who pander to the wishes of early Caesars.[83] And having the right kind of bishop, established after the model of Christ, is essential for rightful governance of the church and the salvation of its people. Through their sacred offices, bishops stand as mediators between God and humans, representing people to God and God to the people: on the one hand showing devotion that they might please Him with oblations, spiritual sacrifice, and prayers; and on the other hand, teaching the ignorant and correcting sinners.[84]

If one considers "De unione" and "De verbo Dei" at once (and in the *PL* they are presented as a continuous work), it seems that Hugh has created a deliberate comparison between symbol and thing symbolized, between the model of the church and the living action of the liturgy, between language and idea. For him, only Christ operates on both sides of these paired relationships: He is both the meaning of the Word and the Word itself; He is the agent of time, but also a character once trapped within it. It is for these reasons that He holds the key to unraveling mysteries, be they of history and its significance or of sacraments and their meanings.[85]

De sacramentis christiane fidei

The several hierarchies found in Hugh's writings were drawn together first through his model of the church as depicted in the ark treatises, and subsequently by developing a history of the church through its sacraments. This second and later mode of explication is the major goal of Hugh's masterwork, *De sacramentis christiane fidei*, now recognized as the first medieval treatise to be called a *summa* by its author.[86] It is in this treatise that one can see most clearly the interconnectedness of Hugh's ideas and the ways in which every individual description of a hierarchy is

---

[82] For the study of this development, see Ladner (1947) and the writings of Stanley Chodorow.

[83] See "De verbo Dei," lines 279–284.

[84] See *ibid.*, lines 289–296.

[85] Zinn (1990, pp. 104–106) describes the Victorine understanding of Christ's power as one which explained both Old Testament and New Testament, but without degrading the Old Testament history. These ideas will be discussed further in Chapters 12 and 13.

[86] The reference is found in the very opening of the prologue. One finds here mention of *Didascalicon* as well as a characteristically Hugonian statement about preparing the summa so that the reader's mind will not be distracted by the great numbers of treatises on the subject: "Since, therefore, I previously composed a compendium on the initial instruction in Holy Scripture, which consists in their historical reading, I have prepared the present work for those who are to be introduced to the second stage of instruction, which is allegory. By this work they may firmly establish their minds on that foundation, so to speak, of the knowledge of faith, so that such other things as may be added to the structure by reading or hearing may remain unshaken. For I have compressed this brief *summa*, as it were, of all doctrine into one continuous work, that the mind may have something definite to which it may affix and conform its attention, lest it be carried away by various volumes of writings and a diversity of readings without order or direction."

related to all the others. Hierarchical models described in a wide range of Hugh's writings can be unified with this work as a guide, and (although the correspondences are far from exact) when these models are placed one on top of the other, a vision of the church appears. In Chapters 12–14, it will be seen that the sequences as sung at the Abbey of St. Victor formed yet another of these visions of the church, and that they did so by adapting Hugh's ideas to liturgical song.

De sacramentis is, then, two things at once: it is both a history of the church through its sacraments, and an explanation of how sacraments have worked throughout history to restore humankind.[87] It is also, as I said earlier (p. 215), a fusion of two standard types of medieval treatise, the Genesis commentary and the liturgical commentary. Through this action, Hugh offers a statement about the church in time and the endless perimeters of its existence. He uses two complementary means of organizing his ideas:

First, he moves from an explanation of God's reason for creating the world and human beings to a discussion of the Trinity and free will and predestination; these are followed by a brief discussion of the angels, and in turn by the most important and by far the longest part of the book, an explanation first of the Fall, and secondly, and most extensively, of the means of restoration, the church and its sacraments.[88] *De sacramentis* outlines the Dionysian hierarchy, pictured from the top downward, from the triune God, to angels, to men, but Hugh's emphasis is on the lowest level, the stage of initiation and the persons who make it possible, the bishops and the priesthood.

Secondly, Hugh unfolds this picture of the means of salvation against a history of the sacraments. This history expounds the parallel between the acts of creation and the acts of restoration, an idea found in many of his writings, but worked out most fully here. According to this view, one finds three kinds of sacraments: those expressed by the creative force during the establishment of the world, those sacraments in Old Testament time which foreshadow sacraments to come, and the sacraments of the church, established by Christ during his years on earth and lasting in efficacy until the end of time.

In Book I of *De sacramentis* Hugh defines sacramental action and explains its history before the fall and afterwards in Old Testament time. In Book II, Hugh focuses upon the sacraments instituted by Christ, identifying them, explaining their various types, and ordering them hierarchically. Hugh talks at length of the incarnation as the great first sacrament in New Testament time. Then he moves within the church, where he is to remain for the rest of the treatise. Here are explained the ranks of the clergy, the significance of their robes and ornaments, and finally the meanings of the sacraments they administer. This is Hugh's commentary upon the allegorical and tropological meanings of the ecclesiastical hierarchy and the actions its members perform in church. It is written, of course, to instruct and inspire the

---

[87] McGonigle (1977) has demonstrated the importance of the incarnation in Hugh's sacramental theory.

[88] Hugh's organizational plan is discussed openly at several places in *SCF*, most notably in Book I, Chapter 1, pp. 28–29 (*On the sacraments*, trans. Deferrari, pp. 26–27; subsequent page references are to this edition). He admits that the major subjects of his book are the works of restoration rather than the works of foundation.

clergy that they may understand the tasks before them and perform them in the proper spirit.

Hugh's treatise is famous among theologians as one of the first attempts to identify and standardize the major sacraments – here baptism, confirmation, communion, marriage, penance, and extreme unction – and give these special prominence.[89] This is a valid description; yet it is crucial to remember that his definition of sacraments and sacramental action attempts to broaden the meanings as much as constrain them. Hugh's discussion of the acts of creation described in the first part of *De sacramentis* will serve here as an example of his working method throughout the entire treatise and demonstrate how Hugh finds sacramental action in all the events of Biblical history.

God's creation of light is interpreted as representative of the ways humans are restored. For God created light first, three days before he created the sun. This is symbolic of the ways in which humans must first rise from the darkness and chaos of their sin, and then discover the rarefied light of the divinity that shines within them, a description reminiscent of the "De unione."

First, therefore, light is created in that rational world of the human heart, and its confusion is illumined that it may be reduced to order. After this, when the interior of this confusion has been purified, the clear light of the sun comes and illuminates it.[90]

Hugh calls this the "recommendation" of a great sacrament. But here, as elsewhere in his discussion of the hexameron, he does not line up acts of creation with specific sacraments. Rather, Hugh believes that the created natural world, as described in the Bible, contains the single meaning of human redemption. And the ways in which God chose to bring the earth into being and to inspire humans to describe these things are representative of sacramental action. Thus, in the passage quoted above, Hugh describes the creation of light and subsequently the sun as a procession of events, moving from chaos to order. And by demonstrating the sacramental significance of this and other creative acts of God, Hugh shows how all the events of time were foreknown by God and that time, in its very beginning, was pregnant with the history of the church to be.[91]

But the sacramental action found in the acts of foundation is not identical to the sacraments themselves. These were instituted after the Fall for the specific purpose of restoration.[92] For sacraments, one needs people. And thus it is only after humans have come into time and fallen from grace that sacraments became necessary. Thus Hugh's famous definition of the term "sacrament" is found in this treatise after his discussion of the Fall:

[89] Hugh discusses ordination in the section on the ranks of the clergy.

[90] *SCF*, p. 17.

[91] Hugh says later in *SCF* (p. 148): "And so then from the very beginning of the world He proposed to man the sacraments of his salvation with which He might sign him with the expectation of future sanctification . . ."

[92] Thus Hugh says: "The time of the institution of the sacraments is believed to have begun from the moment when the first parent, on being expelled by merit of disobedience from the joys of paradise into the exile of this mortal life, is held with all posterity liable to the first corruption even to the end. For from the time when man, having fallen from the state of first incorruption, began to ail in body through mortality and in soul through iniquity, God at once prepared a remedy in His sacraments for restoring man" (p. 150).

Now if anyone wishes to define more fully and more perfectly what a sacrament is, he can say: "A sacrament is a corporeal or material element set before the senses without, representing by similitude and signifying by institution and containing by sanctification some invisible and spiritual grace" . . . For every sacrament ought to have a kind of similitude to the thing itself of which it is the sacrament, according to which it is capable of representing the same thing; every sacrament ought to have also institution through which it is ordered to signify this thing and finally sanctification through which it contains that thing and is efficacious for conferring the same on those to be sanctified. Now it is looked upon as important, that every sacrament indeed has a similitude from the first instruction, institution from superadded dispensation, sanctification from the applied benediction of word or sign.[93]

More than by any other writer, Hugh's definition has been inspired by Augustine.[94] For Augustine, as for Hugh, the sacrament contains not only representations, but also reality: "the *res sacramenti* is the reality symbolized by the sacrament while the *virtus sacramenti* is the effect produced by the presence of the symbolized reality."[95] But in Hugh's hands, this understanding of sacramental action becomes a means of promoting the goals of religious reform. Hugh explains not only what sacraments are, but also why they were instituted: "on account of humiliation, on account of instruction, on account of exercise."[96]

First of all, according to this explanation, humans must venerate the elements of the sacraments, water, ashes, wine, bread, to demonstrate that they lost their absolute superiority over "mute and insensible elements" after the Fall.[97] Now they must stumble blindly, seeking their invisible maker amidst the cold rocks of experience, devotedly believing, nonetheless, that traces of His glory will somehow be revealed in these dumb things.[98] And this seeking takes place in church, for it is only here that the elements are charged with invisible meaning.

Secondly, the sacraments afford humans the opportunity to grow through instruction, and this type of growth is essential to their salvation. From instruction about the sacraments in church, humans can learn the inner value or "thing" of the sacrament: "For man who knew visible things and did not know invisible could by no means have recognized divine things unless stimulated by human." Sacraments

---

[93] See p. 155.

[94] McGonigle (1977, p. 145) breaks down the influences of Hugh's definition as follows: "The first part of Hugh's definition, 'representing by similitude,' has Augustinian roots and was often quoted by Berengar. The second part of the definition, 'signifying by institution,' although it corresponds to Augustine's basic sacramental outlook, gives more emphasis to the role of Christ as the one who actually instituted the sacraments than had the Bishop of Hippo. The third and final part of the definition, 'containing grace by sanctification,' combines Augustine's notion of the sacraments as healing remedies with the Isidorian concept of the sacramental elements as veiling the *res*. Thus for Hugh the sacraments become vessels which contain God's healing power."

[95] See McGonigle (1977), p. 116.

[96] "Sacraments are known to have been instituted for three reasons: on account of humiliation, on account of instruction, on account of exercise." *SCF*, p. 156.

[97] *Ibid.*

[98] McGonigle (1977, p. 102) says: "The symbolism of nature and history merged in the liturgy. Here, water, bread, oil, and salt, everyday things of the natural world, became the means for entering into communion with the divine. And the events of sacred history recorded in the scripture become present reality through their proclamation and celebration in the divine office and Mass. This ritual representation of historic mystery could draw upon the sacramental character of nature since even before it was consciously incorporated into any symbol system, the sacramental universe was filled with God."

prove that humans need each other to come to know the invisible God and the ways in which God works. Sacramental action is a model for the way of restoration, proving to humans that they too, like the sacraments, have hidden worth buried within the elements of their flesh. By learning and believing, they can find the divine within themselves as surely as they can find the divinity within the waters of baptism or the bread of the altar.

Thirdly, the sacraments require constant practice to be understood and appreciated properly. This exercise is of great benefit to the learning and development of humans. Practicing the sacraments requires manifold trials and experiences and challenges humans to seek the one God through the varied medium of liturgical action. The sacraments established by Christ are all institutional, and must be enacted immediately outside or inside a church building.

Now in these pursuits of virtues by wonderful dispensation God provided multiplicity and variety and intermission, that the human mind in multiplicity might find exercise, in variety delight, and in intermission recreation. Certain places were consecrated, churches built, and certain times appointed at which the faithful should assemble together in order as a group to be urged to render thanks, offer prayers, fulfill vows. There God is now sought simply in silence, now praised devotedly with harmonious voices, so that in turn the hearts of the faithful are now composed for rest, now excited to devotion. Also in these divine laudations themselves the same form of praise is not always exhibited; now psalmodies fire to devotion, now hymns and songs excite to divine joy, now lessons are read for the formation of character and the instruction of a good life. Even our actions themselves in divine services do not always proceed according to the same form of institution; now erect, now prostrate, now by bending, now by turning, we express by the gesticulation of the body the state of the mind.[99]

Thus for Hugh the sacraments are not only signs of the things they represent. But they are also, like the many hierarchies found in his writings, symbolic of the process of finding God. Like the Bible and history, they too require "teachers," in their case, administrators who are always members of the ecclesiastical hierarchy. Within their hands, the sacraments become the touchstones of faith, for sacraments are empty, ludicrous even, without belief.

For the first time in the treatises studied in this chapter Hugh faces up to the problem of reconciling his constant plea for learning and understanding with the conditions of the uneducated masses of medieval Christians who could not read and had no time for study. He remains firm in the belief that sacraments require understanding, for "he who understands nothing believes nothing."[100] But whereas in the ark treatises Hugh wants *all* humans to be instructed, here he admits that many people worshiping in church cannot understand the complicated discussions he offers of the mysteries represented by the sacraments. Yet even though these believers cannot know themselves, they can and should be encouraged to believe in those who do know. They have come to church to observe the ecclesiastical hierarchy and to be inspired by their actions. Such simple worshipers are not

---

[99] *SCF*, p. 158.
[100] *SCF*, p. 169.

ultimately left out; rather, they are like the asses who feed alongside the oxen in Job 1:14 – they cannot plow and work, but at least they can eat:

> For he who believes in the believer, not unfittingly is said to believe what he believes in whom he believes, and if he does not know what it is that he believes, he does know in whom he believes. Such are the simple-minded in Holy Church who believe in the more perfect believers and knowers, who are truly saved in their simplicity ... For the simple-minded in Holy Church, although they are unable together with the perfect to search out the hidden things of the sacraments of God, yet, since they do not separate themselves from their society, placed as it were near them they feed themselves on the same faith and hope by operating well.[101]

Hugh has admitted that his elaborate hierarchies of understanding have been created for a select group: the clerics, the learned, the reformed churchmen who attempt to live perfectly according to the model of Christ. These are the humans whom Hugh feels called to see transformed and alive with divine light without and within. Yet he believes that this transformation is vital not only for clerics and the sakes of their own souls, but rather for the benefit of all humankind. Priests and prelates celebrating the sacraments within the church form the teaching image required to draw the rest of humankind upward toward God. These perfect ones reflect the light as it filters down from Christ to his angels and saints. The liturgy and the buildings that contain it magnify the glory of God as seen through his priesthood, through those human beings (living, dead and to come) who will form the Body of Christ at the end of time and who have proclaimed and are proclaiming his death and resurrection. If the clerics cannot be believed in, are not worthy, the "simplices" are left without the means to worship God.[102]

In *De sacramentis* Hugh brings his model of the church to life and explains it not as a drawing, but as a sacrament with the liturgy at its very center. For him the mechanisms of human perception are deliberately ordered so that humans can both receive symbolic representations of this great mystery, be they sacraments or artistic models, and use them to uncover the light within. The agents of this process are the members of the ecclesiastical hierarchy, especially the bishops, whose task it is to insure that all humans receive the rightly ordered images necessary for salvation. The bishops must perform the sacraments, they must pray, and they must teach and admonish. In an idealized picture of a cathedral liturgy, the bishop is the guide leading the journey from building, to ceremony, to sacrament, to God. The worshiper's vision must become ever sharper as the senses are directed from the many to the one, from the symbol to its essence, from the scriptural texts and their history to the single meaning of human redemption. Thus the very act of worship involves the process of Dionysian ascent: during Mass, the worshiper watches the ecclesiastical hierarchy at work, and is led from its actions to belief, to foretaste the sounds of the heavenly hierarchy, and, perhaps, through the administration of the sacraments, to sense the divine reality within.

The *De sacramentis* joins the idea of renovation and re-creation as found in

---

[101] *Ibid.*

[102] It is here that Hugh attempts a fusion of the Pseudo-Dionysius' understanding of "hierarch" or priest and his own ideals of an Augustinian canon regular.

salvation history with the sacraments of the church, making the renewed hierarchy of priests and prelates central to the purpose of the whole. This vision of the church takes the ideas of the *Confessions*, of renewal through the offices of the church, and draws them into the churches and rituals of the twelfth century. It makes one church of the priests of Old Testament time, the church of the Apostles, and the church of Hugh's own time, and all are a hierarchy which must be seen.

Conclusion to Part IV: Augustinian and Benedictine attitudes toward the Dedication compared

Every church was dedicated in the Middle Ages by a bishop in accordance with an ornate and venerable ceremony which has only been substantially modified since the Second Vatican Council.[103] The particular date of this historic occasion became of primary importance in the calendar of the community and was celebrated each year by the Mass and Office for the feast of the Dedication of the Church. Both Hugh of St. Victor and Suger of St. Denis described the ceremony of church dedication in their writings, Hugh in a general sense, and Suger in a specific one. Although the writings of both men are well known, as is the fact that they were contemporaries and lived in the same city, their discussions of this subject have not previously been compared. Comparison of the two accounts is especially useful here because it reveals significant differences in attitude toward the liturgy and its meanings as well as different interpretations of the relationship between the liturgy and the building in which it took place. And since these are differences between an Augustinian canon and a Benedictine monk during the first half of the twelfth century, the comparison provides a further explanation for the differences between Augustinian and Benedictine sequence repertories studied in Parts II and III of this book.

The first of the major sacraments for Hugh is not baptism or communion, as one might expect, it is rather the Dedication of the Church. In Hugh's long discussion of the sacraments in the *De sacramentis*, this comes first, forming a kind of preface to the entire section. And it is at this point in his treatise when all his pictures of the church fold one upon the other, and are explained within the context of an actual church building and religious ceremony.

In this brief section Hugh explains what a church building is and how the liturgy, clergy, and people relate to it. Here the church building becomes a outer shell for the inner significance of its contents: people, clergy, altar and host. And taken altogether, the building and its liturgy form a sacrament of the history of the church in time.

Hugh claims priority for the dedication ceremony on two counts. It must come first because until a church has been dedicated, no other sacraments can take place.[104]

---

[103] Aspects of the medieval feast and theories of its origins are described in Bowen (1941), Willis (1968), Martimort *et al.* (1986), pp. 100–101, Sheerin (1980), and Powell (1983).

[104] "It seems that we must speak first about the sacrament of the dedication of a church, in which all the other sacraments are celebrated" (*SCF*, p. 279). This idea is found in Ivo of Chartres as well in his sermon on the feast of the dedication. See *PL* CLXII, col. 531.

But, much more importantly, the dedication of a church is its baptism, and baptism is the first of the sacraments.[105] And therefore in discussion of the dedication, Hugh seizes an opportunity to make yet another parallel between the church and the human soul.

First, as has been said, we must speak of the dedication of a church just as of the first baptism by which the church itself in a manner is baptized, that in it after a fashion men may be baptized to be regenerated unto salvation. For the first sacrament, as it were, is recognized in baptism through which all the faithful are computed among the members of the Body of Christ through the grace of the new regeneration.[106]

The church building and its dedication are representative of the entire process of restoration. In it, the visible truth of the invisible process of salvation is made manifest. And the church, like Hugh's drawings of Noah's ark, is set before the human senses so that the single meaning of the sacraments and their history may be understood and the beholders may be initiated into the process necessary for their salvation. In a key statement Hugh says:

For what is expressed visibly in a figure in this house is exhibited entirely through invisible truth in the faithful soul.[107]

Thus the church building made of many stones is like both the faithful soul made of many virtues and the Body of Christ made of many saints. Its purpose is to show forth these things that they may be understood, to witness to the "faith formed in it."[108] In his description of the church building and its dedication, Hugh is specific about how this happens, explaining floor, walls, altar and the sacramental actions of the bishop. Throughout, he emphasizes that the bishop is a representative of Christ, a fully religious figure who acts as mediator between God and humankind – the opposite of the stereotypical worldly bishop so frequently attacked by reformers in the early twelfth century.

Hugh singles out three areas of the building for commentary, each of which is represented in the ark treatises as well. First he concentrates upon the pavement. The bishop processes from the left corner of the east to the right corner of the west, inscribing the Latin alphabet on the floor, and then from the right corner of the east to the left of the west, inscribing the Greek alphabet on the floor.[109] In so doing, he traces a giant cross made of matters. For Hugh this action "expresses the form of the cross which is impressed upon the minds of the people by the faith of the evangelical preaching." Letters of the simple alphabet, the basic tools of reading and writing, demonstrate that "carnal and rude people are initiated by the first and simple

---

[105] See *SCF*, p. 282: "The sacrament of baptism is the first among all the sacraments upon which salvation is proven to rest."

[106] *SCF*, p. 279.

[107] *Ibid.*

[108] *Ibid.*

[109] For Ivo of Chartres, the inscribing of the alphabet represents that the teaching of the church must be expressed in simple terms by bishops and other ministers. See his sermon "De sacramentis dedicationis," cols. 530–531. The origins of the alphabet ceremony have been disputed in scholarly literature, and an early suggestion that the ceremony derived from the methods used by Roman surveyors has not found favor.

teaching of faith." Furthermore, the two different alphabets represent that the Jews came first and then the Gentiles, and both are united by Christ. The cross drawn in the bottom of Noah's ark also represents the people of the Old Testament and the New Testament joined, and bears a similar interpretation, although here in *De sacramentis* the emphasis on teaching is much stronger.

The altar is the most important part of the church, and is doubtless represented in the ark treatises by the single cubit to which the entire vessel tends. In the ark treatises, this cubit, inscribed with a cross and a picture of the Lamb, sits atop the great pillar representing the Book of Wisdom and the tree of life. In *De sacramentis* the altar is the Son, upon whom gifts to the Father are offered. When the bishop dedicates the altar with crosses of oil, he shows "the grace of the Holy Spirit whose fullness preceded on the head, then in participation flowed to the limbs."[110] Just as in the ark treatises, this is the metaphorical center point from which all meaning comes.

In *De sacramentis* this flowing-out of the meaning and power from Christ to his Apostles and then to the people is represented by the drawing of the twelve dedication crosses on the walls of the church. Hugh says:

Now the oil demonstrates the grace of the Holy Spirit whose fullness preceded on the head; then participation flowed to the limbs. From the consecrated altar twelve crosses are anointed on the walls, because spiritual grace descended from Christ upon the apostles, so that they proclaimed the mystery of the cross with the faith of the Trinity through the four parts of the world.[111]

In Paris, this was one of the most dramatic parts of the dedication ceremony, marked by the symbolic singing of the twelfth-century sequence "Laudes crucis."[112]

In the ark treatises, the three nesting compartments of the vessel each have four ladders in their corners reaching up to the top. These ladders are then twelve in number and each of them has ten stairs. All must struggle upward to the lamb at the top through "twelve ladders, that is through the apostolic teaching, through ten steps, that is through the ten precepts of the law, from the four corners of the world filled with the faith of the trinity and the evangelical teaching."[113] The walls of the ark and the walls of the church represent the teaching of the faith and show the ways to rise upward from the simple truth to the mystery at the center of it all.[114] The church building as Hugh describes it is a teaching machine, representing history and its single meaning, and showing how to understand the mystery and be changed by it. It is a carefully organized history book, but it is also a similitude of the human soul and, most importantly, a sacrament. And it is peopled by teachers and preachers

[110] *SCF*, p. 282.

[111] *Ibid.*

[112] The singing of "Laudes crucis" at this point in the dedication ceremony is notated in several northern French pontificals and made its way into the pontifical of Durandus of Mende, Book II, Chapter 3; in Andrieu, ed., *Le Pontifical romain*, III, p. 491.

[113] ". . . per duodecim scalas, id est per apostolicam doctrinam, per decem tramites, id est per decem praecepta legis, a quatuor angulis mundi fide Trinitatis imbuti et doctrina evangelica." *The Mystical Ark*, Chapter VII, cols. 692–693.

[114] A treatise on the allegorical significance of systems of ladders was attributed to Hugh by Baron (1963), pp. 225–244. The work exists in a single known copy from the thirteenth century, Brussels, Bibl. R., 9878, fols. 39v–49r.

from the Old Testament and the new who witness the faith. These men and women are joined in a common purpose which is explained by the teacher in the present time, the bishop, who functions with the teaching power and authority of Christ.

Hugh's vision of the church is a reformer's vision on several counts. The church and its well-ordered clergy are the central witnesses to the heavenly hierarchies of the angels and the Trinity. Great emphasis is given in Hugh's writings to the clerical responsibility for teaching and preaching, much more, in fact, than is assigned to prayer. For even as they pray and administer the sacraments, the bishops and clergy teach, and those who cannot know, know through them. Thus the episcopal figure in the dedication ceremony described by Hugh "goes around the altar verbo et exemplo" – with the very cry of reformed clergy throughout the twelfth century. And he shows himself "common to all, both by sprinkling the entire church, as it were, by purifying all and giving care to all." Hugh's bishop teaches by demonstration, as does the teacher in Augustine's early treatise *De magistro*.

Abbot Suger, like Hugh of St. Victor, was deeply interested in history.[115] But whereas Hugh writes histories of the Church Universal, Suger writes them of contemporary kings of France and of his own church, and especially for the purposes of perpetuating the rights, properties, monies, goods, and fame of that church, long after he could no longer look out for them himself. In fact, Suger's treatises on the building and consecration of the new church at St. Denis are the legalistic writings of an administrator, filled with the language of medieval charters.[116] Chief among Suger's purposes in writing them were to ensure that the community would pray in perpetuity for his soul, and to teach the monks how to remember and care for the legacy entrusted to them by Suger.[117] Suger's most famous description of the power of liturgical art is to be found in the *Liber de rebus*. In this passage, there is a love of the bejeweled glare of religious objects as understood within a general Dionysian framework.[118] The lights seize attention and draw the soul upwards through their material splendor to a foretaste of the glories of heaven, the meditator remaining, of course, earthbound, unable to sustain the vision. Yet, still in the midst of a Dionysian reverie, Suger veers off suddenly in another direction, wondering "Do they really have more and better jewels than we do at Hagia Sophia?" Subsequently, as the passage continues, Suger decides that if

[115] For discussion of the Pseudo-Dionysian aspects of Suger's historical writings, see Gabrielle M. Spiegel, "History as Enlightenment: Suger and the *Mos Anagogicus*," in *ASSD*, pp. 151–158.

[116] Panofsky, ed., *On the Abbey Church*, pp. 141–145, provides the following information regarding the dates of Suger's two treatises, related directly to Suger's three-stage building campaign (west facade, by 1140; choir, dedicated in 1144; nave, begun in the 1140s but not completed). The *Liber de rebus in administratione sua gestis* was written over a great number of years, having been begun around 1122 and not completed until 1149. The *Libellus alter de consecratione ecclesiae Sancti Dionysii* was written soon after the consecration of the choir, between 1144 and 1147. Both treatises are contemporary with Hugh of St. Victor's *De sacramentis*.

[117] Suger, as might be expected, was remembered lavishly at St. Denis. The death notice itself is terse, as is typical of necrology as a whole, but Suger's anniversary was celebrated on January 4, as was Charles the Bald's, and on the second of Nones in each month both men were commemorated in the liturgy. See *ODSP*, vol. I, p. 306. A monthly commemoration is very unusual and betokens the highest esteem.

[118] *De rebus in administratione*, Chapter XXXIII; in Suger, *On the Abbey Church*, ed. Panofsky, pp. 62–64. For Panofsky's explication of this passage, see *On The Abbey Church*, p. 21. Subsequent page references are to Panofsky's edition of *De rebus*.

the Greeks seem to have fewer treasures, it may be only because they have hidden their wealth away to protect it during troubled times. Suger thinks, then, if treasures are had, they should be exposed so that all can see them, as his are. And finally he speaks of how the communion vessels should be of the finest materials to honor Christ properly, and praises his Lord, citing passages from the Apocalypse.

This alternating pattern of gloating, worrying, and praising occurs repeatedly throughout Suger's writings of his church, enough to make one suspect that here is the real Suger: perhaps in passages such as this, one glimpses how he would have talked when showing a respected friend his improvements.[119] He would have seemed a man of worldly interests, caught up in the monkish life because it served his ambitions well, and devoted to increasing his revenues, to promoting the glory and splendor of his "estate," St. Denis, and its alliance with the Capetian dynasty. Yet he would also have appeared as a wise and reflective administrator, a believing man, one who suspected that his treasure lay too much in things of this earth, and feared, perhaps, for his own salvation as a consequence.[120]

The opening of *Liber de rebus in administratione* forms a telling contrast with the opening of Hugh's treatise on the moral meaning of Noah's ark. In Hugh's work, the brethren beseech him to explain how they may rise above the floods of time, of mutability, and come to the stability of God. In Suger's work, the brethren entreat him to record the fruits of his labor, the munificence of God toward the abbey, and "the multiplication of improved possessions, in the construction of buildings, and in the accumulation of gold, silver, most precious gems and very good textiles."[121] As a teacher and reformer, Hugh is concerned with his elaborate group of textbooks and the force they will have in shaping and instructing members of the clergy. As abbot and overseer, Suger wishes to keep his ecclesiastical kingdom intact, protected against the inaction of "bad successors."[122] Hugh's writings proclaim "learn!" and Suger's "hold on!": the difference between masters and administrators, then as now.

Suger's attitude toward the liturgy at St. Denis, freely expressed in his histories of the building, contrasts markedly with that of Hugh of St. Victor. Of course, Suger was no bishop and his church was no cathedral. He was a monk, albeit a very special one, his church was a monastic church, and he wrote history in the monastic tradition. It should not be surprising, then, that the understanding of the liturgy and the church contained in his writings is thoroughly Benedictine, and of the older order, far removed from Hugh's view. Hugh wrote for clerics and bishops-to-be; Suger wrote to promote the venerable Dionysian monasticism of the Benedictines

[119] Robert W. Hanning says of Suger, "If time – relentless, wearing time – stands as one great enemy of Suger's self-appointed role as guardian and improver of the patrimony of Saint Denis, it does not stand alone. Suger worries constantly in his writings about another enemy: theft (with its related evils of loss and vandalism)." See his "Suger's Literary Style and Vision," *ASSD*, p. 148.

[120] The extent to which Suger's requests for prayers and his penitential utterances supersedes mere convention is described in Clark Maines, "Good Works, Social Ties, and the Hope for Salvation: Abbot Suger and Saint-Denis," *ASSD*, pp. 77–94.

[121] See *De rebus*, p. 41.

[122] Suger was well aware of the losses incurred through bad administration. When describing the fabrication of his great chalice, he recalls that it was necessary as a substitute for "another one which had been lost as a pawn in the time of our predecessor." See *De rebus*, p. 77.

at St. Denis. And he was far prouder of its age and long-standing tradition than of anything else. Suger's understanding of the liturgy goes hand in hand with Anne Robertson's explanation of the chant and ceremony at St. Denis: the chant repertory was filled with allusions to the patron saint from the beginning and the monks jealously guarded this tradition, not changing it in the twelfth century in any major way.[123] Yet this reluctance to introduce new music existed at twelfth-century St. Denis in spite of the new church and in spite of the striking new changes introduced into other twelfth-century Parisian liturgies, most notably at the Cathedral of Notre Dame and at the Abbey of St. Victor.

When Suger thinks of the liturgy, he thinks of angels:

Certe nec nos nec nostra his deservire sufficimus. Si de sanctorum Cherubim et Seraphim substantia nova creatione nostra mutaretur, insufficientem tamen et indignum tantae et tam ineffabili hostiae exhiberet famulatum.[124]

(Surely neither we nor our possessions suffice for this service. If, by a new creation, our substance were reformed from that of the holy cherubim and seraphim, it would still offer an insufficient and unworthy service for so great and so ineffable a victim;)

Men are not worthy celebrants; their implements are unworthy as well. The ideal celebration of the angels cannot be seen on earth, and could not even if men could somehow be recast in angelic molds. The liturgical celebration must, however, try to reflect as best it can the glorious beauties of the heavenly host. And it is when this happens that Suger thinks the liturgy is most successful.[125]

When Suger described the chapel of St. Romanus at St. Denis, he claimed those who served Mass within it were pleased to feel "as though they were already dwelling, in a degree, in Heaven while they sacrifice."[126] It was the atmosphere of this place that made such feelings possible: the chapel was quiet and secluded. In the church of St. Denis during the magnificent dedication ceremony of the new chevet, Suger found heavenly parallels as well, but these were created by the splendid building, the shining robes, and the host of clergy invited to dedicate the twenty altars. The bishops, representing the major sees of France, consecrated all the various altars at once, and then all sang Mass at the same time, each at his respective altar.[127] For Suger, the effect was sublime:

Qui omnes tam festive, tam solemniter, tam diverse, tam concorditer, tam propinque, tam hilariter ipsam altarium consecratione missarum solemnem celebrationem superius inferiusque peragebant, ut ex ipsa sui consonantia et cohaerente harmoniae gratae melodia potius angelicus

---

[123] See Robertson (1991). The changes Suger did institute are described on pp. 235–248.

[124] *De rebus*, pp. 64–66.

[125] In this same passage, Suger speaks of the "detractors," those who would claim that "a saintly mind, a pure heart, and a faithful intention" are what one really needs for a communion service. The abbot concedes their importance, but gives no ground: "we must do homage also through the outward ornaments of sacred vessels . . ." See *De rebus*, p. 67. Surely Suger realized how little merit some of his arguments had with religious reformers.

[126] See *De rebus*, p. 45.

[127] And where, one wonders, was the Bishop of Paris? Perhaps the dedication occurred too close to the death of Stephen of Senlis for his successor to have been functioning.

quam humanus concentus aestimaretur, et ab omnibus corde et ore acclamaretur, "Benedicta gloria Domini de loco suo," (Ez. 3:12).[128]

(After the consecration of the altars all these [dignitaries] performed a solemn celebration of Masses, both in the upper choir and in the crypt, so festively, so solemnly, so different and yet so concordantly, so close [to one another] and so joyfully that their song, delightful by its consonance and unified harmony, was deemed a symphony angelic rather than human; and that all exclaimed with heart and mouth: "Blessed be the glory of the Lord, from his place," [Ez 3:12].)

This famous passage, well known to historians and students of the arts, demonstrates Suger's Dionysian view of the liturgy and its chant. the celebrants are angelic through the solemn beauty of their songs and actions and are empowered to "Bless the Lord from his place." Here Suger uses the quotation from Ezechiel to join his own description of the ecclesiastical hierarchy to a parallel description in the Pseudo-Dionysius, *The Celestial Hierarchy*, Book VII:

Hence, theology has transmitted to men of earth those hymns sung by the first ranks of the angels whose gloriously transcendent enlightenment is thereby made manifest. Some of these hymns, if one may use perceptible images, are like the "noise of many waters" (Ez. 1:24) as they proclaim "Blessed be the glory of the Lord, from his place." (Ez. 3:12).

Hugh of St. Victor also commented upon the passage from Ezechiel as found in the Pseudo-Dionysius. When he expounded Ez. 3:12, "Blessed be the glory of the Lord from his place," Hugh drew a parallel between the sublime praising of the highest rank of angels and human praise.[129] According to him, our human praise necessarily leads to our having God within us, for when we praise, we are in the right state to receive his light. Mortals shine most radiantly when they give praise from the heart, for it is then that God is most fully within them, and the action is circular: the more we praise the more we know God, the more we know God the better we praise, and the circle draws worshipers upward toward the divine light. It is by praising the Lord that humans become "his place," a divine dwelling.[130] In his discussion of praise, Hugh tightened the analogy between the ecclesiastical hierarchy and the individual soul, an analogy central to his entire vision of the church.

The clergy and the ceremony as Suger has arranged them and described them form an image of the angelic liturgy. Through the sacramental action of anointing and of the eucharist, the "material is joined to the immaterial" and God both "reforms the purer ones to their original condition" and thereby "restores and miraculously transforms the present into the heavenly kingdom."[131] Although it is worked out on an elementary level, Suger's theological explanation of the ceremony and its power is firmly rooted in his understanding of a Dionysian liturgy: it is a liturgy that looks and sounds in accordance with the Biblical and Pseudo-Dionysian depictions of the angelic hosts. The more closely human liturgy is able to

---

[128] *Libellus alter de consecratione*, Chapter VII; in Suger, *On the Abbey Church*, ed. Panofsky, pp. 118–120. The text from Ezekiel was sung as a responsory at Matins for the Feast of the Dedication of the Church.
[129] See Hugh of St. Victor, *Commentary upon the Celestial Hierarchy*, cols. 1067–1072.
[130] *Ibid.*, col. 1069.
[131] See *Libellus*, Chapter VII; Panofsky edn., p. 121.

mirror the revealed splendor of the heavenly Jerusalem, the better it is able to praise God.

But Suger is interested in creating the parallel between men and angels for the very sake of its beauty and its fittingness for the worship of God. He has little to say about the things that concern Hugh, about morality, purity of life, the ability to preach and teach successfully. Suger evidences none of Hugh's concern for the outward actions of the celebrants witnessing the inward conditions of their souls. And Suger shows less interest than Hugh in the effect of the liturgy on the people (although, in truth, neither shows much). He is instead relieved to report that while the splendid display of multiple consecrations was beginning, the king and his men were outside the church keeping the people at bay:

> how so glorious and admirable men celebrated the wedding of the Eternal Bridegroom so piously that the king and the attending nobility believed themselves to behold a chorus celestial rather than terrestrial, a ceremony divine rather than human. The populace milled around outside with the drive of its intolerable magnitude; and when the aforesaid chorus sprinkled the holy water onto the exterior, competently aspersing the walls of the church with the aspergillum, the king himself and his officials kept back the tumultuous impact and protected those returning to the doors with canes and sticks.[132]

Thus although both Suger and Hugh think of the liturgy in Dionysian terms they watch the dedication ceremony with different eyes: Suger is most interested in the ways the human liturgy demonstrates the unseen splendors of Paradise. The ancient chant of his monastery was a capable vehicle for the liturgical expression of this ideal. Hugh, on the other hand, cares about the liturgy as a model for human behavior and as a picture of present and past realities fused together. It must preach and teach; it must demonstrate that the celebrating clergy are a reformed clergy, part of the vast ecclesiastical network beginning with Christ and spreading out through the Apostles to all teachers and preachers to come. Hugh's liturgical ideal was not sufficiently served by the monastic tradition, its chants and ceremonies. It required liturgical change, in this case, a new kind of texts and music. These would be found in sequences of the sort written in abundance in twelfth-century Paris, and championed by Augustinian canons throughout northern Europe in the second half of the twelfth and the early thirteenth centuries. The Victorines designed the unique music of their sequences so that they formed a sounding image of the church, of the church as envisioned by their master.

---

[132] *Ibid.*, p. 115.

Part V

The church, the ceremony, and the sequences at St.
Victor in the late twelfth century

11

Themes of reform in the Victorine church and the sequence repertory

Introduction

The great period of development at the Abbey of St. Victor during the second half of the twelfth century was founded upon an understanding of the history of the abbey, the intentions of its founders and the first generation, and the writings of Hugh of St. Victor. There is no surer way to demonstrate this than through study of the church (what little can be known of it), the liturgy, the sermon literature, and, particularly, the sequence repertory. In the designs of these, it is possible to witness the many ways in which a religious community expressed its historical, political, and religious identity, celebrating daily at Mass, in the Office, and in the chapter, and with many processions through the church and its immediate environs, where it came from, what it stood for, who it was. And, indeed, it is through knowledge of these things that medieval artifacts, be they buildings, texts and music, relics, or even manuscripts, come to life, revealing the complex meanings they once held for those who created them and subsequently used them.

The reasons for the interconnectedness between Victorine theology and Victorine liturgical and religious life may well be related to the continuity provided by the first abbot, Gilduin. Throughout the first forty-seven years of the abbey's existence he was there, and from 1113 to his death in 1155 he bore the responsibility of chief administrator. He had been one of the original band of men coming from the Cathedral of Notre Dame with Archdeacon William in 1108; he doubtless welcomed the young Hugh, is probably the unnamed figure who pressed him to organize his writings into textbooks,[1] and surely was present at Hugh's death in 1141; he was called to Louis VI's deathbed to hear his last confession; and he witnessed several charters in his lifetime demonstrating his active role in securing rights and properties for his abbey and in promoting the goals of religious reformers

---

[1] In *SCF*, p. 7, Hugh says, "Prevailed upon by your frequent entreaty, I am truly entering upon an arduous and laborious task, not merely by compression to reduce to a compendium the whole content of Divine Scriptures, but also by explanation to bring to light the secrets of their profundity. I, indeed, offer the beginning of this work with ready devotion; and I hopefully promise its completion." Preparing editions of the writings of their master theologians was a major task of the Victorine scriptorium. See Gasparri (1991), pp. 132–133.

throughout Paris.[2] Thus Gilduin created a bond between the first and second generations of Victorines. One can suppose the history of the abbey in the second half of the century would have been quite different if he had been replaced by a long-lived man of comparable administrative talents and dedication to this single place.[3]

Yet, even though the abbey had various administrative crises during the second half of the century, this was also an active period, a time for the organization and production of a wide array of materials, both liturgical and educational, some of which were of sufficient general interest to be circulated throughout France and even beyond.[4] Projects that were begun with the blessings of Gilduin, and sometimes undoubtedly with those of Hugh and Adam as well, were continued: Victorine scholars produced theology and scriptural exegesis of major significance, and had in Richard of St. Victor a worthy successor to Hugh.[5] Among the other writers working alongside Richard and after his death in 1174 were Achard, Andrew, and Godefroy.[6] During this time also, Richard's sermons were collected and translated into Old French, forming the first vernacular homiliarium, and were transmitted throughout the kingdom;[7] two major organs of governance (both of which were undoubtedly begun by Abbot Gilduin), the Victorine *Liber ordinis*, a customary, and the Victorine *Liber ordinarius*, an ordinal, were completed;[8] initial steps were taken in establishing what was to become the most important library in Paris;[9] and the Victorine scriptorium was of major importance in copying books and charters for the king and other religious institutions.[10] Additions were made to the Victorine church and monastic buildings, although the major portions of these seem to have been not only begun but also completed by Abbot Gilduin.[11] And the

[2] Abbot Gilduin was in the small group of men who negotiated the peace between Bishop Stephen and the canons of Notre Dame. See *CEND*, vol. I, p. 338.

[3] He was, in fact, replaced by Achard of St. Victor, who, although certainly capable, only stayed with the office until 1161 when he became Bishop of Avranches. See Châtillon (1969).

[4] The most significant crisis took place during the abbacy of Ervisius and inspired Richard of St. Victor to plead to the pope for the abbey. For a full description of these events, see Richard of St. Victor, *L'Edit d'Alexandre*, ed. Châtillon and Lohrmann (1991).

[5] For an introduction to the works and thought of Richard of St. Victor, see Châtillon (1952) and *The Twelve Patriarchs*, ed. Zinn, a translation of various of Richard's writings. Apparently Richard came to the Abbey of St. Victor in the early 1150s; thus he did not know Hugh, except through his writings, but did know Abbot Gilduin. For an investigation of Richard's sources and his uses of them, see Feiss (1979).

[6] Of the three, Andrew has received the greatest attention, and his works are now appearing in the *CCCM*. The pioneer in the study of Andrew was Beryl Smalley. See Smalley (1938, 1939, and particularly 1983). Godefroy's *Microcosmus* has been edited, but his other writings, most notably his sermons, have not been, an unfortunate lack for twelfth-century studies. Achard's sermons have been edited by Jean Châtillon. A discussion of the Victorine exegetical tradition is found in de Lubac (1961), Part II, vol. I, pp. 361–435.

[7] See Robson (1952).

[8] *Liber ordinis*, ed. Jocqué and Milis; the *Liber ordinarius*, which exists in a copy from the late twelfth or early thirteenth century (Paris, BN lat. 14506), has, unfortunately, never been edited. Later copies of the ordinal are found in Paris, BN lat. 14455, 14456, and 15064 as well as Paris, Bibl. Mazar. 3356. The customary will be referred to as LO and the twelfth-century ordinal as Ord. The question of authorship of the LO is discussed in Jocqué (1991), pp. 56–57, note 7.

[9] Gilbert Ouy has edited the sixteenth-century catalog of Claude de Grandrue. There remains much work to be done on the history of the collection itself. The pioneering work on the history of the library is Franklin (1865). For recent introduction to the subject, see Nebbiai-Dalla Guardia (1986).

[10] See especially Gasparri (1991).

[11] The Victorine necrology states that the beginnings of the building took place during the tenure of Bishop Gilbert (1117–1123). See *ODSP*, p. 538.

Victorines consolidated their position, inherited from Gilduin, as confessors to the clerics of Paris.[12]

It is in the midst of such activity that the Victorine sequence repertory was expanded and a new set of melodies developed for many of the texts, both old and new. As with so many other projects representative of Victorine enterprise during the second half of the twelfth century it was begun in the first half. Like Abbot Gilduin, the sequence repertory looked both backwards and forwards at the same time. But it did not die; rather, it remained in place, and thirteenth-century Victorines were demonstrably reluctant to change it. Even after certain aspects of its design were no longer understood, the community undoubtedly recognized it as the only major part of the liturgy that was uniquely and powerfully Victorine. It was designed with the twelfth-century church in mind, and served to enliven the meanings that the architectural space and its decoration had for the community as a whole. And it promoted the Victorine ideals of teaching, preaching, and the common life, all within a complicated system of textual and musical interrelationships that exhibit Hugh's ideas about the church, the sacraments, and religious art and its instructive purposes.

To introduce the liturgical statement created by the Victorine sequence repertory, I will first concentrate upon the major themes developed in the church and liturgy in the twelfth century. In the discussion to follow, the claim is not that the features of the liturgy described are unique to the Abbey of St. Victor. All occurred commonly enough, some more frequently than others. I would argue, however, that ordinals and customaries from particular churches do often suggest which aspects of the liturgy were of greatest interest to their institutions and communities. Since the recipe for such books was not standard, it follows that those aspects of the liturgy described by the compilers in the richest detail were those which mattered most in their particular use. The parts of the liturgy examined below (pp. 260–266) stand out in the Victorine ordinal and customary; the description of the foot-washing ceremony, for example, is especially detailed when compared with most other contemporary accounts.[13]

The church at St. Victor

Of the twelfth-century church of St. Victor, not one known stone remains; all surviving parts of the church were destroyed during the Revolution and its aftermath. On the left bank, down toward the river from the Montagne Ste.

---

[12] Several important penitentials were produced at the Abbey of St. Victor in the early thirteenth century, those by Peter of Poitiers (ed. 1980), Robert of Flamborough (ed. 1971), and Thomas of Chobham (ed. 1968). In addition to the introductions to these editions, see also Bonnard (1904–07), vol. I, pp. 194–199, Cheney (1937), and, especially, Longère (1991), pp. 300–312. An evaluation of the Victorine penitential writers is found in Baldwin (1970), vol. I, pp. 48–49. The influence of Peter the Chanter upon these Victorine writers from the early thirteenth century is emphasized.

[13] For an overview of the medieval foot-washing ceremony (mandatum) and its implications for modern liturgical practices, see Jeffery (1992).

Plate 11.1   The Abbey Church of St. Victor, after an illustration in the Atlas of Jean-Baptiste de Saint-Victor, "The church at St. Victor"

Geneviève, one finds the Parisian church of St.-Nicolas-du-Chardonnet. This building stands on land donated to the parish centuries ago by the Abbey of St. Victor, and recently contained in its relic chapel the foot of St. Victor (stolen around 1960);[14] elsewhere in the church hung a painting of the Pentecost by the School of Jean Restout (stolen from the church in 1972) which once belonged to the Abbey of St. Victor as well;[15] nearby is an infirmary dedicated to St. Victor.[16] A few blocks away, one can find the rue St. Victor and the rue Jussieu, the latter cutting through the area where the Victorine church once stood.[17] In the various *Procès-verbaux* of the Commission du Vieux Paris are reports of minor excavations and investigations into the area: a report of 1898 contains a photograph of an "ancient" door of St. Victor, describing it as located at the rue de Varenne;[18] the most important report

[14] The foot of St. Victor was procured for the abbey by Jean, duc de Berry in 1402 (see Perdrizet [1933], p. 178) and became one of the Abbey's most cherished relics. A feast was established in the fifteenth century in honor of its reception. The relic came to the church of St. Nicholas-du-Chardonnet after the Revolution.

[15] Mention of these objects and their thievery are in Châtillon (1975), p. 63. He reports that a "tres beau parement d'autel" which once belonged to St. Victor and was in the church of Saint-Spire in Corbeil has also disappeared.

[16] L. 893, no. 12 of the French National Archive is a charter from 1230. It states that William, Bishop of Paris and the abbot of St. Victor, gave land in Chardonnet to construct a chapel.

[17] See details from the map of excavations made in 1931 in Willesme (1981), p. 102. The excavations were made in conjunction with preparing the area for the Métro stop at the place Jussieu.

[18] See Sellier (1902) and Bautier (1991), pp. 36–37. I have been unable to ascertain whether this door still exists, and publish this information in the hope that it may inspire someone with long periods of time in Paris to try to find it.

described the activities of 1931, when the area of the church was excavated to make way for the métro station at the place Jussieu. The article contains a map (1791) of the abbey, with details of the excavation drawn in as well as a photograph of tombs in the excavated crypt.[19] The tombs indicated in the map are Carolingian sarcophagi, attesting to the importance of the ancient oratory upon which the original Victorine church was built.[20] The site of the church is now covered over by massive modern buildings (belonging to the Nouvelle Faculté des Sciences) whose presence dampens any hope of future excavation.[21] When they were built in the 1960s, another Carolingian tomb and some Victorine tombs were uncovered as well, but these were, unfortunately, neither saved nor studied in any detail.[22] According to Jean Châtillon, the western part of the church and its portal were situated at 1–5, place Jussieu; the nave covered 17–19, rue Jussieu, and the choir and apse stood where one now finds the enclosure of the Nouvelle Faculté des Sciences.[23]

These excavations of the church at St. Victor are, however, not of the twelfth-century church but of its replacement, built in the first half of the sixteenth century with funds provided by King Francis I.[24] Various aspects of the work on the second church are recorded in the chronicle of Pierre Driart of St. Victor, whose informative journal covers the years from 1522 to 1535.[25] The cornerstone of the new church was laid in 1517 and the building continued intermittently thereafter.[26] In 1524 the first stone of the new choir was laid.[27] In May 1525, on the feast of Pentecost, High Mass was said by the Abbot of St. Victor at the great altar erected in the new church;[28] Mass was sung in the new church in July 1530, by which time only the choir was done.[29] Subsequent work was interrupted in 1540, and appar-

---

[19] See A. Grimault, "Compte rendu de la visite effectuée aux fouilles de la place Jussieu," *Procès-Verbaux de la Commission du Vieux Paris, 1931* (Paris, 1937). Willesme (1981) provides many citations of the *Procès-verbaux* which are of interest to Victorine scholars: Charles Sellier (1902), pp. 169–171, (1907), p. 95; Charles Magne, "Fouilles place de Jussieu et dans la Halle aux vins" (1913), p. 244; M. Fleury, "Fouilles à l'emplacement de l'abbaye de Saint-Victor" (1974), pp. 34–36.

[20] See further discussion in Bautier (1991), pp. 26–27.

[21] See Moreau-Lalande (1979).

[22] This sad neglect of historical treasures is described in Moreau-Lalande (1979). In the first half of the twentieth century, little work had been done on the Abbey of St. Victor and its school, and scholars could not guess the great interest medievalists would one day have in the history of this particular church. Furthermore, the Victorines never became a major order, even during their great heyday in the twelfth and early thirteenth centuries, and they were not reestablished after the French Revolution. Unlike the Benedictines, Dominicans, Franciscans, Cistercians, and other medieval orders, they had no institutional historians to research and preserve the glories of their past.

[23] See Châtillon (1975), p. 62.

[24] Little survives from the sixteenth-century church either. A baptismal font dated 1542 is in the chapel of the Ecole des Beaux-Arts. Most important, however, are the choir stalls made for the new church. Surviving Victorine stalls are in the churches of Fontenay-en-Parisis (Val d'Oise), Soignolles-en-Brie (Seine et Marne) and Brottereaux (Eure), and in the chapel of the lycée in Evreux; twenty other stalls are in the church of Valenton (Val de Marne). All these sixteenth-century stalls were sold by the Victorines in 1779 in the hopes of replacing them. This preserved them from the inevitable destruction of the revolution. See Châtillon (1975), pp. 63–64.

[25] For discussion of the building at St. Victor during the sixteenth century, see Willesme (1991), pp. 100–102.

[26] See Driart, *Journal*, ed. Bournon, p. 77.

[27] *Ibid.*, pp. 89 and 96.

[28] *Ibid.*, p. 96.

[29] *Ibid.*, p. 145.

ently never finished, yet during this time not only the church, but other monastic buildings, too, had been significantly, if not completely, restored or rebuilt.[30]

From early engravings and historical reports, one can tell that the sixteenth-century church incorporated some parts of the original twelfth-century building.[31] A twelfth-century tower stood at one corner.[32] The original choir was retained as a chapel and was dedicated to St. Denis. Jean-Baptiste de Saint-Victor, writing in 1822, recalls that this chapel stood at the extreme end of the chevet and was an elegant Gothic structure. His description claims that this twelfth-century chapel, which must have been built before the mid century, was lighted by two bays, high and narrow, offering at their summit very well-made keystones.[33] Its original doors stood behind the main altar of the new church. It is reasonable to suppose that some glass from the original church remained in this chapel: according to E. H. Langlois (1832), twelfth-century stained glass existed in the church on the eve of the Revolution; Thiery (1788) mentions that the chapel was "ornés des peintures charmantes."[34] Jean-Baptiste de Saint-Victor reports that the original twelfth-century crypt, dedicated to the Virgin Mary, survived in the new building beneath the main altar, and a twelfth-century portal was retained in the new structure, but was replaced in 1760.[35] According to this same author, one wall of the great cloister had columns from the late twelfth or early thirteenth century, and at the end of the second cloister was the chapel called "the infirmary," which "by the elegance of its colonnades and the work of its glazing," could be dated to the thirteenth century.[36]

Willesme posits that the original Victorine church would have resembled numerous other twelfth-century rural churches in the Ile-de-France, composed of an apse flanked by two minor apses on either side of the choir, a plan similar to the churches at St.-Martin-des-Champs and St.-Pierre-de-Montmartre.[37] We have further evidence of its character, decoration, and design in Victorine necrologies and liturgical books. To begin with, it is possible to say with some assurance that the twelfth-century Victorine church, though small when compared with the Cathedral of Notre Dame, was a splendid building, having little to do with the kind of architecture and minimal decoration espoused by the Cistercians. The obituary of Hugh of Halberstadt, who gave the money for the church, testifies to its lavishness:

---

[30] See Châtillon (1985), p. 62.

[31] Châtillon (1975, p. 63) lists the following engravings as containing views of the church: (1) By Marot, as produced by Merian in the *Topographia Galliae*; (2) In a view of Paris by Pierre-Denis Martin, as found in the Musée Carnavalet; (3) A view by an unknown artist of around 1760, found in the Musée Carnavalet. The reconstruction of the church in the sixteenth century is also discussed in Willesme (1991), pp. 102–106.

[32] For a picture of this tower as found in an engraving from 1660, see Willesme (1981), p. 103 and p. 246 above.

[33] Saint-Victor (1822–27), vol. III, p. 479: "Elle étoit éclairée par deux croisées en ogives, hautes et étroites, offrant à leur sommet des arrières-voussures très-bien executées." (Professor Walter Cahn helped to prepare the translation of this passage offered in the text. The rendition is tentative. There were not clearly established terms for many architectural features in the early nineteenth century.)

[34] See further description in Paul and Marie-Louise Biver (1970). The tower at the west and the protrusion of the old choir in the chevet proves that the twelfth-century church was fairly large.

[35] Saint-Victor (1822–27), vol. III, p. 478.

[36] See Willesme (1981), p. 104. For further discussion of the kinds of churches built by the canons regular, see Hubert (1962), Bonde (1984), and especially Untermann (1984).

[37] One object survives from before the restoration: the tomb cover of William of Chanac, Bishop of Paris (1332–1348), which decorated the chapel of the infirmary at St. Victor, is in the Louvre.

Hic rebus suis magnifice satis locum nostrum ampliauit in auro et argento et uestibus pretiosis, tapetibus et cortinis et alia supellectili varia. De quo hoc specialiter commendare et memorie tradere volumus quod eius sumptibus et impensis huius ecclesie nostre edificium factum et constructum est.[38]

Did this ornate church have a thematic program? From what is known of the abbey's early history, it seems that the first generations of Victorines intended the church to celebrate their special relationship with bishops, especially the bishops of Paris, and to demonstrate that the Victorines were the conscience, the moral guide and fortificaion of the secular clergy of Paris. Here at St. Victor was a haven where reform-minded bishops and other high-ranking reformers of any town or city could come for renewal and fellowship, could find suitable lodging when visiting Paris, and could spend their final days, or could, at the last, be buried. The Victorines kept a house for the Bishop of Paris.[39] It was at St. Victor that St. Bernard supposedly quartered when he visited the city, as did other great reformers, including the exiled Thomas of Canterbury. Many clergy retired to St. Victor at the end of their lives in the twelfth and early thirteenth centuries, leaving handsome bequests as payment. A list of the bishops of Paris is found in the important Victorine manuscript Paris, BN lat. 14673;[40] seven of these men (from the twelfth through the thirteenth centuries) were buried at St. Victor. Another list, made in the sixteenth century, contains the names of eighteen bishops buried at St. Victor, from Paris and other places as well, further demonstrating that the Victorines consistently thought of their church as an episcopal memorial. Henri Sauval, writing of the ancient western portal of St. Victor in 1724, claims that the door was "of an architecture the most Gothic and the most bold in Paris: there were three great pendentives of stone, made in arcs, suspended in the air, which were not badly representative of a mitre."[41]

The altars and chapels of the twelfth-century church and their connections to the sequence repertory

The emphasis upon the relationship between the Victorines and the bishops of Paris suggested above is borne out by the study of Victorine altars as established in the twelfth century. The late-twelfth- or early-thirteenth-century ordinals from St.

---

[38] Found in the fourteenth-century Victorine necrology, Paris. BN lat. 14673, fol. 194. This necrology forms the basis for the edition found in *ODSP*. Baron (1963, pp. 17–23) believed that this notice was a later addition, that is, not written in the twelfth century. But even if this were so, and the notice was written in the thirteenth century, it is still a witness to the appearance of the church.

[39] Following an apparently lost document, Jean de Toulouse recorded the rules governing the use of this house. It was located on the northern side of the church and had its own chapel. Bishop Stephen of Senlis was responsible for creating this situation. See discussion in Bonnard (1904–07), vol. I, p. 251. For further discussion of the chapel, see below.

[40] This book contains in its several sections the *LO*, the Victorine version of the Martyrology of Usuard with an important calendar from the late twelfth or early thirteenth century, a fifteenth-century necrology, and numerous other Victorine documents and writings. A full table of contents and bibliography is found in *LO*, ed. Jocqué and Milis, pp. xxxii–xxxvi.

[41] See Sauval (1724), vol. I, p. 409. ("Le portail est d'une architecture de plus gothique et la plus hardie de Paris: ce sont 3 gross pendentifs de pierre, faits en arcs, suspendus en l'air, qui ne ressemblent pas mal à une mitre.")

Victor, Paris, BN lat. 14506, contains a detailed list of the altars.[42] This passage in fact constitutes a kind of guide to the church, explaining locations of altars and mentioning various chapels and other parts of the church.[43] Yet although it is the richest surviving source of information about the twelfth-century building, it has not been studied before, even by Fourier Bonnard (who must have known about the list because he mentions elements of it occasionally).[44] It also shows the kinds of saints and historical figures the Victorines favored. Because the community and church were completely new in the twelfth century, there were few traditions to dictate such choices. St. Victor was the patron of the oratory upon which the church was built; that much was established at the outset. But the rest they could plan themselves: with a greater degree of freedom than was usually possible, they could make a church reflective of their own ideals and history.

The establishment of these particular altars, oratories, and chapels in the twelfth century (listed on pp. 251–254) proceeded along with the development of the liturgy. Once a particular saint had been chosen for such an honor, relics were obtained or selected from among those already possessed (and the relic trade being what it was, the selection was as wide as the list of saints was long), the feast was raised to a high rank, an office for him or her was composed from a preexisting vita (if a standard office did not already exist), and a sequence was written in his or her honor for the Mass liturgy. There is enough evidence from other churches, both in England and in France, to demonstrate that the sequence was commonly sung at the Office as well as the Mass, thus creating a bond between the various parts of the liturgy.[45] In English churches, sequences were sung at the procession made to the altar following first vespers.[46] This was undoubtedly the case at St. Victor and other northern French churches as well.[47]

---

[42] The list is found on fols. 329r and 329v.

[43] Through the study of subsequent versions of the ordinal, the fourteenth-century copy, Paris, BN lat. 14455, and the sixteenth-century copy, Paris, BN lat. 14456, one can trace the program of expansion that took place at St. Victor in subsequent centuries. As would be expected, new altars were added and greater numbers of patrons assigned to earlier altars. As this happened, feasts of relevant saints were upgraded or added, as the case might be.

[44] Throughout this century, scholars have turned their attention to ordinals and other liturgical documents to reconstruct medieval altar plans and other features of destroyed or heavily renovated church buildings. Pelt's (1937) voluminous work on the Cathedral of Metz makes parallels between liturgical sources and architecture; Delaporte (1953) reconstructed the altars of Chartres Cathedral with the help of ordinals; the pioneering work of Kurzeja (1970) provided inspiration for Stansbury O'Donnell's (1990) fine study of Trier; Robertson (1984 and 1991) has identified and situated the altars of St. Denis using ordinals and other liturgical sources; Baltzer (1992) has sketched out the plan of the altars of the cathedral of Notre Dame in Paris and suggested their locations using ordinals and other liturgical sources. The altars of the twelfth-century church at St. Victor were not identified by Willesme (1991), although he does provide (figure 3) a useful plan of the interior of the seventeenth-century church from Paris, Arch. nat. Q2 121. Further bibliography concerning ordinals in general and other Augustinian ordinals is found in Jocqué (1991), pp. 55–56, note 6.

[45] The most extensive and well-documented witness to the extensive use of sequences in the Office in France is Laon 263, a late twelfth-century troper-proser from Laon cathedral.

[46] See Harrison (1963), pp. 67–68. "If the church had an altar dedicated to the saint concerned, the prose was sung there on the arrival of the procession after first Vespers."

[47] The Ord., although usually mute on this subject, states that the sequence "Victime paschali" was sung at vespers throughout Easter week: see fol. 291. The Victorines must have had the festive Easter vespers service that originated in Rome and was common in northern French churches. A gradual, alleluia, and sequence was sung at vespers each day of the week. For discussion of this service, see Oury (1972 and 1973).

The sequence texts provided a carefully designed synopsis of each saint's vita, and served to interpret the meanings his or her relics had for the worshiping community. As was explained in Parts II and III of this book, Augustinian canons favored the late sequence in the twelfth and early thirteenth centuries, and the Victorines wrote and used more of them than any other house. Thus, in their particular liturgy, it was deemed essential for every major altar patron to have a proper sequence, and a comparison with the list of altars and the list of sequences in Paris reveals that all of them did. In fact, of all the seventy-two sequences in the late-twelfth-century Victorine sequence repertory, twenty-five were for feasts of the Lord (Easter and Pentecost each having a sequence for every day of the octave) and three were for the dedication of the church. All the rest, with but one exception (the early sequence "Celsa pueri" for the feast of the Holy Innocents), were for saints in whose honor the altars were dedicated.

Clearly, for those designing the twelfth-century Victorine church, sequences, especially those they wrote themselves, and altars and their relics were essential and interrelated features of an architectural and liturgical program. If the sculpture and glass had survived, one can suppose with some confidence that it would have been as carefully organized as were the altars and sequences to express Victorine ideals, and would have served the grand design common to altars, chapels, and sequences. Table 11.1 (on pp. 254–255) demonstrates the parallel development between altars and sequences in the twelfth-century church and the Victorine liturgy from the same period.

The altars in the twelfth-century church at St. Victor

Following the plan of the ordinal, and using its descriptive language, one can tell that the Victorine church by the early thirteenth century contained these altars:

1. The main altar was dedicated to St. Victor, the martyr of Marseilles, and to St. Augustine, Bishop of Hippo, and to Ste. Geneviève, virgin.
2. The second altar was dedicated in honor of St. Denis the Areopagite, and to St. Nicholas.
3. The single altar which was in the southern part was dedicated in honor of all the Apostles.
4. The altar which was in the northern part was dedicated to St. John the Baptist and to St. John the Evangelist.
5. The altar which was in the oratory of St. Leger was dedicated in the honor of this saint, the martyred bishop of Autun, and to St. Benedict, abbot, and to St. Aurea, virgin.
6. The altar which was behind the back of the choir was dedicated in honor of the Holy Cross and to Saint Martin of Tours, and to St. Agatha, virgin.
7. The altar in the chapel of the Bishop of Paris was dedicated in honor of St. Stephen the Protomartyr.
8. The altar in the oratory of St. Thomas was dedicated in honor of the martyred Archbishop of Canterbury, and to the holy martyrs Lawrence and Pope Urban and Christopher. And the holy confessors Nicholas and Hilary of Poitiers and Bernard of Clairvaux, and blessed virgins Anastasia and Catherine.
9. The main altar in the crypt was dedicated in honor of the Genetrix of God, Mary, and of St. Vincent, and Pope Gregory, and St. Agnes, virgin.

10   The altar that was in the southern part was dedicated in honor of the holy and individual Trinity and to Mary perpetual virgin, and to the vivifying cross, and to blessed Michael the Archangel, and all the saints of God.

11   The altar which was in the northern part was dedicated in honor of St. Mary Magdalene, and St. Sebastian, and St. Marcellus, Bishop of Paris.

12   The altar in the chapel of the infirmary was dedicated in honor of the Blessed Virgin Mary, and St. Maurice and His companions, and St. Silvester, pope.

13   The altar which was in the chapel of the Bishop of Lisieux was dedicated in honor of the Transfiguration of Christ, and in honor of the Apostles Peter, James, and John.

The plans of the altars and their locations, as well as the stature of the saints honored thereby within the liturgy, created both a memorial to political events and historical persons and an endorsement of the reform theology championed by Hugh of St. Victor. Clearly the Victorines planned to give primary honors to the hierarchy of Christ and his apostles, popes, bishops, and other ecclesiastical officials (especially deacons), and to the symbolic power of the cross. Except for Mary, virgins were less prominent than members of the hierarchy, and the great abbots, monks, and martyrs favored by Benedictine houses were, with the exception of St. Bernard and St. Benedict, not represented.

Every altar (with the sole exception of that dedicated to the Trinity in the crypt) had at least one apostle, bishop, or deacon as first or second patron. Standing close by the main altar dedicated to Sts. Victor and Augustine was an altar for St. Denis, the first Bishop of Paris. Altars in the rest of the upper church were dominated by apostles and clergymen: one altar was dedicated to all the Apostles as a group, another to John the Baptist and John the Evangelist, and another to the famous Bishop of Autun, St. Leger, whose eyes were preserved in Paris (one at St. Denis and the other at St. Victor itself).[48] The altar of the Holy Cross had as its second patron St. Martin, Bishop of Tours.

All chapels and oratories, except for the chapel of the Infirmary, which was dedicated to Mary, were built to honor bishops, and there is a history behind each of them; it is here that the political history provided in Chapters 8 and 9 becomes necessary for understanding the sequences and their original meanings.

Perhaps the earliest of these chapels was that named for the Bishop of Paris. It was established by Bishop Stephen of Senlis as part of a house he had built on the northern side of the church, and thus must have been in existence well before his death in 1142. Here the reforming bishop, the man who secured prebends throughout Paris for the Victorines and accompanied Prior Thomas of St. Victor during the ambush of 1133, could escape the world, and worship among his friends. Undoubtedly at his own request, Stephen of Senlis was buried in the choir at St. Victor, the very place where he sang his last Psalms with Abbot Gilduin and Adam of St. Victor.[49] He left handsome gifts to the abbey upon his death, including

---

[48] The eye is listed in a fourteenth-century inventory of relics from the abbey. It is edited by Bonnard (1904–07), vol. II, pp. 289–291. See also Perdrizet (1933), p. 234, who claims St. Victor also possessed a lock of the saint's hair.

[49] The list of bishops in Paris, BN lat. 14673 states that Stephen was buried in the choir.

treasured books, and was solemnly commemorated before Mass upon his anniversary of July 29 (by happenstance, the day after the octave of St. Victor).[50] In fact, the ordinal states that the Mass for the day was to be "Sacerdotes," undoubtedly "Sacerdotes tui," for a confessor bishop.[51] Because the saint commemorated on this day was St. Felix of Nola, a priest but not a bishop, the selection of pericopes was undoubtedly made in honor of Stephen of Senlis.

It is no coincidence that the chapel of the Bishop of Paris at St. Victor was dedicated to St. Stephen the Protomartyr. And because the chapel was established by Stephen during his lifetime and the feast of St. Stephen probably became duplex during this period, it may be supposed that the sequence honoring this same saint was written by Adam himself, and with his friend the bishop in mind.[52] The connection between the chapel and the Bishop of Paris was made all the stronger through this dedication because the original cathedral of Paris (whose ruins still existed at this time) was dedicated to Stephen. The cathedral of Paris, therefore, would have required a special sequence for St. Stephen:[53] Adam, the cantor of the cathedral, may have composed the sequence for the cathedral liturgy as well. With its indictment of St. Stephen's attackers, and its proclamation of him as a shining model of perfection, "protomartyr and Levite, bright with his life, bright with his faith," "Heri mundus" would have reminded the canons of St. Victor of their patron on the feast of the protomartyr.[54]

The oratory to St. Leger, probably located in the north-eastern part of the church, may also have been built to honor reforming bishops of Paris, and Stephen of Senlis in particular. St. Leger's story parallels that of Stephen of Senlis in several ways, except that the saint's life was not spared. According to the vita, Leger was of noble birth and came to be held in high esteem by the royal family, which included Clothar III and his mother St. Balthides (foundress of the abbeys of Corbie and Chelles). In the mid seventh century, Leger was nominated Bishop of Autun, a see fraught with political strife. Leger brought harmony, but was also an advocate of reform. He was particularly concerned that the monks of his diocese follow the rules of St. Benedict strictly: that they work in common, hold no property, and ignore the world's pleasures. The saint's reforming spirit and his loyalty to the legitimate heirs of Clothar III brought him many enemies, of whom the worst was Ebroin, mayor of the palace. In and out of favor with the king, and sometimes supporting

---

[50] See *ODSP*, p. 573: "[July 29] Anniv. pie recordationis domni Stephani, Parisiensis episcopi [1142], qui in vita sua hanc nostram ecclesiam mirabili affectu sincere dilectionis amplectens, multa et magna et beneficia conferens, dignum et perpetuum sui et nominis et amoris memoriale posteris dereliquit . . . Libros quoque optimos quos sibi paraverat nobis moriens dereliquit. Hujus itaque tanti viri, tam specialis amici, anniversarium per singulos annos specialiter et sollempniter celebrandum et cum magna devotione faciendum est et ante missam commendatio . . ."

[51] See fol. 312r.

[52] The language describing St. Stephen's tormentors is particularly strong. Victorine sequences are not usually critical of Jews and the bitter language used here seems rather to refer to contemporary events and the great troubles Bishop Stephen had with his accusers. See "Heri mundus," strophes III and IV, M&A, p. 172.

[53] Appendix 5, p. 408, shows that two sequences were available for St. Stephen in the early-thirteenth-century liturgy of Notre Dame Cathedral: a tenth-century piece, the widespread "Magnus deus," and the late sequence "Heri mundus." See Baltzer (1992), pp. 59–60.

[54] See strophe II, M&A, p. 172.

Table 11.1. *Status of feasts and of sequences for altar patrons in the twelfth century*

Although various levels of double feasts were not fully worked out (nor were they always expressed) in these early calendars, the following hierarchy, from highest to lowest, is generally followed:

Total Duplex
Duplex
9 lectiones (at Matins)
3 lectiones (at Matins)
Memorial (short commemoration with a verse and a prayer)

Saint	Feasts	Rank	Proper sequence	fol. in 14506
I. Main altar				
1. St. Victor	Reception	Duplex	yes	397v–308r
	Anniversary	Total Duplex with octave	yes	310v–311r
2. St. Augustine	1 feast	Total Duplex with octave	yes	315r
3. St. Geneviève	1 feast	Duplex	yes	301v
	1 memorial			319r
II. Second altar				
1. St. Denis	Anniversary	Duplex with octave	yes	318r
	Finding	3 lectiones	no	304r
2. St. Nicholas	Anniversary	Duplex	yes	322v
III. Altar in the southern part				
1. All Apostles	Anniversaries	Duplex or 9 lectiones[a]	yes	
IV. Altar in the northern part				
1. St. John, Baptist	Birthday	Duplex with octave	yes	308r–v
	Decapitation	9 lectiones	no	
2. St. John, Evangelist	Anniversary	Duplex	yes	271v
	Latin gate	3 lectiones	no	305v
V. Altar in the oratory of St. Leger				
1. St. Leger, bishop	Anniversary	Duplex[b]	yes	318r
2. St. Benedict	Anniversary	9 lectiones	no	calendar
3. St. Aurea	Anniversary	3 lectiones	no	318r
VI. Altar behind the back of the choir				
1. Holy Cross	Finding	Duplex	yes	305
	Exaltation	Duplex	same	316
2. St. Martin, bishop	Anniversary	Duplex	yes	321
	Ordination	9 lectiones	no	310
3. St. Agatha	Anniversary	9 lectiones	no	303v
VII. Altar in the chapel of the Bishop of Paris				
1. St. Stephen, first deacon	Anniversary	Duplex	yes	271
St. Stephen	Finding	9 lectiones	same	312v
VIII. Altar in the chapel of St. Thomas of Canterbury				
1. St. Thomas, archbishop	Anniversary	Duplex	yes[c]	272
2. St. Lawrence, deacon	Anniversary	Duplex	yes	313

3. St. Urban, pope	Anniversary	3 lectiones	no	306v
4. St. Christopher	Anniversary	Memorial	no	313
5. Nicholas and Hilary, bishops	Anniversary	Memorial	no	301v
6. Bernard of Clairvaux, abbot	Anniversary	unspecified	no	314v
7. St. Anastasia	Anniversary	Memorial	no	calendar
8. Catherine	Anniversary	Memorial?[d]	yes	322

IX. Main altar in the crypt

1. Virgin Mary	Purification	Total Duplex	yes	302v–303r
	Annunciation	Total Duplex	(Lent)	304
	Assumption	9 lectiones[e]	yes	313v–314r
	Birth	Duplex[f]	yes	316
2. St. Vincent, deacon	Anniversary	Duplex	yes	302
3. St. Gregory, pope	Anniversary	9 lectiones	no	304
4. St. Agnes	Anniversary	9 lectiones	no	302

X. Altar in the southern part of the crypt

1 The Trinity	Trinity Sunday	Total Duplex	yes	297v–298
2. Blessed Virgin Mary (as above)				
3. The Vivifying Cross (as above)				
4. St. Michael	Feast day	Duplex	yes[g]	317
5. All Saints	Anniversary	Total Duplex	yes	319v–320r

XI. Altar in the northern part of the crypt

1. St. Mary Magdalene	Anniversary	Duplex	yes	311
2. St. Sebastian	Anniversary	9 lectiones	no	302
3. St. Marcellus, Bishop of Paris	Deposition	9 lectiones	no	320v–321r

XII. Altar in the chapel of the Infirmary

2. Blessed Virgin Mary (as above)				
2. St. Maurice and His Companions	Anniversary	9 lectiones[h]	no	317
3. St. Silvester, Pope	Anniversary	9 lectiones	yes[i]	272v

XIII. Altar in the chapel of the Bishop of Lisieux

1. Transfiguration	Feast	Duplex	yes	312v–313r
2. St. Peter	Anniversary	9 lectiones[j]	yes	309r–310v
	Octave	9 lectiones	yes	310v
Peter's Chair	Commemoration	9 lectiones	no	303v
Peter's Chains	Commemoration	9 lectiones	no	312
3. St. James	Anniversary	9 lectiones	no	311v–312r
4. St. John, Evangelist (as above)				

[a] most have octaves   [b] may have been upgraded
[c] rubric added   [d] raised to Duplex by mid-century
[e] raised in early 13th century to Duplex with complete octave   [f] raised to Total Duplex
[g] added   [h] appears to have been raised to this status soon after ordinal was prepared
[i] added   [j] in calendar; being raised at time ordinal was prepared

his enemies, Ebroin detested his opposite, the loyal and saintly Leger, and arranged for his death.[55]

The sequence for St. Leger, "Cordis sonet," was probably written by the Victorines at the time they established this altar.[56] The text honors the saint in precisely the way one might expect: he is revered for holding out against the wicked minister Ebroin, and his eyes, one of which was believed to lie beneath his altar at St. Victor, are mentioned.[57] The piece is a hymn to reform in which the Victorines transformed a seventh-century saint into a comrade-at-arms who fought and won the same kinds of political battles that they and Bishop Stephen had when the abbey was still young.[58] However, it is not easy to determine from the sequence when the altar was dedicated to Leger. In the Victorine ordinal, the main heading and the feast's rank were written in the margin, but by the main hand. The sequence rubric appears to have been written in over an earlier title, perhaps that of a common sequence.[59] Thus although an earlier date is not improbable, there is some reason to suspect that the altar was dedicated in the late twelfth century.

The twelfth-century church also had a chapel originally for St. Lawrence, which became dedicated to Archbishop Thomas of Canterbury soon after his martyrdom and canonization (in 1170 and 1172 respectively).[60] Its precise location is difficult to determine, but because the procession for the foot-washing ceremony on Holy Thursday went from the southern altar (dedicated to the Apostles) to this chapel before arriving at the altar of St. John in the northern part of the church, it may have been in the western end.[61] The task of understanding the Victorine choices first of St. Lawrence and subsequently of St. Thomas as the patrons of this chapel is easier. St. Lawrence was honored within the Roman liturgy as the first deacon, standing in the same relationship to Rome as St. Stephen did to Jerusalem. Here was a saint exemplifying clerical excellence, an early high ecclesiastical authority who would not weaken when challenged. For refusing to succumb to the demands of the Roman prefect Decius, Lawrence was roasted to death. The Victorine sequence "Prunis datum" ("Given to the coals"), the text of which may well be by Adam of St. Victor, turns the fire imagery into light imagery, describing Lawrence as capable

---

[55] For a synopsis, see Butler (1981), vol. IV, pp. 9–11. Two versions of the life of St. Leger can be found in *Acta Sanctorum*, ed. Bolland *et al.*, October, vol. I. The matins readings for the feast of St. Leger (October 2) at St. Victor emphasize the events described in our discussion. See, for example, the Victorine breviary, Paris, BN lat. 14811 (fourteenth century), fols. 500–501v.

[56] In strophe VI, "Venerando presuli," reference is made to the tearing out of the martyred bishop's eye (see M&A, p. 216). Of course the Victorines believed that one of these was beneath their altar.

[57] See especially strophe V, "Maior domus regiae," M&A, p. 216.

[58] This sequence was sung only at the Abbey of St. Victor; no other Parisian churches picked it up. The only other concordance is in Assisi 695.

[59] Blume believed the piece to be one of the weakest of the Victorine sequences and was, therefore, reluctant to assign it to Adam. See *AH* LV, p. 251. The opening and closing are typical of Adam's style, but the rest does seem crabbed.

[60] The chapel of St. Lawrence was, according to later Victorine historians, the place where Thomas of Canterbury celebrated Mass when he visted the abbey. See Bonnard (1904–07), vol. I, p. 225.

[61] Bonnard (1904–07) claimed, however, that it was near the crypt, (whatever this may mean): see vol. I, p. 225, n. 2. Bonnard is a difficult source to use in some ways: he knew a great deal, but much of his information came from Victorine chroniclers, especially from the prolific Jean de Thoulouse, who wrote in the mid seventeenth century.

of illuminating others.[62] The flame of God burns in Lawrence and he transmits its light to all who know about his martyrdom.[63] Through the pen of the sequence poet, Lawrence becomes a Dionysian hierarch, one of the sort described at length by Hugh of St. Victor.

Legend has it that it was in the chapel of St. Lawrence that Archbishop Thomas of Canterbury celebrated Mass when he visited the Abbey of St. Victor in 1169. It was during this occasion, on the octave of St. Augustine, that he preached a sermon in chapter before the entire community.[64] The relationship between the Victorines and St. Thomas has been rigorously explored during the last few decades. Thomas's library contained copies of Hugh of St. Victor's writings, and his religious thinking and extreme ideas regarding the reform of the English church were perhaps inspired by them.[65] Richard of St. Victor was himself English, and helped to nourish a colony of Englishmen at the Abbey of St. Victor.[66] The Victorines were among the earliest in France to establish an altar in honor of St. Thomas, and may have named the chapel even before he was canonized.[67] The powerful alliance of French bishops, Rome, and the Capetian kings could appear, under the banner of the triumphant reform movement, as protectors of the saint from the English king. The sequence "Gaude syon et letare" was probably written at St. Victor for St. Thomas. The piece commemorates the saint's exile in France, refering to his prolonged stay in Sens, and emphasizes the pastoral and liturgical role of the bishop.[68] Here, as in other sequences written by canons in his honor, Thomas becomes the victim on the altar.[69] In strophes VI and VII, the Victorine song praises the transformation of

---

[62] The text of "Prunis datum" is translated in the anthology (pp. 438–439).

[63] See especially strophes VI and VII:

VI.1 Nescit sancti nox obscurum	(The night of the saint does not know darkness,
ut in penis quid impurum	Such that in torments
fide tractet dubia;	He might consider something base with wavering faith,
VI.2 Neque cecis lumen daret	Nor would he give light to the blind
Si non eum radiaret	If the presence of light
luminis presentia.	Did not illuminate him.
VII.1 Fidei confessio	The confession of faith
lucet in Laurentio	Shines in Lawrence;
non ponit sub modio	He does not put it under a bushel;
statuit in medio	He sets up the light,
lumen coram omnibus;	Openly, before all.
VII.2 Iuvat Dei famulum,	It pleases the servant of god,
crucis suae baiulum,	The bearer of His Cross,
assum quasi ferculum	As if a roast dish,
fieri spectaculum	To be made a spectacle
angelis et gentibus. (M&A, p. 206)	For angels and pagans.)

[64] See Foreville (1975), pp. 168–169 and Bonnard (1904–08), vol. I, p. 225. The sermon, which does not survive, was on the text "In pace factus est locus eius," (Psalm 75:3 [76:2]). See Châtillon (1975), pp. 95–96.

[65] See Smalley (1973 and 1951).

[66] See Châtillon (1980), pp. 95–98.

[67] See Foreville (1975), pp. 168–169. Other early chapels and churches established in France are listed in this same article, pp. 172–187.

[68] Some have supposed that the reference to Sens means the sequence was composed there. But it was not sung in the cathedral of Sens in the early thirteenth century. See Paris, BN lat. 10502, a gradual with sequences from the period: here are included two sequences in honor of the martyred bishop of Canterbury: "Pia mater plangat ecclesia," and "Spe mercedis et corone."

[69] See especially the opening strophes, M&A, p. 175.

Thomas from "first within the courtly crowd and fighting for the royal palace," to "a new person, restored."[70] The "novus homo" is, of course, Augustine's new man who has been renewed by Christ, a theme which appears elsewhere as well in the Victorine sequence repertory. Through their commemoration, the Victorines were able to transform the difficult personality and sometimes questionable motives of Thomas of Becket to fit their own mythography, making him the ideal bishop, a man who, patterned after the model of Christ, the high bishop of the universal church, was willing to sacrifice himself for the good of his flock.[71]

The Chapel of the Bishop of Lisieux was part of the establishment of Arnulf, Bishop of Lisieux, and, according to Fourier Bonnard, was constructed to the east of the abbey, near the cloister of the novices, in the early years of the 1180s (Arnulf died in 1184).[72] Arnulf of Lisieux was a reformer and a friend to the Abbey of St. Victor. He was originally from Sées and had studied in the cathedral school there under the venerable Serlon, bishop until 1122. In 1124, his older brother became Bishop of Sées, introducing the Victorines into the cathedral chapel in 1131. Subsequently Arnulf protected this community whenever it was threatened.[73] As a young man, Arnulf established his reformer's credentials by composing a treatise in defense of Pope Innocent II during the schism of the early 1130s;[74] the preface of this work was addressed to Geoffrey of Chartres, at one point Arnulf's teacher, and one of the French bishops who supported Innocent II most strongly.[75] Arnulf, who had struggled with the difficult task of keeping allegiances to the kings of England and France, chose to spend the final part of his life at St. Victor and was buried there as well, near the choir.[76]

The dedication of the altars in his chapel was carefully planned: the major dedication is in honor of the Transfiguration of the Lord; the minor dedications are to the Apostles Peter, James, and John. Thus the altar commemorates the moment that Jesus revealed his divinity to these three apostles, as described in the Synoptic Gospels and the Second Epistle of Peter.[77] Although the feast was widely celebrated

[70] Quondam cetu curiali
    primus eras et regali
        militans palatio . . .

    Consequenter es mutatus,
    presulatu sublimatus,
    novus homo reparatus
        felici commercio. (M&A, p. 175)
[71] For recent evaluations of Becket's success as a reformer, see Alexander (1970), and Foreville (1981).
[72] See Bonnard (1904–07), vol. I, p. 260, n. 1. Bonnard undoubtedly found this information in his favored source, the chronicle of Jean de Thoulouse. Arnulf's house was also described in Monumenta Germaniae Historica, vol. VI, p. 531, by Robert of Tourigni.
[73] See Schriber (1990), pp. 2–3 and Bonnard (1904–07), vol. I, pp. 143–144.
[74] See discussion in Chapter 9.
[75] For discussion of this work and its history, see de Formeville (1873), vol. II, pp. 47–48 and Schriber (1990), pp. 3–4.
[76] See Bonnard (1904–07), vol. I, p. 260. Carolyn Schriber's interpretations of Arnulf's life, based on careful study of his many letters, depict him as an old-style reformer who tried to keep close contacts with royalty and retain the splendor of his own entourage, and yet who wished to upgrade the moral life of the clergy under his control. In the second half of the twelfth century, this position failed with both kings and clergy. See Schriber (1990), pp. 120–122.
[77] See Matt. 17:1–13; Mark 9:2–13; Luke 9:28–36 and 2 Peter 1:16–19.

in the West by the eleventh century, and Peter the Venerable wrote an Office for it, it did not come into the Roman calendar until the fifteenth century.[78] The Victorines showed their devotion to the feast through this altar and by a sequence written for the Transfiguration, a piece that may have been composed around 1180, the time Arnulf built his chapel.

The bishop most closely allied with the Victorines during the second half of the twelfth century, was, however, Maurice of Sully, Bishop of Paris, who reigned from 1160 to 1196. Maurice was the true successor of Stephen of Senlis in his attempt to strengthen the Parisian church and carry through the plans laid earlier by reformers. Bishop Maurice, who was responsible for beginning the building of a new cathedral dedicated to the Virgin Mary in 1163, took up residence at St. Victor in around 1170 and signed several charters while in residence there.[79] As part of his plan of improving the preaching of clerics in his diocese and throughout France, Maurice of Sully wrote a series of sermons in the vernacular.[80] His major source in this work was, as Charles Robson has pointed out, the popular *Liber exceptionum* by Richard of St. Victor. The Victorine church and liturgy were marked by this historic alliance: Maurice of Sully was buried in the choir of the church.[81] The feast of St. Maurice and His Companions appears to have been raised to nine readings soon after the ordinal was prepared, and therefore, perhaps soon after the bishop's death in 1196.[82] St. Maurice was also a secondary patron for the altar in the Chapel of the Infirmary.

Although the Victorine church was built first and foremost to honor bishops and other members of the ecclesiastical hierarchy, two other subjects for devotion were important. One was the cross: the altar at the back of the choir was dedicated to it, and the Altar of the Trinity, located in the southern part of the crypt, had "the vivifying cross" as a tertiary patron. The other was the Virgin Mary. The main altar in the crypt was dedicated to her, but with St. Vincent as a second patron. She was the second patron for the Altar of the Trinity; the altar in the Chapel of the Infirmary was also dedicated to her. Mary, who was not a subject of great importance to Hugh of St. Victor, became increasingly revered by the Victorines during the second half of the twelfth century, as she did throughout France, and her veneration in the Victorine liturgy will be studied at greater length in Chapter 14 of this book.

All altars in the Victorine church and late sequences chosen from elsewhere or written at the abbey served to promote the reformers' emphasis upon the ecclesiastical hierarchy – all but one, the altar for Mary Magdalene located in the northern part of the crypt. The sequence for the saint, "Mane prima sabbati," was probably

---

[78] In 1457, to be precise, upon the occasion of a Christian victory over the Turks.

[79] See Bonnard (1904–07), vol. I, pp. 252–253 and Longère (1991), p. 106. According to Longère, the bishop rarely resided in his palace in the Cité, and spent most of his time at St. Victor. For a tentative description of the building at St. Victor, see Crepin-Leblond (1987), pp. 249–251.

[80] See Longère (1991).

[81] See Bonnard (1904–07) vol. I, pp. 266–267. The list of bishops and their burial places found in Paris, BN lat. 14673 (a sixteenth-century copy) states that Maurice of Sully lies in the middle of the choir on the right of Stephen of Paris.

[82] See Paris, BN lat. 14506, fol. 317. The rubric "IX lc.' is squeezed in the margin.

taken over by the Victorines from the cathedral use at an early stage. As mentioned in Chapter 7, it was written in the second half of the eleventh century and was sung in liturgies throughout northern Europe by the third quarter of the twelfth century. This text offers no immediate clues to the popularity of Magdalene's cult at St. Victor, at least, not in the direct way that an original sequence would have done. Yet one can guess why the Victorines would have honored this saint so lavishly, aside from her general popularity in Paris at this time. The Victorines, it must be remembered, were in charge of administering penance and hearing confessions for the clerics of Paris. Mary Magdalene was the patroness of those who were sorry for their sins and asked forgiveness. The several churches dedicated to her in medieval Paris demonstrate not only her popularity, but the chief qualities for which she was remembered.[83] The Church of Mary Magdalene the Penitent, for example, was on the Ile de la Cité, and was built by Maurice of Sully in 1183 upon the site of the razed synagogue.[84] In the Church of Mary Magdalene built in 1360 by Bishop Jean de Meulan, the sisters were called "les Dévotes." They walked barefoot in all seasons and ate exceedingly meager meals. It was their task to serve the last meals to the condemned, and their church had an altar dedicated to "St. Abraham."[85] Identification with Mary Magdalene through an altar would have served to intensify the Victorines' image as the chief confessors of Paris.

Symbolic expressions of hierarchy in the medieval liturgy and at St. Victor

The liturgy of the Western church in the Middle Ages included a variety of ceremonies that may have inspired and certainly would have heightened the carefully organized themes unifying the altars and sequences of the Abbey of St. Victor. Hugh's description of the liturgy as expressed in *De sacramentis christiane fidei* (and quoted in Chapter 10) must be recalled here. He considered liturgical action as deliberately varied, the many types of texts, music, and activities found there symbolizing the meaning of the whole.[86] And the twelfth-century ordinal and customary, through their precise and detailed descriptions of liturgical action, demonstrate the primary importance the Victorines assigned to certain of their liturgical ceremonies and to the movement and position of the worshipers during their services. All liturgical action at St. Victor (as in all other medieval churches) was hierarchically ordered, and one can see why Hugh was inspired to think of it in such strongly Dionysian terms. As was customary throughout Europe, the brethren sat, processed, and carried out their duties according to their rank; all feasts and various aspects of feasts were ranked as well: vestments, numbers of candles, the nature of the processions, all these were carefully worked out according to degree. The manner of celebrating the three Masses of Christmas exemplifies the variation

[83] For a list of these, see Perdrizet (1933), pp. 178–179.
[84] Philip Augustus expelled the Jews from Paris during this time. See Perdrizet (1933), p. 178.
[85] See Perdrizet (1933), p. 179.
[86] *SCF*, p. 158.

in detail. Not only did each Mass have proper texts and music, but the physical circumstances were different as well. The first Mass, which took place at midnight, was celebrated by the prior at the matutinal altar.[87] Very precious vestments were used, but the sequence was not sung. The subprior celebrated the Mass at dawn, using precious vestments, at the altar of St. John.[88] The abbot celebrated the third Mass, the main Mass, after terce at the main altar.[89] Only for this Mass was a sequence sung ("In natale saluatoris").[90] Thus the third Mass was given priority over the other two, and the Mass at midnight was more splendid than the Mass at dawn.

The matins service at St. Victor was lavish and carefully ordered, even more than might be expected of Augustinian canons during this period,[91] and only they had the right to keep singing during periods of interdict. This privilege was won for them by Bishop Maurice of Sully, and was undoubtedly invoked during the time of King Philip Augustus's excommunication, when all the Parisian churches fell silent for several months.[92] At the opening of the night office (or matins), all the brethren were ordered in the middle of the choir, opposite the step in front of the altar;[93] all bowed low toward the altar. There they said three prayers; after each of these they prostrated themselves. Subsequently, they took their seats and there said the fifteen Gradual Psalms, with a Kyrie and Pater noster after each. After every group of five, they prostrated themselves again, although how this was possible in the stalls is difficult to understand. During the office psalmody immediately following this opening section, the brethren rose and sat in alternation as each new psalm was sung. Hence half of the entire group got to rest physically half of the time, although all continued to sing antiphonally throughout the entire service.[94]

Periods of respite may have been necessary: the Victorine Office was known in the Middle Ages as being sung very slowly, with long pauses at the middle and close of each psalm verse. When the Trinitarian order adopted the Victorine customary and liturgy in the late thirteenth century, Pope Urban IV stated that the long rests,

---

[87] It was customary for there to be two Masses during the day in Benedictine and Augustinian churches. The first Mass, the matutinal Mass, was celebrated in choir by the assembled community in the early morning, just after prime. At St. Victor, it was usually a Mass for the dead. See discussion in Bonnard (1904–07), vol. I, p. 72 and a description of the Mass in LO, pp. 234–236. Apparently, the Mass was celebrated at the second altar in the choir, rather than the main altar.

[88] A correction in the main hand states that the vestments at the second Mass should be conducted "in vestimentis preciosis," since "vestimenta" of the first Mass ought to be "preciosiora." See Ord., fol. 270v.

[89] Although the abbot, prior, and subprior had important liturgical roles to play throughout the entire year, it was the armarius (the librarian and cantor) who orchestrated the elaborate liturgical practice at St. Victor. LO contains one of the most specific and lengthy descriptions of this official and his numerous duties. One can tell from comparison of various monastic customaries that the armarius's office at St. Victor was inspired by the late-eleventh-century customaries from Cluny. For further discussion, see Fassler (1985).

[90] As Appendix 5, p. 391 shows, the Victorines were unusual in not having sequences for all three Masses of Christmas. They abandoned earlier, well-established pieces, and used only their own for the major Mass.

[91] See the description in LO, pp. 224–230, from which the following details are taken.

[92] See Bonnard (1904–07), vol. I, pp. 272–273. For the details of the king's difficult relationship with his young Queen, Ingeburge of Denmark, see Baldwin (1986), pp. 80–86.

[93] As in any church, the seating in choir was carefully ordered, seniority and rank determining where and with whom one sat.

[94] Among Godefroy of St. Victor's unedited sermons is a long discussion of the proper spirit in which to say the Office. This sermon will be a subject of central concern in my forthcoming paper on the Victorine Office.

prolixities, and vigils characteristic of the Victorine practice were to be omitted.[95] The Victorines remained vigilant throughout their arduous psalmody, however: one of the brethren circulated constantly with a book, and if he came face to face with a canon who neither sang nor bowed in acknowledgment, he bumped the dozing brother, who, once he had roused himself, in his turn began to carry the book through the choir.[96] The sick and infirm did not have to carry the book if they were caught sleeping, but they were awakened. The customary also stipulated how many times the book was circulated; this varied according to the length of the service and the particular demands of the day.[97]

The powerful communal sense created by the strenuous group effort of the psalmody was underscored through several symbolic ceremonies, three of which will be described here in some detail. All such ceremonies have structural parallels with the dedication ritual, which Hugh of St. Victor named as the first sacrament in his commentary upon the liturgy. At the dedication of the church, the altar was consecrated first and then it was possible to consecrate the entire building. The power of the altar, which symbolized the crucified Christ, was carried by the apostles and the teachers and preachers who followed them throughout the world. The cross of the altar symbolized the message to be borne, and the members of the hierarchy were to speak it with their lives as well as with their words. The message of the dedication was commemorated at St. Victor on the feast of the Dedication, June 5: during matins and the major Mass of the day, twelve candles were burned beside the dedication crosses on the walls of the church.[98] These represented the light brought to the world by the apostolic teaching, and symbolized the mission of the Victorines themselves. The ceremonies described below, like the dedication ceremony, demonstrate the symbolic power of the altar to represent Christ and the importance of liturgical acts that manifested the motion of this saving power: from the source to the Apostles, to the ministers, and ultimately (although this is usually not so important) to the rest of the people.

The first ceremony to be described here is the Veneration of the Cross, which took place throughout Christian churches during the Middle Ages during the solemn liturgy of Good Friday.[99] On this day, the altar died symbolically, and the clergy and people adored the cross in its stead. Just before the reading of the passion during the special service of this day (often called the Mass of the Presanctified; see p. 263 below), the sacristan placed two stoles upon the altar. When the deacon came to the words "partiti sunt vestimenta mea" (John 19:24), two other deacons, who had been told beforehand about their role, removed the stoles from the altar as if preparing to divide them.[100] In this dramatic ceremony, the vestments were divided like the garments of Christ before the crucifixion.

---

[95] See Bonnard (1904–07), vol. I, p. 72.

[96] See LO, pp. 137–138 for the many details of this practice.

[97] See LO, p. 138. In a nine-readings matins service, for example, it went through the choir once for each nocturn. Clearly the motion of the circulator was not random.

[98] See Ord., fol. 306v.

[99] See Vogel and Elze, *Pontifical romano-germanique*, vol. II, pp. 86–93.

[100] See Ord., fol. 287. This same ceremony took place in other churches as well. See Reynolds's "Cluny' in the *DMA*.

While the solemn prayers following the passion were said, two priests vested in albs, stoles, and maniples, and two subdeacons in albs took up a station by the altar. Following the prayers, the abbot and the ministers removed their vestments and their shoes, and the rest of the community took off their shoes and copes. Then the two priests stood on either side of the altar and placed the cross upright upon it while the verse "My people, what have you done to me?" was sung.[101] With the cross held upon the altar, the two subdeacons, standing on the step of the sanctuary, sang the Trisagion in Greek; after a pause of undetermined length, the choir sang the same piece in Latin, and another pause followed. Then the abbot took the cross from one of the priests and intoned the antiphon "Behold the wood of the cross," after which it was placed on the step of the altar and the abbot and the ministers assisting in the ceremony adored it. Subsequently it was carried to the step of the sanctuary, and, while antiphons and psalms were sung, the rest of the community adored it in order, each man prostrating himself and then kissing it. During the adoration by the community, another cross was reverently carried by the sacrist and another brother to the oratory of St. John so that it might be presented to servants and any guests who had come for the adoration. After this, the cross was elevated again, and then ceremonially replaced. The host used in the communion service which followed had been presanctified on another day (hence the title of the Mass): the ministers were unable to consecrate on the altar on Good Friday, as it was symbolically "dead."

The ceremonies of Good Friday, signifying the cultic remembrance of the passion, are unique in the medieval liturgy. The altar was usually a focal point for the presence rather than the absence of the divine, the source of sacramental gifts. The second ceremony to be described, the Asperges, uses the altar in this way. Commonly held by religious communities each Sunday, it recalled the sprinkling rite found in the dedication of the church. At St. Victor, the ceremony took place just before terce and the major Mass of the day. Here, as for other large, closely ordered community rituals, the customary stresses the importance of participation by all: hearing the sound for convocation, "immediately at the same time let all go into the choir, with no diversion in other things."[102] Through the action of the ceremony, the entire community, its buildings and its actions, were ritually cleansed, and baptism was renewed.[103] The elements of salt and water, both purifying agents with symbolic powers, were mixed in the choir by the celebrating priest and the text of the exorcism was said, with the assembled brethren turned toward the altar. The cantor then began to sing the "Asperges me," and the priest ascended to the main altar, sprinkling water first in front of the altar and subsequently all around it.[104] After this, he asperged the altars of St. Peter and St. John,

---

[101] For further background to the texts and ceremonial, see Baumstark (1922), Drumbl (1973), and Tryer (1932).

[102] See the description in the LO, pp. 200–203. Discipline at the Abbey of St. Victor has been discussed by Feiss (1988).

[103] The Asperges in Milis, ed., *Constitutiones* is described in less detail, and only in connection with the Palm Sunday processional.

[104] The text of the antiphon was taken from Psalm 50:9 [51:7]: "Asperges me Domine hyssopo, et mundabor: lavabis me, et super nivem dealbabor." It was also sung at the feast of the Dedication.

crossed over to the abbot and, bowing to him, gave him the sparsorium. The abbot sprinkled the priest, himself, and those around him. Then the priest took the sparsorium back from the abbot and sprinkled the brethren assembled in choir, first those on the right and then those on the left, beginning with the most senior members. After the choir, its altars, the abbot, and the brethren had been asperged, the procession descended into the crypt, singing an antiphon to Mary, while the priest sprinkled the altars there; it continued into the cloister, the dormitory, the refectory, back through the cloister, and finally into the choir again, singing an antiphon to St. Victor. A prayer was said and terce was begun, but while it was sung, the priest who had officiated at the matutinal Mass vested and asperged the remaining altars and the people in the church.[105]

The asperges ceremony, like that of the dedication, creates a powerful image. The purifying elements flowed, through priestly action, from the altar representing Christ, first to altars dedicated to the apostles and then to those for other saints, to the ecclesiastical hierarchy represented by the assembled canons, and finally to the people. The motion, like that explained in Hugh's ark treatises, was from the head to the members of the body. Through it, all were gathered up into the hierarchical structure and ordered, in the hope that divine power could thereby flow smoothly through them all, unite them, restore them, cleanse and heal them. The emphasis was on the men who transfer Christ's power to the people – the prelates and priests of the church – and on the saints who typified them historically – the apostles and the Virgin Mary.

The third ceremony, found at many churches including that of St. Victor, was the elaborate washing of the altars. At St. Victor and elsewhere, it was connected thematically with a special foot-washing and a ritual meal which followed immediately after it.[106] Taking place on Holy Thursday, these events marked the opening of the solemn three-day period just before Easter and commemorated Christ's preparation for His death and the Last Supper.[107] The altar-washing ceremony, like the Asperges, used the symbolic power of water, but here the accompanying element was wine rather than salt. At St. Victor, the ceremony apparently took place after Mass.[108] Immediately after the Benedicamus domino (sung in place of the Ite missa est during Lent and other solemn feast-days), the sacristan stripped the altars and the abbot removed his chasuble, the deacon his dalmatic, and the subdeacon his tunicle, all dropping them in front of the altar. Then the deacon took up the book of prayers, which he held before the abbot so that he could read aloud, and the subdeacon took up the jar of wine which was to be poured upon each altar.[109] First the main altar and

---

[105] At duplex feasts when time was shorter, a different version of the ceremony was used. Most of the ceremony took place after terce; only the most important part of the ceremony took place as terce was beginning: the asperging of the main altar, of the brethren, and of the people. See LO, pp. 203–204.

[106] For a recent discussion of the foot-washing, or mandatum, as it was called in the Middle Ages (following the incipit of the accompanying antiphon), see Jeffery (1992).

[107] A comparison with the description of the altar-washing ceremony as found in the twelfth-century customary of Arrouaise reveals similarities, but less detail. See Milis, ed., *Constitutiones*, p. 104.

[108] See Ord., fol. 184v.

[109] Thus each official carried out the traditional duties of his office: the abbot, as chief priest and celebrant, blessed and consecrated, the deacon was in charge of the book, and the subdeacon of the vessel.

then all the other altars were, in their turn, scrubbed and wiped dry with a clean linen cloth. Immediately afterwards, the abbot poured wine on the altar in the shape of a cross; then a responsory (without the verse) from the matins service of Holy Thursday was sung, followed by an antiphon for the major patron, and a prayer as well.[110] Because the chant texts of the responsories for Holy Thursday tell the story of Christ on the Mount of Olives and the Last Supper, the themes of penance and preparation were mingled with the honoring of the saints. The water and the wine used in the service were emblematic not only of the water and blood that supposedly flowed from the crucified, but also of baptismal water and communion wine.

Immediately after the altars were washed, the brethren entered the choir silently, took off their choir copes, and, in surplices only, awaited the foot-washing cere-mony.[111] While the Mass and the altar-washing had been going on, the almsman (the elemosinarius) had assembled poor men in the cloister (taking care not to choose men whose feet were ulcerous or excessively calloused), as many as there were brethren (both lay and clerical) at St. Victor. He had them seated on benches against the wall of the church in a place that might allow them first to hear the Mass and subsequently to have their feet washed.[112] Once the men were ready and the vessels and cloths prepared, the almsman went near the wall of the church and struck a wooden tablet three times. The brethren proceeded from the choir in order and, while prayers were said, stood opposite the poor and then bowed to them. Then, beginning with the abbot, the members of the Victorine community, kneeling in turn, washed and kissed the hands and feet of the paupers. Coins were distributed, and the almsman instructed the poor men about the meal they were to receive. Tables were set up and the poor were served the same bread and other food that the canons were served in the refectory.

These Holy Thursday ceremonies, like the Asperges, represent the sacramental power of the church, linking historical events associated with the institution of the sacraments with the reality of present time. The ministers of the altar renewed the power of consecration and dedication in the altar-washing ritual, a power believed by them to have first been created by Christ's redemptive act on the cross.[113] In the actions that followed, it was transferred to the people, as the Victorine community went solemnly forth to adore the lowest members of society and to offer them gifts, not only of washing, food, and money, but also of instruction, both through the hearing of Mass and through the example of the canons' humility. This particular commemoration of the Last Supper did not attempt a realistic portrayal; rather, it searched for the spirit of the original event and challenged the participants to experience charity and humility in their everyday lives. Thus through their par-ticular interpretation of this standard ceremony, the Victorines emphasized their

---

[110] The order of the altars is presented in Ord., fol. 329v. Altars which were added in the thirteenth and fourteenth centuries are written in the margin.

[111] The twelfth-century foot-washing ceremony at St. Victor is described in Ord., fols. 284v–286r, and in LO, pp. 244–250. The washing of the poor took place daily during Lent at St. Victor.

[112] The office of elemosinarius is described in LO, pp. 52–55.

[113] Ord. states that only consecrated altars may be washed in this ceremony.

ideals of instruction through deeds and words, attempting to teach through symbolic, ritualized action. But, as always, they were concerned primarily that their actions inspire understanding and excellence in themselves and other clerics, and more interested in the righteous behavior of the shepherds than in the lives of the sheep.

All the ceremonies described above took place in churches and cathedrals throughout Europe. The great detail with which twelfth-century Victorine books described these particular ceremonies, however, suggest the special importance they had for the Victorines. These ceremonies, when placed in the context of Hugh's liturgical commentaries, explain the kinds of ceremonial language at the heart of the liturgical observance at the Abbey of St. Victor in the twelfth century. And the themes embodied in the liturgical action of the abbey were central as well to both Victorine sermons and to the Victorine sequence repertory.

The Victorine sequences desired, above all else, perhaps, to take the worshipers who sang them and heard them to church, to explain the ceremony, the functions of the clergy, the medicine of the sacraments. They are poetic versions of liturgical commentaries. In their singing, clerics were to find both the understanding and inspiration necessary to carry out their duties fervently. It is probably not a coincidence that the number of altars in the Victorine church numbered 13 at the time the liturgical books discussed here were prepared: the main altar and twelve others, a number symbolizing Christ and the apostles. The same symbolism is used in the contemporary sequence "Cor angustum," which was written at the Abbey of St. Victor. The poem has thirteen strophes, usually one per apostle.[114]

---

[114] The first and last strophes do not mention anyone by name; Paul is mentioned among the twelve as the poem proceeds, the two Jameses have one strophe, and Mathias and Barnabas share a strophe. Otherwise, each apostle has a single strophe of poetry. The text is filled with sacramental imagery.

12

Sequences for the temporale: unity through the cornerstone

Introduction

We saw in Chapter 9 how during the 1120s, the canons regular in Paris, in concert with Bishop Stephen of Senlis, attempted to convert the clergy of Notre Dame Cathedral to the common life and the Rule of St. Augustine. During this same decade, perhaps in support of this political goal, but certainly to celebrate the common life advocated in the Rule of St. Augustine, Hugh of St. Victor developed the model of the church, focusing upon Old Testament and New Testament types of the clergy, discussed in Chapter 10. Through contemplation of the history depicted in the model, clerics and, ultimately, those they taught would be instructed in God's love for the Jews and Gentiles, and, inspired by this love, would both reform themselves and be able to carry out their tasks with greater zeal and efficacy. Study of the Victorine church in Chapter 11 suggests that the canons planned their building to manifest their ideals and to celebrate the ecclesiastical hierarchy of apostles, bishops, and clerics, of whom they believed themselves to be the heirs. Hugh's writings about the liturgy emphasize that the great stone in the center of the church, the main altar, was the source of sacramental power, and the link between what he saw as the two branches of the Judeo-Christian tradition.[1] The understanding that this power was transmitted first through the apostles, then to the clergy, and finally, through them, to the people was a part of the ritual life at St. Victor, as, indeed, it was in churches throughout the Latin West, but both Victorine exegetical writings and Victorine liturgical books emphasize ceremonies in which this idea is prominent.

This transferral of power is the central theme of the Victorine sequences as well, just as it was in the writings of St. Augustine, and subsequently of Hugh. In these songs, the Victorines attempted to arrange and interrelate the texts through the music to make yet another hierarchy, a hierarchy of praise. This hierarchy, by its very nature, both reflected the structure of the church and a particular mode of

---

[1] Modern scholars instead emphasize the great diversity within pre-destruction (70 CE) Judaism. In contemporary Christian scholarship, the Jewishness of Jesus and of Paul are now taken for granted. For an overview, see Charlesworth (1990).

ritual action, and created a system of musical and textual interaction which was sacramental in character. The symbolic power of the music sustained the words, much as the power of the spirit was believed to fill the sacramental elements of oil, water, wine, and bread. The sequence texts are about the Christian Messiah, the divine source of the sacraments, symbolized for the Victorines by the cross in both texts and music, and about his twelfth-century apostles, the canons themselves. The texts fuse the image of the cross with that of the keystone at the apex of a building, and find in both a joining of Old and New Testament priesthoods under the governance of one supreme archbishop.[2] The sequence music as sung at the abbey, a significant part of it written by the Victorines themselves, is symbolic of the cross, and spreads out through the repertory as the messages of the preachers were believed to spread through the people.[3] The sequences are best discussed according to their hierarchical arrangement, beginning with the pinnacle of the edifice as described in texts for feasts of the temporale. Sequence poets began with texts, sometimes with music for them in mind, sometimes not, and then composed – or recomposed – the music (in the case of the Victorine sequences, an essential aspect of theological meaning). (See pp. 295–296.) To begin with the texts is not to say music was unimportant, only to claim that texts were often written first in this tradition. The music, which usually came later, was the more individual and personal dimension of the repertory: each center had its own, and at the Abbey of St. Victor, the musical dimension of the sequences contributed in a major way to establishing uniqueness.

Parisian sequences for the temporal cycle, especially those for Easter and Pentecost, doubtless include some texts by Adam himself (see pp. 161–170). Within these texts, ideas of ecclesiastical unity are strongly represented: they describe the very summit of the ecclesiastical hierarchy, a central feature of Hugh's drawings of the church as described in *The Moral Ark of Noah* and *The Mystical Ark of Noah*.[4] Within this apex of the church, called the builder's cornerstone after New Testament interpretations of Psalm 117:22 [118:22], is positioned the source of sacramental power.[5] Likewise, sequences for feasts of the Lord emphasize this same part of Hugh's drawings, the part which he inscribed first, the small square in the center with the Lamb and a cross drawn within it. Hugh's description of the feast of the Dedication suggests that this small "cubit" is the altar in his figural representation, for, of course, the altar was the main focus of Christian worship in the Middle Ages, and in several liturgical ceremonies it was marked with a cross.[6] In the sequence poetry, the altar joins and sustains the entire edifice of the church, as it remakes the elements used in the sacraments dispensed to the people.

---

[2] This image was central to the drawing of the church presented by Hugh of St. Victor. Its most important scriptural source is the Pauline Letter to the Hebrews.

[3] This action was symbolized during the feast of the Dedication during the singing of "Laudes crucis." See Chapter 4.

[4] Discussion of *De diversis ordinibus* in Chapter 9 shows that a call for church unity was paramount among the canons regular during the early twelfth century.

[5] The "stone which the builders rejected" (Psalm 117:22 [118:22]) was a central image in several early Christian writings found in the New Testament. See Matthew 21:42, Acts 4:11, 1 Corinthians 3:11, Ephesians 2:20, and 1 Peter 2:7–8.

[6] See Chapter 11, pp. 264–265.

In a study of the symbolism of the Biblical cornerstone, Gerhart Ladner demonstrates the several meanings the image had for Biblical exegetes. It is clear that the Victorines, following Hugh, interpreted it as a coping-stone, the final stone of an arch or wall, and consistently thought of it as joining the Jews and Gentiles.[7] Ladner says,

The interpretation of that stone as being exclusively a coping-stone is rare and represents a special trend, different from the main current of biblical exegesis and of liturgical symbolism, a trend which goes back to the era of Hellenistic, Jewish and Christian syncretism.[8]

In his discussion, Ladner traces the idea of the coping-stone as the stone topping a building and used to complete the temple of Solomon to a passage in the *Historia scholastica* by Peter Comestor, who studied at the Abbey of St. Victor in the second half of the twelfth century.

Key scriptural sources for many of the sequence poems – and the Rule of St. Augustine alike – are the Acts of the Apostles and the Pauline Epistles. The emphasis upon these texts and the ideas of typology within them was undoubtedly stirred by a profound interest on the reformers' part in the early Christian church, in its first priests and preachers, and, of course, in their Jewish counterparts in Old Testament time; they concentrate more upon these texts and descriptions of early Judeo-Christian communities than upon events in the life of Christ as depicted in the Gospels. What all these texts have in common is the main ideal of church unity, and connections between the Old and New Testaments through typology, especially following themes of Augustine and Hugh of St. Victor, are made throughout.

The sequence texts described below are all taken from feasts of the temporale: Christmas, Easter, Pentecost, Ascension. The sequence texts are not paraphrases of liturgical texts from the Mass and Office, although they sometimes quote from them (as will be seen below).[9] More important are a group of common themes from the Victorines) favoured sources: Acts, the Pauline Epistles, the commentaries on the Psalms and other sermons by Augustine, and the writings of Hugh of St. Victor; the *Liber exceptionum* of Richard of St. Victor often contains succinct explanations of typology found in the sequences.[10] All the sequences attempt to draw the singing clergy into the world of the primitive Christian church, the world they believed Augustine wished them to emulate. Some, however, are more elaborate than others, and seem to use scriptural sources in more sophisticated ways. It may not be a coincidence that these texts all fall in the early family of pieces studied in Chapter 8. Special attention will be paid to three of these texts here, one for Pentecost, "Lux iocunda, lux insignis," and two for Easter, "Ecce dies celebris" and "Zima uetus." The correspondences between their themes and choices and

---

7 See Ladner (1942 and 1983) for references to other traditions.
8 Ladner (1942 and 1983), p. 173.
9 They do, however, reflect the great attention given to the sermons of St. Augustine in the Victorine breviary.
10 For discussion of Richard's exegesis and his use of typology, see van Zwieten (1987).

orderings of words suggests that they were by the same poet, who may have been Adam of St. Victor.

Texts for Pentecost and Ascension: Apostles as canons

Several Parisian sequence texts from this period emphasize the importance of the Jewish tradition and its extension to a new group of people, the Gentiles; the sequences usually follow ideas about typology found in the Pauline Epistles, and then incorporate these into the model of the church as found in Hugh of St. Victor. Even though the Pauline Epistles are consistently of primary importance, Parisian sequences found in the Victorine tradition do not echo Paul's habitual attitude toward the Jews: they never argue polemically against them, or single them out for castigation, as many medieval hymns and sequences did, as even Augustine often does.[11] The mid twelfth century in Paris was a time of rare and significant cooperation between Jewish and Christian Biblical scholars, and the Victorines were in the forefront of this exchange.[12] The desire to learn from the Jewish tradition, foreshadowed in Hugh of St. Victor's interest in typology, became central to his disciple Andrew in the second half of the twelfth century, who knew Hebrew and was apparently interested in Jewish exegesis for its own sake.[13] Yet the twelfth century was a difficult one for European Jewry, especially in the Rhineland. unofficial pogroms were carried out, most intensely during the many Crusades. Although Jews were better treated west of the Rhine than east of it during much of the twelfth century, King Philip Augustus did great harm by expelling them briefly from his territories in the final decades of the century and the thriving Jewish community in Paris diminished during this time.[14]

The sequence texts reflect the varying attitudes of the Victorine community toward Jewish traditions and Old Testament figures and stories. Although Hugh is never directly and sharply critical of the Jews, he – predictably – considered their

[11] Augustine's point of view was that Jews, although not believers in Christ, should be protected. Very unfortunately for the history of the Jews and of Jewish–Christian relations, he associated them with Cain, the slayer of Abel, and with the slayers of Christ. See, for example, his sermon on Psalm 58 [59] for a full exposition of this position. For further discussion of exegesis on Cain, see Dahan (1982). The idea of Jews as the slayers of Christ has long been attacked by modern Christian theologians and scriptural scholars, and it was officially repudiated by the Second Vatican Council in "Nostra aetate" art. 4, promulgated on October 28, 1965. See *Vatican Council II: The Conciliar and Post-Conciliar Documents*, ed. Austin Flannery (Collegeville, 1975), pp. 738–742.

[12] See Zinn (1990), Berndt (1991), and Hailperin (1963). Professor Zinn (p. 111) mentions an unpublished paper by Michael Signer which demonstrates that concern with "narrative units of text in historical interpretation was a distinctive element of not only Victorine exegesis but the practice of Jewish exegetes in northern France as well." For discussion of the meaning of Judaism in Rupert of Deutz, see Timmer (1982). Influence of later exegetical traditions upon Christian art is discussed in A. Belkin (1988).

[13] The bibliography on Andrew referred to in Chapter 11, note 3 is to be supplemented by Grabois (1983). For discussion of the disapproval Andrew met at St. Victor, especially from Richard of St. Victor, see van Zwieten (1987). The extent to which Andrew was influenced by Jewish exegesis is evaluated by Berndt (1991), who says that 78 percent of the Jewish interpretations found in Andrew's commentary on the *Heptateuch* appear there for the first time in Christian exegesis.

[14] See Baldwin (1986), pp. 230–233, M. Roblin (1952), B. Blumenkranz, and Chazan (1973), pp. 63–99 and 154–205. Philip Augustus expelled the Jews in 1182, primarily for financial reasons, but allowed them to return again in 1198.

theological position inferior to his own. In one of the most negative passages in his writings, he claimed that there have always been three types of people: those who follow natural law, those who follow written law, and men of grace, typified by pagans, Jews, and Christians:

men of the natural law are openly evil, men of the written law fictitiously good, men of grace truly good . . . and both of the first two kinds of men always persecute the truly good.[15]

Throughout his writings Hugh emphasized the idea of Jews who believed in the Messiah to come in Old Testament time, focusing, in this way, upon the historical continuity of the Christian tradition. His admiration for the forefathers was undeniable, but he viewed them as proto-Christians rather than as Jews, as was typical of his age.[16] The Jewish tradition is interpreted in the same way in the sequences. Although it is commonly praised rather than reviled, it is misunderstood and denied its own identity.

The Pauline Letter to the Ephesians is a short treatise, now believed to have been written sometime during the second half of the first century CE, after the corpus of Paul's original writings had been collected and studied; its authorship is disputed.[17] Recent scholarship emphasizes "its connections with the world of Hellenistic Judaism and, in particular, its close contact with a type of Judaism represented by the *Dead Sea Scrolls*."[18] The text would have appealed to Parisian reformers and to students of Hugh of St. Victor's writings because of its dual purpose:

1. to celebrate the unity of Jews and Gentiles into one group, as found in the church of the Apostles, and

2. to exhort Christians to be deserving of membership in the church through devout lives.

The passages quoted below from Ephesians contain the themes most important to several early sequence texts for feasts of the temporale, and especially for the magnificent "Lux iocunda, lux insignis" for Pentecost, with which discussion will begin.

Eph. 2:3–4

In which also we all conversed in time past, in the desires of our flesh, fulfilling the will of the flesh and of our thoughts, and were by nature children of wrath, even as the rest:

Eph. 2:12–22

That you were at that time without Christ, being aliens from the conversation of Israel, and strangers to the testament, having no hope of the promise, and without God in this world. But now in Christ Jesus, you, who some time were afar off, are made nigh by the blood of Christ. For He is our peace, who hath made both one, and breaking down the middle wall of partition,

---

[15] *SCF*, p. 149.

[16] In his discussion of this subject in *SCF* (p. 174), Hugh quoted Augustine to support his arguments, but Hugh is more conciliatory than his master.

[17] See *JBC*, pp. 884–885, and Brown (1984), pp. 47–60.

[18] This position is described in *JBC*, p. 885, with reference to two articles, one by K.G. Kuhn and the other by F. Mussner, both found in Murphy-O'Connor, ed. (1968).

the enmities in His flesh: Making void the law of commandments contained in decrees; that He might make the two in Himself into one new man, making peace; And might reconcile both to God in one body by the cross, killing the enmities in Himself. And coming, He preached peace to you that you were afar off, and peace to them that were nigh. For by Him we have access both in one spirit to the Father. *Now therefore you are no more strangers and foreigners; but you are fellow citizens with the saints, and the domestics of God, Built upon the foundation of the apostles and prophets, Jesus Christ himself being the chief corner stone: In whom all the building, being framed together, groweth up into an holy temple in the Lord. In whom you also are built together into an habitation of God in the Spirit.*

Eph. 4:11–12

And He gave some apostles, and some prophets, and other some evangelists, and other some pastors and doctors, For the perfecting of the saints, for the work of the ministry, for the edifying of the body of Christ:

Eph. 4:22–24

To put off, according to former conversation, the old man, who is corrupted according to the desire of error. And be renewed in the spirit of your mind: And put on the new man, who according to God is created in justice and holiness of truth.

Eph. 5:5–8

For know you this and understand, that no fornicator, or unclean, or covetous person (which is a serving of idols), hath inheritance in the kingdom of Christ and of God. Let no man deceive you with vain words. For because of these things cometh the anger of God upon the children of unbelief. Be ye not therefore partakers with them. For you were heretofore darkness, but now light in the Lord. Walk then as children of the light.

In Ephesians and its close textual companion, the Pauline Letter to the Colossians, an early community of Judeo-Christians is enjoined to "be not drunk with wine, wherein is luxury; but be ye filled with the Holy Spirit, speaking to yourselves in psalms, and hymns, and spiritual canticles, singing and making melody in your hearts to the Lord."[19] In earlier chapters of this book the suggestion has been made that through their sequences the Augustinians were following the command in their own Rule to "pray to God in psalms and hymns, ponder in your heart what your lips are saying."[20] In their sequences the canons tried to make music in accordance with the ideal of early Christian music described in the Bible and the related (and sole) statement about music in their own Rule. As will be seen below, the power of their new music is to be their wine, and they the grace-drunken Apostles and early Christians.

"Lux iocunda, lux insignis" for Pentecost Monday was very likely written by Adam of St. Victor. As Table 7.1 (p. 156) and the chart in Appendix 5 (p. 394) show, it was found at Notre Dame, St. Victor, and Ste. Geneviève by the early thirteenth century; it was also found at St. Leonard's in Limoges. It is one of the very few sequences for which the canons at Ste. Geneviève adopted the Victorine

---

[19] Eph. 5:17–18 and the parallel passage in Col. 3:16.
[20] *The Rule of St. Augustine*, Book II, Chapter 3.

musical setting rather than that of the cathedral: both places used the melody "Laudes crucis" (analyzed on pp. 72–77) for "Lux iocunda," whereas at the cathedral it was set to other music. This sequence is an excellent representative of the workings of a twelfth-century Parisian sequence text, and through analysis of it one can explain the structure underlying both other sequences for Pentecost and those for Easter. It is also the sequence which manifests most fully the text of Ephesians/ Colossians, parts of which are quoted above.

In "Lux iocunda" the sacramentally empowered elements work together to unify and strengthen the worshiping community through an elaborate analogy which compares the assembled disciples upon the first Pentecost with the Jewish Feast of Weeks (Shavuot) and draws both the Old Testament and the New Testament celebrations into the present. Like the Letter to the Ephesians, this sequence celebrates the coming of Christians into their Jewish patrimony, and remembers with sadness the pagan days of darkness and pursuits of the flesh.

The light of the first strophes of the sequence is the fiery tongues of the Holy Spirit, shooting out "from the throne" onto the disciples; it is also the light of grace, as mentioned in Eph. 5.[21] Simultaneously, it stirs the tongues and fills the hearts of the assembled worshipers, and invites them to a harmonious modulation of heart and tongue. The Christ who sends down the fiery light onto his bride, the church, is the rock of Deut. 32:13, pouring forth first sweet honey and then, when it is harder, oil.[22] This rock which pours forth honey and oil has an Old Testament type in the stone tablets of the law. Because the Feast of Weeks commemorates Moses' reception of the Ten Commandments, the sequence contrasts the giving of the Old and New Laws, concentrating upon the coming together and harmonizing of both. The Christian elements are here grafted onto the Jewish ones; both traditions for once receive equal emphasis. The two loaves of bread to be offered on the Feast of Weeks (Lev. 23:17) here become a single loaf, and this loaf, in turn, the single stone joining two sides of a building.[23] Half-way through, the sequence poet moves from the unifying stone that exudes various sacramental liquids to the vessels that catch the liquid. These are new wine jars, ready for new wine, an oblique reference to the description of the Apostles in Acts 2:13 as men who had "been drinking too much

[21] The reference here is to a great responsory for Pentecost, sung at the Office of St. Victor, and elsewhere as well: "Spiritus sanctus precedens a throno, apostolorum pectora invisibiliter penetravit novo sanctificationis signo; Ut in ore eorum ominium genera nascerentur linguarum, alleluia."

[22] In the vulgate the text reads "constituit eum super excelsam terram ut comederet fructus agrorum ut sugeret mel de petra oleumque de saxo durissimo . . ." And the sequence: "Post dulcorem melleum / Petra fudit oleum / Petra iam firmissima." The sequences are made up of interlocking scriptural allusions, several for each strophe. I have been selective in my identifications, focusing upon those of particular relevance to the themes discussed. Many specific scriptural sources are provided in Legrain (1989), *Adam de Saint Victor: Sämtliche Sequenzen*, ed. Wellner (1955), and Hegener (1971), and, with the use of a standard concordance, other sources can be readily identified as well.

What is new about my work are the interpretive readings of the texts, and the understanding of how they manifest the canons' communal identity.

[23] First appearing in Psalm 117:22 [118:22], this "stone which the builders rejected," which "is become the head of the corner," is referred to in both the Old and New Testaments: Isa. 28:16; Zach. 3:9; Matt. 21:42; Acts 4:11; 1 Cor. 3:11; Eph. 2:20; and 1 Peter 2:7–8. The commentary is most extensive in 1 Peter 2:4–8. Here the once-rejected cornerstone is Christ, beloved by God, and now a "living stone" and the model for a "holy priesthood," one made of living stones who are like the cornerstone itself.

new wine."[24] These jars are also the vessels collected by the widow of Elisha's disciple to receive oil;[25] and they are the five jars of the Pentateuch into which Moses poured the law.[26]

The rest of the poem concentrates on the vessels of the contemporary church, the clerical heirs of the first Apostles, men who stand under the descending spirit (strophe VIII). The oil given by Elisha (symbolic of clerical anointing) can be given to the sequence singers too, if their hearts are pure. But this oil, the sacred dew, the new wine, will not fill vessels whose "customs are discordant." The calling (the Greek abstract noun "paraclisis" [rather than the usual "paraclete" or Holy Spirit]) cannot dwell in hearts which are darkened and divided. The sequence pleads for the common life and for a unified clergy, as advocated by the Rule of St. Augustine. The sacramental liquids running down from the rock filled the men and women of the early church and will now, according to this sequence, fill the assembled singers too, but they must be properly prepared to receive them.

Strophe IX emphasizes that this is the time of grace, the time after Christ, and none of these sacramental miracles can take place without his operation, not even praise.[27] At the close, then, the sequence presents yet another sacrament, the most immediate of them all: the act of singing as representing the rightful operation of grace. The canons giving praise become one of the transformed elements of God's creation, living stones which sing and which allow the divine power to flow through them, to unify them, to renew and recreate them, as they sing. The model for unity through singing "Alleluia" was found in Augustine, as can be seen, for example, in a long sermon preached for the Ascension which describes at its very close the main event of Pentecost:

Venit Spiritus sanctus: quos primum implevit, linguis omnium gentium loquebantur. Unusquisque homo loquens omnibus linguis, quid aliud significavit, quam unitatem in omnibus linguis? Hoc tenentes, in hoc firmati, in hoc roborati, in hoc inconcussa caritate defixi, laudemus pueri Dominum, et dicamus alleluia.[28]

(The Holy Spirit came: those whom He filled first spoke with the tongues of all nations. What else did this incident where each man spoke all tongues signify except unity in all speech? Holding fast to this, confirmed in this, strengthened in this, implanted, as it were, in this by indestructible charity, let us as children praise the Lord and let us sing "Alleluia.")

In the sequence, the images of sound and of tongues refers, of course, to the description of Pentecost in Acts 2. But here the great sound is the sequence, and the tongues are those of the inspired clergy filled with the restorative grace of God. Through their singing, they attempt to recreate the historical event, not through a realistic reenactment but by a representation which captures the spirit of the

---

[24] See also Matt. 9:17, Christ's statement that new wine requires new skins, for its force would break old ones.

[25] See 4 Kings [2 Kings] 4:1–7 for the story of the widow who collected empty jars at Elisha's bidding, and then, in a closed room, miraculously was able to fill them all with the oil from a single flask.

[26] An interpretation followed by Godefroy of St. Victor in the *Fons philosophiae*.

[27] The time of grace is described at length in *SCF*, especially in the chapters at the beginning of Book II. The primary emphasis placed on grace in Hugh's writings is reflected in many of the sequence texts as well.

[28] *PL* XXXVIII, col. 1224; Muldowney trans., p. 420.

original. If the clerics sing in the right way, with common laws and moral lives, they come into their heritage, that of the Old Testament and of the primitive church of the Pauline Epistles.

"Lux iocunda, lux insignis"
Feria II, Pentecost
Text transcribed from Paris, BN lat. 14819, fols. 81–83.

I.1   Lux iocunda, lux insignis
qua de throno missus ignis
    in christi discipulos;
I.2   Corda replet linquas didat
ad concordes nos inuitat
    cordis lingue modulos.

(I   The delighting, glorious light,
by which fire is sent from the throne
    on the disciples of Christ;
strengthens hearts, enriches tongues,
invites us to concordant modes
    of heart and tongue.

II.1   Christus misit quem promisit
pignus sponse quam reuisit
    die quinquagesima;
II.2   Post dulcorem melleum
petra fudit oleum
    petra iam firmissima.

II   Christ sent whom He promised,
a pledge to the bride to whom He returns
    on the fiftieth day;
after the sweet honey,
the rock poured forth oil,
    the rock very strong at that time.

III.1   In tabellis saxeis
non in linguis igneis
    lex de monte populo;
III.2   Paucis cordis nouitas
et linguarum unitas
    datur in cenaculo.

III   In stone tablets,
not in tongues of fire,
    the law came from the mountain to the people;
the newness of heart
and the unity of tongues
    is given to a few in an upper room.

IV.1   O quam felix quam festiua
dies in qua primitiua
    fundatur ecclesia;
IV.2   Viue sunt primitie
nascentis ecclesie
    tria primum milia.

IV   O how happy, how festive,
the day on which the early
    church is founded;
the living first fruits
of the church being born
    are the three thousand (Acts 2:41).

V.1   Panes legis primitiui
sub una sunt adoptiui
    fide duo populi;
V.2   Se duobus interiecit
sicque duos unum fecit
    lapis caput anguli.

V   The loaves of the early law
are two peoples adopted
    under one faith;
and thus the stone, the headstone of the angle,
they interposed between the two
    and made the two one.

VI.1   Ultres noui non uetusti
sunt capaces noui musti
    uasa paret uidua;

VI.2   Liquorem dat helyseus
nobis sacrum rorem deus
    si corda sunt congrua.

VI   The new wineskins not the old
are full with new must,
    the widow makes ready the jars; (4 Kings
      [2 Kings] 4:1–7)
Elisha gives a liquor,
God gives to us a sacred dew,
    if our hearts are concordant.

VII.1 Non hoc musto uel liquore	VII We are not fitting for the must
non hoc digni sumus rore	or the liquor or the dew
si discordes moribus;	if we are discordant in customs;
VII.2 In obscuris uel diuisis	the calling cannot
non potest hec paraclisis	dwell in darkened
habitare cordibus.	or divided hearts.

VIII.1 Consolator alme ueni	VIII Come nourishing consoler,
linguas rege corda leni	rule our tongues, soften our hearts;
nichil fellis aut ueneni	there is nothing of gall or venom
sub tua presentia.	in your presence;
VIII.2 Nil iocundum nil amenum	nothing joyful, nothing pleasing,
nil salubre nil serenum	nothing wholesome, nothing serene,
nichil dulce nichil plenum	nothing sweet, nothing complete,
sine tua gratia.	without your grace.

IX.1 Tu lumen es et unguentum	IX You are the light and the oil,
tu celeste condimentum	you, heavenly seasoning,
aque ditans elementum	enriching the element of water
uirtute mysterii;	by the power of the mystery;
IX.2 Noua facti creatura	made in a new creation,
te laudemus mente pura	let us praise you with pure mind,
gratie nunc sed natura	now sons of grace, but formerly,
prius ire filii.	by natural order, sons of wrath (Eph. 2:4).

X.1 Tu qui dator es et donum	X You who are giver and gift,
nostri cordis omne bonum	you are all that is good in our hearts,
cor ad laudem redde pronum	render the heart ready for praise,
nostre lingue formans sonum	forming the sound of the tongue
in tua preconia;	in your preaching,
X.2 Tu purga nos a peccatis	you, the very source of piety,
auctor ipse pietatis	purge us from sins,
et in christo renouatis	and give
da perfecte nouitatis	the full joys of complete newness
plena nobis gaudia. Amen.	to us renewed in Christ.

"Simplex in essentia," sung on Pentecost Thursday at St. Victor, is also structured around parallels between the Jewish Feast of Weeks with its celebration of the reception of the Law and Pentecost with the descent of the Holy Spirit. Although "Simplex in essentia" bears the strongest resemblance to "Lux iocunda" among the sequence texts for Pentecost, it is very different from it as well. Rather than exploring continuity between Jewish and Christian traditions, this poem expounds supposed differences between the Old Law as received by Moses and the New Law believed to have been given to the Apostles by the fiery tongues of the spirit. A probable source for this interpretation is Augustine's sermon on Psalm 90 [91]:

The Lamb was slain, the Passover was celebrated, the fifty days were completed, and the Law was given. But that Law was to cause fear, not love: but that fear might be changed into love, He who was truly righteous was slain . . . He released the faithful from the guilt of the Law . . .[29]

[29] Trans. in *Expositions*, ed. Coxe, p. 451.

Following Augustine's interpretation, typologies are used as contrasts, serving the larger purposes of the sequence: (1) to emphasize the unity which comes to the church through the Holy Spirit and the Spirit-filled sacraments, and (2) to describe the role of the Apostles in the administration of the sacraments, especially that of penance (see Chapter 11, p. 245), over which the Victorines had special charge in the city of Paris. As priests of the new covenant, they are to nurture love and to consider themselves able to bind and loose with a newly won freedom. This freedom brings the joy of the jubilation, as found at the end of the text.

In strophe IV, the giving of the Old Law is characterized by the fear God's presence inspired in the people.[30] The anointing is that of Aaron described soon after the Law was given.[31]

IV Ignis, clangor buccine	(The fire, the clamor of the horn,
fragor cum caligine	a crash with darkness,
lampadum discursio;	a scattering of lights,
Terrorem incutiunt	inspire terror:
nec amorem nutriunt	they do not foster love
quem infundit unctio.	which the anointing pours on us.)

Strophe VII, by contrast, describes the priests under the New Law.

Exhibentes egris curam	(Showing forth the cure to the sick,
morbum damnant, non naturam;	they condemn the affliction, not the nature;
persequentes scelera	punishing evil deeds,
Reos premunt et castigant	they subdue the accused and chastise,
Modo soluunt modo ligant	now binding, now loosing,
potestate libera.	with a free authority.)

The sequence suggests the attitudes priest-confessors should have toward the sin and the sinner, and refers to the authority given first to Peter and then to the rest of the Apostles to bind and loose.[32] The concept of freedom referred to here is described in John 8:34–39, where once again the ability to forgive sins is described.[33] The poem also mentions the jubilation of the fiftieth year (Leviticus 25) and the jubilant day soon after Pentecost (Acts 2:40–41) when Peter and the apostles baptized three thousand in one day, an event also described in "Lux iocunda." It is the early Apostles' ability to minister successfully that the sequence poet admired and wished to see restored in his own time.

Themes found in "Qui procedis ab utroque" for Pentecost Tuesday, though related to the two sequences discussed above, are strongly reminiscent of the writings of Richard of St. Victor, and indeed, this text may be from his generation rather than from Adam's. The opening pleads for praisers and preachers, asking that the Holy Spirit render tongues eloquent and minds fervent by the power of its fire;

---

[30] The text is a version of Exodus 19:16 and 20:18.
[31] See Exodus 29:7.
[32] See Matt. 16:19 and Matt. 18:18.
[33] John 8:36: "If therefore the son shall make you free, you shall be free indeed." For a later interpretation, see Romans 6:20.

the second strophe concentrates upon the theme of three-way love, that exemplified by the Trinity and praised by Richard in his treatise *De trinitate*.[34]

I.1 Qui procedis ab utroque	(I You, Paraclete, who proceed from both
genitore genitoque	begotten and begetter
pariter paraclite;	equally,
I.2 Redde linguas eloquentes	render our tongues eloquent,
fac ferventes in te mentes	make our minds fervent in you,
flamma tua diuite.	by your precious flame.
II.1 Amor patris filiique	II Love of father and of son,
par amborum et utrique	the peer of both,
compar et consimilis;	equal and totally similar to each,
Cuncta reples cuncta foues	you fill the whole, you nurture everything,
astra regis celum moves	you rule the stars, you move the heavens,
permanens immobilis.	remaining unalterable.)

The love shared between the elements of the Trinity was, in Richard's thought, as in this sequence text, a model for the love between the members of a religious community, and for living the common life:

And so sharing of love cannot exist among any less than three persons. Now, as has been said, nothing is more glorious, nothing more magnificent, than to share in common whatever you have that is useful and pleasant.[35]

Although "Qui procedis" is based upon Richard's trinitarian doctrine, it also continues in the Victorine tradition of commenting upon the sacraments and the priest's office. In strophe VI the spirit is revered for the powers it has to change elements and give efficacy to the sacraments.

VI Tu commutas elementa	(VI You alter wholly the elements,
per te suam sacramenta	through you the sacraments
habent efficaciam;	have their efficacy;
Tu novicam vim repellis	you drive back the noxious force,
tu confutas et refellis	you confute and disprove
hostium nequitiam.	the immoral ways of the enemies.)

The Spirit is not only necessary for ritual life in the sacraments, it also aids in preaching. In the first half of strophe XI, the Spirit teaches and comforts the fearing disciples; in the second half, the poet pleads that it visit the sequence singers, and then, in a rare mention of them, the believing people as well.

---

[34] Richard's work begins with Augustine's own treatise on the same subject, but with the latter, the treatise becomes a study of interpersonal relationships. Richard of St. Victor was the master student of the human psyche at the Abbey of St. Victor in the twelfth century. For further discussion, see Fernand Guimet (1948), Zinn (1977b), and Bell (1980).

[35] See Richard of St. Victor, *De trinitate*, Book III, Chapter 15; Zinn trans., p. 388.

XI Tu qui quondam uisitasti	(XI You who formerly visited,
docuisti confortasti	taught, and comforted
timentes discipulos;	the fearing disciples,
visitare nos digneris	may you deign to visit us;
nos si placet consoleris	if it pleases you, may you comfort us
et credentes populos.	and the believing people.)

The subject of the Apostles as the first priests and administrators of the sacraments is found as well in the sequence "Postquem hostem et inferna" for Ascension. In this text, the Apostles are given their mandate by Christ: they are to teach "verbis et miraculis," that is, as the canons regular should, "verbo et exemplo." The story expounded here is central to the Augustinian canons regular of St. Victor: the mandate is symbolized by the drawing of twelve crosses on the church walls during the feast of the Dedication. It is a central mystery of the cult of the cross, as discussed in the text of "Laudes crucis" and referred to repeatedly in the writings of Hugh of St. Victor.

IV Cum recessit ita dixit	(IV When He withdrew, thus He said,
intimauit et infixit	made known, and impressed
talia discipulis;	the following things on his disciples:
Ite mundum circuite	"Go, encircle the world,
universos erudite	teach all people
verbis et miraculis . . .	by words and miraculous deeds."

VI Super egros et languentes	VI Laying your hands
manus uestras imponentes	on the sick and languishing,
sanitatem dabitis;	you will give healing;
Universas res nocentes	you will rout all harmful things,
inimicos et serpentes	enemies, snakes,
et morbos fugabitis.[36]	and diseases.")

Patriarchs and Apostles at Easter

In the sequences for Pentecost, the theme of a unified church, made of two walls (the Jews and the Gentiles) and joined in the cornerstone, is expounded in terms of the canons' special goals: the praise of the common life, and the instruction of the clergy. These themes are also found, although in slightly different guises, in the sequences for Easter, and once again the emphasis is upon the importance of unity within the church.

"Ecce dies celebris," sung on Easter Monday at St. Victor, associates the imagery of the wine and of the stone found in "Lux iocunda" with the cross, drawing both into one cubit, as in the apex of Hugh's model of the church. Christ is first typified by Samson, who achieved a kind of salvation in his own death.[37] In strophe VI, the

---

[36] Here most importantly as in Mark 16:15–18, but also in Matt. 28:19–20. These texts are not mentioned in the description of the Ascension in Acts 1:9–12.

[37] The several ways in which Samson was believed to foreshadow Christ are cataloged in Richard of St. Victor's *Liber Exceptionum*, Part II, Book IV; Châtillon edn., pp. 278–279.

wine flows from the cross into the innermost part of the beloved church.[38] Through this reference to the Song of Songs (Cant. 1:13 [1:14]) the Church, the beloved, receives the sacramental liquid flowing from the crucified Christ, the bridegroom and lover.[39] Then, as in "Lux iocunda," reference is made to the Apostles drunk with new wine on Pentecost. The wine is made of blood, and the flesh is the straining-cloth, first punctured and slashed, but then glorified.[40] Here again, the sacrament flows from the head to the apostles to the sequence singers, and offers the promise of binding them together. In strophe VIII, the stone rejected by the builders appears again, but described standing erect in victory, with reference to the cross. The idea of conformity to the cornerstone at the apex of the building persists through the end of this piece. The cross becomes a symbol of the joining of Old and New Testament figures, as it does in Hugh's model of the church.[41]

Ecce dies celebris
Feria seconda
From Paris, BN lat. 14819, fols. 64r–65v

I Ecce dies celebris	(I Behold the celebrated day,
lux succedit tenebris	light follows after darkness,
morti resurrectio.	resurrection after death.
II.1 Letis cedant tristia	II Let sad things give way to joyful ones,
cum sit maior gloria	since the glory is greater
quam prima confusio;	than the first confusion;
II.2 Umbram fugat ueritas	truth puts to flight shadow,
uetustatem nouitas	newness antiquity,
luctum consolatio.	consolation grief.
III.1 Pascha nouum colite	III Revere the new Paschal Lamb
quod preit in capite	which leads the way in the head,
membra sperent singula;	let individual members hope;
III.2 Pascha nouum christus est	Christ is the new Passover,
qui pro nobis passus est	who suffered for us,
agnus sine macula.	the lamb without blemish.
IV.1 Hosti qui nos circuit	IV From the enemy who encircles us,
predam christus eruit	Christ snatches up the prey,
quod sanson preinnuit	which Samson foreshadows
dum leonem lacerat;	when he tears the lion in pieces;

[38] Iam de sacro crucis vecte
botrus fluit in dilecte
   penetral ecclesie;
Iam, calcato torculari,
musto gaudent debriari
   gentium primitie. (M&A, p. 184)

[39] The blood and water said to have come from side of Christ on the cross (John 19:34) were commonly interpreted in medieval exegesis as the types of the sacramental wine and water. For a classic exposition of this theme, see Augustine's sermon on Psalm 126 [127], *CCSL* XL, p. 1862.

[40] See also *Proses d'Adam de Saint-Victor*, ed. Legrain, p. 23.

[41] See Hugh's commentary on the Feast of the Dedication in *SCF*, II, v, 3; p. 281: "Therefore, these two verses arranged in the sign of the cross signify the gathering of both peoples . . ."

IV.2   Dauid fortis uiribus
a leonis unguibus
et ab ursi faucibus
    gregem patris liberat.
	David, with great strength,
	frees the flock of his father
	from the claws of the lion
	    and the jaws of the bear.

V.1   Quod in morte plures strauit
sanson christum figurauit
    cuius mors uictoria;
V.2   Sanson dictus sol eorum
christus lux est electorum
    quos illustrat gratia.
	V Since in death he laid many low,
	Samson prefigured Christ,
	    whose death is victory;
	Samson is called their sun,
	Christ is the light of the elect,
	    whom He illuminates by grace.

VI.1   Iam de sacro crucis uecte
botrus fluit in dilecte
    penetral ecclesie;
VI.2   Iam calcato torculari
musto gaudent ebriari
    gentium primitie.
	VI Now from the sacred bar of the cross
	the grape flows
	    into the inner chanbers of the beloved church;
	now the winepress has been trodden,
	and the first fruits of the Gentiles
	    rejoice to be made drunk by this must.

VII.1   Saccus scissus et pertusus
in regales transit usus
saccus fit soccus glorie
    caro uictrix miserie;
VII.2   Quia regem peremerunt
rei regnum perdiderunt
sed non deletur penitus
    caym in signum positus.
	VII The torn straining cloth full of holes
	passes over into royal uses:
	the straining cloth becomes made a cover of glory,
	    the flesh the conqueror of misery;
	because they destroyed the king,
	those guilty lost the kingdom,
	but Cain is not destroyed utterly,
	    made into a sign of his order.[42]

VIII.1   Reprobatus et abiectus
lapis iste nunc electus
in tropheum stat erectus
    et in caput anguli;
VIII.2   Culpam delens non naturam
nouam creat creaturam
tenens in se ligaturam
    utriusque populi.
	VIII The very stone rejected and cast off,
	now chosen,
	stands erect in glory,
	    and as the headstone of the corner;
	abolishing fault, not nature,
	He creates a new creature,
	holding in Himself the joining
	    of both people.

IX Capiti sit gloria membrisque concordia. Amen.	IX Let there be glory to the head, and concord to the members. Amen.)

A call for unity within the church is also found in the sequence "Lux illuxit dominica." In strophe III the joyful light of grace, which illuminates many of these religious poems, finds the members of the body in conformity with the "head."

III In spe perennis gaudii lucis exsultent filii Vindicent membra meritis conformitatem capitis.	(III I hope in everlasting joy, let the sons of light exult; let the members claim likeness with the merits of the head.)

---

[42] For discussion of Cain, see note 11 above.

Advocating unity within the contemporary church was not sufficient. The Easter texts turn also to the theme of a single church existing throughout all time and containing both Jews and gentiles, illustrating it by the story of the harrowing of hell. The harrowing is one of the most dramatic of all the episodes in Christian history, and although very little is said about it in the Bible, it grew into a myth of great proportions during the Middle Ages.[43] The earliest full account is found in the apocryphal Gospel of Nicodemus, which dates from the early fifth century but contains earlier material.[44] This version was retold in the thirteenth-century *Golden Legend* by Jacobus de Voragine, who emphasized the tale's popular aspects and liturgical resonances.[45] It tells how the Devil was fooled into believing that Christ had died and was going to join the other captives in their dungeon of the lower world, and how instead Christ broke down the gates of hell, quoting from Psalm 23:7 [24:7]: "Lift up your gates, O ye princes, and be ye lifted up O eternal gates: and the King of Glory shall enter in," and led all the Old Testament "saints," beginning with old Adam, to Paradise.[46]

The harrowing underlies several of the sequences for Easter, the most important being "Zima uetus expurgetur," a sequence by Adam, the music of which will be discussed further in Chapter 13. "Zima uetus," like the Pentecost sequences discussed above, draws upon the traditions of an Old Testament feast – in this case, of course, the feast of Passover, rather than the Feast of Weeks.[47] It attempts throughout to show the Christian Easter as a new Passover, a feast to celebrate the salvation of the Gentile church, seen here as the foreign bride of an Israelite.[48] The language chosen is liturgical and sacramental, as would be expected from a Victorine sequence, and the historical events depicted are from the Old Testament, presenting, for the most part, defeated heroes who turned their failures into triumphs, especially those seen as prefigurations of the harrowing. The stories are of reversals, placed in parallel, at the end, with the resurrection. But reference is made also to the parallel meals of Passover and communion, and to liturgical texts as well.[49]

The opening strophe presents all these themes at once, woven into a dense introduction which the rest of the sequence will unravel.[50] As was described in Chapter 4, in any strophe of a late sequence, the second hemistrophe is immediately related to the first because of the repetition of the music. Thus, in minds keenly attuned to this repertory, the text of the first part of every strophe replays in the memory while the second half is sung. This structural feature was often utilized by

---

[43] See 1 Peter 3:19 for the only New Testament reference to Christ's ministering to the dead before his resurrection. A statement that Christ descended into hell before he rose is found in the Apostles' Creed, which dates from the fourth century.

[44] See Quasten (1962–67), vol. I, pp. 115–118.

[45] For recent bibliography on the *Legenda aurea*, see Dunn-Lardeau (1986). Reames (1985) provides the necessary historical context for the collection.

[46] This passage was stated dramatically by the bishop during the dedication ceremony.

[47] For text and music, see Example A.3 in the anthology (pp. 421–424 and 438).

[48] See strophe VI, second half. To his parents' dismay Samson married a Philistine woman, Judges 14:14.

[49] On the new Passover as a communion meal, see Hugh of St. Victor, *SCF*, pp. 306–308.

[50] An English translation of the text is found in the anthology (p. 438).

the poets who knew as they wrote that the first and second halves of individual strophes would be intimately interrelated through music.

In the opening hemistrophe of "Zima uetus" a command is given to celebrate Passover: worshipers are to throw out their old leaven that they might feast properly.[51] But the allusion here is not only to the Jewish feast, but also to Paul's words in 1 Cor. 5:7: "Expurgate vetus fermentum, ut sitis nova consparsio, sicut estis azymi. Etenim Pascha nostrum immolatus est Christus," which was the Epistle proper to Easter day.[52] Hence, as in Paul, the old leaven represents sin, now redeemed through the new sacrifice. the reference is also to another meal, however, to the Christian communion: a version of this same text from Paul (and its continuation) was sung at communion on Easter day: "Pascha nostrum immolatus est Christus, alleluia: itaque epulemur in azymis sinceritatis et veritatis, alleluia, alleluia, alleluia." The second half of the first strophe proclaims that this is Easter as well as Passover: "This is the day" refers not only to Psalm 117:24 [118:24], but also to the Gradual at Easter Mass, "Haec dies," which has the same text and was the scriptural verse most closely associated in the Roman liturgy with the Easter celebration.[53] The last two lines claim that the day is "marvelous by the testimony of the law."

Superimposition of Easter upon Passover continues in strophe II. In the opening, the "haec" of the Easter gradual becomes immediately the "haec" of the Exsultet, the magnificent poem intoned at the ceremony of the blessing of the Paschal candle,[54] a central event in the so-called vigil Mass of Holy Saturday (which originally opened the Easter celebration during Saturday night, but by the later Middle Ages was being celebrated on Saturday morning).[55] The Exsultet, which describes the harrowing of hell, makes the liberation of Adam and his ancestors one with the crossing of the Red Sea. This reference to the night and the harrowing persists for the several strophes of the middle part of the poem. The free voice ("vox libera") which bursts forth in Strophe III is Christ at the gates of hell thundering "Lift up your gates" (from Psalm 23:7 [24:7], as above). In the story of the harrowing as found the Gospel of Nicodemus, the loudness of the voice and the text of the Psalm are a major feature of the attack on hell.

[51] At Passover time, all old leaven and foods containing it must be removed from a dwelling. Only unleavened bread is eaten during the feast. See Exodus 12:6, 18–20.

[52] "Throw out the old yeast so that you can be the fresh dough, unleavened as you are. For our Passover has been sacrificed, that is Christ."

[53] It was also sung as the response of the Gradual throughout Easter week and the opening was used as an Office antiphon.

[54] The passage which repeats "haec" as a rhetorical device is as follows: "Haec sunt enim festa paschalia, in quibus verus ille Agnus occiditur, cuius sanguine postes fidelium consecrantur.

Haec nox est, in qua primum patres nostros, filios Israel eductos de Egypto, mare rubrum sicco vestigio transire fecisti.

Haec igitur nox est, quae peccatorum tenebras, columnae illuminatione purgavit.

Haec nox est, que hodie per universum mundum in Christo credentes, a vitiis saeculi et caligine peccatorum segregatos, reddit gratiae, sociat sanctitati.

Haec nox est, in qua destructis vinculis mortis, Christus ab inferis victor ascendit. Nihil enim nobis nasci profuit, nisi redimi profuisset."

[55] The passage referred to directly in the sequence reads "O vere beata nox, quae exspoliavit Egyptos, ditavit Hebraeos. Nox, in qua terrenis caelestia, humanis divina junguntur."

The descriptions of reversals which follow are filled with imagery of hell – snakes and serpents (who represent the Devil) – and the harrowing: in strophe IV Joseph is seen leaving the well (Gen. 37:28). In strophe V the serpents of Pharoah are devoured by the rod of Aaron, which turns into a snake itself (Exodus 7:8–12); the young child puts his hand harmlessly into the serpent's den (Isa. 11:8). In strophe VI those who mocked Elisha are punished (4 Kings [2 Kings] 2:23–24); Samson smashes the gates of Gaza and climbs up the mountain (Judges 16:3). In strophe VIII Jonah emerges living from the darkness of the whale's belly (Jon. 2:11). The night before Easter morning is depicted as the climax of the cosmic struggle between good and evil, between Christ and Satan, with all the characters of the Old Testament who understood the struggle and were on the right side being led from the jaws of their captivity to Paradise. Christ is the hook that pierces the jaw of the great serpent (strophe V), wounding him mortally and permanently containing the power of his reign.

In the final two strophes, the poet leaves the harrowing of hell and returns to the subject of Easter, with which he began. Reference is made in the penultimate strophe to the popular Easter sequence "Victime paschali laudes," and to Psalm 29:6 [30:5], which tells of sorrowing at night, followed by joy in the morning.[56] Life and death have fought their last major battle. The final strophe shows Christ in triumph, victorious and living, and presiding over His own Passover meal, both as the priest and as the offering. He invites the worshipers to the table, offering the communion bread, the wine, and the baptismal waters. He feeds and saves through the very sacraments which first flowed from the cross. At the end of the sequence, the sacraments themselves become the ultimate symbols of death turned to life. As is always the case in the poems thought to be by Adam, explaining the power of the sacraments is a major purpose, just as it was with his contemporary Hugh of St. Victor.

Yet another way of promoting the ideal of unity in the Easter sequences, an ideal central to the political purposes and spirituality of the regular canons, is through reference to the Alleluia, the song of unity between the church on earth and the church in heaven. The act of singing the sequence becomes a showing forth of oneness, of joining both heaven and earth and Old Testament and New through the power of a Hebrew word in Christian mouths.[57] The final strophes of "Salue dies dierum" and of "Sexta passus feria" describe singing and praising, as did "Lux iocunda," except that here the sound is proper to Eastertide.[58] It was on Easter that the Alleluia made its dramatic return to the Mass liturgy. Although by the mid twelfth century it is no longer their major purpose, sequences continue to provide commentary upon the meaning of Alleluia, announcing that in this song mother church joins the angels, issuing forth a praise that is both sound and symbol.

---

[56] And which begins "I praise you to the heights, Yahweh, for you have raised me up, you have not let my foes make merry over me . . . You have lifted me out of Hell."

[57] See *Proses d'Adam de Saint-Victor*, ed. Legrain, p. 32, note 43.

[58] See M&A, p. 185, strophe VI, and p. 186, strophe VIII.

"Salue dies dierum," strophe VI

Harmonie celestis patrie	(Let the voice of mother church
vox concordet matris ecclesie	join with the harmony of the heavenly fatherland,
alleluia frequentet hodie	let the faithful people repeat
plebs fidelis.	the Alleluia today;
Triumphato mortis imperio	in the triumph over the domination of death,
triumphali fruamur gaudio	let us delight with triumphant joy,
in terra pax et jubilatio	let peace be on earth and jubilation
sit in celis.	in heaven.)

The description of the singing invokes the liturgical practices of Augustine's time, when the people sang Alleluia as a respond to the soloist's psalm verses:

Nam et nos diximus Alleluia, et cantatum est mane hic, et cum jam adessemus, paulo ante diximus Alleluia.[59]

(But we too have sung Alleluia. It was sung here early in the morning, and when we were present, we sang Alleluia a little while ago.)

Conclusion: themes of unity at Christmas

The themes of unity, especially through the symbols of the cornerstone joining two sides of a building and the cross representing the joining of two peoples, have been shown to operate throughout Easter and Pentecost sequences, and to be central to those texts probably by Adam of St. Victor. This is also true of Christmas texts, one of which, "In excelsis canitur," will serve as an example and a conclusion to this discussion of texts for the temporale. Although the now familiar ideas of unity are present, here the typology has been changed to evoke the season of Christmas, emphasizing the Old Testament lineage of Christ. At Christmas, the genealogies of Christ found in the New Testament (Matthew and Luke) were read at the Office, and sermons describing the line of Judah and the house of David, from which it was believed Christ descended, were commonly preached.[60] From the late eleventh century on, some churches had dramatic readings or plays of the prophets, both of which demonstrated what was held to be Old Testament typology for the coming of Christ.[61] The plays and readings were based upon a sermon now known to be written by the Carthaginian Quodvultdeus, but which was thought throughout the Middle Ages to have been written by Augustine himself. The poet of "In excelsis canitur" draws upon this tradition, expanding it through further use of Old

---

[59] Sermon 252, *PL* XXXVIII, col. 1176; Muldowney trans., p. 333.

[60] There are problems with the genealogies presented in both New Testament accounts. Instead of reflecting accurate or historically consistent accounts of the lineage of Christ, the genealogies rather demonstrate where early Christians thought he came from. Brown (1977, p. 94) says, "while the two NT genealogies tell us how to evaluate Jesus, they tell us nothing certain about his grandparents or his great-grandparents. The message about Jesus, son of Joseph, is not that factually he is also (grand) son of either Jacob (Matthew) or of Eli (Luke) but that theologically he is 'son of David, son of Abraham' (Matthew), and 'Son of God' (Luke)."

[61] Young's (1933) introduction to the prophets' plays remains standard.

Testament typology and thereby making "the law and the psalms harmonize with the pages of the prophets" (strophe IX).

The sequence begins with reference to the infancy narrative as found in Luke 2, claiming concord between heaven and earth at the time of birth, and emphasizing the New Law of grace, a theme of major importance in sequences for other seasons as well. Soon after the mention of grace comes a description of the light of the star, which here becomes associated with the miraculous light of newness.[62] In Easter and Pentecost sequences, the light of grace found in the Pauline Epistles was a major subject. Strophes V–IX are built around Old Testament types of the divine birth, and all the persons involved were found in the medieval prophets' plays proper to the Christmas season. Instead of the stone the builders found wanting (Psalm 117:22 [118:22]), used as a central image throughout the Easter and Pentecost sequences, here the stone is the one which Nebuchadnezzar saw in his dream (Dan. 2:34–35):

videbas ita donec abscisus est lapis sine manibus et percussit statuam in pedibus eius ferreis et fictilibus et comminuit eos . . . lapis autem qui percusserat statuam factus est mons magnus et implevit universam terram

(Thus thou sawest, till a stone was cut out of a mountain without hands: and it struck the statue upon the feet thereof that were of iron and of clay, and broke them in pieces . . . but the stone that had struck the statue became a great mountain, and filled the whole earth.)

Nebuchadnezzar is one of the "Prophets" in the traditions of the prophets' plays, and his dream was commonly seen as a foretelling of the Messiah in the Christian tradition. Here the image is particularly apt, not only because of its Christmas resonances, but because it overlaps in meaning with the central idea of the power of the source filling the world, which was developed fully by Augustine and his disciple Hugh of St. Victor, and, of course, by the sequences.[63]

Strophes VI and VII expound the most common of all Christmas typologies, the root of Jesse which brings forth flower, from Isa. 11:1.[64] There is nothing unusual about the treatment of this image except that the typology is explained: a common feature of Victorine sequences. The final strophes are, like the beginning, about the many unities represented by the Christmas miracle: heaven and earth, Old Testament and New, eternity and the world of time.

In excelsis canitur
Transcribed from Paris, BN lat. 14819, fols. 50r–51v

I.1 In excelsis canitur	(I Glory is sung in the heights
nato regi gloria;	to the new-born king;
I.2 Per quem terre redditur	through whom concord is restored to earth
et celo concordia.	and to heaven.

[62] See Eph. 5:8.
[63] Hugh of St. Victor (*SCF*, p. 254): "One head, many members, and one body consists of head and members and in one body is one spirit whose fullness in the head is, indeed, participation in the members."
[64] The text resonates too with image of the rod of Aaron as described in Num. 17 and mentioned again in Hebr. 9:4.

II.1   Jure dies colitur
christi natalicia;
II.2   Quo nascente nascitur
noue legis gratia.

III.1   Mediator nobis datus
in salutis precium
non nature sed reatus
    refugit consorcium;
III.2   Non amittit claritatem
stella fundens radium
nec maria castitatem
    pariendo filium.

IV.1   Quid de monte lapis cesus
sine manu nisi ihesus
    qui de regum linea.
IV.2   Sine carnis opere
de carne puerpere
    processit uirginea.

V.1   Solitudo floreat
et desertum gaudeat
    uirga iesse floruit;
V.2   Radix uirgam uirga florem
uirgo profert saluatorem
    sicut lex precinuit.

VI.1   Radix dauid typum gessit
uirga matris que processit
    ex regali semine;
VI.2   Flos est puer nobis natus
iure flori comparatus
    pre mira dulcidine.

VII.1   In presepi reclinatur
cuius ortus celebratur
    celesti preconio.
VII.2   Celi ciues iubilant
dum pastores uigilant
    sub noctis silentio.

VIII.1   Cuncta laudes intonant
    super partum uirginis;
VIII.2   Lex et psalmi consonant
    prophetarum paginis

IX.1   Angelorum et pastorum
stelle simul et magorum
    concordant indicia;
IX.2   Reges currunt orientis
ad presepe uagientis
    gentium primordia.

II   Justly the birth day
of Christ is revered
by whose birth
the grace of the new law is born.

III   The mediator given to us
for our salvation
escaped participation
    not in our nature but in our sin;
the star pouring forth the beam of light
does not lose brightness
nor Mary her chastity
    in bearing a son.

IV   What is the stone hewn from the mountain
without human hand except Jesus,
    who from a line of kings,
without need of the flesh,
came forth from the virginal flesh
    of a woman in childbirth?

V   Let the wilderness bloom
and the desert rejoice;
    the rod of Jesse has blossomed;
the root brings forth the rod,
the rod the flower, the virgin the saviour,
    just as the law foretold.

VI   The root manifested the type of David,
the rod the type of the mother
    who came from royal seed;
the flower is the boy born for us,
justly compared to a flower
    for its marvelous sweetness.

VII   In the stable He is laid down
whose birth is celebrated
    by celestial proclamation;
the citizens of heaven rejoice
while the shepherds keep watch
    beneath the silence of night.

VIII   All praises resound
    over the offspring of the virgin;
the law and the Psalms sound together
    with the pages of the prophets.

IX   The signs of angels, shepherds,
star, and kings
    are concordant;
the kings hasten from Eastern lands
to the stable of the crying baby,
    to the beginning reign of the Gentiles.

X.1 Ihesu puer immortalis	X Jesus, immortal boy,
ex eterno temporalis	from eternity belonging to time,
nos ab huius uite malis	according to your powers,
tu potenter erue.	rescue us from the evils of this life;
X.2 Tu post uitam hanc mortalem	You, after this mortal life,
siue mortem hanc uitalem	or this living death,
uitam nobis immortalem	by degrees
clementer restitue.	restore immortal life to us.

A significant number of sequence texts created in twelfth-century Paris have a particular structure and develop a series of themes which can be readily identified with the reform theology of Hugh of St. Victor: they combine images drawn from the Bible into a composite picture of the institutional church. Using theological arguments, Hugh explained the parallels between the works of creation and restoration and the ways in which the church is the instrument of a new creation; the sequences assume understanding of the explanations and reach directly for the evocative natural elements of God's creation, the rocks, the water, the fire, and transform them into sacraments, blazing and dripping with the power they are given by the church and its liturgy. The church with head and members is united in two ways, by the preaching of the ministers and by the administration of the sacraments, and both of these are constantly described in the sequence texts.[65]

Again and again, in almost every sequence, we have seen that the underlying idea is the motion of power from the source throughout the members, and great emphasis is given to the state of the members. They must be pure, and they must be unified in custom and intention so that the light from the head may shine in them. These members are the clerics, the canons of the cathedrals and priories, those whose lives must shine forth that the people may see them and learn from them. The emphasis in these works, as in the writings of Hugh of St. Victor, is constantly upon the unity of outward appearances and inward spirituality which reformers believed necessary both for good bishops and priests and for a strong and effective church.[66] These texts bear the message of reform as developed in the writings of Hugh, but in a different language and medium. Their ultimate goal is the same as his, however: to inspire the clergy. The stockpiling of sacramental imagery in the sequences develops a strong sense, particularly at the closing of pieces, that the singing itself has become a sacrament of communal unity, creating a place in the liturgy for the worshiping clerics to emit the light of well-lived lives, the sound of tongues that harmonized with pure hearts. It is such people, an anonymous twelfth-century Victorine sermon says, who are "fit to be preachers of God who acknowledge with their lives what they preach with their mouths."[67]

---

[65] Hugh of St. Victor, *SCF*, p. 24: "Through faith we are made members, through love we are vivified. Through faith we receive union, through charity we receive vivification. Now in the sacrament through baptism we are united; through the body and blood of Christ we are vivified."

[66] Hugh says in *SCF*, p. 269: "After all these matters regarding the sacerdotal office have been treated briefly, the priests of Christ are to be admonished in order that, just as they excel by the dignity of their order, so they may excel by the sanctity of life, so that the people committed to them and taught by their teachings may obey them gladly and profit by imitating them from day to day."

[67] Walter of St. Victor and others, *Sermones*, ed. Châtillon, p. 265.

This same sermon goes on to state the constant message of the Victorine liturgy and its sequences:

If therefore you wish to praise God in the right way, first you must be upright of heart through love of God, secondly you must treat God as holy by living soberly and justly, and finally your tongue will break forth in praise of God.

In the writings of Hugh of St. Victor, the church building came to have a sacramental relationship with the liturgy within it. Through the plan of their church and the messages of the sequence repertory, the Victorines strove to demonstrate the dynamic relationship between exterior and interior. The church was their vessel, the liturgy their wine, and both were designed to proclaim their ideals and purposes.

13

The Victorine sequence music: an art of memory

Introduction: hierarchy and melody

As has been explained in Chapters 11 and 12, many of the sequence texts written in twelfth-century Paris seem designed in support of Hugh of St. Victor's vision of the church, and were also well suited to the building and ceremony of the Abbey of St. Victor. In spite of this, it is not possible to know absolutely that Parisian texts and melodies which appear both at the abbey and the cathedral were written by Victorines, even though it is probable that many of them were. Of the majority of texts belonging to both traditions one can say only this for now: they were written in Paris, by theologians in sympathy with Hugh's ideas and with Augustinian ideals of reform in general.[1]

In three of its aspects, however, the Victorine sequence repertory is unique: first, as established in Chapter 8, it contains more families of sequences in proportion to its total number of texts than any other Parisian repertory; secondly, it contains a small group of sequence texts which do not appear in other Parisian centers, some of which were undoubtedly created for the abbey itself; thirdly, many of the musical settings from St. Victor, whether or not for texts uniquely Victorine, are not found elsewhere in Paris.[2]

As I have said earlier (in Chapter 8), it must be assumed that their music was different because they made it that way, and not because of either coincidental circumstances or latent inertia. The Victorines lived in a world of bookmaking and copying, having, in the twelfth century, an important scriptorium of their own, and sending orders to copy shops or ateliers when they desired.[3] Their cantor was a highly trained specialist, in charge of the library and the scriptorium.[4] It was his job as well to correct and emend all liturgical books;[5] musical performances and

---

[1] More specific information regarding attribution will be forthcoming once the edition of the Parisian texts and melodies is completed.

[2] With the occasional exception of the sequences found at the Abbey of Ste. Geneviève, as explained in Chapters 7 and 8.

[3] A book on the Victorine scriptorium by Françoise Gasparri (*Scriptorium et scribes à Saint-Victor au XIIe Siècle*) is forthcoming in the Bibliotheca Victorina.

[4] See Fassler (1985).

[5] See LO, Chapter 19, pp. 81–82.

liturgical readings were rehearsed in his presence and corrected if they did not follow what was written.[6] It was doubtful that any Victorine music was ever transmitted exclusively through an oral tradition. Liturgists there could have adopted cathedral melodies for their texts; they knew the cathedral repertory intimately, many of their members having been cathedral canons at one time in their lives. Victorine individuality in regard to sequences during a period when all other churches followed the melodic use of the cathedral testifies first to their early adoption of many late sequences, and secondly to the importance they gave to this part of their liturgy.[7]

Because it is primarily through the music they selected and designed that the Victorines distinguished their own sequence repertories from those of all other Parisian churches, it must be assumed that the melodies intensified the particular meanings the sequences had for their community. In Chapter 8 of this book, I suggested that the Victorines wrote so many contrafacta because they wished to promote the melodies created by or associated with Adam of St. Victor. But there is more to the Victorine sequence repertory than nostalgic conservatism. As might be expected, similar amounts of energy have been expended on the sequences and on church design, and the themes developed through and within the sequentiary are the same as those operating in Victorine liturgical and theological writings.

Explaining the Victorine sequence music requires an understanding of the various layers within the music, and an identification of those parts of the repertory singled out for the greatest attention; it also requires some understanding of how the repertory developed, and a framework for this has been provided in Chapter 8. Clearly, the repertory evolved gradually and was shaped by many hands. The texts came first, along with a small group of melodies, and then more texts and, as a consequence, more melodies. Adam played a role in the first stage: some of the most magnificent and carefully worked out exegesis is found in those texts thought to be early and probably by Adam.[8] The second stage was the work of his disciples, men who may either have known him or at least have known about him.[9] There was a late stage, too, in the very late twelfth or early thirteenth century, when it is clear that the vision sustaining the creation of the Victorine texts and music had blurred, and yet when there was great interest in standardizing the repertory.[10]

The "plan" or "system" underlying the Victorine sequence repertory is not, then, informed by a rigid and carefully ordered set of principles. One can identify the system operating only in certain layers of the repertory and not in others, as would be expected of an art created by at least three generations. When this system works most forcefully, it is clear that there was an attempt (or attempts) to make the Victorine sequence repertory an art for meditation. At these times, the sequences through which the system operates embody, more perfectly than any other surviv-

---

[6] See LO, pp. 83–84.

[7] A point which can be made with some confidence because of the nature of variants found in the Parisian and Victorine sequence manuscripts.

[8] See Chapter 12 for discussion of a few pieces which may be by Adam.

[9] The reasons for assuming this second stage are presented below.

[10] The nature of corrections to Arsenal 197, a Victorine gradual with sequences from the late thirteenth century, are particularly instructive in this regard.

ing art, the ideals of Hugh of St. Victor and of the Augustinian canons regular of Paris. In the sequences, the pictograms described in Hugh's treatises on Noah's ark have been turned into another medium.

To describe such a complicated artistic phenomenon is not an easy task. It is best to begin by remembering that only certain texts were supplied with the music the Victorines wrote themselves. These texts and their music, clearly, are the most important for this study: if there is a system of sorts standing behind some of the Parisian sequence music, it is here that it will operate. Texts with Victorine music fall into several families, as described in Chapter 8. For the sake of facilitating comparison, the tables below will use the same system of numbers and letters followed there.

Any sequence melody in the twelfth century is made up of small units ("melodic units", as I call them; "timbres," as Misset and Aubry called them), each serving for an individual strophe of poetry. As demonstrated in the analysis of "Laudes crucis" in Chapter 4, many melodies that were famous in the late eleventh and early twelfth century, especially "Mane prima," "Congaudentes," "Hodierne lux diei," and, a few decades later, "Laudes crucis," are demonstrably more than the sum of their parts; other less successful melodies seem to be just a collection of individual units, with little care given to choice and arrangement. The best and most famous melodies each have a tonal plan and a way of exploring their range and they each present a series of dramatic climaxes, offering singular, long-tested, and highly revered ways of organizing the melodic units they contain into wholes. Each of them, therefore, could serve as a compositional model in two ways: first for the collection of individual melodic units it provided, and secondly for its plan of organization. Each geographic area (and even many centers) had its own versions of the most famous melodies, plus a store of other melodies that it favored. "New" melodies for twelfth-century sequence texts were often formed by reusing the elements found in a popular fund of preexisting material.[11]

Much of the work on late sequence melodies has proceeded without sufficiently acknowledging their composite nature, treating each melody as if it were a fixed entity with little opportunity for variation and development.[12] Actually, the reverse is true. To understand late sequence melodies, one must pay close attention both to the melodic units and to the plans of the melodies as wholes. What is needed to understand how the music works are catalogs of the melodic units of individual regions along with analyses of modes of combination. If this work were done, it might well be possible to study the melodic dialects of different regions of Europe in the twelfth and thirteenth centuries through their sequence repertories. This study begins such an investigation through examining the Victorine sequence music, the melodies the Victorines wrote themselves, a music not found, for the most part, in

---

[11] An introduction to the differences between the text of "Laudes crucis" in various centers is found in Weisbein (1947).

[12] Just because the music for a given text begins and ends like "Congaudentes," for example, there is no reason to suppose that its middle part will be like "Congaudentes" too. Husmann, for example, treated all Victorine melodies with common incipits as if they were all identical, when actually, as the tables below will demonstrate, many are not.

Table 13.1. *Plans of "Laudes crucis" and of twelfth-century Victorine sequence melodies*

Underscored melodic units occur only in the family; bold units only in the piece. For convenience, sequence numbers and numbers of melodic units follow M&A whenever possible

Sequence	Melodic units
Family IIA. "Laudes crucis"	
No. 18. "Laudes crucis"[a]:	61 70 <u>168</u> 83 84 85 <u>95</u> <u>102</u> 96 144 <u>137</u> 160
Family IVA: "Zima uetus"	
No. 17 "Zima uetus" (for the octave of Easter):	60 <u>69</u> <u>169</u> 89 <u>171</u> 173 104 **138** 140 <u>165</u>
No. 1 "In natale saluatoris" (for Christmas):	60 <u>69</u> <u>169</u> 89 <u>171</u> 173 139 104 100 **12**
No. 34 "Gratulemur in hac die" (for the octave of the Assumption):	60 <u>69</u> <u>169</u> 89 <u>171</u> 173 104 **139** 140 <u>165</u>
Family IVB	
No. 29 "Ecce dies triumphalis" (St. Victor):	62 <u>71</u> 72 <u>126</u> 88 80 <u>74</u> <u>133</u> <u>166</u>
No. 31 "Prunis datum" (St. Lawrence, deacon):	62 <u>71</u> 72 <u>126</u> 88 163 84 80 156 <u>133</u> <u>74</u> **106** <u>144</u> <u>160</u>
No. 4 "Gaude syon" (St. Thomas of Canterbury, bishop):	62 <u>71</u> 72 <u>126</u> 88 87 88 <u>133</u> <u>166</u> **98**
No. 28 "Roma petro" (Sts. Peter and Paul):	62 <u>71</u> 72 <u>126</u> 88 81 **76** **93** 163 **143** **147** **161**
No. 38 "Cordis sonet" (St. Leger, bishop):	62 <u>71</u> 72 88 84 80 <u>74</u> <u>133</u> **94** 87
No. 43 "Stola regni" (Apostles):	62 <u>71</u> 72 88 87 64 91 **97** 100 73
Family IVC	
No. 25 "Ex radice caritatis" (St. Victor):	63 64 <u>65</u> 81 **78** **155** 149 **135** **159** **164**
No. 3 "Gratulemur ad festivum" (St. John the Evangelist):	63 64 <u>65</u> 81 **82** 73 156 **90** **153**
No. 26 "Gaude Roma" (Sts. Peter and Paul):	63 64 <u>65</u> **127** **172** 85 181 **142** **145**
No. 42 "Cor angustum" (Apostles):	63 64 <u>65</u> 144 77 70 176 85 101 105 **107** **108** **111**
No. 47 "Ecce dies preoptata" (St. Vincent, deacon)[b]:	63 64 <u>65</u> 81 125 **153.1** 140v Par 181v <u>149</u> <u>181</u> 140v 165
Family IVD	
No. 14 "Salue dies dierum" (within the Easter octave):	<u>122</u> <u>123</u> <u>152</u> <u>125</u> <u>131</u> 132
No. 40 "Gaude, syon, que diem" (St. Martin, bishop):	<u>122</u> <u>123</u> <u>152</u> <u>125</u> <u>131</u> ★★[c] 129 132
Family IVE	
No. 9 "Virgo mater saluatoris" (for the octave of the Epiphany):	<u>121</u> <u>150</u> <u>151</u> <u>124</u> <u>130</u> 72 64 <u>134</u> 140
No. 33 "Ave uirgo . . . mater saluatoris" (within the octave of the Assumption):	<u>121</u> <u>150</u> <u>151</u> <u>124</u> <u>130</u> 72 64 <u>134</u> 140
No. 46 "Iocundare plebs fidelis" (St. Matthew)[d]:	<u>121</u> <u>150</u> <u>151</u> <u>124</u> <u>130</u> 72 64 <u>134</u> 140

[a] Eight other texts are set with very little variation   [b] not edited by M&A   [c] not in M&A   [d] not edited by M&A

any other church.[13] The first goal has been to identify and separate out the melodies the Victorines created themselves. The second task is to understand how these melodies were organized, how larger groups of them were created, and, most importantly, the relationships of the melodies to the texts and the ultimate meanings they may have had for the Victorines who expended such great energy upon them.

Fortunately, for the sake of this discussion, two scholars who worked on Victorine sequences recognized the importance of studying the melodic units and their modes of combination. Pierre Aubry provided the first (and still the only) catalog of melodic units within a late sequence repertory as a prologue to his edition of the Victorine melodies. Today, one can find faults with the catalog: Aubry left out many melodies; he failed to organize the units in any consistent and meaningful way; and he did not recognize the interrelationships between many of the units. Still, his work was a giant step in the right direction, and the only study of its type. Hans Spanke realized, apparently even better than Aubry himself, the importance of such a catalog. In his admirable attempt to explain the way Victorine sequences work, Spanke used Aubry's "timbre" numbers to create plans of the various Victorine sequences, to organize them into families, and to show the variation within individual families.[14] Table 13.1, above, is modeled upon his work.

Table 13.1 presents a concentrated overview of the music written by the Victorines themselves in the twelfth century. It can be seen at a glance that individual families have fairly consistent musical characters. In some families, the music is set in a straightforward manner with very little variation; in others it is quite freely adapted. When melodies are not varied greatly within the same family, variation usually appears to occur for the sake of the length of the texts and new music is tacked on at the end. In the freer families, IVB and IVC, although the opening few units are the same (and this is what defines the family), variation often occurs when it would not be required by the length of the text, even in the middle units of a piece.

Although one could not tell from the tables, all the melodies the Victorines wrote themselves are in fact interrelated, and they are all modeled, to a greater or lesser degree, upon "Laudes crucis."[15] In fact, the Victorines generated a musical language of their own out of a single famous song. They probably did so not only because they associated the melody "Laudes crucis" and its creation with the early history of the Augustinians and the formation of their own order, but also because they came to see the melody as pregnant with a host of symbolic meanings; and the more texts they set to it, or to variations upon it, the more meaningful it became.

Through their music and the saints commemorated, one well versed in Victorine writings and liturgy might imagine that the sequences fall into a hierarchy which contains the same broad categories found in Hugh's picture of the church. At the top of the edifice is "Laudes crucis" and the texts set to it; this is the source from

---

[13] The melody for "Zima uetus" is an exception. Although it was not sung in the cathedral and in most other Parisian churches, it was sung at Ste. Geneviève, and many churches outside Paris, at Chartres, for example.

[14] See Spanke (1941).

[15] I pointed this fact out in my Ph.D. dissertation (Fassler [1983]), but did not realize the full implications of the discovery at the time.

which all the Victorine melodies are generated. Its melismatic counterpart is "Zima uetus," a piece which becomes a source for other Victorine melodies generated from this material. These two melodies are older than the others and have priority because they become the models for all other melodies composed at St. Victor. Because of their venerability and musical prominence, the pair forms a pinnacle at the height of the repertory. Their subjects make the picture of the cross and the Lamb described by Hugh at the pinnacle of his pictogram: a singer having both melodies securely in the memory would be aware of the strong musical connections between them; yet the text of one is about the mystery of the cross and the other about the sacrifice of the Christian pasch.

The hierarchy includes the other sequences with melodies related to "Laudes crucis.' The families of sequences found in families IVB and IVC, most of which are for Apostles and members of the church hierarchy, would follow next. Below these are yet other families, IVD and IVE, some of which have texts for Apostles or bishops, but others of which are for Mary. The melodies for these texts were drawn through direct quotation upon the two source melodies "Laudes crucis" and Victorine "Zima uetus." The hierarchy as I have arranged it can be represented visually as follows:

"Laudes crucis" (Concentration on temporale)
"Zima uetus" (Concentration on temporale)

Family IVB	Family IVC
(Apostles and Clerics)	(Apostles and Clerics)
Family IVD	Family IVE
(Bishop and Mary)	(Apostles and Mary)

After years of singing the Victorine repertory, I have come to believe that at least some persons at the Abbey of St. Victor worked with such a structure in mind. I would not want to insist upon this, however, and present the arguments to the reader realizing that my own imagination may have played too active a role in uncovering this structure. It seems more responsible to explain the possibility of these correspondences and to offer meanings for them than to ignore them, however. Surely, in so far as this hierarchy exists, history and liturgical change intrude constantly upon it, and each level has some sequence texts which fit the categories exactly and some which do not. One cannot prune away the parts which seem to fit only imperfectly into the structure; nor should one expect to. Clearly there was a constant reevaluation of the repertory throughout the course of the twelfth century. Yet Adam's generation seems to have had an idea of the structure of this "church" embodied within its sequence repertory, although much of the effort in making it went into the texts. The generation or so after Hugh and Adam, which included Richard and Godefroy, was responsible for erecting much of the "building." The third generation put on the final touches, but these men were less attuned to the mystical meanings of the whole. The fourth generation had forgotten what the underlying structure was about, but it still knew that sequences were somehow interrelated, that there was an underlying system sustaining at least some of them, and that the repertory should remain intact.

It is impossible to say how many Victorines came to understand the interlocking features of the melodies and their art as related to many of the texts. All members of the community memorized the sequence repertory, and, as will be shown below, this art will only operate within minds already filled with the texts and music. It is not an art which can be "read" at a single glance; it requires the work of memory.[16] As with Hugh's depictions of history, only when all events are placed in the mind can the singer – and it is for the singers these texts and their music were written – understand the unity found in diversity, and be drawn more deeply into the center of the "edifice."[17]

The musical cornerstone: "Laudes crucis" and "Zima uetus"

The significance the "Laudes crucis" would have had for twelfth-century Augustinians in general has been discussed in Chapter 4 of this book. Its music would, of course, have been charged symbolically not only by the words of the sequence, but also by the fact that its opening eight notes are closely modeled upon the Alleluia for feasts of the cross, "Dulce lignum." This sequence was heard as the song of the cross, the "dulce melos" which the canons regular of St. Victor clearly believed was particularly connected with their order. Their devotion to the cross is shown not only by the dedication of a choir altar to it, but also, and more importantly, through the writings of Hugh of St. Victor and later Victorines as well. The sequence melodies based upon "Laudes crucis" are yet another aspect of this cult, presented in music that was capable of symbolizing the transferral of the power of the cross through the preachers to all believers.

The Victorine settings of the "Laudes crucis" melody to other texts are all very similar. They were not, however, content to use the melody for the same group of texts as at the cathedral. As the list (on pp. 178–181 of Chapter 8) shows, when the Victorines differed from the cathedral use, they increased the number of pieces for the temporale ("Lux iocunda," "Postquam hostem," "Profitentes") and removed pieces for the sanctorale ("Gaude syon," "Prunis datum," "Roma petro"). Thus, at some point in the development of the repertory, there was an attempt to make "Laudes crucis" a melody for temporal feasts, which celebrate Christ. This work resulted in a greater number of texts for the temporale set to "Laudes crucis," but some saints' feasts continued to be sung to "Laudes crucis": "Corde uoce" for St. Paul, "Heri mundus" for St. Stephen, "Laus erumpat" for St. Michael, and "Vox sonora" for St. Catherine. It is likely that only two of these saints' texts belong to an early layer: the Victorines had an altar dedicated to St. Stephen before the mid

---

[16] For Victorine attitudes toward memory, see Zinn (1974).

[17] Zinn (1972–73) has related Hugh's drawings of the ark to the Tibetan mandala. The Victorines did believe in meditation upon their religious art, as did many other religious during the Middle Ages; one should not be surprised to find that many ways of heightening this experience were designed.

twelfth century; St. Paul was counted among the apostles, who had their own altar. Other saints' sequences probably entered later, after the repertory had been put in order by Victorines of Richard's generation: the revisions in the ordinal show that "Laus erumpat" for St. Michael may have been an addition, while "Vox sonora" for St. Catherine (set to "Laudes crucis" at both the cathedral and St. Victor) was certainly one, coming into the Victorine repertory late (probably well after the major redaction had taken place).

When were the four sequences of the temporale not set to "Laudes crucis" at the cathedral assigned to it at St. Victor? Two of them may have been set early, "Lux iocunda" and "Postquam hostem," but "Profitentes" came in later.[18] "Letabundi iubilemus" for the Transfiguration is probably later, too. One can suppose that this sequence was added to the Victorine repertory in the years after an altar was dedicated to the Transfiguration in the chapel of the Bishop of Lisieux, that is, sometime after 1180.[19] The Parisian calendar with sequences in Appendix 5 (pp. 390–411) shows that "Letabundi iubilemus" was not transmitted even to those repertories that incorporated great numbers of Victorine pieces in the early thirteenth century; it remained isolated in Victorine manuscripts.[20] This too suggests tht it was a later piece standing outside the mainstream of the tradition. The two melodic units in "Laudes crucis" that use Bᵇs to illustrate a point in the original text are not usually found in the contrafacta, those responsible for resetting the melody apparently deciding that they would be out of place. The single exception to this rule at St. Victor is "Letabundi iubilemus": its melody employs unit 102 just as in the original "Laudes crucis," with Bᵇs, but for a part of the poem praising Christ as the king of all and the light of the saints,[21] a theme very different from the one that first occasioned Bᵇs (see the discussion of "Laudes crucis" on pp. 72–77). This suggests that the setting of "Letabundi iubilemus" was made at a somewhat later time, by people who no longer remembered the conventions of Adam's generation.

The Easter sequence "Zima uetus" was attributed to Adam of St. Victor in the late twelfth century.[22] It shows every indication of having come into the Victorine repertory early and having been especially favored by the Victorines: the incipit is one of the few for late sequences written in the ordinal by the original hand; its melody, which was not sung at the cathedral (there the text was set to "Laudes crucis"), was sung at Ste. Geneviève, and its centers outside Paris as well. It is not unreasonable to suppose that this melody represents Adam's own gift to the Abbey of St. Victor, and that here one finds the Parisian master's own reworking of the melody "Laudes crucis." Whoever wrote this melody, whether Adam or not, had meditated long upon "Laudes crucis," had great respect for it, and deliberately and boldly transformed it into a new song, one which could represent musically the triumph of the cross on Easter day.

---

[18] The text is scholastic in its mode of development and does not sound like the "Victorine" sequences. See Fries (1983).

[19] See Chapter 11.

[20] See Appendix 5 (p. 402).

[21] It should be noted that M&A's edition has the ♭ in the wrong place, on F! See p. 288.

[22] See Fassler (1984).

Both the text and the music of "Zima uetus" depict transformations: the poem is about the adversity and defeat of the Crucifixion turned to Easter victory through the action of the harrowing of hell;[23] the music is a variation upon "Laudes crucis," changed to a piece with a different character, the familiar shapes and contours of the lines made more florid and dramatic. Through this music, emblematically, the song of the cross is changed into a new song. The composer has taken "Laudes crucis" for his model, using direct quotations throughout, particularly at the beginning. Although he has also freely reworked well-known melodic units into new state-ments, he has great respect for the total structure of "Laudes crucis," dividing his own melody into three sections which are reminiscent of those found in the original, and borrowing material from the model in order. This composer clearly felt free to transform his model in any way he chose, yet it was important to him that the connections between the old and new works remained direct and perceiv-able, especially at the beginning. If this were not true, the symbolic power of the original would be lost, as would the major thematic idea of the new music, that this is a new cross, now beautified through triumph over death. The voice that sings of its glories is free, crossing customary cadence points, running lines of text together rhapsodically.

In Example A.3 in the anthology (pp. 421–424), the melody of "Zima uetus" is presented alongside the appropriate melodic units from "Laudes crucis." A cursory glance reveals that there is a concentration of directly borrowed music in the early part of the melody. Yet, even when "Zima uetus" is directly modeled upon "Laudes crucis," the original melody is freely adapted and greatly changed. Unit 1 (t. 60) provides an excellent example of the way the composer works. "Laudes crucis," Unit 1A (t. 61), is comprised of two small cells, the first consisting of an ornamented g, and the second of a leap up to c′ and a stepwise descent back to g. Each cell accommodates four syllables of text, and the break between them matches the caesura found in the poetry. An identical situation prevails in "Zima uetus," except that in the first cell the g is decorated with both upper and lower neighbor notes, in the second cell the c′ is ornamented with upper and lower neighbors, and the descent hovers just above the expected g. Thus the music pushes forward, toward the next unit, and away from the weak cadence closing the first unit. In the second unit, the first cell is identical to that of unit 2A of "Laudes crucis" and the rest of the phrase in "Zima" is calmer and more staid at the close than that of the model. In Unit 2B, however, the melody of "Zima" seems to rush ahead of "Laudes," using material from 3B and C but breaking the alignment between the accentual pattern and the position of the text: t. 168B begins in the middle of the line (at the word "liberavit"), spills over into the next line, and then closes at what is the middle of the phrase in "Laudes crucis." The text here describes freedom from servitude. The music, with an unusual violation of customary patterns, may be underscoring the meaning of the text.

Although the opening three units of "Zima uetus" are strongly dependent upon

---

[23] The text is discussed in Chapter 12, pp. 282–284.

direct quotation from the model, the rest are freer. They resembled "Laudes crucis" because they seek to restate its style, reworking familiar contours and utilizing musical cells found early in the piece but not containing great amounts of note-for-note quotation. Middle phrases, as in "Laudes crucis," tend to be very alike in contour, even when the pitches are not the same. Units 4B (t. 89B), 5B (t. 171B), 5E (t. 171E), 6B (t. 173B), 7B (t. 104B), and 8B (t. 138B) all begin with a melodic cell which descends, followed by a cell which ascends briefly, only to move even lower than the first cell of the phrase. The original model for all these phrases is "Laudes crucis" 4B (t. 84B), which is referred to strongly in the fourth unit of "Zima uetus" (t. 89B) and thus initiates the entire set. The tone painting found in "Laudes crucis" is also found in "Zima uetus," B♭s being used in strategic places to sneer at the devil in 5F (t. 171F) and 7B (t. 104B).

"Zima uetus" is also like "Laudes crucis" in its overall structure: three distinct sections, each of which resembles the sections of the model. The first three units, the textual introduction, are served by melodic phrases which follow "Laudes crucis" carefully, and which explore, for the most part, only limited parts of the G scales at one time. The middle section, which extends from the fourth through the eighth units, is ever more complicated, both in the range and complexity of the lines and in the extent of the ornamentation. The final section, which consists of two units (t. 140 and t. 160), corresponds to the final section of "Laudes crucis," either quoting from it directly or adopting the same musical style. The lines are calmer, and phrases are often made up of short sequential phrases or cadential formulas. There is an emphasis on the chain of thirds g–d–d′–f′, perhaps to establish firmly the tonality of the piece.[24]

The creator or creators of "Zima uetus" expended much effort to make an Easter sequence whose text and music fit the occasion thematically and liturgically. That the text was not sung at Easter, either at the cathedral (Easter Tuesday) or St. Victor (the Easter Octave), seems unfortunate, for its author and composer certainly had that intention. But even "Zima uetus" was not able to unseat the early sequence traditionally sung on Easter day in Paris, "Fulgens preclara." The Victorines, however, who realized the power and beauty of their particular version of "Zima uetus," used the melody elsewhere in their liturgy, and by studying these occasions, more information can be gained about the Victorine attitude toward "Zima uetus" and their method of setting sequence texts to music.

"Zima uetus" and the two other sequences set to the same melody ("In natale saluatoris" and "Gratulemur in hac die") formed a small family of pieces at the Abbey of St. Victor. In a general sense, the purpose of the three works was to celebrate three major feasts of the late medieval Roman church: Easter, Christmas, and the Assumption of the Blessed Virgin Mary. By assigning the melody to these three feasts only, the Victorines demonstrated their high regard for it, and through its use, they were able to interrelate the themes of the three sequence texts. Each of these feasts commemorates what O. B. Hardison (following Aristotle) described as

---

[24] See discussion of chains of thirds and the G-tonality in twelfth-century music in Treitler (1967).

a "peripeteia: a reversal causing the action to 'veer around in the opposite direction,'" a dramatic change from one state to another.[25] It has already been demonstrated how both the text and melody of "Zima uetus" are about night turning to
day, grief to joy, death to life. The two other sequence texts set to this same melody
are deliberately constructed to follow a similar plan and to discuss the same themes
of change and transformation, but, of course, within the context of different feasts.

A brief examination of "In natale" and "Gratulemur" reveals that the older
sequence melody remains essentially the same (see p. 293). Since each melodic unit of
"Zima uetus" recalled a particular strophe of poetry, the new texts were, inevitably,
sometimes written with the original strophes in mind. It was possible, with such a
system of contrafacta, to make the meaning of each text richer in this way, because
the music linked them together. And when the music itself was of symbolic
significance, as in the case of "Zima uetus," the entire interrelated complex
resonated with a host of associations. A mind which contained all three sequences
would hear all three of them each time any one of them was sung.

Of the two other pieces set to "Zima uetus" at St. Victor, "In natale" is probably
the earlier: it shows a far better understanding of the contrafacta technique described
above, and may have been written by the direct descendants of Adam or even by
Adam himself. The opening strophe alone is enough to demonstrate the interplay of
meanings possible in this combination of text and music: first of all one hears a song
which is clearly and deliberately a transformed "Laudes crucis," the song of the
Cross made new. Yet the text is for the Christmas season, and describes the sound
which angels and humans make together when celebrating the coming of the
Redeemer into the world. They sing triumphantly at this moment, as one would
expect, but they sing the song of the cross, and of the death and victory to come at
the end. All time crushes into one dense instant of meaning, and Christmas, Passion,
and Easter become one. The use of the word "dulce" here refers back to the sweet
wood and to the sweet "melos" of "Laudes crucis," which is ever present, of course,
in the music itself.

In strophe 2 the poet of "In natale" seizes upon the "haec dies" used in "Zima
uetus" and depicts yet another day, the "felix dies," on which the man coeternal
with the father was born. Just as strophe II of "Zima" alluded to the "Haec nox" of
the Holy Saturday Exsultet, so strophe II of "In natale" alludes to another famous
phrase for the Exsultet, the "O felix culpa." Strophe III continues the same idea as
strophe I: the infinite, the timeless, the immense, the divinity which no place can
contain, is translated into a single space, localized in both time and place, so that all
might be redeemed. The emphasis upon themes of time and timelessness is particularly appropriate to Christmas, the season in which Christian exegetes
throughout the centuries have been most inspired to address these subjects.[26] But the
text corresponds here to that of "Zima uetus" as well, which, at this very point,
describes how the past is the shadow of the future.

---

[25] Hardison (1965), p. 139.
[26] Especially important are Augustine's sermons written for the Christmas season.

"In natale saluatoris," strophes I and II

I	In natale saluatoris	(I	On the birthday of the saviour,
	angelorum nostra choris		let our condition sing together with
	succinat condicio;		the choirs of angels;
	Harmonia diuersorum		the harmony of diverse things
	sed in unum redactorum		reduced into one
	dulcis est connectio.		is a sweet union.
II	Felix dies hodiernus	II	How happy the present day
	in quo patri coeternus		On which the one coeternal with the father
	nascitur ex uirgine;		is born from the virgin;
	Felix dies et iocundus		Happy and joyful day,
	illustrari gaudent mundus		the world rejoices to be illuminated
	ueri solis lumine.		by the light of the true sun.)

Other parallels between the texts appear as well: the climactic unit 7 (t. 104), whose text in "Zima uetus" describes Christ breaking hell's dire gates, is sung in "In natale" with a text describing the devils who vex mortals violently and fraudulently. Although the B♭ of t. 104 is retained in the music of "In natale unit 7B (7b: "quam nos vexant violenter") because the text is appropriate for such tone painting, "In natale," strophe IV has a revised ending of "Zima uetus" unit 5F (t. 171F), and the B♭ is eliminated.[27] Here the text describes the unity of word, flesh, and spirit in the singular person of Christ, not the sort of subject that, to the Victorine sensibility then prevailing, calls for B♭s. "In natale," then, was written at a time when various Victorine musical conventions of the mid twelfth century were still understood. This is not the case for the sequence to be discussed below.

"Gratulemur" is one of the few pieces in the Victorine repertory which, like "Letabundi iubilemus" for the Transfiguration, was sung in no other Parisian churches and in none of the centers that incorporated a large repertory of Victorine sequences.[28] It too, therefore, is probably a very late piece, one written substantially after the greatest part of the repertory was formed. It suggests that the Octave of the Assumption and the pieces found there may have been late in being organized and standardized at St. Victor. Accordingly, the attempt at creating a parallel between the texts operates only in a general sense. There is a reference to the text of "Zima uetus" in the opening with the "hac die" and "dies ista," and the verb "expurgemus" of strophe III recalls "expurgetur." Yet "Gratulemur" has B♭s in unit 7 (t. 104), even though there is nothing in the melody or the text to call for them (cf. "Letabundi," p. 297).[29] The piece was probably created to be a member of this group because its theme and liturgical position provide a well-drawn parallel with those of "Zima uetus." But the art of closely drawn correspondences between

[27] See M&A, pp. 228–288. Strophe IV is labeled "5–6" and begins with the text "Non peccatum, sed peccati." Strophe VII is labeled 11 and begins "O maria, stella maris."

[28] In addition to these two, there is only one other such piece, "Ave uirgo . . . porta," sung on Saturday after the Assumption.

[29] M&A have mistranscribed the piece, leaving the B♭s out. Compare their version of strophe VII ("De te uirga"), p. 298, with the Victorine sequentiary, lat. 14819, fol. 87. In the manuscript the accidentals are clearly indicated for each versicle.

musically related texts is not found here, and the original reason for B♭s has been quite forgotten.

The relationship between "Zima uetus" and the two later pieces set to its melody is not consistent. The work of interrelating is not exact; rather the texts sometimes seem in close agreement and sometimes not. The character of the relationship is symbolic, rather than neatly reasoned, as might be expected; understanding would have come after meditation upon the material. Sometimes the messages burst forth clearly, as in the opening of the pieces; at other times they are elusive, and modern interpretations should not be pushed too hard. This is to be expected of an art designed by exegetes whose main task was to allegorize the Bible and the liturgy.

"Laudes crucis" and "Zima uetus" and their texts reflect the common twelfth-century practice of creating contrafacta to build families of interrelated texts and melodies. It is, of course, no coincidence that Hugh of St. Victor's theology and his vision of the church constantly strove to create an impression of simultaneous unity and diversity, and that he believed humans could be transformed by meditating upon subjects which, like his model of the church, worked in this way. To understand more completely how Hugh's ideas are made manifest in the sequence repertory, one must look at the remaining families of texts set to uniquely Victorine music.

The Apostles and the cross

Analysis of "Laudes crucis" and "Zima uetus" leads to the heart of the Victorine sequence repertory, that is, to the melodies known to have been created by the Victorines exclusively for their own liturgy. Although the Victorine melody for "Zima uetus" was most likely written by Adam for the abbey, it does survive in other early collections frequently enough to raise doubt.[30] The rest of the sequences whose texts are listed in Chapter 8, pp. 180–181 (Family IV) and whose melodies are outlined in Table 13.1 were definitely set to music by the Victorines themselves; in all cases, this was music of their own design. Several of these texts were written at the abbey as well. It is through these pieces that the Victorines reveal most clearly what their great book of sequences signified to them, for it is here that the work is most directly their own.

In Chapter 12, it was shown how several Parisian sequences written for feasts of the temporale emphasize the sacraments and the transferral of their power from the head to the members. This major theme continues to prevail in the rest of the repertory as well, but in a different way. Here the emphasis is upon the receiving of the power and the ways in which each who would transfer it to the people must bear his own cross as an example. Thus, "Laudes crucis" is redefined once again by this group of texts as well, all of which are set to yet other versions of it.

---

[30] Among other places, the Victorine "Zima uetus" is found in Rome, Bibl. Ang. 435 from St. Chèron in Chartres, in the sequentiary from Aix-la-Chapelle (in an incomplete version because of the lacuna in the manuscript), and in Rouen 249 from Eu in Normandy.

There is no better introduction to these four smaller families of sequences, which, taken together, make up an entire group, than one of the two texts written for the Apostles at the Abbey of St. Victor, "Stola regni" (no. 43, family IVB). Whereas "Laudes crucis" itself represented Christ to the Victorines and "Zima uetus" symbolized first Christ and, later, his mother in glory, "Stola regni" represents the medium levels of the hierarchy, whose saints carried the message of the cross throughout the world "verbo et exemplo." Hugh of St. Victor wrote to inspire those who followed in the Apostles' footsteps, the clergy of his own time. These sequences for the Apostles are meant to dispose this same group of people toward chastity, the common life, and fervent praise, by making them feel at one with the ecclesiastical hierarchy as it was believed to have existed throughout the history of the Church.

The opening of "Stola regni" urges the singers to make their hearts and mouths one, to make the inner self match the words they speak, to be, as Hugh so often demanded, both pious within and holy without.[31] The sequence as prized at St. Victor is a measure of this state: it cannot be sung properly by anyone who is not chaste, by anyone whose deeds and inner thoughts are not trained to the message of the words.[32] In "Stola regni" the collective mind and mouth harps (the verb is "psallere") for the gathering of apostles in heaven.[33] The sonorous sound of the pure mind becomes the angelic hymn itself. The apostles wear the "stola" or stole, the garment worn by ordained clerics from the deacons on up.[34] The opening challenges the worshipers to mean what they sing, to be what they claim to be.

In its second and third strophes, the poet of "Stola regni" depicts Christ surrounded by this new senate: Christ is the apex of the church and the Apostles, the outstanding Nazarenes, create the building by telling the world of the battles of the cross and the glory of victory.[35] The next strophes show the apostles constructing the church through their actions of proclaiming and dispensing the word of God, referring to Psalm 17 [18] ("Caeli enarrant"), the so-called "Apostolic Psalm." Several of the opening strophes of the sequence are based on this Psalm, and particularly on its opening verses.

---

[31] This theme is found, of course, in sequences from other repertories and times as well. But the Victorines use it so often that it becomes a hallmark of their style.

[32] In "Cor angustum," another Victorine sequence for the Apostles, reference is made to the first strophe of "Laudes crucis," a reference which, it will be demonstrated shortly, is in the music as well. The worshiper's narrow heart must swell so the community can "raise the praises of the apostolic senate": "Cor angustum dilatemus / Ut senatus exaltemus / Laudes apostolici." The "laudes" and "exaltare" are prominent in the first lines of "Laudes crucis" as well.

[33] The gathering of apostles in both Victorine sequences is called "senatus," a reference to the Notkerian sequence "Clare sanctorum" which was sung in centers throughout Europe (including Paris) for feasts of the apostles. At St. Victor, "Clare sanctorum" was the work these new pieces were replacing. The opening reads "Clare sanctorum / senatus apostolorum / princeps orbis terrarum / rectorque regnorum." See von den Steinen *Notker der Dichter*, Editionsband, p. 80.

[34] Hugh of St. Victor says in *SCF*, p. 277: "The stole, which by another name is called napkin, is that which is placed upon the neck of the priest to signify that he has assumed the yoke of the Lord." In the sequence, the stole of strophe I becomes the yoke of strophe IV.

[35] With reference to the feast of the Dedication of the Church: see *SCF*, p. 281.

Caeli enarrant gloriam Dei	(The heavens shew forth the glory of God,
et opera manuum eius adnuntiat	and the firmament declareth the work of
firmamentum	his hands.
dies diei eructat verbum	Day to day uttereth speech,
et nox nocti indicat scientiam	and night to night sheweth knowledge.
non sunt loquellae neque sermones	There are no speeches or languages
quorum non audiantur voces eorum	where their voices are not heard.
in omnem terram exivit sonus eorum	Their sound hath gone forth into all the earth:
et in fines orbis terrae verba eorum	and their words unto the ends of the world.
in sole posuit tabernaculum suum	He hath set His tabernacle in the sun:
et ipse tamquam sponsus	and He, as a bridegroom coming out of His
procedens de thalamo suo	bride chamber,
exsultavit ut gigans ad	hath rejoiced as a giant to run the way:)
currendam viam suam:	

By spreading the seed, the Apostles bear the light yoke of Matt. 11:30 and evoke the parable of the good sower (Matt. 13:4–23, Mark 4:3–20, and Luke 8:5–15); they become the bridesmen of the New Law, bringing the queenly spouse (the church) to the embrace of the new king.[36] They are the foundation of the temple, the living stones, the cement holding the building together;[37] they are the joining between two things, Jews and Gentiles, which makes the edifice – replicas of the cornerstone itself.[38] Piling up images from the Old Testament the poet finds other groups of twelve to represent them: the twelve gates of Jerusalem (Apoc. [Rev.] 21:12–14) and the twelve patriarchs; and particularly those whose imagery relates to the Old Testament temple and liturgy: the twelve oxen who support the sea in the temple (strophe VIII.2),[39] the loaves of the tabernacle (strophe IX.1),[40] the twelve gems on Aaron's priestly garments (strophe IX.2).[41] He says, "with these recognizable figures, the new leaders of the people portend." The twelve build the church, they preach in it, they administer its sacraments. Like the discussion of the priesthood, its *ordines*, its garments, found in Hugh of St. Victor's *De sacramentis*, Book II, parts

---

[36] As in Eph. 5:25–27, "Husbands love your wives, as Christ also loved the church, and delivered himself up for it: That he might sanctify it, cleansing it by the laver of the water in the word of life: That he might present it to himself a glorious church, not having any spot or wrinkle, or any such thing; but that it should be holy, and without blemish."

[37] The reference to 1 Peter 2:5 is especially apt, since the text is about the priesthood: "Be you also as living stones built up, a spiritual house, a holy priesthood, to offer up spiritual sacrifices, acceptable to God by Jesus Christ." Also important as a source is 1 Cor. 3:9–10, "For we are God's coadjutors: you are God's husbandry; you are God's building. According to the grace of God that is given to me, as a wise architect, I have laid the foundation; and another buildeth thereupon . . ."

[38] See Exodus 26:23–24, "et rursum alias duas quae in angulis erigantur post tergum tabernaculi eruntque coniunctae a deorsum usque sursum et una omnes conpago retinebit duabus quoque tabulis quae in angulis ponendae sunt similis iunctura servabitur." (And again other two which shall be erected in the corners at the back of the tabernacle. And they shall be joined together from beneath unto the top, and one joint shall hold them all. The like joining shall be observed for the two boards also that are to be put in the corners.)

[39] See *JBC*, p. 1264, for discussion of the laver supported by the oxen as found in 3 Kings [1 Kings] 7:23–26. This large basin was used for ritual purification.

[40] See Lev. 24:5–9 and commentary in *JBC*, p. 1270.

[41] See Sirach 25:11–12. According to this passage, the jewels are one for each of the twelve tribes.

2–4, the language and imagery explain the Christian priesthood in terms of the Levites, and draw both Jewish and later Christian traditions into the early Judeo-Christian church of the first century CE. Thus the apostles become the canons regular of olden times, just as the canons are the new Levites and the new Apostles.

"Stola regni" for the Apostles as found in Paris, BN lat. 14452

I.1 Stola regni laureatus	(I Decorated with the stole of authority
summi regis est senatus	is the senate of the highest king,
cetus apostolicus;	the apostolic throng
I.2 Cui psallant mens et ora	to whom let the mind and mouth sing.
mentis munde uox sonora	The sonorous voice of the pure mind
hymnus est angelicus.	is the angelic hymn [the sequence].
II.1 Hic est ordo mundi decus	II This order is the glory of the world,
omnis carnis iudex equus	the fair judge of all flesh,
noue preco gratie;	the herald of new grace;
II.2 Ab eterno preelectus	eternally preelected,
cuius floret architectus	the master builder flourishes
ad culmen ecclesie.	at the apex of his church.
III.1 Hii preclari nazarei	III There the glorious Nazarenes
bella crucis et trophei	tell the world
mundo narrant gloriam;	the struggles of the cross and the glory of the victory;
III.2 Sic dispensant uerbum dei	thus they distribute the word of God,
quod nox nocti lux diei	so that night to night, light to the day,
indicant scientiam.	demonstrate knowledge.
IV.1 Honus leue iugum mite	IV Advertising the light burden and the easy yoke,
proponentes semen uite	let them sow the seed of life
mundi spargunt terminis;	to the ends of the world;
IV.2 Germen promit terra culta	the cultivated earth sends forth the shoot;
feneratur fruge multa	faith in the God-man
fides dei hominis.	repays much fruit.
V.1 Paranimphi noue legis	V Bridesmen of the new law,
ad amplexum noue regis	they will lead the queenly bride
sponsam ducent regiam;	to the embrace of the new king;
V.2 Sine ruga sine neuo	without blemish or wart,
permansuram omni euo	the bride who will remain for all the age,
uirginem ecclesiam.	the virgin church.
VI.1 Hec est uirgo gignens fetus	This is the virgin bringing forth the young,
semper noua tamen uetus	ever new, yet old,
sed defectus nescia;	but unknowing of defect;
VI.2 Cuius thorus mens sincera	whose marriage bed is a pure mind,
cuius partus fides uera	whose bringing forth is true faith,
cuius dos est gratia.	whose dowry is grace.

VII.1 Hii sunt templi fundamentum	VII These are the foundation,
uiuus lapis et cementum	the living stone and mortar
ligans edificium;	binding the edifice;
VII.2 Hii sunt porte ciuitatis	These are the gates of the city,
hii compago unitatis	these the joining of the unity
israhel et gentium.	of Israel and the Gentiles.
VIII.1 Hii triturant aream	VIII These thresh the field,
uentilantes paleam	winnowing straw
uentilabri iustitia;	by the justice of the winnowing fork [Matt.3:12];
VIII.2 Quos designant erei	whom the copper oxen
boues maris uitrei	of the glassy sea appointed
salomonis industria.	through the effort of Solomon.
IX.1 Patrarche duodeni	IX The twelve patriarchs,
fontes aque gustu leni	the fountains of water with the sweet taste,
panes tabernaculi;	the loaves of the tabernacle,
IX.2 Gemme uestis sacerdotis	the jewels on priestly clothing:
hoc figuris signant notis	so signify this with well-known figures,
noui duces populi.	the leaders of the new people.
X.1 Horum nutu cedat error	X Let error withdraw with their nod,
crescat fides absit terror	let faith increase, let terror
finalis sententie;	of the last judgment be removed,
X.1 Ut soluti a delictis	so that, freed from our crimes,
sociemur benedictis	we may join together with the blessed
ad tribunal glorie.	at the judgment seat of glory.

In "Cor angustum" the Apostles are once again seen as carrying the message of the cross throughout the world, but this sequence is a catalog, usually with a strophe for each Apostle, and lacks the exegetical force of "Stola regni."[42] At a guess, "Stola regni" would seem the older of the two sequences for the apostles and the one more likely by Adam or his immediate disciples. In "Cor angustum" Peter with his keys is described in language which makes him both apostle and Bishop of Rome: he is head of "the sacred college," and the keeper of the sheepfold. One senses here the great hope of many twelfth-century reformers for church unity through stronger ties to a more powerful pope. Although Peter's crucifixion is not mentioned, those

---

[42] Opening of "Cor angustum" for the Apostles, as found in Paris, BN lat. 14452:

I.1 Cor angustum dilatemus	(I Let us swell the narrow heart
ut senatus exaltemus	so that we may raise praises
laudes apostolici;	to the apostolic senate;
I.2 Leta lingue mens collaudet	let the joyful mind extol together with the tongue:
que si laude se defraudet	if it might defraud itself of praise,
fructus laus est modici.	the praise is of middling worth.
II.1 Petro laudis sit primatus	II Let the primacy of praise be to Peter,
cui prouenit principatus	to whom the first place falls
in sacrum collegium.	in the sacred college;
II.2 Petro tradit claues celi	to Peter, Christ assigns the keys of heaven,
petro credit ut fideli	to Peter, as to a loyal servant,
curam christus ouium;	he entrusts the care of the sheep.)

of Andrew and Philip are.[43] Other Apostles are shown performing sacraments and sowing the seeds of doctrine.

These two sequences, in two very different ways, advanced the same ideas: (1) the mystery and meaning of the cross is transmitted through the Apostles, who are types of the members of the ecclesiastical hierarchy, and (2) the history of this transmission and the people responsible creates a picture of the church. These ideas have been met before in the pages of this book: in Chapter 10, Hugh of St. Victor's vision of the church was seen to have centered upon a history of the sacraments, with Christ as the link between the sacramental power of nature and the sacraments within the liturgy; it was demonstrated, too, in this same chapter that Hugh believed in the importance of meditating upon works of art which embodied a history of the Church and its sacraments; in Chapter 11, one discovers the several ways in which the Victorine church, liturgy, and selected sequence texts for the temporale were designed in concert to promote the ideals of a reformed clergy serving to unify and strengthen the church by continuing the apostolic mission. To find these ideas in sequence texts for the sanctorale as well underscores their fundamental importance to this community of canons regular. One should not be surprised, therefore, to find that the Victorines sought ways of making not only their sequence texts but also their sequence music resound with the song of the cross and depict the history of the transmission of its powers.

With "Stola regni" and "Cor angustum" as guides, it is now possible to turn to the families of sequences to which they belong, those listed in Table 13.1, families IVB–E. These sequences commemorate Apostles, other important members of the ecclesiastical hierarchy, and (in the more recent layers) the Virgin Mary. In the midst of this illustrious company, the inner circle upon which the holy spirit descended at Pentecost and the teachers and preachers who followed after them as bishops and other high-ranking officials, is St. Victor. With one sequence in each of the two primary families, Victor is honored as is no other non-clerical saint and his presence within these particular families attests to the Victorine belief that they belonged with the apostolic senate, whose work was to teach and spread the faith. The music works to underscore and further develop the meanings of the texts and the Victorine liturgy in two ways:

(1) Since all the music written by the Victorines themselves is based upon the melodies of "Laudes crucis" and (to a lesser extent) "Zima uetus," it thus depicts through its very notes the process of transmission of the power of the cross from the head of the church to the teachers and preachers who form the ecclesiastical hierarchy. By using this particular music for families IVB–E, the entire section of the sequence repertory completely designed and created by the Victorines themselves became a sounding representative of the idea of transmission and building; when they sang the pieces, they proclaimed their vocation, becoming part of a complex liturgical and musical symbol.

---

[43] For Andrew's crucifixion, see strophe IV: "Gaudens sequi Christum ducem / fert andreas promptus crucem, / promptus ad suspendium;" (Rejoicing to follow Christ the leader, Andrew readily bears the cross, goes readily to hanging).

(2) Individual melodic units were manipulated in two major ways to complement and deepen the meanings of the texts:

(a) Certain units were used to interrelate specific strophes of poetry, particularly when the subject of the strophe was the cross. The use of small sections of melody in this way was possible because the total structure of "Laudes crucis" was so important as to become a kind of organizational paradigm wherein the units were modular, existing in predictable positions and behaving in expected fashions. By disrupting these modes of organization, the composer could focus attention upon the text.

(b) Certain melodic units were altered within themselves, independently of the overall structure, to underscore specific words. Sometimes these changes were "pictorial," what is called "tone painting" in later music. An example is the quotation in "Zima uetus" from "Laudes crucis" unit 3 (t. 168), as described above: the borrowed music, although in the expected position in the sequence, is used in a highly unusual and fluid fashion, and the text at this point describes liberation and freedom from servitude. The use of B♭s later in the piece when the text describes the Devil and his offices can also be counted as an example of slight alteration for the sake of underscoring, although its meaning depends upon convention rather than graphic representation. Although the examples of Victorine "tone painting" are not numerous, they are plentiful enough to demonstrate that composers had begun to experiment with the idea.

The sequence melodies representing families IVB–E are printed in the anthology (Examples A.4–A.7, pp. 425–435) so that borrowings from "Laudes crucis," "Zima uetus" (family IVA), and "Prunis datum" (family IVB) – found in IVB and in "Gaude Roma" (family IVC), "Gaude, syon, que diem" (family IVD), and "Iocundare plebs fidelis" (family IVE) – are written above on smaller staves and can therefore be easily observed (as was the case for the source of "Mundi renouatio"). From such examples it is possible to suggest a tentative chronology for the formation of the groups: the earliest families of the four are IVB and IVC, represented here by "Prunis datum" for St. Lawrence (No. 31 in family IVB) and "Gaude Roma" (No. 26 in family IVC). These two families are similar in their use of borrowed material and in the relative freedom with which they operate after the opening units. Their subject matter is unified as well, and several of the melodies share material not found in "Laudes crucis," suggesting that they are contemporary and perhaps designed by the same person or group of people. Families IVD and IVE are later. Less free in their adaptations of preexisting melodies, they also draw upon material found in families IVB and IVC and were almost certainly created after them.

Thus the most significant families of Victorine music are IVB and IVC, and it is with them that discussion should begin. As can be seen from the examples in the anthology, the opening few units of "Prunis datum" and "Gaude Roma" are adaptations of "Laudes crucis," sometimes using direct quotations from the model, and sometimes not. Unit 1 of "Prunis datum" (t. 62) is quite free, built for the most part by varying the second cell of "Laudes crucis," unit 1 (t. 61) (see p. 425). Comparison between t. 62 of "Prunis datum" and t. 61 of "Laudes crucis" shows that the opening cell of t. 62 is also comprised of a decorated g, but the two gs are on the first and third syllables of text rather than the second and fourth as in "Laudes crucis." (The B♭ here is to avoid the tritone.) The characteristic leap up to c′ and the stepwise descent back down to g, found in the second cell (or half phrase) of t. 61A in "Laudes crucis," is in position in t. 62A as well, except that the c′ is missing. This lack is accounted for, however, in the B or middle phrase of t. 62: it is nothing more than an ornamented version of the second cell of t. 61A, the stepwise descent from c′ to g which was left out of the first phrase in t. 62A by the omission of the c′. The cadential formula is like the model (t. 61C) for the last five notes, but different for the first two.

The next two units of "Prunis datum" are variations and adaptations of the familiar cells and phrases of "Laudes crucis," with occasional short quotations placed in the corresponding position. But then unit 4 (t. 88) follows the model more closely, and unit 5 (t. 84) is borrowed note for note from "Laudes crucis." Thus one finds, as in "Zima uetus," varying degrees of dependence upon the model, "Laudes crucis," but a strong tendency to quote from it in order, to follow the design of the whole piece. One could say the same thing about "Gaude Roma," from family IVC: "Laudes crucis" is clearly used as the model for the opening melodic units of this piece, sometimes by free adaptation, sometimes through direct quotation, but always with respect for the position of the borrowed material in the original. (See pp. 429–431.)

These examples, which represent only a small proportion of the total number, point to the major feature of this repertory mentioned earlier: virtually all the uniquely Victorine music, even when it is free and not a direct contrafactum, remains connected in one way or another, either to the ultimate source, "Laudes crucis," or to other pieces following this model. By contrast, the smaller-scale interrelationships heightening the meanings of particular strophes of text, described on p. 308 above, were not developed in all sequences and are therefore difficult to decipher. As far as can be told, two rules were observed. First, the original text of a melodic unit had staying power, charging it with the meanings of its specific words. This is, of course, especially true of melodic units in "Laudes crucis," so well known and highly valued were each of them. Secondly, Victorine composers were therefore able to put their new melodies in parallel with "Laudes crucis" through exact quotation and draw the meanings of the original text into the new piece. The example below has been chosen from many to show how this procedure works.

The plan for "Gaude Roma" (No. 26 in family IVB, p. 293) illustrates the apparent freedom with which the final melodic units were composed. In fact, from t. 127 forward, all save one of the melodic units are what I call "composite." A composite unit is one whose individual phrases are selected from more than one pre-existing unit. "Gaude Roma," t. 172 is an example: its A phrase is found in t. 73 (from No. 3, "Gratulemur ad festiuum," found in family IVC, and No. 43, "Stola regni," found in family IVB); its B and C phrases are the same as the B and C phrases of t. 83, found in "Laudes crucis;" its D and E phrases are similar but not identical to the A and B phrases of t. 84, found in "Laudes crucis," and its F phrase is identical to the C phrases of t. 84. The notated version of "Gaude Roma" as explained here shows how easy it is to miss quotations when using M&A's list of melodic units ("timbres") alone.[44] All of this "free" music is related to other material in the Victorine repertory: t. 181 of "Gaude Roma" is made up of some direct quotations from the "Zima uetus" family, t. 140 (phrases A, B, and C) and t. 139 (phrases A and C). And t. 142, the penultimate melodic unit of "Gaude Roma," shares music with the sequence for St. Peter in family IVB, "Roma petro." The final melodic unit of "Gaude Roma," t. 145, opens with music very similar to the opening of t. 106 of "Prunis datum" (found near the end) of family IVB.

In the midst of these composite units whose phrases are borrowed from a variety of places is one long, direct quotation of t. 85 from "Laudes crucis." Why, all of a sudden, this strong and immediate reference to "Laudes crucis" in a piece that is made up of so many composite melodic units? The reason has to do with the text. The texts set to t. 85 in "Laudes crucis" and t. 85 in "Gaude Roma" both describe being spared miraculously from the sword. "Laudes crucis" tells of the Passover and the deliverance from the sword of the avenger (Exodus 12:1–28), "Gaude Roma" of Peter's deliverance from the sword of execution during the Passover (Acts 12:1–12). Although the New Testament passage refers directly to the one in Exodus (Peter is told to put on his belt and sandals, a reference to the traditional dress of Passover night), the sequence text itself does not make the parallel. It is rather the music which draws the texts together and points to the similarities between these two events. (Other sequences in the "Gaude Roma" family do not, of course, quote the entire t. 85 from "Laudes crucis" in the equivalent place.)

The use of direct melodic quotation to make exegetical points is frequent in this repertory. But on rare occasions quotations use more graphic details as well to expand upon textual meaning. Of the few examples, the most dramatic has been chosen for discussion. It has already been mentioned above that the two sequences for St. Peter, "Roma petro" (also for St. Paul) of family IVB and "Gaude Roma" of family IVC, share musical material. But the composers of these two pieces did not relate the texts through shared music just because they were for the same saint: both the texts emphasize Peter's martyrdom and his cross. But the music makes a further point not actually found in the text of "Gaude Roma": Peter was believed to have been crucified upside down, and in both pieces, exactly at the reference to his cross, phrases from the common closing melodic unit of "Laudes crucis" (t. 144) are inverted. These particular phrases occur in no other place in the repertory, and clearly this is an attempt to enliven both Peter sequences: in "Roma petro" by

---

[44] It also shows how artificially constructed Aubry's "timbres" are. In my forthcoming edition of these works, I will offer a table of melodic units for the Parisian sequences, both those at the cathedral and those from St. Victor, which better suits the nature of the repertory. The idea of having such a catalog was a good one, however, for reasons I have explained above. Aubry, like Spanke, had brilliant insights into how this music should be studied. But he simply did not know the Victorine repertory well enough to understand how it worked, and its various intricate complexities were completely lost on him. He worked quickly, pioneering the study of a great number of medieval French manuscripts and the music they contain, and, of course, he died too young. His analyses are not the results of painstaking investigation or of long contact with the music and its texts.

making the music and text express the same idea in different media, and in "Gaude Roma" by letting the music carry the idea left out by the poet. (See t. 142, p. 431.)

Later adaptations of Victorine music

The symbolic power of the Victorine sequence music and the variety of ways it has been used to interrelate texts and comment upon them can be seen once again in the two final small families making up group IV. The music of these two families (IVD and IVE) relates to its texts most clearly through statement of general themes rather than strophe by strophe, unit by unit (as is often the case in families IVB and IVC). Yet the music of both of these families was created by Victorines who recognized the symbolic power of their own musical language and wished to extend it to yet more texts. The interrelationships between texts and melodies in these families shows the last stage in the development of the Victorine musical language, and through them one can gain not only a fuller understanding of the vision behind it but also a suggestion of what person or group of persons may have sustained and developed it in the decades following the deaths of Hugh and Adam. In the case of both these families, sequences for Apostles or clerical saints seem to have been written first; the music parallels the text in a meaningful way. The other pieces, lacking clear text – music parallels, seem to be later; the fact that these seemingly later texts are Marian lends weight to the hypothesis, since the Victorines were engaged in adding these works after a repertory honoring Christ and the Apostles was basically in place.

Family IVD consists of two sequences, No. 14, "Salue dies dierum" for within the Easter octave (Easter Wednesday at St. Victor), and No. 40, "Gaude, syon, que diem" for St. Martin. Clearly the Victorines knew the melody used at the cathedral for both these texts: their own melody uses notes from it in the first unit. Yet evidently the Victorines were not satisfied with the cathedral melody, for they created new music as well, music which underscores the poetry and would enrich the meaning it had in their church. They doubtless worked with both the texts in mind, a difficult task because the two poems are not intrinsically related.[45]

Although one could not tell it from using M&A's timbres and Spanke's charts, the melody used for "Gaude, syon, que diem" and "Salue dies dierum" draws upon the Victorine music for family IVB (which includes "Prunis datum"), the music of "Laudes crucis," and the Victorine music for "Zima uetus." The text of "Gaude, sion, que diem" parallels the symbolism of each group of melodic quotations and

---

[45] It was not unusual to find texts which do not seem related set to the same music at the cathedral, even though, as suggested in Chapter 3, Adam seems to have favored interrelating texts through their music. The reasons Victorines kept "Salue dies" and "Gaude syon" as a pair probably has to do not only with tradition (they were willing enough to break this for others of their texts), but also with the poetic form of the two pieces. The texts are identical in syllable count and versification, except that "Gaude syon" is two strophes longer. Most of the lines are ten syllables in length, as opposed to the eight syllables which predominate in most Parisian sequence poetry.

seems to have inspired the composer's choice of melodic units. The opening cell of phrase A in t. 122 is the familiar opening of "Laudes crucis," but the second cell of the same phrase is taken from the cathedral melody. (See p. 432.) Phrase C of t. 122 again resembles the opening notes of "Laudes crucis," and this is true both at the cathedral and at St. Victor. But because the Victorine quotation has the bistropha on g that characterized the melody of "Laudes crucis" in most places (and undoubtedly at St. Victor in the mid twelfth century) it creates a stronger musical association than that of the cathedral melody.[46] As Example A.6 in the anthology (p. 432) shows, phrases B and C of t. 122 are taken almost note for note from the Victorine melody used for family IVB, strophe II (t. 71). Thus the music shifts to the IVB melody, that is, to music associated with the Apostles at St. Victor, just when the text says that Martin is comparable to the Apostles ("qua martinus compar apostolis"). The next two strophes of text, which describe Martin first leaving the military vocation and then performing the sacramental offices of priest and bishop, offering the host at communion, healing the sick, purging demons, are also set to music borrowed from IVB. T. 71 becomes t. 123; t. 72 becomes t. 152.[47] But in strophe IV, when the text describes Martin's lack of fear regarding death, the music is borrowed from "Laudes crucis." In strophe V ("Hic Martinus qui phana destruit") the music quotes the penultimate unit of "Zima uetus," t. 140. The reason for the music is less apparent with this particular strophe of text.[48] "Salue dies dierum," the other text set to the family IVD melody, has this unit at the same point, and its inclusion here may well be simply to complete the Easter theme of the piece. But "Gaude, syon, que diem" is longer by two strophes than "Salue dies," and so it needs more music. The extra units, t. 129 (for "Hic Martinus cuius est obitus") and the one before it, which is unlisted in M&A's catalog, are both fashioned after "Laudes crucis," unit 3, t. 168. (The ending of t. 129, however, quotes the music for "Zima uetus," strophe IX, t. 140B.) The usual custom of retaining the quotation's original position is thus violated by quoting music from early in "Laudes crucis" late in a piece. But the rule can be broken if it happens to deepen the meaning of the text, and here the Martin sequence describes the saint's death. The association of text and music is particularly well drawn in strophe VII: the opening two lines of the poetry describe Martin's last minutes; in the last two lines the heavenly choirs sing the "dulce melos" as he dies. As Example A.6 in the Anthology (p. 433) shows, "Laudes crucis" is used for the death itself and "Zima uetus" for the triumphant song of victory over death. The "dulce melos" is the sweet song of the cross, the only song which, according to an

---

46 Although the Victorines were one of the few places that did not sing "Laudes crucis" with the bistropha on the G of the first phrase, when they quote this section of the melody in other melodies, they usually do use the bistropha. I take this to mean that the Victorine version of "Laudes crucis" once did have the bistropha. At the time the Victorine melodies were formed, it prevailed. Later, sometime before the sequentiaries of lat. 14452 and 14819 were copied, the bistropha dropped out in "Laudes crucis" itself, but remained in the quotations from "Laudes crucis" found in a melody such as that used in family IVD.

47 The music is altered slightly because each of the phrases of "Gaude syon que diem" has ten syllables as opposed to the eight found in texts set to the IVB melody.

48 In this discussion, as in others presented here, only the best examples of the Victorine methods of interrelating texts and commenting upon them through music are given. Attempting to second-guess medieval poets and composers is treacherous, but, fortunately, the Victorines responsible for many of these sequences were clear in their intentions.

anonymous Victorine sermon, could be heard by the ears of God and Father.[49] Here, with text and music, St. Martin plays this sweet melody on the harp of his martyred flesh. The final description of his triumph is sung to t. 132, a version of the glorious t. 165, the closing melodic unit of "Zima uetus." (See p. 433.)

In "Gaude, syon, que diem," we see that by following the poem almost strophe by strophe, the Victorine music not only transforms individual strophes, but also ingrafts the text into the larger world of Victorine sequences and their multiple symbolic meanings. It is no wonder the Victorines often chose not to adopt the music of the Cathedral of Notre Dame for their sequence repertory during the second half of the twelfth century. Adam's early attempts to relate text and music, especially as described in Chapter 8, apparently were not continued at the cathedral. It was only the Victorines who persisted in interrelating sequence texts through the melodies chosen for them. At the abbey, the development of sequence music kept pace with the writing of new texts, and Adam's ideals of musical and textual interplay were respected even after his death.

The last family of sequences to be discussed here, family IVE, demonstrates yet another Victorine melody at work. Here too the composers responsible chose very familiar and beloved music and combined it with their own to create lively new meanings both for the original model and for the new pieces. The melody comes from a famous twelfth-century sequence, one which was not yet in their own repertory, "Verbum bonum et suaue" for the Blessed Virgin Mary. Both the text and the melody of the piece clearly interested them, and the fact that they admitted it only in a kind of disguise demonstrates that their canon of texts was well-established at the time the sequence repertory went through its final major redaction.[50] The melodies were what needed further attention.

"Verbum bonum" appealed to the Victorines primarily because its melody, at least as it survives in Parisian sources, relates to "Laudes crucis," and, indeed, as Example A.7 in the Anthology (p. 434) shows, quotes from it in several places.[51] Through such a well-known tune, the Victorines could expand their own musical language, gaining as well a series of new melodic units charged with the associations of a very popular text, and yet remain faithful to their tradition.[52] The text of "Verbum bonum" describes the moment of Christ's conception within the womb of the Blessed Virgin. In this view of the Annunciation the Word, Christ, is associated with the word "Ave" spoken to Mary as a greeting by the angel Gabriel.[53] In this elaborate conceit, word begets Word and praise is offered to the language which inspired Mary's consent to become pregnant with a divine son. The sequence singers are charged to resound the "Ave" themselves, hailing Mary with

---

[49] See Walter of St. Victor, *et al.*, "Sermon on the three-fold Glorying ...," p. 255.

[50] In fact, because the repertory was so large, it was probably usual to add new sequences only if someone gave the money for a new altar or chapel (or both) and the ranks of the dedicatees were raised. See Chapter 11.

[51] The melody of "Verbum bonum" is, as indicated in "Iocundare," the first three units of the Victorine melody for family IVE.

[52] For an edition of this text, see AH LIV, p. 343. The popularity of the piece is attested by the numerous manuscript sources listed on pp. 343–345.

[53] See the Vulgate Bible, Luke 1:28.

the words "good and sweet." Addressing her as "Mother of the highest word," they beg her to change them, and once they are changed, to commend them to her son.

The brief text of "Verbum bonum" uses the process of understanding as a metaphor for salvation. The importance of this idea will be demonstrated in subsequent discussions of the "O Maria, stella maris" sequence and the other Victorine texts set to the same melody.[54] The Victorines, with their emphasis upon inner transformation, were concerned with the ways the Word is begotten within the human person. Their interest in Mary grew from the popular understanding of her as the ultimate Word-bearer, the model of the faithful soul. The hope was, of course, that those who shared in her faith and obedience would themselves hear an "Ave" and acquiesce to its call.

As reference to "Iocundare plebs fidelis," the Group IVE sequence in the anthology, shows, the Victorines used the "Verbum bonum" melody for this text by extending it with several melodic units taken from their own repertory. In the melody for "Iocundare plebs fidelis," three of the families of music modeled after "Laudes crucis" are referred to, as is "Laudes crucis" itself: "Laudes crucis" provided the music for units 4 and 5; family IVB (represented in the anthology by "Prunis datum") for unit 6; family IVC (represented in the examples by "Gaude Roma") for unit 7; and "Zima uetus" for units 8 and 9. The creators of the Group IVE melody fashioned a pastiche using opening materials from a variety of Victorine sources. Yet rather than positioning borrowings so they correspond closely to their positions within the originals, the borrowings all come from the early sections of their models, at least for the first two thirds of the text of "Iocundare." Perhaps these musical "beginnings" were seen as proper extensions of "Verbum bonum," whose text is about the annunciation and conception of Christ, the beginning of his life on earth. The ending shifts abruptly, however, to the final units of "Zima uetus" just as the text in "Iocundare" begins to speak of the joys of heaven ("Paradisus hiis rigatur") and the end of time. (See p. 435.)

Of the three sequences in family IVE, "Iocundare plebs fidelis" seems to be best suited to the Victorine melody made up of "Verbum bonum," "Laudes crucis," and Victorine music modeled after the latter; it was probably the original text chosen. It describes the four Evangelists, viewing them through the standard imagery of Ez. 10:14 as reinterpreted in Apoc. [Rev.] 4:7.[55] In strophe VII, the types of the Evangelists make up a history of Christ's life on earth: the man declares His birth into time, the bull represents His sacrifice, the lion His triumph over death, and the eagle His ascension to the heavenly kingdom. The fourfold imagery tells the story of the cross, the symbol of Christ. And in this sequence, as in so many other

---

[54] See Chapter 14.

[55] Apoc. [Rev.] 4:7: "And the first living creature was like a lion: and the second living creature like a calf: and the third living creature, having the face, as it were, of a man: and the fourth living creature was like an eagle flying." Since the time of Irenaeus in the second century, these four creatures have been interpreted as types of the Evangelists: eventually the lion became identified with Mark, the bull with Luke, the man with Matthew, and the eagle with John.

Victorine settings, the final music of "Zima uetus" beautifies the description of paradise at the end. In the text, the Evangelists are the four streams coming from the fountain, and they flood paradise and the church on earth with their doctrinal waters. Through the Victorine melody, the Word incarnate and the message of the cross flows like undercurrents, sustaining the poetry with their mystical meanings.

The two Marian texts, No. 9, "Virgo mater salvatoris," and No. 33, "Ave virgo . . . mater," relate to "Verbum bonum," also in honor of Mary, in a general way. In addition, the text of "Ave virgo . . . mater" has Mary as bearer of the Word as one of its themes – a closer link with the original text:

Tu perfusa celi rore,	(You, sprinkled with heavenly dew,
Castitatis salvo flore,	By the saving power of chastity,
Novum florem novo more	Brought forth to the world
Protulisti seculo.	The new flower in a new way.
Verbum patri coequale	The Word, coequal with the Father,
Corpus intrans virginale	Entering the virginal body,
Fit pro nobis corporale	Is made corporeal for us
Sub ventris umbraculo.	Under the shade of the womb.)

This part of the text, however, occurs after the "Verbum bonum" part of the melody is over and the "Laudes crucis" part has begun. "Virgo mater saluatoris" is probably a very late text: there was no rubric for it in the Victorine ordinal lat. 14506, and it is one of the few sequence titles actually added in the margin. Clearly this piece was not part of the repertory at the time the ordinal was compiled, and its relationship to the purposes most often served by the uniquely Victorine music is tenuous.

Conclusion: "Let this church sing"

The best conclusion for this long discussion of the uniquely Victorine sequence music and its mode of operation comes from Hugh of St. Victor himself:

This is it that, in a wonderful manner, all of sacred Scripture is so suitably adjusted and arranged in all its parts through the wisdom of God that whatever is contained in it either resounds with the sweetness of spiritual understanding in the manner of strings; or, containing utterances of mysteries set here and there in the course of a historical narrative or in the substance of a literal context, and, as it were, connecting these up into one object, binds them together all at once as the wood does which curves under the taut strings; and, receiving their sound into itself, it reflects it more sweetly to our ears – a sound which the string alone has not yielded, but which the wood too has formed by the shape of its body.[56]

Hugh's sounding harp of Scripture, whose strings reverberate in different ways, yet harmoniously and miraculously make the same tune, exemplifies the Victorine ideal of the many and the one, diversity reducing to unity. For Hugh, although he does not say so specifically but only hints at it, the wooden harp frame and the

---

[56] *Didascalicon*, Book V, Chapter 2; Taylor edn., p. 121.

strings are Christ on the cross. The song they make is the message of salvation and expiation, the meaning of history and of Scripture.

The Victorines created a sequence music that conformed to Hugh's ideal and that promoted the cult of the cross within their own abbey. Their music, which along with settings of "Laudes crucis" itself accounts for thirty late sequence texts, makes the texts interact in precisely the way Hugh described Scripture: underlying all of the texts in one meaning, redemption through sacrifice, and one symbol, the cross. And because of the way the texts interact through the music, one finds a constant interplay of meanings. Old Testament passages are related to New Testament passages, the preaching and teaching of the Apostles is fused with the ecclesiastical hierarchy, past and present.

At St. Victor, where some of the most important twelfth-century scriptural commentators made their home, a new exegesis was born: one which depended upon the power of musical symbolism and the abilities of a single melody to accomodate several texts, and, in the process, to interrelate them. In "Laudes crucis" the text presents an Old Testament typology of the cross and its powers. In subsequent adaptations, the melody was used for texts describing events in the life of Christ. Melodies modeled upon "Laudes crucis" were then set to texts honoring the Apostles, the Evangelists, and bishops, deacons, and other members of the ecclesiastical hierarchy. Mary, in her role as genetrix of the Word, was seen as a parallel to the Evangelists. To a musically sensitive canon, any one of these sequences could bring a number of others to mind. As he sang and listened, groups of texts would sound at once in his mind, all exploring similar themes, all related through symbolic music.

The Victorine sequences depended upon an art of memory, but not of individual memory alone. As Mary Carruthers has stated, "Hugh of St. Victor's particular genius in 'De arca Noe morali' is to bring together the processes of Scriptural reading, moral development, and memory training in the single image of Noah's Ark."[57] By creating a particular image in the individual memory, a person could be transformed. So, too, by creating a particular image within the collective "memory" of the community through liturgical singing, that community could be converted more profoundly to the common life. Although the art of the Victorine sequences called to the common life by techniques described throughout Hugh's writings, the art was different from anything in Hugh. It depended upon music and it was liturgical and fully communal. The singing of their sequences was a time for the community to make a statement of their ideals, and when they made this statement in any of their sequences, the music caused the texts of others to resound at the same time, caused the "compounding with interest" described in Hugh's writings.[58]

That the sequence was a communal statement of unity is forcefully expressed by the Victorines themselves in "Ex radice caritatis," the sequence sung on the feast of

---

[57] Carruthers (1990), p. 44.
[58] See Chapter 10, p. 217 above.

the Reception of St. Victor's Relics.[59] The command in the early strophes of the sequence is for the community to match the praise of the mouth to the condition of the heart. Praise is meant to enlarge the "inner sanctuary," that is, following the commands of the Rule of St. Augustine and Hugh of St. Victor's teachings, to build a church within, a place for the divinity to dwell. Just as the flesh and the heart are to play in harmony within each individual during the act of singing, so too are both halves of the choir to sing together with one melody, and this is representative of the unity of their customs and of the common life. God will tune this communal instrument so that it will play a unified tune. The sweetness is the odor of Christ, which becomes here like must to be stored in the "cellar of the heart." This unity will free those who make room for it from the cares of the world.

As Table 13.1 (p. 293) shows, this text was sung at St. Victor to a melody from family IVC, but its final units are unique. This melody, which may very well have been written by Adam of St. Victor because of its early date (the relics were received at the time Hugh entered the abbey), far exceeds the usual range of melodies in this repertory, soaring upwards to a'. At the end, it resembles "Zima uetus" in its florid style.[60] And, in fact, the two final units, t. 159 and t. 164, are related to "Zima uetus," t. 140 and t. 165. The composer of this piece adapted "Zima uetus" freely, and designed t. 159 to show the closest relationship. T. 159A, although lying far up the scale, has a similar contour to that of t. 165A and it also repeats, just as the model does. The D and E phrases of t. 159 are similar to "Zima uetus," t. 140B in their shape and style. The creator of this melody adapted the source material from "Zima uetus" more freely here than in the sequence melodies comprising families IVD and IVE. This wholesale reworking of earlier musical material recalls the relationship between "Laudes crucis" and "Zima uetus" and suggests that this melody was composed by Adam. It also shows how well this composer, if he was indeed the great Adam, understood both the conventions within the musical language and its symbolic power. Here the glory of the Easter celebration is extended and made more dramatic for the patron saint. "Ex radice" is not primarily about St. Victor; it is rather about the Victorines and the spirit in which their sequences were to be sung. "Ex radice" demonstrates that the sequence was a time for the entire community to be put in tune, incorporated through its special music within the vast ecclesiastical hierarchy to which the members believed they belonged.

"Ex radice caritatis"
In susceptione reliquiarum
As found in Paris, BN lat. 14819, fols. 96v–98v

I.1 Ex radice caritatis	(I From the root of charity,	
ex affectu pietatis	from the state of piety,	
psallat hec ecclesia;	let this church sing;	
I.2 Psallat corde psallat ore	let it sing with the heart, let it sing with the mouth,	
et exsultet in uictore	and let the household of Victor	
uictoris familia	rejoice in Victor.	

[59] A Mass was sung on this day in commemoration of Magister Hugo, who procured the relics for the church. This reference is probably to Hugh's uncle, whose name was also Hugh.

[60] The end of "Ecce dies triumphalis," the sequence for St. Victor, also soars into an upper range. See M&A, p .286. There are also parallels between the final melodic units, creating musical links between the two pieces. This same technique was used to interrelate the sequences for St. Peter discussed above.

II.1   Pars istius nobis data
per fideles est allata
   ab urbe massilia;
II.2   Cuius prius spiritali
nunc ipsius corporali
   fruimur presentia.

III.1   Hec est summa gaudiorum
dilatemus animorum
   ipsa penetralia;
III.2   Martyris reliquie
laudis et leticie
   nobis sunt materia.

IV.1   Nostri cordis organum
nostre carnis tympanum
   a se dissidentia;
IV.2   Armonia temperet
et sibi confederet
   pari consonantia.

V.1   Choris concinentibus
una sit in moribus
   nostris modulatio;
V.2   Vocum dissimilium
morum dissidentium
   grauis est collisio.

VI.1   Ex diuersis sonitus
fiet incompositus
nisi dei dignitus
cordas aptet primitus
   dulci magisterio;
VI.2   Nisi dulcor spiritus
cor tangat medullitus
nichil uocis strepitus
nichil sapit penitus
   carnis exsultatio.

VII.1   Dulcor iste non sentitur
in scissuris mentium
nec in terra reperitur
   suaue uiuentium;
VII.2   Hunc dulcorem sapiat
et pregustans sitiat
donec plene capiat
   unitas fidelium.

VIII.1   Pregustemus cordis ore
ut interno nos sapore
reuocemur ab amore
   mundi seductorio;

II   The part of that saint given to us
was brought by faithful men
   from the city of Marseilles;
first we enjoyed his spiritual presence,
but now we enjoy
   his bodily presence.

III   This is the summit of joys:
let us enlarge the innermost sanctuary
   of our souls;
the relics of the martyr
are the subject of praise and gladness
   for us.

IV   The organ of our heart,
the drum of our flesh
   are diverse from one another;
let harmony temper
and unite to each other
   with suitable consonance.

V   With our choirs singing together,
let the modulation be one
   in our customs;
harsh is the clash
of dissimilar voices,
   of diverse customs.

VI   From diverse things
the sound will be disordered
unless the finger of God
first adjust the strings
   with sweet instruction;
unless the sweetness of the spirit
touch the heart of the marrow,
the noise of the sound and
the exultation of the flesh
   tastes nothing deeply.

VII   This sweetness is not felt
in dividings of minds
nor is it agreeably found
   in the land of the living;
may the unity of the faithful
taste this sweetness,
and foretasting, thirst
   until it may seize it fully.

Let us foretaste with the mouth of the heart,
so that by internal savor,
we may be recalled
   from the seductive love of the world;

VIII.2 Hic est sapor salutaris | this is the wholesome taste,
hic est gustus singularis | this is the unique taste,
per quem cure secularis | through which forgetfulness of worldly care
   subrepit obliuio. | advances by degrees.

IX.1 Ut hic mundus amarescat | So that this world may grow bitter,
odor christi preculcescat | let the odor of Christ become very sweet;
hec dulcedo semper crescat | may this sweetness ever grow
   cordis in cellario; | in the wine cellar of the heart;
IX.2 Ubi spirat fragor talis | where such a fragrance breathes forth,
feruor crescit spiritalis | spiritual fervor increases
et frigescit temporalis | and love of temporal life
   uite delectatio. | grows cold.

X.1 Victor miles triumphalis | Victor, triumphant soldier,
christi martyr specialis | special martyr of Christ,
nos a mundi serua malis | preserve us from the evils of the world,
ne nos amor mundialis | that worldly love
   mergat in flagicia; | not drown us in sins;
X.2 Una uoce mente pari | with one voice, with like mind,
nos honore singulari | with singular honor,
te studemus uenerari | we are zealous to worship you
dum uersamur in hoc mari | while we are tossed in this sea,
   exhibe suffragia. | confer your assistance.

XI. Ne permittas spe frustrari | May you not permit those for whom you are able to plead
quibus potes suffragari | to be deceived in their hope:
fac nos christo presentari | make us to be presented to Christ
ut hunc tecum contemplari | so that we may contemplate Him
   possimus in gloria; | with you in glory;

XI.2 Ad honorem tuum christe | to your honor, Christ,
decantauit chorus iste | this choir has sung repeatedly
tui laudes agoniste | the praise of your fighter
quo presente nichil triste | in whose presence let nothing sad
nostra turbet gaudia. Amen. | disturb our joys. Amen.)

Through the large group of pieces set to their own music, the Victorines built a huge harp, each of the individual sequences being one of the strings. Yet all were harmoniously tuned; all played the same song, the song of the cross. And although the texts explored several layers of time, Old Testament time, New Testament time, and present time, and created historical, allegorical, and tropological levels of meaning, the music served to reduce all these to a single truth and a single meaning for all of history. This was what Hugh of St. Victor attempted to do in his ark treatises as well, the drawings of which do not survive.[61] The sequences do survive, however, and they are an embodiment of Hugh's call for an art that would represent the church and encourage conversion to the common life as described by

[61] See Chapter 10.

St. Augustine. Thus the sequences operate as Hugh said Scripture did, but, like his drawings of Noah's ark, they extend the meanings of Scripture to all the saints and to the present age. And like Hugh's picture of the church, they were designed to draw those who sang them ever deeper into the midst of the structure they attempted to depict.

14

Mary and the microcosm

The lateness of the Marian emphasis

In Chapter 13 it has been shown that the music the Victorines wrote themselves (found in families IVB–E of Chapter 8, pp. 180–181 and Table 13.1) and the texts set to this music develop themes found consistently in the writings of Hugh of St. Victor. Many of these sequences were well suited to the Victorine church and liturgy as built and developed during the abbacy of Gilduin, several seeming as if they were designed for them. Thus, even though the surviving copies of these works date from the second quarter of the thirteenth century, one needs to understand the Abbey of St. Victor of the mid twelfth century to appreciate how and why the texts and melodies were made as they are. There is, however, one part of the Victorine sequence repertory which cannot be fully understood in the context of Hugh's thought and the early Victorine liturgy: the Marian sequences. In Chapter 13, it has been suggested that the Marian sequences with music by the Victorines themselves are later additions: apparently, the first goal in the development of the repertory was to celebrate Christ, the Apostles, the early church, and the common life as the continuation of this tradition.

Thus among the large group of some thirty sequences set to Victorine music there is only a small number of Marian texts, and even those few texts which are found in families IVA–E seem to be latecomers, the texts not interacting with the music in any sophisticated way. Comparison of the sequences listed in the Victorine ordinal from the late twelfth century with those in the sequentiary of some three decades later reveals that the only substantial difference in the two repertories is in regard to Marian sequences and sequences for the Dedication.[1] Taken together, these facts suggest that the veneration of Mary was not of major importance during the first half of the twelfth century at the Abbey of St. Victor.[2] It was only in the second half of the twelfth century that Marian devotion became more fervent there,

---

[1] "Aue uirgo . . . porta" for Saturday in the octave of the Assumption and "O Maria, stella maris" for Marian feasts in general are not in the ordinal; missing also are "Rex salomon" for the octave of the Dedication, and "Quam dilecta tabernacula," also for the Dedication.

[2] And this in spite of the fabled devotion of Adam of St. Victor to the Blessed Virgin. See Fassler (1984).

as it did in many other churches throughout France, and the number of sequences in her honor was increased.[3] Yet even at the time the Victorine sequence book was put together in the thirteenth century, it was significantly poorer in Marian sequences than was the sequentiary of Notre Dame, a church dedicated, after all, to the Assumption of the Blessed Virgin Mary.[4]

Through study of Marian sequences and Victorine sermons written in honor of the Virgin, one can observe how the theological ideals of these canons regular were expanded during the late twelfth century to include this saint, who was neither apostle, evangelist, bishop, nor priest. All the saints especially revered at the abbey were, with but few exceptions, members of the ecclesiastical hierarchy. How did Mary come to fit into this structure?

The best way to answer this question is by examining a family of six sequences listed in Table 8.6. Family IIB, all of whose texts are set to the melody "O Maria, stella maris," is the only complicated exegetical exploration of Marian themes in the Victorine repertory. Here one finds the interaction between texts and music which characterizes the Victorine pieces in family IV, but in a particularly clear plan of organization. And when the pieces are studied in the context of Victorine sermons from the second half of the twelfth century, a picture of Mary as a symbol for both the reformed church and the reformed clergy comes into view. Family IIB forms a conclusion to this study of Victorine sequences, providing an overview of techniques for the integration of texts and music.

The themes of family IIB's texts also point to the persons who may have been responsible for assigning many of them to their melody. Of the several Marian sermons to be mentioned here, those of primary importance are by Richard of St. Victor and Godefroy of St. Victor. Because their work sometimes seems to form a commentary upon the meaning of the "O Maria, stella maris" family, it adds weight to the suggestion made in Chapter 8 that both men were involved in standardizing the Victorine repertory in the decades after the death of Adam.

A family of Marian sequences at St. Victor

Family IIB: "O Maria, stella maris"

No. 45   "O Maria, stella maris" (Feasts of the Virgin Mary):
<u>23</u> <u>24</u>   <u>25</u> 26 <u>46</u> <u>28</u> <u>27</u> <u>39</u>

No. 24   "Rex salomon" (For the octave of the Dedication):
<u>23</u> <u>24</u> 9 <u>25</u> 26 <u>46</u> <u>28</u> <u>27</u> <u>39</u>

No. 6   "Iubilemus saluatori quem" (Sunday in the octave of Christmas):
<u>23</u> <u>24</u>   <u>25</u> 26 <u>46</u> <u>28</u> <u>27</u> <u>39</u>

---

[3] See Chapter 10.
[4] Comparison between the octaves of the Assumption at the two churches in Appendix 5 (pp. 402–403) reveals, as would be expected, major differences.

No. 11   "Templum cordis" (Feast of the Purification):
          <u>23</u> <u>24</u>   <u>25</u> 26 <u>46</u> <u>28</u> <u>27</u> <u>39</u> 154 + 162

No. 32   "Aue uirgo . . . porta" (Saturday in the octave of the Assumption):
          <u>23</u> <u>24</u>   <u>25</u> 26 <u>46</u> <u>28</u> <u>27</u> <u>39</u> 52 38 37 58 59 53 55

No. 15   "Sexta passus' (Within the octave of Easter):
          <u>23</u> <u>24</u>   <u>25</u> 26 <u>46</u> <u>28</u> <u>27</u> <u>39</u> 162a

The six texts set to "O Maria, stella maris" were found as a family only at the Abbey of St. Victor.[5] In Chapter 13 above, the music studied was all by Victorine composers. That is not the case here: instead, this is a family created by the Victorines using a melody that was sung at the cathedral as well. But through the arrangement and development of the melody, by setting other texts to it and adding new music when necessary, those responsible represented the various exegetical levels of interpretation commonly used to explain the importance of the Blessed Virgin Mary at the Abbey of St. Victor in the second half of the twelfth century. These levels are clearly laid out in "Sacram et salutiferam," Godefroy's sermon for the Nativity of the Virgin, and demonstrate the threefold system of exegesis championed by Hugh of St. Victor:[6]

For in three ways, as we learn from Holy Scripture, is the virgin the bride of the King and mother. The first is the singularly blessed Mary, who is born today, virgin bride of the King and mother. The second is the generally blessed Church, in like manner having its beginning today, virgin bride of the King and mother. The third is the specially blessed faithful soul, which is born every day, virgin bride of the King and mother. Thus the first is defined historically, the second allegorically, and the third tropologically.[7]

Five of the sequences found in Family IIB have been set to "O Maria, stella maris" because they are all related to this particular exegetical complex of meanings.[8] On the simplest level, several of the texts are Marian: they are therefore well suited to the melody and help establish the family as Marian. But, as was the case in the families studied in Chapter 13, some of the texts seem to work better than others, and in some examples the redactor has improved the fit through the music chosen for strophes of poetry which could not be accommodated by the original melody. Beginning with the original sequence, the discussion will cover each text and its music in turn, and then the meaning of the family as a whole.[9]

The Victorines were not interested in sequence melodies without symbolic

---

[5] As Appendix 5 (pp. 390–411) shows, only two of the texts in this family besides the original were sung in Paris: "Rex salomon" and "Sexta passus feria." And of these two, only one, "Rex salomon," was sung to this melody at the cathedral. In other sources such as Assisi 695 and the sequentiary from Aix-la-Chapelle, only "O Maria, stella maris" has this melody; other texts set to it at the Abbey of St. Victor are not set to it outside Paris.

[6] The antecedents for Hugh's threefold interpretations are analyzed in de Lubac (1959–64).

[7] See Beumer (1960), p. 255.

[8] The sixth text, "Sexta passus feria," is more difficult to understand, but an attempt will be made at the close of this discussion.

[9] The text (also in translation) and melody of "O Maria, stella maris" are found in the anthology, Example A.8, pp. 436–437 and 441.

content, and used only those which, like "Laudes crucis," "Zima uetus" and "Verbum bonum," could both relate to the themes of individual texts and serve to draw thematically similar texts into meaningful families of pieces. In these families the melodies both organize the pieces into groups and sustain the sense of the group as a whole. "O Maria stella maris" undoubtedly became the matrix for a large group of sequences because its melody was, at least in its opening, modeled upon the ninth-century hymn "Ave maris stella," one of the most beloved and best known of all medieval melodies and one long associated with the veneration of Mary through its presence in the medieval office.[10] As Example A.8 in the anthology (p. 436) demonstrates, the sequence composer remodeled both the text and the melody of the hymn to create the first strophe of the new piece, fusing the second and third phrases of the hymn tune into a single phrase.[11] And, like "Laudes crucis," the melody of "O Maria, stella maris" refers back to the opening melodic unit in several places, the sequence becoming a kind of "theme and variations" on the hymn tune.[12]

Ideas presented in the analysis of "Laudes crucis" found in Chapter 4 can be developed further through this Parisian sequence. Here too music not only supports and underscores the theme and structure of the poem as a whole but also reflects the structure of its lines and strophes. In every three-line hemistrophe the first two lines rhyme and are of the same accentual pattern and syllable count. The third line of each half strophe introduces a new rhyme and has a strong–weak–strong cadence. The music has been composed with this same design: phrases A and B parallel each other in some way. Most often these related phrases have similar melodic contours (phrases 3A and 3B, or 4A and 4B), but they also occasionally contain similar music at different pitch levels (phrases 5A and 5B).[13] C phrases, however, are usually distinguished from the type of phrase found in the A or B position of any given hemistrophe.

The influence of position within the hemistrophe upon musical style operates throughout the piece. Although each melodic unit has unique characteristics that set it apart from all the others, A phrases consistently relate to other A phrases, echoing the shape of line 1A; B phrases persist in swooping downward, much as does phrase 1B (see phrases 2B, 3B, 4B, and 8B). C phrases are usually simple cadential formulae. Thus against the rhythmic gridwork of the text, the tightly controlled syllable count, line length, strophic shapes, accentual patterns, and rhyme, the composer constantly varied the music, and played with motivic development. In each half strophe the composer can continue to explore subtle difference between A and B phrases, both in relation to each other and to the "originals," 1A and 1B. The ear comes to anticipate this subtle variation and to delight in it.

The appeal of "O Maria stella maris" for the Victorines does not rely only upon its melodic sophistication. Because of the strong association with the hymn tune

---

[10] See Lausberg (1976).
[11] In Fassler (1987) an analysis of the formal properties of this melody is given. The similarities between the hymn melody and the sequence melody are discussed in Wagner (1911–21), vol. III, and in Fassler (1983).
[12] The hymn tune is the Parisian version, here as transcribed from Paris, BN lat. 10482.
[13] This last illustrates the principle of "affinitas." For further discussion, see Pesce (1989).

built into the sequence melody, one must also study first their understanding of "Ave maris stella," the hymn upon which the sequence is based, and secondly the reworking of these Marian themes within the sequence text.[14] Richard of St. Victor wrote a sermon on the meaning of "Ave maris stella."[15] The most striking thing about Richard's exposition is how little he has to say about Mary. Instead, the entire sermon is about the sea and the ship and what they stand for. The allegory is developed so that one sees how the ship was built: it swells and grows first with Old Testament characters, and then, after the coming of Christ, with the ranks of the Gentiles, inspired in all the earth by hearing the sound of the apostolic preaching."[16] The ship, of course, is the church, and the troubled sea the world with its distractions.[17] Although this is a popular medieval allegory for the church, the later Victorines were particularly drawn to it, undoubtedly because of its extensive use in Hugh's ark treatises. The ship, in Richard's sermon, as in the writings of Hugh, contains all the ages and is, therefore, a defense against time made possible through the power of understanding history. The ship and the sea also represent those who live rightly and can, by clinging to the mast of doctrine, be saved from the swirling floods of sin. With its most recent occupants collected by the power of the cross as preached by the apostles, the Victorine ship is peopled most prominently by members of the ecclesiastical hierarchy, by those men who have reformed themselves and carried out their duties as pastors to the spiritual needs of their flocks, teaching not only by words but by example as well. The ship is staffed by hearty sailors who sing as they row, preaching and praising:

Debemus igitur, fratres carissimi, habere navem per fidem, malum per spem, velum per caritatem, galliculum per probationem spirituum, cordas per exercitationem virtutum, remos per exhibitionem bonorum operum, gubernaculum per discretionem, anchoram per humilitatem, escam per Scripturarum lectionem, rete per predicationem, et celeuma debemus cantare per laudis Dei jubilationem.[18]

(We ought, dear brothers, to have the ship through faith, the mast through hope, the sail through charity, the crow's nest through the testing of spirits, the ropes through the exercise of virtue, the oars through the public production of good works, the rudder through discretion, the anchor through humility, the food through the reading of Scripture, the net through preaching, and we ought to sing the celeuma [the call given by the chief oarsman to help the other rowers keep time] through the jubilation of the praise of God.)

It is only at the very end of the sermon that there is mention of the Virgin Mary. "And so that we might cross this sea salubriously, very often we salute the star of the sea, that is blessed Mary, and saluting her, we invoke her saying 'Hail star of the

---

[14] Stäblein (1958–61) has explored the adaptation of "Ave maris stella" to serve for a Troubadour poem.

[15] See *Liber exceptionum*, ed. Châtillon, pp. 381–385.

[16] *Ibid.*, p. 382.

[17] Students of the Middle Ages must always be careful not to think that all symbols are the same every time they are used. It is the different ways which particular communities and thinkers had of treating popular images that matters, and indeed studying these differences, however subtle they may seem to us today, is one of the surest methods we have of distinguishing individual strains of thought and emphasis.

[18] *Liber exceptionum*, ed. Châtillon, p. 384.

sea.'"[19] These are the clergy whose ship is the church, and like their secular counterparts who cross the Mediterranean and other seas, they ask for the help of Mary and her son. Here Mary seems a guide for the ship and no more. But then, as a final touch, Richard expands his commentary, quoting at length from the sequence "Ave uirgo . . . mater."[20] Richard concentrates upon those strophes with sea imagery: here the sailors are about to be shipwrecked, and they pray to Mary as the "Mother of the spirit," who can save them when the "animal" part of the human cannot not triumph. (The celeuma which they sing was associated with the Alleluia by the fourth-century Carthaginian Quodvultdeus, whose writings were commonly assigned to Augustine in the Middle Ages.[21]) Thus, at the end of the sermon, through the quotation of a sequence by Adam, Mary becomes a special guide for the human soul.[22]

The sequence "O Maria, stella maris" is a companion for Richard's sermon, and he could well have quoted from it, although the storm imagery is not as vivid as that of "Ave virgo . . . mater." Beginning with the powerful image of the star as an "eye," the sequence develops the theme of Mary as guide. The sailors in this storm are held captive by the nets of sin and wracked by the waves of their own desires. As they battle the Devil, lord of the world, Mary gives hope through goodness and tenderness, through her chaste example.

By themselves, Richard's sermon and "O Maria, stella maris" are imperfect introductions to the complexities of Victorine Mariology. Mary is seen as a guide in these two works, as a foil for the entanglements of the world, but her abilities to serve as a model are not thoroughly explicated, and Godefroy's three levels of interpreting Mary are not found. Here she is the historical Mary, mother of Christ, and only weakly Mary, the model for the faithful soul. The sequence family as a whole, however, shifts the emphasis from the first level, the historical, to the second and third, the allegorical and the tropological.

Mary: type of the reformed church

It appears that presenting Godefroy's second theme, the allegorical one of Mary as a type of the church, may have been the first purpose of the Marian sequence family and the intention of Adam himself. "Aue uirgo . . . mater" was not the only Parisian sequence quoted by Richard of St. Victor: he also refers extensively to "Rex salomon fecit templum." Although this does not prove the piece was sung at St. Victor at this time, it suggests that it was. In any case, Richard knew and revered

---

[19] *Ibid.*

[20] This sequence is part of family IVE, discussed above.

[21] See his short treatise *De Cantico novo*, Book II; Braun edn., p. 383. As McKinnon (*Music in Early Christian Literature*, p. 167) points out, Augustine also mentioned the *celeuma* in his *De opere monachorum*: "In fact those working with their hands are easily able to sing the divine songs also and to lighten the labor itself with a kind of divine *celeuma*."

[22] This is the one sequence attributed by Richard to a certain "outstanding poet." See discussion above in Chapter 10.

the text, which was certainly circulating in Paris by the mid twelfth century.[23] Because "Rex salomon" was set to the "O Maria, stella maris" melody both at the cathedral and at St. Victor, it was probably associated with this music from the very beginning. The text was highly favored by Richard of St. Victor because it describes the building of the Church in Old Testament typology.[24] It has been shown earlier that many sequences favored by the Victorines and perhaps written by Adam describe their own liturgical ceremonies, feasts, and the sacraments in Old Testament terms.[25] The building of the temple was perfectly suited to the expression of Victorine ideals because it is about construction, growth, development, and the process by which a religious edifice is made. The Victorines, of course, were most concerned with the ways in which the institutional church was built throughout time by the preaching and teaching of the apostles, the men whose heirs they believed themselves and all reformed clergy to be. Richard's sermon draws these parallels with a heavy hand: Solomon is Christ (the one man built the temple, the other builds the church);[26] the twelve administrators of Solomon are the twelve Apostles;[27] the temple was built in the fourth year of Solomon's reign to represent the four Evangelists.[28] The sequence text parallels the sermon in its use of Old Testament imagery from 3 Kings, sometimes down to the very details. And the opening strophe of the sequence proclaims the parallel between the two builders, one from the Old Testament, one from the New, and their edifices. The middle strophes of "Rex salomon" are especially to be noted for their concentration upon aspects of the temple liturgy as foreshadowing the sacraments of the Christian faith and the priests who administered them. The reference here is to Exodus 30, where God continues with instructions to Moses for constructing and setting up the tabernacle. In this passage, the spices required for the temple become the good odor of lives rightly lived, and the golden dishes are suited to the actions of the Spirit-filled clergy. One sees how closely the parallel could be drawn between praising the clergy to make them better trained and more zealous, and praising them for the magnificence of their office.

From "Rex salomon" for the octave of the Dedication

VI.1	Templi cultus extat multus	(VI	The great cult of the temple stands forth:
	cinnamomus odor domus		cinnamon, the scent of the house,
	myrrha stactis cassya;		myrrh, cassia,
VI.2	Que bonorum decus morum		which signify
	atque bonos precum sonus		the dignity of good customs
	sunt significantia.		and the good sounds of prayer.

---

[23] "Rex salomon" is one of the few sequences found in the sequentiary that is not listed in the ordinal. See Paris BN lat. 14506, fol. 307: neither Sunday within the octave or the octave itself has a sequence listed here. This, of course, does not definitely mean that one was not sung.

[24] Richard also wrote a long exposition of the ways of meditation based upon an allegory of the ark of the covenant. It has been translated by Zinn (1979).

[25] See discussion of "Lux iocunda" in Chapter 12 and of "Zima uetus" in Chapters 12 and 13.

[26] *Liber exceptionum*, ed. Châtillon, p. 314.

[27] See 3 Kings [1 Kings] 4:7.

[28] 3 Kings [1 Kings] 6:1 and Richard of St. Victor, *Liber exceptionum*, ed. Châtillon, p. 314.

VII.1 In hac casa cuncta uasa	VII In this house all dishes
sunt ex auro de thesauro	are of gold forechosen
preelecto penitus;	from the inner recesses of the treasury:
VII.2 Nam magistros et ministros	it befits the superiors, the ministers,
decet doctos et excoctos	learned and refined
igne sancti spiritus.	by the fire of the Holy Spirit.

While the text of the sequence was sung, however, the music that sustained it symbolized the Church on another exegetical level. The melody is a Marian one, and by pairing it with this text the Old and New Testament types of the church, Solomon's temple and the Virgin Mary, became one, and time stood still. It was expected that the singer would make the connection between text and music through the action of memory.

The person who adapted "Rex salomon" to "O Maria, stella maris" pursued this idea even further. Because the original text has but eight strophes and the second text nine, more music was needed. Whoever set "Rex salomon" took the third unit of its music (t. 9 in M&A) from another Parisian sequence for the feast of the Dedication, "Quam dilecta tabernacula." The music was borrowed from "Quam dilecta" at the point where the poem describes the tabernacle built by Christ as an edifice safe from the elements of wind and water. Thus, charged by the meaning of its original text, the melody suits the meaning of both "O Maria, stella maris" and "Rex salomon."[29]

The idea of Mary as a type of the church was developed in another text belonging to family IIB, "Iubilemus saluatori quem" for the Sunday after Christmas.[30] This short sequence serves to honor Mary during the Christmas octave and is essentially a commentary upon the standard Old Testament types of the Incarnation and the virgin birth: the burning bush (Ex. 3:2–4), the flowering branch of Aaron (Num. 17:22–24), and the root of Jesse.[31] Mary is called the "templum Dei"; at the end the singers hope to have a flower recreated in themselves, so that they, like Mary and like the temple, may have the divinity within.

Mary: model of the faithful soul

With the texts of "O Maria, stella maris" and "Rex salomon" paired through their music, two of Godefroy's exegetical levels are present. But what of the third, Mary as a type of the faithful soul?[32] To understand the importance this tropological level had for the Victorine, one must return to Hugh of St. Victor. Hugh did not write

---

[29] "Quam dilecta" was not edited by M&A, but can be found in the Prévost, ed., *Recueil complet*. Although the melodies of "Quam dilecta" are quite different at the cathedral and St. Victor, they are identical for this unit.

[30] For the text see M&A, pp. 177–178 and AH LIV, pp. 152–153.

[31] In the Vulgate, this scion from the root of Jesse is also described as a flower: "et egredietur virga de radice Iesse et flos de radice eius ascendet . . ." Isa. 11:1.

[32] Matter (1990, p. 106) says that commentaries upon the "Song of Songs" began to place greater emphasis upon the idea of love between Christ and the individual soul during the twelfth century. The idea had a long history before this time, however, which she outlines.

extensively about Mary, but what he did have to say served as a springboard for later ideas found in Victorine sermons and sequences.[33] For Hugh, the Incarnation was the turning point in the history of the church: he discusses its meaning at the very beginning of the second half of the *De sacramentis*. The Incarnation marks the coming of "the time of grace," and begins a new order of divine works, the works of restoration.[34] Although Hugh is most concerned with the Christological implications of the Incarnation, he also questions, far into his discussion of the subject, how it was exactly that the word became flesh in Mary's womb. "How must we understand that it was written, 'He was conceived of the Holy Spirit?," Hugh asks in the title to Book II, Chapter 1.[35]

Mary conceived of the Holy Spirit not because she received the seed of the fetus from the substance of the Holy Spirit, but because through the love and operation of the Holy Spirit, nature provided the substance for the divine fetus from the flesh of the virgin. For since in her heart the love of the Holy Spirit was especially ardent, on this account in her flesh the virtue of the Holy Spirit worked marvelous things . . . Accordingly, the lust of the flesh did not operate conception in the virgin, who neither received seed from the flesh of man nor conceived from her own flesh through love of man, but conceived through the love and operation of the Holy Spirit. Nor is the Holy Spirit himself to be called father of Christ because His love operated the conception of the virgin, since He did not contribute the seed of the fetus of His own essence to the virgin but provided substance to the virgin herself from her own flesh through His love and virtue.[36]

Hugh's Mary is an active agent in her own impregnation, working under the inspiration of the Spirit to do God's will. Hugh explains that no semen is involved (the triune God, acting through the spirit, does not operate like the pagan Zeus to impregnate human woman with his offspring). The emphasis here is, as in so many others of Hugh's writings, upon the power of love and understanding to generate God within, a view of human change and psychology which was explained in Chapter 10. It is through this love that Mary conceives Christ, that the invisible deity becomes visible. This action of Mary's is the model for all of human Christ-bearing, for change and conversion, subjects which became of primary importance in the writings of Hugh's disciple Richard.

Godefroy of St. Victor extends Hugh's idea of virgin as Christ-bearer in "Sacram et salutiferam," saying that Mary is like other virgins who would also bear Christ within themselves.[37] Godefroy's virgins are clerics, who bring forth their young by preaching, teaching, and doing good works. Mary is the model, not only for faithful souls in general, but more particularly for the fruitful members of the

---

[33] See Baron (1955) for an introduction to Hugh's understanding of Mary. The sermon for the Assumption sometimes accredited to Hugh is discussed by Matter (1990), p. 158.

[34] See *SCF*, p. 206.

[35] From the Apostles' Creed.

[36] Hugh of St. Victor, *SCF*, pp. 229–230. The passage commented on is Luke 1:31–38. The angel replies to Mary's query about how she can conceive without intercourse: "The Holy Ghost shall come upon thee, and the power of the most High shall overshadow thee" (Luke 1:35).

[37] "Cetere namque sancte et caste virgines anime Verbum divinum sibi celitus inspiratum spiritualiter quidem concipere et gignere merentur, concipere audiendo, discendo, meditando, gignere docendo, predicando, operando." See Beumer (1960), pp. 250–251.

ecclesiastical hierarchy, who would propagate the faith and have "wombs" filled with Christ.

These ideas are developed in the family of texts set to "O Maria, stella maris" by the Victorine sequence for the Purification, "Templum cordis adornemus." This sequence both explains how Mary can serve as a model for human "Christ-bearers" and suggests the feelings proper to the celebration.[38] Taken together, its text and music form a guide for worshipers during the Feast of the Purification.[39] As a treatise by Richard of St. Victor states, this feast was distinguished by one of the three major processions of the Church year,[40] during which the participants carried recently blessed and lighted candles throughout the church to the singing of the antiphon "Lumen ad revelationem gentium."[41] The candles recall the words of the aged Simeon, who, present at the temple when Mary arrived with her child, recognized the baby as the Christ and called him a "light to enlighten the nations."[42]

The feast commemorates the story recounted in Luke 2:22–38, of the Blessed Virgin submitting to the rites of purification after birth, and presenting her child in the temple.[43] In his attempt to signify the fulfillment of the Old Testament religion in Christ, Luke conflated two different practices, neither of which, as a matter of historical fact, was customarily celebrated in the temple itself.[44]

"Templum cordis" falls into two parts: the first is about models for praise and for the soul, and the second describes Mary as a type of the church. The opening is about Simeon and the coming of the "light" into the temple. Simeon embraced the baby, and thus held him as the processors in the medieval feast held their candles.[45] They are like Mary, who brought the baby to the temple; they are also like Simeon, who embraced him and recognized him as the redeemer. Thus the first line asks the singers to make beautiful their hearts that they might receive Christ within the internal temple, "tenens per amorem," holding Christ through love in their hearts as they hold the candle in their hands. The joy of receiving should be that of Simeon, the old man who had been promised he would not die without seeing the redeemer. The adorning of the inner temple of the worshiping soul is effected by

---

[38] Though the original feast, as it was celebrated in the Eastern church, focused primarily on the coming of Christ to the temple, Western theologians emphasized instead the Virgin's role. See discussion and further bibliography in Joseph Crehan, "Candlemas" in *A Catholic Dictionary of Theology*, 3 vols. (London, 1962–71), vol. I, pp. 317–321; and in Bruno Kleinheyer, "Maria in der Liturgie," in *Handbuch der Marienkunde*, ed. Wolfgang Beinert and Heinrich Petri (Regensburg, 1984), pp. 404–439.

[39] A substantial part of the next few pages is a revised version of the discussion of "Templum cordis" found in Fassler (1983). It is the only part of that work which is directly used in this book.

[40] The other two were the processions of Palm Sunday and of the Ascension. Richard explains these three processions allegorically in *Super exiit edictum seu De tribus processionibus* (*L'Edit d'Alexandre*, ed. Châtillon).

[41] An early account of the feast is found in a document known as Ordo Romanus 20; see Andrieu, ed., *Les Ordines Romani*.

[42] The text Simeon speaks when recognizing Jesus as the Saviour (Luke 2:29–32) is called the "Nunc dimittis" from its Latin incipit. This canticle was sung at Compline, the final hour of the Divine Office, in the Western church.

[43] See Lev. 12. According to this passage, the woman was to bring a lamb for a burnt offering and a dove as a sacrifice for sin. If she were poor, she could bring two doves instead, one for a burnt offering and the other for the sacrifice for sin.

[44] For a critical study of Luke's account, and the theological reasons for his departures from historical accuracy, see Brown (1977), pp. 447–451, and *JBC*, pp. 683–684.

[45] For background to the medieval feast, see Waddell (1991).

renewal, a process which, Godefroy says, takes place constantly.[46] As the light of the procession comes into the church, all are filled, with love, with light, with praise.

The second half of the sequence is about the model Christ-bearer, the Virgin Mary. Here she begins as the beautiful spouse of Christ (strophes VI–VIII), becomes the star of the sea, the guide for human beings (strophe IX, first half), and then is immediately transformed from the star into the church (strophe IX, second half and strophe X). In this conclusion, Mary, as church, is the watercourse through which Christ flows, the duct for the wine, the bearer of the medicine. Because she represents the actions of the sacramental church, she becomes a mighty priest, who floods the people with the wine of communion and the waters of sanctification.

"Templum cordis"
As found in Paris, BN 14819, fols. 60r–61r

I.1　Templum cordis adornemus
nouo corde renouemus
　　nouum senis gaudium;
I.2　Quod dum ulnis amplexatur
sic longeui recreatur
　　longum desiderium.

(I　Let us adorn the temple of the heart,
let us renew with new heart
　　the new joy of the old man:
while he embraces it with his arms
thus is fulfilled the long-standing desire
　　of the aged man.

II.1　Stans in signum populorum
templum luce laude chorum
　　corda replens gloria;
II.2　Templo puer presentatus
post in cruce uir oblatus
　　pro peccatis hostia.

II　Standing as a sign for the peoples,
he fills the temple with light, the choir with praises,
　　hearts with glory;
now a boy presented in the temple,
later a man offered on the cross,
　　the sacrifice for sins.

III.1　Hinc saluator hinc maria
puer pius mater pia
　　moueant tripudium;
III.2　Sed cum uotis perferatur
opus lucis quod signatur
　　luce luminarium.

III　Therefore the saviour, therefore Mary:
let the holy boy, the holy mother
　　begin this ceremonial dance,
and with prayers
let the work of the light be carried out,
　　the work signified by the light of lights.

IV　Verbum patris lux est uera
uirginalis caro cera
　　christus splendens cereus;
IV.2　Cor illustrat ad sophiam
qua uirtutis rapit uiam
　　uiciis erroneus.

The word of the father is the true light:
the virginal flesh is the wax,
　　Christ is the shining candle;
He lights up the heart to wisdom,
by which the one straying in sins
　　seizes the path of virtue.

V.1　Christum tenens per amorem
bene iuxta festi morem
　　gestat lumen cereum;
V.2　Sicut senex uerbum patris
uotis strinxit pignus matris
　　brachiis corporeum

V　Everyone holding Christ through love,
properly, according to the custom of the feast,
　　bears a lighted candle;
just as the old man embraced with his prayers
the word of the father and with his arms
　　the corporeal pledge of the mother.

---

[46] The faithful soul is "born every day."

VI.1	Gaude mater genitoris	Rejoice, mother of the creator,

VI.1   Gaude mater genitoris
simplex intus munda foris
  carens ruga macula;
VI.2   A dilecto preelecta
ab electo predilecta
  deo muliercula.

VII.1   Omnis decor tenebrescit
deformatur inhorrescit
  tuum intuentibus;
VII.2   Omnis sapor amarescit
reprobatur et sordescit
  tuum pregustantibus.

VIII.1   Omnis odor redolere
non uidetur sed olere
  tuum odorantibus;
VIII.2   Omnis amor aut deponi
prorsus solet aut postponi
  tuum nutrientibus.

IX.1   Decens maris luminare
decus matrum singulare
uera parens ueritatis
uie uite pietatis
  medicina seculi;
IX.2   Vena uiui fontis uite
sitienda cunctis rite
sano dulcis et languenti
salutaris fatiscenti
  confortantis poculi;

X.1   Fons signate sanctitate
riuos funde nos infunde
fons ortorum internorum
riga mentes arescentes
  unda tui riuuli;
X.2   Fons redundans sis inundans
cordis praua queque laua
fons illimis munde nimis
ab immundo munda mundo
  cor mundani populi. Amen.

Rejoice, mother of the creator,
guileless within, pure without,
  free from wrinkle or stain;
chosen before by the beloved,
loved before by the chosen,
  handmaiden to God.

Every beauty is clouded over,
deformed, made hideous,
  to those contemplating your beauty;
all flavor grows bitter,
is rejected and grows foul,
  to those foretasting your savor.

VIII   Every smell seems not to smell
but to stink
  to those smelling yours;
every love is wont to be put aside
immediately, or neglected
  by those fostering your love.

IX   Beautiful light of the sea,
beauty singular among mothers,
true parent of truth,
of the way, of life, of piety,
  medicine of the ages;
watercourse of the living fountain of life,
rightfully thirsted for by all,
draught of the strengthening cup,
sweet to the healthy and the sick,
  health-bearing to the fainting.

X   Fountain sealed with sanctity,
pour out streams, flood us;
fountain of inner gardens,
water thirsting minds
  with the flood of your streams;
abounding fountain, may you overflow,
wash all that is corrupt in our hearts;
mudless fountain, totally pure,
purify the heart of worldly people
  from the impure world. Amen.

In "Templum cordis," Hugh's vision of the church as the historical purveyor of sacraments, the actual building, and the model of the human soul and divine worship becomes united in a single person, a person capable of representing all three things at once. Mary, like the Apostles, is here interpreted as a model for clerics, for reformed members of the ecclesiastical hierarchy. She is pure, her life is a source of

inspiration causing others to follow after her, and she offers the sacraments instituted by Christ. In an Assumption sermon by Walter of St. Victor, Mary is seen
sitting on her heavenly throne next to Christ. First Christ takes up the whole of the
power of the Father within himself, and then he offers it to his mother. As Mary
accepts his gift, she becomes the church, receives the power of the sacraments, and
offers them to the people. "Look at this with me," Walter says:

Intuemini una mecum unde tanta matris Domini procedat exultatio. Ipse Pater, qui est "fons
vitae," origo summi boni, emittit vocem suam, profert verbum suum, generat unigenitum suum.
Homo vero assumptus excipit illud verbum Patris ex ore eius secundum plenitudinem; fontem
vitae totum exhaurit, totum bibit, nihil de eo relinquit, totum in se suscipit, deinde genitrici suae
poculum vitae porrigit. Illa vero, tanquam proxima et immediate coniuncta, accipit illud poculum
vitae de manu filii sui, et apponit labiis suis, et bibit prima post filium suum, et bibens tota
absorbetur a gloria Dei. Deinde ceteris propinat de illo tanquam "ab ubertate domus" Dei, omnes
inebrians illo vino optimo quod protulit vitis illa, quae dicit: "Ego sum vitis." (John 15:1)

(Behold with me whence comes the singular, great exultation of the Mother of God. The Father
himself, who is the fountain of life, the origin of the greatest good, emits his voice, brings forth his
word, generates his only-begotten. And the man taken up receives the word of the Father from
His mouth fully. He drains the whole fountain of life, and drinks the whole, leaving nothing from
it, and takes the whole within Himself. Then to His mother He extends the cup of life, and she, as
though next to and immediately joined with him, receives that cup of life from the hand of her
son and takes it to her lips and drinks first after her son, and drinking is totally absorbed by the
glory of God. Then she administers to others from the cup as if "from the abundance of the
house" of God, intoxicating all with that fine wine which that vine itself brought forth which said
"I am the vine."

The four sequence texts examined so far, taken together, present a multidimensional
exegetical exposition of the meanings of the Virgin Mary at the Abbey of St. Victor.
Two other texts extend this meaning, although in very different fashions. "Ave uirgo
... porta" is the longest sequence in the Victorine repertory, a late piece, probably
added in the early thirteenth century. Its opening strophes describe the historical
Mary, mother of Christ. In strophes III and IV, the poet describes his difficulty in
finding the right words to express a miracle beyond human comprehension.[47] The
poet then chooses an allegorical exposition of the mystery of the divine birth (strophes
V–IX). Strophes X–XIII switch to the tropological level of explanation. And the
end of the sequence is, as sequences usually are, about the joys of heaven.[48]

The music of this sequence represents a conscious attempt to integrate the piece
fully into the family of works to which it belongs. It contains several more strophes
of poetry than can be accommodated by the original melody, "O Maria, stella
maris," and so several units of music were borrowed from other well-known
sequences to make up the difference, but they were borrowed with thematic
considerations firmly in mind. The final three melodic units were taken from
"Hodierne lux diei," a late-eleventh-century piece which was very popular
throughout northern Europe in the twelfth century. The music comes from the

[47] See Chapter 3 for discussion of this common topos.
[48] SEe M&A, pp. 207–208.

place in "Hodierne" where the text best fits the words of "Ave virgo . . . porta": it describes Mary as the way through the sea, the door to heaven, and the splendor of the firmament.[49] Another melodic unit comes from the popular "Mane prima sabbati," an Easter sequence also written in honor of Mary Magdalene. The borrowed music is taken from the place where the poem honors Mary by comparing her to the mother of God.[50] The borrowed music has been chosen because of the themes of its texts, as was the case in the setting of "Rex salomon." By using music from popular sequences to extend their own, Victorine composers were able to deepen the power of the exegesis.

The final sequence set to "O Maria, stella maris" is the only one whose text does not immediately seem right for this family. "Sexta passus feria" is a sequence for Easter Friday, and has nothing about the Virgin Mary or the church in its text. This fact, however, may have troubled the Victorines. The liturgical representation of the founding of the church and its sacraments and the ongoing transmission of sacramental power from priest to people was a major theme for them, as has been demonstrated in Chapter 11. Easter Friday, celebrating these themes, must have been a special day in their liturgy. The Gospel from Matthew 28:16–20 tells the story of Christ's meeting the assembled eleven disciples in Galilee.[51] The Victorines would have believed that this event was essential to the founding of the church and the establishment of the ecclesiastical hierarchy of teachers and preachers.[52] In the liturgy as celebrated at St. Victor and in most other places on this day, this text provided the words for the communion antiphon and for antiphons of the office; at the Abbey of St. Victor, it was read during the hours of the day with appropriate scriptural commentaries. Easter Friday, therefore, was a day for commemorating Christ's command to the assembled Apostles that they baptize and teach, that they build the church. The choice of "O Maria, stella maris" as the sequence melody for this day may have been the Victorine way of introducing the subject of the church into a sequence text which did not mention it and thereby of making the sequence a better preparation for the Gospel.

Conclusion to Part V: Godefroy of St. Victor, redactor of the Victorine sequentiary?

Through the themes of their texts and the symbolic power of their melodies, the six sequences of family IIB exemplify Godefroy's multi-layered explanation of Mary as mother of Christ, as type of the church, and as model for the faithful soul. This

---

[49] "Porta clausa post et ante . . . via viris invia . . . splendor firmamenti . . ." For an edition of the text of "Hodierne," see AH LIV, p. 346. Timbres 59, 53, and 55 come from "Hodierne."

[50] "O Maria mater pia / Stella maris appellaris / Operum per merita. / Matri Christi coequata / Dum fuisti sic vocata / Sed honore subdita." See AH LIV, p. 215. Timbre 58 is borrowed from "Mane prima."

[51] This meeting is known among students of the Bible as "The Great Commission," for it was here that Jesus commanded his disciples to go forth into all nations. See *JBC*, p. 674.

[52] Medieval commentators often referred to the establishment of the church when they wrote about this text. In the *Glossa ordinaria*, for example, the text is said to refer to the apostolic succession of the universal church. The early-twelfth-century reformer St. Bruno of Segni wrote in a homily for Easter Friday that in this passage Galilee, the place to which Christ called the disciples, represents the church.

Mary is also designed to speak to the special concerns of the canons regular, for she is a model priest, pure inside and out, and a worthy dispenser of the sacraments. Each time any of these six sequences was sung, the texts of all of them would be heard, for music has this power to bring all its texts to a singer's mind at once.

The sequence family as developed by the Victorines is a kind of motet, but it is a motet which must be played within the person, perhaps changing him as he plays it within, challenging him to make the sound of the mouth one with internal understanding.[53] In the families described in Chapters 13 and 14, the Victorines created a new kind of exegesis, one which depended upon the power of music, as used in contrafacta, to interregulate texts. The general idea – of setting two or more Easter texts, for example, to the same Easter melody – was not new; although there has been no careful study of the subject, numerous examples of this technique have been pointed out. Adam of St. Victor was surely deeply interested in relating texts in just this simple way, as his setting of "Ecce dies celebris" to the Easter melody "Mane prima" or his setting of "Mundi renouatio" to "Victime paschali laudes" demonstrates. But if we believe that the melody for "Zima uetus" is his own, he also went beyond this. Here he increased the symbolic power of the music by modeling it upon a well-known tune and yet transforming it to make a statement about the original and its meaning. Other texts set to this melody could then pick up on this symbolism and use it to underscore their own themes, as was the case with "In natale saluatoris."

The second generation of composers and sequence poets after Adam took this idea further, extending it to a larger body of texts and music, allowing their combination in the sequences to become a sounding replica not only of the church, but also of the process by which the church, according to their Augustinian ideals of preaching by word and example, should be built. If one searches for the person responsible for organizing the texts and music of the Victorine repertory into a book dependent upon ideas begun by Adam during the mid twelfth century, Godefroy of St. Victor emerges as a likely candidate. He explained in his own words what it meant to be a canon regular at the Abbey of St. Victor during the third quarter of the twelfth century. In the beginning of his autobiographical poem *Fons philosophiae*, Godefroy describes the study of the liberal arts in Paris at mid-century. From this information and other evidence, Philippe Delhaye has sketched out the main events of Godefroy's life.[54] He was born around 1125–30, studied the liberal arts in Paris (perhaps with Adam of Balsham, one of the masters who had rooms on the famous "Petit-Pont"), and began the study of theology around 1150. Soon after this time, although the precise date is not known, he became a canon regular at the Abbey of St. Victor. His life at the abbey was not always easy, and around 1180 his quarrels with Abbot Gautier became so intense that he was asked to leave. In 1185, however, he seems to have completed his masterpiece, the *Microcosmos*, and by 1194

---

[53] The thirteenth-entury motet in its classic mid-century form was a three-voice piece. The top two voices most often had different texts which expounded different, yet sometimes interrelated themes, while the bottom voice, the tenor, sang a textless melisma taken from a well-known liturgical chant.

[54] See Delhaye (1951), pp. 13–33.

he was back at the Abbey of St. Victor, holding the office of sacristan. He died in 1198.

Godefroy, like his older contemporary Richard of St. Victor, was a disciple of the ideas of Hugh of St. Victor. His *Fons philosophiae* clearly owes much to the *Didascalicon*; his *Microcosmos*, a story about the creation within the human soul, uses the writings not only of Hugh but also of Richard as sources.[55] The second part of the *Fons philosophiae* is about the church as the City of God (as borrowed from St. Augustine), and types of ceremonies and the priesthood in the Old Testament; there is a section devoted to the disciples and evangelists and their actions as belonging to the priestly order of Melchisedeck; there is reference to the fathers of the church, to Augustine above all the others and finally to the canons regular. Of the canons he says:

> At exemplis alii grandibus accensi
> Semitam preambuli pergunt inoffensi,
> Nec excedunt regulam tramitis ostensi,
> Patris ad uestigia filii suspensi.
>
> Hii sunt quos canonicos uocant regulares
> Docti sacre regule uias salutares,
> Vita, uotis, habitu, uictu, gestu pares;
> Omnia communia: nulli propria res.
>
> Et nunc ad officium uacant clericale,
> Nunc ad exercitium pergunt manuale,
> Nunc ad patris pocula recurrentes, quale
> Cuique placet aliquid bibunt spiritale.
>
> (But by great examples some, all on fire are burning;
> Faultless do they walk that path, never miss a turning,
> Never wander from the Rule of the norm they're yearning
> To fulfill as faithful sons, from their Father learning.
>
> "Canons regular" they're called, holy life constructed;
> In that salutary Rule they have been instructed:
> Peers by habit, gestures, food, life by vows conducted,
> All is common – nothing for private use deducted.
>
> Now they cleric's role fulfill by the recitation
> Of the Office, now their hands find much occupation,
> Now their Father's cups they seek, make their application
> For a drink their spirits need, a desired potation.)

The canons have the liturgical functions of Mass and Office, but these are supported by the work of their hands. As Godefroy describes them subsequently, the drinks the canons imbibe are not only those of Mass, but also those of ethics, and of preparing for the ascent to ecstasy as taught at the school of St. Victor by Richard during the time of Godefroy's first fifteen or so years at the abbey.

[55] For an evaluation of the many sources used by Godefroy, see Delhaye (1951), pp. 150–177.

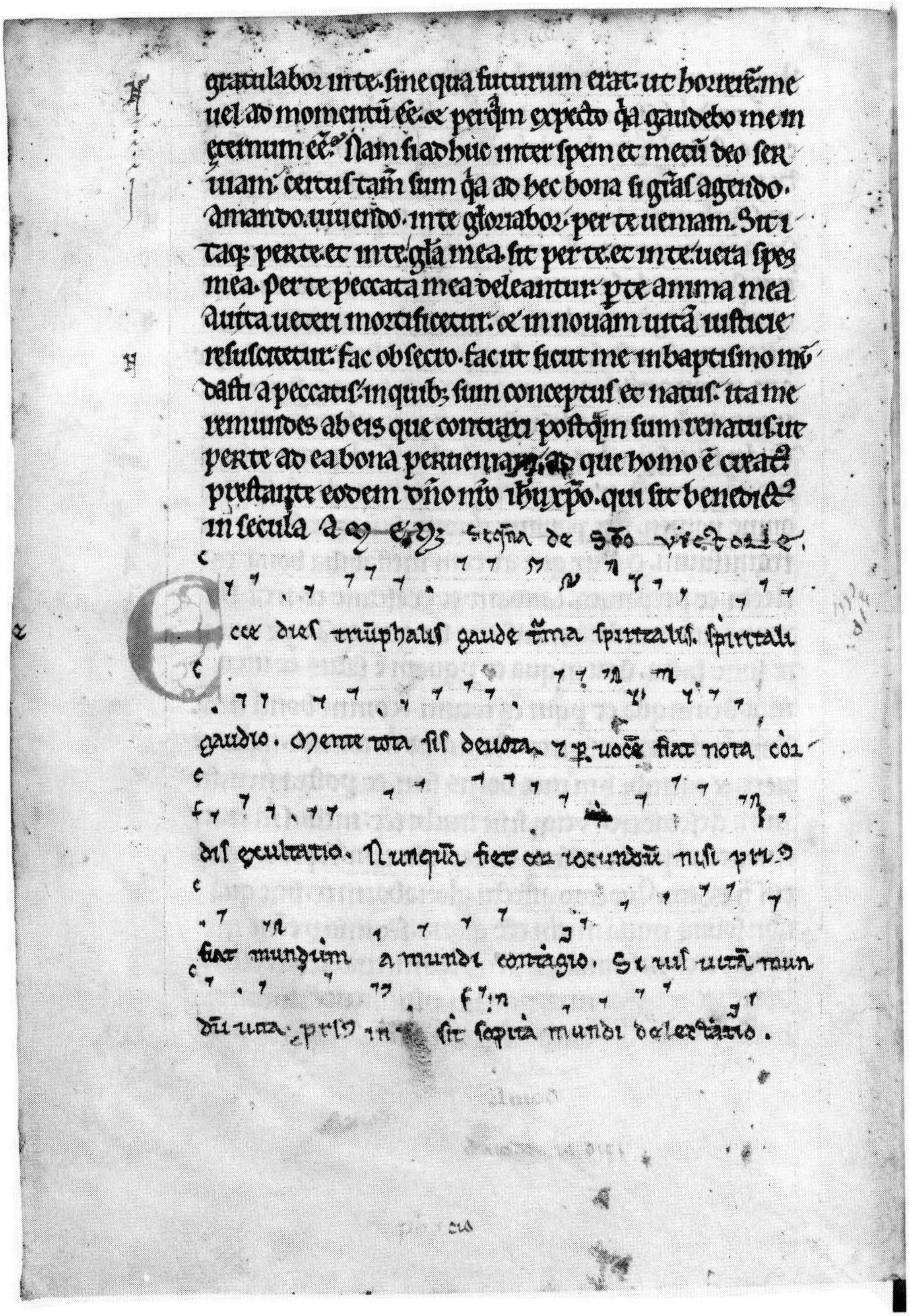

Plate 14.1 Opening of the sequence "Ecce dies triumphalis" in the hand of Godefroy of St. Victor. Paris, BN lat. 15045, fol. 84v

Godefroy's writings are supported completely by themes found in the sequences as well, but the best reason for supposing his connection with the formation of the repertory during the second generation is the fact that he was both a poet and a musician and had an interest in writing sequences.[56] It has already been observed that the sequence "Ecce dies triumphalis" exists in a copy made in his own hand, demonstrating that he knew the melodic tradition of the second generation and suggesting involvement in it; the possibility that he wrote the piece and its music cannot be denied (see Plate 14.1). He wrote other music as well, including the relatively well-known planctus for the Virgin Mary, sometimes seen as the first of its type in the twelfth century.[57] In one of his two self-portraits, an unusual genre in the twelfth century, Godefroy holds a book on his knees with the inscription "prosaice, rithmice, metrice, melice," thereby announcing that he wrote prose works, rhythmic poetry, metrical poetry, and songs.[58] His other self-portrait exists in two copies, the less well-drawn in Paris, Mazarine 1002, fol. lv (see Plate 14.2) and the better in Paris, BN lat. 14515, fol. 106v.[59] In his hand, he carries a banner with the inscription "Aspicio cantans, aspiciensque cano" ("I look singing and looking I sing"), with reference to the first great responsory of the Office, "Aspiciens a longe."[60] Here he wears the full attire of the regular canons and is ready to preach; he stands in a watchtower above Sion, above the temple. The inscription above him announces who he is, and, by implication, who the canons regular are according to his interpretation. With his expansion of Isa. 21:8, and within this pictorial context, they become the watchmen who guard the temple:

Super specula domini sum stans iugiter per diem et super custodiam meam sum stans totis noctibus, speculator castrorum Dei.[61]

(Upon the watchtower of the Lord I stand continually by day, and on my guard I stand all night, a watchman of God's encampment.)

The canons saw themselves as the "watchmen" of the church, especially as the interpreters of its liturgy. Their goal was to inform the clergy about their liturgical roles and, whenever possible, to promote conversion to the common life and to encourage well-informed preaching. Their sequences were designed to serve all these purposes, and allowed for their celebration within the liturgy. Clearly, Godefroy of St. Victor understood all these ideas and accepted a role in strengthening and developing them.

In Richard of St. Victor's description of the church as a great boat (see p. 325), the

---

[56] In the *Fons philosophiae*, Godefroy acknowledges tarrying long over the art of music. See lines 361–364; Michaud-Quantin edn., p. 47. His role as a composer is also discussed in Gasparri (1982 and 1985).

[57] See discussion in Delhaye (1951), pp. 251–259.

[58] See Delhaye (1951), p. 229.

[59] Photographs of both of these are found in Delhaye (1951) as the frontispiece and facing p. 228.

[60] Godefroy's sermon on the divine office will be discussed at length in my forthcoming article on the Victorine office.

[61] See Isa. 21:8: "et clamavit leo super specula Domini ego sum stans iugiter per diem et super custodiam meam ego sum stans totis noctibus." (And a lion cried out: I am upon the watchtower of the Lord, standing continually by day: and I am upon my ward, standing whole nights.)

Plate 14.2   Copy of the self-portrait of Godefroy of St. Victor, Paris, Bibl. Maz. 1002, fol. 1v

clergy are the oarsmen, who sing as they row. Godefroy sings as he watches over Sion, using music as a metaphor for understanding and service. Throughout the sequence poetry too, singing is described as the measure of the reformed life: those who lived well, would sing well, and their communal song was the only one which would rise up to the ears of God.[62] Those who were fit to be canons, fit to teach and preach and administer the sacraments, were to know the secrets of scriptural exegesis. The sequences offer examples of scriptural exegesis, with an emphasis on clerical office and the sacraments; they also attempt to explain how their own exegesis works and what it means. They proclaim and teach at the same time, encouraging minds to flow freely between the various levels of exegetical understanding, and hearts to rise and fall in their various contemplative states. The Victorine sequence melodies were designed to promote knowledge of the Bible in a liturgical way: by linking one text to another, one level of meaning to another, and sustaining the symbolic meanings of the parts and the whole simultaneously. "Whoever carries out the function of Moses," says Richard of St. Victor, "whoever accepts the pastoral office, this person certainly ought to move about by means of free flight everywhere among those three kinds of contemplation."[63] Those who sang the sequences were to move joyfully through memory's storehouse, revealing their inner states in the singing, just as the clergy were to delight in their work and in their offices through their knowledge of sacred history and Scripture, and contemplation upon their meanings.

Here without a doubt we cause a minstrel to sing when on account of great dancing of the heart we shout in divine celebration and while rising up in thanksgiving we reecho in divine praises with a great shout of the heart from the innermost parts of ourselves . . . And so by singing and praising the way is prepared for the Lord, the way by which He judges it worthy to come to us and show us some marvelous showings of his mysteries.[64]

[62] See especially the anonymous Victorine sermon "On the praises of divine praise," Walter of St. Victor and others, *Sermones*, ed. Châtillon, pp. 263–269.
[63] *The Mystical Ark*, Zinn trans., p. 301. For a discussion of ascent in Richard and the sources of this idea, see Feiss (1979).
[64] See Richard of St. Victor, *The Mystical Ark*, Zinn trans., p. 341.

EPILOGUE

Sacred history and the common life

I once wrote: "the Cathedral of Notre Dame was the first great center for the production of late sequences in twelfth-century Paris."[1] This book has been written, in part, as a modification of that statement, explaining that the sequences were Victorine in spirit and created originally to serve the ideals of the Augustinian canons regular. My long rethinking of the evidence surrounding the late sequences in twelfth-century France included exploration of sources from outside Paris. I found that only Augustinians showed great interest in bringing substantial repertories of late sequences into their liturgies. Other religious groups remained content with earlier sequence styles, at least until the late twelfth and early thirteenth centuries, when many cathedrals and monastic churches in France (with the exception of those belonging to Cistercians, Franciscans, and Carthusians) began to adopt great numbers of late sequences. Thus the rise of the late sequence was the only major liturgical change in the twelfth century effected almost single-handedly by canons regular.

Paris, where, as Husmann and others have argued, the Cathedral of Notre Dame apparently had great numbers of late sequences by the end of the twelfth century, would seem to be an exception. But I think this situation existed only because the cathedral administration was strongly influenced by the canons regular of St. Victor and their ideals throughout most of the century. The sequence composer and poet Adam served as Precentor of the cathedral for most of his life, but he was, at heart, a Victorine; indeed, as soon as the revenues from his prebend could be legally assigned to St. Victor, he took up residence there. The two most powerful and long-serving bishops of the century, Stephen of Senlis and Maurice of Sully, both fought for the rights of the canons regular throughout their tenures, lived at the abbey in a specially appointed house, and ended their lives as Victorines. I have argued here that the late sequences of Paris were, for the most part, written as calls to the common life and the Rule of St. Augustine; and of course, a Parisian bishop such as Stephen of Senlis, who had the conversion of secular canons as a major goal, would have wished to hear them sung in the Mass liturgy.

There are many kinds of evidence available for assigning priority to the Abbey of

---

[1] See Fassler (1987), p. 348.

St. Victor in the creation of the Parisian sequence texts. It is worth noting that their manuscript tradition is firm, and that their use of liquescent neumes to underscore the sounds of certain consonants is strikingly consistent. The sequence repertory often seems designed for their church (built in the mid twelfth century): vitae of saints chosen for altar dedicatees and sequence subjects support their ideals in a variety of ways. Most significant, however, is the fact that the Victorines seem to have understood both the sequence texts and Adam's original intentions as composer-poet so well. Only they reorganized a core of commonly-circulating Parisian sequence texts to create meaningful families of sequences, each bonded by particular, symbolically charged melodies.

The exegesis they created through their unique joining of text and melody was inspired by the writings of Hugh of St. Victor. Hugh designed vast pictograms capable of organizing the major events of salvation history. Individuals who memorized such a scheme could take the divine plan within themselves and be transformed by it, much as a believing person could receive the sacrament of faith. The Victorines organized their sequence texts through interrelated melodies, forming a representation of the church and its history. Because the songs were liturgical, they were taken into the communal memory, and could be used to inspire, teach, and transform the group who sang them. Theories about the memory and its actions were expanded in new ways, serving the needs of a religious community.

Adam of St. Victor died just before the mid twelfth century, never knowing that his texts and music, and those of his disciples, would set the style for the songs soon to fill the new cathedrals and other churches of northern France. In Paris, Chartres, Sens, Laon, Rheims, Lisieux, Rouen, new sequences and new buildings went together. Although each new building had its own themes and ways of developing these themes, each was dependent upon a program depicting salvation history through Old Testament and New Testament typology; when each bishop and chapter built a church, therefore, they had in mind models similar to those explained in the ark treatises and the *De sacramentis*, and also as first carried by the sequences of Victorine inspiration throughout France and beyond. Like the sequences, each new building defined the clergy and clerical functions by revealing the sacred history that stood behind them.

There is an irony in the history of these Gothic songs, the Parisian sequences. They, and the model of the church which inspired them, were designed to convert the clergy to the common life, and to help those who had already adopted it to celebrate their conversion. Hugh believed that by contemplating religious art the beholder would change, would be reformed, and become like the art he meditated upon. Speaking in the exegetical mode of Augustine, singing with a music symbolic of the Augustinians' cult of the cross, these sequences were originally created to promote change through liturgical action. Yet, in spite of the fact that the Augustinian canons' vision of religious art became a model followed, first in Paris and the Ile-de-France but later elsewhere, by a large and diverse number of religious groups, the canons failed in one of their primary goals. For cathedral clergy in France were never won in large numbers to the common life during the Middle Ages. The art which was originally designed to teach the clergy and strengthen their ideals, and to encourage and celebrate conversion to the Rule of St. Augustine, came instead to promote and sustain the power of the clergy in a secular world.

Appendices

Key to the appendices

Only the first occurrence of each sequence is listed, with the exception that Common Sequences are listed at the end of each Appendix.

★	without notation
★★	occurs out of liturgical order in the MS
★★★	in a hand different from and later than the main hand(s)

AH	*Analecta Hymnica*
BVM	Blessed Virgin Mary
NS	new-style sequence
TR	transitional-style sequence

Abbreviations used at the heads of the columns (Appendix 5 only):

Augus.	The MS represents the use of Augustianian canons
Bene.	The MS represents the use of Benedictine monks
Cath.	The MS represents the use of a cathedral chapter
Den	St. Denis
Gen	Ste. Geneviève
Mag	St. Magloire
ND	Notre Dame
Vic	St. Victor
c1, c2, etc.	various collections or series found in a given manuscript
vel	or: the sequence was offered as an optional replacement for the first sequence listed
F and G	French and German and refer to the two major sections of Aix 13

Abbreviations used for identifying manuscripts:

Gen.	Paris, Bibliothèque Ste. Geneviève
lat.	Paris, Bibliothèque Nationale, fonds latins
Maz.	Paris, Bibliothèque Mazarine
lat. n.a.	Paris, Bibliothèque Nationale, nouvelles acquisitions latines

Abbreviations used throughout the columns:

@	The source has this sequence with a comparable liturgical assignment (in Appendix 5)
10 7:1/53:28	This sequence dates from the tenth century; the text was published in *AH* VII, beginning on p. 1, and *AH* LIII, beginning on p. 28 (supplied only in Appendix 5)
11ex	This sequence dates from the late eleventh century
add	The sequence is added in a different hand
alia	The rubric "alia" in the MS means that this sequence is offered as an alternative to the preceding one
Circ	Circumcision
Cras	Crastina die (the next day)
CS	The source has a "common sequence" for this feast (common sequences are listed at the end)
E	The source has this sequence, but elsewhere, assigned to a different feast
Fer	Feria (weekday); number indicates which feria
frag	fragmentary
Mel:P	In this manuscript, the text is set to the Parisian melody
Mel:Vic	In this manuscript, the text is set to the Victorine melody
o	The relevant folios are missing
Oct	Octave
Sab	Saturday
Sun	Sunday
X	The source does not have this sequence at all (in Appendix 5)

When no century is supplied, it means that a time frame for the piece has not yet been established. The volume and page of *AH* will be given instead. The rubrics supplied (for Paris, lat. n.a. 1235 in Appendix 2, and for Paris, lat. 778 in Appendix 4) have been placed in parentheses. For an alphabetical listing, which includes titles in these appendices, see the Index of sequence incipits (pp. 473–478).

Appendix 1. Three Norman sequence repertories from the first half of the twelfth century (main hands only; see p. 96 for further discussion of addenda)

Cathedral	Augustinian	Benedictine	Century (or *AH* vol. and first page)
		Paris, BN lat. 10508 St. Evroult	
Ordo veridicus Notre Dame/Chartres Ordinal	Paris, BN lat. 1794 St.-Jean-en-Vallée Ordinal	Gradual with Sequences and ordinary chants, some with tropes	
Temporal cycle			
Advent			
Salus eterna	Salus eterna	Salus eterna	10
Regantem	Regantem	Regantem	10
Qui regis	Qui regis	Qui regis	10
	Advent and Christmas		
	Iubilemus	Iubilemus	10
Christmas			
		Nato canunt	10
	Nostra tuba		10
Sonent regi	Sonent regi		11
		Christi hodierna	10
	Lux fulget		12
		Eia recolamus	10
Epiphany			
Epiphaniam	Epiphaniam	Epiphaniam	10
Easter			
Fulgens preclara	Fulgens preclara	Fulgens preclara	10
(Also Pentecost in Chartrian sources)			
Easter ferias			
Dic nobis	Dic nobis		10
Ecce uicit	Ecce uicit		10
Prome casta	Prome casta	Prome casta	10
		Concurrat urbs	13: 261
		Laudes christo	10
Octave			
		Sempiterno	9: 32
Finding of the Cross			
Alte uox	Alte uox		11
		Salve crux	10
Ascension			
Rex omnipotens	Rex omnipotens	Rex omnipotens	9

Appendix 1 (*cont.*)

Cathedral	Augustinian	Benedictine	Century
		Paris, BN lat. 10508	
		St. Evroult	
Ordo veridicus	Paris, BN lat. 1794	Gradual with Sequences	
Notre Dame/Chartres	St.-Jean-en-Vallée	and ordinary chants,	
Ordinal	Ordinal	some with tropes	
Pentecost			
		Sancti spiritus	9
Pentecost, ferias			
		Resonat sacrata	11
		Eia musa	11
		Alma chorus	10
Alia		Christe salvator	8: 37
Trinity			
	Benedicta sit	Benedicta sit	10
		O alma trinitas	10
Sanctoral cycle			
St. Stephen, Dec. 26			
Gloriosa			10
	Magnus deus	Magnus deus	10
St. John, Evan., Dec. 27			
		Johannes Jesu	late 10
Innocents, Dec. 28			
		Rex magne	10
St. Evroult, Dec. 29			
		Solemnis erit	9: 143
St. Vincent, Jan. 22			
	Precelsa seclis		11
Purification, Feb. 2			
Claris vocibus	Claris vocibus		10
Hac clara die		Hac clara die	10
	(*Purification or Annunciation*)		
Annunciation, March 25			
		Salve porta	10
St. John, Baptist, June 24			
	Gaude caterna		11
		Exsulta celum	9: 181
Sts. Peter and Paul, June 29			
Laude iocunda	Laude iocunda	Laude iocunda	10

St. Benedict, July 11			
		Laudum carmina	11
St. Mary Magdalene, July 22			
		Laudum christo	9: 217
Alia, Mary Magdalene			
		Gaudete fidelium	9: 127
Mary Magdalene, if feast falls on a Sunday			
	Mane prima		late 11
St. Peter's Chains, August 1			
		Psallat vox	44: 241
St. Lawrence, August 11			
		Laurenti David	9
Assumption, BVM, August 15			
Aurea virga	Aurea virga	Aurea virga	11
Salve porta	Salve porta		10
		Congaudent angelorum	9
St. Augustine, August 28			
	Interni festi		early 12
	Adest nobis		late 10
St. John, Baptist, Beheading, August 29			
		Sancti Baptiste	9
Nativity, BVM, Sept. 8			
	Alle celeste	Alle celeste	10
St. Maurice, Sept. 22			
		Alludat letis	11
St. Michael, Sept. 29			
Ad celebres	Ad celebres	Ad celebres	10
St. Denis, Oct. 9			
		Super armonie	11
Feast of the Dedication			
	Clara chorus		late 11
Salue porta			10
All Saints, Nov. 1			
Ecce pulchra	Ecce pulchra	Ecce pulchra	10
		Laus honor	37: 287
St. Martin, Nov. 11			
		Sacerdotem	10
St. Nicholas, Dec. 6			
		Christo regi	11

Appendix 1 (*cont.*)

Cathedral	Augustinian	Benedictine	Century
		Paris, BN lat. 10508	
		St. Evroult	
Ordo veridicus	Paris, BN lat. 1794	Gradual with Sequences	
Notre Dame/Chartres	St.-Jean-en-Vallée	and ordinary chants,	
Ordinal	Ordinal	some with tropes	
Common sequences			
(*Martyred saint*)			
		Resultet tellus	11
Martyr or confessor			
	Adest nobis	Adest nobis	late 10
Confessors			
		Alma cohors	
Apostles			
	Clare sanctorum	Clare sanctorum	9
		Concelebremus sacrum	10
Martyrs			
Mirabilis	Mirabilis	Mirabilis	10
Confessors			
Organicis	Organicis	Organicis	10
		Rex celice	
Sundays			
Stans a longe	Stans a longe	Stans a longe	10
Octaves			
		Gande uirgo	

Appendix 2. Three sequence collections of the third quarter of the twelfth century from Nevers and the vicinity

Cathedral	Augustinian	Benedictine
Paris, BN lat. n.a. 1235	Paris, BN lat. n.a. 3126	Paris, BN lat. 10511

Thirteenth-century supplement at the beginning contains alleluias and sequences necessary for updating the cults of Mary, Nicholas, and St. Cyr.

2–5 Alleluias;
5 Res. and Verse: "Benedictus es domine"
6 (Prosa de beato cyrico:)
"Puer natus est Cyricus"

7v "Ordo iste prosarum que secuntur continentur in uno psalterio ex utraque parte chori et sunt de Beata Virgine"

Incipits:

Ave maris stella dei mater alma porta spei
Ave maris stella mellis celi cela precellens
Ab arce syderea decendens uix aurea virg.
Vergente mundi vesperi sereno fusus sydere
Veneremur uiginem per cuius dulcedinem
Mundamini mundamini laudantes matrem
Laudes claras canticorum sacer chorus ante
(In the margin) Memoriania
Res est admirabilis uirgo uenerabilis parit
Tibi cordis in altari decet preces
Aue uirgo uirginum aue lumen luminum

Appendix 2 (*cont.*)

Cathedral Paris, BN lat. n.a. 1235	Augustinian Paris, BN lat. n.a. 3126	Benedictine Paris, BN lat. 10511
		Thirteenth-century supplement added in the front contains: Aue maria gratia plena Gabriheli celesti nuntio Aue mundi spes maria Salue sanctorum sanctissima Stella maris o maria
Aue uirgo regia regis regum filia Aue uirgo insularis mater nostri saluatoris Salue sancta puritas salue pure santitas Salue sancta uerbi parens uirga yesse flos De sancto Martino: Gaude syon que diem Ant. (for the BVM) Speciosa facta es et Alia Aue stella matutina Alia O maria mater De Sancto Guillielmo: Gaude prole gallia		
Sequences found in the main body of Paris, BN lat. n.a. 1235	Concordances found in the main body of Paris, BN lat. n.a. 3126; rearranged in order of lat. 1235 for comparison. Rubrics provided only when substantially different from lat. 1235.	Sequences found in the main body of Paris, BN lat. 105111; rearranged in order of lat. 1235 for comparison. Rubrics provided only when substantially different from lat. 1235.
	c2 = supplement in the main hand c3 = thirteenth-century additions	c2 = continuation in a later hand
fol. 164r (Prosa Pro hinno ad completorium In die ascensionis) Qui scandis		
Advent fol. 178r (Dominica I in aduentu domini) Salus eterna	Salus eterna	

Appendix 2 (*cont.*)

Cathedral Paris, BN lat. n.a. 1235	Augustinian Paris, BN lat. n.a. 3126	Benedictine Paris, BN lat. 10511
fol. 186 Celica resonant	Celica resonant	
		Eya recolamus/piis 10
		Christi hodierna 9
St. Stephen, Dec. 26 fol. 189v (Prosa) Enarmonia uoce	Prosa in natale S stephani Enarmonia uoce	
fol. 190 (Prosa (Stephani)) Magnus deus	Alia prosa de sco stephano Magnus deus	Magnus deus
St. John, Evan., Dec. 27 fol. 193 (Prosa (De Sancti iohanne)) Ecce pulchra	Prosa sci iohannis evangeliste Ecce pulchra	Iohannes Iesu
Holy Innocents, Dec. 28 fol. 194v (Sanctorum Innocentum) Agmina tibi sonora		

St. Sylvester, Dec. 31	Prosa de innocentibus	
fol. 196r	Celsa pueri	Celsa pueri
(Sancti silvestri)		
Candida concio melos		
fol. 197v	Candida concio melos	
(In Octabas domini)		
Nato canunt (incipit only)		
Epiphany, Jan. 6		
fol. 199v		
(Epiphany)		
Psalle turbe canora	(3) Psalle turbe	
	(Listed third)	
fol. 200r		
(Epiphany)	(1) Epiphaniam domino	
Epiphaniam domino	(2) Letabundus exaltet	Epiphaniam domino
	11	
St. Vincent, Jan. 22	Prosa de sco Vincentio	
(See below for Precelsa)	Precelsa seclis	Precelsa seclis
	(c2)	
	Ecce dies preoptata	

Appendix 2 (cont.)

	Cathedral Paris, BN lat. n.a. 1235	Augustinian Paris, BN lat. n.a. 3126	Benedictine Paris, BN lat. 10511
Purification, BVM, Feb. 2 fol. 202v (Prosa Purificacio sancte marie) Rex laudes criste		(2) Rex laudes criste	
fol. 203r (Prosa Purificacio sancte marie) Claris uocibus inclita		(1) Claris uocibus	(2) Claris uocibus (1) Salue porta
Annunciation, March 25 fol. 204r (Prosa in annunciacione sancte marie) A(u)rea uirga		Salue porta	
			O beata theotochos
			St. George, April 23 Aue stella gloriosa
Easter and octave fol. 209r (Easter) Fulgens preclara		In pascha domini prosa Fulgens preclara	Fulgens preclara

fol. 211r
(Feria II)
Dic nobis quibus

fol. 211v
(Feria III)
Prome casta

fol. 212r
(Feria III)
Adest namque

fol. 212v
(Feria V)
Angelica roboat

fol. 213r
(Feria VI)
Ecce uicit radix

(Feria II)
Dic nobis quibus

Feria III
Prome casta

Feria III
Adest namque

Feria V
Angelica roboat

Feria VI
Ecce uicit radix

(c2)
Epithalamica dic
(Peter Abelard)

(c2)
Zima uetus expurgetur
12 NS

Feria IV
Dic nobis quibus

Feria III
Prome casta

Feria II
Laudes christo

Appendix 2 (cont.)

Cathedral Paris, BN lat. n.a. 1235	Augustinian Paris, BN lat. n.a. 3126	Benedictine Paris, BN lat. 10511
Finding of the Cross, May 3		
fol. 215r		
(Prosa Invencio sancte crucis)		
Laudamus te rex		
	Laudes crucis attollamus	Nunc crucis
	12 NS	11
Ascension		
fol. 217v		
(In ascencione)		
Rex omnipotens	Rex omnipotens	Rex omnipotens
fol. 218v		
(Ad vesperos prosa)	Alia prosa	
Qui scandis astra	Qui scandis astra	
Pentecost and octave		
fol. 219v		
(In pentecostem)		
Almiphona iam gaudia	Almiphona iam gaudia	(2) Almiphona
(Place for rubric left empty)		
fol. 220r	Feria II	
Resonat sacrata	Resonat sacrata	
(Place for rubric left empty)		

fol. 221r	Feria III	(1) Sancti spiritus adsit
(Sancti spiritus adsit)	Sancti spiritus adsit	
(Place for rubric left empty)		
	Feria V	(3) Alma chorus domini
fol. 221v	Alma chorus domini	
Alma chorus domini		
(Place for rubric left empty)		
	Benedicta sit beata trinitas	Benedicta sit beata trinitas
fol. 223r		
(De sancta trinitate)		
Benedicta sit beata trinitas	(c2)	
(Place for rubric left empty)	Profitentes unitatem	
	12 NS	
	(c3)	
	Veni sancte spiritus	
	12 NS	
St. Cyr, June 15		
fol. 225r		
(Sancti Cyrici)	Organicis canamus modulis	
Deus quoniam magnus		
	(c2)	
fol. 225v	Quam ammirabile	
(Sancti Cyrici)		
Organicis canamus modulis		

Appendix 2 (*cont.*)

Cathedral Paris, BN lat. n.a. 1235	Augustinian Paris, BN lat. n.a. 3126	Benedictine Paris, BN lat. 10511
St. John, Baptist, June 24 fol. 227v Prosa (Sancti iohannis baptiste)		
Gloriosa dies adest	Gloriosa dies adest	
fol. 228r		
Gaude caterua (Place for rubric left empty)	Gaude caterua	Gaude caterua
fol. 229r (Prosa De sancto Petro)		
Laude iocunda	Laude iocunda	Laude iocunda
		Petre summe
		St. Benedict, Trans., July 11
		Quem superne
St. Mary Magdalene, July 22		
	Fulget dies preclara	
	Mane prima	Mane prima
	St. James, July 25	
	Gratulemur et letemur	
	12 NS	

St. Lawrence, August 11
fol. 230v
(De sancti Laurentii)
Gloriosa dies adest*

Stola iocunditatis
12 NS

Laurenti dauid
9

Assumption, August 15, and octave
fol. 231v
(Prosa In assumptione sancte marie)
Hac clara die

Hac clara die
A(u)rea uirga

Aurea uirga
Iubilemus collaudantes
12 NS

Clemens et benigna
12 NS

Congaudent angelorum
9

St. Mames, August 17
Omnipotens deus salus

St. Augustine, August 28
Interni festi
12 NS

Appendix 2 (cont.)

Cathedral Paris, BN lat. n.a. 1235	Augustinian Paris, BN lat. n.a. 3126	Benedictine Paris, BN lat. 10511
		St. John, Baptist, Beheading, August 29 Sancti baptiste late 10
Nativity, BVM, Sept. 8 fol. 232r (Prosa De Natiuitate sancte marie) Alle celeste	Alle celeste	Alle celeste
Exaltation of the Cross, Sept. 14 Laudamus te rex		Salue crux late 10 (c2) Laudes crucis
St. Denis, October 9 (An error: sequence is really for St. Maurice) fol. 233r (Dionisii Rustici et eleutherii) Alludat letus	Alludat letus	(c2) Alludat letus

St. Michael, Sept. 29 fol. 235r (Sancti Michaelis) Ad celebres	Ad celebres	(c2) Ad celebres
St. Maurice, Sept. 22 fol. 236r (This is the sequence for St. Denis) ("Retro in Sancti maurici solliter") Mirabilis deus	Mirabilis deus	(c2) Mirabilis deus
Dedication (position differs in each source) fol. 236v (Prosa In dedicatione ecclesia [*sic*]) Obseruanda habunde		
fol. 237v Ad templi huius	Ad templi huius	
	Rex salomon 12 NS	(c2) Clara chorus 11 TR
	Quam dilecta 12 NS	
All saints, Nov. 1 fol. 238r (In festiuitate omnium sanctorum) O alma trinitas deus	O alma trinitas deus	

Appendix 2 (*cont.*)

Cathedral Paris, BN lat. n.a. 1235	Augustinian Paris, BN lat. n.a. 3126	Benedictine Paris, BN lat. 10511
Christo inclita	Christo inclita	Christo inclita
	(c2) De profundis ad te clamantium (Peter Abelard)	
	(c2) Dolorum solatium, laborum remedium (Peter Abelard)	
		St. Florentinus, Nov. 7 Adest namque
	Exultet nunc omnis	
	Sacerdotem christi martinum	
	(c3) Ecce dies specialis 12 NS (Adapted for St. Martin)	
	St. Cecilia, Nov. 22 Sponso sacrarum	
St. Martin, Nov. 11 fol. 241r (Prosa Sancti martini) Exsultet nunc omnis		

365

St. Andrew, Nov. 30
fol. 242r
*Ecce pulchra
*Laude iocunda

Sacrosancta hodierne
12 NS

Common of Apostles
Clare sanctorum
9

BVM, Unspecified
(c2)
Aue maria, gratia plena
12 NS
(c2)
Mater clemens ac benigna
(c2)
Salue mater saluatoris, uas
(Melody from Nevers)
(c3)
Salue mater saluatoris, uas
(Melody as in Paris)
(c2)
Orbis totus unda lotus
(Peter the Venerable)

Clare sanctorum

Appendix 2 (*cont.*)

Cathedral Paris, BN lat. n.a. 1235	Augustinian Paris, BN lat. n.a. 3126	Benedictine Paris, BN lat. 10511
	(c2) Iesse uirgam humidauit 12 NS (c2) Hodierne lux diei 12 NS (c3) Lux aduenit ueneranda 12 NS (Also added to 1235, see below)	
fol. 242r (★★Sancti Vincencii) Precelsa seclis colitur		
fol. 243r ★★Sonent regi (?)		
	(Added in the 14th century) *St. Firmin* Triumphanti cruore proprio	
(Supplement from the thirteenth century)		
fol. 245v (Katherine uirgines et martyris prosas) Christi sponsa katherina		

(In yet another thirteenth-century hand is the office for St. Anne)

fol. 250r
(Prosa ad missam)
Mater matris domini

(Back to the hand which wrote "Christi sponsa")

fol. 251v
(Sancti martini prosa)
Pater noster pastor bonus

fol. 252r
(In natalis sancti stephani prothomaris prosa)
Alabaustrum frangitur nardus

(Yet another thirteenth-century hand)

fol. 253r
Beate Marie Virginis
Lux aduenit ueneranda

(And in yet another hand from the late thirteenth century)

fols. 254r–258v
Office for St. Augustine

(Yet another hand, this from the fourteenth century)

Office for Corpus Christi
fols. 259r–262v

(Incipit officium de corpore domini nostri ihesu christi ad missam)

fol. 259v
Prosa: Lauda syon

Appendix 3. Five southern French Benedictine sequence libelli from St. Martial of Limoges: late eleventh to early thirteenth century

			Series 4
Series 1	Series 2	Series 3	Paris 1139
Paris 1132	Paris 1132	Paris 1132	fols. 9v–31
fols. 113v–131	fols. 132–144	fols. 149–199	various hands;
late 11th c.	mid 12th c.	late 12th c.	early 13th c.

Temporal cycle
Precamur
10

Advent
Salus eterna		Salus eterna	
10		10	
(Alia)		(Sunday 1)	

Regantem		Regantem	
10		10	
(Alia)		(Sunday 2)	

Qui regis		Qui regis	
10		10	
(Alia)		(Sunday 3)	

Christmas
Nato canunt
10

Celeste organum
12 TR
(John, *sic*)

Celica resonant
10
(Alia)

Celebranda
10
(Major Mass)

Epiphany
Epiphaniam
10

Easter
Fulgens
10

Easter ferias

	Dic nobis	Dic nobis	
	10	10	
	(Feria 2)	(Feria 3)	
	Prome casta	Prome casta	
	10	10	
	(Feria 3)		
	Letabunda	Letabunda	
	10	10	
	(Feria 4)		
		Victime paschali	
		late 10 TR	
			Salve dies dierum
			12 NS

Ascencion
Rex omnipotens
10

			Postquam hostem
			12 NS

Pentecost
Sancti Spiritus

		Sancti spiritus	
		(Feria 4)	
		(Rubric only)	

Ferias
Ad te summe
(Alia)

		Ad te summe	
		(Feria 3)	
	Almiphona	Almiphona	
	(Feria 4)	(Feria 3)	
	late 10	late 10	
			Qui procedis
			12 NS
			Lux iocunda
			12 NS

Trinity
O Alma trinitas deus
10

	Benedicta sit	Benedicta sit	
	10	10	

Appendix 3 (*cont.*)

Series 1 Paris 1132 fols. 113v–131 late 11th c.	Series 2 Paris 1132 fols. 132–144 mid 12th c.	Series 3 Paris 1132 fols. 149–199 late 12th c.	Series 4 Paris 1139 fols. 9v–31 various hands; early 13th c.
			Patrem natum paraclitum 12 NS
Holy Cross	Laudes crucis 12 NS	Laudes crucis 1 NS	
Sanctoral cycle *St. Stephen* Dec. 26	Gloriosa dies 10	Gloriosa dies 10 ★★Magnus deus 10	
St. John, Evangelist Dec. 27	Organicis canamus 10	Organicis canamus 10	
Holy Innocents Dec. 28	Rex magne 10	Rex magne 10	
St. Vincent Jan. 22 ★★Precelsa seclis 10	Sacra vincentii 12 NS	Sacra vincentii 12 NS	
Annunciation March 25	Ave maria gratia 12 NS		Ave maria gratia 12 NS (BVM, not specific)

St. John, Baptist (Birth) June 24 ★★Gaude caterua 10			
Sts. Peter & Paul June 29	Laude iocunda 10		
St. Martial June 30 Valde lumen 10			
	Omnis mundus letabundus 11 TR	Omnis mundus letabundus 11TR	
		★★Puer purus beniamita 12 NS	
			★★Lux preclara lemouix 12 NS
			★★Celi enarrant 12 NS
		★★★Veneranda veneretur 12 NS	★★Veneranda veneretur 12 NS
			★★Dissoluto carnis luto 12 NS
St. Benedict (Trans.) July 11	Quem superne 10	★★Quem superne	
St. Mary Magdalene July 22	Mane prima late 11 NS	★★Mane prima late 11 NS	
Assumption, BVM Aug. 15 Hac clara die 10		Hac clara die 10	

Appendix 3 (*cont.*)

Series 1 Paris 1132 fols. 113v–131 late 11th c.	Series 2 Paris 1132 fols. 132–144 mid 12th c.	Series 3 Paris 1132 fols. 149–199 late 12th c.	Series 4 Paris 1139 fols. 9v–31 various hands; early 13th c.
	Aurea virga (Octave) 11		
St. John, Baptist (Beheading) Aug. 29			
			★★Precursorem summi 12 NS
Nativity, BVM Sept. 8 Alle celeste 10			
Claris uocibus 10 (Alia)			
St. Michael Sept. 29 Ad celebres 10			
St. Maur Oct. 5 ★★Alludat letus 10			
All Saints Nov. 1 Ecce pulchra 10			
St. Martin Nov. 11 Exsultet nunc late 10 (fragment)		Exsultet nunc late 10	
			Letabundi iubilemus late 12 NS

St. Andrew
Nov. 30
Prefulgida
10

Prefulgida
10

Exsultet nunc
late 10
(Fragment)

St. Nicholas
Dec. 6
★★Congaudentes
11 TR

Congaudentes
11 TR

Dedication
Letetur et concrepet
10

★★★Quam dilecta
12 NS

Quam dilecta
12 NS

Rex salomon
12 NS

BVM
(Specific feast not indicated)

★★Ave mundi spes
12 NS

★★Hodierne
late 11 NS

★★Ave iesu fili david
late 12 NS

★★Imperatrix gloriosa
12 NS

★★Missus gabriel
late 12 NS

★★Iubilemus collaudantes
early 13

★★Contra casum
early 13

★★Gaudens gaude

Appendix 3 (*cont.*)

Series 1	Series 2	Series 3	Series 4
			Paris 1139
Paris 1132	Paris 1132	Paris 1132	fols. 9v–31
fols. 113v–131	fols. 132–144	fols. 149–199	various hands;
late 11th c.	mid 12th c.	late 12th c.	early 13th c.

Series 5
Paris 1139
fols. 10–20v
early 13th c.

Proser of William la Concha, made for St. Martial in the early thirteenth century

St. Martial
Exsultemus sic
early 13

St. Peter
Gaude Roma
12

St. Paul
Corde uoce
12

St. Andrew
Exultemus et letemur
12

For Virgins
Virgines egregie

St. Lawrence
Prunis datum
12

Easter
Morte christi
early 13

St. Stephen
Mundus heri
12

St. Martin
Velud topazion ex ethiopia
early 13

Appendix 4. Two late-twelfth- or early-thirteenth-century sequence repertories from southern France

Cathedral	Augustinian
Paris, BN lat. 778	Paris, BN lat. 1086
A late-twelfth- or early-thirteenth-century collection of ordinary chants with tropes and sequences from Narbonne	A late-twelfth- or early-thirteenth-century collection of ordinary chants with sequences from St. Leonard in Limoges

[BVM]
★★★Hodierne
late 11
(In a blank space near the beginning)

Masses of Christmas and its octave
HAND I
fol. 41r Venit rex in eternum
(In Nocte)
10

fol. 41v Celeste organum	fol. 28v Celeste organum
(In Prima missa)	(In luce)
12 NS	

fol. 42v Nato canunt omnia	fol. 27r Nato canunt
(In missa de luce)	(In galli cantu)
10	

fol. 43v Age nunc mitis
(Alia)
(Adapted from "Prome uerba")
Only witness in *AH*

fol. 44v Adest una
(In missa maiori)
10

fol. 45v Pangat uox humana
(Alia)
10 (Same melody as Adest una)

fol. 49r Christi hodierna
(Alia)
10

fol. 48v Hec dies est sancta
(Alia)
10

fol. 49r Potestate non natura
(Alia)
12 NS

Appendix 4 (*cont.*)

Cathedral	Augustinian
Paris, BN lat. 778	Paris, BN lat. 1086
A late-twelfth- or early-thirteenth-century collection of ordinary chants with tropes and sequences from Narbonne	A late-twelfth- or early-thirteenth-century collection of ordinary chants with sequences from St. Leonard in Limoges

fol. 50v Ante thorum virginalem
(Alia)
12 NS

fol. 52v Quia uerbum hodie
(In die ad Vesperas)
NS

fol. 53r Celebranda satis   fol. 30r Celebranda satis
(In octave)   (In natali ad maiorem missam)
10

St. Stephen Dec. 26
fol. 54v Celsa polorum
10

fol. 56v Gloriosa dies
(Alia)
10

fol. 59r Enharmonica uoce sonora
10

fol. 32r Mundus heri
12 NS

St. John, Evangelist Dec. 27
Organicis canamus
10 (2 versions)
fol. 58v Version 1: HAND I
10
fol. 59v Version 2: HAND II
10

fol. 34r Christo laudes
12 NS First witness in *AH*

HAND II TAKES OVER FROM HERE

Holy Innocents Dec. 28
fol. 60v Rex magne deus
10

fol. 61r Qui regis
11 TR

fol. 62r ★Christe sacra serenat
(In octave)
11

fol. 63r ★Celica resonent
(Alia)
10

fol. 35r Misit herodes
late 11 NS

Thomas of Canterbury Dec. 29
fol. 36r Aquas plenas
12 NS

Epiphany Jan 6
fol. 64v Epiphaniam domino
10

fol. 39r Epiphaniam domino

fol. 65v Letabundus exsultet
(Ad vesperas)
11 TR

fol. 38r Letabundus exsultet
(In circumcisione)

fol. 41r Christi hodierna
(In oct epiphanie)
10 (See 778, fol. 47r)

St. Vincent Jan. 22
fol. 67r ★Precelsa intonent
11

fol. 68r ★Post apostolicus
(Alia)
TR   Only source in *AH*

St. Hilary Jan. 14
fol. 69r ★ and ★★Noua gratia
10

Conversion of St. Paul Jan. 25
fol. 42v Corde uoce
12 NS

Purification Feb. 2
fol. 70v Virgo Israhel decus
10

fol. 71v ★Egregia plebs una
(Alia)
11 TR

fol. 73r Hac clara die
10

fol. 44r Hac clara die
10

Appendix 4 (*cont.*)

Cathedral	Augustinian
Paris, BN lat. 778 A late-twelfth- or early-thirteenth-century collection of ordinary chants with tropes and sequences from Narbonne	Paris, BN lat. 1086 A late-twelfth- or early-thirteenth-century collection of ordinary chants with sequences from St. Leonard in Limoges

Annunciation March 25
fol. 74r Ave salutata
11 (?) TR First source in *AH*

Easter
fol. 75r Fulgens preclara (Ad missam maiorem) 10	fol. 45v Fulgens preclara 10
fol. 77r Clara gaudia festa (Ad vesperas) 10	
fol. 77v Adsunt (commonly Adest) enim festa (Alia) 10	fol. 53r Adsunt enim festa (In Octava Pasche)
fol. 78r Precelsa admodum 11	
fol. 79v ★★Splendent ecce noui (Dominica 5 in Octava Pasche)	
fol. 81v ★★Laudent ecce per orbem (Dominica 1 in Octava Pasche)	
fol. 83r Adest pia ac salutifera 11	
fol. 83v Victime pascali late 10 TR	fol. 48r Victime pascali late 10 TR
	fol. 48v Mane Prima Sabbati (Feria 2) late 11 NS
	fol. 50r Sexta passus feria (Feria 3) 12 NS
	fol. 51r Salue dies dierum (Feria 4) 12 NS

fol. 84r Dic nobis quibus
10

fol. 84v ★Cuncta simul
11

fol. 85r Gaudeat eccelesia
(In octabas pasche)
Only source in *AH*

Holy Cross
fol. 86v Laudes crucis   fol. 54r Laudes crucis
12 NS   12 NS

fol. 88r Vexilla regis
(Alia)
11

                                         fol. 56v Si uis uera
                                         (Alia)
                                         12 NS

Thomas of Canterbury Dec. 29
★★ and ★★★Spe mercedis
13 NS

Cross, cont.
★Hec est uera
10 (Opening is missing)

Ascension
fol. 90r Rex omnipotens   fol. 57v Rex omnipotens
10   10

fol. 91v Laude Letabunda
(Ad vesperas)
Only source in *AH*

                                         fol. 59v Postquam hostem
                                         (In Octave ascensionis)
                                         12 NS

Pentecost
fol. 93v Sancti spiritus adsit   fol. 61r Sancti spiritus adsit
(Major Mass)   (In die pentecoste)
9   9

fol. 95r Cantantibus hodie
(Ad vesperas)
Only source in *AH*

fol. 96v ★★★Veni sancti spiritus
(Alia) (Added mid 13th century)
12 NS

Appendix 4 *(cont.)*

Cathedral	Augustinian
Paris, BN lat. 778	Paris, BN lat. 1086
A late-twelfth- or early-thirteenth-century collection of ordinary chants with tropes and sequences from Narbonne	A late-twelfth- or early-thirteenth-century collection of ordinary chants with sequences from St. Leonard in Limoges

fol. 96v Orbis conditor
10
(Veni sancti is written over this piece)

fol. 97v Laudiflua cantica
(Alia)
10

Pentecost, Ferias
fol. 100r Dic queso preclara
(Feria 2)
late 10

fol. 63r Qui procedis
(Feria 2)
12 NS

fol. 65v Lux iocunda
(Feria 3)
12 NS

Trinity
fol. 101r O alma trinitas deus
10

fol. 102r O alma trinitas deitas
10

fol. 103r Benedicta sit beata
10

fol. 68r Profitentes
12 NS

Sundays
fol. 104r Adest nempe
(In dominicis diebus alia prosa)
10

fol. 105v Alma chorus	fol. 69v Alma chorus
(Prosa de nominibus christi)	(For the Transfiguration,
10	usually August 6)

fol. 106r *Omnipotens Deus fortis
(Alia)
10

fol. 107r *Benedictus es domine
(Alia)
Only source in *AH*

fol. 108r Benedicta semper
(Alia)
11

Dedication
fol. 109r *Ad templi huius/supra
10

fol. 110r Ad templi huius/fundata
11

fol. 111r Letemur (commonly Letetur)
et concrepat (Alia)
10

fol. 112r Clara chorus
(Alia)
late 11 TR

fol. 70r Rex salomon
12 NS

fol. 72r Quam dilecta
12 NS

St. John, Baptist June 24
fol. 113r Hodierna dies ueneranda
10

fol. 114r Precursor christi
(Partially erased)
10

fol. 115r Nostra promat herilia
TR   Only source in *AH*

fol. 117r Gaude chaterua
(Alia)
11

fol. 74v Precursorem summi regis
12 NS

St. Peter June 29
fol. 119r Pulchra prepollens
10

Appendix 4 (*cont.*)

Cathedral	Augustinian
Paris, BN lat. 778	Paris, BN lat. 1086
A late-twelfth- or early-thirteenth-century collection of ordinary chants with tropes and sequences from Narbonne	A late-twelfth- or early-thirteenth-century collection of ordinary chants with sequences from St. Leonard in Limoges

fol. 120r Sanctus petrus (Alia) 10	
fol. 121r Laude iocunda (Alia) 10	
fol. 122r Ecce pulcra canorum (Peter on the Feasts of Other Apostles) 10	
	fol. 76r Summa summi luminis 12 NS Only source in *AH*
St. Martial June 30 fol. 123r ★Observanda abunde 11	
fol. 125r ★Alle-sublime 11	
	fol. 77r Superne matris gaudia 12 NS (This is a sequence for All Saints, sung here for St. Martial)
St. Benedict (Translation) July 11 fol. 125v ★Quem superne 10	
St. Mary Magdalene July 22 fol. 127v ★Laudes deo Only source in *AH*	
fol. 128v Mane prima late 11 NS	fol. 78r Mane prime late 11 NS
St. James July 25 fol. 129v Gratulemur et letemur 12 NS	
St. Nazarius July 28 fol. 132v Laude summa deo psallat 11 TR	

St. Peter's Chains Aug. 1
fol. 133r ★Summa culmina
TR   Only source in *AH*

St. Stephen (Finding) Aug. 3
fol. 79r O athleta gloriose
12 NS   Only source in *AH*

St. Felix July 29
fol. 134v ★★Concrepet simbolica
TR   Only source in *AH*

St. Just Aug. 6
fol. 136v Virtutum deus
Only source in *AH*

St. Lawrence Aug. 10
fol. 137v Alme martyr domini
10

fol. 138v Stola iocunditatis
(Alia)
early 12 TR

For Lawrence
(Opening erased)

fol. 82r Prunis datum
12 NS

Assumption, BVM Aug. 15
fol. 140v Hodie maria uirgo
(Ad Vesperas)

fol. 141r Aurea flore (usually Aureo flore)
(Alia)
10

fol. 142v Virgo dei maria
(Alia)
10

fol. 84v A(u)rea virga

fol. 86v Aue maria gratia
(Alia beate marie)
12 NS

fol. 88r Aue mundi spes maria
12 NS

fol. 89r Hodierne lux diei
(Alia beate marie in sabbatis)
late 11 NS

Appendix 4 (*cont.*)

Cathedral	Augustinian
Paris, BN lat. 778	Paris, BN lat. 1086
A late-twelfth- or early-thirteenth-century collection of ordinary chants with tropes and sequences from Narbonne	A late-twelfth- or early-thirteenth-century collection of ordinary chants with sequences from St. Leonard in Limoges

	fol. 90r Missus gabriel (Alia) 12 NS
	fol. 91v Salue mater saluatoris (Alia) 12 NS
	fol. 94r Verbum bonum (Alia) 12 NS
	St. Augustine Aug. 28 fol. 94v Interni festi 12 NS
St. John, Baptist (Beheading) Aug. 29 fol. 143v ★Plebs redempta Only source in *AH*	
fol. 145r ★Ecclesia deuota	
	fol. 96v Cum iohannis sanctitatem 12 NS Only source in *AH*
Nativity, BVM Sept. 8 fol. 145v ★★★Natiuitas marie uirginis 13 NS	
fol. 146v Alle celeste 10	fol. 98v Alle celeste
fol. 148r Christo inclita candida 10 (All Saints)	
St. Maurice Sept. 22 fol. 149r ★Alludat letus ordo 10	
St. Michael Sept 29 fol. 150v Has celebres (Usually Ad celebres) 10	

fol. 100v Laus erumpat
12 NS

fol. 152r ★Laudat Christum
(Alia) (Not in *AH*)
(Erased to make way for Letabundus francisco)

★★★*Francis of Assisi Oct. 4*
fol. 152v ★★★Letabundas francisco
13 NS

All Saints Nov. 1
fol. 153v Adonay sabat
10

fol. 154v Mirabilis deus
(Alia ad vesperas)
10

fol. 155r Vexilla martirum
(Alia)
10

fol. 102v Ecce pulchra
10 (see 788, fol. 122r)

St. Leonard Nov. 6
fol. 104r Anni nobis
12 NS   Only source in *AH*

fol. 105v Exultet uox sonora
12 NS   Only source in *AH*

St. Martin Nov. 11
fol. 156v Hec est dies veneranda
10

157v ★O Martine
(Alia)
10

fol. 158v Digna cultu dies
(Alia)
TR   Only source in *AH*

fol. 106v Lux illuxit triumphalis
NS 12

St. Saturninus Nov. 29
fol. 159v ★Hodiernus sacratior
early 11

fol. 160v ★Angelica turba
(Alia)
TR   Only source in *AH*

Appendix 4 (*cont.*)

Cathedral	Augustinian
Paris, BN lat. 778 A late-twelfth- or early-thirteenth-century collection of ordinary chants with tropes and sequences from Narbonne	Paris, BN lat. 1086 A late-twelfth- or early-thirteenth-century collection of ordinary chants with sequences from St. Leonard in Limoges

St. Andrew Nov. 30
fol. 162v Adest beata precelsa
11

fol. 162v Nostra promat
(Alia)

fol. 163v ★Prefulgida dies
(Alia)
10

                                           fol. 108v Exsultemus et letemur
                                           12 NS

St. Nicholas Dec. 6
fol. 164v Congaudentes   fol. 110r Congaudentes
late 11 NS

St. Eulalia Dec. 10
fol. 165v Psallat plebs egregia
NS   Only source in *AH*

Confessors (Common)
fol. 167r ★Celsa celorum
11

fol. 168v ★Alle uox promat
11

St. Maur Oct. 5
fol. 169v ★ and ★★Auriflua chaterua

Virgins (Common)
fol. 170v ★En uirginum
10

                                           Common for Evangelists
                                           fol. 112r Iocundare plebs
                                           12 NS

                                           Common for Apostles
                                           fol. 114r Celi solem
                                           12 NS

Common for Apostles
fol. 115r Laus sit patri
NS 12   Only source in *AH*

For an apostle or a martyr
fol. 117r Letabundi iubilemus
12 NS   *AH*

For one confessor
fol. 119r Assunt festa
11   One of 2 sources in *AH*

For Virgins
fol. 120v Virgines egregie
12 NS

For Mary in Paschal Time
fol. 121v Virginis marie laudes
12 NS

HAND I AGAIN
Supplemental series in liturgical order
Dom 2 in Oct. Pasche
fol. 171v Gaudeat tellus
(Should be Dom. II post Pascha)
10

Sundays
fol. 173r Rex eterne dominator
10

Sunday after Ascension
fol. 173v Creator poli rexque terre
10

John the Baptist, ad vesperas
fol. 174r Aue dei dilecte
(In double notation)

St. Just and Pastor
fol. 175r Laudes deo persolvamus
12 NS

Assumption
fol. 176v A(u)rea virga

St. Augustine
fol. 178r Laude preclara reboat
TR   Only source in *AH*

Several Martyrs
fol. 179v Febus nunc pollens
10

Appendix 4 *(cont.)*

Cathedral	Augustinian
Paris, BN lat. 778	Paris, BN lat. 1086
A late-twelfth- or early-thirteenth-century collection of ordinary chants with tropes and sequences from Narbonne	A late-twelfth- or early-thirteenth-century collection of ordinary chants with sequences from St. Leonard in Limoges

fol. 181r Festum martyrum
TR   Only source in *AH*

End of Supplemental Series in liturgical order
fol. 182r Aue mundi spes maria
12 NS

fol. 83r Aue maria gratia plena
12 NS

fol. 184r Salue mater saluatoris, uas
12 NS

Dedication
fol. 185v Sancte Sion adsunt
12 NS

(St. Vincent)
fol. 186v Ecce dies preoptata
12 NS

fol. 187v Missus gabriel de celis
12 NS

fol. 189v Aue plena singulari gracia
12 NS

NEW HAND AND NOTATOR
fol. 190v Gaude Roma
NS 12

fol. 192r Sonent plausus
(Conversion of St. Paul)
NS 12   Only source from this era in *AH*

fol. 193v Laus erumpat
(St. Michael)
NS 12

ANOTHER HAND
fol. 195R Zyma uetus
12 NS

fol. 196v Exultemus salventes

YET ANOTHER HAND
St. Nazarius et Celsius (or All Saints)
Superne matris
12 NS

YET ANOTHER HAND
Verbum bonum et suave
12 NS

Appendix 5. The earliest sequence repertories of Paris compared: status of Parisian sequences in first major collections of late sequences

| Church | Parisian sources | | | | | Sources from outside Paris | | | | |
| Use | ND Cath. | Vic Augus. | Gen Augus. | Den Bene. | Mag Bene. | Nevers Augus. | Limoges Augus. | Laon Cath. | Aix Augus. | Paris/ Rheims Cath. |
MS	lat. 1112	lat. 14819 and 14452	Gen. 1259	Maz. 526	lat. 13252	lat. n.a. 3126	lat. 1086	Laon 263	Aix 13	Assisi 695
Temporale										
Advent I										
Gaudia mundo										
37:44	×	×	×	@	×	×	×	×	×	×
Salus eterna										
10 7:1/53:28	@	@	×	×	×	c1	×	×	×	c1
Advent II										
Regnantem										
10 7:30/53:5	@	@	@	@	×	c1	×	×	×	c1
Advent III										
Qui regis										
10 7:31/53:8	@	@	@	@	×	c1	×	×	×	c1
Advent IV										
Iubilemus omnes										
10 7:33/53:9	@	@	@	@	×	c1	×	×	×	c1

Nativity [Dec 25]: Three Masses (Nat1, Nat2, Nat3); sequences vary in Parisian churches

Sequence / AH ref			Nat 2	Nat1						
Salus eterna★	Nat1									
Regnantem★	Nat 2									
Nato canunt — 7:49/53:41	×	×	Nat1	Nat1	×	@	c1	@	×	c1
Christi hodierna — 7:42/53:25	×	×	Nat3	Nat3	×	@	×	@	×	c1
Letabundus exultet fidelis — 11 54:5	Nat3	×	Nat2	Nat2	×	c1	@	×	F	c1
In natale salvatoris — 12 54:150	×	Nat	×	×	×	×	×	×	F	c2
Hac clara die — 10 7:115–53:168	Nat:Vespers	×	E	E	E	@	c1	@	×	c1
(See *Common sequences* [p. 410] for other appearances)										
Celeste organum — 11 7:51	×	×	×	×	@:add	×	@	@	×	c1
Sequences for the octave of the Nativity										
Splendor patris — 12 54:154	Sun in Oct. Mel:P	Cras S. Thom Mel:Vic	×	×	×	×	×	×	F	c2
In excelsis canitur — 12 54:160	Vel	Circ	Circ	×	×	×	×	×	×	c2
Eya recolamus — 10 53:23	×	×	Circ	×	@:add	×	×	×	G	c1
Nato nobis — 12 54:155	Vel	×	×	×	×	×	×	×	×	c2
Ante torum — 12 54:148	Vel	×	×	×	×	×	×	×	×	c3

Appendix 5 (*cont.*)

	Parisian sources					Sources from outside Paris				
Church	ND Cath.	Vic Augus.	Gen Augus.	Den Bene.	Mag Bene.	Nevers Augus.	Limoges Augus.	Laon Cath.	Aix Augus.	Paris/Rheims Cath.
Use MS	lat. 1112	lat. 14819 and 14452	Gen. 1259	Maz. 526	lat. 13252	lat. n.a. 3126	lat. 1086	Laon 263	Aix 13	Assisi 695
Epiphany [Jan 6]										
Epyphaniam										
10 7:53/53:47	@	@	@	@	×	c1	@	×	×	c1
Virgo mater saluatoris										
12 54:161	×	Oct	×	×	×	×	×	×	F	c2
Epiphany, octave										
Letabundus	(See above)				@					

Easter and the octave: Number and order of pieces vary;
    Fer2 = Feria II (Monday), etc.
    Sun = Sunday; Sab = Sabbato or Saturday

	ND	Vic	Gen	Den	Mag	Nevers	Limoges	Laon	Aix	Paris/Rheims
Fulgens preclara										
10 7:57/53:62	@	@	@	@	O	c1	@	@	F	c1
Mane prima										
11 52:214	Fer2	Fer5	Fer2	Fer2	×	c1	@	@	F	c1
Prome casta										
10 7:61/53:89	×	×	×	×	@	c1	×	×	×	×
All. Dic nobis										
10 53:69	×	×	×	×	@:alia	c1	×	×	×	×
Zima uetus										
12 54:227	Fer3	Oct	Oct	×	×	c2	×	@:add	F	c2

		1	2	3	4	5	6	7	Final	Clef
Ecce dies celebris	12 54:218	Fer4	Fer2	Fer3	×	×	×	×	×	c2
Lux illuxit	12 54:220	Fer5	Fer3	Fer4	×	×	×	×	F	c2
Sexta passus	12 54:223	Fer6 Mel:P	Fer6 Mel:V	×	×	×	@: Mel:P	×	×	c3
Mundi renouatio	12 54:224	Sab	Sab	Fer5	×	×	×	×	×	c2
Salve dies dierum	12 54:222	Sun in oct Mel:P	Fer4 Mel:V	Fer6	×	×	@	×	F	c2
Agnus redemit		Part of Victime		Notre Dame only: Sundays until Ascension						
Victime paschali	11 54:7	×	Alia	Suns until Ascen	Suns until Ascen	@:add c3	@	@	F	c1
Ascension										
Rex omnipotens	10 7:83/53:111	@ Mel:P	@	@	@	@	@	@	F	c1
Sunday in the octave										
Postquam hostem	12 54:231	@ Mel:Vic	@ Mel:Vic	Rex frag	Rex	×	@	×	×	c3
Summi triumphum	9 53:114	×	×	×	×	@2	×	×	G	×

Appendix 5 (*cont.*)

	Parisian sources					Sources from outside Paris				
Church	ND	Vic	Gen	Den	Mag	Nevers	Limoges	Laon	Aix	Paris/Rheims
Use	Cath.	Augus.	Augus.	Bene.	Bene.	Augus.	Augus.	Cath.	Augus.	Cath.
MS	lat. 1112	lat. 14819 and 14452	Gen. 1259	Maz. 526	lat. 13252	lat. n.a. 3126	lat. 1086	Laon 263	Aix 13	Assisi 695
Pentecost										
Fulgens preclara★ Frag										
Sancti spiritus 9 53:119	Fer2	@	@	@	@	c1	@	@	F	c1
Resonat sacrata 11 7:91	×	×	×	×	@	c1	×	×	×	×
Days in the octave of Pentecost										
Lux iocunda 12 54:239	Fer3 Mel:P	Fer2 Mel:Vic	Fer2 Mel:Vic	×	×	×	@	×	O	c2
Lux iocunda Frag			Fer5							
Simplex in essentia Frag										
12 54:243	Fer4	Fer5	Fer3	×	×	×	×	×	O	c2
Almiphona 10 7:73/53:132	×	Fer4	×	Fer4	@	c1	×	×	O	×
Qui procedis 12 54:241	Fer5 Mel:P	Fer3 Mel:Vic	×	×	×	×	@	×	O	c3

Feast / Piece									O	CS
Alma chorus — 10 53:152	Fer6	Sab	Fer4	×	@	c1	@	@	○	c1
Veni sancte — 12 54:234	Vel	Fer6	Fer6	×	×	c4	×	@:add	○	c3
Laudes deo — 11ex 54:21	×	×	Sab	Oct	×	×	×	@	○	×
Eia musa — late 10 · 7:90/53:130	×	×	×	×	@	×	×	×	○	×
Rex celice — 11? 9:288	×	×	×	×	@	×	×	×	○	×
O alma trinitas — 10 7:239	×	×	×	×	@	c1	×	@	○	×

Trinity

Feast / Piece									O	CS
Profitentes — 12 54:249	@	@	×	@2	×	c2	@	×	○	c2
Benedicta semper sit — 10 7:108	@2	×	@	×	ck	×	×	×	○	×
Benedicta sit beata trinitas — 10 7:109/53:143	×	×	×	×	@	c1	×	×	○	×
Benedicta semper sancta sit — 7:108/53:139					@:add					
Laudes deo deuotas — 11ex 54:21 (See above)			Sab	@1						

Sanctorale (Only saints with special sequences written for these feasts are included.
Saints assigned common sequences are listed under the appropriate pieces at the end.
CS: Means that instead of the listed piece, a "common" sequence, a piece used repeatedly for a particular category of saint, is present. This information is provided only for the five Parisian manuscripts).

Appendix 5 (*cont.*)

		Parisian sources					Sources from outside Paris				
Church		ND	Vic	Gen	Den	Mag	Nevers	Limoges	Laon	Aix	Paris/ Rheims
Use		Cath.	Augus.	Augus.	Bene.	Bene.	Augus.	Augus.	Cath.	Augus.	Cath.
MS		lat. 1112	lat. 14819 and 14452	Gen. 1259	Maz. 526	lat. 13252	lat. n.a. 3126	lat. 1086	Laon 263	Aix 13	Assisi 695
JANUARY											
3 St. Geneviève											
Genovefe sollempnitas											
12	55:167	@	@	@:add	×	×	×	×	×	×	c2
19 Dagobert											
De profundis											
10	40:69	×	×	×	@	×	×	×	×	×	×
21 St. Agnes											
Animemur ad agonem											
12	55:60	@	×	×	CS	×	×	×	×	×	c2
22 St. Vincent											
Ecce dies preoptata											
12	55:377	@ Mel:P	@ Mel:Vic	×	CS	×	c2	×	×	×	c2
Precelsa seclis											
11	7:226/53:359	×	×	×	CS	@:add	c1	×	@	×	×
Martyris egregii											
12	55:379	×	×	@	×	×	×	×	×	F	c3

25 *Conversion of St. Paul*										
Jubilemus . . . qui										
12 55:313	×	×	CS	CS	×	×	×	×	×	×
Corde uoce										
12 55:308	@	E	×	×	×	×	@	×	×	c2
FEBRUARY										
2 *Purification of the BVM*										
Templum cordis										
12 54:307	CS	@	CS	CS	×	×	×	×	F	c2
Lux advenit										
12 54:309	@2	×	×	×	×	c4	×	×	×	c3
Hac clara★	@1	(See above, Nativity)								
Regina uirginum	@3	(Only at Notre Dame)								
Letabundus				@						
(See above, Nativity)										
MARCH										
21 *St. Benedict (Nativity)*										
Laudum carmina										
7:145/53:223	×	×	×	@	E	×	×	×	×	c1
25 *Anunciation of the BVM*										
Salve mater saluatoris										
12 54:383	If on Sunday	E	CS	×	×	c2 & c3	@	@:add	F	c2
Ave maria gratia										
11/12 54:337	Vel	×	×	×	×	c2	@	@	×	c1
Hac clara★ (See above)										

Appendix 5 (cont.)

Church Use MS	Parisian sources					Sources from outside Paris				
	ND Cath. lat. 1112	Vic Augus. lat. 14819 and 14452	Gen Augus. Gen. 1259	Den Bene. Maz. 526	Mag Bene. lat. 13252	Nevers Augus. lat. n.a. 3126	Limoges Augus. lat. 1086	Laon Cath. Laon 263	Aix Augus. Aix 13	Paris/ Rheims Cath. Assisi 695
APRIL										
22 St. Denis (Finding)										
Gaude prole										
12 55:130	@	E	E	@3	×	c3	×	×	F	c2
Super armonie										
9:141	×	×	×	@1	E	×	×	@	×	×
Gaude turma										
9:140	×	×	×	@2	×	×	×	×	×	×
25 St. Mark	Frag Victime	Victime or Zima Add:Iocundare								
MAY										
May 3 Finding of the Cross										
Laudes crucis										
12 54:188	@	@	@	@	×	c1	@	@:add	F	c1

All. nunc crucis											
11 53:146	×	×	×	×	@1	×	×	×	×	×	
Laudamus te											
11 9:28	×	×	×	×	@2	c1	×	×	×	×	
Alle uox psallat											
11 7:107	×	×	×	×	@3	×	×	×	×	×	
May 29 St. Germanus											
Lux illuxit							(for Martin)				
12 8:137	@	@	×	×		×	@	×	×	c3	
Candida cantio											
10 7:184/53:392	×	×	×	×	@	c1	×	×	×	×	
JUNE											
17 Reception of St. Victor											
Ex radice caritatis											
12 55:375	×	@	×	×	×	×	×	×	×	c2	
20 St. Leufredus											
Mundi etate											
12 8:93	@	×	×	×	@:add	×	×	×	×	c1	
24 St. John, Baptist (Nativity)											
Precursoris											
12 8:151	@1	×	×	×	×	×	×	×	×	c3	
Ad honorem											
12 55:200	@2	@	@	CS	×	×	×	×	×	c2	
Gaude caterua											
10 7:161/53:270	×	×	×	×	@:add	c1	×	×	×	×	

Appendix 5 (*cont.*)

	Parisian sources					Sources from outside Paris				
Church	ND	Vic	Gen	Den	Mag	Nevers	Limoges	Laon	Aix	Paris/Rheims
Use	Cath.	Augus.	Augus.	Bene.	Bene.	Augus.	Augus.	Cath.	Augus.	Cath.
MS	lat. 1112	lat. 14819 and 14452	Gen. 1259	Maz. 526	lat. 13252	lat. n.a. 3126	lat. 1086	Laon 263	Aix 13	Assisi 695
29 Sts. Peter and Paul										
Gaude Roma										
12 55:313	@	@	×	×	×	×	×	×	F	c2
Laude iocunda										
7:201/53:339	×	×	@	@	×	c1	×	×	×	c1
30 Conversion of St. Paul										
Corde voce										
12 55:308	CS	@	×	CS	×	×	@	×	×	c2
Sacre Paule	×	×	×	×	@	×	×	×	×	c1
(latter part of "Laude iocunda")										
30 St. Martial										
Valde lumen										
11 7:177	×	×	×	×	@	×	×	×	×	×
JULY										
5 St. Martin (*translation*)										
Christo inclita										
10 7:132/53:201	@	×	E	×	E	c1	×	@:add	×	c1

Date	Feast / Incipit										
	6 Octave of Peter and Paul										
	Roma petro										
12	55:321	@	CS	@	×	×	×	×	×	F	c2
	11 St. Benedict (Translation)										
	Laudum carmina	CS	×	×	×	@	(See above, March 21)				
	21 St. Victor										
	Ecce dies triumphalis										
12	55:374	CS	@	×	×	×	×	×	×	F	c2
	22 St. Mary Magdalene										
	Mane prima	@	E	E	@	×					
	(See Easter octave)										
	26 St. Marcellus										
	Gaude superna										
	44:194	@	×	×	×	×	×	×	×	×	c2
	AUGUST										
	1 St. Peter's Chains										
	Ecce dies digna										
	39:249	×	CS	CS	@:add	×	×	×	×	×	
	3 St. Stephen (Finding)										
	Organicis canamus										
10	53:385	@	×	E	×	c1	×	×	×	×	c1

("Organicis" is a common sequence, usually sung for martyrs.)

6 Transfiguration

Appendix 5 (*cont.*)

	Parisian sources					Sources from outside Paris				
Church	ND	Vic	Gen	Den	Mag	Nevers	Limoges	Laon	Aix	Paris/Rheims
Use	Cath.	Augus.	Augus.	Bene.	Bene.	Augus.	Augus.	Cath.	Augus.	Cath.
MS	lat. 1112	lat. 14819 and 14452	Gen. 1259	Maz. 526	lat. 13252	lat. n.a. 3126	lat. 1086	Laon 263	Aix 13	Assisi 695
Letabundi iubilemus										
12 54:163	×	@	×	×	×	×	×	×	×	×
Benedicta semper sancta (See Trinity Sunday)	E	×	@	×	E:add			×	×	×
10 St. Lawrence										
Prunis datum										
12 55:245	@1 Mel:P	@ Mel:Vic	×	×	×	×	@	×	F	c2
Stola iocunditatis										
12 54:86	@2	×	@	@	×	c1	×	@	F	c1
Laurenti david										
10 53:283	×	×	×	×	@	×	×	×	G	×
15 Assumption BVM, and its octave										
Letabundus* (See above, Nat.)	Assump.		Assump.	Assump.	Assump.					
Aurea virga										
11 7:122/53:186	Sun in oct	Assump.	Assump.	Assump.	Assump.	c1	@	@:add	F	c1

Chant	No. / AH									
Hodierne	11 54:346	Fer2	BVM	E	×	BVM:add c2	@	×	F	c1
O maria stella maris	12 54:386	Fer3	BVM	×	×	×	×	×	F	c2
Aue Maria★		Fer4	×	×	×	(See above)	×	×	F	c2
Aue uirgo . . . mater	12 54:323	Fer5 Mel:P	Sun in oct Mel:V	×	×	×	×	×	×	c2
Ave mundi spes maria	12 54:340	Fer6	×	×	×	×	@	@:add	×	c1
Vergente mundi	12 9:61	Vel	×	×	×	×	×	×	×	×
Ave virgo . . . porta	12 54:326	×	Sab	×	×	×	×	×	×	×
Salve mater★		In oct	Nat BVM (As below)	(As below)	×	×	×	×	×	×
Gratulemur in hac die	12 54:325	×	In oct	×	×	×	×	×	×	×
Regine nunc	7:124	×	×	×	Fer4	×	×	×	×	c1
Salve porta perpetue	10 7:123/53:188	×	×	×	×	Alia c1	×	@	×	c1
Hec clara die	10 7:115/53:168	Vesp	×	E	Fer2	@ (See above)		@	×	
24 St. Bartholomew Laudemus omnes inclita	12 55:104	@2	@	CS	CS	×	×	×	×	c2

Appendix 5 (cont.)

Church	Parisian sources					Sources from outside Paris				
	ND	Vic	Gen	Den	Mag	Nevers	Limoges	Laon	Aix	Paris/Rheims
Use	Cath.	Augus.	Augus.	Bene.	Bene.	Augus.	Augus.	Cath.	Augus.	Cath.
MS	lat. 1112	lat. 14819 and 14452	Gen. 1259	Maz. 526	lat. 13252	lat. n.a. 3126	lat. 1086	Laon 263	Aix 13	Assisi 695
28 St. Augustine (octave at St. Victor as well)										
Interni festi										
12 55:89	CS	@	@ and oct	×	×	c1	@	×	×	×
29 John the Baptist (Beheading)										
Precursorem summi regis										
12 55:202	@	×	×	CS	×	×	@	×	F	c2
Sancte baptiste										
9 53:267	×	×	×	×	@	×	×	×	G	×
SEPTEMBER										
1 St. Egidius										
Promat pia										
39:86	@	×	×	×	×	×	×	×	×	c3
8 Nativity of the BVM and Octave (Complete octave only at ND)										
Hac clara die*	@	×	E	E	E	(See above)	@	E	×	
Salve mater saluatoris	E	@	×	×	×	(See above)	@	×	×	
Alle celeste										
10 7:111/53:166	×	×	@	@	@	c1	@	@	×	c1

	1	2	3	4	5	6	7	8
Aue mundi★			(See above)					
Rex est admirabilis	Fer2							×
12 54:397	Fer3	×	×	×	×	×	×	c2
Ave mater ihesu								
12 54:394	Fer4	E1	×	×	×	×	@	c2
Ave uirgo★	Fer5	×	(See above)	×	×	×	×	×
Inuiolata intacta	Sun in oct	×	×	×	×	×	G	×
(Originally a trope for the great responsory, "Gaude maria virgo")								
Hodierne								
11 54:367	E	E	Oct	E:add	(See above)	×	×	
Gaude eia unica								
9:54	×	×	×	Alia	×	×	×	c1
14 Exaltation of the Cross								
Salve crux								
12 54:192	@	×	×	×	×	×	F	c2
Laudes crucis	E	@	@	(See above)	×	@		
21 St. Matthew								
Jocundare plebs								
12 55:11	@ Mel:P	@ Mel:V	CS	CS	×	c3	c3	@ Mel:P c3
22 St. Maurice								
Alludat letus								
10 7:193/53:305	CS	×	@	@	c1	@	×	×
29 St. Michael								
Laus erumpat								
12 55:288	@	@	@	×	×	@	F	c2
Ad celebres rex	×	×	×	@	c1	@	×	c1

Appendix 5 (*cont.*)

Church Use MS	Parisian sources						Sources from outside Paris			
	ND Cath. lat. 1112	Vic Augus. lat. 14819 and 14452	Gen Augus. Gen. 1259	Den Bene. Maz. 526	Mag Bene. lat. 13252	Nevers Augus. lat. n.a. 3126	Limoges Augus. lat. 1086	Laon Cath. Laon 263	Aix Augus. Aix 13	Paris/ Rheims Cath. Assisi 695
OCTOBER										
2 *St. Leger* Cordis sonet 12 55:249	×	@	×	×	×	×	×	×	×	ck
4 *St. Aurea* Virginis egregie 12 55:28	@	×	×	×	×	×	@	×	×	×
9 *St. Denis* (ND and Den have full octave with sequences)										
Gaude prole★	@	@	@	@3	× (See above)	(See above)				
Super armonie	×	×	×	@2	@ and oct	(See above)				
18 *St. Luke* Psallat chorus corde mundo 12 55:9 (A version of 'Plausu chorus")	@	×	×	×	×	×	×	×	F	c3
25 *Hilary of Mende* Laudis odas 9:283	×	×	×	@	@: For martyrs	×	CK	×	×	×

NOVEMBER

1 All Saints									
Christo inclita									
10 7:132/53:223	@	@	×	@2	c1	×	@:add	×	c1
Ecce pulchra									
10 7:130/53:200	×	×	×	@1	c1	@	×	×	×
11 St. Martin									
Gaude syon que diem									
12 55:278	oct / Mel:P	@ / Mel:Vic	CS	×	×	×	×	×	c3
12 St. Gendulf									
Ecce magno sacerdoti									
40:193	@	×	×	×	×	×	×	×	c3
23 St. Clement									
Organicis	@	(Notre Dame only, see above)							
25 St. Catherine									
Vox sonora									
12 55:236	@	@:add	×	×	×	×	×	×	c3
26 Miracles of the Ardents									
Genovefe sollempnitas	CS	E	@	(See above)	×	×	×	×	
30 St. Andrew									
Exsultemus et letemur									
12 55:68	@	@	CS	×	×	×	@	×	F	c2

Appendix 5 (*cont.*)

	Parisian sources					Sources from outside Paris				
Church	ND	Vic	Gen	Den	Mag	Nevers	Limoges	Laon	Aix	Paris/ Rheims
Use	Cath.	Augus.	Augus.	Bene.	Bene.	Augus.	Augus.	Cath.	Augus.	Cath.
MS	lat. 1112	lat. 14819 and 14452	Gen. 1259	Maz. 526	lat. 13252	lat. n.a. 3126	lat. 1086	Laon 263	Aix 13	Assisi 695
DECEMBER										
6 St. Nicholas										
Congaudentes										
11 54:95	@	@	@	×	×	c1	@	@	×	c1
21 St. Thomas, Apostle										
Congaudeant hodie										
12 55:353	CS	@	CS	CS	×	×	×	×	×	×
26 St. Stephen, Protomartyr										
Heri mundus										
12 55:341	@	@	×	×	×	×	@	×	F	c2
Magnus deus										
10 7:221/53:353	Vel	×	@	@	×	c1	×	@	×	c1
27 St. John, Evangelist										
Gratulemur ad festivum										
12 55:215	@ Mel:P	@ Mel:Vic	×	×	×	×	×	×	○	c2
Alma cohors										
7:238/53:329	×	×	×	@	@:add	×	×	×	○	×
Organicis		@								

28 Holy Innocents

	1	2	3	4	5	6	7	8	9	10
Celsa pueri 10 53:264	@	@	@	@	×	×	@	×	×	c1

29 St. Thomas of Canterbury

	1	2	3	4	5	6	7	8	9	10
Gaude syon / et letare 12 55:361	@	Mel:P	@	Mel:V	×	×	×	×	×	c3
Mundo christus 40: 297	×	×	@	×	@	×	×	×	×	×

30 St. Silvester

	1	2	3	4	5	6	7	8	9	10
Iubilemus . . . quem 12 54:152	CS	CS	@	@	CS	×	×	×	×	c2

Feast of the Dedication

(Each church celebrates this feast on the anniversary of its own dedication.)

	1	2	3	4	5	6	7	8	9	10
Ierusalem et syon 28:106	Ded	×	×	×	×	×	×	×	O	c3
Rex salomon 12 55:35	Vel	oct	×	×	×	×	@×	×	F	c2
Quam dilecta 11/12 55:33	Vel	oct	×	×	@	×	@	×	O	c2
Clara chorus 11 54:138	Item	@	@	@:add	×	×	×	@	O	c1
Sancte syon 12 55:40	Item	×	×	×	×	×	×	×	O	×
Christo inclita	Ded	(see above: Nov. 1)								

Common sequences in the earliest Parisian sources

I. Hac clara die
10 7:115/53:168 Summary: Used generally for the BVM at ND; not at St. Victor; occasionally elsewhere.

II. Mirabilis deus
10 7:231/53:372 Summary: Used frequently at ND, and occasionally at St. Denis; not at all at St. Victor and Ste. Geneviève. St. Magloire used this piece "for martyrs," and this is its use at ND and St. Denis as well.

III. Superne matris
12 55:45 Summary: Used extensively in all sources with the exception of Mag. Assigned to a variety of saints. At St. Victor the rubric read "De quolibet sancto."

IV. Clare sanctorum
9 53:367 Summary: Used here, as throughout Europe, to celebrate Feasts of the Apostles. All the earliest Parisian sources have it, including St. Magloire, where it is listed with common sequences under the rubric "De apostolis."

V. Christo inclita
10 7:132/53:201 Summary: The final strophes of this sequence were written for Apostles. These were not used in other Parisian churches.

VI. At St. Victor, two common sequences were written for Apostles. These were not used in other Parisian churches.

Cor angustum
12 55:4
(Also found in the French section of Aix 13 and in Assisi 695: c2)

Stola regni
12 55:3
(Also found in Assisi 695: c2)

VII. Common sequences used at St. Magloire but not found in the other earliest Parisian sources

In omnem terram
40:49 "Alia de apostolis"

A solis occasu
50:274

Stans a longe
7:254/53:158

"De uno confessore"

"Prosa ubi uolueris"

Anthology

The examples in this anthology of sequences have been discussed at length in the text of the book. The source for all of them but one has been Paris, BN lat. 14819. Because the manuscript is incomplete at the end, "O Maria, stella maris" was copied from Paris, BN lat. 14452. Small inserts have been used to identify many of the numerous borrowings found within these melodies. Accidentals found in the manuscripts have been positioned where they occur in the originals. Slur lines are used only for liquescent neumes; ligated notes are written closely together and not slurred. Spellings are those found in the manuscripts. In the manuscripts, each sequence was originally followed by a simple "Amen," which was crossed out at a later time in the sources' history. The "Amen" would have added to the hymn-like form of these pieces.

The texts of Examples A.3–A.8 are translated on pp. 438–441 below; those of Examples A.1 and A.2 are translated on pp. 70–72 and 165–166 above.

Example A.1

Laudes Crucis   Paris, BN lat. 14819, fols. 74r–76v
de sancta cruce

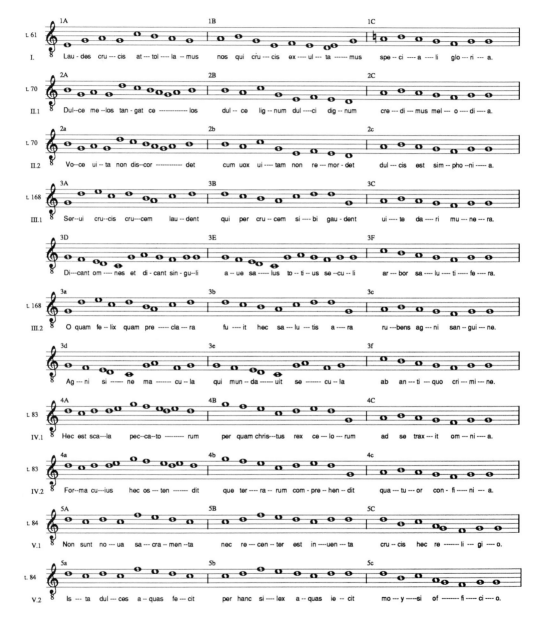

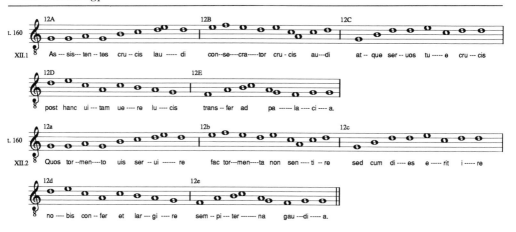

t. 160

XII.1   As --- sis--- ten -- tes cru -- cis lau ----- di con--se----cra-----tor cru - cis au---di at -- que ser -- uos tu ----- e cru --- cis

post hanc ui --- tam ue ---- re lu ---- cis trans -- fer ad pa ----- la ---- ci ---- a.

t. 160

XII.2   Quos tor --men----to uis ser -- ui ------ re fac tor---men----ta non sen --- ti -- re sed cum di --- es e ----- rit i ---- re

no ---- bis con -- fer et lar --- gi ---- re sem -- pi --- ter ------- na gau ---di ----- a.

Example A.2

Mundi Renouatio   Paris, BN lat. 14819, fols. 70v–71r

I.1 Mun —— di re —— no —— ua —— ti ——— o no —— ua pa —— rit gau — di —— a;

I.2 Re ——— sur —— gen —— ti do —— mi —— no con — re —— su —— gunt om — ni ——— a;

I.3 E — le — men —— ta ser —— ui —— unt et auc — to —— ris sen — ti —— unt quan — ta sit po — ten — ti — a.

II.1 Ce — lum fit se — re — ni —— us et ma — re tran-quil — li — us spi — rat au — ra mi — ti — us ual —— lis nos — tra flo — ru —— it;

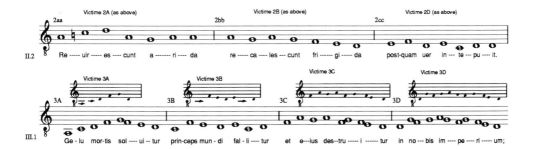

II.2 Re —— uir —— es —— cunt a ——— ri —— da re —— ca — les —— cunt fri —— gi —— da post-quam uer in — te — pu — it.

III.1 Ge - lu mor-tis sol —— ui — tur prin-ceps mun - di fal - li —— tur et e —— ius des—tru —— i ——— tur in no — bis im —— pe —— ri —— um;

III.2 Dum te — ne —— re uo ——— lu —— it in quo ni —— chil ha —— bu —— it ius a —— mi - sit pro — pri —— um;

III.3 Vi — ta mor-tem su — pe — rat ho — mo iam re — cu — pe — rat quod pri-us a — mi —— se —— rat pa — ra —— dy — si gau —— di — um;

III.4   Vi ----- am   pre ----- bet   fa ----- ci ------ lem   che ------ ru --------bin   uer ------ sa -----ti ---- lem   a --- mo ------ uen -- do   gla --- di -- um.

IV.1   Chris -- tus   ce - los   re - se -- rat   et   cap ----ti - uos   li --- be-rat   quos cul--pa   li ---- ga - ue --rat   sub mor--tis   in --- te - ri ---- tu;

IV.2   Pro   ta ----- li   uic ----- to ------ ri ------- a   pa -------- tri   pro --- li   glo --- ri ----- a   sit   cum   sanc -- to   spir --- i --- tu.

Example A.3

Zima uetus
in oct. pas.

Paris, BN lat. 14819, fols. 71v–73v

L.1 Zi - ma ue - tus ex - pur - ge - tur ut sin - ce - re ce - le - bre - tur no - ua re - sur - rec - ti - o.

L.2 Hec est di - es nos - tre spe - i hu - ius mi - ra uis di - e - i le - gis tes - ti - mo - ni - o.

II.1 Hec e - gyp - tum spo - li - a - uit et he - bre - os li - be - ra - uit de for - na - ce fer - re - a.

II.2 Hiis in ar - to con - sti - tu - tis op - us e - rat ser - ui - tu - tis lu - tum la - ter pa - le - a.

III.1 Iam di - ui - ne laus uir - tu - tis iam tri - um - phi iam sa - lu - tis uox e - rum - pat li - be - ra

Hec est di - es quam fe - cit do - mi - nus di - es nos - tri do - lo - ris ter - mi - nus di - es sa - lu - ti - fe - ra.

III.2 Lex est um - bra fu - tu - ro - rum chris - tus fi - nis pro - mis - sor - um qui con - sum - mat om - ni - a.

chri - sti san - guis ig - ne - am he - be - ta - uit rum - phe - am a - mo - ta cus - to - di - a.

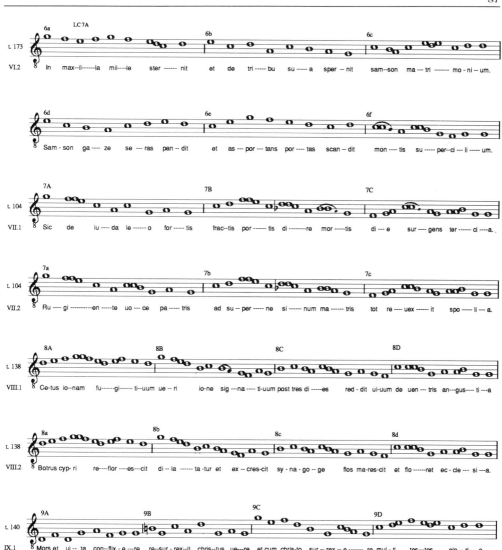

t. 165

X.1   lhe ---- su   vic ---- tor   ihe ---- su   ui ------ ta   ihe ---- su   ui ----- te   ui ------ a   tri ---- ta   cu --- ius   mor---te   mors   so ----pi -- ta

ad   pas --------- ca -------- lem   nos   in --------- ui -------------- ta   men ---- sam   cum   fi ----- du ------- ci ------ a.

t. 165

X.2   Vi ---- ue   pa ---- nis   ui -- uax   un ---- da   ue ----- ra   ui ----- tis   et   fe ---cun ----- da   tu   nos   pas -- ce   tu   nos   mun-da

ut   a   mor --------- te   nos   se -------- cun ------------- da   tu ---- a   sal ----- uet   gra ------- ti ----- a.

Example A.4

Prunis Datum
De sancto laurentio

Paris, BN lat. 14819, fols. 111v–113v

t.62 / I.1 Pru -- nis da -- tum ad -- mi -- re -- mur lau - re - a -- tum ue -- ne -- re - mur lau -- di -- bus lau -- ren -- ti --- um.

t.62 / I.2 Ve -- ne -- re -- mur cum tre -- mo -- re de-pre -- ce -- mur cum a -- mo -- re mar -- ty -- rem e --- gre --- gi -- um.

t.71 / II.1 Ac -- cu -- sa -- tus non ne -- ga -- uit sed pul -- sa -- tus re -- sul -- ta -- uit in tu -- bis duc -- ti -- li -- bus.

t.71 / II.2 Cum in pe -- nis uo -- to ple -- nis ex -- ul -- ta -- ret et so -- na -- ret in di -- ui -- nis lau -- di -- bus.

t.72 / III.1 Sic – ut cor -- da mu -- si -- co -- rum tan--dem so -- num dat so -- no -- rum plec -- ti mi -- ni -- ste -- ri -- o.

t.72 / III.2 Sic in che -- li tor -- men -- tor -- um me -- los chris -- ti con -- fes -- sor -- um de -- dit hu -- ic ten -- si -- o.

t.88 / IV.1 De -- ci ui -- de qui -- a fi -- de stat in -- uic -- tus in -- ter ic -- tus mi -- nas et in -- cen -- di -- a.

IV.2 Spes in -- ter -- na uox su -- per -- na con -- so -- lan -- tur et hor -- tan -- tur ui -- rum de con -- stan -- ti -- a.

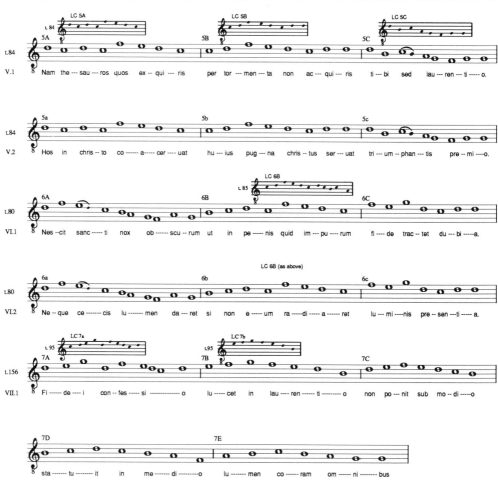

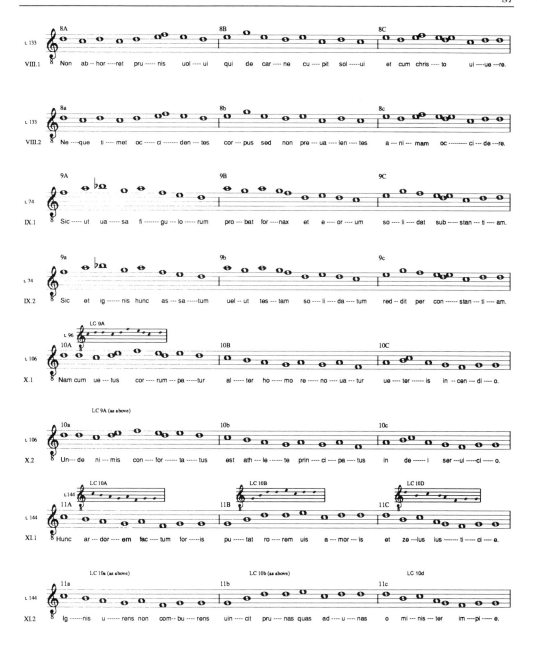

XII.1   Par--um sa---pis uim sy-----na-pis si non tan--gis   si non fran-gis et plus fra-grat quan-do fla--grat thus in--iec-----tum   ig---ni---bus.

XII.2   Sic ar--ta--tus   et as-----sa-tus sub la--bo--re   sub ar--do---re dat o--dor--em ple----ni--o--rem   mar--tyr de   uir----tu----ti----bus.

XIII.1   O   lau--ren----ti   lau----te   ni--------mis   re----ge   uic---to   rex sub-----li-----mis   re---gis re--gum for---tis   mi---les

qui   dux-----is------ti   pe----nas   ui------les   cer----tans   pro   ius---------ti------ci------a.

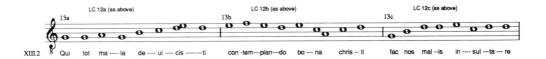

XIII.2   Qui   tot ma----la   de----ui----cis--------ti   con--tem---plan---do   bo---na   chris--ti   fac nos mal--is   in----sul--ta---re

fac   de   bo-----nis   ex---sul----ta------re   me-----ri------to---------rum   gra-----ti--------a.

Example A.5

Gaude Roma
De sancto Petro

Paris, BN lat. 14819, fols. 100v–102v

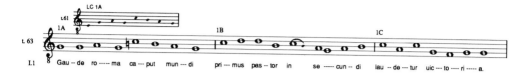

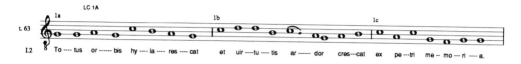

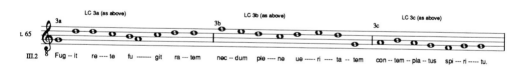

Zima 9A (as above) Zima 9B (as above) Zima 9C (as above)

7a 7b 7c 7d

t. 181

VII.2 Hic a pe tra chris-to dic--tus in con-flic---tu stat in---uic--tus li -- cet iu - gis sit con--flic ------ tus et gra--uis con --- gres-si ----- o.

from t. 139 from t. 139

7e 7f 7g 7h

Dum uo ---- la -- re ma --- gus que ----- rit to ---- tus ru -- ens to ---- tus pe -- rit quem di-ui --na dig -ne f e-rit et condempnat ul -- ti --- o.

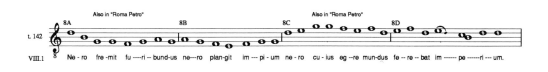

Also in "Roma Petro" Also in "Roma Petro"

8A 8B 8C 8D

t. 142

VIII.1 Ne - ro fre -mit fu --ri -- bund-us ne---ro plan-git im --- pi - um ne - ro cu - ius eg --re mun-dus fe -- re -- bat im ------ pe ------ri --- um.

Also in "Roma Petro" Also in "Roma Petro"

8a 8b 8c 8d

t.142

VIII.2 Er---go pe -- tro crux pa - ra - tur a mi -- nis--tris sce -- le -- rum cru--ci --- fi ---- gi se tes--ta - tur in hoc chris-tus i -------- te -- rum.

LC 10D, t. 144

9A 9B 9C 9D

t. 145

IX.1 Pe--tro sunt o --- ues cre - di -- te cla--ues-que reg --ni tra--di-- te pe--tri pre--it sen--ten-- ti -- a li--gans ac sol --uens om --- ni --- a.

LC 10D, t. 144 LC 10D (as above) LC 10D, t. 144

9a 9b 9c 9d

t. 145

IX.2 Pas--to---ris nos--tri me--ri ---tis ac pre--ce sa - lu ---ti -- fe -- ra nos a pec-ca ---- ti de -- bi -- tis e -- ter - ne pas-tor li --- be - ra.

Example A.6

Gaude, Syon, que diem recolis   Paris, BN lat. 14819, fols. 137v–139r
Sancti Martini

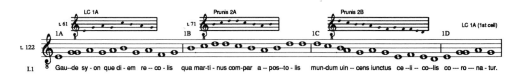

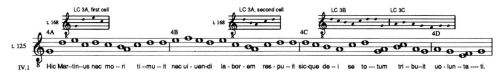

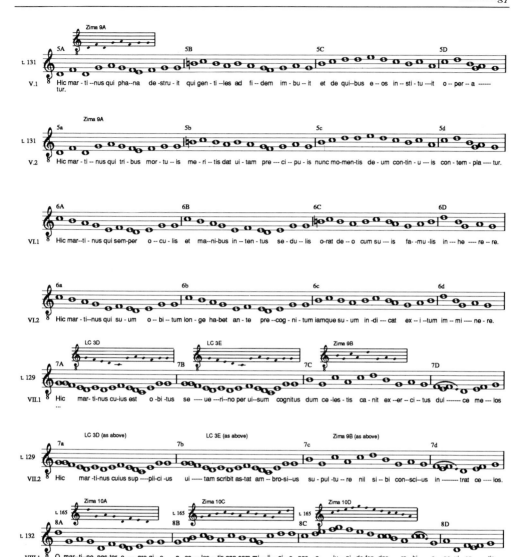

Example A.7

Iocundare plebs . . . cuius   Paris, BN lat. 14819, fols. 128v–130r
Mathei apostoli

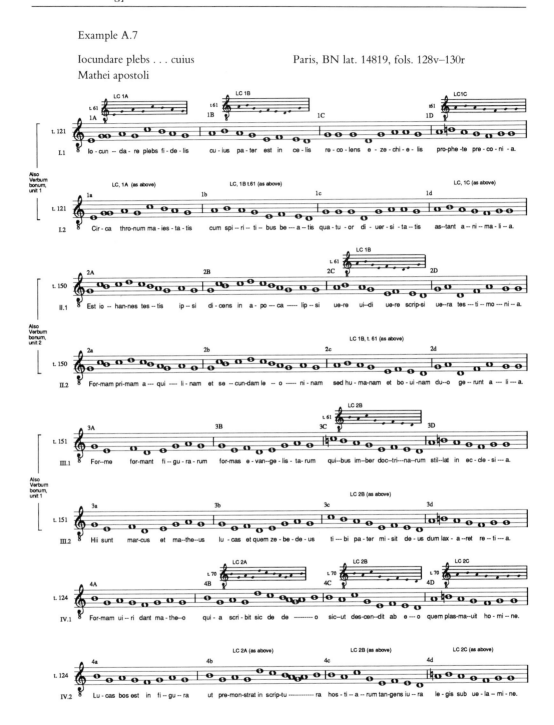

Example A.8

O, Maria stella maris
alia de beata maria

Hymn melody   Paris, BN lat. 10482

Paris, BN lat. 14452, fols. 127r–127v

Translations

"Zima uetus," for the octave of Easter (Example A.3)

I.1   Let the old leaven be purged so that the new resurrection may be celebrated without taint; I.2 This is the day of our hope: the power of this day is marvelous by the testimony of the law.

II.1   This day despoiled Egypt and freed the Hebrews from the cruel kiln; II.2 When they were established in the labor of their servitude, there was mud, brick, and straw.

III.1   Now the praise of divine virtue, now of triumph, now of salvation, an unimpeded voice breaks out: this is the day which the Lord has made, this day is the end of our pain, the healing day; III.2 The law is the shadow of future things: Christ is the end of promises who fulfills all things: Christ's blood has dulled the fiery sword; the watchmen are driven away.

VI.1   The boy, form of our laughter, for whom the wether was slain, represents the joy of life. IV.2 Joseph went out from the well, Christ returned on high after the pain of death.

V.1   This serpent devours the serpents of Pharaoh, immune from the evil of the serpent: the presence of the brazen snake makes free those whom the fiery one wounds. V.2 Christ the hook and buckle pierces the serpent in its jaw; the weaned child puts his hand in the basilisk's den and thus the ancient guest of this world flees in confusion.

VI.1   The mockers of Elisha, when he goes up to the house of God, feel the anger of the bald one: David is inspired, the scapegoat sent, and the sparrow flees away. VI.2 Samson levels a thousand with a jawbone and rejects marriage from his own tribe; Samson throws open the doorbars of Gaza and, lifting up the city gates, climbs the summit of the mountain.

VII.1   Thus from Judah the strong lion, with gates of dire death broken, rising on the third day, VII.2 as the voice of the father roared, carried back so many spoils to the bosom of the celestial mother.

VIII.1   The whale restores the fugitive Jonah, significant of the true Jonah, alive after three days, from the narrow straits of his stomach; VIII.2 the cluster of henna blooms again, it is enlarged and swells, the flower of the synagogue droops and the church flourishes.

IX.1   Life and death have fought, Christ has risen truly, and with Christ many witnesses to the glory have risen. IX.2 Let the new morning, the joyful morning, wipe away the evening weeping: because life conquered death, it is time for joy.

X.1   Jesus victor, Jesus life, Jesus, common way of life, by whose death, death is put to sleep, invite us to the paschal table with confidence; X.2 living bread, living water, vine true and fertile, feed us, cleanse us, so that your grace may save us from the second death. Amen.

"Prunis datum," for St. Lawrence (Example A.4)

I.1   Let us admire the one given to the hot coals; let us venerate the laureate Lawrence with praise; I.2 Let us venerate with trembling; let us pray with love to the excellent martyr.

II.1   The accused did not deny, but, struck, resounded in long trumpets; II.2 when in torments full of prayers he exulted and sounded in divine praise.

III.1   Just as the musician's string at length gives the sonorous tone by the action of the quill; III.2 thus stretching out on the harp of torments this man gave the song of the confessors of Christ.

IV.1   Decius, see, that with faith he stands unconquered amid blows, threats, and flames; IV.2 internal hope, celestial voice, console and exhort the man to constancy.

V.1   For the treasures that you search for through these torments, you acquire not for yourself, but for Lawrence; V.2 his struggle stores up these treasures in Christ; Christ saves them for the reward of the triumphing one.

VI.1   The night of the saint does not know darkness, such that in torments he might consider something base with wavering faith; VI.2 nor would he give light to the blind if the presence of light did not illuminate him.

VII.1   The confession of faith shines in Lawrence; he does not put it under a bushel; he sets up the light openly before all. VII.2 It pleases the servant of God, the bearer of his Cross, as if a roast dish, to be made a spectacle for angels and pagans.

VIII.1   He does not refuse to be turned in flames who desires to be freed from the flesh and to live with Christ; VIII.2 nor does he fear those killing the body, but not able to kill the soul.

IX.1   Just as the furnace tries the vessels of potters and hardens their substance, IX.2 so the fire makes solid this roasted one through his fortitude, just like a vessel made solid.

X.1   For, while the old man is ruined, the other man is renewed by the fire of the old; X.2 whence the preeminence of the martyr was strengthened greatly in the service of God.

XI.1   The power of love and the zeal of justice consider this external fire as dew; the fire burning without consuming conquers the coals which you pile up, O impious minister.

XII.1   Too little you know the power of mustard if you do not touch it, if you do not bruise it, and incense thrown into fire, smells more sweetly when it burns. XII.2 Thus the martyr, pinned down and roasted, beneath the toil and heat, gives the fuller odor for his virtues.

XIII.1   O Lawrence, most splendid, having conquered the king, king sublime, brave soldier of the king of kings, you made light of torments, fighting for the sake of justice. You who vanquished so many evils by contemplating the blessings of Christ, make us scoff at evil things, make us exult because of good things by the grace of your merits. Amen.

"Gaude Roma," for St. Peter (Example A.5)

I.1   Rejoice, Rome, head of the world: let the first shepherd be praised in the victory of the second; I.2 let all of the world be glad and let the ardor of virtue grow from the memory of Peter.

II.1   Peter, flame of sacred love, light of doctrine, salt of sweetness: Peter mountain of justice; II.2 Peter is the fountain of the saviour, wood of productivity and good odor, wood free from decay.

III.1   And what will you say worthy of Peter? Seeing no sign from Christ, at the first warning, III.2 he left the net, left the boat, not yet fully observing the truth by the spirit.

IV.1   Lacking gold and silver, he shines with wondrous deeds: in a moment he loosened the lame man from his sinews' bonds; IV.2 Aeneas, free from paralysis, stood erect; the attendant will of God follows Peter in the promise.

V.1   Peter gives life to Tabitha and returns the youth to life with untrammeled power. On foot he treads the waves of the sea and the saving hand guides him when he hesitates. V.2 When the question of Christ has been posed, he encompasses the requisite faith with a brief speech: he calls Christ one person, but does not ignore the meet distinction of nature.

VI.1   Although he sinned by denying three times, simple love and threefold confession expiate. An angel boldly released Peter, destined for the sword, from prison.

VII.1   With his shadow, he heals the sick, heals limbs, heals minds; the power of the physician leaves diseases powerless. Simon the magician detests Peter, Peter exposes Simon Magus; he warns the people and defends them from the craft of the magician. VII.2 He, given his name by Christ the rock, stands unconquered in conflict, although the conflict be long and the attack severe; when the Magus seeks to fly, altogether falling down, he perishes entirely, he whom divine vengeance rightly kills and condemns.

VIII.1   Raging Nero roars, Nero laments, Nero, whose impious rule the world bore with grief; VIII.2 therefore the cross was prepared for Peter by the ministers of wickedness; in him Christ shows Himself to be crucified again.

IX.1   To Peter the sheep are entrusted and the keys of the kingdom delivered; the sentence of Peter goes before, binding and loosing all things.

X.1   By the merits and the healing prayer of our shepherd, free us, eternal shepherd, from the debts of sin. Amen.

"Gaude syon, que diem recolis," for St. Martin (Example A.6)

I.1   Rejoice, Zion, you who celebrate the day, in which Martin, peer of the apostles, conquering the world, joined to the angels, is crowned. I.2 May Martin, poor and modest, the wise servant, the faithful steward, is raised wealthy to heaven, an angelic citizen.

II.1   This Martin, a catechumen, clothes a naked man; and forthwith, in the following night, the Lord Himself is clothed by this garment. II.2 This Martin, leaving military service, prepares to go unarmed against the enemy, having acquired the grace of Baptism.

III.1   This Martin, when he offers the host, glows within through the grace of God: and above appears a globe of fire. III.2 This Martin, who unlocks heaven, is set over the sea, and rules the earth, cures diseases, and conquers monsters, an extraordinary man.

IV.1   This Martin neither feared to die nor rejected the labor of living, and thus offered his whole self to God's will; IV.2 This Martin who injured no one, this Martin who did good to all, this Martin who pleased the triune majesty.

V.1   This Martin who destroyed the heathen temples, who inspired gentiles to the faith, and according to what he teaches them, he acts. V.2 This Martin who gave life to three dead by his outstanding merits, now contemplates God constantly.

VI.1   This Martin, whose eyes and industrious hands are always purposeful, prays to God to remain with his servants. VI.2 This Martin, who has long foreknown his death, and now indicates that his death is imminent.

VII.1   This Martin, whose death is known to Severinus through a vision, while an army of angels sing the sweet melody; VII.2 This Martin (whose life Sulpicius writes, Ambrose standing near the tomb) enters heaven, with no wrongdoing on his conscience.

VIII.1   O Martin, glorious shepherd, member of the heavenly host, may you defend us from the savagery of the ravening wolf. VIII.2 O Martin, do now what you have done: may you offer prayers to God for us; be mindful of your people, that you may never desert them. Amen.

"Iocundare plebs fidelis," for the Evangelists (Example A.7)

I.1   Be glad, faithful people, whose father is in heaven, recalling the proclamation of the prophet Ezechiel; I.2 around the throne of majesty, with the blessed souls, stand four living beings of a different type.

II.1   John is witness for himself, writing in the Apocalypse: "Truly I have seen, truly I have written the true evidence." II.2 The first bears an eagle's form, the second a lion's, but the two others bear a man's and an ox's.

III.1   The forms of the figures form the shapes of the Evangelists, by whom the rain of teachings flows into the church; III.2 These are Mark and Matthew, Luke, and he whom Zebedee his father sent to you, God, while he spreads out his nets.

IV.1   They give the form of man to Matthew because he writes about God, just as he descended from him whom he fashioned – man. IV.2 Luke is the ox in figure as he shows in Scripture, speaking of the rites of sacrifice under the veil of the law.

V.1   Mark, the lion crying through the desert, roars in the open: let the way be made sure for God, let the heart be made clean of offense. V.2 But John, in eagle's form, is carried by the double wing of charity, by a purer light into things divine.

VI.1   Behold, the bestial form which prophetic writing indicates, but this is the literal reading: they run with wheels, they fly with wings. A spiritual sense is seen: the wheel is the equal course, the wing, contemplation.

VII.1   These four describe the quadriform actions of Christ and represent them, as you have heard, each by its condition: VII.2 the man is declared a son, the young bull is made a sacrifice, the lion ravages death, and the eagle ascends.

VIII.1   By these Paradise is watered, made verdant, blooms, is made fruitful; with these four rivers it overflows, with them it is made glad; VIII.2 Christ is the fountain, these the streams; the fountain is on high, these descend, so that they may pour out the taste of the living fountain to the faithful.

IX.1   Let their teaching draw us up from the bilge of errors that we not be condemned by sudden death with the impious; IX.2 for those who have drunk deeply from its stream, let the thirst for charity grow so that we may enjoy fully the joys of heavenly splendor. Amen.

"O Maria, stella maris," for the Blessed Virgin Mary (Example A.8)

I.1   O Mary, star of the sea, uniquely compassionate, with your eye of tenderness, I.2 Deem us worthy to be looked upon, lest you delay in pitying this shipwrecked race.

II.1   In this valley of tears, nothing is sweet, nothing is loving; all things are uncertain; II.2 What is safe for us here when even the very triumph of virtuousness is unsure?

III.1   The flesh is against us, the world of the flesh favors our destruction; III.2 The enemy harasses, infesting us, now showing himself openly, now hiding the savagery.

IV.1   And we sin and we are punished, and from all sides we are snared by the nets of the hunters. IV.2 O Mary, mother of God, you, after God, are the summit of hope, you, the sweet refuge.

V.1   Enmeshed by so many and such [snares], we are not strong enough to resist, neither by force nor by effort. V.2 Consoler of the wretched, reviver of the dead, break the nets of death.

VI.1   Attend to us pouring forth your praise, hear us, listen to us, free us from death. VI.2 You who are seated first after Christ among those belonging to Christ, assign us to Christ.

VII.1   Jesus, sweet and good, whose name is a sign, the sweet salvation-bearing name; VII.2 Give to us the gift of salvation, the fullness of gifts to us in our state of sin;

VIII.1   Father, consoler of the son, one God, one giver of sevenfold grace: VIII.2 With a single nod of affection, make us, according to our hope, enjoy the vision of the undivided Trinity.

Bibliography

The bibliography is divided into primary and secondary sources, with reference works included among the secondary sources. Primary sources are cited in the footnotes as author (or editor) and short title, secondary sources as author and date. Because of limitations of space, not all the works listed in the bibliography have been referred to in the notes; nevertheless, the bibliography should provide a useful and otherwise unavailable introduction to the canons regular, their liturgy and ideals in the twelfth century, and especially to the twelfth-century Victorines.

Primary sources

Modern editions and translations of the Victorine sequence repertory
Adam of St. Victor: Liturgical Poetry. Notes and translations by Digby S. Wrangham. London, 1931. 3 vols.
Adam de Saint-Victor: Sämtliche Sequenzen, lateinisch und deutsch. Notes and translations by Franz Wellner. Munich, 1955.
Adam of St. Victor: Sequentiae. PL XCCCVI, cols. 1423–1534.
Dreves, Guido and Clemens Blume. AH LIV and LV. Leipzig,, 1915 and 1922.
Gautier, Léon. Oeuvres poétiques d'Adam de Saint-Victor, précédées d'un essai sur sa vie et ses ouvrages. Paris, 1858–89.
    Adam de Saint Victor: Oeuvres poétiques. 2nd edn. Paris, 1881.
    Oeuvres poétiques d'Adam de Saint-Victor. Paris, 1894.
Legrain, Modest, ed. Proses d'Adam de Saint-Victor. Collection de classiques latins comparé, second series: Auteurs chrétiens et paiens. Rome, 1889.
Misset, Eugène and Pierre Aubry, eds. Les proses d'Adam de Saint-Victor: texte et musique précédées d'une étude critique. Paris, 1900.
Prévost, Hildebrand, ed. Recueil complet des célèbres séquences du maître Adam le Breton. Ligugé, 1910.
Vecchi, Giuseppe, ed. Adam de S. Victor: Liriche sacre. Bologna, 1953.

Other primary sources
Abelard, Peter. Historia calamitatum, ed. J. Monfrin. Paris, 1959.
Acta sanctorum . . . Ed. Jean Bolland, et alii. 63 vols. in 65 (through mid-November). 1643–.
Amalar of Metz. Amalarii episcopi opera liturgica omnia. Studi e testi CXXXVIII–CXL. Ed. I. M. Hanssens. 3 vols. Vatican City, 1948.
Andrieu, M. Les Ordines Romani du haut moyen âge. Spicilegium sacrum Lovaniense XI, XXIII, XXIV, XXVIII, XXIV. 5 vols. Louvain, 1931–61.
    Le Pontifical Romain moyen âge. 4 vols. Vatican, 1938–44.

Andrew of St. Victor. *Andreae de Sancto Victore opera.* CCCM LIII, A–F (so far). Several editors. Turnhout, 1986–91.

Annales Nivernaises. Monumenta Germaniae Historica Scriptores XIII, pp. 88–91.

Augustine. *Confessiones.* CCSL XXXVII. Ed. Luke Verheijen. Turnhout, 1981.

    De civitate dei [*The City of God*]. CCSL XLVII and XLVIII. Turnhout, 1955.

    De doctrina Christiana. CCSL XXXIII. Turnhout, 1962.

    On Christian Doctrine. Trans. D. W. Robertson, Jr. Indianapolis, 1958.

    De magistro. Ed. K.-D. Daur. CCSL XXIX, pp. 138–203. Turnhout, 1970.

    De musica. Trans. R. C. Taliaferro. The Fathers of the Church Series. Writings of Saint Augustine. II. New York, 1947.

    Enarrationes in Psalmos. Ed. E. Dekkers and J. Fraipont. CCSL XXXVIII–XL. Turnhout, 1956.

    Expositions on the Book of Psalms. Edited and condensed from the Oxford Translation by A. Cleveland Coxe. Nicene and Post-Nicene Fathers of the Christian Church VII. Reprint. Grand Rapids, MI, 1979.

    Quaestiones in heptateuchum. CCSL XXXIII. Turnhout, 1958.

    Sermones de Vetere Testamento. Ed. C. Lambot. CCSL LI. Turnhout, 1961.

    Sermones de Scripturis. PL XXXVIII and XXXIX.

    Sermons on the Liturgical Seasons. Translated by Sr. Mary Muldowney. Fathers of the Church XXXVIII. New York, 1959.

Writings of Augustine pertaining to the religious life are gathered (and translated by Edmund Colledge) in Adolar Zumkeller, *Augustine's Ideal of the Religious Life* (New York, 1986). The following have been especially useful in this study, and are followed by the Latin editions used by Zumkeller:

    Rule (the *Praeceptum*). Zumkeller, pp. 289–300; Luc Verheijen, *La règle de Saint Augustin.* Paris, 1967.

    From *De opere monachorum.* Zumkeller, pp. 323–330; *CSEL* XLI (00).

    From *Epistolae* 5, 48, 60, 78, 83, 111, 157, 210, 211, 243. Zumkeller, pp. 340–382; *CSEL* XXXIV, XLIV, LVII.

Bernard of Clairvaux. *Life and Works of Saint Bernard, Abbot of Clairvaux.* From the edition of Mabillon, but translated and edited by Samuel J. Eales. 4 vols. London 1889–1896. Vol I: Preface, Chronology, List of Dates of Bernard's Letters, and English translations of letters 1–145. London, 1889.

Bernold of Constance. *Micrologus de ecclesiasticis observationibus.* PL CLI, cols. 974–1022.

Boutillier du Retail and Piétresson de Saint-Aubin. *Obituaires de la Province de Sens: Diocèses de Meaux et de Troyes.* In *Recueil des Historiens de la France: Obituaires.* 7 vols.

Chevalier, Cyr Ulysse. *Repertorium, hymnologicum: catalogue des chants, hymnes, proses, séquences, tropes.* 5 vols. Louvain, 1889; Louvain, 1897–1912; Paris, 1919.

La Chronique de Morigny (1095–1152). Ed. Leon Mirot. Paris, 1909.

Contemporary Chronicles of the Middle Ages: Sources of Twelfth-Century History. Translated from the Latin by Joseph Stephenson. Dyfed, 1988.

Crosnier, A., ed. *Sacramentarium ad usum aeclesiae nivernensis.* Société nivernaise VIII. Nevers, 1873.

Delaporte, Yves, ed. *Fragments des manuscrits de Chartres.* Paléographie musicale Ser. I, vol. XVII. Solesmes, 1958.

    L'Ordinaire chartrain du XIIIe siècle. Mémoires de la Société archéologique d'Eure-et-Loir XIX (1953).

Dinter, Peter, ed. *Liber tramitis aevi Odilonis Abbatis.* Corpus Consuetudinum Monasticarum X. Siegburg, 1980.

Driart, Pierre. *Journal*. Ed. Fernand Bournon. Mémoires de la Société de l'Histoire de Paris et de l'Ile-de-France XXII, pp. 67–178. Paris, 1895.

Eeles, Francis, ed. *The Holyrood Ordinal: a Scottish Version of a Directory of English Augustinian Canons, with Manual and other Liturgical Forms*. Edinburgh, 1916.

Foley, Edward B., ed. *The First Ordinary of the Royal Abbey of St.-Denis in France (Paris, Bibliothèque Mazarine 526)*. Fribourg, 1990.

Fredborg, Karin Margareta, ed. *The Latin Rhetorical Commentaries by Thierry of Chartres*. Pontifical Institute of Medieval Studies: Studies and Texts LXXXIV. Toronto, 1988.

Fulbert of Chartres. *The Letters and Poems of Fulbert of Chartres*. Ed. F. Behrends. Oxford, 1976.

Gallia Christiana, vol. VII, cols. 656–699. Paris, 1744.

Garner of St. Victor. *Gregorianum. PL* CXCIII, cols. 1–462.

Gillingham, Bryan, ed. *Paris, Bibliothèque Nationale, fonds latin 1139*. [Facsimile of the manuscript.] Institute of Mediaeval Music: Publications of Mediaeval Music XIV. Ottawa, 1987.

Godefroy of St. Victor. *Fons philosophiae*. Ed. and annotated by Pierre Michaud-Quantin. Namur, 1956.

The Fountain of Philosophy. Trans. Edward A. Synan. Toronto, 1972.

Microcosmos. Ed. Philippe Delhaye. Lille, 1951.

de Goede, Nicholas, ed. *The Utrecht Prosarium: Liber sequentiarum ecclesiae capitularis sanctae Mariae Ultraiectensis, saeculi XIII*. Monumenta Musica Neerlandica VI. Amsterdam, 1965.

Grocheo, Johannes de. Ed. Ernst Rohloff. *Die Quellenhandschriften zum Musiktraktat des Johannes de Grocheio*. Leipzig, n.d.

Guérard, M. *Cartulaire de l'église de Notre-Dame*. Collection des Cartulaires de France IV–VII. Paris, 1850.

Guido of Arezzo. *Micrologus*. Ed. Josef Smits van Waesberghe. Rome, 1955.

Helgaud de Fleury. *Vie de Robert le Pieux*. Ed. and trans. R.-H. Bautier and G. Labory. Paris, 1965.

Hesbert, René-Jean, ed. *Antiphonale missarum sextuplex*. Brussels, 1935.

Le Prosaire d'Aix-la-Chapelle, XIIIe siècle, début. Monumenta musicae sacrae III. Rouen, 1961.

Le Prosaire de la Sainte-Chapelle: manuscrit de Saint-Nicholas de Bari (Vers 1250). Monumenta musicae sacrae I. Macon, 1952.

Le tropaire-prosaire de Dublin. Monumenta musicae sacrae IV. Rouen, 1966.

Honorius Augustodunensis. *Gemma animae. PL* CLXXII, cols. 541–738.

Sacramentarium seu de causis et significatu mystico rituum divini in ecclesia officii liber. PL CLXXII, cols. 737–806.

Speculum ecclesiae. PL CLXXII, cols. 813–1108.

Hucbald, Guido, and John on Music: Three Medieval Treatises. Ed. Claude V. Palisca, trans. Warren Babb. New Haven, 1978.

Hugh of St. Cher. *Tractus super missam seu speculum ecclesiae*. Ed. G. Sölch. Münster, 1940.

Hugh of St. Victor. *De archa noe morali. PL* CLXXVI, cols. 618–680.

On the Moral Ark of Noah. Trans. by a Religious of CSMV. New York, 1962.

De archa noe mystica. [*The Mystical Ark of Noah*]. *PL* CLXXVI, cols, 681–704.

De scaramentis christianae fidei. PL CLXXVI, cols. 173–618.

On the sacraments of the Christian faith. Trans. Roy Deferrari. Cambridge, MA, 1951.

"De unione spiritus et corporis." Ed. Ambrogio Piazzoni in "Il 'De unione spiritus et corporis' di Ugo de San Vittore." *Studi Medievali*, 3rd series, 21 (1980), pp. 861–888. *PL* CLXXVII, cols. 285–294.

Didascalicon de studio legendi: a Critical Text. Ed. Charles H. Buttimer. Washington, DC, 1939.

The Didascalicon of Hugh of St. Victor: a Medieval Guide to the Arts. Ed. and trans. Jerome Taylor. New York, 1961.

Explicatio in canticum beate Marie. PL CLXXV, cols. 413–431.

Expositio in hierarchium coelestum S. Dionysii [*Commentary on the Celestial Hierarchy*]. *PL* CLXXV.

Six opuscules spirituels. Ed. Roger Baron. Paris, 1969.

Isidore of Seville. *De ecclesiasticis officiis. CCSL* CXIII.

Iversen, Gunilla, ed. *Tropes du Sanctus.* Corpus Troporum VII. Stockholm, 1990.

Ivo of Chartres. *Epistolae. PL* CLXII, cols. 11–290.

(Jacobsson) Jonson, Ritva, ed. *Cycle de Noël.* Corpus Troporum I: *Tropes du propre de la messe 1.* Stockholm, 1975.

Johan Beleth. *Summa de ecclesiasticis officiis.* Ed. H. Douteil. *CCCM* XLI–XLIA. Turnhout, 1976.

John of Avranches. *De officiis ecclesiasticis. PL* CXLVII, cols. 27–1216.

Kaemmerer, Walter, ed. *Aachener Quellentexte.* Veröffentlichungen des Stadtarchivs Aachen I. Aachen, 1980.

Kurzeja, A., ed. *Der älteste "Liber ordinarius" der Trier Domkirche.* Münster, 1970.

Lemaître, Jean-Loup, ed. *Répertoire des documents nécrologiques français.* In *Recueil des historiens de la France: Obituaires.* 7 vols. Paris, 1902–87. Vol. VII, Parts I and II and supplement. Paris, 1980–87.

Lespinasse, René de, ed. *Cartulaire de Saint Cyr de Nevers.* Nevers, 1916.

Libellus de diversis ordinibus et professionibus qui sunt in aecclesia. Ed. Giles Constable, trans. B. Smith. Oxford, 1972.

Liber ordinis sancti victoris parisiensis. Ed. Luc Jocqué and Ludo Milis. *CCCM* LXI. Turnhout, 1984.

Mansi, J. D., ed. *Sacrorum conciliorum nova et amplissima collectio.* 31 vols. 1759–1798.

Marcusson, Olof, ed. *Tropes de l'alleluia.* Corpus Troporum II: *Prosules de la messe 1.* Stockholm, 1976.

McKinnon, James, ed. *Music in Early Christian Literature.* Cambridge, 1987.

Merlet, Lucien. *Cartulaire de l'abbaye de la Madeleine de Châteaudun.* Châteaudun, 1896.

Merlet, René, ed. *Cartulaire de Saint-Jean-en-Vallée de Chartres.* Paris, 1906.

Meuthen, Erich, ed. *Aachener Urkunden 1101–1250.* Bonn, 1972.

Milis, Ludo, ed. *Constitutiones canonicorum regularium ordinis arroasiensis. CCCM* XX. Turnhout, 1970.

Molinier, Auguste, ed. *Obituaires de la Province de Sens: Diocèses de Sens et de Paris.* In *Recueil des Historiens de la France: Obituaires.* 7 vols. Paris, 1902–87. Vol. I, parts 1 and 2. 1902.

Monumenta Germaniae Historica. Auctores antiquissimi. 15 vols. in 17. Berlin, 1877–1919.

Notker the Stammerer. *Notker der Dichter und seine geistige Welt.* Ed. Wolfram von den Steinen. 2 vols. Bern, 1948.

Odelman, Eva, ed. *Les Prosules limousines de Wolfenbüttel.* Corpus troporum, VI. Stockholm, 1986.

Ordericus Vitalis. *Historia ecclesiastica.* Ed. Marjorie Chibnall. 6 vols. Oxford, 1968–1980.

Petrus of Poitiers. *Summa de confessione, compilatio praesens.* Ed. Jean Longère. *CCCM* LI. Turnhout, 1980.

Petrus Pictor. *Carmina.* Ed. L. van Acker. *CCCM* XXV. Turnhout, 1972.

Pseudo-Alcuin. *De divinis officiis. PL* CI, cols. 1173–1286.

Pseudo-Dionysius. *The Complete Works.* Trans. Colm Luibheid. Foreword, Notes, and Collaboration by Paul Rorem. Mahwah, NY, 1987.

Pseudo-Germanus. *Expositio antiquae liturgicae Gallicanae.* Ed. E. C. Ratcliffe. Henry Bradshaw Society XCVIII. London, 1971.

Pseudo-Hugh of St. Victor. *Speculum ecclesiae. PL* CLXXVII col. 335–79.

Quodvultdeus. "De Cantico Novo." In *Opera Quodvvltdeo carthaginiensi episcopo tribvta*. R. Braun, ed. *CCSL* LX, pp. 3379–392. Turnhout, 1976.

Recueil des historiens des Gaules et de la France. Paris, 1738–1904. 24 vols. in 25.

Richard of St. Victor. *L'Edit d'Alexandre ou les trois processions* [*Super exiit edichum seu De Tribus processionibus*]. Ed. Jean Châtillon. Bruges, 1951.

   Liber exceptionum: texte critique avec introduction, notes et tables. Ed. Jean Châtillon. Paris, 1958.

   De trinitate: texte critique avec introduction, notes et tables. Ed. Jean Rabaillier. Paris, 1958.

   The Twelve Patriarchs; The Mystical Ark; Book III of the Trinity. Trans. and Introduction by Grover Zinn. New York, 1979.

Richard of Wedinghauser. *Libellus de canone mystici libaminis*. PL CLXXVII, cols. 455–70.

Sicard of Cremona. *Mitrale seu de officiis ecclesiasticis summa*. PL CCXIII, cols. 13–436.

Suger, Abbot of St. Denis. *Abbot Suger On the Abbey Church of St.-Denis and its Art Treasures*. Ed., trans., and ann. Erwin Panofsky. Includes editions and English translations of *Liber de rebus in administratione*, pp. 40–81, and *Libellus alter de consecratione ecclesiae sancti dionysii*, pp. 82–121. Second edn. prepared by Gerda Panofsky-Soergel. Princeton, 1979.

   Vita Ludovici grossi regis (Vie de Louis VI, Le Gros). Ed. and trans. Henri Waquet. Paris, 1929.

Vogel, Cyrille and R. Elze, eds. *Le Pontifical romano-germanique du Xe siècle*. Studi e testi CCXXVI, CCXXVII, CCLXIX. Vatican City, 1963–72.

Walter of St. Victor and others. *Galteri a Sancto Victore et quorumdam aliorum: sermones ineditos triginta sex*. Ed. Jean Châtillon. *CCCM* XXXCI. Turnhout, 1975.

Weiss, Günther, ed. *Introitus-Tropen I: das Repertoire der südfranzösischen Tropare des 10. und 11. Jahrhunderts*. Monumenta Monodica Medii Aevi III. Kassel, 1970.

William Durandus of Mende. *Le Pontifical de Guillaume Durand*. ed. M. Andrieu. In *Le Pontifical romain au moyen âge*. 4 vols. 1938–41. Vol. III. Studi e testi LXXXVIII. Vatican City, 1940.

   Rationale divinorum officiorum. Naples, 1859.

Zumkeller, Adolar. *Augustine's Ideal of the Religious Life*. New York, 1986. (See also under Augustine, above.)

Selected secondary sources

Alexander, James W. 1970. "The Becket Controversy in Recent Historiography." *Journal of British Studies* 10:1–26.

Alford, John A. 1982. "The Grammatical Metaphor: a Survey of Its Use in the Middle Ages." *Speculum* 57:728–760.

Alverny, Marie-Thérèse d'. 1962. L'Ecriture de Bernard Itier et son évolution." *Medievalia et Humanistica* 14:47–54.

Anfray, M. 1964. *La cathédrale de Nevers et les églises gothiques du Nivernais*. Paris.

Apel, Willi. 1958. *Gregorian Chant*. Bloomington, IN.

Arlt, Wulf. 1982. "Zur Interpretation der Tropen." In *Aktuelle Fragen der musikbezogenen Mittelalterforschung. Texte zu einem Basler Kolloquium des Jahres 1975*. Forum musicologicum III. Winterthur.

   1986. "Zu einigen Fragen der Funktion, Interpretation und Edition der Introitustropen." In *LitTrop*, pp. 131–150.

Asztalos, Monika, ed. 1986. *The Editing of Theological and Philosophical Texts from the Middle Ages: Acts of the conference arranged by the Department of Classical Languages, University of Stockholm, 29–31 August, 1984*. Stockholm.

Atchley, Cuthbert F. 1900. "Notes on a Bristol Manuscript Missal." *Transactions of St. Paul's Ecclesiological Society* 4:277–292.

Auvray, L. 1892. "Documents parisiens tirées de la bibliothèque Vatican." *Memoires de la Société de l'Histoire de Paris* 19:17–35.

Bailey, Terence. 1983. *The Ambrosian Alleluias*. Englefield Green, Surrey.

Baldwin, John W. 1970. *Masters, Princes and Merchants: the Social Views of Peter the Chanter and His Circle*. 2 vols. Princeton, NJ.

1986. *The Government of Philip Augustus*. Berkeley.

Baltzer, Rebecca. 1988. "Another Look at a Composite Office and Its History: the Feast of *Susceptio Reliquiarum* in Medieval Paris." *Journal of the Royal Musical Association* 113:1–27.

1992. "The Geography of the Liturgy at Notre-Dame of Paris." In *Plainsong in the Age of Polyphony*. Ed. Thomas Forrest Kelly, pp. 45–64. Cambridge.

Baron, Roger. 1955. "La Pensée mariale de Hugues de Saint-Victor." *Revue d'Ascétique et de Mystique* 31:249–271.

1957. *Science et sagesse chez Hugues de Saint Victor*. Paris.

1958. "Le 'sacrement de foi' selon Hugues de Saint-Victor." *Revue des Sciences Philosophiques et Théologiques* 00:50–78.

1959. "Rapports entre Saint Augustin et Hugues de Saint-Victor: trois opuscules de Hugues de Saint-Victor." *Revue des Etudes Augustiniennes* 5:391–429.

1962. "Note sur la succession et la date des écrits de Hugues de Saint-Victor." *Revue d'Histoire Ecclésiastique* 57:88–118.

1963. *Etudes sur Hugues de Saint-Victor*. Paris.

1969. "Hugues de Saint-Victor." *Dictionnaire de spiritualité*, vol. VII, pp. 901–939. Paris.

Barstow, Anne L. 1982. *Married Priests and the Reforming Papacy: the Eleventh-Century Debates*. Texts and Studies in Religion XII. New York.

Baumstark, Anton. 1922. "Die Orient und die Gesänge der *Adoratio crucis*." *Jahrbuch für Liturgiewissenschaft* 2:1–17.

Bautier, Geneviève. 1971. "L'Envoi de la relique de la vraie Croix à Notre Dame de Paris en 1120." *Bibliothèque de l'Ecole des Chartres* 122/2:387–397.

Bautier, Robert-Henri. 1978. "Quand et comment Paris devint capitale." *Bulletin de la Société de l'Histoire de Paris*, 105:17–46.

1981. "Paris au temps d'Abélard en son temps: actes du colloque international organisé à l'occasion du 9e centenaire de la naissance de Pierre Abélard (14–19 Mai, 1979), pp. 21–77. Paris.

1991. "Les Origines et les premiers développements de l'abbaye Saint-Victor de Paris." In *APS-V*, pp. 23–52.

Becker, Hansjacob. 1979. "Peregrinus Coloniensis O.P. und die sequenz 'omnes gentes plaudite': ein Hymnologischer Beitrag zur literarischen und liturgischen Bedeutung von St. Jacques in Paris im 2. Viertel des 13. Jahrhunderts." *Archivum Fratrum Praedicatorum* 40:39–77.

Becquet, Jean. 1960. "Les Chanoines réguliers en Limousin aux XIe et XIIe siècles." *Analecta Premonstratensia* 36:193–236.

1972. "Bulletin d'histoire de la spiritualité: chanoines réguliers et érémitisme clerical." *Revue d'Histoire de la Spiritualité* 48:361–370.

1974. "Chanoines réguliers en Limousin au XIIe siècle: sanctuaires régularisés et dépendances étrangères." *BSHAL* 101:67–111.

1977. "La Réforme des chapitres cathédraux en France aux XIe et XIIe siècles." *BPH* 1975):31–41.

1979. "Le Mouvement canonial en Limousin aux Xe–XIIe Siècles." *BPH* (1977):2–43.

1982. "L'Election épiscopale de Limoges et l'abbé de Saint-Martial au XIIe siècle." *Revue Mabillon* 60:193–200.

1983. "La Préchantre Hélie et les chroniques de la cathédrale de Limoges au XIIIe siècle: la translation du corps de S. Just." *BSHAL* 110:89–101.

1985. *Vie canoniale en France aux Xe–XIIe siècles.* London.

Belkin, A. 1988. "Suicide Scenes in Latin Psalters of the 13th Century as Reflective of Jewish Midrashic Exposition." *Manuscripta* 32:75–92.

Bell, David N. 1980. "The Tripartite Soul and the Image of God in the Latin Tradition." *RTAM* 47:16–52.

Benton, John F. 1962. "Nicholas of Clairvaux and the Twelfth-Century Sequence, with Special Reference to Adam of St. Victor." *Traditio* 18:149–180.

1986. "Introduction: Suger's Personality." In *ASSD*, pp. 3–15.

Bennett, Camille. 1985. "Historiography as Religious Event: Otto of Freising's Use of the Past for Religious Restoration." Ph.D. dissertation, Cornell University.

Bergner, Heinz. 1983. *Lyrik des Mittelalters: Probleme und Interpretationen.* 2 vols. Stuttgart.

Bernard, Madeleine, ed. 1965. *Bibliothèque Sainte-Geneviève, Paris. Répertoire de manuscrits médiévaux contenant des notations musicales.* General editor, Solange Corbin. Paris. 3 vols., 1965–74. Vol. I.

ed. 1974. *Bibliothèques Parisiennes Arsenal, Nationale (Musique), Universitaire, École des Beaux-Arts et Fonds Privés. Répertoire de manuscrits médiévaux contenant des notations musicales.* General editor, Solange Corbin. Paris. 3 vols., 1965–74. Vol. III.

Berndt, Rainer. 1991. "La Pratique exégétique d'André de Saint-Victor: Tradition victorine et influence rabbinique." In *APS-V*, pp. 271–290.

Beumer, Johannes. 1960. "Die Parallele Maria–Kirche nach einem ungedruckten Sermo des Gottfried von St.-Viktor." *RTAM* 27:248–266.

Birkner, Günter von. 1962. "Notre-Dame Cantoren und Succentoren vom Ende des 10. bis zum Beginn des 14. Jahrhunderts." In *In Memoriam Jacques Handschin*, ed. Higini Anglès *et al.*, pp. 107–126. Strasbourg.

Bischoff, Bernhard. 1935. "Aus der Schule Hugos von St. Viktor." In *Aus der Geisteswelt des Mittelalters*, ed. A. Lang, J. Lechner, and M. Schmaus. Beiträge zur Geschichte der Philosophie des Mittelalters, ed. A. Lang, J. Lechner, and M. Schmaus. Beiträge zur Geschichte der Philosophie des Mittelalters, suppl. vol. III/1, pp. 246–250. Münster.

Bishop, Edmund. 1918 and 1962. "The Genius of the Roman Rite." In *Liturgica Historica: Papers on the Liturgy and Religious Life of the Western Church*, pp. 1–19. London.

Biver, Paul and Marie-Louise. 1970. *Abbayes, monastères, et couvents de Paris, des origines à la fin du XVIIIe siècle.* Paris.

Bloomfield, Morton, ed. 1981. *Allegory, Myth, and Symbol.* Harvard English Studies IX. Cambridge, MA.

Blume, Clemens. 1908. "Inviolata: der älteste Marien-Tropus im Brevier. Geschichte des Textes und der Melodie." *Die Kirchenmusik* 9:41–48.

Blumenkranz, B. 1960. *Juifs et Chrétiens dans le monde occidental, 430–1096.* Paris.

Blumenthal, H. J. and R. A. Markus, eds. 1981. *Neoplatonism and Early Christian Thought: Essays in Honour of A. H. Armstrong.* London.

Boblitz, Hartmut. 1972. "Die Allegorese der Arche Noahs in der frühen Bibelauslegung." *Frühmittelalterliche Studien* 6:159–170.

Bogdanos, Theodore. 1983. *Pearl: Image of the Ineffable. A Study in Medieval Poetic Symbolism.* University Park, PA.

Bonde, Sheila, Edward Boyden, and Clark Manies. 1991. "Centrality and Community: Liturgy and Gothic Chapter Room Design at the Augustinian Abbey of St.-Jean-Des-Vignes, Soissons." *Gesta* 29:189–213.

Bonnard, Fourier. 1904–07. *Histoire de l'abbaye royale et de l'ordre des chanoines réguliers de St.-Victor de Paris*. 2 vols. Paris.

Bony, Jean. 1986. "What Sources for the Chevet et Saint-Denis?" In *ASSD*, pp. 131–142.

Bosl, Karl. 1979. *Regularkanoniker (Augustinerchorherren) und seelsorge in Kirche und Gesellschaft des europäischen 12. Jahrhunderts*. Munich.

Bournazel, Eric. 1975. *Le Gouvernement capétien au XIIe siècle (1108–1180): structures sociales et mutations institutionnelles*. Limoges.

1986. "Suger and the Capetians." In *ASSD*, pp. 55–72.

Boussard, Jacques. 1976. *Nouvelle histoire de Paris: de la fin du siège de 885–886 à la mort de Philippe Auguste*. Paris.

Boutet, Dominque and Strubel, Armand. 1979. *Littérature, politique et société dans la France du moyen âge*. Paris.

Boutillier, F. 1872. "Chronique ou histoire abrégée des 'Evêques et des Comtes de Nevers,' écrite en Latin au seizième siècle et publiée pour la première fois." *BSN* 7:10–241.

1880. "Drames liturgiques et rites, figurés ou cérémonies symboliques dans l'Eglise de Nevers." *BSN* 8:441–521.

1890. "Le Trésor de la Cathédrale de Nevers." *BSN* 13:213–281.

Bowen, Lee. 1941. "The Tropology of Mediaeval Dedication Rites." *Speculum* 16:469–479.

Bower, Calvin. 1978. "The Origins and Fate of Notker's Easter Week Cycle." Annual Meeting of the American Musicological Society, Minneapolis, MN. Oct. 1978.

Boyle, Leonard E. 1970. "The Emergence of Gothic Handwriting." In *Y1200*, vol. II, pp. 173–178.

1981. *Pastoral Care, Clerical Education and Canon Law, 1200–1400*. Collected Studies Series CXXXV. Variorum Reprints. London.

Branner, Robert. 1969. "Two Parisian Capella Books in Bari." *Gesta* 8:14–19.

1970. "Manuscript Painting around 1200," in *Y1200*, vol. II, pp. 173–178.

1971. "The Sainte-Chapelle and the Capella Regis in the Thirteenth Century." *Gesta* 10:19–22.

1977. *Manuscript Painting in Paris during the Reign of Saint Louis: a Study in Styles*. Berkeley, CA.

Braswell, Laurel Nicholas. 1981. *Western Manuscripts from Classical Antiquity to the Renaissance: a Handbook*. Garland Reference Library of the Humanities CXXXIX. New York and London.

Brémond, Claude, Jacques le Goff, and Jean Claude Schmitt. 1982. *L'exemplum*. Typologie des sources du moyen âge occidental XL. Turnhout.

Brereton, Georgine E. and Janet M. Ferrier, eds. 1981. *Le Menagier de Paris*. Oxford.

Brinkmann, Hennig. 1976. "Voraussetzungen und Struktur religiöser Lyrik im Mittelalter." *Mittellateinisches Jahrbuch* 3:37–54.

1980. *Mittelalterliche Hermeneutik*. Tübingen.

Brooke, Christopher. 1985. "Monk and Canon: Some Patterns in the Religious Life of the Twelfth Century" in *Monks, Hermits and the Ascetic Tradition*, ed. W. J. Sheils. Studies in Church History XXII. Oxford.

Browe, P. 1967. *Die Verehrung der Eucharistie im Mittelalter*. Rome.

Brown, Raymond E. 1977. *The Birth of the Messiah: a Commentary on the Infancy Narratives in Matthew and Luke*. New York.

1984. *The Churches the Apostles Left Behind*. New York.

Bruyne, Edgar de. 1946. *Etudes d'esthétique médiévale*. 3 vols. Bruges.

Bubacz, Bruce. 1982. *St. Augustine's Theory of Knowledge: a Contemporary Analysis*. Studies and Texts in Religion XI. New York.

Bur, Michel,. 1986. "A Note on Suger's Understanding of Political Power." In *ASSD*, pp. 73–76.

Burke, Kenneth. 1961, 1970. *The Rhetoric of Religion*. 1961. Reprint. Berkeley, CA.

Buschhausen, Heide and Helmut Buschhausen. 1979. "Studien zu den typologischen Kreuzen der Ile-de-France und des Maaslandes." In *Zeit der Staufer: Geschichte, Kunst, Kultur*. 5 vols. Vol. V, *Supplement: Vorträge und Forschungen*, pp. 247–277.

Buschhausen, Helmut. 1974. "The Klosterneuburg Altar of Nicholas of Verdun: Art, Theology, and Politics." *Journal of the Warburg and Courtauld Institutes*, 37:1–32.

1975. "The Theological Sources of the Klosterneuburg Altarpiece." In *Y1200S*, pp. 119–138.

1980. *Der Verduner Altar: das Emailwerk des Nikolaus von Verdun im Stift Klosterneuburg*. Vienna.

Butler, Alban. 1981. *Butler's Lives of the Saints*. Complete edition: edited, revised and supplemented by Herbert J. Thurston and Donald Attwater. 4 vols. Westminster, MD.

Bynum, Carolyn Walker. 1973. "The Spirituality of Regular Canons in the Twelfth Century: a New Approach." *Medievalia et Humanistica*, n.s. 4:3–24.

1979. *Docere Verbo et Exemplo: an Aspect of Twelfth-Century Spirituality*. Harvard Theological Studies XXXI. Missoula, MT.

Cabié, R. 1972. "Les Lettres attribuées à Saint Germain de Paris et les origines de la liturgie gallicane." *Bulletin de Littérature Ecclésiastique* 73:183–92.

Cahn, Walter. 1975. "St. Albans and the Channel Style in England." In *Y1200S*, pp. 187–230.

1976. "Architectural Draftsmanship in Twelfth-Century Paris: The Illustrations of Richard of Saint-Victor's Commentary on Ezekiel's Temple Vision." *Gesta* 15:247–54.

1981. "Three Eleventh-Century Manuscripts from Nevers." In *Études offertes à Louis Grodecki*, pp. 63–78. Paris.

1982. *Romanesque Bible Illumination* Ithaca, NY.

Callahan, D. F. 1976. "The Sermons of Adémar of Chabannes and the Cult of St. Martial of Limoges." *RB* 86:251–295.

Camargo, Martin. 1984. "The *Libellus de arte dictandi rhetorice* Attributed to Peter of Blois." *Speculum* 59:16–41.

Camille, Michael. 1989. "Visual Signs of the Sacred Page: Books in the *Bible moralisée*." *Word and Image* 5/1:111–130.

Carruthers, Mary J. 1990. *The Book of Memory: a Study of Memory in Medieval Culture*. Cambridge.

Chailley, Jacques. 1955. "Les Premiers Troubadours et les Versus de l'Ecole d'Aquitaine." *Romania* 76:212–239.

1957. "Les Anciens Tropaires et sequentiaires de l'école de Saint-Martial de Limoges (Xe–XIe siècles)." *Etudes grégoriennes* 2:163–188.

1960. *Ecole musicale de Saint-Martial de Limoges jusqu'à la fin du XIe siècle*. Paris.

Champeval, M. J.-B. 1894. "Chroniques de Saint-Martial de Limoges: supplement." *BSHAL* 42:303–391.

Chaponnel, Raimond. 1699. *Histoire des chanoines au recherches historiques – critiques sur l'ordre canonique*. Paris.

Charlesworth, James H. 1990. "Exploring Opportunities for Rethinking Relations Among Jews and Christians." In *Jews and Christians: Exploring the past, Present, and Future*. Ed. James H. Charlesworth, pp. 35–59. New York.

Châtillon, Jean. 1949. "Une ecclésiologie médiévale: l'idée de l'église dans la théologie de l'école de Saint Victor au XIIe siècle." *Irènikon* 22:115–138, 395–411.

1952. "De Guillaume de Champeaux à Thomas Gallus: chronique d'histoire littéraire et doctrinale de l'école de St.-Victor." *Revue du Moyen Age Latin* 8:147–162, 247–272.

1965. "Sermons et prédicateurs victorins de la seconde moitié du XIIe siècle." *Archives d'Histoire Doctrinale et Littéraire du Moyen Age* 32:7–60.

1968. "La Culture de l'école de Saint Victor au 12e siècle." In *Entretiens sur la Renaissance du 12e siècle*, ed. Maurice de Gandillac and Edouard Jeanneau, pp. 147–178. Paris.

1969. *Théologie, spiritualité, et métaphysique dans l'œuvre oratoire d'Achard de Saint-Victor*. Études de philosophie médiévale LVIII. Paris.

1973. "Les Anciennes Stalles de l'Abbaye de Saint-Victor: Iconographie et théologie." *Bulletin Archéologique du Comité des Travaux Historiques et Scientifiques*, n.s. 9A: 99–114.

1975. "L'abbaye de Saint Victor." *Montagne Ste-Geneviève* 183:60–64.

1977a. "La Crise de l'Eglise aux XIe et XIIe siècles et les origines des grandes fédérations canoniales." *Revue d'Histoire de la Spiritualité* 53:3–45.

1977b. "Hugues de Saint-Victor critique de Jean Scot." In *Jean Scot Erigène et l'histoire de la philosophie*. Colloques Internationaux du CNRS, No. 561: Laon, 1975, pp. 415–431. Paris.

1979. "Guillaume de Saint-Thierry, le monachisme et les écoles: à propos de Rupert de Deutz, d'Abélard et de Guillaume de Conches," in *Saint-Thierry: une abbaye du VIe au XXe siècle. Actes du colloque international d'histoire monastique: Reims-Saint-Thierry, 11 au 14 octobre 1976*, pp. 375–394. Saint-Thierry.

1980a. "La Méthode théologique d'Alain de Lille." In *Alain de Lille, Gautier de Châtillon, Jakemart Giélée et leur temps. Actes du Colloque de Lille, Octobre, 1978*, ed. H. Roussel and F. Suard, pp. 47–60. Lille.

1980b. "Thomas Becket et les Victorins." In *TB*, pp. 89–101 and 127–29.

1980c. "La Transmission de l'œuvre de Hugues de Saint-Victor: à propos d'un livre recent de Rudolf Goy." *Mittellateinisches Jahrbuch* 15:57–62.

Chazan, Robert. 1973. *Medieval Jewry in Northern France*. Baltimore.

Cheney, C. R. 1937. "La Date de composition du 'liber poenitentialis' attribué à Pierre de Poitiers." *RTAM* 9:401–404.

Chenu, Marie-Dominique. 1968. *Nature, Man, and Society in the Twelfth Century*. Ed. and trans. Jerome Taylor and Lester Little. Chicago.

1980. "Un témoin médiéval de l'épistemologie pluridisciplinaire." In *Esistenza, mito, ermeneutica: scritti per Enrico Castelli*, ed. Marco M. Olivetti. pp. 211–212. Padua.

Chibnall, Marjorie. 1988. "Fakes, Identity and the Real Thing." In *Fälschungen im Mittelalter*, vol. IV, pp. 331–346. Internationaler Kongress der Monumenta Germaniae Historica, Munich, 16–19 September 1986. 5 vols. Hannover.

Chidester, David. 1983. "The Symbolism of Learning in St. Augustine." *Harvard Theological Review* 76:73–90.

Chodorow, Stanley. 1972. *Christian Political Theory and Church Politics in the Mid-Twelfth Century: the Ecclesiology of Gratian's Decretals*. Berkeley, CA.

1989. "Paschal II, Henry V, and the Origins of the Crisis of 1111." In *Popes, Teachers, and Canon Law in the Middle Ages*, ed. James Ross Sweeney and Stanley Chodorow, pp. 3–25. Ithaca, NY.

Chydenius, Johan. 1960. *The Theory of Medieval Symbolism*, Helsingfors.

Cobban, Alan B. 1975. *The Medieval Universities: Their Development and Organization*. London.

Coenegracht, M. Pia. 1963. "De Kloosterwetgeving van de Victorinen." *Ons Geestelijk Erf* 37:291–328.

Colish, Marcia. 1978. "St. Augustine's Rhetoric of Silence Revisited." *Augustinian Studies* 9:15–24.

1983. *The Mirror of Language: a Study in the Medieval Theory of Knowledge*, 2nd edn. Lincoln, NB.

1987. "Gilbert, the Early Porretans, and Peter Lombard: Semantics and Theology." In *Gilbert de Poitiers et ses contemporains aux origines de la "Logica Modernorum,"* ed. Jean Jolivet and Alain de Libera, pp. 229–250. Naples.

1988. "Systematic Theology and Theological Renewal in the Twelfth Century." In *Rewriting the Middle Ages*, ed. Lee Patterson. Durham, NC.

Congar, Yves. 1983. "Modéle monastique et modèle sacerdotal en Occident de Grégoire VII (1073–1085) à Innocent III (1198)." In *Etudes d'ecclésiologie médiévale*, pp. 153–160. London.

Conomos, Dimitri E. 1974. *Byzantine Trisagia and Cheroubika of the Fourteenth and Fifteenth Centuries*. Salonika.

Constable, Giles. 1964. "Reformatio." In *Ecumenical Dialogue at Harvard: the Roman Catholic–Protestant Colloquium*, ed. Samuel H. Miller and G. Ernest Wright, pp. 330–343. Cambridge, MA.

1971a. "The Popularity of Twelfth-Century Spiritual Writers in the Late Middle Ages." In *Renaissance Studies in Honor of Hans Baron*, ed. Anthony Molho and John A. Tedeschi, pp. 5–28. DeKalb, IL.

1971b. "Twelfth-Century Spirituality and the Late Middle Ages." *Medieval and Renaissance Studies* 5:27–60.

1979. *Religious Life and Thought (11th–12th Centuries)*. Collected Studies Series LXXXIX. London.

1980. *Cluniac Studies*. Collected Studies Series CIX. London.

1982. "Renewal and Reform in Religious Life: Concepts and Realities." In *Renaissance and Renewal in the Twelfth Century*, ed. Robert Benson and Giles Constable, pp. 37–67. Cambridge, MA.

1983. "Forgery and Plagiarism in the Middle Ages." *Archiv für Diplomatik, Schriftsgeschichte, Siegel und Wappenkunde* 29:1–41.

1985. "Baume and Cluny in the Twelfth Century." In *Tradition and Change: Essays in Honor of Marjorie Chibnall*. Ed. D. Greenway *et al.*, pp. 35–61. Cambridge.

1987. "The Ceremonies and Symbolism of Entering Religious Life and Taking the Monastic Habit, from the Fourth to the Twelfth Century." In *Segni e rita nella chiesa altomedioevale occidentale*. Settimana di studio del Centro italiano di studi sull'alto medioevo XXXIII. 2 vols. Vol. II, pp. 771–834. Spoleto.

1989. "Past and Present in the Eleventh and Twelfth Centuries: Perceptions of Time and Change." In *L'Europa dei secoli XI e XII. Fra novità e tradizione: Sviluppi di una cultura. Atti della decima Settimana internazionale di studio. Mendola, 25–29 agosto 1986*. Pubblicazioni dell'Università cattolica del Sacro Cuore: Miscellanea del Centro di Studi medioevali XII, pp. 135–170. Milan.

1990. "A Living Past: the Historical Environment of the Middle Ages." *Harvard Library Bulletin* n.s. 1, 3:49–70.

Costa, Eugenio, Jr. 1979. *Tropes et sequences dans le cadre de la vie liturgique au moyen âge*. Rome.

Cottineau, Laurent Henri. 1939–70. *Repertoire topo-bibliographique des abbayes et prieures*. Macon. 3 vols.

Cowdrey, H. E. J. 1978. *Two Studies in Cluniac History, 1049–1126*. Studi Gregoriani per la storia della *Libertas Ecclesiae* XI. Rome.

Crepin-Leblond, Th. 1987. "Recherches sur les palais épiscopaux" (Unpublished dissertation, École des Chartes).

Crocker, Richard. 1957. "The Repertoire of Proses at Saint Martial de Limoges (Tenth and Eleventh Centuries)." Ph.D. dissertation. Yale University.

1969. "The Troping Hypothesis." *Musical Quarterly* 52:183–203.

1973. "The Sequence." In *Gattungen der Musik in Einzeldarstellung: Gedenkschrift Leo Schrade*, ed. Wulf Arlt *et al.*, pp. 269–322. Bern.

1977. *The Early Medieval Sequence*. Berkeley, CA.

1990. "Medieval Chant" in *The New Oxford History of Music*, vol. II (new edn.): *The Early Middle Ages to 1300*, ed. Richard Crocker and David Hiley, pp. 225–309. Oxford.

Crocker, Richard and John Caldwell. 1980. "Sequence." *NG* 17:141–153.

Crosnier, Augustin-J. 1860. *Hagiologie Nivernaise ou vies des saints.* Nevers.

1868. *Études sur la liturgie Nivernaise.* Nevres.

1877. *Les Congregations réligieuses dans le diocèse de Nevers.* Nevers.

Crouse, Robert D. 1987. "A Twelfth-Century Augustinian: Honorius Augustodunensis." In *Atti III, sezioni di studio V–VI: congresso internazionale su. s. Agostino nel XVI centenario della conversione, Roma, 12–20 settembre 1986,* pp. 167–177. Studia ephemeridis *Augustinianum,* XXVI. Rome.

Crozet, René. 1967. "Le Rôle du clergé épiscopal dans la vie artistique en France (Xe–XIIe siècles)." In *21. internationaler Kongress für Kunstgeschichte, Bonn, 1964,* vol. III, pp. 19–29. Bonn.

Cunnar, Eugene R. 1987. "Typological Rhyme in a Sequence by Adam of St. Victor." *Studies in Philology* 89:394–417.

Dahan, G. 1982. "L'Exégèse de l'histoire de Cain et Abel du XIIe au XIV siècle en Occident." *Bulletin de Théologie Ancienne et Médiévale* 49:21–89.

Damme, Jean van. 1972. "La 'summa cartae caritatis,' source des Constitutiones Canoniales." *Cîteaux* 23:5–54.

Danielou, Jean. 1956. *The Bible and the Liturgy.* Notre Dame.

Davis, Hugh H. 1966. "The 'De rithmis' of Alberic of Monte Cassio: a Critical Edition." *Mediaeval Studies* 28:198–227.

Delhaye, Philippe. 1951. *Le Microcosmos de Godefroy de Saint-Victor: étude théologique.* Lille.

1954. "Les Sermons de Godefroy de Saint-Victor." *RTAM* 21:194–210.

1988. *Enseignement et morale au XIIe siècle.* Fribourg.

Delisle, Léopold. 1860. "Rapports faits au comité section d'histoire et de philologie." *Revue des Sociétés Savants,* 2nd series, 3:559–563.

1868–81. *Le Cabinet des manuscrits de la bibliothèque impériale.* Paris. 4 vols.

1869. "Inventaire des manuscrits latins de Saint-Victor conservés à la bibliothèque impériale sous les numéros 14232–15175." *Bibliothèque de l'Ecole des Chartes* 30:1–79.

1895. "Les MSS de Saint-Martial de Limoges – réimpression textuelle du catalogue de 1730." *BSHAL* 43:1–64.

1896. *Notice sur les manuscrits orginaux d'Adémar de Chabannes.* Paris.

1912. *Orderic Vital et l'abbaye de Saint-Evroul: notices et travaux en l'honneur de l'historien normand, moine de cette abbaye.* Alençon.

Dereine, Charles. 1948. "Les coutumiers de Saint-Quentin de Beauvais et de Springiersbach." *Revue d'Histoire Ecclésiastique* 43:411–442.

1951 and 1959. "Coutumiers et ordinaires des chanoines réguliers." *Scriptorium* 5 (1951):107–113 and 13 (1959):244–246.

1952. *Les Chanoines réguliers au diocèse de Liége avant Saint Norbert.* Académie Royale de Belgique: Classe des Lettres et des Sciences Morales et Politiques, *Mémoires* XLVII. Brussels.

1959. "La spiritualité 'apostolique' des premiers fondateurs d'Afflegem (1083–1100)." *Revue d'Histoire Ecclésiastique* 54:41–65.

Dickinson, John C. 1950. *The Origins of the Austin Canons and their Introduction into England.* London.

Dictionnaire d'Histoire et de Géographie Ecclésiastique. 1912– Paris. Vols. I–XXIV [1990, "Haegy-Herlemundus"] have appeared so far.

Diehl, Patrick S. 1985. *The Medieval European Religious Lyric: an Ars Poetria.* Berkeley, CA.

Dolbeau, François. 1983. "Une séquence inédite de Guibert de Nogent." *RB* 93:323–326.

Dondaine, H. F. 1953. *Le Corpus dionysien de l'université de Paris au XIII siècle.* Rome.

Douglas, Mary. 1986. *How Institutions think.* Syracuse, NY.

Douteil, Herbert. 1969. *Studien zu Durantis "Rationale divinorum officium" als Kirchenmusikalischer Quelle.* Regensburg.

Dreves, Guido Maria. 1885. "Adam von St. Victor: Studien zur Literaturgeschichte des M. A." *Stimmen aus Maria Laach* 29:278–295.

Dronke, Peter, 1965. "The Beginnings of the Sequence." *Beiträge zur Geschichte der deutschen Sprache und Literatur* 87:43–73.

    1977. "'Theologia veluti quaedam poetria': quelques observations sur la fonction des images poétiques chez Jean Scot." In *Jean Scot Erigène et l'histoire de la philosophie*, pp. 242–252. Colloques Internationaux du CNRS, No. 561: Laon, 1975. Paris.

    1984. *The Medieval Poet and His World.* Storia e Letteratura, Raccolta di Studi e Testi CLXIV. Rome.

    1985. "Types of Poetic Art in Tropes." In *LitTrop*, pp. 1–23.

Drumbl, J. 1973. "Die Improperien in der lateinischen Liturgie." *Archiv für Liturgiewissenschaft* 15:68–100.

Dubois, Gérard. 1690–1710. *Historia Ecclesiae Parisiensis.* 2 vols. Paris.

Dubois, Jacques. 1982. *Histoire monastique en France au XIIe siècle: les institutions monastiques et leur évolution.* Collected Studies CLXI. London.

Dufrasne, Jean. 1959. *Les Ordinaires manuscrits des églises seculières conservés à la Bibliothèque nationale de Paris.* Paris.

Duggan, Anne. 1980. *Thomas Becket: a Textual History of His Letters.* Oxford.

Dumiege, Gervais. 1952. *Richard de Saint-Victor et l'idée chrétienne de l'amour.* Paris.

Duminy, E. 1900. "Notice sur la bibliothèque de Nevers." *BSN* 18:145–172.

Dunlop, Ian. 1982. *The Cathedrals; Crusade: the Rise of the Gothic Style in France.* New York.

Dunn-Lardeau, Brenda, ed. 1986. "Legenda aurea: sept siècles de diffusion. Actes du colloque international sur la *Legenda aurea*: texte latine et branches vernaculaires à l'Université du Québec à Montréal, 11–12 mai 1983. Cahiers d'Etudes Médiévales, Cahier Spécial vol. II. Montreal.

Edwards, Robert. 1989. *Ratio and Invention: a Study of the Medieval Lyric and Narrative.* Nashville, TN.

Ehlers, Joachim. 1972. "Arca significat ecclesiam: Ein theologisches Weltmodell aus der ersten Hälfte des 12. Jahrhunderts." *Frühmittelalterlichen Studien* 6:171–187. Wiesbaden.

    1973. *Hugo von St. Viktor: Studien zum Geschichtsdenken und zur Geschichtsschreibung des 12. Jahrhunderts.* Frankfurter historische Abhandlungen VII.

Elfving, Lars. 1962. *Etude lexicographique sur les séquences limousines.* Stockholm.

Ernst, Ulrich and Peter-Erich Neuser. 1977. *Die Génèse der europäischen Endreimdichtung.* Darmstadt.

Esmeijer, Anna C. 1978. *Divina quaternitas: a Preliminary Study in the Method and Application of Visual Exegesis.* Amsterdam.

Evans, G. R. 1980. *Old Arts and New Theology: the Beginnings of Theology as an Academic Discipline.* Oxford.

    1983. "Hugh of St. Victor on History and the Meaning of Things." *Studia Monastica* 25:223–234.

Evans, Paul. 1970. *The Early Trope Repertory of Saint Martial de Limoges.* Princeton, NJ.

Eynde, Damien van den. 1960. *Essai sur la succession et la date des écrits de Hugues de Saint-Victor.* Spicilegium pontificii athenaei antoniani XIII. Rome.

Falconer, Keith. 1989. "Some Early Tropes to the Gloria." Ph.D. dissertation, Princeton University.

Fanning, Steven. 1988. *A Bishop and His World before the Gregorian Reform: Hubert of Angers, 1006–1047*. Transactions of the American Philosophical Society LXXIX 1. Philadelphia.

Fassler, Margot E. 1983. "Musical Exegesis in the Sequences of Adam and the Canons of St. Victor." Ph.D. dissertation, Cornell University.

    1984. "Who was Adam of St. Victor? The Evidence of the Sequence Manuscripts." *JAMS* 37:233–269.

    1985. "The Office of the Cantor in Early Western Monastic Rules and Customaries: a Preliminary Investigation." *Early Music History* 5:29–51.

    1987a. "Accent, Meter, and Rhythm in Medieval Treatises 'De rithmis.'" *Journal of Musicology* 5:164–190.

    1987b. "The Role of the Parisian Sequence in the Evolution of Notre-Dame Polyphony." *Speculum* 62:345–374.

    1991. "The Feast of Fools and *Danielis Ludus*: Popular Tradition in a Medieval Cathedral Play." In *Plainsong in an Age of Polyphony*, ed. Thomas F. Kelly, pp. 65–99. Cambridge.

    1992. "The Disappearance of the Proper Tropes and the Rise of the Late Sequence: New Evidence from Chartres." In *Cantus planus: the Conference Report of the Chant Study Group of the International Musicological Society, Held in Pécs, Hungary, Sept., 1990*, pp. 319–335. Budapest.

Feiss, Hugh Bernard. 1979. "Learning and the Ascent to God in Richard of St. Victor." Unpublished manuscript. Portland.

    1988. "*Circatores* in the *Ordo* of St. Victor." In *The Medieval Monastery*, ed. Andrew MacLeish. pp. 53–58. St. Cloud, 1988.

Félibien, Michel. 1725. *Histoire de la ville de Paris*. 5 vols. Paris.

Feret, Pierre. 1883. *L'Abbaye de Sainte-Geneviève et la congrègation de France*. 2 vols. Paris.

Ferguson, Chris D. 1989. *Europe in Transition: a Select, Annotated Bibliography of the Twelfth-Century Renaissance*. New York.

Ferruolo, Stephen. 1985. *The Origins of the University: the Schools of Paris and their critics 1100–1215*. Stanford, CA.

Fischer, Balthazar. 1987. "Liturgiesgeschichte und Exegesegeschichte: interdisziplinäre Zusammenhänge." *Jahrbuch für Antike und Christentum* 30:5–13.

Fischer, L. 1917. "Ivo von Chartres, der Erneuerer der Vita canonica in Frankreich." In *Festgabe A. Knöpfler*, pp. 67–88. Freiburg-im-Breisgau.

Fleury, Michel. 1961. "Paris du Bas-Empire au début du XIIIe siècle." In *Paris: croissance d'une capitale*, pp. 73–96. Paris.

Fliche, Augustin. 1912. *Le Règne de Philippe Ier, Roi de France (1060–1108)*. Paris.

Flint, Valerie J. 1970. "The True Author of the 'Salonii commentarii in Parabolas Salomonis et in Ecclesiasten.'" *RTAM* 37:174–186.

    1972. "The Chronology of the Works of Honorius Augustodunensis." *RB* 82:215–42.

    1975. "The 'Elucidarius' of Honorius Augustodunensis and the Reform in Late Eleventh Century England." *RB* 85:178–189.

    1981. "World History in the Early Twelfth Century: the 'Imago mundi' of Honorius Augustodunensis." In *The Writing of History in the Middle Ages: Essays Presented to Richard William Southern*, ed. R. H. C. Davis and J. M. Wallace-Hadrill, pp. 211–238. Oxford.

    1982. "Heinricus of Augsburg and Honorius Augustodunensis: Are They the Same Person?" *RB* 92:148–58.

Foley, Edward B. 1988. "The 'Libri ordinarii': an Introduction." *Ephemerides Liturgicae* 102:129–139.

Foley, John Miles. 1986. *Oral Tradition in Literature: Interpretation in Context*. Columbus, OH.

Folz, Robert. 1974. *The Coronation of Charlemagne, 25 December 800.* Trans J. E. Anderson. (First published in French in 1964.) London.

Foreville, Raymonde. 1980. "Monachisme et vie commune du clergé dans les conciles œcuméniques et généraux." In *Istituzioni monastiche e istituzioni canonicali in Occidente (1123–1215).* Atti della settimana internazionale di studio Mendola, 28 agosto – 3 settembre, 1977. Milan.

   1981. *Thomas Becket dans la tradition historique et hagiographique.* Variorum Reprints. London.

Formeville, H. de. 1873. *Histoire de l'ancien évêché-comté de Lisieux.* 2 vols. Lisieux.

Forshaw, Helen. 1972. "St. Edmund's 'speculum': a Classic of Victorine Spirituality." *Archives d'Histoire Doctrinale et Littéraire du Moyen Age* 39:7–40.

Franklin, Alfred. 1865. *Histoire de la bibliothèque de l'Abbaye Saint Victor à Paris d'après des documents inédits.* Paris.

Fredborg, Karin Margareta. 1976. "The Commentaries on *De Inventione* and *Rhetorica ad Herennium* by William of Champeaux." *Cahiers de l'institut du Moyen Age Grec et Latin* 17:1–39.

Freedman, Paul H. 1983. *The Diocese of Vic: Tradition and Regeneration in Medieval Catalonia.* New Brunswick, NJ.

Freytag, Hartmut. 1982. *Die Theorie der allegorischen Schriftdeutung und die Allegorie in deutschen Texten besonders des 11. und 12. Jahrhunderts.* Bibliotheca Germanica XXIV. Bern.

Fried, Johannes, ed. 1986. *Schulen und Studium im sozialen Wandel des hohen und späten Mittelalters.* Vorträge und Forschungen XXX. Sigmaringen, 1986.

Fries, A. 1983. "Die Trinitätssequenz 'Profitentes' und Albertus Magnus. "*Archiv für Liturgiewissenschaft* 25:276–296.

Fuehrer, M. L. 1979. "The Principle of Similitude in Hugh of St. Victor's Theory of Divine Illumination." *The American Benedictine Review* 30:80–92.

Fuller, Sarah Ann. 1969. "Aquitanian Polyphony of the Eleventh and Twelfth Centuries." Ph.D. dissertation, University of California at Berkeley.

   1979. "The Myth of 'Saint Martial' Polyphony: A Study of the Sources." *Musica Disciplina* 30:5–26.

   1981. "Theoretical Foundations of Early Organum Theory." *Acta Musicologica* 53:52–84.

   1990. "Early Polyphony." In *The New Oxford History of Music,* vol. II (new edn.): *The Early Middle Ages to 1300,* ed. Richard Crocker and David Hiley, pp. 485–556. Oxford.

Funkenstein, Amos. 1982. "Nahmanides' Symbolical Reading of History." In *Studies in Jewish Mysticism,* ed. Joseph Dan and Frank Talmage, pp. 129–150. Cambridge, MA.

Galbraith, V. H. 1937. *The St. Albans Chronicle, 1406–1420.* Oxford.

Gallacher, Patrick J. and Helen, Damico, eds. 1989. *Hermeneutics and Medieval Culture.* Albany, NY.

Garrigues, M.-O. 1977. "Honorius était-il benedictin?" *Studia Monastica* 19:27–46.

Gasparri, Françoise, 1973. *L'Ecriture des actes de Louis VI, Louis VII et Philippe-Auguste.* Paris.

   1976. "Un copiste lettré de l'abbaye de Saint-Victor de Paris au XIIe siècle." *Scriptorium* 30:232–237.

   1979. "La Chancellerie du roi Louis VII et ses rapports avec le scriptorium de l'abbaye de Saint-Victor de Paris." *Studi in onore di Giulio Battelli, 1979.* Vol. II, pp. 151–158.

   1982. "Observations paléographiques sur deux manuscrits partiellement autographes de Godefroid de Saint-Victor." *Scriptorium* 36:43–50.

   1985. "Godefroid de Saint-Victor: une personnalité peu connue du monde intellectuel et artistique parisien au XII siècle." *Scriptorium* 39:57–67.

   1991. "'Scriptorium' et bureau d'écriture de l'abbaye Saint-Victor de Paris." In *APS-V,* pp. 119–139.

Gastoué, Amédée. 1912. "Une prose inédite contre les Normands pour la fête de la Toussaint," in *La Tribune de Saint-Gervais* 18:220–225, 257–262.

Gaussin, P.-R. 1984. *L'Europe des ordres et des congrégations: des Bénédictines aux Mendiants (VIe–XVIe siècle)*. Saint-Etienne.

Gérard, P. 1982. "La Reforme grégorienne et ses problèmes: transformations des mentalités de la société aux XIe et XIIe siècles." *Mémoires de l'Academie des Sciences . . . Toulouse* 144:103–18.

Gerz von Büren, Veronika. 1986. "Études des classements de bibliothèques anciennes pour essayer de comprendre le rôle culturel de la bibliothèque de St. Victor à Paris." *Codices manuscripti* 12:1–26.

Gerz von Büren, Veronika and Donatella Nebbiai-Dalla Guardia. 1985. "Les Catalogues de bibliothèques comme sources pour l'histoire intellectuelle: le cas de trois bibliothèques monastiques françaises à la fin du XVe siècle" in *colloques internationaux CNRS: La France de la fin du XVe siècle*, pp. 282–299. Paris.

Giroud, Charles. 1961. *L'Ordre des chanoines réguliers de Saint Augustin et ses diverses formes de régime interne: essai de synthèse historico-juridique*. Martigny.

Giusberti, Franco. 1982. *Materials for a Study on Twelfth-Century Scholasticism*. Naples.

Godding, Robert. 1982. "Vie apostolique et société urbaine à l'aube du XIIIe siècle: une œuvre inédite de Thomas de Cantimpré." *Nouvelle Revue Théologique* 104:602–721..

Goetz, H.-W. 1978. "Die 'Summa Gloria': ein Beitrag zu den politischen Vorstellungen des Honorius Augustodunensis." *Zeitschrift für Kirchengeschichte* 89:307–353.

Gold, Penny Schine. 1985. *The Lady and the Virgin: Image, Attitude, and Experience in Twelfth-Century France*. Chicago.

Gössman, Elizabeth. 1981. "Dialektische und rhetorische Implikationen der Auseinandersetzung zwischen Abaelard und Bernard von Clairvaux um die Gotteskenntnis." *Sprache und Erkenntnis im Mittelalter; Akten des VI. Internationalen Kongress für Philosophie, Bonn, 29 August – 3 Sept., 1977.* Ed. Jan P. Beckman *et al.*, pp. 890–902. Berlin.

Gould, Karen. 1981. "The Sequences 'De Sanctis Reliquiis' as Sainte-Chapelle Inventories." *Medieval Studies* 43:315–341.

Goy, Rudolf. 1976. *Die Überlieferung der Werke Hugo von St. Viktor: ein Beitrag zur Kommunikationsgeschichte des Mittelalters*. Monographien zur Geschichte des Mittelalters XIV. Stuttgart.

Graboïs, Aryeh. 1975. "The *Hebraica veritas* and Jewish-Christian Intellectual Relations in the Twelfth Century." *Speculum* 50:613–634.

1983. "Le Non-Conformisme intellectuel au XIIe siècle: Pierre Abélard et Abraham Ibn Ezra." *Modernité et non-conformisme en France à travers les âges. Colloque, Haifa, 1978*, pp. 3–13. Haifa.

Green, Patrick J. 1989. *Norton Priory: the Archaeology of a Medieval Religious House*. Cambridge.

Green-Pedersen, N. J. 1974. "William of Champeaux on Boethius' Topics according to Orléans Bibl. Mun. 266." *Cahiers de l'Institut du moyen âge grec et latin* 13:13–30.

Grégoire, Réginald. 1980. *Homéliaires liturgiques médiévaux: analyse de manuscrits*. Biblioteca degli Studi Medioevali XII. Spoleto.

Grévy-Pons, Nicole and Ezio Ornato. 1976. "Qui est l'auteur de la chronique latine de Charles VI dite du Religieux de Saint-Denis?" *Bibliothèque de l'Ecole des Chartes* 139:85–102.

Grier, James. 1988. "The Stemma of the Aquitanian Versaria." *JAMS* 41:250–288.

Grimes, Ronald. 1990. *Ritual Criticism*. Columbia, SC.

Gros, Miguel. 1966. "El ordo romano-hispanico de Narbona para la consagracion de iglesias," *Hispania sacra* 19:312–401.

1976. "La Liturgie narbonnaise: témoins d'un changement rapide de rites liturgiques." In *Liturgie de l'église particulière et liturgie de l'église universelle*, pp. 127–154. Rome.

1982. "Le Pontifical de Narbonne." In *Liturgie et musique (IXe–XIVe siècle): cahiers de Fánjeaux 17* pp. 97–113. Toulouse.

Guérout, Jean. 1949. "Le Palais de la Cité, des origines à 1418." In *Mémoires de la Fédération des Sociétés Savantes de Paris et de l'Ile-de-France*1:57–212.

Guenée, Simone. 1981. *Bibliographie de l'histoire des universités francaises des origines à la revolution, 1: Généralitiés. Université de Paris*. Paris.

Guimet, Fernand. 1948. "*Caritas ordinata et amor discretus* dans la théologie trinitaire de Richard de Saint-Victor." *Revue du Moyen Age Latin* 4:225–236.

Gut, Christian. 1967. "Les Actes de Maurice de Sully relatifs aux possessions parisiennes de Saint-Victor (1180–1198)." In *Huitième Centenaire de Notre-Dame de Paris (Congrès des 30 Mai–3 Juin 1964)*, pp. 35–52. Paris.

Gy, M-D. 1981, 1990. "Rapports entre sources liturgiques et sources non liturgiques au moyen âge." First published in 1981 and reprinted in *La Liturgie dans l'histoire*, pp. 141–143: see 1990 below.

1982. "L'Ordinaire de Mende, une œuvre inédite de Guillaume Durand l'Ancien." In *Liturgie et musique (IXe–XIVe siècle): cahiers de Fanjeaux 17*, pp. 239–249. Toulouse.

1983. "Les Tropes dans l'histoire liturgique et de la théologie." *Research on Tropes: Proceedings of a Symposium Organized by the Royal Academy of Literature, History and Antiquities and the Corpus Troporum, Stockholm, June 1–3, 1981*. Ed. Gunilla Iversen, pp. 7–16. Stockholm.

1984, 1990. "L'influence de chanoines de Lucques sur la liturgie du Latran." *Revue des Sciences Réligieuses* 58:31–41 and reprinted in *La Liturgie dans l'histoire*, pp. 127–139: see 1990 below.

1990. *La Liturgie dans l'histoire*. Paris.

Haberl, F. 1984. "Origine e sviluppo dell'Alleluia gregoriano." *Rivista Internazionale di Musica Sacra* 5:92–100.

Hagiographie, cultures et sociétés, IXe–XIIe siècles: actes du colloque organisé à Nanterre et à Paris (2–5 mai 1979). 1981. Centre de recherches sur l'Antiquité tardive et le haut Moyen Age, Université de Paris X. Paris.

Hailperin, H. 1963. *Rashi and the Christian Scholars*. Pittsburgh.

Halphen, Louis. 1909. *Paris sous les premiers Capétiens (987–1123): études de topographie historique*. paris.

Hammerstein, Reinhold. 1962. *Die Musik der Engel: Untersuchungen zur Musikanschauung des Mittelalters*.Bern.

Handschin, Jacques. 1929–30, 1930–31. "Über Estampie und Sequenz." *Zeitschrift für Musikwissenschaft* 12:1–20: 13:113–132.

1935. "Das Weihnachts Mysterium von Rouen als Musikgeschichtliche Quelle." *Acta Musicologica* 7:98–110.

1954. "Trope, Sequence, and Conductus." In *The New Oxford History of Music*, vol. II: *Early Music up to 1300*, ed. Anselm Hughes. Oxford.

Hardison, Osborne Bennett. 1965. *Christian Rite and Christian Drama in the Middle Ages*. Baltimore.

Häring, Nikolaus. 1982. "Commentary and Hermeneutics." In *Renaissance and Renewal in the Twelfth Century*, ed. Robert L. Benson and Giles Constable, pp. 173–200. Cambridge, MA.

Harrison, Frank. 1963. *Music in Medieval Britain*. 2nd edn. London.

1972. "Music and Cult: the Functions of Music in Social and Religious Systems." In *Perspectives in Musicology*, ed. B. S. Brook *et al.* New York.

Haug, Andreas. 1987. *Gesungene und schriftlich dargestellte Sequenz: Beobachtungen zum Schriftbild der ältesten ostfränkischen Sequenzenhandschriften*. Neuhausen–Stuttgart.

1991. "Ein neues Textdokument zur Entstehungsgeschichte der Sequenz." In *Festschrift Ulrich Siegele zum 60. Geburtstag*. Ed. Rudolf Faber, Anton Förster, *et al.*, pp. 10–19. Kassel.

Häusler, Martin. 1980. *Das Ende der Geschichte in der mittelalterlichen Weltchronistik*. Cologne.

Hearn, M. F. 1981. *Romanesque Sculpture: the Revival of Monumental Stone Sculpture in the Eleventh and Twelfth Centuries*. Ithaca, NY.

Hegener, Eckhard. 1971. *Studien zur "zweite Sprache" in der religiösen Lyrik des zwölften Jahrhunderts: Adam von St. Viktor – Walter von Chatillon*. Ratingen.

Héliot, Pierre. 1967. "La Diversité de l'architecture gothique à ses débuts en France." *Gazette des Beaux-Arts*, a. 109 période 6, tome 69:269–306.

Hiley, David. 1981. "The Liturgical Music of Norman Sicily: a Study Centred on Manuscripts 288, 289, 19421 and Vitrina 20-4 of the Biblioteca Nacional, Madrid." Ph.D. dissertation, University of London, King's College.

1987. "The Rhymed Sequence in England: a Preliminary Survey," in *Musicologie médiévale: notations et séquences*, ed. Michel Huglo, pp. 227–246. Paris.

1989. "Rouen, Bibliothèque Municipale, MS 249 (A. 280) and the Early Paris Repertory of Ordinary Mass Chants and Sequences." *Music and Letters* 70:467–482.

1990. "Cluny, Sequences, and Tropes," in *La tradizione dei tropi liturgici: Atti dei convegni sui tropi liturgici Parigi–Perugia organizzati dal Corpus Troporum*. Ed. Claudio Leonardi and Enrico Menesto, pp. 125–138. Spoleto.

Hodl, L. 1963. "Sacramentum et res – Zeichen und Bezeichnetes." *Scholastik* 38:161–182.

Hoeppner, J. A. 1984. "A 'Common Profit' Library in Fifteenth-Century England and Other Books for Chaplains." *Manuscripta* 28:17–25.

Hofmeier, Johann. 1963. *Die Trinitätslehre des Hugo von St. Viktor dargestellt im Zusammenhang mit den trinitarischen Strömungen seiner Zeit*. Munich.

Holdsworth, Christopher. 1985. "Orderic, Traditional Monk and the New Monasticism." In *Tradition and Change: Essays in Honor of Marjorie Chibnall*. Ed. D. Greenway *et al.*, pp. 21–34. Cambridge.

Hoppin, Richard. 1966. " 'Exsultantes collaudemus': a Sequence for Saint Hylarion." In *Aspects of Medieval and Renaissance Music: a Birthday Offering for Gustave Reese*, ed. Jan La Rue, pp. 392–405. New York.

Hubert, Jean, 1962. "La vie commune des clercs et l'archéologie." In *La vita comune del clero nei secoli XI e XII: atti della settimana di studio, Mendola, settembre 1959*. 2 vols. Vol. I, pp. 90–111. Milan.

Hufgard, Kilian. 1990. *Saint Bernard of Clairvaux: a Theory of Art Formulated from His Writings and Illustrated in Twelfth-Century Works of Art*. Lewiston, NY.

Hughes, Andrew. 1983. "Modal Order and Disorder in the Rhymed Offices." *Musica Disciplina* 37:29–51.

1985. "Research Report: Late Medieval Rhymed Offices." *Journal of the Plainsong and Medieval Music Society* 8:33–49.

Hughes, Anselm. 1934. *Anglo-French Sequelae, Edited from the Papers of the Late Dr. Henry Mariott Bannister*. Nashdom Abbey.

Huglo, Michel. 1957. "Un nouveau prosaire nivernais." *Ephemerides Liturgicae* 71:3–30.

1979. "On the Origins of the Troper-Proser." *Journal of the Plainsong and Medieval Music Society* 2:11–19.

1984. "Musicologie et codicologie à l'Institut de Recherch et d'Histoire des textes," in *Aspects de la recherche musicologique au Centre National de la Recherche Scientifique*, ed. Hélène Charnassé, pp. 85–98. Paris.

1986. "Les *Libelli* des tropes et les premiers tropaires-prosaires," in *Pax et Sapientia: Studies in*

Text and Music of Liturgical Tropes and Sequences in Memory of Gordon Anderson, ed. Ritva Jacobsson, pp. 13–22. Stockholm.

1987. "Origine et diffusion de la séquence parisienne (ou séquence de second époque)," in *Musicologie médiévale: notations et séquences*, ed. Michel Huglo, pp. 209–212. Paris.

1988. *Les livres de chant liturgique*. Typologie des sources du moyen âge occidental LII. Turnhout.

Huguenin, A. 1857. *Suger et la monarchie française*. Paris.

Husmann, Heinrich. 1956. "Alleluia, Vers und Sequenz." *Annales musicologiques* 4:19–53.

1961. "Notre-Dame Epoch." *Musik in Geschichte und Gegenwart*, vol. IX.

1964. "Notre-Dame und Saint-Victor: Repertoire-Studien zur Geschichte der gereimten Prosen." *Acta musicologica* 36:98–123, 191–221.

Imkamp, Wilhelm. 1983. *Das Kirchenbild Innocents III*. Stuttgart.

Iversen, Gunilla. 1981. "Problems in the Editing of Tropes." In *Text: Transactions of the Society for Textual Scholarship*, ed. D. C. Greetham and W. Speed Hill, pp. 95–132. New York.

1985. "Music as 'Ancilla Verbi' and Words as 'Ancilla Musicae': On the Interpretation of the Musical and Textual Forms of two Tropes to 'Osanna in excelsis': 'Laudes deo' and 'Trinitas, unitas, deitas.'" In *LitTrop*, pp. 45–66.

1986. "Pax et Sapientia: a Thematic Study on Tropes from Different Traditions (Based Primarily on Sanctus and Agnus Dei Tropes.) In *Pax et Sapientia: Studies in Text and Music of Liturgical Tropes and Sequences in Memory of Gordon Anderson*. pp. 23–58. Stockholm.

1992. "Splendor patris, on Influence and Genre Definition: Victorine Props Reflected in the Sanctus." In *Cantus planus: the Conference Report of the Chant Study Group of the International Musicological Society, Held in Pécs, Hungary, Sept., 1990*.

(Forthcoming) "On the Iconography of Praise in the Sanctus and its Tropes." In *Festschrift Helmut Hucke zum 60. Geburtstag*. Frankfurt.

Jackson, W. T. H. ed. 1980. *The Interpretation of Medieval Lyric Poetry*. New York.

(Jacobsson) Jonson, Ritva. 1973. "Amalaire de Metz et les tropes du "Kyrie eleison" in *Classica et mediaevalia: F. Blatt*, ed. O. S. Due, H. Friis Johansen and B. Dalsgaard Larsen, pp. 510–540. Copenhagen.

Jacobsson, Ritva and Leo Treitler. 1986. "Tropes and the Concept of Genre." In *Pax et Sapientia; Studies in Text and Music of Liturgical Tropes and Sequences in Memory of Gordon Anderson*, pp. 59–89. Stockholm.

Jaeger, Stephen. 1980. "Peter Abelard's Silence and the Council of Sens." *Res publica litterarum* 3:31–54.

Janson, Tore. 1975. *Prose Rhythm in Medieval Latin from the 9th to the 13th Century*. Stockholm.

Javelet, Robert. 1967. *Image et ressemblance au 12e siècle: de Saint Anselm à Alain de Lille*. 2 vols. Paris.

Jeauneau, Edouard. 1987. "Le Renouveau érigénien du XIIe siècle." In *Eriugena Redivivus: zur Wirkungsgeschichte seines Denkens im Mittelalter und im Übergang nur Neuzeit*, ed. Werner Beierwaltes, pp. 26–46. Heidelberg.

Jeffery, Peter. 1984. "A Four-Part *In seculum* Hocket and a Mensural Sequence in an Unknown Fragment." *JAMS* 37:1–48.

1992a *A New Commandment: toward a Renewed Rite for the Washing of Feet*. Collegeville, MN.

1992b *Re-Envisioning Past Musical Cultures: Ethnomusicology in the Study of Gregorian Chant*. Chicago.

(Forthcoming) *Prophecy Mixed with Melody: from Early Christian Psalmody to Gregorian Chant*.

Jocqué, Luc. 1991. "Les Structures de la population claustrale dans l'ordre de Saint-Victor au XIIe siècle: un essai d'analyse du 'Liber ordinis.'" In *PAS-V*, pp. 53–95.

Johnson, Penelope D. 1981. *Prayer, Patronage, and Power: the Abbey of La Trinité, Vendôme, 1032–1187*. London and New York.

Johnstone, John G. 1986. "Appendix II: the Musical Notation." In *Les Prosules limousines de Wolfenbüttel*. Corpus troporum VI: *Prosules de la messe 2*, ed. Eva Odelman, pp. 144–152. Stockholm.

Jolivet, Jean. 1991. "Données sur Guillaume de Champeaux: dialecticien et théologien." In *APS-V*, pp. 239–251.

Jounel, Pierre. 1963. "Le Culte de la Croix dans la liturgie romaine." *La Maison-Dieu* 75:68–91.

Kahles, Wilhelm. 1960. *Geschichte als Liturgie: die Geschichtstheologie des Ruperts von Deutz*. Münster.

Kahn, J.-C. 1987. *Les moines messagers: la religion, le pouvoir et la science saisis par les rouleaux des morts, XIe–XIIIe siècles*. Paris.

Kaske, Robert, with Arthur Groos and Michael Twomey. 1988. *Medieval Christian Literary Imagery: a Guide to Interpretation*. Toronto.

Kelly, Thomas. 1986. "Melisma and Prosula: the Performance of Responsory Tropes." In *LitTrop*, pp. 163–180.

Kimpel, Dieter and Robert Suckale. 1985. *Die gotische Architektur in Frankreich 1130–1270*. Munich.

King, Archdale A. 1955. *Liturgies of the Religious Orders*. London.

Kitzinger, Ernst. 1972. "The Gregorian Reform and the visual Arts: a Problem of Method." *Transactions of the Royal Historical Society*, 5th series, 22:87–102.

Kleinz, John. 1944. *The Theory of Knowledge of Hugh of St. Victor*. The Catholic University of America Philosophical Studies LXXXVII. Washington, DC.

Klewitz, H. W. 1939. "Das Ende des Reformpapstums." *Deutsches Archiv für Erforschung des Mittelalters* 3:372–412.

Klopsch, Paul. 1980. *Einführung in die Dichtungslehren des lateinischen Mittelaters*. Darmstadt.

Knape, J. 1984. "Zur Benennung der Offizien im Mittelalter: das Wort 'historia' als liturgischer Begriff." *Archiv für Liturgiewissenschaft* 26:305–20.

Kohrs, Klaus Heinrich. 1978. *Die apparallelen Sequenzen: Repertoire, liturgische Ordnung, musikalischer Stil*. Munich.

Kraus, Henry. 1979. *Gold Was the Mortar: the Economics of Cathedral Building*. Boston.

Ladner, Gerhart B. 1942. "The Symbolism of the Biblical Corner Stone in the Medieval West." Reprinted in *Images and Ideas*, pp. 171–196: see 1983 below.

    1947. "Aspects of Mediaeval Thought on Church and State." Reprinted in *Images and Ideas*, pp. 435–456: see 1983 below.

    1954. "St. Augustine's Conception of the Reformation of Man to the Image of God." Reprinted in Images and Ideas, pp. 595–608: see 1983 below.

    1955. "St. Gregory of Nyssa and St. Augustine on the Symbolism of the Cross." Reprinted in *Images and Ideas*, pp. 197–208: see 1983 below.

    1959. *The Idea of Reform: Its Impact on Christian Thought and Action in the Age of the Fathers*. Cambridge.

    1963. "Gregory the Great and Gregory VII: a Comparison of Their Concepts of Renewal." *Viator* 4:1–27.

    1971a. "Aspects of Patristic Anti-Judaism." Reprinted in *Images and Ideas*, pp. 867–876: see 1983 below.

    1971b. "Reform: Innovation and Tradition in Medieval Christendom." Reprinted in *Images and Ideas*, pp. 533–588; see 1983 below.

    1979. "Medieval and Modern Understanding of Symbolism: a Comparison." Reprinted in *Images and Ideas*, pp. 239–282: see 1983 below.

1982. "Terms and Ideas of Renewal in the Twelfth Century." Reprinted in *Images and Ideas*, pp. 687–726: see 1983 below.

1983. *Images and Ideas in the Middle Ages: Selected Studies in History and Art.* 2 vols. Rome.

Lambot, C. 1935. "Texte complété et amendé du 'Psalmus contra partem donati' de Saint Augustin." *RB* 47:312–330.

Langlois, Eustache H. 1832. *Essai historique et descriptif sur la peinture sur verre.* Rouen.

Langosch, Karl. 1969. *Mittellateinische Dichtung.* Darmstadt.

Lasteyrie, Charles de. 1901. *L'Abbaye de Saint-Martial de Limoges.* Paris.

Lausberg, Heinrich. 1967. *Der Hymnus "Jesu dulcis memoria."* Hymnologische und hagiographische Studien I. Munich.

1976. *Der Hymnus "Ave maris stella."* Opladen.

1979. *Der Hymnus "Veni creator spiritus."* Opladen.

Lawless, George, 1987. *Augustine of Hippo and his Monastic Rule.* Oxford.

Leach, Mark. 1986. "The Gloria in Excelsis Deo Tropes of the Breme-Novalesa Community and the Repertory in North and Central Italy." Ph.D. dissertation, University of North Carolina.

Lebeuf, Jean. 1883–93, rpt. 1969. *Histoire de la ville et de tout le diocèse de Paris.* 7 vols. Paris; rpt. Brussels.

Leclercq, Jean. 1958. "La Crise du monachisme aux XIe et XIIe siècles." *Bollettino dell'Istituto Storico Italiano* 70:19–41.

1962. "La spiritualité des chanoines réguliers." In *La vita comune del clero nei secoli XI e XII: atti della settimana di studio, Mendola, settembre 1959.* 2 vols. Vol. I, pp. 117–141. Milan.

1966. "The Bible and the Gregorian Reform." *Concilium: Theology in the Age of Renewal* 17:63–77.

LeFèvre, Placide F. 1957. *La liturgie de Prémontré histoire, formulaire, chant et cérémonial.* Louvain.

Le Goff, Jacques. 1980. *Time, Work, and Culture in the Middle Ages.* Trans. Arthur Goldhammer. Chicago and London.

Lehmann, P. 1922. *Die Parodie im Mittelalter.* Munich.

Le Jay, Paul, 1899. "Les traités attribués à Adam de Saint-Victor." *Revue d'histoire et de littérature religieuse* 4:161–166.

Lemaître, Jean-Loup. 1985. "Une Chronologie de Bernard Itier." *Bulletin de la Société Nationale des Antiquaires de France, 1983,* pp. 135–147.

1989. *Mourir à Saint-Martial: la commémoration des morts et les obituaires à Saint-Martial de Limoges du XIIe au XIIIe siècle.* Paris.

Lespinasse, René de. 1908. "Les Chartes de Saint-Etienne de Nevers." *BSN* 22:51–130.

Lettinck, Nico. 1984. "Comment les historiens de la première moitié du XIIe siècle jugeaient-ils leur temps? *Journal des savants*: 51–77.

Levy, Kenneth. 1987. "Charlemagne's Archetype of Gregorian Chant." *JAMS* 40:1–30.

Lewis, Andrew W. 1981. *Royal Succession in Capetian France: Studies on Familial Order and the State.* Harvard Historical Studies C. Cambridge MA.

Limouzin-Lamothe, Roger. 1951. *Le Diocèse de Limoges des origines à la fin du moyen âge.* Strasbourg–Paris.

Liver, R. 1982. "Der singende Schwan: Motivgeschichteliches zu einer Sequenz des 9. Jahrhunderts." *Museum Helveticum* 39:146–56.

Lohrmann, Dietrich. 1991. "Ernis, abbé de Saint-Victor (1161–1172): rapports avec Rome, affaires financières." In *APS-V*, pp. 181–193.

Lokrantz, Margareta. 1964. *L'opera poetica di s. Pier Damiani.* Stockholm.

Lombard-Jourdan, Anne. 1976. *Aux origines de Paris: la genèse de la rive droite jusqu'en 1223.* Paris.

Longère, Jean. 1987. "La prédication et l'instruction des fidèles selon les conciles et les statuts syno-daux depuis l'antiquité tardive jusqu'au XIIIe siècle." In *Etudes bourguignonnes: finance et vie économique dans la Bourgogne médiévale*, Congrès national des sociétés savantes (109th: Dijon, 1984), pp. 391–418. Paris.

    1991. "La Fonction pastorale de Saint-Victor à la fin du XIIe et au début du XIIIe siècle." In *APS-V*, pp. 291–313.

Lottin, Odon. 1959. "Les 'sentences' de Guillaume de Champeaux." In *Psychologie et morale aux XIIe et XIIIe siècles*. 6 vols., 1948–60; Vol. V, Chapter 2, pp. 189–227.

Lourdaux, W. and D. Verhelst, eds. 1979. *The Bible and Medieval Culture*. Mediaevalia Lovaniensia, Series I, Studia 7. Louvain.

Louth, Andrew. 1981. *The Origins of the Christian Mystical Tradition: from Plato to Denys*. Oxford.

Lubac, Henri de. 1959–64. Exégèse médiévale. 4 vols in 2 parts, 2 vols. each. Paris.

Luchaire, Achille. 1883. *Histoire des Institutions monarchiques de la France sous les premiers Capétiens (987–1180)*. Paris.

    1890. *Louis XI le Gros: annales de sa vie et de son règne*. Paris.

    1899. "Une correspondance inédite des abbés de Saint-Victor sous Louis VII." *Académie des Sciences Morales et Politiques, Séances et Travaux (Institute de France)* 59/2:547–569.

Lynch, Joseph. 1976. *Simoniacal Entry into Religious Life: 1000–1260*. Columbus, OH.

Lyons, John D. and Stephen G. Nichols, Jr. eds. 1982. *Mimesis: from Mirror to Method, Augustine to Descartes*. London and Hanover, NH.

Macy, G. 1976. "A Biographical Note on Richardus Praemonstratensis." *Analecta Praemonstraten-sia* 52:64–9.

Madec, G. 1978. "The Notion of Philosophical Augustinianism: an Attempt at Clarification." *Mediaevalia* 4:125–46.

Maître, Claire. (forthcoming) "A propos des séquences cisterciennes." In *Mélanges offerts à M. Huglo*. Stockholm.

Marcusson, Olaf. 1979. "Comment a-t-on chanté les prosules? Observations sur la technique des tropes de l'alleluia." *Revue de Musicologie* 65:119–159.

Marshall, Judith M. 1961. "A Late Eleventh-Century Manuscript from St. Martial de Limoges: Paris, Bibliothèque Nationale, Fonds Latin No. 1139." Ph.D. dissertation, Yale University.

Martimort, Aimé-Georges. 1970, rpt. 1983. "Origine et signification de l'alleluia de la messe romaine," in *Kyriakon, Festschrift Johannes Quasten*, ed. Patrick Granfield and Josef A. Jung-mann, vol. II, pp. 811–834. 2 vols. Munich. Rpt. in *Mens concordet voci*, pp. 95–122. Tournai.

Martimort, Aimé-Georges. 1991. *Les "Ordines", Les Ordinaires et les Cérémoniaux*. Typologie des sources du moyen âge occidental LVI. Turnhout.

Martimort, Aimé-Georges, R. Cabié, *et al.* 1986–88. *The Church at Prayer: an Introduction to the Liturgy*, trans. Matthew O'Connell. 4 vols. Collegeville, MN.

Matter, E. Ann. 1990. *The Voice of My Beloved: the Song of Songs in Western Medieval Christianity*. Philadelphia.

Mayer, Cornelius. 1969. *Die Zeichen in der geistigen Entwicklung und in der Theologie des jungen Augustinus*. Würzburg.

McCormick, Michael. 1987. *Eternal Victory: Triumphal Rulership in Late Antiquity, Byzantium, and the Early Medieval West*. Cambridge.

McGonigle, Thomas Declan. 1977. "Hugh of St. Victor's Understanding of the Relationship between the Sacramental and Contemplative Dimensions of Christian Life." Ph.D. disserta-tion, Harvard University.

McKinnon, James. 1988. "The Origins of the Roman Alleluia." Unpublished paper presented at the American Musicological Society Meeting in Baltimore.

1990. "The Patristic Jubilus and the Alleluia of the Mass." In *Cantus planus: Papers Read at the Third Meeting, Tihany, Hungary, 12–14 September, 1988*. Budapest.

McKitterick, Rosamund. 1977. *The Frankish Church and the Carolingian Reforms, 789–895*. London.

Mellor, Jean E. and Terry Pearce. 1981. *The Austin Friars, Leicester*. London.

Mensbrugge, A. van der. 1959. "L'Expositio missae gallicanae est-elle de St. Germain de Paris?" *Messager de l'Exarchat du Patriarche Russe en Europe Occidentale* 8:217–249.

Merlet, R. 1895. "Les origines du monastère de St.-Magloire de Paris." *Bibliothèque de l'Ecole des Chartes* 56:237–273.

Michel, Alain. 1976. *In hymnis et canticis: culture et beauté dans l'hymnique chrétienne latine*. Louvain.

Milis, Ludo. 1969. *L'Ordre des chanoines réguliers d'Arrouaise*. Rijksuniversiteit te Gent: werken uitgegeven door de Faculteit van de Letteren en Wijsbegeerte CXLVII. Bruges.

1972–73. "Le Coutumier de Saint-Quentin de Beauvais." *Sacris eruditi* 21:435–481.

1979. "Hermits et chanoines réguliers au XIIe siècle." *Cahiers de Civilization Médiévale* 22:39–80.

Miquel, Dom Pierre. 1989. *Le Vocabulaire latin de l'expérience spirituelle dans la tradition monastique et canoniale de 1050 à 1250*. Paris.

Mitchell, Nathan. 1982. *Cult and Controversy: the Worship of the Eucharist outside Mass*. New York.

Mittler, Placidus. 1965. *Melodieuntersuchung zu den dorischen Hymnen der lateinischen Liturgie im Mittelalter*. Siegburger Studien II. Sieburg.

Molinier, E. 1882. *Fragments d'un inventaire du trésor de l'abbaye de Saint Victor de Paris*. Paris.

Moreau-Lalande, Hyacinthe. 1979. "Société historique et archéologique du Ve arrondissement: de l'abbaye Saint-Victor à la nouvelle faculté des Sciences." Bulletin of the Société, no. 218.

Morris, Colin. 1989. *The Papal Monarchy: the Western Church from 1050 to 1250*. Oxford History of the Christian Church. New York.

Morrison, Karl F. 1982. *The Mimetic Tradition of Reform in the West*. Princeton, NJ.

Muller, H. F. 1924. "Pre-history of the Medieval Drama: the Antecedents of the Tropes and the Conditions of Their Appearance." *Zeitschrift für Romanische Philologie* 44: 544–575.

Murphy-O'Connor, Jerome, ed. 1968. *Paul and Qumran: Studies in New Testament Exegesis by Pierre Benoit [and others]*. Chicago.

Narbonne, Louis. 1901. *La Cathédrale Saint-Just de Narbonne*. Narbonne.

Nebbiai-Dalla Guardia, Donatella. 1985. *La Bibliothèque de l'Abbaye de Saint-Denis du IXe au XVIII siècle*. Paris.

1986. "Les listes médiévales de lectures monastiques: contribution à la connaissance des anciennes bibliothèques bénédictines." *RB* 96:271–326.

Nelson, Janet L. 1971. "National Synods, Kingship as Office, and Royal Anointing: an Early Medieval Syndrome." In *Studies in Church History 7: Councils and Assemblies*, ed. G. J. Cuming and Derek Baker, pp. 41–59. Cambridge.

Nichols, Stephen G. Jr. 1983. *Romanesque Signs: Early Medieval Narrative and Iconography*. New Haven, CT.

Nielsen, Lauge Olaf. 1982. *Theology and Philosophy in the Twelfth Century: A Study of Gilbert Porreta's Thinking and the Theological Exposition of the Doctrine of the Incarnation during the Period 1130–1180*. Acta Theologica Danica XV. Leiden.

Norberg, Dag. 1968. *Manual pratique de latin médiéval*. Connaissance des langues IV. Paris.

1988. *Les vers latins iambiques et trochaïques au Moyen Age et leurs répliques rhythmiques*. Stockholm.

Novelli, Silvana Casartelli. 1987. "Segno *Salutis* e segno 'iconico': dalla 'invenzione' costantiniana ai codici astratti del primo altomedioevo." In *Segni e riti nella chiesa altomedioevale occidentale*. Settimane di studio del centro italiano di studi sull'alto medioevo XXXIII. Vol. I, pp. 103–173 and plates. 2 vols. Spoleto.

Oakley, Francis. 1979. *The Western Church in the Later Middle Ages*. Ithaca, NY and London.

O'Daly, G. J. P. 1981. "Augustine on the Measurement of Time: Some Comparisons with Aristotelian and Stoic Texts." In *Neoplatonism and Early Christian Thought: Essays in Honour of A. H. Armstrong*, ed. H. J. Blumenthal and R. A. Markus, pp. 171–179. London.

Odelman, Eva. 1975. "Comment a-t-on appelé les tropes? Observations sur les rubrics des tropes des Xe et XIe siècles." *Cahiers de Civilization Médiévale* 18:15–36.

Odier, Jeanne B. 1973. "'Membra Disiecta' du fonds de la reine dans le fonds latin de la Bibiothèque Vaticane: notes inédites de Bernard Itier," *Mélanges de l'Ecole Française de Rome: Moyen Age – Temps Modernes* 85:588–610.

Ohly, Friedrich. 1958. *Hohelied-Studien: Grundzüge einer Geschichte der Hoheliedauslegung des Abendlandes bis um 1200*. Wiesbaden.

  1972. "Die Kathedrale als Zeitenraum: zum Dom von Siena." *Frühmittelalterliche Studien* 6:94–158.

Olsen, Glenn. 1969. "The Idea of the 'Ecclesia Primitiva' in the Writings of the Twelfth-Century Canonists." *Traditio* 25:61–86.

Ong, Walter J. 1947. "Wit and Mystery: a Reevaluation in Medieval Latin Hymnody." *Speculum* 20:310–431.

Orme, Nicholas. 1989. *Education and Society in Medieval and Renaissance England*. London.

Ostler, Heinrich. 1906. *Die Psychologie des Hugo von St. Viktor: ein Beitrag zur Geschichte der Psychologie in der Frühscholastik*. Münster.

Otto, Rudolf. 1958. *The Idea of the Holy*, trans. John W. Harvey. New York.

Oury, G. 1971 and 1972. "Les matins solennelles aux grandes fêtes dans les anciennes églises françaises." *Études Grégoriennes* 12:155–162; "La structure cérémonielle des vêpres solennelles dans quelques anciennes liturgies françaises. *Études Grégoriennes* 13:225–236.

Ouy, Gilbert. 1982. "Manuscrits entièrement ou partiellement autographes de Godefroy de Saint-Victor." *Scriptorium* 36:29–42.

  1983. *Le catalogue de la bibliothèque de l'abbaye de Saint-Victor de Paris de Claude de Grandrue 1514*. Paris.

Overton, J. H. 1958. "The Fifth and Sixth Degrees of Contemplation Studied in the Context of the Sequences Community from Some Newly Edited Texts of Richard of St. Victor." Ph.D. dissertation, Duke University.

Parsons, S. C. 1983. "The 'Hierarch' in the Pseudo-Dionysius and its Place in the History of Christian Priesthood." *Oxford Patristics Conference* 1:187–190.

Pelt, J. B. 1937. *Etudes sur la cathédrale de Metz. La liturgie I (Ve–XIIIe siècle)*. Metz.

Perdrizet, Paul. 1933. *Le Calendrier parisien à la fin du Moyen Age d'après le bréviaire et les livres d'heures*. Paris.

Pesce, Dolores. 1989. *The Affinities and Medieval Transposition*. Bloomington, IN.

Petit, François. 1968. *La Réforme des prêtres au moyen âge, pauvreté et vie commune*. Paris.

Petit-Dutaillis, Charles Edmond. 1936. *The Feudal Monarchy in France and England from the Tenth to the Thirteenth Century*. London.

Pintard, Jacques. 1960. *Le Sacerdoce selon Saint Augustin: le prêtre dans la cité de dieu*. Paris.

Planchart, Alejandro. 1977. *The Repertory of Tropes at Winchester*. 2 vols. Princeton, NJ.

  1988. "On the Nature of Transmission and Change in Trope Repertories." *JAMS* 41:215–249.

Poerck, Guy de. 1969. "Le MS Paris, B.N. lat. 1139: étude codicologique d'un recueil factice de pièces paraliturgiques c. XIe–XIIIe siècles." *Scriptorium* 23:298–312.

Polheim, J. 1963. *Die lateinischen Reimprosa*. Berlin.

Pontet, Maurice. 1946. *L'Exégèse de S. Augustin, prédicateur*. Paris.

Powell, James M. 1983. "Honorius III's 'Sermo in Dedicatione Ecclesie Lateranensis' and the Historical-Liturgical Traditions of the Lateran." *Archivum Historiae Pontificiae* 21:195–209.

Prache, Anne. 1990. "Remarques sur la Bibliothèque du Chapitre de Notre-Dame de Paris au XVe Siècle." In *Medieval Architecture and its Intellectual Context: Studies in Honour of Peter Kidson*, ed. Eric Fernie and Paul Crossley, pp. 203–208. London.

Prassl, Franz Karl. 1987. *Psallat Ecclesia Mater: Studien zu Repertoire und Verwendung von Sequenzen in der Liturgie österreichischer Augustinerchorherren vom 12. bis zum 16. Jahrhundert*. Klagenfurt.

Pullen, Brien. 1981. *Sources for the History of Medieval Europe from the Mid-Eighth to the Mid-Thirteenth Century*. Oxford.

Quasten, Johannes. 1962–67. *Patrology*. 3 vols. Westminster, MD.

Raby, F. J. E. 1953. *A History of Christian-Latin Poetry from the Beginnings to the Close of the Middle Ages*. Oxford.

   1959. *The Oxford Book of Medieval Latin Verse*. Oxford.

Rado, Polycarp. 1945. *Répertoire hymnologique des manuscrits liturgiques dans les bibliothèques publiques de Hongrie*. Budapest.

Ray, Roger. 1972. "Orderic Vitalis and His Readers." *Studia Monastica* 14:17–33.

Reames, Sherry L. 1985. *The Legenda aurea: a Reexamination of its Paradoxical History*. Madison, WI.

Reckow, Fritz. 1975. "Organum-begriff und frühe Mehrstimmigkeit." In *Forum musicologicum 1. Basler Studien zur Musikgeschichte I*, pp. 32–167. Bern.

Régnier, Louis. 1921. "Les Stalles de l'abbaye de Saint-Victor." *Bulletin archéologique du comité des travaux historiques et scientifiques*:165–222.

Reier, Ellen J. 1981. "The Introit Trope Repertory at Nevers: MSS Paris, B.N. lat. 9449 and Paris, B.N. n.acq. 1235." Ph.D. dissertation, University of California at Berkeley.

Reijners, G. O. 1965. *The Terminology of the Holy Cross in Early Christian Literature*. Nijmegen.

Reinhold, H. A. 1972. "The Pyrrhic Victory of Florus of Lyons." In *Liturgy for the People*, ed. W. J. Leonard. Milwaukee, WI.

Reinke, D. R. 1987. "'Austin's Labour': Patterns of Governance in Medieval Augustinian Monasticism." *Church History* 56: 157–171.

Resnick, Irven M. 1990. Lingua dei, Lingua hominis: Sacred Language and Medieval Texts." *Viator* 21:51–74.

Reynolds, Roger E. 1981. "A Visual Epitome of the Eucharistic 'Ordo' from the Era of Charles the Bald: the Ivory Mass Cover of the Drogo Sacramentary." In *Charles the Bald: Court and Kingdom*, ed. Margaret Gibson and Janet Nelson, pp. 265–289. Oxford.

   1983. "Image and Text: a Carolingian Illustration of Modification in the Early Roman Eucharistic 'Ordines.' *Viator* 14:59–75.

Rigg, A. G. 1977 and 1978. "Medieval Latin Poetic Anthologies." *Mediaeval Studies* 39:281–330; 40:387–407.

Robert, Michel. 1967. "Les adieux à l'alleluia." *Etudes Grégoriennes* 7:41–51.

Robertson, Anne Walters. 1984. "Music and Liturgy at the Abbey of Saint-Denis, 567–1567: a Survey of the Primary Sources." Ph.D. dissertation, Yale University.

   1985. "The Reconstruction of the Abbey Church at St-Denis (1231–81): the Interplay of Music and Ceremony with Architecture and Politics." *Early Music History* 5:187–238.

   1988. "'Benedicamus domino': the Unwritten Tradition," *JAMS* 41:1–62.

1991. *The Service Books of the Royal Abbey of St. Denis: Images of Ritual and Music in the Middle Ages.* Oxford.

Robinson, I. S. 1979. *Authority and Resistance in the Investiture Contest: the Polemical Literature of the Late Eleventh Century.* Manchester.

Roblin, M. 1952. *Les Juifs de Paris: démographie, economie, culture.* Paris.

Robson, Charles Alan. 1952. *Maurice of Sully and the Medieval Vernacular Homily.* Oxford.

Roetzer, Wunibald. 1930. *Des heiligen Augustinus Schriften als liturgie-geschichtliche Quelle.* Munich.

Rohrig, Floridus. 1984. *Stift Klosterneuburg und seine Kunstschätze.* St. Pölten.

Rosenwein, Barbara. 1982. *Rhinoceros Bound: Cluny in the Tenth Century.* Philadelphia.

Rouse, Richard H. and Mary A. 1979. *Preachers, Florilegia, and Sermons: Studies on the "Manipulus florum" of Thomas of Ireland.* Studies and Texts XLVII. Toronto.

Rudolf, Conrad. 1987. "The 'Principal Founders' and the Early Artistic Legislation of Cîteaux." In *Studies in Cistercian Art and Architecture 3*, ed. Meredith P. Lillich, pp. 1–45. Cistercian Studies Series LXXXIX. Kalamazoo, MI.

1990. *Artistic Change at St.-Denis: Abbot Suger's Program and the Early Twelfth-Century Controversy over Art.* Princeton, NJ.

Ryan, Christopher. 1989. *The Religious Roles of the Papacy: Ideals and Realities, 1150–1300.* Papers in Mediaeval Studies VIII. Toronto.

Ryle, Stephen. 1977. "The Sequence: Reflections on Literature and Liturgy." In *Papers of the Liverpool Latin Seminar, 1976: Classical Latin Poetry/Medieval Latin Poetry/Greek Poetry*, ed. Francis Cairns, pp. 171–182. Liverpool

Saint-Victor, Jean-Baptiste de. 1822–27. *Tableau Historique et Pittoresque de Paris depuis les Gaulois jusqu'à nos Jours.* Second edition. 7 vols. in 4 tomes plus an atlas, which is not numbered or paginated. Paris.

Samaran, Charles and Robert Marichal. 1959–81. *Catalogue des manuscrits en écriture latine portant des indications de date, de lieu, ou de copiste.* Paris. 6 vols.

Sauval, Henri. 1724. *Histoire et recherches des antiquités de la ville de Paris.* Paris. 3 vols.

Saxer, Victor. 1973. "Épaves d'un antiphonaire de la messe médiévale à l'usage de Narbonne." In *Narbonne: archéologie et histoire: Narbonne au Moyen-Age.* Fédération historique du Languedoc méditerranéen et du Roussillon XLV, part 2, pp. 179–198. Montpellier.

Sayce, Oliver. 1982. *The Medieval German Lyric, 1150–1300: the Development of Its Themes and Forms in Their European Context.* New York.

Schaefer, Mary M. 1982–83. "Twelfth-Century Latin Commentaries on the Mass: the Relationship of the Priest to Christ and to the People." *Studia liturgica* 15:76–86.

1983. "Twelfth-Century Commentaries on the Mass: Christological and Ecclesiological Dimensions." Ph.D. dissertation, University of Notre Dame.

Schapiro, Meyer. 1973. *Words and Pictures: on the Literal and the Symbolic in the Interpretation of a Text.* The Hague.

Schlager, Karl-Heinz. 1984. "Beobachtungen zur frühen Sequenz in ost- und westfränkischer Überlieferung." In *Gordon Athol Anderson (1921–1981) in Memoriam*, ed. Nancy van Deusen, vol. II, pp. 531–543. 2 vols. Henryville, PA.

Schlette, Heinz Robert. 1961. *Die Nichtigkeit der Welt: der philosophische Horizont des Hugo von St. Viktor.* Munich.

Schmale, F. J. 1961. *Studien zum Schisma des Jahres 1130.* Cologne.

Schmidt, Rudolf Wolfgang. 1983. "Die Frage nach der Herkunft des Cod. Vindob. palat. 13314 und die Problematik seines Sequenzenrepertoires." *Jahrbuch des Stiftes Klosterneuburg*, n.s. 12:43–62.

Schmitz, Philibert. 1960. "La Liturgie de Cluny." In *Spiritualità Cluniacense*. Convegni del Centro di studi sulla spiritualità medioevale II, pp. 83–99. Todi.

Schnith, Karl. 1980. "Ordericus Vitalis – ein Sympathisant der normannischen Kirchenreform in England?" In *Reformatio Ecclesiae: Beiträge zu kirchlichen Reformbemühungen von der Alten Kirchen bis zur Neuzeit, Festgabe für Erwin Iserloh*, ed. Remigius Bäumer, pp. 77–87. Paderborn.

Schriber, Carolyn Poling. 1990. *The Dilemma of Arnulf of Lisieux: New Ideas versus Old Ideals.* Bloomington, IN.

Schueller, Herbert M. 1988. *The Idea of Music: an Introduction to Musical Aesthetics in Antiquity and the Middle Ages.* Kalamazoo, MI.

Schumann, Otto. 1979–1989. *Lateinisches Hexameter-Lexikon: Dichter. Formelgut von Ennius bis zum Archipoeta.* Monumenta Germaniae Historica: Hilfsmittel IV. 6 vols. and a supplement by Dirk Kottke. Munich.

Sedlmayr, Hans. 1950. "Die gothische Kathedrale Frankreichs als europäische Königskirche," *Anzeiger der Phil.-Hist. Klasse der Österreichischen Akademie der Wissenschaften* 17:390–409.

1988. *Die Entstehung der Kathedrale.* Second edition, with an introduction by Bernhard Rupprecht. Graz.

Seeberg, Reinhold. 1920–33. *Lehrbuch der Dogmengeschichte.* 4 vols. in 5. Leipzig.

Seidel, Linda. 1981. *Songs of Glory: the Romanesque Facades of Aquitaine.* Chicago.

Sellier, Charles. 1902 and 1931. "Vestiges de l'ancienne église de Saint-Victor." In *Procès-verbal de la Commission du Vieux Paris*: (1902) pp. 169–71; (1931) 87–92.

Servatius, Carlo. 1979. *Paschalis II. (1099–1118): Studien zu seiner Person und zu seiner Politik.* Päpste und Papsttum XIV. Stuttgart.

Sery, André. 1902. *L'Abbaye St. Martin de Nevers de chanoines réguliers de Saint-Augustin.* Nevers.

Sheerin, Daniel. 1982. "The Church Dedication 'Ordo' Used at Fulda, 1 Nov., 819." *RB* 92:304–316.

Siegwart, Josef. 1962. *Die chorherren und Chorfrauengeminschaften in der deutschsprachigen Schweiz vom 6. Jahrhundert bis 1160 mit einem Überblick über die deutsche Kanonikenreform des 10. und 11. Jahrhunderts.* Studia Friburgensia n.s. XXX. Freiburg.

Sigal, L. 1921. "Contribution à l'histoire de la cathédrale Saint-Just de Narbonne," in *Bulletin de la Commission Archéologique de Narbonne* 15:11–153.

Signer, Michael. n.d. "Peshat, Sensus Litteralis, and Sequential Narrative: Jewish and Christian Exegesis in the Twelfth Century." Unpublished paper.

Simpson, Otto von. 1962. *The Gothic Cathedral.* Princeton, NJ.

Skubiszewski, Piotr. 1988. "Une vision monastique de l'Eglise au XIIe s. A propos d'un livre récent sur les peintures murales de Prüfening." *Cahiers de Civilization Médiévale* 31:361–376.

Smalley, Beryl. 1938. "Andrew of St. Victor, Abbot of Wigmore: A Twelfth-Century Hebraist." *RTAM* 10:358–373.

1939. "The School of Andrew of St. Victor." *RTAM* 11:145–167.

1951. "A Commentary on the Hebraica by Herbert of Bosham," *RTAM* 18:29–65.

1973. *The Becket Conflict and the Schools.* Oxford.

1981. *Studies in Medieval Thought and Learning.* History Series VI. London.

1983. *The Study of the Bible in the Middle Ages.* 3rd edn. Oxford.

Smith, Norman. 1972. "Interrelationships among the Alleluias of the *Magnus liber organi*." *JAMS* 25:175–202.

Smits van Waesberghe, Josef. 1959. "Zur ursprünglichen Vortragsweise der Prosulen, Sequenzen und Organa." In *Berricht über den Internationalen Musikwissenschaftlichen Kongress, Köln 1958*, pp. 251–253. Kassel.

1976. "De glorioso officio . . . dignitate apostolica . . ." (Amalarius): zum Aufbau der Gross-Alleluia in den päpstlichen Ostervespern" in *Dia-Pason de omnibus: ausgewählte Aufsätze von Joseph Smits van Waesberghe*, ed. C. J. Maas *et al.*, pp. 117–146. Buren.

Somerville, Robert. 1977. *Pope Alexander III and the Council of Tours (1163): a Study of Ecclesiastical Politics and Institutions in the Twelfth Century.* Berkeley, CA.

Sorrell, Alan, 1981. *Reconstructing the Past*, ed. Mark Sorrell. Totwa, NJ.

Sot, Michel. 1981. *Gesta episcoporum, gesta abbatum.* Typologie des sources du moyen âge occidental XXXXVII. Turnhout.

Southern, Richard. 1971. "Aspects of the European Tradition of Historical Handwriting: Hugh of St. Victor and the Idea of Historical Development." *Transactions of the Royal Historical Society*, 5th series, 21:211–234.

Spanke, Hans. 1931 and 1932. "St. Martial-Studien: ein Beitrag zur frühromanischen Metrik." *Zeitschrift für Französische Sprache und Literatur* 54:285–317; 385–422; 56:450–478.

1932. "Fortschritte in der Geschichte mittelalterlicher Musik: zur Geschichte der Sequenz und ihrer Nebenformen." *Historische Vierteljahrschrift* 27:374–389.

1941. "Die Kompositionskunst der Sequenzen Adams von St. Viktor." *Studi Medievali*, n.s. 14:1–29.

Spicq, C. 1944. *Esquisse d'une histoire d l'exégèse latine au moyen âge.* Paris.

Stäblein, Bruno. 1958–61. "Eine Hymnusmelodie als Vorlage Einer Provenzalischen Alba." In *Miscelánea en homenaje a Monseñor H. Anglés*, vol. II, pp. 889–894. 2 vols. Barcelona.

1961. "Zur Frühgeschichte der Sequenz," *Archiv für Musikwissenschaft* 18:1–33.

1962. "Zum Problem Lai–Planctus–Sequenz." In *Festschrift Karl G. Fellerer*, ed. Heinrich Hüschen, pp. 491–502. Regensburg.

1964. "Die Sequenzmelodie 'Concordia' und ihr geschichtlicher Hintergrund." In *Festschrift H. Engel*, ed. Horst Heussner, pp. 364–392. Kassel.

1975. *Schriftbild der Einstimmigen Musik. Musikgeschichte in Bildern*, ed. Werner Bachmann, vol. III: *Musik des Mittelalters und der Renaissance*, part 4. Leipzig.

Stansbury O'Donnell, Mark. 1990. "The Shape of the Church: The Relationship of Architecture, Art, and Liturgy at the Cathedral of Trier." Ph.D. dissertation, Yale University.

Steigman, Emero. 1988. "Analogues of the Cistercian Abbey Church." In *The Medieval Monastery*, ed. Andrew MacLeish, pp. 17–33. St. Cloud.

Steiner, Ruth. 1969. "The Prosulae of the Ms Paris BN F. lat. 1118." *JAMS* 22:367–393.

Stiefel, Tina. 1985. *The Intellectual Revolution in Twelfth-Century Europe.* New York.

Stirnemann, Patricia. 1990. "Fils de la vierge: l'initiale à filigranes parisienne: 1140–1314." *Revue de l'Art.* 90:58–73.

1991. "La Production manuscrite et la bibliothèque de Saint-Victor: 1140–1155." In *APS-V*, pp. 140–141.

Stock, Brian. 1983. *The Implications of Literacy: Written Language and Models of Interpretation in the Eleventh and Twelfth Centuries.* Princeton, NJ.

Stotz, Peter. 1978. "Die Gedichte des Hoheliedkommentars und der 'Expositio de muliere forte' Brunos von Segni: mit einem Beitrag von Andreas Wernli zur musikalischen Fassung eines Hoheliedgedichts von Bruno von Segni." *Zeitschrift für Schweizerische Kirchengeschichte* 72:1–53.

Suntrup, R. 1978. *Die Bedeutung der liturgischen Gebärden und Bewegungen in lateinischen und deutschen Auslegungen des 9. bis 13. Jahrhunderts.* Munich.

Szövérffy, Josef. 1957. "Der Investiturstreit und die Petrus-Hymnen des Mittelalters." *Deutsches Archiv für Erforschung des Mittelalters* 13:228–240.

1965a. *Die Annalen der lateinischen Hymnendichtung: ein Handbuch.* Berlin. 2 vols.

1965b. "A Mirror of Medieval Culture: St. Peter Hymns of the Middle Ages." *Transactions of the Connecticut Academy of Arts and Sciences* 42:97–403.

1976. *Hymns of the Holy Cross: an Annotated Edition with Introduction*. Brookline, MA.

1979. "False Use of Unfitting Hymns: Some Ideas Shared by Peter the Venerable, Peter Abelard, and Heloise." *RB* 89: 187–199.

1983a. "Religiöse Dichtung als Kulturphänomen und Kulturleistung." In *Repertorium hymnologicum novum*. Vol. I, Part I: *Einführung und alphabetisches Verzeichnis. Religiös Dichtung als Kulturphänomen und Kulturleistung*, pp. 24–62. Berlin.

1983b. "Zur Frage der Kontrafaktur in Hymnodie: 'Victime paschali.'" In *"Psallat Chorus Caelestium": Religious Lyrics of the Middle Ages, Hymnological Studies and Collected Essays*, pp. 484–499. Berlin.

1985a. *A Concise History of Medieval Latin Hymnody: Religious Lyrics between Antiquity and Humanism*. Leiden.

1985b. *Marianische Motivik der Hymnen: ein Beitrag zur Geschichte der marianischen Lyrik im Mittelalter*. Leiden.

1989. *Latin hymns*. Typologie des sources du moyen âge occidental LV. Turnhout.

Tanon, L. 1883. *Histoire des justices des anciennes églises et communautés monastiques de Paris*. Paris.

Tartarkiewicz, Wladyslaw. 1970. *History of Aesthetics*, vol. II: *Medieval Aesthetics*. Warsaw.

Tellenbach, Gerd. 1940. *Church, State, and Christian Society in the Investiture Contest*. Oxford.

Teske, Roland. 1985. "'Vocans Temporales, Faciens Aeternos': St. Augustine on Liberation from Time." *Traditio* 41:36–58.

Teviotdale, Elizabeth. 1991. "The Cotton Troper (London, British Library, Cotton MS Caligula A.xiv, ff. 1–36): a Study of an Illustrated English Troper of the Eleventh Century." Ph.D. dissertation, University of North Carolina.

Thiery, Luc Vincent. 1788. *Guide des amateurs et des étrangers . . . aux environs de Paris*. Paris.

Thiry, C. 1985. "L'histoire immédiate, une invention du moyen âge?" In *L'histoire aujourd'hui*. Liège.

Thomson, Rodney M. 1982. *Manuscripts from St. Albans Abbey, 1066–1235*, vol. I: *Text*; vol. II: *Plates*. Woodbridge, Suffolk.

Tierney, Brian. 1964. *The Crisis of Church and State, 1050–1300*. Englewood Cliffs, NJ.

Timmer, David Ernest. 1982. *The Religious Significance of Judaism for Twelfth-Century Exegesis: a Study in the Thought of Rupert of Deutz*. Ann Arbor, MI.

Toubert, Hélène. 1990. *Un art dirigé: réforme grégorienne et iconographie*. Paris.

Treitler, Leo. 1967. "The Aquitanian Repertories of Sacred Monody in the Eleventh and Twelfth Centuries." Ph.D. dissertation, Princeton University.

1982. "Observations on the Transmission of some Aquitanian Tropes." *Forum musicologicum* 3:11–60.

Tryer, John W. 1932. *Historical Survey of Holy Week, its Services and Ceremonial*. Alcuin Club Collections XXIX. London.

Untermann, Matthias. 1984. *Kirchenbauten der Praemonstratenser: Untersuchungen zum Problem einer Ordensbaukunst im 12. Jahrhundert*. Cologne.

La vita comune del clero nei secoli XI e XII: atti della settimana di studio: Mendola, settembre, 1959. 1962. 2 vols. Milan.

van Deusen, Nancy. 1908a. *Music at Nevers Cathedral: Principal Sources of Medieval Chant*. Institute of Medieval Studies: Musicological Studies XXX. Stroudsburg, PA.

1980b. "The Sequence Repertory of Nevers Cathedral." In *Basler Studien zur Interpretation der alten Musik*, Forum musicologicum vol. II, pp. 44–59. Winterthur.

1986. "The Use and Significance of the Sequence." *Musica Disciplina* 40:45–47.

van Deusen, Nancy. 1987. "Polymelodic Sequences and a 'Second Epoch' of Sequence Composition." In *Musicologie Mediévale: Notations et Séquences*, ed. Michel Huglo, pp. 213–225. Paris.

van Deusen, Nancy. 1988. "Medieval Organologies: Augustine Vs. Cassiodor On the Subject of Musical Instruments." In *Augustine on Music: an Interdisciplinary Collection of Essays*. Ed. Richard R. La Croix, pp. 53–93. Lewiston, NY.

Van Dijk, Stephen. 1969–70. "The Medieval Easter Vespers of the Roman Clergy." *Sacris erudiri* 19:261–363.

Van Dijk, Stephen and Joan H. Walker. 1960. *The Origins of the Modern Roman Liturgy*. London.

Van Engen, John, 1983. *Rupert of Deutz*. Berkeley, CA.

1986. "The 'Crisis of Cenobitism' Reconsidered: Benedictine Monasticism in the Years 1050–1150," *Speculum* 61:269–304.

Vauchez, André, 1981. *La Sainteté en Occident aux derniers siècles du Moyen Age d'après les procès de canonisation et les documents hagiographiques*. Bibliothèques des Ecoles Françaises d'Athènes et de Rome, vol. 241. Rome.

Vaughn, Sally N. 1981. *The Abbey of Bec and the Anglo-Norman State, 1034–1136*. Woodbridge, Suffolk.

1987. *Anselm of Bec and Robert of Meulan: the Innocence of the Dove and the Wisdom of the Serpent*. Berkeley, CA.

Verbraken, Pierre-Patrick. 1976. *Etudes critiques sur les Sermons Authentiques de Saint Augustin*. Wetteren.

Verger, Jacques and Jean Folivet. 1982. *Bernard–Abélard, ou le cloître et l'école*. Douze Hommes dans l'Histoire de l'Eglise. Paris.

Vernet, André. 1965. "Un manuscrit autographe de Bernard Itier (1202) et le "Liber de sacramentis" de Jean Maréchal." *Bulletin de la Société Nationale des Antiquaires de France, 1983*, pp. 161–163.

Vert, Claude de. 1709–18 and 1970. *Explication simple, littérale et historique des cérémonies de l'église*. 2nd edn. 4 vols. Paris; reprinted in Farnborough.

Vezin, Jean. 1990. "L'Évolution du culte des saints à Paris aux XIIIe et XIVe siècles." In *Rituels: mélanges offerts au Père Gy*, ed. Paul de Clerck and Eric Palazzo, pp. 473–479. Paris.

Vogel, Cyrille. 1978. *Les "Libri Paenitentiales."* Typologie des sources du Moyen Age occidental, vol. 27. Turnhout.

1982. "Histoire du culte chrétien: histoire d'un cérémonial ou d'une institution?" In *La liturgie; son sens, son esprit, sa méthode*. Conférences Saint-Serge 28 and Semaine d'études liturgiques, Paris, June 30 – July 3, 1981. pp. 339–348. Rome.

1986. *Medieval Liturgy: an Introduction to the Sources*. Trans. and Rev. William Storey and Niels K. Rasmussen. Washington, DC.

Vroom, H. 1933. *Le Psaume abécédaire de s. Augustin et la poésie rythmique*. Latinitas christianorum primaeva IV. Nijmegen.

Vulliez, Charles, 1990. "Etudes sur la correspondance et la carrière d'Etienne d'Orléans dit de Tournai (†1203)." In *APS-V*, pp. 195–231.

Waddell, Chrysogonus. 1976. "Peter Abelard's *Letter 10* and Cistercian Liturgical Reform." In *Studies in Medieval Cistercian History Vol. II: Papers*, ed. John R. Sommerfeldt, pp. 75–86. Cistercian Studies Series XXIV. Kalamazoo, MI.

1980. "St. Bernard and the Cistercian Office at the Abbey of the Paraclete." In *The Chimaera of His Age: Studies on Bernard of Clairvaux*, Studies in Medieval Cistercian History, vol. V, ed. E. Rozanne Elder and John R. Sommerfeldt, pp. 76–121. Cistercian Studies Series LXIII. Kalamazoo, MI.

1986. "'Epithalamica': an Easter Sequence by Peter Abelard." *Musical Quarterly* 72:239–271.

1989. "A Monk's Christmas Carol: Christmas at Marmoutier and at Cîteaux, 24–25 December, 1113." *Liturgy* 23:46–103.

1991. "Notes on the Early Cistercian Blessing of Candles and Candlemas Procession." *Liturgy* 25:43–86.

Wagner, Peter. 1911–21. *Einführung in die gregorianischen Melodien*. Leipzig. 3 vols.

Waldman, Thomas. 1985. "Abbot Suger and the Nuns of Argenteuil." *Traditio* 41:239–272.

Ward, Benedicta. 1982. *Miracles and the Medieval Mind: Theory, Record and Event, 1000–1215*. Philadelphia.

Ward, John O. 1979. "Gothic Architecture, Universities and the Decline of the Humanities in Twelfth Century Europe." In *Principalities, Powers, and Estates: Studies in Medieval and Early Modern Government and Society*, ed. L. O. Frappel, pp. 75–85. Adelaide.

Warren, H. B. de 1953. "Bernard et l'ordre de Saint-Victor. In *Bernard de Clairvaux*. Paris.

Weimar, Peter, ed. 1981. *Die Renaissance der Wissenschaften im 12. Jahrhundert*. Zürcher Hochschulforum II. Zurich.

Weinfurter, Stefan. 1975. *Salzburger Bistumsreform und Bischofpolitik im 12. Jahrhundert: der Erzbischof Konrad I. von Salzburg und die Regularkanoniker* Kölner Historische Abhandlungen XXIV. Cologne.

1978. "Vita canonica und Eschatologie: eine neue Quelle zum Selbstverständnis der Reformkanoniker des 12. Jahrhunderts aus dem Salzburger Reformkreis." In *Secundum regulam vivere: Festschrift für Norbert Backmund*, ed. Gert Melville, pp. 139–67. Windberg.

Weinstein, Donald and Rudolph M. Bell. 1982. *Saints and Society: the Two Worlds of Western Christendom, 1000–1700*. Chicago and London.

Weisbein, Nicholas. 1947. "Le 'laudes crucis attollamus' de Maître Hugues d'Orleans le Primat." *Revue du Moyen Age latin* 3:35–26.

Weisweiler, H. 1957. "'Sacramentum fidei': Augustinische und Ps.-Dionysische Gedanken in der Glaubenauffassung Hugos von St. Viktor." In *Theologie in Geschichte und Gegenwart*, ed. J. Auer and H. Volk, pp. 433–456. Munich.

Weitzmann-Fiedler, Josepha. 1981. *Romanische gravierte Bronzeschalen*. Berlin.

Wilcox, D. J. 1985. "The Sense of Time in Western Historical Narratives from Eusebius to Machiavelli." In *Classical Rhetoric and Medieval Historiography*, ed. Ernst Breisach. Kalamazoo, MI.

Wilmart, André. 1932. *Auteurs Spirituels et textes dévots du Moyen Age latin*. Paris.

1933. "Un florilège carolingien sur le symbolisme des cérémonies du baptême, avec un appendice sur la lettre de Jean Diacre." In *Analecta Reginensia: Extraits des manuscrits latins de la reine Christine conservés au Vatican*. Studi e testi LIX. Vatican City.

Williams, Paul L. 1980. *The Moral Philosophy of Peter Abelard*. Lanham, MD.

Willesme, Jean-Pierre. 1979. "Les origines de L'Abbaye de Saint-Victor de Paris à travers ses historiens des XVIIe et XVIIIe siècles." *Bulletin Philologique et Historique* (Année 1977): 101–114.

1981. "Saint-Victor au temps d'Abélard." In *Abélard en son temps: Actes du Colloque International organisé a l'occasion du 9e Centenaire de la naissance de Pierre Abélard (14–19 mai 1979)*, pp. 95–106. Paris.

1991. "L'Abbaye Saint-Victor: l'église et les bâtiments, des origines à la Révolution." In *APS-V*, pp. 97–115.

Willis, Geoffrey G. 1968. "The Consecration of Churches down to the Ninth Century." In his *Further Essays in Early Roman Liturgy*, pp. 133–73.

Wright, Craig. 1989. *Music and Ceremony at Notre Dame of Paris (500–1550)*. Cambridge.

Young, Karl. 1933. *The Drama of the Medieval Church*. 2 vols. Oxford.

Yudkin, Jeremy. 1989. *Music in Medieval Europe*. Englewood Cliffs, NJ.

Zephirin, Yolande. 1984. "Deux documents concernant l'abbaye de Saint-Victor." *Montagne Ste.-Geneviève* 258:20–21.

Ziezulewicz, William. 1986. "'Restored' Churches in the Fisc of St. Florent-de-Saumur (1021–1118): Reform Ideology or Economic Motivation?" *RB* 96:106–117.

Zinn, Grover A. 1969. "History and Contemplation: the Dimensions of the Restoration of Man in Two Treatises on the Ark of Noah by Hugh of St. Victor." Ph.D. dissertation, Duke University.

    1972–73. "Mandala Use and Symbolism in the Mysticism of Hugh of St. Victor." *History of Religions* 12:317–341.

    1974a. "Book and Word: the Background of Bonaventure's Use of Symbols." In *S. Bonaventura 1274–1974*, ed. Jacques Guy Bouger, pp. 143–169. Rome.

    1974b. "Historia fundamentum est: the Role of History in the Contemplative Life according to Hugh of St. Victor." In *Contemporary Reflections on the Medieval Christian Tradition: Essays in Honor of Ray C. Petry*, ed. George H. Shriver, pp. 135–158. Durham, NC.

    1974c. "Hugh of St. Victor and the Art of Memory." *Viator* 5:211–234.

    1975. "'De gradibus ascensionum': the Stages of Contemplative Ascent in Two Treatises on Noah's Ark by Hugh of St. Victor." *Studies in Medieval Culture* 5: 61–80.

    1977a. "The Influence of Hugh of St. Victor's Chronicon on the *Abbreviationes chronicorum* by Ralph of Diceto." *Speculum* 52: 38–61.

    1977b. "Personification Allegory and Visions of Light in Richard of St. Victor's Teaching on Contemplation." *University of Toronto Quarterly* 46: 190–214.

    1986. "Suger, Theology, and the Pseudo-Dionysian Tradition." In *ASSD*, pp. 33–40.

    1990. "History and Interpretation: 'Hebrew Truth,' Judaism, and the Victorine Exegetical Tradition." In *Jews and Christians: Exploring the Past, Present, and Future*, ed. James H. Charlesworth, pp. 100–127. New York.

    n.d. "The Seraphic Mysticism of Hugh of St. Victor." Unpublished paper.

Zumkeller, Adolar. 1987. *Augustine's Rule: a Commentary*. Villanova, PA.

Zwieten, J. W. M. van. 1987. "Jewish Exegesis with Christian Bounds: Richard of St. Victor, 'De Emmanuele,' and Victorine Hermeneutics." *Bijdragen Tijdschrift voor filosofie en theologie* 48: 327–335.

Indices

Index of sequence incipits

If the piece is in *AH*, the volume number and the first page are provided in parentheses immediately following the incipit

Index of manuscripts

1993